KENNEDY
JUSTICE

VICTOR S. NAVASKY

KENNEDY
JUSTICE

ATHENEUM   *NEW YORK*

1971

Copyright © 1970, 1971 by Victor S. Navasky
All rights reserved
Library of Congress catalog card number 77–145633
Published simultaneously in Canada by McClelland and Stewart Ltd.
Manufactured in the United States of America by
Kingsport Press, Inc., Kingsport, Tennessee
Designed by Kathleen Carey
First Printing September 1971
Second Printing October 1971
Third Printing October 1971

To
M & M

CONTENTS

AUTHOR'S NOTE

Kennedy Justice is neither a personal portrait nor an attempt at chronological reconstruction of the historical high and low points of the Justice Department under Robert F. Kennedy. Rather, it is a series of forays into what is forbiddingly known as the Decision-making Process, a look at how an institution makes up its mind, a tracing of one man's attempt to translate policy values into results, an inquiry into how justice is or isn't done. It is the premise of this book that as the President's brother, Robert Kennedy had a chance to be the maximum Attorney General, to explore the outermost reaches of that office, and that therefore Robert Kennedy's Attorney Generalship provides a unique opportunity to focus on the points at which the pursuit and exercise of power meet bureaucratic resistance—and to ask what are the consequences of that conflict.

Toward that end I have resisted the temptation to cover such extracurricular activities as the Cuban missile crisis, Robert Kennedy's post-Bay of Pigs role as CIA watchdog and promoter of counterinsurgency in Vietnam, and his trips around the world, which collectively took up about half of Kennedy's time during his years at Justice. Consistent with that end—but in addition because I did not know Robert Kennedy well—I have also done my best not to indulge any long-range psychoanalysis or motivation-spelunking, except where it seemed essential to develop the issue under investigation, as in the discussion of bugging and wiretapping. Nor have I pretended to any sort of systematic coverage of those areas of the Justice Department's business such as anti-trust and internal security that did not have Robert

Kennedy's interest. Finally, I have not dealt at any length with the period after President Kennedy's assassination but before Robert Kennedy's resignation as Attorney General (November 22, 1963–September 3, 1964), when the conditions for Robert Kennedy's exercise of optimal power no longer applied. This has meant omitting extended consideration of his role in what many may consider a hallmark of his Attorney Generalship—others give Lyndon B. Johnson the major credit—the Civil Rights Act of 1964, which was formulated largely on RFK's initiative in the spring of 1963 but not passed until the spring of 1964.

Kennedy Justice is not an insider's book, but neither is it an outsider's. When I started my research in early 1966, Kennedy tried to discourage me from writing it, and one of his old Justice Department colleagues went so far as to inform my then-publisher that I would receive no cooperation. Then, when they became persuaded that I was proceeding anyway, I received arm's-length cooperation, which in a way was worse than none, since I would travel great distances only to be told what I could have found out in the local library. After about a year and a half of that, I started running into Senator Kennedy at various functions, and although he had not yet agreed to an interview, he would say, "Have you found out anything good about me yet?" or "I understand you saw so-and-so last week—you're working very hard, aren't you?" Eventually he told me he would be happy to help in any way he could, and by that time—late 1967—I had my guard up, so I suggested we commence serious interviews as soon as I had completed my basic reading and research. By March 1968, when I was ready to interview him, he was ready to run for President, and although we did have some talks which were quite useful to me, we never really got to know each other. I did get to know some of the Kennedy Justice people, though, and after his sad death many of them were imprudently helpful in their reminiscences and in guiding me through the random source material to which they had access.

My experience with the FBI was more consistent. From the day I started till the day I finished, the FBI declined to assist me in any way. When Clifford Sessions, then Director of Public Information of the Justice Department, called his FBI counterpart in Crime Records (the FBI's public relations office) to arrange an appointment, he was told that they preferred not to talk with me. When he asked why, he was told that I might ask questions they did not want to answer. I have tried not to let issues of access prejudice matters of substance, but inescapably my perspective has been shaped by my experience. For instance, my hypothesis that to understand the FBI it helps to think of it as a secret society was stimulated in part by my own exposure to the quaint rituals of the Bureau's Crime Records office, which considers its job more to withhold than to provide information.

Because this is not an authorized account, I have had only *ad hoc* access to confidential memoranda, files and correspondence. Thus I have occasionally resorted to speculation (identified as such when used) where reportage would have been preferable. Because this is an interim report rather than a definitive one (which can be undertaken only after both the Kennedy and J. Edgar Hoover papers, among others, are made available) I have felt no compulsion to rehash old material except where it contributes to understanding the new, nor have I gone out of my way to document the original with the familiar. Unless otherwise indicated in the text or notes, the sources of all direct quotes or paraphrases are personal interviews which I have conducted over the past five years. In some cases interviewees requested anonymity and I, of course, have respected that. Upon publication of *Kennedy Justice,* I am turning my papers over to the John F. Kennedy Library, where they will be available for inspection after an appropriate interval.

A note on usage: Because that is what they were called in the U.S. Department of Justice, 1961–1964, I call the Attorney General "General," the Director of the FBI "the Director," and blacks "Negroes."

.V.S.N.

PROLOGUE

The Attorney General

THE TENSION between law and politics dominates what little literature there is on the United States Department of Justice, and it was not absent from the Kennedy Justice Department, which was headed by the President's political campaign manager but staffed at the top with an elite corps of lawyer's lawyers. The current and previous Attorneys General—John Mitchell with his political commitment to "law and order" (code words for cracking down on crime at the expense of traditional procedures) and Ramsey Clark, with his purist commitment to procedural integrity—symbolize the polar tendencies that coexisted in Kennedy Justice. Robert Kennedy's personal appointment was in the political tradition, but he staffed the Department in the legal tradition.

The tension between private values and public standards is as old as Aristotle's question about whether the virtue of a good man is the same as that of a good citizen. How, for instance, did a man of Robert Kennedy's incorruptible self-image reconcile conflicts between loyalty (ranked high in the Kennedy value hierarchy) and duty? Conversely, consider Kennedy's prosecution—his critics call it persecution—of Jimmy Hoffa. To what extent may a public law enforcer permit his private estimate of evil to intrude on that legal no man's land known as "prosecutor's discretion"?

Nor is there anything new in the tension between the policy maker and the bureaucracy—except that in this case the policy maker happened to be a Kennedy and the bureaucracy happened to include the FBI. Kennedys, as the ongoing flood of Kennedy literature attests, are good copy, and the fascination they hold for analysts of the American political system—even those who consider the Kennedys a triumph of style over substance—cannot be explained by reference to Kennedy glamour or to the public's remarkable appetite for Kennedy gossip. Rather, Kennedys make interesting case studies at least in part because the conflicts that defined them to some degree anticipated the tensions that surrounded them. They embodied the dilemmas that confronted them. Robert Kennedy at the Justice Department was a prime example. He commuted between idealism and expediency. He valued toughness but was inhabited by compassion. He had a sense of purpose informed by Harvard and a sense of method informed by the ward politics of Irish Boston. Puritanism coexisted with pragmatism; he always knew what he wanted, yet his values were ever evolving.

The FBI was, of course, the ultimate bureaucracy, and—a fact unknown to the general public—constitutes almost half of the Justice Department. The clash between the maximum Attorney General, the President's brother, and the ultimate bureaucrat, J. Edgar Hoover, could be expected to reverberate throughout the government.

The Justice Department that Robert Kennedy took over had almost 32,000 employees, a budget of $400 million, seven divisions whose titles describe their work (Anti-Trust, Civil, Civil Rights, Criminal, Internal Security, Lands and Natural Resources, Tax), three offices (Solicitor General, Legal Counsel, Pardon Attorney), three bureaus (Prisons, Immigration and Naturalization and the FBI), and ninety-two U.S. attorneys each heading up a Justice Department field office scattered across the land, plus a vast force of U.S. marshals who could be augmented by special deputy marshals whenever the occasion required.

As the nation's chief prosecutor, the Attorney General, who presides over the Justice Department, had come to enjoy a variety of formal and informal power, not the least of which was the power of patronage since he had the most to say about who would serve as U.S. attorney, a powerful office in its own right but also a traditional jumping-off point for state and local political careers; and about more than 500 federal judgeships—with salaries that started at $22,500 a year—whose importance cannot be underestimated. As Attorney General he would in effect decide whether and when to indict, prosecute, deport, enjoin, settle, commute or litigate in cases affecting tens of millions of Americans and hundreds of billions of dollars in cases prosecuted and adjudicated by men he had appointed.

Three additional factors, not mentioned in the textbooks or visible on the organization charts, conspired to give the Kennedy Justice Department its significance and centrality. First, Robert Kennedy's blood line to the White House meant that the Attorney General's office became a strategic way station for petitioners on the road to persuading the President, and simultaneously Justice served as a 32,000-man addition to the White House staff for random Presidential business.

Second, Justice's Civil Rights Division had jurisdiction over the onrushing movement for equal justice that increasingly preoccupied the Administration and the country as crisis built on crisis—the freedom-rider bus burning, the rioting at the University of Mississippi, the murder of Medgar Evers, the near race riot in Birmingham and the bombings there, Governor Wallace standing in the schoolhouse door, the murder of three civil rights workers in Philadelphia, Mississippi.

Third was the strategic situation which the Justice Department, as clearinghouse (or stumbling block) for all government litigation and as watchdog over the federal establishment, had come to occupy by the early Sixties. It transcended the relationship of the Attorney General to the President, so far had the Attorney General's job evolved from the days when George Washington had to talk Edmund Randolph, his lawyer in private life, into taking the $1,500-a-year job by arguing that it would "confer pre-eminence" and give him "decided preference in professional employment"—i.e., it was only a part-time job but would bring some business his way. Indeed, when President Madison introduced legislation to require the Attorney General to reside in the capital while Congress was in session, William Pinckney, his Attorney General, expressed great alarm and shortly thereafter resigned.

The Justice Department itself was not invented until 1870, the FBI got its full name only in 1935, there was no Internal Security Division until 1950, and the Civil Rights Division did not exist until 1957, less than four years before the Kennedys came to power. Nevertheless, by the early Sixties not only was every federal agency required to clear cases and rulings with the Justice Department ("the largest law firm in the world with the richest client—the U.S. government," went the standard description), but wherever private parties were involved in Constitutionally significant litigation, the Justice Department generally stepped in at the Supreme Court level and appeared as *amicus* (a friend of the court). The increasing political significance of the post was underlined by the number of recent Attorneys General who came to their jobs via deep involvement in Presidential politics. Among Kennedy's predecessors were Harry Daugherty, President Harding's political campaign manager, who barely escaped jail for his role in the Teapot Dome scandal; Homer Cummings, who had served as national chairman of the Democratic Party under Woodrow Wilson and seconded Franklin D. Roosevelt's nomination at the 1932 convention (his subsequent observation that the Constitution doesn't mandate nine Supreme Court Justices gave Roosevelt the idea for his court-packing plan); Howard McGrath, Truman's campaign manager, who also resigned under a moral cloud as the result of an aborted conflict-of-interest investigation by New York reformer Newbold Morris; and Herbert Brownell, President Eisenhower's campaign manager, who came close to accusing former President Truman of treason when he charged that Truman had promoted Harry Dexter White to the International Monetary Fund despite his knowledge of allegations that White was a spy. No other agency of government with the possible exception of the Bureau of the Budget would have offered a President's brother such a panoramic view of what was happening or so many levers to do something about it.

Does the Internal Revenue Service want to prosecute Sherman Adams for not paying taxes on moneys allegedly given by Boston industrialist Bernard Goldfine in the form of cashier's checks to pay Adams' rent? The matter was turned over to Justice's Tax Division.

Can the President ban segregation in all publicly assisted housing with the stroke of his pen, as John Kennedy promised in his Presidential campaign? Justice's Office of Legal Counsel will draft a memorandum.

Did Peter Minuit really buy Manhattan island for $24 from the Indians or did he merely lease it to make beer, as a spokesman for the Kent Indians of Connecticut claimed? Justice's Lands and Natural Resources Division argued the matter before the Indian Claims Commission.

Are the Hearst and Chandler publishing empires guilty of a conspiracy to monopolize the newspaper business in the Los Angeles area by permitting Hearst's *Herald Examiner* to monopolize the afternoon market and Chandler's Los Angeles *Times* to monopolize the morning market? Justice's Anti-Trust Division will recommend whether to proceed under the Sherman Act.

Does the State Department want to bar Carlos Fuentes, pro-Castro Mexican novelist and intellectual leader, from a lecture tour of the United States? State personnel will work through Justice's Immigration and Naturalization Service.

Is Ralph Ginzburg, proprietor of *Eros*, which describes itself as a magazine "devoted to the joys of love and sex," publishing pornography before its time? The case will be tried by the U.S. attorney in Pennsylvania in consultation with Justice's Criminal Division.

Will the government intervene in a Supreme Court proceeding on behalf of a privately financed integrated housing project in the lily-white suburb of Deerfield, Illinois? The man to convince is Justice's Solicitor General, whose office handles all litigation before the U.S. Supreme Court.

Will the U.S. government be liable for accidents incurred during the massive March on Washington in the summer of 1963 by newsmen while on government property? Justice's Civil Division will draft an exculpatory clause to be stamped on all press passes.

Such were the institutions, issues and power awaiting the new Attorney General. As for the man himself, it was his inexperience rather than his experience that made the headlines. He had never practiced law, never argued a case. After graduating law school in 1951, he took a job in the Criminal Division of the Justice Department that lasted less than six months and then resigned to manage JFK's successful Senatorial campaign against Henry Cabot Lodge.

Next came his service on Senator Joseph R. McCarthy's Permanent Investigations Subcommittee, where he worked under Francis Flanagan, an ex-FBI agent, and made headlines when he documented the number of Allied ships trading with Communist China. William V. Shannon, a severe McCarthy critic, has observed, "This was the only major episode of McCarthy's tenure in which Kennedy was involved and it was not an example of McCarthyism," involving primarily the traditional split between the executive, which has to negotiate with foreign countries, and the legislature, whose belligerents traditionally take a hard line in times of "national emergency" like the Korean "police action."

Kennedy quit the committee when Roy Cohn, with whom he had personality differences, was made staff director. Characteristically, his main objections to Cohn at the time were not that Cohn's witness-badgering tactics were careless with other people's lives but that he didn't do his homework. Kennedy worked briefly for the Hoover Commission (his father was a member) studying the reorganization of the government, and a few months thereafter rejoined the McCarthy subcommittee as Minority Counsel to the Democrats, who had walked out and returned in time for the Army–McCarthy hearings. Six years later, when it was politically congenial to do so but before he had an inkling that he might be named Attorney General in his brother's

Administration, he wrote of the McCarthy committee in *The Enemy Within*:

> With two exceptions no real research was ever done. Most of the investigations were instituted on the basis of some preconceived notion by the chief counsel or his staff members and not on the basis of any information that they had developed. Cohn and Schine claimed they knew from the outset what was wrong; and they were not going to allow the facts to interfere. Therefore no real spadework that might have destroyed some of their pet theories was ever undertaken. I thought Senator McCarthy made a mistake in allowing the Committee to operate in such a fashion and I told him.

Kennedy's service on the McCarthy committee, then, was nothing to be ashamed of. But neither was it a qualification for the office of Attorney General. The issue it raises is not how he behaved but why he took the job in the first place, especially since his brother Jack had argued against it. Joe McCarthy was a family friend, had dated sister Pat and had even cracked a rib in a Kennedy family touch football game. But he had also—prior to Robert Kennedy's joining him—waved his famous piece of paper in Wheeling, West Virginia ("I have here in my hand . . ."), with the names of "205 card-carrying Communists and fellow travelers," had maligned General George C. Marshall, had hinted that Adlai Stevenson was a traitor and had generally behaved in a way that should have put young Kennedy on notice as to the Senator's character. Undoubtedly the prospect of headline investigations, joining the holy crusade against Communism and going to work for a family friend were too much to resist. It should be noted that even in his after-the-fact critique, Kennedy objected not to the shabby treatment of witnesses and possible violation of individual rights but rather to the hit-and-miss nature of the investigations and the sloppiness of the staffwork.

With the election of 1954, Senator John McClellan inherited the committee chairmanship from McCarthy and named the 29-year-old Kennedy as Chief Counsel of what became known as the Rackets Committee two years later when McClellan launched his nationally televised probe into crime and corruption in the union movement. By most measurements the investigation was a smashing success. It uncovered corruption in fifteen unions and fifty companies and led to the passage of a major piece of labor-reform legislation—the Landrum–Griffin bill. Among those toppled as a direct result of its finds were Dave Beck of the Teamsters, Dave Cross from the Bakers, William E. Maloney of the Operating Engineers, and the president and secretary-treasurer of the Textile Workers Union. It alerted the country to what Robert Kennedy called "the conspiracy of evil," it made the name Kennedy a household word, and it helped John F. Kennedy obtain the Democratic nomination (he was one of the Senators on the committee and instrumental in drafting parts of the labor-reform bill). In supervising a staff of fifty-five, compiling a record of 11,000,000 words at a cost of $1,500,-000, Robert Kennedy displayed energy, drive, zeal, imagination, the ability to get a job done—qualities that were, of course, confirmed by his work in his brother's various political campaigns. He won the loyalty of his staff, whom he inspired to a round-the-clock effort.

Old Joe Kennedy had been the chief lobbyist urging a skeptical John Kennedy to appoint his brother Robert Attorney General. The senior Kennedy's arguments were that nobody knew more about organized crime and labor corruption than Bobby, that his work on the McClellan committee was superb training for using the anti-trust laws to manipulate the business structure, that a Cabinet officer's main job is to administer and organize (Bobby's specialty) and that the President needed somebody outside the White House who wouldn't be afraid to tell him the truth.

Robert Kennedy himself was not enthusiastic. He had talked of a job in the Defense Department, where he could "ramrod the missile program through" (one of JFK's big campaign themes was the Republican-made "missile gap"), but his brother-in-law Sargent Shriver pointed out that Robert McNamara, the new Secretary of Defense but a stranger to the Kennedys, did not seem like the kind of fellow who would take kindly to the President's brother looking over his shoulder. There was talk of a White House job, but that was unpopular with JFK's staff, who correctly judged that their direct access to the President might be compromised, since Robert would be the natural communications channel. When Connecticut's Governor Abraham Ribicoff, who had first refusal rights on the Attorney Generalship, let it be known that he wasn't really interested (he foresaw the civil rights turbulence and didn't think there was much social utility in a Jew serving in the least popular political job in the country), Ambassador Kennedy went to work on the President-elect and suggested he float a trial balloon on Robert's behalf via *The New York Times*. A couple of days later, JFK went golfing in Palm Springs with *New York Times*man William Lawrence, now with ABC-TV; a page-one story followed, and when the negative outcry was loud but not deafening, he decided to heed his father's advice.

Early on the morning of December 20, Robert Kennedy, accompanied by his friend John Seigenthaler, a reporter for the Nashville

Tennessean who had exposed Teamster corruption, helped Kennedy write *The Enemy Within* and taken a leave of absence from his paper to work on the JFK campaign, made his way through the deep Georgetown snow to the John Kennedy house, where he would tell his brother his decision. But when they arrived John Kennedy started saying he didn't really know anybody in the Cabinet. Of all of them, the closest was Ribicoff, who the President-elect said "is a friend but we were never intimate." He said it was going to take a strong man to tell the President what he needed to be told. He mentioned that as long as he was going to take the rap for civil rights he might as well get the credit. He started to tell how Stevenson had agreed to the UN post when Robert said, "Let's talk about me." Then, says Seigenthaler, "the two brothers had a very personal conversation, brother to brother, man to man. And Johnny said, 'I've got to have you. I need the help of my brother more than I need anyone else.' It was almost a direct order. When he finished he said, 'All right, General, let's grab our b---- and go,' and they went into the kitchen. Then he said, 'So okay? Dillon is going to be here at two o'clock, and we want to announce both together. Will you be here?' And it was settled."

There were a lot of jokes about how the announcement would be made at two A.M. and JFK would tell the press, "I need him" (echoing Ike's famous ineffective lament for the outgoing Sherman Adams); later, the President asked as a quip what was wrong with giving Bobby a little legal experience before he practiced law. The TV commentators talked "nepotism," satirist Richard R. Lingeman reported that Assistant U.S. Attorney Edward M. Kennedy (then under thirty) had turned down the post of Chief Justice of the U.S. Supreme Court, and Yale law professor Alexander Bickel, who in 1968 was to campaign for Presidential candidate Robert Kennedy in California, wrote in *The New Republic* that "On the record, Robert F. Kennedy is not fit for the office." *The New York Times* editorialized that "The one appointment thus far that we find most disappointing is Mr. Kennedy's choice of younger brother Robert as Attorney General. . . ." He had, by most accounts, been an overzealous prosecutor and an underexperienced attorney, without the breadth to take on so important a post. His affection for the late Senator Joe McCarthy and his closeness to the Catholic Church were further grounds for suspicion in the non-Catholic intellectual community. The Attorney General, after all, said Bickel, is the "keeper of the executive conscience," the nation's chief law officer.

In fact, Kennedy's work with the Rackets Committee, like his work with the McCarthy committee, served as a warning signal rather than a stop sign, and the issue was soon academic as old Joe's logic won the day and Robert Kennedy became the sixty-fourth Attorney General of the United States. But the objections raise the question: By what criteria should an Attorney General be judged? Since the purpose of what follows is to explore a process rather than rate a performance, the issue is not central, although it raises a nice point where Robert Kennedy is concerned. Any checklist of what to look for in an Attorney General would have to include the quality of his executive and judicial appointments, his legal and administrative expertise, his personal integrity, his impact on the development of law and on the office itself, his record with Congress and the courts, his response to crises, the quality of his opinions, his sense of national priorities, his sense of justice.

But ultimately the test of any Cabinet officer—usually as a result of his ranking high on most of the above—is his ability to win the confidence of and exert influence on the President, qualities with which Robert Kennedy started out in the first place. As a result, the natural tendency was to focus on his status as the President's brother and to overlook the fact that he was also beset by the same conflicts and confrontations that greet any policy-maker who tries to influence the bureaucracy, with its vested interest in the status quo. He had to face the same collision of principles as any law enforcement officer who tries to adjust the demands of law-in-the-abstract with the realities of politics and power. And he had the same dilemmas as any public servant who tries to reconcile his private values and personal loyalties with public standards.

The tendency, on the eve of his attorney generalship, was to assume that Robert Kennedy would do his brother's bidding. A clue to what lay ahead, however, was available in the event that some analysts credit with putting JFK over the top. It will be recalled that in October 1960 Dr. Martin Luther King was sentenced without bail to six months in a Georgia prison on a traffic violation. Candidate John F. Kennedy called Dr. King's pregnant wife, Coretta, to express his sympathy and good will. Campaign manager Robert Kennedy called the judge, and Dr. King was released the next day.

PART ONE

The Code of
the FBI

CHAPTER ONE

Secrecy:
The Director and the General

Each had a law degree but neither had practiced law. J. Edgar Hoover, armed with a degree from George Washington University's night school (he worked days cataloguing new books at the Library of Congress), began his career by securing a clerkship in the Justice Department. Robert F. Kennedy, 56th in his class of 123 at the University of Virginia Law School, where his major academic achievement was a term paper attacking the "sell out" at Yalta, went to work in the Justice Department's Internal Security Section, then a part of the Criminal Division.

Each got his real start fighting subversion. In one hundred days in 1919 Hoover helped put together 60,000 political dossiers on radicals and anarchists—a prelude to the notorious "Red raids" of Attorney General A. Mitchell Palmer. Kennedy, restless at the Justice Department, where an office mate reports he would leave his pay checks uncashed in his desk drawer, thus forever fouling up the departmental budgetary system, soon moved over to the Communist-hunting (Joe) McCarthy Committee. While neither Hoover nor Kennedy either condoned or can be blamed for the excesses of their respective superiors, both found the super-patriotic environment of the work congenial.

Each had assumed a position of high responsibility at an early age.

In 1924 Attorney General Harlan Fiske Stone, at the recommendation of Herbert Hoover, asked J. Edgar Hoover (no relation) to head the FBI—then called the Bureau of Investigation—at age twenty-nine. Don Whitehead, the FBI's official biographer, confirms the legend that he accepted on "certain conditions": "The Bureau must be divorced from political hacks. Appointments must be based on merit. Second, promotions will be made on proved ability and the Bureau will be responsible only to the Attorney General." Attorney General Stone is reported to have replied, "I wouldn't give it to you under any other conditions. That's all. Good day."

Robert Kennedy was sworn in as Attorney General at age thirty-five. Before he agreed to take the job he conferred with his former Rackets Committee boss, Senator John McClellan (who pointed out that if he took the job it could hurt his brother), his friend Supreme Court Justice William O. Douglas, with whom he had journeyed through the Soviet Union (who said he might find more fulfillment doing something else and suggested a sabbatical), Attorney General William Rogers (who told him it was a lousy job—"You spend all your time arguing about who's going to be a judge and worrying about what anti-trust cases to bring") and J. Edgar Hoover, who encouraged him to take it (but Kennedy told his aide John Seigenthaler that he didn't really think Hoover meant it).

Each made his name chasing gangsters and hoodlums. In the Thirties, Hoover went after and bagged such public enemies as John Dillinger, Baby Face Nelson, Ma Barker and Machine Gun Kelly. Kennedy, aiming his sights at *The Enemy Within*, the title of his first book, used his position as Chief Counsel of Senator McClellan's Rackets Committee (on which Senator John F. Kennedy served) to expose such public enemies as Tony "Ducks" Corallo, Johnny Dio, Jimmy Hoffa, Dave Beck, the Gallo brothers, Tony Provenzano.

Each had what others might—and did—call an obsession about personal toughness and courage. In April 1936, when Senator Kenneth McKellar accused Hoover of taking the glory but not the risks, the FBI chief flew to New Orleans and personally supervised the capture of Alvin "Creepy" Karpis. (But when he gave the command "Put the cuffs on him, boys," it turned out, to the embarrassment of all, that the boys had forgotten the handcuffs, so they ended up using an agent's tie. Today that tie is available for viewing in the FBI museum.) Kennedy, who once offered to punch it out with one of the Gallo brothers and continuously engaged in a variety of physical endurance contest against the elements, characteristically ruminated on the way home from a specially arranged dinner meeting (his first) with Jimmy Hoffa at the home of a law associate of Edward Bennett Williams that Hoffa wasn't so tough after all:

> I thought of how often Hoffa had said he was tough: that he destroyed employers, hated policemen and broke those who stood in his way. It had always been my feeling that if a person was truly tough, if he actually had strength and power; if he really had the ability to excel, he need not brag and boast of it to prove it.

Hoover was a super-administrator and Kennedy was fast becoming one. Hoover took the Bureau of Investigation, an agency shot through with corruption, apathy and demoralization after the Teapot Dome scandals of the Harding Administration, and built it into what is generally regarded as the least corruptible and most sophisticated investigative agency in the world, the Federal Bureau of Investigation (the "Federal" was added to the title in 1935). His first year on the job he set up the Identification Division, including the Central Fingerprint Repository, which now contains over 81 million American fingerprints. In 1932 he established the FBI Crime Laboratory, in 1935 the FBI Academy at Quantico, and in 1939, at the direction of President Franklin D. Roosevelt, he inaugurated from scratch America's efficient and effective wartime internal-security and counter-espionage program. He set up such effective information retrieval systems as the National Fraudulent Check File, the National Automobile Altered Numbers File, the National Paint Standards File and the National Typewriter File. Kennedy, after piloting JFK to a series of record-breaking Congressional and Senatorial victories, created, organized and managed the juggernaut political organization which won for his brother the Democratic Party's Presidential nomination on the first ballot in Los Angeles in August 1960 and elected the nation's first Catholic President in November.

Both were puritanical and moralistic in their pronouncements about vice, prostitution and obscenity. Hoover made speeches about "smut peddlers" and Kennedy gave the green light to the prosecution of Ralph Ginzburg, publisher of "The Housewife's Handbook of Selective Promiscuity" and *Eros*, "A magazine devoted to the joys of love and sex."

Hoover was a long-time friend of Robert Kennedy's father, Ambassador Joseph P. Kennedy. Hoover had cooperated (with Special Agent Courtney Evans as liaison) with Robert Kennedy's Rackets investigations and in 1960 sent the young Chief Counsel an adulatory telegram on the occasion of his first "Meet the Press" appearance, advising

him that he was destined for great things. After the election it was
Ambassador Kennedy who advised the President-elect that if he were
going to keep Hoover (and Allen Dulles, head of the CIA) he might
as well make a virtue of it. Along with Kennedy family friend James M.
Landis, commissioned to do a study of federal regulatory agencies (he
was later criminally prosecuted by Robert Kennedy on tax-evasion
charges), they were President Kennedy's first appointments.

Yet it was inevitable that thirty-five-year-old Robert Kennedy, the
maximum Attorney General, should clash with sixty-six-year-old J. Edgar Hoover, the ultimate bureaucrat. For Kennedy, prevailing clichés
to the contrary, was less result-oriented than action-oriented. And
Hoover, as Joseph Kraft shrewdly observed in *Profiles in Power*, was
less ideologically motivated than bureaucratically motivated—an insight subsequently documented by Tom Wicker of *The New York
Times* and Richard Harwood of the Washington *Post* and a small but
growing band of Hoover-watchers in the press. Inaction is, of course, the
last refuge of the professional bureaucrat. "You can't get in trouble by
doing nothing," says Jack Miller by way of partial explanation. Miller
was the Republican, anti-Hoffa member of the Teamster's Board of
Monitors * whom Kennedy named Assistant Attorney General in
charge of the Criminal Division.

The dimensions of the encounter should not be underestimated.
Robert Kennedy had behind him much of the power of the Presidency.
But to take on Hoover meant to take on the whole Federal Bureau
of Investigation, since Hoover, more than any other man in Washington, is identified with—indeed, is indistinguishable from—his agency.
"Let me reiterate my oft-stated position," Hoover wrote in response to
a remark of Governor Grant Sawyer of Nevada that he had not attacked Hoover but just the local FBI, "that as long as I am Director
of this Bureau, any attack upon an FBI employee who is conscien-
tiously carrying out his official duties will be considered an attack on
me personally." It is not a unique strategy, but it is an effective one.
As Robert Michels observed in his classic study *Political Parties:*

> The Bureaucrat identifies himself completely with the organization,
> confounding his own interests with its interests. All objective criticism
> of the organization is taken by him as a personal affront . . . the
> leader declares himself personally offended, doing this partly in good
> faith, but in part deliberately, in order to shift the battleground, so
> that he can present himself as the harmless object of an unwarrantable

* A court-appointed, three-man board to supervise Teamster Union activities,
established in 1958.

attack. . . . If on the other hand the leader is attacked personally, his first care is to make it appear that the attack is directed against the party as a whole. He does this not only on diplomatic grounds, in order to secure for himself the support of the party and to overwhelm the aggressor with the weight of numbers, but also because he quite ingenuously takes the part for the whole.[1]

Not many people realize, moreover, that the FBI accounts for 41 percent of the Justice Department's budget and 42 percent of its manpower. Since it can plausibly be argued that the Bureau's influence exceeds its numbers by at least 10 percent, as much as one half of the Attorney General's job has to do with making the traditionally autonomous Bureau responsive to the will of the Administration. By the same token, it is the Director's job to resist political pressures and to maintain the professionalization of his agency. When James V. Bennett, retired Director of the Justice Department's Bureau of Prisons, was asked to pinpoint the greatest single problem confronting an Attorney General, he stated, "They all have the same problem—the control and management of J. Edgar Hoover." By 1961, when Robert Kennedy became Attorney General, the FBI was charged with investigating more than 160 federal matters ranging from anti-trust and auto theft to espionage. So how it sees itself, what it *chooses* to emphasize, what cases it puts its best agents on, become critical.

The psychological aspect of the relationship Kennedy and Hoover shared is perhaps best left to those who knew both men,* but two observations are nevertheless worth offering at the outset. First, Mr. Kennedy and Mr. Hoover had different styles, different values, differ-

* I would be remiss, however, if I did not take note even at this remove, perhaps *because* of this remove, that Mr. Hoover seems to possess a constellation of those traits which usually are thought to come together in the authoritarian personality. (I use the term in a value-neutral sense rather than as an index to ideology.) It is worth remarking only because it may give some insight into the structure of the FBI with which Mr. Hoover is so closely identified. Certainly he is, in Else Frenkel-Brunswick's phrase, "intolerant of ambiguity." In the Bureau, everything is by the numbers and everything is on paper.

As Professor Fred Greenstein lists authoritarian character traits they include: ". . . dominance of subordinates; deference toward superiors; sensitivity to power relationships; need to perceive the world in a highly structured fashion; excessive use of stereotypes; and adherence to whatever values are conventional in one's setting."

The authoritarian is also said to be preoccupied with virility, his assumptions about human nature are pessimistic, he tends to be cynical about the motives of others and he is disposed to believe that "wild and dangerous things go on in the world"—that the world "is a jungle." He shows a puritanical preoccupation with "Sexual 'goings on' " and he is impatient with the tender-minded, the subjective.

Mr. Hoover's world is bounded on the left by the menace of "atheistic Communism" and on the right by muggings, murders and rapes, which are ticked off second by second on the FBI crime clocks. He literally has a direct line from his home to the White House and insists on absolute discipline in FBI ranks.

ent power bases and different commitments, which likely predetermined the tension that characterized their relationship. Second, while Mr. Kennedy, as a vast literature on the subject indicates, was in transit, Mr. Hoover and his Bureau were implanted. This was true institutionally, but it was also true personally. Robert Kennedy was evolving. Hoover was encrusted. Besides, the Director and his organization were there first. As the FBI Tour Guide used to say (until Kennedy found out about it), "Mr. Hoover became the Director of the Bureau in 1924, the year before the Attorney General was born." So the burden was always on Kennedy. Did he wish to intrude on existing Bureau practices? How much innovation would he strive for, how much accommodation would he accept? In other words, differences of personality as well as differences of policy, from the Kennedy perspective, surfaced as questions of tactics. To understand what Kennedy was up against, it is less important to psychoanalyze Hoover than to analyze his organization, the FBI.

When he resigned as Attorney General to run for Senator from New York in September 1964, the informed consensus of the working press was that one of the more singular aspects of Robert Kennedy's reign had been his success in harnessing J. Edgar Hoover and the FBI. James F. Clayton wrote in the Washington *Post*: "No other Attorney General in 30 years has been able to impose his will on Hoover. Kennedy was able to do so largely because of his relationship to the President. . . ." Anthony Lewis reported in *The New York Times* that "He made the first real effort in years to bring the Federal Bureau of Investigation and its powerful Director, J. Edgar Hoover, under effective direction and to turn the FBI's attention to such law enforcement problems as civil rights and organized crime." Lewis added, "Whatever ability Mr. Kennedy had to move Mr. Hoover stemmed obviously from the fact that his brother was President. . . ." James Wechsler said in the New York *Post* that "During the regimes of several distinguished Attorneys General, the Justice Department's subservience to J. Edgar Hoover was a local joke. Robert Kennedy changed all that. . . ."

The truth of the proposition is beyond doubt. Kennedy pushed the Bureau past the point of no return in civil rights and organized crime. Burke Marshall, Kennedy's introspective Assistant Attorney General in charge of civil rights, stresses that by 1963 the whole federal government had changed its attitude toward civil rights, but recalls, "When I got there the FBI had three agents in Mississippi. When I left there were 153." When Kennedy arrived, Hoover did not believe there was such a thing as a national crime syndicate. In 1962 he stated that "no single individual or coalition of racketeers dominates organized crime across the nation." When Kennedy left, Hoover was taking credit for the discovery of the Cosa Nostra. In September of 1963, he wrote in the FBI's *Law Enforcement Bulletin* that the sensational Valachi disclosures merely "corroborated and embellished the facts developed by the FBI as early as 1961 which disclosed the makeup of the gangland hordes." "At first it was like pulling teeth to get the Bureau to enter these areas," recalls a Kennedy assistant, "but by 1963 all that had changed."

It is arguable, however, that the influence of Hoover and the Bureau on the Department and Kennedy was at least as great as, if less visible than, the influence of Kennedy and the Department on Hoover and the Bureau. And although Kennedy and his "riot squad," as his energetic staff were once termed, were resourceful in making the Bureau more responsive to Justice Department policy, ultimately the FBI was equally successful in limiting and perhaps even diminishing Robert Kennedy's vision of the possible. When militant critics of Kennedy's civil rights policy like Pat Watters and Reese Cleghorn write in *Climbing Jacob's Ladder*, their moving and passionate study of the anti-segregation movement, that Kennedy "made a decision . . . to keep the FBI away from the kind of apprehension and arrest actions [in civil rights cases] that it constantly engaged in when bank robberies or auto thefts were involved . . ." [2] they are telling only a three-quarter truth. The FBI always had that policy. What Kennedy & Co. really decided, consciously or otherwise, was *not to attempt to change the Bureau's pre-existing policy*. This is a distinction that is not without a difference.

Organizations—public and private—tend to develop purposes and "bureaucratic truths" of their own. John Kenneth Galbraith has eloquently reminded us, "What is done and what is believed are, first and naturally, what serve the goals of the bureaucracy itself." [3] The FBI is no exception to Galbraith's rule. Robert Kennedy's strategy in attempting to cope with those situations where the Bureau's interests conflicted with the Kennedy interests was a policy of unconfrontation. Collision-avoidance was in the Administration's interest. "Bob never sat down with the Director and read him the riot act—that's not the way it worked," says a colleague.

The General didn't fear to challenge the Director to specific skirmishes, but none of them was of a magnitude to change the essential balance of power within the Department. Mr. Hoover was the hedgehog (to borrow Isaiah Berlin's useful terminology) with one big idea, the preservation of business as usual. Mr. Kennedy was the fox, with lots of little ideas, like halfway houses for juvenile delinquents (Hoover called them "young punks" [4]), sentencing and bail reform (Hoover thought they were the "maudlin proposals" of "misguided sentimentalists"), closing Alcatraz because it was outmoded, expensive and a penological anachronism (Hoover believed we needed a maximum-security hellhole as a deterrent to crime), commuting the sentence of convicted ex-Communist Junius Scales (Hoover believed that the litmus test of repentance was to "name names," a confidence Scales wouldn't violate), surfacing Cosa Nostra informer Joseph Valachi (Hoover believed that the identity of an informant should never be revealed) or setting up an independent national crime commission (Hoover thought it would lead to a national police force). Sometimes Kennedy prevailed and sometimes he didn't, but always his policy decision was made in the environment of the Bureau's organizational preferences.

Once, at the suggestion of a number of liberal Democrats (including Senator Paul Douglas of Illinois and California Attorney General Stanley Mosk), the Kennedy Justice Department suggested to the FBI that in compiling criminal records it indicate whenever an arrest had grown out of a non-violent racial demonstration. That way "innocent" college kids would not have to go through life with the stigma of an unexplained police record. A Civil Rights Division memorandum describing what happened gives a good picture of the way in which the Bureau was able to frustrate action when it chose to:

> On July 12 we conferred with Mr. Rosen and other officials of the FBI including Assistant Director Trotter, who is in charge of the Bureau's identification Division concerning the suggestion that the Bureau, in compiling criminal records, include appropriate notations regarding arrests and convictions growing out of non-violent racial demonstrations. . . .
> Mr. Barrett suggested that since the names of most of those persons arrested in racial demonstrations are already contained in memoranda supplied by the FBI to the Civil Rights Division, the task involved seemed only to compile a list of arrested demonstrators together with the dates and locations of their arrests and convictions. . . .
> The FBI officials present were uniformly opposed to undertaking any such project. They made the following specific observations:
> 1) The furnishing of such information by this Department is unnecessary since it could be supplied by the person involved when he listed his background on whatever application he submitted that led to the inquiry concerning his criminal record. . . . The FBI representatives contended that all local authorities (including Jackson, Mississippi, where hostility to racial demonstrators is great . . .) will disclose the circumstances of an arrest. They also observed that the

criminal identification service is designed only to provide "leads" whereby agencies can be guided to more complete sources of information.

2) The identity of persons listed in racial information memoranda provided this Division is not based upon fingerprint data as are all other FBI reports therefore you couldn't correlate with certainty.

3) Lists are incomplete therefore it's a disservice to the demonstrator whose arrest has not come to the Bureau's attention.

4) The Bureau would have to interpret whether a demonstration was "violent" or not and this would change the character of the information supplied. It would involve a qualitative judgment.

5) The Bureau objected to the administrative burden. They said the Civil Rights Division had the information therefore the Civil Rights Division could make it available.

As an alternative, the Bureau official suggested that local officials might be requested to include a notation "C.R. Dem" beside a report of an arrest submitted to the FBI, in which event the Bureau would in turn so report to any inquiry . . . it usually being the Bureau's practice to transmit the record exactly as received.

The merits aside, it was a typical encounter between the Department and the Bureau—an ostensibly simple request engulfed in a morass of organizational resistance. Multiply that a few thousand times and one gets some idea of what happened when the much publicized Kennedy charisma confronted the little-understood Hoover organization. But to understand the chemistry of that confrontation one must inspect the organization—its structure, its style, its assumptions, its sources of power.

Even before Kennedy took the job, Mr. Hoover's negative attitude toward Kennedy's proposal for a national crime commission, which was advanced by the McClellan Committee and which he had included in his book *The Enemy Within*, put him on notice as to what he was up against. Robert Kennedy's only credential to be Attorney General was his experience as an investigator of organized crime and labor corruption. And his only program was a result of that experience, which he set forth in *The Enemy Within*, published in late 1960:

In my opinion . . . our first and most urgent need is for a national crime commission. This commission would serve as a central intelligence agency, a clearinghouse to which each of the seventy-odd Federal agencies and the more than ten thousand local law enforcement agencies throughout the country would constantly feed information on the leading gangsters. The commission would pool and correlate all its information on underworld figures and disseminate it to the proper authorities. . . .

This was not the top-of-the-head plan of an amateur author in search of a sensational ending. It was a thoughtful proposal, born out of months of frustration at the nationwide shortage of information in the crime field, and it had the support of men like the captain of the Los Angeles Police Department and New York's distinguished District Attorney, Frank Hogan. His message was clear and ominous:

> Only through a national network can we fight the widespread penetration by criminals into our economy. Its members, appointed by the President, should be nationally prominent, of unquestionable integrity, and experienced in opposing crime. It would not be a national police, but a national information service for local police. . . . The point I want to make is this: If we do not on a national scale attack organized criminals with weapons and techniques as effective as their own, they will destroy us.

Yet less than a year later, when Senator Estes Kefauver asked at Robert Kennedy's confirmation hearing whether he would be in favor of a bill to establish "some kind of a National Crime Advisory Committee" that would "not interfere with or supersede but will work with the FBI and as a clearinghouse and study group to get information and coordinate it," Robert Kennedy said:

> I have felt for some time that such an institution is necessary; an intelligence group to attack organized crime as we deal with Communism and subversion here and in the U.S.
> Mr. Hoover, for whom I have tremendous respect, has not been enthusiastic for the idea as it has been proposed. I had some conversations and discussions with him, as well as Mr. Anslinger from the Bureau of Narcotics and some of the people who will be over in the Internal Revenue Service. And I think that we have worked out an arrangement whereby we can all work together to attack organized crime here in the U.S., and I would hope that this would go along, would evolve over the period of the next year or so, and we could then see what was necessary as far as any supplemental legislation to set up a crime commission.

What had happened was that Robert Kennedy had unwittingly challenged one of the Bureau's favorite bureaucratic truths: that there is no such thing as a national crime syndicate. If there is no national criminal conspiracy, then there is no need for a national crime commission. Besides, according to official rationale, such a commission could lead to a national police force, and as Mr. Hoover told the International Association of Chiefs of Police in 1960, "nothing could be more dangerous to our democracy."

Nobody has yet satisfactorily explained why, after the revelations of the Kefauver Committee in the early Fifties and the shock of the mass mobster gathering at Apalachin, New York, in 1957, the Bureau was so seemingly unconcerned about the prevalence and effect of organized crime that it was still relying on a clipping service for its information on the subject when Kennedy took over. Among the hypotheses: The Bureau was not structured to deal with organized crime. It was structured to investigate complaints, but there are few organized-crime complaints because of *omerta* (the underworld code of silence) and the fact that most people injured by organized crime (vice, gambling, narcotics) are already implicated in something illegal and therefore reluctant to report it. A second theory is that the Bureau's preoccupation with impressive statistical batting averages for display at appropriations time led to the avoidance of the long-drawn-out investigations organized crime requires and concentration instead on such easily quantifiable, open-and-shut crimes as auto thefts and bank robberies. Third, it is suggested that Hoover, whose Bureau had an almost perfect record of incorruptibility, was reluctant to expose his agents to the blandishments of fixers and corrupters—the hallmark of syndicated crime. Fourth, there is the matter of *hubris*—if the Bureau, with its ultra-effective detection apparatus, didn't know about it, how could it exist? Finally, the Bureau's jurisdiction in the area was not explicit. A by-product of the anti-crime legislation which Kennedy pushed through in 1961 was that the new, explicit authorization gave the FBI a face-saving rationalization for past inactivity. Until then the implicit organizational truth on the subject was that if it is outside our jurisdiction, as far as we are concerned it doesn't exist.

The real reason for Mr. Hoover's attitude can only be conjectured on here, but the fact was indisputable. The late Luther Huston, Public Information Director under then Attorney General (and now Secretary of State) Rogers and former Washington correspondent for *The New York Times,* recalled stopping off to say goodbye to Hoover, whom he had come to know and admire, around the time Kennedy was moving in. "I had arranged to see him at a particular time but I had to wait because the new Attorney General was there. He hadn't called or made an appointment. He had just barged in. You don't do that with Mr. Hoover. Then my turn came and I'll tell you the maddest man I ever talked to was J. Edgar Hoover. He was steaming. If I could have printed what he said, I'd have had a scoop. Apparently Kennedy wanted to set up some kind of supplementary or overlapping group to take over some of the investigative work that the FBI had been doing. My surmise is that Mr. Hoover told Bobby, 'If you're going to do that, I can retire tomorrow. My pension is waiting.' Robert Kennedy wouldn't want to be responsible for being the man who caused Hoover to leave the Justice Department."

Kennedy quickly abandoned his proposed commission, but at the same time undertook to transfer its functions to a relatively anonymous unit in the Criminal Division, the Organized Crime Section. It was symbolic that in his only area of unquestioned expertise and commitment, the General—on the surface—had yielded to the Director.

At the height of the freedom-rider crisis, the General buzzed the Director on the intercom which connected their two offices. "Edgar," he asked, "how many agents do we have in Birmingham?" "We have enough," Hoover answered, "we have enough." And then, according to one Assistant Attorney General sitting in Kennedy's office at the time, "A torrent of words came out. Mr. Hoover is a filibusterer. This torrent of words would keep coming but he didn't tell us how many agents he had there. I don't know if he knew, but he never wanted us to know. It was his secret."

The FBI, like the Mafia and the Ku Klux Klan, is a secret society. Like all secret societies, its organization is rigidly hierarchical—all communications go up from the agents (there were about 6,000 of them) to the Special Agent in Charge (there are field offices in fifty-eight larger cities and "resident agencies" in about five hundred smaller cities) to the "seat of government," as both Hoover and FBI literature refer to his Washington headquarters on the fifth floor of the U.S. Department of Justice building.

This caused a problem. "If Bob Kennedy wanted to know something," says a former agent, "he'd call you and ask you. That violated the system. No Attorney General had ever done that before. You weren't supposed to communicate with the Attorney General. You were supposed to send a memo to your SAC [Special Agent in Charge], he would pass it on to the Director, and Mr. Hoover would communicate with the Attorney General." As Nicholas Katzenbach noted, the FBI system meant that the radio and "ticker" (jargon for the AP and UPI wire services) were often as much as thirty minutes ahead of the Director—a constant source of irritation to the fast-moving Kennedy team.

Like other secret-society members, FBI personnel adhere to a strict code of personal conduct, enforced by the threat of swift, unappealable punishment. With the exception of the Director of the CIA, Hoover is alone in the federal bureaucracy in possessing the power to fire at will. All other agencies are under Civil Service and/or have to give thirty days' notice, can dismiss only for cause and must provide appeals procedures. The FBI novice is instructed in the art of silence—a twelve-week training course at Quantico, Virginia, teaches, among other things, that an agent never volunteers information. And the official manual advises moderation in alcohol (Hoover takes one Jack Daniel's before dinner [5]), gambling (Hoover, a racing fan, claims never to bet more than $2), sex (one FBI man, who contested the matter in court, was summarily dismissed when it was discovered that he spent the night with a girl in his room) and credit. Agents are expected to dress in conservative suits with color-coordinated tie and socks and to report anything that might embarrass the Bureau (such as divorce, an auto accident, the indiscretion of a fellow agent). Agents are always accountable for their time, and when he comes to work as well as when he departs, the FBI man signs a "number 3" card on which he writes the file number of the case he is working on, his time of departure, his expected time of return and the name of the contact he is making. Ronald Goldfarb, a young attorney with the Organized Crime Section of Justice, recalls that in order to put in a respectable amount of out-of-office time for the record, one agent would do his in-office paperwork on a bench outside Goldfarb's office. When asked why, the agent said, "So I can get credit for out-of-office contacts."

The late Georg Simmel, the leading authority on the sociology of secret societies ranging from the Gallic Druids to the Italian Carbonari to the Elks, reported that "There are perhaps no other external traits which are so typical of the secret society . . . than the high valuation of usages, formulas, and rites." He added that "Sometimes the contents [of a group's activities] are less anxiously guarded than is the secret of the ritual." FBI codes and usages (see Chapter II) help explain the misunderstanding between the Director and the General over the Bureau's electronic eavesdropping practices. From mid-1961 to 1964 and after, the Bureau furnished the Department with detailed intelligence reports, some of which are just now finding their way into print, in the organized-crime area. They would often commence: "T-1, a usually reliable informant whose identity cannot be disclosed . . ." or "T-2, a reliable informant who is not available for reinterview . . ." The reports would then spell out gory tales of treachery, extortion and brutality. In 1966 William O. Bittman, a young government lawyer, advised Mitchell Rogovin, chief of the Tax Division, that these cryptic references were, at least in the case at hand (which involved Bobby

Baker's associate Fred Black), occasionally code words for electronic eavesdropping. Thurgood Marshall, then the Solicitor General, confessed the bugging to the U.S. Supreme Court, which was considering the case, and the Court sent the matter back to the Justice Department asking for full disclosure of who had authorized what and when.

The Bureau employs two separate languages. The first, for internal and interdepartmental communications, may be called Bureau-speak. It is cryptic, telegraphic and routine and its purpose is less to communicate than to anticipate, to make a record for future protection. "You can have a conversation with an agent," says Edwin O. Guthman, Kennedy's press secretary, "and when it is over he will send a memo to the files. Any relation between the memo and what was said in the conversation may be purely coincidental. You would think you were at different meetings."

Bureau-speak is often prepackaged on forms and rubber stamps. At the bottom of an FBI memorandum on the racial situation in Mississippi will appear the admonition

> This document contains neither recommendations nor the conclusions of the FBI. It is the property of the FBI and is loaned to your agency; it and its contents are not to be distributed outside the agency.

Or, at the close of a long memorandum signed by Hoover (as are all interagency Bureau memoranda) about the alleged interracial sexual indiscretions of a young Civil Rights Division lawyer, the reader who continues to the end may find that

> These allegations were not made directly to representatives of the FBI but were received through a third person. Thus the FBI is not in any position to comment upon the reliability of the source; however the source has furnished some other information, some of which is of a questionable nature which leaves considerable doubt as to the credibility of the source.

When the Attorney General asked the Bureau for background information on the anonymous sit-inners who walked in and occupied his office early in 1962 (one was a twenty-two-year-old named Stokely Carmichael), six reports came back and each was stamped

> Since neither fingerprints nor an identifying number which is indexed in our files accompanied your request, FBI cannot guarantee in any manner that this material concerns the individual in whom you are interested.

The corollary of Bureau-speak is Bureau-hear, wherein the FBI places a literalistic interpretation on anything said about it by an unauthorized person. For instance, in February 1967, when E. Barrett Prettyman, Jr., a Kennedy assistant who was by then a private attorney, asked a policeman on the witness stand, in a case he was trying, to define profligacy, Prettyman said, "Would . . . a person who gambles regularly . . . [be] leading a profligate life?" Yes, the policeman answered. Said Prettyman: "J. Edgar Hoover, for example, out at the race track on numerous occasions; would you consider that he's leading a profligate life?" "Yes," the policeman replied, "I would." The indefatigable Mr. Hoover read the exchange in the next day's paper and hastily dispatched a letter to Prettyman pointing out that he was not profligate and that the $2 bet was in the American tradition.

In striking contrast, the Bureau's second language, which we may call Hoover-speak, is distinguished by its clarity and is intended primarily for external consumption. An example would be Mr. Hoover's suggestion that the term "juvenile delinquency" be banished from the national vocabulary. "There are still among us," he wrote in the January 1961 issue of the FBI's *Law Enforcement Bulletin,* "muddle-headed sentimentalists who would wrap teenage brigands in the protective cocoon of the term 'juvenile delinquency' with emphasis upon all its connotations of youthful prankishness. . . . As a representative of law enforcement, I would like to see the term 'juvenile delinquency' banished forever from our language as a description for vicious acts. Such teenager gangsterism should be labeled for exactly what it is—'youthful criminality.' " In June 1961 Hoover came out against "misguided do-gooders," "maudlin viewers of the death penalty" and "Bible quoters who object to capital punishment." In November 1962 he called teen-age criminals "beastly punks" who laugh at "scholarly theories and misguided sentiment." His message: Punish, don't "coddle," which "is an appeasement of justice." A year later he told 4,500 CYO teenagers at a Hilton Hotel convention in New York that Communists should be banned from campus because their presence "has nothing to do with academic freedom."

It would not, of course, be fitting for a secret society to have a public-relations office, so the Bureau denies that it has one. It does, however, maintain something called the Office of Crime Records (one of ten FBI divisions, each headed by an Assistant Director), which prepares all of the Bureau's press releases, publishes a monthly *Law Enforcement Bulletin* (including a page 1 editorial from Mr. Hoover) and the controversial but useful Uniform Crime Reports (controversial because critics say they artificially inflate the level of criminal activity, useful because nobody puts out any more accurate ones), and

manages the famed FBI tours, which accommodate an estimated 700,-
ooo visitors annually. On one such tour, *Life* magazine's Loudon Wain-
right was provided a twenty-eight-page document,* which suggests one
of the differences between an Office of Crime Records and an Office
of Public Information. "During the past 30 years," it read, "the entire
complexion of law enforcement throughout the United States has
been changed primarily because of the principles advocated by Mr.
Hoover and successfully tried by law enforcement agencies." The last
twenty-two pages list Mr. Hoover's honorary degrees and include such
citations as: "Fearless fighter and implacable foe of the godless tyranny
of cancerous Communism . . . inspirational leader, champion of the
people, outstanding American."

While the Office of Crime Records will hand out this and other
literature, its primary job is to refuse requests for information from
all but a select few. During the Kennedy years the Bureau routinely
refused interviews to papers such as *The New York Times* and the *Wall
Street Journal* or to free-lance writers, while granting interviews to others
whose sympathies were less in doubt. Information is a commodity to be
exchanged for favors or a weapon with which to threaten; it is not something to be indiscriminately handed out on request.†

The secret society confers on its members both material and spiritual
rewards. New FBI agents start at a $11,517-per-annum salary. The
Secret Service and the Internal Revenue Service generally start their
new investigative agents at $6,981. The usual starting salaries for law-
yers throughout the government is $8,462. The CIA is said to start its
MAs and Ph.D.s at $8,000. (Although the numbers change with the
years, the ratio has remained constant.) The FBI pension system, which
took a great leap forward in 1947 when Congress unanimously passed a
special FBI Retirement Bill over the opposition of the Bureau of the
Budget, the Treasury Department, the Civil Service and the President,
is generous. When Courtney Evans, Hoover's liaison to the Attorney

* All I ever got was a used bullet.
† Note: In 1970 Mr. Hoover, started, for the first time, to experiment with
hostile media, granting interviews to *Time* magazine and the Washington *Post*. Subsequently Hoover suffered a deluge of press criticism, partly because he called Ramsey
Clark a "jellyfish"; partly because the extent of FBI surveillance activities—including
participants in Earth Day, 1970—was revealed; partly because at seventy-six he had
long since passed retirement age; partly because the FBI office in Media, Pennsylvania, was raided and its copious confidential files duplicated and to its escalating
embarrassment mailed to journalists throughout the country; partly because he forced
ex-agent Jack Shaw out of the Bureau for criticizing Hoover in a letter to one of
his professors. In addition, as Hoover became less of a sacred cow, more politicians
found the courage to oppose him openly; it has become something of a litmus test
among liberal Democratic Presidential hopefuls to call for his retirement.

General's office during the Kennedy years, retired from the Bureau (he was rumored to have been eased out after Kennedy's departure) his pension had an actuarial value of over a quarter of a million dollars.* Had he stayed on, it would have been worth close to half a million. This helps explain why an extraordinary 67 percent of the agents have been with the Bureau more than ten years. In the pre-pension days, the average length of service was under three years.

In addition, the Bureau advertises these and other of its benefits throughout the law-enforcement community through such institutions as the FBI National Academy, which trains law-enforcement officers from all fifty states on modern police procedure. "More than one quarter of all policemen who have taken this course," says the Office of Crime Records literature, "and remained in police work, are now executive heads of their own departments"—a statistic, one might note in passing, which *really* suggests the possibility of an informal national police force, in contrast to the official (but probably unwarranted) fears of a formal national police force inevitably growing out of FBI participation in such areas as civil rights.

Of course the real rewards the secret society holds out are psychological—namely, inclusion in the secret. "The secret gives one a position of exception," says Simmel. "From secrecy, which shades all that is profound and significant, grows the typical error according to which everything mysterious is something important and essential." In the Bureau's case, inclusion in the secret means access to five million individual files, including 426,000 "internal security" cases. Douglas Kiker, a former Washington correspondent and later a television newscaster, has pointed out that this is enough material to blackmail "or thoroughly embarrass half of America, and there are many who feel that the files would be extremely dangerous if they ever got into the wrong hands. . . . But the fact is that their size, their mystery and their very nature provide a built-in safeguard against any Gestapo-like use of them." [6] As Kiker notes, with a file on virtually every politician, it is not at all difficult to imagine what the reaction would be to evidence that the files were being improperly used.

The Director himself is, of course, the ultimate insider and his anecdotal style is admirably suited to his role as custodian of the oldest established permanent floating gossip column in town, the Bureau's

---

* An FBI agent may retire at age fifty after twenty years of service as an agent, and he receives about 40 percent of the average annual salary he was paid during his three highest salary years. The maximum retirement pay is 80 percent at the end of forty years of service. (See Don Whitehead, *The FBI Story: A Report to the People*, p. 128). This policy holds true for all federal law-enforcement positions.

files. As former Attorney General Francis Biddle recalls in his autobiography:

> I sought to invite his confidence and before long, lunching alone with me in a room adjoining my office, he began to reciprocate by sharing some of his extraordinary broad knowledge of the intimate details of what my associates in the Cabinet did and said, of their likes, their weaknesses and their associations. . . . I confess that within limits, I enjoyed hearing it. His reading of human nature was shrewd, if perhaps colored with the eye of an observer to whom the less admirable aspects of behavior were being constantly revealed.[7]

Secrecy surrounds the Bureau like a boundary. As a result, says one former career attorney at Justice, "When you deal with the Bureau it is like dealing with a foreign power, the Soviet Union. You never really know where you stand." A closer look at the freedom-rider episode helps uncover the causes for tension and the possibilities for cooperation between the Director, who was running a secret society, and the General, who was running a more or less open one.

It will be recalled that in May of 1961 the Congress of Racial Equality (CORE) organized an integrated group, dubbed them "freedom riders" and sent them forth on Trailways and Greyhound buses bound for points south. Their intention was to test and challenge segregation in bus terminals and facilities all the way from the District of Columbia to New Orleans.

Before it was over, twelve other freedom rides had commenced; a bus had been burned, windows broken and tires slashed in Anniston, Alabama; a mob of 1,000 met the riders with pipes, sticks and clubs and rioted in Montgomery, Alabama, where the Attorney General's special assistant, John Seigenthaler, who was doubling as the President's representative, had been knocked unconscious while trying to help Diane Nash, a Negro freedom rider, escape into a car; 600 federal marshals (including some specially deputized from the Border Patrol, the Alcohol and Tobacco Tax Unit, the Immigration and Naturalization Service and the Bureau of Prisons) were dispatched to Montgomery under the direction of Deputy Attorney General (now Supreme Court Justice) Byron White; Martin Luther King, Jr., flew in, only to find himself and his followers surrounded in a Montgomery church by an angry mob that was out to kill (U.S. marshals dispersed the crowd with tear gas and billy clubs); the Department of Justice asked for and obtained unprecedented court orders from Eisenhower appointee Judge Frank Johnson, enjoining the Ku Klux Klan, the National States Rights Party and the Birmingham and Montgomery police from interfering with interstate travel.

The Attorney General, after much telephoning to Alabama Governor John Patterson, who was mostly unavailable, Lieutenant Governor Albert Boutwell, who was mostly unbelievable, and the Director of Highway Safety, who was responsible but without much power, even called the Greyhound bus dispatcher and after a frustrating exchange suggested: "I think you should—had better be getting in touch with Mr. Greyhound or whoever Greyhound is and somebody better give us an answer to this question. I am—the government is—going to be very much upset if this group does not get to continue their trip. In fact I suggest that you make the arrangements to get a driver immediately and get these people on the way to Montgomery. . . ." [8] He also called Senator James Eastland, who personally guaranteed the physical safety of the riders in Mississippi, where they were peacefully arrested in Jackson, thus obviating the necessity for federalizing the Guard or calling in the Army. And finally he called for a "cooling-off period" and was seconded by *The New York Times* and the Washington *Post*. Martin Luther King agreed to "a lull but not a cooling-off period." James Farmer, originator of the rides and Executive Director of CORE, points out that "We had been cooling off for 100 years. If we got any cooler we'd be in a deep freeze."

Then, in an extraordinary proceeding, the Justice Department petitioned the Interstate Commerce Commission, an independent regulatory agency not inclined to act on its own, requested an order banning segregation in interstate bus terminals and provided them with a blueprint on how it might be done. When the ICC balked, the Attorney General set up a communications system with ICC Commissioner William Tucker, whom the political-science texts would describe as an "independent" and "autonomous" Commissioner, an inhabitant of "the headless fourth branch of the government." But he also happened to be a Democrat, he happened to be from Massachusetts, and he happened to have been appointed some three months earlier by President Kennedy. With Mr. Tucker's assistance, the Department anticipated all of the ICC's reservations; in September the ICC issued the order and by that time the Attorney General and his staff had helped convince the civil-rights-oriented Taconic and Field Foundations to subsidize a voter registration drive on condition that civil rights agencies across the board (from the Urban League and NAACP to CORE, SNCC and SCLC) agree to redirect their energies from buses to ballots, from civil disobedience to the Voter Education Project, thereby diverting the energy of civil rights workers from direct confrontation with Southern "law."

What did the Bureau have to do with this hurricane of anti-bureaucratic, unconventional, spontaneous activity? As John Seigenthaler lay unconscious in a Montgomery gutter for twenty-five minutes, an FBI man across the street, true to his rigid code ("The FBI is strictly an investigative agency"), took highly accurate notes on a little pad provided for such occasions. Why hadn't he come to Seigenthaler's aid? For the same reason he hadn't come to Diane Nash's or anyone else's aid. According to the FBI position on such matters:

> The agents are present for the specific purpose of observing and reporting the facts to the Department of Justice in order that the Department will have the benefit of objective observations. If the agent should become personally involved in the action, he would be deserting his assigned task and would be unable to fulfill his primary responsibility of making objective observations.[9]

Seigenthaler has a more subjective view: "It galls me to think that the FBI stood there and watched me get clubbed and was close enough so that they could positively identify my assailant. If I had been looking the other way, my assailant would be suing me. I'm not non-violent, you know." Granting the logic of FBI policy, one may note in passing that Seigenthaler had no more and probably less statutory authority than did the Bureau for helping Miss Nash into a waiting car. Yet one may assume that he acted as the Attorney General would have expected, which is why he was dispatched in the first place. "Secret societies above all others," says Simmel, "carry through the division of labor and the gradation of their members with great finesse and thoroughness. . . . This rationalistic nature of their organization finds no more visible expression than in its clear-cut and well-balanced structure."

Howard Glickstein of the Appeals Section of the Civil Rights Division recalls sitting in the Attorney General's office when a call came from Byron White in Montgomery. Apparently there was a communications problem. The Bureau's vertical, closed communications system didn't mesh with the Kennedy Department's *ad hoc*, on-the-spot trouble-shooting. White and his people were having difficulty getting information in time to use it. Kennedy arranged a conference call: White, Marshall, Hoover, himself. White wanted someone in Alabama he could talk to. Hoover said it couldn't be done, but shortly thereafter Assistant Director Alex Rosen was dispatched to Montgomery and communications improved.*

---

* Rosen was the Bureau's civil rights liaison. Here it might be noted that the Bureau had liaisons to each of the Department's divisions—Civil Rights, Criminal, Tax, Lands and Natural Resources, Civil, Internal Security and Anti-Trust—so that in effect the Bureau had a shadow Department going.

Some years later William Orrick, an efficient San Francisco lawyer who headed the Civil Division * but in addition volunteered for extracurricular civil rights duty, told a group of Notre Dame law students that "Fifteen minutes before the bus arrived in Montgomery, the FBI was advised by the Montgomery police that there would be no violence in Montgomery. At the same time, a member of the Montgomery Police Department told a reporter . . . that the police would not lift a finger to protect the freedom riders."

Today, Burke Marshall still gets agitated as he recalls that "When the bus arrived in Montgomery and the local police—as the courts later found—were purposely not there to meet it, I realized for the first time that we didn't have any spy system, we didn't have any information." What happened in Montgomery was simply that the Bureau's traditional information-gathering routine—checking with local police— turned out to be an empty, if not a counter-productive, ritual. Marshall complained bitterly to Rosen, and the General complained to the Director. But the Bureau's immediate response was (a) to send a memorandum complaining about Marshall's dedicated first assistant, John Doar (who had himself expressed his impatience with the Bureau's procedures while helping to prepare the brief on the case enjoining the Klan), and (b) to start calling Marshall at two or three A.M. with reports of racial unrest in a Shreveport, Louisiana, diner and other trivia. The trick, of course—and this was worked out with ingenuity over the next few years—was to get the Bureau to devise a new set of routines which would bypass discriminatory Southern law enforcers.

That the Department had learned something about how to maximize the Bureau's talents is evident from the appendix contained in ICC Docket No. M-C-3358, the Attorney General's official statement urging a rule banning segregation in interstate bus facilities, filed on June 21, 1961, less than a month after the freedom rides. It included an FBI survey (conducted at the Civil Rights Division's request) of 297 terminals, which featured FBI photographs of 97 violations (discriminatory signs). The Attorney General said the survey confirmed "the persistence of racial discrimination in interstate bus transportation." It also confirmed that they also can serve who only take notes and photographs, if you know how to use them.

The great accomplishment of the freedom riders was that they succeeded in desegregating the bus terminals. As Farmer says: "I am convinced to a moral certainty that if it hadn't been for the rides there

---

* Kennedy later moved him over to Anti-Trust.

would have been no ICC order. That was our strategy, to create crises and apply pressure." The great accomplishment of the Justice Department was the overnight mobilization and coordination, deputization and deployment of six hundred men borrowed from a variety of agencies, scattered all over the country, on behalf of law and order in Montgomery. "If we hadn't been lucky enough to get those marshals collected and ready," says Marshall, "I'm just sure that Dr. King and all those people would have been killed."

Because of the impressive performance by Justice personnel, no outside commentator thought to question the need for such chaotic if inspired improvisation when the FBI, with its thousands of agents on twenty-four-hour call, might have done the job by itself. Surely the answer that the FBI "is not a protection agency," which became a recurring rejoinder of the Kennedy years, was insufficient. Neither are the Border Patrol, nor the Alcohol and Tobacco Tax Unit, nor the Bureau of Prisons protection agencies. Yet they responded to the exigencies of this crisis. And if six hundred FBI men were not available, a smaller number—say, twenty-five, detailed to work as part of the marshals' operation—would have helped.

The fact was that the General accepted the Bureau's self-image as the reality. He was willing to move through, around and beyond organization charts. He had won the war against bus segregation without having to call out the troops. He didn't hesitate to trade the freedom riders' constitutional right to interstate travel for Senator Eastland's guarantee of their right to live. He operated without undue deference to abstract theories about checks and balances, the separation of powers, the role of the regulatory agencies, the wall of separation between the public and private sector. He did all these things, but when it came to the FBI, he left it alone and thereby further solidified its inflexibility in ways he could not foresee. Now there are undoubtedly good reasons why the Bureau should stay out of the protection business. One would be the difficulty of establishing criteria to decide who should and who shouldn't be protected. But to accept the Bureau's self-determination of its role so early in his administration had the unintended result of limiting the General's future options.*

---

* On non-fundamentals, however, the Attorney General did intervene. Thus when Carl Eardley of the Civil Division complained, in the course of trying to prepare a motion for a mandatory injunction commanding the police to keep the peace, that "I can't do a thing. I can't get any help at all. The FBI won't do a thing," Bill Orrick, Assistant Attorney General in charge of the Civil Division, but also helping Byron White during the freedom-rider crisis, called Robert Kennedy at midnight to pass on Eardley's complaint. Kennedy spoke to the President, the

If the Bureau thrived on hierarchies, systems, routines, paperwork, accountability, regularity and anonymity (except at the top), Robert Kennedy's style, which was quickly transmitted to the Department, was anti-bureaucratic, informal, impulsive, chaotic, spontaneous and personal. He roamed the marble corridors of the Department, opened doors unannounced and interrupted astounded civil servants with an outstretched hand, "I'm Bob Kennedy, the Attorney General," asking men twenty years his senior where they had gone to law school, how they had stood in their class and what they were working on. "When he came down the hall, you'd know it," recalls one lawyer. "The buzz was all over the Division." Take the case of the Civil Division, which had about three hundred lawyers, ten sections and thousands of cases. William Orrick, the San Francisco lawyer and JFK delegate to the 1960 convention who had accepted the job as Assistant Attorney General in charge of the Civil Division, remembers, "Bob would say, 'What do your people *do?*' I said, 'I don't know—they've got three or four thousand cases down there.' He said, 'Aren't you going to find out?' I said, 'Give me time.' He said, 'You'd better get with it.' So I said, 'Do you know how to run your part of the operation?' He said, 'Yes, I found out I could come here every day or I could go skiing and nobody would know and nobody would *care*—but *you're* supposed to *do* something.' "

He let his gigantic dog Brumus have the run of the fifth floor and thereby violated Section 201, Chapter 8, Title II of the Rules and Regulations for Public Buildings (which read "Dogs . . . shall not be brought upon property for other than official purposes"). He let Ethel pipe music into the courtyard, where she set up umbrellaed tables.

He had young attorneys up to his office for beer and briefings. Even the FBI started dispatching agents (consciously selected from his own age group) to meet him at the airport on his frequent travels and escort him to town. "It was the first time I ever felt I was part of the Department of Justice," says one agent who would pick up the Attorney General and Courtney Evans whenever they came to town.

Kennedy designated Louis Oberdorfer, the Alabama-born head of the Tax Division, to direct the government side of the effort to ransom the Bay of Pigs prisoners with $53 million worth of drugs. Oberdorfer, on leave from the prestigious Washington law firm of Wilmer, Cutler &

President spoke to Mr. Hoover and an hour later three agents and the commanding general of Maxwell AFB appeared in front of Orrick's desk and asked whether he had complained about the FBI. When he said yes, they said, "Please don't do it again" and offered their services.

Pickering whose senior partner, Lloyd Cutler, was Washington counsel for the drug industry, correctly anticipated that the drug industry would need tax and anti-trust rulings before they would commit themselves to contributions.

He sent Ramsey Clark, then head of the Lands and Natural Resources Division, on tours of the South to anticipate and prevent violence and assess and promote the progress of school desegregation. Clark came back and wrote memos urging a total overhaul of the Administration's school desegregation strategy.

In the midst of the Hoffa trial in Tennessee, he dispatched Civil Rights Chief Burke Marshall to advise the government's attorneys on how and when to disclose to the court the existence of a government informant (Partin) in the Hoffa camp. Marshall's advice was subsequently ratified by the Supreme Court when it upheld Hoffa's conviction, although Chief Justice Warren wrote a blistering dissent.

Kennedy named a non-lawyer, former FBI man Walter Sheridan, who had worked for him on the Rackets investigations, to head up a group of attorneys technically under the jurisdiction of the Organized Crime Section (actually Sheridan reported directly to the Attorney General), whose mission was to complete the work of the McClellan Committee with regard to Hoffa and the Teamsters. And when Sheridan's group, variously known as "the Hoffa Squad," "the Get-Hoffa Squad" and "the Terrible Twenty," had finished their work on Hoffa, he dispatched them to Mississippi to see what might be done about the Klan.

When Harold Reis, a career attorney in the Office of Legal Counsel, stuck his head in the Attorney General's office on a Saturday afternoon in the midst of the crisis surrounding the admission of James Meredith to the University of Mississippi, he thought he was saying a weekend goodbye. One half hour later he found himself on a plane to Mississippi, where he stayed for the duration of the hostilities.

John E. Nolan, Jr., who had clerked for Associate Justice Tom Clark and became a special assistant to the Attorney General after working as a private attorney on the Bay of Pigs prisoner ransom, enjoyed a characteristic relationship. "The extent to which I operated without instructions—oral or written—and didn't report is unbelievable," he says. "He didn't want reports and he didn't waste time recapping. He wasn't too interested in hearing about it unless you had something that required action or a decision on his part. When you first get into that, it's like being dropped into an ice-cold lake—alone. You learn the method, which is to talk to him whenever you need to, but you never really understand it. I try it with young associates in the firm with indifferent success."

Nolan's experience in Gadsden, Alabama, is typical. "One morning the Attorney General called me in and said there was some trouble in Gadsden and would I go down and see what it was all about. Well, I went down to Gadsden and there were three thousand whites on one side of the street and three thousand blacks on the other. I was there for about a week and talked to Burke [Marshall] a few minutes every day. I think I talked to Bob once. By Saturday it looked like it was okay, so I called Bob and said, 'I'm down here and it looks like it's going to be okay.' He said, 'Are you coming back?' I said yes and he said, 'Why don't you come out to the house on Sunday?' "

Nolan said he would try, but took advantage of Sunday to visit with his own kids. By Monday morning *The New York Times* (which rivaled the FBI as the chief source of civil rights information) reported that the whole thing had fallen apart again, so Nolan talked with Marshall for about half an hour and then went back to Gadsden, where he stayed for another week and again "got it put together." Nolan remembers that "I came back and saw Bob later that same afternoon. There was a story in the *Times* by Claude Sitton about how things had quieted down, so Bob said, 'I see where the papers gave you credit for a good job. How is it?' I said, 'I think it's okay.' And that was it! He never mentioned Gadsden again. I was his administrative assistant and had spent three weeks of my time down there, but he never talked to me about it again. By the same token he was always accessible and could give you a decision whenever you asked for one. He certainly never *explained* to anybody how he wanted this process to work. But it was one of the great marvels and it happened."

It was not a question of right and wrong. The Kennedy Department and the Hoover Bureau were marching to the beat of radically different drummers and discord was inevitable. If the Bureau's job was to gather information, an important part of the Department's job was to process it. If efficient information-gathering requires secrecy, efficient information-processing requires exchange and openness. That is one reason why if Hoover was running a closed society, Robert Kennedy was running a participatory democracy. The system was to gather all the Assistant Attorneys General (except J. Walter Yeagley of the Internal Security Division, a holdover from earlier Administrations who worked in a different building) and whoever else was relevant or passing through, in his baronial fifth-floor office, and then toss around problems much as he and Byron "Whizzer" White, the former All-American from Colorado, tossed around a football while they talked.

And even as his staff people shed their jackets, loosened their ties, rolled up their sleeves and hung their children's scrawls on office walls Kennedy style, so did they tend to solve their *own* problems by calling lesser colleagues into smaller offices for mini-dialogues. It was the rub of unfamiliar styles, the assumption that the Department and the Bureau could participate in these Constitution Avenue town meetings as equals and abide by decisions made that led to a variety of misunderstandings. Such was the situation surrounding the decision to turn over Cosa Nostra informant Joseph Valachi to Senator John McClellan's permanent investigating committee.

Press Secretary Edwin Guthman recalls, "We wanted Valachi to go public. We thought it would help in the fight against organized crime, that it would shake up the mob to know that one of their guys was talking, and we thought it was good public relations. But if Hoover said it would blow the intelligence-gathering mechanism we wouldn't have done it. We didn't know the answer to that one, so it was really his decision to make."

Guthman's solution: He called a meeting, where he assumed the issue was thrashed out. In attendance were Cartha "Deke" DeLoach (Guthman's FBI counterpart), Courtney Evans, Jack Miller and Bill Hundley (of the Criminal Division) and others. The discussion went on for two days, with the Department asking whether it would jeopardize the Bureau's information sources and the Bureau opposed to the idea, but not really saying don't do it. "Finally," says Guthman, "they said 'Go ahead and do it.' * Later they leaked word that it was done against their will. We made the mistake of dealing with them like we dealt with everybody else. You talked something out, reached a decision and carried it out. We didn't understand that they never really said what they were thinking. Dealing with the Bureau was a different deal."

Before Valachi surfaced, DeLoach had routinely submitted for Departmental clearance an article with Hoover's byline intended for the *Reader's Digest*. Guthman read it, and buried in a couple of paragraphs in the middle was a reference to the words "La Cosa Nostra," which had not previously been heard by the American public. "I wouldn't let it through," says Guthman. "The whole purpose of the

---

* DeLoach preferred not to talk to me about the meeting, so I do not have the benefit of the FBI version.

Valachi thing was to focus attention on organized crime through his revelations. I thought this would undermine that. We had an argument, a discussion about it, but the point is when we didn't approve it *with* those two paragraphs, the article never appeared. It was a perfectly good piece, but he just wanted to get those two paragraphs printed so that he could say, 'The FBI knew all along.' "

The epilogue appeared in the September 1963 issue of the *Law Enforcement Bulletin*, featuring one of Hoover's monthly editorials, which said:

> Recent disclosures in the fight against organized crime serve in a larger degree to magnify the enormous task which lies ahead. To know the identities of underworld "bosses" and the intricate composition and operations of their "families" and "regimens" is, of course, not enough. . . .

When the press picked up the word "magnify" and asked whether the Director wasn't criticizing the General, a spokesman for the Department said no, Mr. Hoover was using the word "magnify" to mean that it spotlighted the enormous task. Reporters protested that the dictionary defines it as "to make greater." The truth, of course, was that the editorial was written in Bureau-speak, which made standard dictionaries irrelevant.

It was never a question of the black hats vs. the white hats. The FBI's never-reveal-an-informant policy can be defended as a sensible though rigid security precaution. And from the Bureau's vantage point it has the additional merit of preserving yet another organizational secret. The Department's desire to dramatize an evil as a means of mobilizing public opinion on behalf of related legislation also seems a laudable objective. And it has the additional merit of ventilating an issue on which the average man has scant information. It was a question of conflicting stakes and conflicting styles. It may be observed that the General won the battle but as of this writing, he had lost the war. Six years later, Senator McClellan had evidence for his charge, delivered March 11, 1969, on the floor of the U.S. Senate, that "when Bob Kennedy left the Department of Justice, the organized crime program seemed to leave with him; it just seemed to fall apart."

In the never-ending struggle between the politicians and the bureaucracy, each has an advantage. The bureaucrat's advantage is that he is a statutory tenant while the politician is a transient. The bureaucrat knows or assumes that if he can only delay, evade, postpone and frustrate over a long enough period, eventually the politician will go away.

The politician's advantage comes precisely from his status as one who is only passing through. Whereas the bureaucrat must conserve his power for unknown future confrontations, the politician need have no such inhibitions. He can spend it more or less as he needs it.

Though every Attorney General since Stone has had his problems with J. Edgar Hoover, none has seriously attempted to dethrone him.* Six sources of power, in addition to whatever power may derive from the fact of secrecy itself, help explain why.

First is Hoover's durability itself, which is both a tribute to his power and a generator of it. The Director has served under fifteen Attorneys General and seven Presidents, his term has been indefinitely extended past retirement age, he rides in his own bullet-proof Cadillac (the only man in Washington outside of the President to do so). He has proven, in a word, irreplaceable.

What other figure in Hoover's position could call the Reverend Martin Luther King, Jr., then the nation's number-one civil rights leader, "the most notorious liar in the country," allow Clint Murchison to pay his California health-resort bills at a time when the Murchisons were under FBI investigation in connection with the Bobby Baker case, sit on the Board of the Hertz family foundation while exercising discretion over how many FBI men to assign to interstate auto thefts, accept antique gifts worth thousands from a Florida hotel man ordered through Krupsaws's, Washington's exclusive antique dealer and call Ramsey Clark, his former boss, "a jellyfish"—and not only get away with it but have it go largely unremarked? From the time of the Teapot Dome scandal Hoover had learned his way around Washington, the way it worked. He was Assistant Director when the Bureau reached its nadir, but he survived.

Some observers of Mr. Hoover's durability, such as Cyril Connolly, attribute it primarily to his sense of public relations: "The Federal Bureau of Investigation, the G-Men and Mr. J. Edgar Hoover form one of the most important elements of the American myth—symbols of perfection in detective methods, wholesale anti-communism, ruthless pursuit of gangsters and spies, and of a dedicated puritanical but unselfseeking chief above and outside politics, the nation's watchdog

---

* It is rumored that Senator Tom Walsh, FDR's Attorney General-designate, intended to fire Hoover in 1933. But he died before the inaugural. Homer Cummings was appointed in his stead and retained Hoover. Frank Murphy, who followed Cummings, was an admirer, and Hoover's future was assured.

and the President's counsellor." [10] True. But in addition, the fact of long-term survival itself reinforced the prospects for further survival and thereby consolidated and extended Hoover's power.

He had become such a fixture by the time Kennedy arrived that one Kennedy aide recalls, "The real problem in getting rid of Mr. Hoover was finding a replacement. If you took someone he approved of, what had you gained? If you took someone he disapproved of, there would be chaos. Whatever you may think of Mr. Hoover he has the allegiance of the agents and absolute control of the Bureau. Without that sort of control, it is potentially a highly dangerous organization." Indispensability is hard to argue with.

The combination of Hoover's durability and identity with his organization determined the way his FBI was perceived—as an island of intelligence, not really a part of the Justice Department. Robert Kennedy accepted and respected J. Edgar Hoover's boundary. He didn't really regard the FBI as part of the Department. He had an impact on agents, certainly, he visited FBI offices as he traveled around, and he knew agents by name. He even got them to put up a portrait of the President next to the one of Hoover which decorated FBI offices across the country, although he told Courtney Evans he was convinced that the FBI had one picture of JFK which they kept shipping around the country ten minutes ahead of the Attorney General's stop-off. (Evans pointed out that the frames were different.)

Kennedy won such devotion from men like Evans and Bill Barry that after Kennedy left Hoover couldn't believe they could serve him loyally. They were reassigned and voluntarily resigned. You leave the FBI with a whimper, not a bang, because if you are in the security business—as is Bill Barry, now a bank officer in charge of security—you can't afford the antagonism of the FBI. You rely on its good will and cooperation for the performance of your professional duties in private enterprise.

Second, in addition to Hoover's durability, there is the Bureau's mastery of the new technology. As Max Weber has observed:

> . . . The primary source of bureaucratic administration lies in the role of technical knowledge. . . . The question is always who controls the existing machinery and such control is possible only in a very limited degree to persons who are not technical specialists. . . . Bureaucratic administration means fundamentally the exercise of control on the basis of knowledge. This is the feature of it which makes it specifically rational. . . . Bureaucracy is superior in knowledge, including both technical knowledge and knowledge of the concrete fact within its own sphere of interest.[11]

In the war against crime the technical specialists were the technical surveillance specialists. Nobody not in the business had any idea what was going on—and so the question of whether Kennedy controlled the electronic eavesdroppers was irrelevant. It was never raised. As Henry Ruth, who served in the organized-crime section at the time, reminisces, "You look back and you feel stupid. We'd get furious because we'd propose an investigation and they'd say, 'There's absolutely nothing there!' *Now* I know what this meant—either they knew from bugging that there was nothing there, or they knew that whatever *was* there was tainted—it couldn't be used as evidence in court because it was the result of a bug."

The FBI can tap a phone, bug a martini, analyze a blood stain, track a typewriter, trace a hair, match a fingerprint, conduct a complex ballistics and spectograph analysis. Such expertise further strengthens the alliance between the Bureau and state and local police agencies that rely on "the seat of government" for cooperation and information. Such expertise, at the same time, places the average Justice Department attorney at a disadvantage in his dealings with the Bureau and adds to its mystique.

Third is the Bureau's power to define its own jurisdiction. Hoover's constant warnings about the dangers of a national police force are well taken and reassuring. Without question, as recent revelations involving FBI surveillance practices suggest, an overresponsive secret national police agency is a greater danger to a democratic society than an underresponsive one is an inconvenience. By erring on the side of recalcitrance (except in the national-security area) the Bureau has reinforced its autonomy. Given stereotypical liberal fears about the built-in conservative ideology of investigative organizations, it is reassuring to be told, as the *Law Enforcement Bulletin* has told us:

> In civil rights cases, as in all other matters within our jurisdiction, the FBI functions strictly as a fact-gathering and fact-reporting agency. Our special agents do not express opinions as to guilt or innocence; nor do they make prosecutive recommendations or otherwise assume the role of accuser, prosecutor, jury or judge. The results of every investigation are referred to the civil rights division of the U.S. Department of Justice for a determination of the U.S. Department of Justice for a determination as to whether further action is warranted.

Of course the fact is that the Bureau does, informally, make prosecutive recommendations. But it does so behind the scenes and uses them to pyramid its power still further. As one U.S. attorney points out, "If you cooperate with the Bureau and bring the cases they want you to bring, when you need something—like a Saturday investigation—they'll do it. But if you don't cooperate, they'll tell you they don't work on Saturday." The Bureau was so insistent about the Department prosecuting one grinning college student who told a stewardess that his baggage wouldn't pass "a Geiger counter test" that a local U.S. attorney called the Department of Justice to find out if they were kidding. Rather than alienate the Bureau, the Department advised, "Just tell the grand jury the facts, they'll know what to do." And they did—they dismissed the case.

Some authorities, such as Professor Arthur Selwyn Miller of the George Washington University Law Center, point out that in effect the Bureau, which then administered 160 statutes, already is a national police force. Today the FBI is into not only national security and organized crime but racketeering, labor-management corruption, antitrust, bank robberies, bribery and conflict of interest among government employees, hijacking, crime on the high seas, and in federally assisted housing, illegal wearing of military uniforms, interstate gambling; in other words, in anything that goes across state lines that it wants to be in. Professor Miller concludes: "What is in the making is a true national police force. As federal activity expands, so too does the work of the Department of Justice—and of the FBI. Congress has deemed it necessary to deal with crimes committed in interstate commerce and otherwise to reach down and assert federal responsibility over matters traditionally local in nature. The movement seems to be increasing. At some time, therefore, the FBI will be recognized as a national police force—in fact, if not in theory. . . ." [12] The best case for this view was made as long ago as 1947, when Attorney General Tom Clark wrote Representative Edward Reese (the Bureau undoubtedly drafted the letter, in accordance with Departmental practice) urging passage of the FBI's special retirement bill:

> The Federal Bureau of Investigation is the only general law enforcement body of the Federal Government. Other agencies are specifically charged with the enforcement of a limited number of laws pertaining to federal violations. The FBI has primary jurisdiction over all matters of investigatory nature pertaining to violations of Federal statutes when such matters are not specifically assigned to other Federal investigating agencies. . . . [13]

The Bureau's accordion concept of jurisdiction increases its power. James V. Bennett, former Director of the Bureau of Prisons, remarks, "If they want to do it, it's within the jurisdiction of the FBI. If they don't want to do something, they'll tell you it's outside the jurisdiction of the FBI. A typical example is the Walter Jenkins case. Mr. J. Edgar Hoover appraised it immediately. Within ten days he found that Mr. Jenkins was not in any sense a security risk. It didn't take him long to appraise that. But if he wanted to duck the issue, he could say, we don't evaluate."

Fourth are Hoover's relations with Congress. Through a combination of friendship, generational ties, ideological coincidence, the Senate's seniority system and Hoover's stayability, he has lines out to virtually all the key committee chairmen in Congress. So much so that for most purposes the Bureau is no longer accountable to the national legislature. Indeed, the United States Senate no longer reviews the FBI budget since, as Senator John McClellan acknowledges, whatever Hoover and Rooney want is all right with him. And Representative John Rooney, who never hesitates to slash the Bureau of Prisons budget, or indeed any budget that comes before him, told the Washington *Post*'s Richard Harwood, "I have never cut his [Hoover's] budget and I never expect to. The only man who ever cut it was Karl Stefan, Republican from Nebraska who had this job before me. When Stefan went home for election that year, they nearly beat him because he took away some of Hoover's money. When he came back he told me, 'John, don't ever cut the FBI's budget. The people don't want it cut.' I've always followed that advice. It's a real fine outfit and their budget is tight." [14]

In 1962 when the FBI asked for $127,216,000, Representative Rooney said: "The confidence which the Committee has in the Federal Bureau of Investigation under the highly capable and efficient leadership of Director J. Edgar Hoover is best illustrated by the fact that this is the tenth consecutive year that not one penny of the funds he has requested of the Committee has been denied. . . ."

Hoover has called Rooney "an implacable foe of Communism," and Rooney has singled out Hoover at appropriations time for personally backing up all his money requests with the aid of only two assistants, Clyde Tolson and John Mohr, "in contrast with some of the other agencies which are represented by a retinue of 20 or more witnesses together with a corridor full of back-stoppers. . . . He makes the presentation himself. And I've seen time and again his being asked questions with regard to how many automobiles the FBI has in its Chicago office; and he'll give you the answer accurately and immediately. And then if pursued, he can give you the mileage of every one of those cars as they are that day in the city of Chicago, Illinois. Now that's the kind of an administrator he is, and that's the kind of an impression he makes upon this Subcommittee on Appropriations, and it's the reason why he gets the amount of money that he asks for." Traditionalists might find a conflict of interest in the Bureau's practice of assigning, and the Appropriations Subcommittee's practice of accepting, three FBI agents to run the Subcommittee's Investigations and Surveys staff, which has a Director and two Assistant Directors. Each Special Agent puts in two years as an Assistant Director and one year as a Director before returning to the Bureau. At one time there were twenty agents in that unit, former Attorney General Katzenbach has recalled.

Fifth, although the FBI has by and large been circumspect about file-leaking, any legislator with an inclination to take on the Bureau must assume that the price for doing so may be the admission of his indiscretions into the public domain. That people believe the FBI may have a dossier on them is a deterrent to action that might antagonize the FBI. So the mere *fact* of the FBI's record-keeping, no matter how circumspect the record keeper, is a means of controlling—or at least sharply curtailing—the anti-FBI conduct of those who have anything in their background on which a record might be kept.*

Sixth, and overriding, is the Bureau's involvement in national security, which has escalated its leverage with Congress and given it a privileged position in the intelligence community, an anything-goes assumption in the dealings with those it suspects of disloyalty to the United States, and a perpetual stake in portraying the world as half slave and half free—an ideology authentic with Mr. Hoover as long ago as 1923 when he opposed the recognition of Soviet Russia. A curious footnote in Don Whitehead's *The FBI Story*, published in 1956 with a foreword by J. Edgar himself, reveals that

> The State Department was called in 1923 by a Subcommittee of the Senate Foreign Relations Committee to present its position on the recognition of Soviet Russia. Secretary of State Charles Evans Hughes requested J. Edgar Hoover to prepare the brief for his use on Communist activities in the U.S. Young Hoover's brief, supported by original documents, traced the interlocking relationship and control of Soviet Russia over the Third International and Communist leaders in the U.S. in their preparation and advocacy of the use of force and violence to obtain Communist ends. Hoover sat with Secretary Hughes at the witness table, and their presentation was neither controverted nor denied by Communist leaders in the U.S. or abroad. The Senate Foreign Relations Subcommittee refrained from acting favorably on the Senate Resolution to recognize Soviet Russia.[15]

* Perhaps the most blatant leaks were tapes played for journalists by Cartha DeLoach, in connection with the alleged indiscretions of Martin Luther King. Journalists were told that if they attributed the tapes to DeLoach he would deny it.

FBI power is augmented, moreover, by state and local police force power precisely because of the Bureau's responsibility for the national security. Jerome Skolnick's Study Group of the National Commission on the Causes and Prevention of Violence concluded that J. Edgar Hoover helped spread the view among police ranks that any kind of mass protest is due to a conspiracy promulgated by agitators, often Communists, "who misdirect otherwise contented people." The Skolnick Report said this view was behind much of the politicization of the police as well as widespread use of "police violence" against demonstrators.

Furthermore, the Bureau's involvement with national security makes a mockery of the homily that the FBI is essentially an agency of law-abiding fact collectors. Ever since September 1939, when FDR put the FBI in charge of "espionage, counter-espionage, subversive activities and violations of the neutrality laws," it has combined intelligence activities (infiltration, counter-espionage, preventive law enforcement) with investigatory ones. This was precisely the conjunction that Attorney General Stone had warned against in 1924 when he abolished the old General Intelligence Division which Hoover had headed under Palmer. Intelligence agencies operate at the margins of the law while investigatory ones which require confidence in their integrity should be above suspicion. That is why Great Britain keeps so distinct Her Majesty's Secret Service (intelligence) and Scotland Yard (investigatory). As an augur of things to come, shortly thereafter FDR gave Attorney General Robert Jackson a secret memorandum * empowering him to authorize the Bureau to tap telephones in national-security cases. Two years later, Congress, unaware of the memo, debated and defeated legislation that would have authorized openly what the Bureau was doing and has continued to do (until recent years) secretly.

After World War II the FBI's power ballooned primarily as a result of President Harry S Truman's 1947 government loyalty program, which significantly enlarged the Bureau's scope of operations. The Communist menace loomed large as the Alger Hiss case, the Rosenberg atom-spy case and the Korean war raced across the front pages in swift succession. Instead of throwing out Truman's ill-advised order, Eisenhower expanded it and by 1953 the normally non-partisan Mr. Hoover

---

* On May 21, 1940, FDR wrote Jackson directing him "in such cases as you may approve, after investigation of the need in each case, to authorize the necessary investigating agents that they are at liberty to secure information by listening devices direct to the conversations or other communications of persons suspected of subversive activities against the Government of the United States, including suspected spies. You are requested furthermore to limit these investigations so conducted to a minimum and to limit them in so far as possible to aliens."

announced, "I think well of Senator Joe McCarthy." [16] J. Parnell
Thomas of the House Un-American Activities Committee had announced, before he went to the penitentiary for graft, that "the closest
relationship exists between Mr. Hoover and this Committee." Neither
the McCarthy Committee, the Senate Internal Security Subcommittee,
nor the House Committee on Un-American Activities could have functioned without the cooperation of the FBI and access to its files.

By the time the Kennedys took office, Hoover and anti-Communism
were synonymous. As Senator Frank Lausche, Democrat of Ohio, said
in 1961 in response to rumors that Hoover was on his way out, "I cannot believe it. I hope it is not true. Mr. Hoover has been the most
feared individual in America by Communists and their hirelings. . . .
[They] would shout with joy upon the dismissal of Mr. J. Edgar
Hoover." The applause was so loud and long that Senator Lee Metcalf,
presiding, had to rap his gavel to bring the Senate back to order.

Despite his basic training with Senator Joe McCarthy, by 1961 Robert Kennedy was much more concerned with organized crime than
organized Communists. In his first interview as Attorney General he
told *Look* magazine's Peter Maas that he was thinking of abolishing the
Internal Security Division, which had jurisdiction over enforcing the
Smith Act of 1940 and the Internal Security Act of 1950, and generally
kept the subversives-in-government issue alive, and thereby dealt it a
morale blow from which it never recovered, although it was never abolished either. While Hoover was warning that the Communist Party is
"a Trojan horse of rigidly disciplined fanatics unalterably committed to
bring this free nation under the yoke of international communism,"
Kennedy's view was that "The party does not pose a problem other
than as the Supreme Court held—that it is dominated and directed by
a foreign power—the Soviet Union. But the great menace as far as
communism is concerned is not this group here in the U.S. but the
problems we have overseas." To which Hoover in effect rejoined in a
Law Enforcement Bulletin when he editorialized: "The threat from
without should not blind us to the threat from within."

In December 1962 Robert Kennedy recommended and John Kennedy approved—over the objections of the FBI, the Senate Internal
Security Subcommittee, the House Committee on Un-American Activities, the Justice Department's Internal Security Division and the U.S.
Attorney (who had opposed a court motion on the matter)—the com-
mutation of the seven-year sentence of Junius Scales, who had been
convicted under the Smith Act of active and knowing membership in
the Communist Party. He had been imprisoned since October 1961. "I

was virtually alone on this one," Robert Kennedy said some years later.

At the time, liberal commentators hailed the action as a major victory over the FBI. Joseph Rauh, the Washington civil libertarian attorney who had organized the movement for Scales's release, arguing that he was the only person in jail for the crime of active and knowing membership in the Communist Party, that he had repudiated the Communist movement (because of Khrushchev's revelations about Stalinism and Soviet repression of the Hungarian uprising) four years before his imprisonment commenced, and that his sentence was disproportionately severe—the Party's top leaders had gotten only three to five years in 1949—commented on the true significance of the Attorney General's action:

> . . . [The] test of loyalty for ex-Communists and all others too has been a willingness to give the names and activities of one's associates over the years. But this test has been distasteful and unacceptable to many distinguished Americans who have refused to protect themselves at the expense of others who had committed no crime and might long since have ceased the "suspect" association or activities.
>
> The act of granting clemency to Scales without his "cooperation" by "naming names" is a repudiation of the loyalty test long used by the FBI and these Congressional investigating Committees. For the first time since the rise of McCarthyism an Attorney General has refused to treat a man's unwillingness to inform on others as a ground for withholding favorable government action in his case.

Kennedy probably decided the issue on humanitarian rather than libertarian grounds. His action was consistent with the over-all Kennedy record on pardons, which was much more liberal than Eisenhower's, who believed that as a rule a President should not tinker with decisions arrived at by the courts. Ike commuted forty-seven sentences in eight years, while the Kennedys commuted 155 sentences in three and one half years. A less charitable interpretation would not discount the possibility that at a time when the liberal community was impatient with the Attorney General's failure to push for significant civil rights legislation and disturbed by his zeal in pushing for wiretapping legislation, he needed the credit of clemency for Scales. Whatever his motives, it was not an outright repudiation of the cold-war assumptions which helped rationalize the postwar role of the FBI. As Rauh had written to White House assistant Arthur Schlesinger, Jr.:

> Far from clemency for Scales being a pro-Communist act, it is actually an anti-Communist act. The Communists do not really want Scales out of jail as he is not *their* cause. There are Communist fronts for Morton Sobell, for the Haugs, etc., but there is no front for

Scales. . . . I believe nothing would make the Communists sicker than the release of Scales who has turned away from them.

Mercy, civil liberties and anti-Communism all demand a Christmas release for Scales.

Secret societies guard their rituals as closely as their secrets, so Kennedy's decision to challenge the Bureau's requirement that ex-Communists name names as their ticket back to political acceptability was a serious one. "All of us were saying, 'You have no idea of the problems.' Bob could be too brave for his own good. It was a typical case of everybody trying to save Bob from himself," recalls Katzenbach. "Scales gave the Bureau problems. They had good arguments. Here is the only fellow convicted under this statute, who never cooperated in the slightest or indicated any sorrow at what he did. You may think the Scales case is clear because it's a political case but if he were a bank robber who saw the light but wouldn't name his associates it's not so clear."

But occasional attacks on the trappings of the Bureau's ideology were by no means tantamount to attacking its power. When the Kennedys took over the government there were executive orders, loyalty oaths, complicated and trivial forms to be filled out in triplicate, and long lists of unjoinable organizations. Any serious challenge to the Bureau's authority would have involved, as a minimum, scrapping the whole lot of them. As William Shannon wrote at the time, "Nothing would do more to restore the pure air of American freedom."

Kennedy did not share Hoover's alarmist attitude toward the Communist Party of the United States, but he did accept the cold-war hypothesis of a world split in ideological halves. This put him in a weak position to challenge the FBI hypothesis that every member of the CPUSA, as the Bureau sometimes refers to the Party, was a potential if not a probable enemy agent whose phone was tappable at the stroke of a pen (the Attorney General's). Since this hypothesis was the rock on which the FBI of the early Sixties had been built, not to question it was not to challenge the fundamental power relationship of the Bureau to the Department.

Not to question it was also to sacrifice some of Kennedy's most cherished projects. For instance, there was no piece of legislation he fought for more vigorously than the Administration's pro-wiretapping bill of 1962. This bill included all kinds of libertarian safeguards against abuse (such as a provision against wiretapping without the approval of a federal judge) except in the area of national security, where the bill would have permitted the Attorney General to authorize wiretapping on his own judgment, as he already did under existing practice—a practice many libertarian scholars consider unconstitutional and/or illegal. It was Mr. Hoover who insisted on the national-security exception—threatening to oppose the bill if it were omitted. The Director didn't trust the federal judges, the head of the Organized Crime Section explains.

The official reason, as articulated by Jack Miller, Assistant Attorney General, Criminal Division, when he testified before Congress in the matter, was:

> Although a juridical proceeding is warranted in other situations, I believe it to be absolutely essential to preserve the present authority of the chief executive and the AG to authorize wiretapping in cases involving a threat to the national security. . . .
>
> The need for speed, secrecy and centralized control are too great to permit reliance upon applications to the Federal Courts.

Congressional Republicans and libertarian Democrats, fearing that Robert Kennedy would exploit such powers, provided the added opposition which kept the bill from passage.

If ever an Attorney General was in a position to challenge Hoover's authority in this critical national-security area, Robert Kennedy was, of course, the man. Until Kennedy came along, the Attorney General—a Cabinet officer concerned almost exclusively with domestic matters—was not on the National Security Council, which deals with international affairs. Robert Kennedy was issued so many informal invitations to attend that he became a *de facto* member. "Under Eisenhower," recalls a staff-man carry-over, "there was a planning board which sorted out issues before they reached the NSC, did the staff work and prepared the papers. Under the planning board there were two intelligence subcommittees. One was the subcommittee whose job was to coordinate the intelligence policy among existing investigative agencies, to coordinate investigation of all domestic espionage, counter-espionage, sabotage, subversion and other internal security matters. It was called the Interdepartmental Intelligence Conference, and its chairman was J. Edgar Hoover. The other subcommittee covered non-investigative security problems and was called the Interdepartmental Committee on Internal Security, and its chairman was J. Walter Yeagley, Assistant Attorney General in charge of the Internal Security Division of the Justice Department. Under the Kennedys the two subcommittees of the old Planning Board were continued, but they were ordered to report directly to the Attorney General. So you had Hoover's subcommittee and Yeagley's subcommittee each reporting to the Attorney General. He had the authority to make the decision or refer it to the Council. *This put him in charge of security for the whole executive branch of the government!"*

That Robert Kennedy nevertheless went along with Hoover and indeed bowed to Hoover's will in a matter like the tapping of Dr. Martin Luther King's telephone (explored in Chapter III) suggests the range of Hoover's power as much as the limitations of the Attorney General's civil libertarianism.

Throughout Robert Kennedy's stay there were periodic rumors of a "rift" with Hoover. Curiously—actually, not so curiously in view of the FBI's leak techniques—the rumors were usually surfaced by a journalist friendly to the FBI and were accompanied by a counter-threat or counter-rumor. Thus on February 27, 1961, the Hearst papers reported ". . . the line is that Attorney General Robert F. Kennedy and FBI Director Hoover have fallen out. . . . In fact there has never been as close a team operating in the Justice Department as the new Attorney General and the veteran FBI Director." The report went on to note that Kennedy visited Hoover's office to work out the details of his stepped-up organized-crime program and that "Only this week they walked together from Justice to Treasury for an appointment with Secretary of the Treasury Dillon."

On March 3, 1961, George Sokolsky noted that *"The Insider's Newsletter* says that some DC insiders predict that Hoover will be out by summer. He won't resign," Sokolsky said, "although he might be dismissed. When he does leave he won't want a politician to take over but another FBI man." Sokolsky noted that Hoover had been careful not to expand his jurisdiction. He said that the rumors about Hoover leaving were not a direct attack but "more subtle." They assumed Hoover was old and dead and therefore his retirement was imminent. But, said Sokolsky, these tactics didn't work with those who sought to remove Frankfurter or Rickover, and they wouldn't work with Hoover. "Robert Kennedy is an astute man. . . . It is not likely he will fall for the scheming and plotting which always go on in Washington as they do in every capital. For to dismiss J. Edgar Hoover would start such a fracas as no one needs; surely not a person with political ambitions and political sense. . . ."

On March 4, 1961, Lyle Wilson of UPI wrote that "American Communists and their associates will be displeased with this dispatch." He said that J. Edgar Hoover is not about to retire and that reports of a rift were not true. His advice: "Ask for the source, ask for proof." "The

FBI and its boss are functioning easily in the Justice Department pretty much on the same basis of friendly informality as in other years. The forecast is for more of the same."

A couple of weeks later Robert Kennedy said, "[We] get along extremely well. I have a great deal of admiration for him. I would hope that he would continue to have a long and worthy service. . . ." [17] And so things quieted down until a few months later, when the rumors started all over.

Here then was the Director, impregnable behind his boundary of secrecy, vastly powerful from his involvement in the national security, his possession of the new technology and the old files, his links to the prevailing potentates in Congress—taking no chances. Was it merely the conditioned reflex of the smoothly functioning Crime Records personnel, routinely countering rumor with rumor? Or was the Director really sacred? Cartha DeLoach's repeated inquiries of Guthman as to whether there was any substance to the rumors, which floated as regularly as New Frontiersmen in Bob Kennedy's swimming pool, indicated genuine concern. The Director was a psychological creature of the system he himself had created. The FBI processed rumors about the Director more or less the way they processed rumors about everything else. Once it was on paper—raw and unevaluated though it may have been—the Director cared enough to counter. Putting it on paper is one of the ultimate actions of a paper bureaucracy like the FBI. Thus the FBI's response to the New York *Daily News* editorial entitled "Alarming Crime Statistics" (July 31, 1961) which stated:

> When the President's brother took over the department . . . it took a bit of doing to start the FBI communicating with the Secret Service and Vice Versa, and the Bureau of Narcotics telling either of these units anything."

Countered Hoover:

> Knowing the *News'* reputation for objectivity, I felt you would want me to bring to your attention a glaring inaccuracy in your July 31 editorial. . . .
> Throughout my tenure . . . this bureau has worked in close cooperation with all other investigative and law enforcement agencies of the federal government. There has been an uninterrupted flow of information between these agencies and the FBI. During the past fiscal year we disseminated no less than 101,210 items of criminal information to other agencies. Of this total 38,115 items were furnished to other federal agencies, including the Secret Service, the Bureau of Narcotics, etc . . .

The rumors and counter-rumors, the charges and rebuttals were, of course, expressions of the underlying tension between the secret society and the open one—between the Director and the General. If Hoover read them as tactical problems to be met, Kennedy misread them as irritations to be ignored or surmounted. As the President's brother, he had the last clear chance to fire Hoover. By not doing so he guaranteed the Director at least another ten-year lease on his job. Ironically, the source of Robert Kennedy's power was also his greatest inhibition. For if the Director had merged his ego and his organization, the Attorney General identified, more than any Cabinet officer in history, with the fortunes and reputation of the Administration. He might have done more on his own, but because his brother the President would be inescapably implicated, he couldn't afford to take the chance.

CHAPTER TWO

Organized Crime:
The Bureaucracy and the General

IN THE FALL OF 1958 twenty-five numbered copies of an FBI report on the Mafia—the first and only time the FBI has acknowledged the Mafia's existence—were distributed to the top twenty-five officials in government concerned with law enforcement.

The day after they were circulated, J. Edgar Hoover had each copy recalled and destroyed. He denounced the report as "baloney," and it was never heard of again.

The story of the suppression of this report has never been told. In fact, until now the existence and suppression of this document has apparently not been reported. It is disclosed here only because before it was recalled Attorney General William Rogers "made the mistake of showing his numbered copy to me," says Milton Wessell, a distinguished New York attorney who had been brought to the Department to head a Special Group whose job would be to fight organized crime.

Like the report, the Special Group was also effectively put out of circulation by the FBI, after a year in operation during which it prosecuted an obstruction of justice case arising out of the Apalachin, New York, meeting of seventy-five gangland leaders at Joe Barbara's palatial home in 1957 (convictions were later overturned) and recommended that a separate unit be set up in the Attorney General's office to fight

organized crime. Its recommendations were not followed and the unit
was disbanded. Gerard L. Goettel, Deputy Chief of the group, later
complained:

> It turned out that we were woefully wrong in assuming that various
> law enforcement agencies would be eager to cooperate with us. We
> learned that in Washington there are Republicans, Democrats and
> Bureaucrats, and while the first two come and go, the last are im-
> mutable. Bureaucratic opposition to our work—on grounds totally
> divorced from politics—proved our greatest stumbling block. In-
> credibly, in our battle against organized crime, the obstructionists
> were not merely the gangland leaders whom we sought to destroy, but
> also the public servants entrenched in the federal government, who
> disapproved of and mistrusted our crusade.
>
> Typical was the attitude of a seasoned investigator of the otherwise
> helpful Immigration and Naturalization Service. Declining to work
> overtime on a case he remarked, "I survived the Kefauver investigation
> and a couple of others like it, and I'll still be on the job long after you
> guys are back in your Wall Street law offices."
>
> Similarly a field supervisor for the Food and Drug Administration
> refused to investigate a hoodlum's profitable scheme for adulterating
> olive oil. His budget, he said, was not even large enough to protect
> consumers from poisonous foods. Hence he could not waste valuable
> power on "cops and robbers capers."
>
> The FBI was the coolest agency of all. J. Edgar Hoover at a national
> meeting of U. S. Attorneys denied the need for "special groups" to
> fight organized crime.[1]

Such was the environment confronting the new Attorney General:
twenty-seven independent, non-cooperating intelligence agencies each
going its own separate way * including one immediately under his
jurisdiction—the FBI—which persisted in denying the existence of the
very organized criminal conspiracy which he was intent on putting out
of business. It was apparent that if Robert Kennedy was going to make
any headway in his war on organized crime, he first had to win a
bureaucratic war within the federal government.

The conventional wisdom is that he won that war; that through a
combination of fraternal power and personal dynamism he achieved a

* Federal Bureau of Investigation, Internal Revenue Service, Secret Service,
Alcohol and Tobacco Tax Division, Narcotics Bureau (Treasury), General Accounting Office, Federal Power Commission, Department of the Army, Department
of the Navy, Department of the Air Force, Veterans Administration, Central In-
telligence Agency, Civil Service Commission, Securities and Exchange Commission,
Interstate Commerce Commission, Federal Communications Commission, Civil
Aeronautics Board, Atomic Energy Commission, Department of Health, Education
and Welfare, Department of Labor, Post Office Department, National Security
Agency, Coast Guard, Customs Bureau, State Department, Federal Aviation Agency,
Immigration and Naturalization Service.

degree of cooperation in the federal, state and local law enforcement and intelligence communities previously unknown; and that he pushed, ordered, cajoled and successfully enticed the FBI into the fray so that eventually it was a full-fledged if somewhat eccentric participant in the fight to destroy the syndicates.

If Robert Kennedy won the bureaucratic battle in the sense that he engineered the cooperation of twenty-seven ultracompetitive and independent agencies, he lost the bureaucratic war with the FBI, because although he indeed enlarged the FBI's arena of operations, he did so on the Bureau's own terms and thereby enlarged the Bureau's power. It was, of course, Hoover's bureaucratic genius that he thereby won by "losing."

Ever since Prohibition, when Al Capone was jailed on charges of tax evasion, Attorneys General have been "declaring war" on organized crime, but Robert Kennedy was the first to fight one. James P. McGranery called a valuable conference on organized crime in 1950, but its recommendations were ignored. Herbert Brownell, Jr., responded to the sensational Kefauver hearings (which concluded that the Mafia was the "cement" which held together syndicated crime) by creating an Organized Crime and Racketeering Section within the Criminal Division of the Justice Department, but its strength never exceeded sixteen men, and their performance was indefensibly sloppy (if one accepts the documentation provided by Robert Kennedy himself in *The Enemy Within*, published just prior to his assuming the Attorney Generalship). William Rogers followed up the gathering of seventy-five racketeers at Joe Barbara's Apalachin, New York, home in 1957 by naming Milton Wessel to head the Special Group on Organized Crime, but its report, Wessel tells me, was "unanimously rejected." Hoover, by most accounts, vetoed acceptance of the Wessel report, which had recommended the creation of an Attorney General's Office of Syndicated Crime.

Robert Kennedy changed this pattern. "When you talked about organized crime," recalls Henry Peterson, a career attorney in the Criminal Division (who went on to head up the Organized Crime Section under Attorney General Ramsey Clark), "people would ask you to define what you meant. Robert Kennedy came in and said, 'Don't define it, do something about it.'" His instructions were: "Don't let anything get in your way. If you have problems, come see me. Get the job done, and if you can't get it done, get out." As William Shannon wrote, "His zeal to break up the syndicates was reminiscent of a sixteenth-century Jesuit on the hunt for heresy. . . ."[2]

Robert Kennedy thought he understood the links between political corruption and crime syndicates. He argued that illegal gambling profits of about $7 billion a year were used to bankroll narcotics, loan-sharking, white-slave traffic, infiltration and manipulation of legitimate businesses, and so he conducted a crackdown on illegal gambling. He pointed out that for every $5 lent, shylocks got back $6 a week later, which compounded to a rate of 800 percent over a twelve-week repayment period, and he cited the case of the usurer who increased his net worth from $500,000 to $7,500,000 in a couple of years. He believed that racketeers literally got away with murder—and would cite the fact that of one thousand Chicago gang slayings in less than fifty years only a handful had resulted in *arrests* as compared with the non-organized-crime average of 91 percent arrested, and so he organized the structure of law enforcement so that racketeers became the special target rather than the privileged evaders of justice.

G. Robert Blakey, then a junior member of the Organized Crime Section, now one of the leading authorities on the subject, points out that "Kennedy's experience on McClellan gave him a thorough working knowledge of organized crime. He knew that the traditional division, where the prosecutor prosecutes and the investigators investigate, doesn't work in organized crime. Thomas E. Dewey had innovated the notion of a Rackets Bureau and Kennedy picked it up and adapted it to the federal level. Kennedy said that now the same lawyer would be involved in the investigation, indictment, trial and appeal. He said agents in the field should come together. He said the orientation should be functional—what will do the job—not theoretical, governed by some organization chart. So instead of Kennedy talking to a Deputy who talks to the Assistant Deputy who talks to the Assistant Attorney General who talks to the head of the section who talks to me, he walks into my office and says what are you doing and what can I do for you? This is awesome because he's deadly serious. He *knows* this stuff. He *means* it. And he has these regular meetings every few weeks with our section. I remember Whizzer White used to sit on the window seat with his feet up and not say much except to bring the discussion back to the point. But Bobby would always know the names of the minor hoods we thought we had discovered. He cared. And if I complained about some problem I was having, Kennedy would turn to Courtney Evans and say, 'Do you hear that, Courtney? Can you take care of it?' He exercised charismatic authority rather than bureaucratic authority."

In the same interview that he speculated about abolishing the Internal

Security Division, when *Look* reporter and family friend Peter Maas asked him what areas of law he intended to emphasize, Kennedy said that number one on the list was organized crime. At his first press conference he announced that his organized-crime drive had the President's backing and needed national support. His first (and most successful) effort at legislation resulted in the speedy passage of an anti-crime package which made it a crime to travel in interstate commerce in aid of racketeering or gambling enterprise, to transport gambling paraphernalia in interstate commerce and to transport gambling information by wire in interstate commerce (the first of these bills had been introduced in 1909). "It was one of those little deals with Senator Eastland," recalls Byron White's Deputy William Geoghegan. "He got five anti-crime bills moved through the Judiciary Committee so quickly that nobody had a chance to read them. Eastland mumbled some words on the floor and the bills were passed by unanimous consent. Maybe this was the price for appointing [Judge Harold] Cox in Mississippi," Geoghegan adds in a comment truly revealing of the Administration's ranking priorities.

In other words, having interrogated over 800 witnesses during 270 days of hearings on the McClellan Committee and then written a book on the subject, Robert Kennedy thought he knew what had to be done in the crime and corruption area and set out to do it. He knew how Thomas E. Dewey had created a special Rackets Squad to crack Murder, Inc. He knew that Kefauver had identified the "cement" which helped bind the Costello–Adonis–Lansky syndicate of New York and the Accardo–Guzik–Fischetti syndicate of Chicago. He had testified before the grand jury which investigated the Apalachin meeting to discuss the vacuum created by the murder of Albert Anastasia. He understood the links between local police, local politics, corruption and organized crime. As Byron White recalls, "He was not interested in crimes of desperation, but in the cynical big-time organized-crime operators, he regarded it as a conspiracy of evil. . . ."

One night in the Christmas season of 1961 Ramsey Clark, then Assistant Attorney General in charge of the Lands and Natural Resources Division, and Byron White were heading back to the Department from Caruso's Italian restaurant across Pennsylvania Avenue. White turned to his companion and observed, "You know, we have about as much chance of changing that place as you and I do of walking up to it, putting our shoulders against the building and moving it." Yet for a brief moment that is what happened in the organized-crime field. One need not be a firm believer in crime statistics to note those surrounding

Kennedy's organized-crime drive—especially since they were compiled by the opposition.* In 1960 Criminal Division attorneys spent 283 days in court and 1,963 days in the field. In 1962 Criminal Division attorneys spent 809 days in court and 7,359 days in the field. There were nineteen indictments of organized-crime figures in 1960 and there were 687 in fiscal 1964. As a result of his pressure and coordination, the Internal Revenue Service assessed top racketeers a quarter of a billion dollars in taxes beyond the amount paid when they had filed.

Whatever his intent was, the effect of events such as a February 1961 meeting with the representatives of all twenty-seven intelligence agencies around a Justice Department conference table was not merely inspirational. It was practical. IRS Commissioner Mortimer Caplin, for instance, followed up with a directive to IRS investigative personnel which said:

> I cannot emphasize too strongly the importance I attach to the success of the Service's contribution to this over-all program. . . . The tax returns of major racketeers to be identified by the Department of Justice will be subjected to the "saturation type" investigation, utilizing such man-power on each case as can be efficiently employed. In conducting such investigations, full use will be made of available electronic equipment and other technical aids as well as such investigative techniques as surveillance, undercover work, etc.[3]

Essentially, Robert Kennedy's strategy had four components: (1) to mobilize the country and Congress through speeches, articles, testimony, legislation, publicity stunts (like the Valachi testimony)—all designed to educate the nation to the dimensions and urgency of the threat posed by the Cosa Nostra, membership estimated at 5,000; (2) to motivate and give new status, manpower, money and priority to the Justice Department's own Organized Crime Section and thereby do informally what Hoover had prevented him from doing formally (e.g., setting up a National Crime Commission that would coordinate and

---

* In 1967, three years after Kennedy had gone to the Senate, a group of Republican Congressmen, reporting on the relationship of organized crime to the urban poor, found that with Kennedy's departure the crime drive ended. In addition to the numbers cited above, they noted that "The number of man days in the field of personnel of the Organized Crime and Racketeering Section of the Justice Department has decreased by over 48% since 1964. The investigative activities of the section grew steadily under the Kennedy administration to a high point of 6699 man days in the field by the section personnel in fiscal 1964. In 1966 it was 3480. The number of man days before grand juries by personnel of the Organized Crime and Racketeering Section of the Justice Department has decreased by over 72% since 1963. The number of man days in court . . . has decreased by over 56% since 1964. The number of District Court briefs prepared or reviewed by the Organized Crime and Racketeering Section of the Justice Department has decreased by 83% since 1963."

serve as a national clearinghouse for information on organized crime and racketeers); (3) to win the cooperation of other government agencies through visits, telephone calls, meetings, lunches, the threat, promise and actuality of Presidential intervention, and general behind-the-scenes pressures and promises; (4) to send out a group of centrally based prosecutors who would investigate, indict and try cases against the key rackets figures.

While his public lobbying was visible, as Mortimer Caplin points out, "his private meetings did the trick. When he got the Secretary of the Treasury Dillon and the head of the Narcotics Bureau and me to lunch, and he brought J. Edgar Hoover over to Dillon's office with him to work out coordination problems, that gave the whole thing a blessing. You couldn't have done it without that." His non-public talks also had an impact. On April 13, 1962, for instance, in an unreported address to the graduating class of IRS A Basic School number 14, he typically spoke of the importance of the anti-crime drive ("Unless we are strong here in our country, unless we are able to put our own house in order, we are not going to be able to meet the great problems that are facing us abroad") and referred in passing to the new cooperation between agencies "who until some time ago . . . operated on an independent plane. There was not the exchange of information that was necessary in order to deal with this problem." He told how the new anti-crime legislation was making the difference, and then in the key passage of these remarks he said:

> The reason that this has received such top priority over the period of the last year is not just the fact that Mr. Dillon is interested in it, that other Cabinet members are interested in it, that the Justice Department is interested in it, but the fact that the President himself is personally interested in this effort. He served on the McClellan Committee for three years and became personally interested. He wanted to have something done in this field, he has spoken about it, and he's made efforts along those lines. It's receiving his continued attention, so your work is of great importance.

Robert Kennedy told the 67th graduating class of the FBI National Academy that the old non-sharing information policy of the Bureau no longer applied: "I can report to you that there is a new awareness in law enforcement throughout the country of a greater willingness, a greater need and a greater means for cooperation—by the federal and local authorities in combatting the underworld. We will give information to local police whom we know to be trustworthy. And of course this exchange of information works both ways." That this directive turned out to be as much aspiration as description (at least insofar as the FBI was concerned) did not undercut its symbolic importance.

Under Kennedy, for the first time agents—around his own age and chosen to represent the Bureau in its best light—in each major city he visited were assigned to travel with and brief the Attorney General. One of these agents remembers, "I served under McGranery, Mc-Grath, Brownell and Rogers, but until Bob Kennedy came along the only way I knew that the Attorneys General changed was that they signed our credentials. But then some time in the middle Fifties, Mr. Hoover started signing our credentials, so there was *no* way to know!

"I never felt any connection between the investigative agent and the Attorney General. The Department was remote. I never had any idea that we were part of the Justice Department, and I was in Portland, Oregon, San Francisco and New York over a ten-year period. Robert Kennedy was the first Attorney General to have an impact on the agents in the street. Basically, the administrative idea I accepted was that each agent was directly accountable to Hoover. I never got over that. But Kennedy made inroads. His visits to the FBI offices, his interest in the field, his knowledge of what agents were doing instilled a tremendous gung-ho feeling, a spirit of the chase.

"He wanted to show that he was interested. He wanted to know what was going on. And he remembered from one meeting to the next, he did his homework. I used to kid Kennedy about his pizza [anti-Mafia] squad."

The point was, and nobody in government missed it, that Robert Kennedy's organized-crime drive ranked at the top of the nation's domestic priorities. Eventually civil rights passed organized crime as Robert Kennedy's primary preoccupation. But that was not until well into 1963. It was not aberrational that on the sad afternoon of November 22, 1963, when the Attorney General received the news of his brother's assassination by way of a telephone call from J. Edgar Hoover, he was on a lunch break—with Robert Morgenthau, the U.S. attorney for the Southern District of New York and perhaps the country's leading prosecutor of Mafiosi—from an all-day meeting with the Organized Crime Section. Thomas McBride, whom Kennedy had personally interviewed before signing him up from Hogan's office, recalls, "About forty of us were at the long round-up meeting on assassination day. He never met the section again, and we had met regularly for two and a half years. The round-up meetings didn't accomplish that much, but they were valuable drills. They kept the level of steam up. They proved that this was a serious business." That Robert Kennedy never met with his racket squad again showed that something had died in him. But it also suggests that chasing these fellows was something of a game for the young Kennedy, and now the fun was over. The agency for his re-emergence in early 1964 would be the Civil Rights Division, which had monopolized more and more of his attention even while JFK lived, its content the revolution for social equality. But in the early years a look at the differing assumptions operative in the organized-crime and civil rights areas makes it impossible to mistake the primacy Kennedy gave to catching the hot shots.

First, there was his central assumption that "If we do not on a national scale attack organized criminals with weapons and techniques as effective as their own, they will destroy us." [4] When Hoover success-fully blocked Kennedy's plan to set up a National Crime Commission as a sort of clearinghouse for the nationwide exchange of organized-crime information, Kennedy hired Mrs. Winifred Willse, a veteran of nineteen years in the Narcotics Division of the New York Police De-partment, whose husband had worked as a Kennedy investigator for the Rackets Committee, to set up an information exchange system among all of the twenty-seven intelligence-gathering agencies of government to be coordinated within the Organized Crime and Racketeering Section of the Criminal Division. Not only was Kennedy not interested in centralizing the anti-segregation effort in the same way, but his chief deputy, Byron White, recalls: "I had thought that the Administration ought to locate the primary leadership in the civil rights fight outside the Department of Justice." And as Director of Public Information Ed-win Guthman has recalled, "As Bob and White looked ahead to the role the Justice Department would play in the gathering struggle over civil rights . . . they felt the only proper course for the Department would be to proceed in strict accordance with the law, avoiding any appearance of pitting one social point of view against another."

Second, there was the choice of personnel. Kennedy's subconscious strategy for running the Justice Department seems to have been to employ a two-platoon system. He put an Ivy League intellectual and cautious proceduralist with no civil rights training, Burke Marshall, in charge of the Civil Rights Division—believing that civil rights could await this brilliant anti-trust lawyer's on-the-job training; and he en-couraged other high-minded libertarians like Nicholas Katzenbach, Lou Oberdorfer, Ramsey Clark, William Orrick and, later, John Douglas to get involved in the struggle for civil rights in an *ad hoc* way.

But to head the Criminal Division Kennedy chose Republican Jack Miller, whose paper credentials were not up to those of the Ivy League intellectuals and who, according to an approving colleague, "would not hesitate to indict a man for spitting on the sidewalk if he thought that was the best he could get." Kennedy had worked closely with Miller when the latter was a lawyer for the court-appointed Board of Monitors supervising the Teamsters on a case which generated more than forty appeals, and together Kennedy and Miller had worked to topple Hoffa from his post of power in extracurricular ways which Paul Jacobs, an anti-Hoffa student of the trade-union movement, found "trespassed heavily on the rights of Hoffa and the union." Miller would not raise any procedural obstacles to action.

And to head the Organized Crime and Racketeering Section (whose size increased under Kennedy by 400 percent to sixty lawyers) Kennedy named Edwyn Silberling, a spirited, ultra-aggressive prosecutor who had put in seven years with New York's District Attorney Frank Hogan (where one of his specialties was preparing wiretap evidence, then legal under New York law) and had been appointed a Special Prosecutor for Governor Rockefeller. Silberling brought in a friend and former colleague as an assistant, James Misselbach, who says he also had specialized in the preparation of wiretap testimony in New York.

In charge of the Get-Hoffa Squad (technically the Labor and Racketeering subdivision of the Organized Crime Section) Kennedy named Walter Sheridan, former FBI man, former McClellan Committee investigator. That he chose Sheridan over Carmine Bellino (also a McClellan operative and conceded to be the best investigative accountant in the country) indicated his intent to carry the war against Hoffa beyond the white-collar-investigator stage—to liberate the Get-Hoffa Squad to conduct its own guerrilla war against Teamster corruption. "In any fight I would always want Walter Sheridan on my side," Kennedy said at the time.[5] And as he received the bright young attorneys of the Justice Department in his office for informal gatherings of beer and pretzels he would always wind up the bull sessions by saying, "If any of you guys don't have enough to do, come see me." A number of those who took him up on his offer, such as Bill French, a recent Notre Dame graduate, ended up working for Sheridan as one of the Get-Hoffa Squad.

Thus, while the thinkers ended up in civil rights, the doers—the alumni and friends of the Rackets Committee, the men more likely to short-cut procedural obstacles than to discover them—were enlisted in the organized-crime and corruption chase. This is, of course, part caricature, since it was Kennedy's style to cross-check, to intermingle, to improvise—to send Burke Marshall down to Nashville to consult on one of the Hoffa trials, or to dispatch Walter Sheridan to Mississippi to look into the Klan. Also, Byron White, a tough-minded proceduralist, was actively overseeing the Department. Nevertheless, the split in personalities manning them accurately reflected Kennedy's approach in the two areas. And in the organized-crime area he wanted enthusiasts, not restrainers.

Third, there were the contrasting assumptions about the nature of the federal system. The war on discrimination reflected classic images of the federal system, the assumption that state and local authorities— even those obviously out to undermine the Constitution—had to be given the opportunity to perform. As Burke Marshall said of Kennedy's protracted conversations with Mississippi Governor Ross Barnett about federal protection for James Meredith on registration day at Ole Miss, despite repeated evidence of Barnett's broken promises and bad faith, "You had to assume that the Governor of a sovereign state would do what he told you he would do." The war on organized crime and corruption intentionally reversed such high-school textbook assumptions about the operation of the federal system. "Our idea was to set up a group of centrally based prosecutors who would do everything," recalls Silberling. "They would conduct investigations [traditionally the function of the FBI], they would go before grand juries and try cases [traditionally a function of U.S. attorneys], and where we thought state and local authorities were unreliable, we'd figure out a theory of federal jurisdiction and do the job ourselves." Kennedy made the point shortly after taking office when he observed, "Traditionally, action against the rackets has been mainly the province of local authorities. In many localities they have outgrown the authorities. The rackets have become too widespread, too well organized and too rich."

Thus when the Justice Department satisfied itself that reform mayoral candidate and former football star George Ratterman had been framed (his drink was doped and he was deposited in bed with a stripper named April Showers in time to welcome a police raid) in Newport, Kentucky—a notorious bastion of gambling, vice, prostitution and narcotics—they usurped the role of the U.S. Attorney in Lexington, Kentucky, and two young attorneys from the Organized Crime Section in Washington presented the evidence to the grand jury, which resulted in the conviction of the chief of police, among others. Citizens' groups had been fighting Newport corruption without success for years when Silberling dispatched Ronald Goldfarb, a young attorney fresh from the Arthur Garfield Hayes civil liberties internship at New York University Law School, who got federal jurisdiction by arguing that the framing of

Ratterman was a violation of the Civil Rights Act. "It was ridiculous, but it was the only way we could think of to get the federal government involved. We got jurisdiction, and it worked," says Silberling.

One of Silberling's first actions was to compile the list of top racketeers who had escaped the law. These men were singled out as priority targets in the crime war. The list started at forty and by the time Kennedy left it was up to 2,300. "Our technique," recalls Silberling, "was to circulate the list among twenty-seven different investigative agencies and then to investigate these guys up to their eyeballs." Assisted by eleven typists and three assistants, Mrs. Willse prepared information folders and file cards on such target-list names as Mickey Cohen (convicted of tax evasion), Franky Carbo and Joe Sica (convicted of extortion in a Los Angeles boxing case), Carlos Marcello of New Orleans, Tony "Ducks" Corallo of New York, Carmine Lombardozzi, Trigger Mike Coppola of Miami and many more.

The strategy of cross-referencing and exchanging information plus placing investigations under the jurisdiction of individual members of Silberling's Organized Crime Section, which had regular meetings with Kennedy, was simple—at least in theory. In fact, there was friction between Silberling and local U.S. attorneys who didn't want outsiders coming in and running their cases for them. In New York's Southern District, tough-minded Robert Morgenthau got Kennedy's agreement to leave the traditionally autonomous district alone. There was friction between Silberling and his immediate superior, Herbert Jack Miller, who was Assistant Attorney General in charge of the Criminal Division and had to answer to the FBI for the free-wheeling investigations Silberling's "whiz kids" were carrying on.

There was friction between Silberling and Walter Sheridan, whose Get-Hoffa Squad fell within Silberling's jurisdiction for budgetary purposes but who reported directly to Robert Kennedy for practical purposes. And when Silberling didn't get the expected clear-cut backing from the top in messy political cases—like the Keogh case in New York and the Chacharis case in Indiana (see Chapter VIII)—there was friction between Silberling and the Attorney General. All of this clash of wills and purposes resulted not in a diminution of the organized-crime drive, which remained Robert Kennedy's pet project until his brother's assassination, but rather in Ed Silberling's premature retirement. He was replaced by William Hundley, a pleasant and canny Irishman whose handling of the Section under Eisenhower had drawn Kennedy's fire when Kennedy was running the McClellan investigation but whose performance as Kennedy's confidential emissary in the matter of

Bernard Goldfine, the Boston industrialist accused of gifting Sherman Adams and others for influence, and in the Keogh trial, which he won, earned him Kennedy's respect; also, unlike Silberling—who had antagonized the Bureau most of all—Hundley had good relations with the FBI, which Kennedy considered a major qualification for the job.

The fourth respect in which organized crime and civil rights assumptions differed was the matter of sensitivity to procedural due process. In fighting the war on discrimination, the Justice Department was rigidly scrupulous about protecting the rights of those against whom it did battle and administering justice with the traditional even hand. "The Justice Department kept insisting," complained C. B. King, the militant and radical black attorney of the Albany, Georgia, civil rights movement, "that the sheriff who bludgeoned me over the head with a cane when I went to see him on behalf of a client, and the policeman who kicked my pregnant sister-in-law and caused a miscarriage, were decent citizens to be reasoned with rather than criminals to be dealt with."

No such unadulterated sense of equality before the law prevailed in the organized crime area. Although men like Lou Oberdorfer, head of the Tax Division, fought with some success to have racketeers judged by the same tax standards as everyone else, the fact was that organized-crime folders were routinely moved from the bottom to the top of the tax prosecution pile. This meant that although everybody was treated equally in terms of tax law, administratively some were less equal than others. Mortimer Caplin, who had taught Robert Kennedy as a student at the University of Virginia Law School, recalls that before he was appointed Commissioner of Internal Revenue, "I saw Bob in December. He asked my views on tax and organized crime and whether I wanted to join the Administration. He asked me to write a letter telling how I felt about IRS working closely with Justice in organized crime. I hadn't thought much about it, but I said sure. Then I went back and saw Dean Ribble and concluded, after much thought, that as long as we were making real tax investigations—not sham ones—there was nothing objectionable. I wrote him a long letter, five or six pages, spelling out my philosophy." Caplin's appointment was announced January 24, 1961, IRS detached a special organized-crime squad to work with Justice, and all Organized Crime Drive (OCD) cases got priority treatment. "That meant," says Caplin, "that we tagged them. So if we had a hundred cases and forty were OCD, we'd process those forty first." The result was that 60 percent of all organized-crime cases from 1961–1965 turned out to be revenue cases.

This was consistent with Robert Kennedy's philosophy and his early blueprints of the way he would proceed. "We are going to take a new look at the income tax returns of these people, to spot the flow of crooked money," he announced in his first exclusive interview as Attorney General. "I have been criticized on the ground that tax laws are there to raise money for the government and should not be used to punish the underworld. I think the argument is specious.

"I do believe that tax returns must remain confidential. But I also recognize that we must deal with corruption, crime and dishonesty."

Three cases among many dramatically suggest the way the process worked. That the Department in each case made micro-cases against macro-operators is another example of the different assumptions in the organized-crime and civil rights areas. For instance, it would have been unthinkable to book Governors Barnett or Wallace on speeding charges, but:

The notorious Louis Gallo and his father were indicted for submitting false income statements on a VA loan application for a home mortgage. "The U.S. Attorney told me they'd be laughed out of town on a horse shit charge like that," says Silberling, "but Gallo pleaded guilty."

Racketeer Joseph Aiuppa (number 6 on Mrs. Willse's list of top racketeers), identified before the McClellan Committee as a gambler and gunman for the Capone mob, was apprehended by the Park and Wildlife Service, which discovered that he had in his possession 563 frozen dressed mourning doves (539 over the possession limit of twenty-four per person) that he had transported from Kansas to Chicago. The case was forwarded to the Organized Crime Section and he was convicted under the Migratory Bird Act.*

Because his name was on the list, Chicago racketeer Moses Joseph's application to the FCC for a station license was forwarded to the Organized Crime unit for investigation. Although he had written "none" where the application asked him to list any felony convictions, Willse's files revealed two felony convictions, and the OCS successfully prosecuted him for perjury.

Such cases, of course, raise serious questions about the use and abuse of prosecutor's discretion: The dangers of intergovernmental information exchange should be evident from the countless records, trade secrets and financial data private citizens and business firms now

---

* The conviction was eventually overturned because of illegal search and seizure. In *The Enemy Within*, Kennedy reported that when Committee investigators tried to serve a subpoena on him, "Aiuppa raced his car directly at [one of them] and the Committee investigator barely jumped aside in time to avoid being hit."

deposit with the government, expecting that it will remain uncirculated. "Getting racketeers on a VA application is like getting civil rights workers for speeding," says Howard Glickstein, who was in the Civil Rights Division at the time. "This time it's the Mafiosi, but next time it could be the Black Panthers or Goldwater supporters." "The purpose of the tax laws is to collect revenue," says one tax lawyer. "Once you bend them to catch criminals, you undermine the tax laws and ultimately destroy confidence in them. Justice has to be even-handed. It can't be personal."

Ramsey Clark, who followed Nicholas Katzenbach, Kennedy's successor, as Attorney General, and counts himself among Kennedy's most devoted admirers, agrees: "I don't think justice can be served—unless it's even-handed. Therefore you can't go after people. . . . I disagree with the view that it's okay to select organized-crime cases as long as you apply tax criteria. What you're basically doing in the long run is using tax law to justify judgments about people on other grounds. Lawyers believe you can make a net worth case against anybody with a substantial income. You get people on what the essential violation is. It hurts the tax laws to do anything else."

Supporters of the Oberdorfer–Kennedy policy pointed out that 96 million tax forms were filed annually, 3.5 million were audited and around 800 cases were brought. As long as each and every one of these cases met the requirements of tax law, what was wrong with bringing as many of them as possible against racketeers?

Lou Oberdorfer is adamant that the arrangements worked out under Kennedy were not only proper but preferable because "No prosecution would be authorized unless the reviewing attorneys [in the Tax Division] were satisfied in their own minds that (a) the taxpayer was guilty of violating the Code, and (b) there was some likelihood of victory. There *were* a few dubious cases, but remember, we had a record of 96 percent convictions. We rejected 10 to 20 percent of the IRS-recommended prosecutions."

It was Robert Kennedy's style to delegate administrative problems to his deputy (Byron White), who had a remarkable ability for reconciling the competing claims of the various Justice Department principalities. As Lou Oberdorfer recalls it: "There was a movement led by this fellow Ed Silberling, who came to the Criminal Division before Jack Miller, to take the criminal tax prosecutions away from the Tax Division on the theory that tax cases were just one more criminal case and they should be used to punish criminals. We resisted that. I resisted that and won Byron's blessing to agree that the Organized Crime Section of the Criminal Division would coordinate investigation of all criminal cases, including tax investigations conducted by the Internal Revenue Service. Prior to this if the IRS made a recommendation to prosecute somebody, the file came to the Department of Justice; if they conducted an investigation, the Department had no opportunity to second-guess that. The IRS cut us off. Under the new arrangement, the Organized Crime Section got a look at every one of the investigations in the area in which they were interested. They were sent over even though the IRS did not recommend prosecution. But in order to maintain our control—really the point was to satisfy the court that the criminal tax sanction wasn't going to be used just as a device to get people. We established, and it was a struggle, or re-established our prerogative, that all tax prosecutions, all cases that were actually prosecuted, would be reviewed by our office and the final decision as to whether to prosecute a particular case would be made by the Tax Division . . . the banker and the bookie would be prosecuted and the decision for prosecution would be made by the same people using the same criteria."

"Before Kennedy," Oberdorfer says, "no Tax Division lawyers tried criminal cases. The U.S. attorneys did. We started the practice of sending lawyers from this office out to try the major cases, cases that were in the OCD program. And we also offered assistance to the U.S. attorneys."

The lone exception was in the Southern District of New York. John Reilly, in charge of the U.S. Attorneys' office, recalls traveling to New York with Oberdorfer for a luncheon with Robert Morgenthau in order to alert him to the Tax Division's intent to exercise its jurisdiction over all criminal tax cases. "He looked like a real milquetoast, and I was sure we had made a mistake with his appointment," recalls Reilly. "Then I saw what happened at the lunch." Morgenthau, whose toughness in these matters was legendary, wouldn't budge, and Oberdorfer returned to Washington with no concessions. White's administrative technique in the matter was to let the boys work these things out among themselves.

One should not confuse the issue here—on which reasonable men might disagree—with the other question of the conscious politicization of the tax process. As Oberdorfer recalls, "The whole time Kennedy was here, never once did he try to push me to indict somebody or to push me not to indict somebody or to settle a tax case or not to settle it. . . . Occasionally I would call him up and tell him we were going to indict somebody who was important to him and he would say, 'Well, thanks a lot.' "

And as veteran tax practitioner John Nolan, a conservative Republican (no relation to the Justice Department's John Nolan, Jr.), saw it: "It has been true over the years that in tax cases occasionally you will see the Attorney General step in. Especially on policy matters. But I never saw it happen with Lou. Oberdorfer was thoroughly in command of the Tax Division, he brought in the best men out of the law schools, initiated more extensive use of discovery, selected better cases to appeal, and had special tax dockets in the Districts. It was all very impressive and successful."

Tax enforcement provides another contrast with civil rights enforcement. While the basic strategy with the Southern Governors was to win minimal compliance with the law (in exchange for peace and tranquility), the basic strategy in the organized-crime field was to exploit the maximum zone of play that the law allowed. The Internal Revenue Service, which operates under strict information-hearing restrictions, is a good example. Until Kennedy came along, IRS had historically been reluctant to participate in organized-crime drives because, as Mitchell Rogovin (then Caplin's assistant) notes, "Theologically, IRS has always maintained that its purpose was to collect tax revenue. Historically there had been no formal interchange of information—although as a practical matter agents give information to get information. Conceptually a tax prosecution against an organized-crime figure doesn't really have a tax deterrent value. You don't teach foxes not to eat chickens. So it doesn't meet the primary thrust of tax prosecution. . . ." Besides, there was no appropriation for it, the cases wouldn't bring in revenue so statistics would go down, cases inevitably would be chosen for non-tax reasons and therefore would have less precedential impact, and it would put the IRS in conflict with other agencies. (Which indeed happened after the wholesale bugging engaged in by both the IRS and the FBI was revealed some years after Kennedy had evacuated the Department.)

But Robert Kennedy spoke to Treasury's Douglas Dillon and with J. Edgar Hoover at his side secured the cooperation of *all* the Treasury Department agencies—the Alcohol and Tobacco Tax Service, the Secret Service, the Bureau of Narcotics. He, of course, spoke to Caplin. He spoke to the IRS overseers on the House Appropriations Committee. He got new grades for IRS agents. He arranged for the President to address IRS agents and did so himself. He even got a reference to IRS investigative needs into the President's State of the Union message and that, says Caplin, "can make the morale difference." When Caplin reported non-cooperation by an FBI office in upstate New York, the Attorney General personally bucked Caplin's note to

Hoover with a query (which won Caplin his point, but also a visit from Clyde Tolson, Hoover's Associate Director, and a platoon of agents to find out precisely what his complaint was, and also to suggest that in the future he go through FBI channels). Once, recalls an IRS regional director, "Kennedy got us all into a lecture hall and let us have it. If you know government, you know you can't move IRS with a derrick. Bob Kennedy told us if he thought we were doing a good job he wouldn't have us in the lecture hall." When a member of Silberling's Organized Crime Section complained that a particular regional director of IRS was being uncooperative ("I'd ask to see the file and he'd hold it up tight against his nose and say, 'What do you want to know?' I wanted to know what was in the file!") two weeks later there was a new regional director, and as the Justice Department attorney puts it, "I saw the file."

So on the one side was the Oberdorfer argument that the issue was less one of principle than of policy, and the Kennedy policy was that racketeer-catching was more important than revenue-collecting. While the procedure was legally correct and jurisprudentially arguable, a persuasive case against it was the generalized caveat uttered by Associate Justice (and former Attorney General) Robert Jackson, who told the Second Annual Conference of U.S. Attorneys in April 1940 of the most dangerous power of the prosecutor: "That he will pick people he thinks he should get rather than pick cases that need to be prosecuted."

These issues are more fully explored in Chapter IX. Here the point is that whether or not the information exchange was desirable, it was— to a degree—effective.

Finally, one might observe that while Kennedy went out of his way, at least before the Birmingham race-relations crisis of May 1963, to portray his civil rights role as neutral, law-upholding, even-handed and low-key, a special publicity campaign was mounted to alert the nation to the menace of, and the Justice Department's efforts to ensnare, the nation's top racketeers—the Cosa Nostra, as Joe Valachi was to dub them. Often the publicity effort papered over some real problems within the program. The 1962 raid on the largest dice game on the East Coast in Reading, Pennsylvania, is a case in point. At the time, the *Wall Street Journal* reported: "FBI agents noticed New Jersey license tags outside the [Reading] building and established that customers were being carried back and forth across state lines. That gave the FBI jurisdiction under the new law banning travel to further an illegal enterprise. One hundred FBI agents were brought in for the raid and found $57,000 on the dice tables." [6]

A brilliant publicity coup—since it advertised the new Kennedy anti-crime legislation, the new FBI cooperation and the effectiveness of the Kennedy drive, all in one paragraph. The account seemed credible enough at the time since the new cooperation had also yielded such bonanzas as the Aguichi case, involving the smuggling of $150 million worth of heroin in false trunk bottoms. Brought by the Narcotics Squad, this case involved cooperation by Customs, the Royal Canadian Mounted Police, the Border Patrol, the French Sûreté, the Italian police, the New York City Police Department and the sheriff in Westchester County, New York. "We wanted a simultaneous crackdown on the whole operation," recalls Silberling. "We had the refiners outside Marseilles, the exporters in Italy, the importers in Canada, the distributors—the whole lot. Bob even got the State Department to arrange extraditions from Canada." Before it was all over the bullet-riddled body of one implicated man was found in the Bronx, another was found burned in Rochester during the trial, a third attempted suicide, two jumped the country forfeiting $50,000 bail bonds, and twenty-four were indicted, including Joseph Valachi.

But the Reading raid didn't quite happen that way. Tom McBride, the Hogan-trained attorney who supervised it, remembers things differently. "It was absurd," he says. "The FBI refused to have anything to do with it. I had to go back to Philadelphia and concoct a ludicrous tax theory so that the IRS could get involved. Owen Morris of the IRS supervised the entire investigation. Finally, when IRS had finished its investigation, we turned the information over to the Bureau. By then the Bureau couldn't possibly deny jurisdiction and they took over. Once they got into it, they were superb. They had an efficient, organized systems approach to the thing. But the IRS were a more daring, creative group of investigators."

It was ironic that the FBI—the only intelligence agency directly under the Attorney General's jurisdiction—was the only agency which he did not feel free to bully, pressure, harass and pull rank on. His policy toward the Bureau was essentially one of peaceful coexistence. Nowhere are the mixed fruits of this policy more apparent than in the area of wiretapping and bugging.

Operating with a direct line to the top, the Organized Crime "whiz kids" fanned out across the country and began raiding gambling establishments, closing down bookies' wire services, indicting corrupt mayors and judges, and generally picking off, one by one, the names on the "hit list." Were existing statutes inadequate to do the job? Kennedy pushed through the gambling paraphernalia legislation. Was the Section undermanned? Kennedy tripled the number of attorneys in the Section (to sixty-five). Did the Mafia code of Omerta keep small fry from talking about the big operators? Kennedy's gangbusters had no compunctions about invoking the immunity provisions in, say, the Federal Communications Act in grand-jury investigations where communications facilities in interstate commerce were used in connection with suspected criminal activity. (In the case of the Delaware Sports Service, where a witness was offered immunity and still refused to talk after being directed by the judge to do so, the witness was convicted of contempt of court.)

They also invoked the immunity provision of the Labor-Management Reporting and Disclosure Act of 1959, which authorizes the Secretary of Labor to conduct investigations and to grant immunity to witnesses subpoenaed during these investigations. Once the witness got immunity in a Labor Department proceeding he could be compelled to repeat his testimony before a grand jury. What was extraordinary about the procedure was that the Secretary of Labor—on Kennedy's request—delegated his investigative power to Justice Department attorneys so that they could act both in the capacity of attorneys before grand juries and Labor Department compliance officers.

And where a combination of personality and tradition rendered the centrally based prosecutor approach inappropriate, as in the Southern District of New York, the Kennedy anti-crime program was ably carried forward by the local man in charge, U.S. Attorney Robert M. Morgenthau. As U.S. attorney from the traditionally autonomous, prestigious and independent Southern District—Felix Frankfurter served as an assistant to Henry Stimson in the office—Morgenthau who also specialized in the prosecution of white-collar crime, was responsible for almost half the organized-crime convictions during his time in office (which lasted through 1969, when the Republican Attorney General demanded and received his resignation). When asked to describe the impact of his organized-crime program—given the fact that whenever one syndicate member gets knocked off and goes to jail another is there to take his place—Morgenthau made the following observations:

> I think we've had a significant impact on organized crime in New York. You've got to remember that, really, for pretty close to 25 years, organized crime had a free run. I mean from the end of Prohibition down to 1960. And I think it kind of had woven its way into at least a part of the fabric of society. . . . It really wasn't until Robert F. Kennedy became Attorney General that an organized program was developed.

I think one of the reasons that people are so much more aware of the Mafia now than before is that we've made a lot of cases and people now have court records which show exactly what happens, and I think we've slowed them up a lot. I mean, for instance, take the Bonanno family, where we had a major grand jury investigation and then Bonanno was kidnapped and disappeared. First they had one man appointed to succeed him—Gasper DiGregorio—and he was thoroughly investigated and he couldn't hold on to the leadership. And then you had somebody else appointed—Paul Sciacca—and you had a split in the family. So that I don't think that they ever regained their strength, because we also convicted the underbosses like Carmine Galante. Take the Lucchese family, where we had an extensive grand jury investigation, had over 100 members of the family in and picked quite a large number out and as a result, when Lucchese died they hadn't really been able to establish a strong leadership. It's kind of like a good football team. You know, they can lose a few of their top players, and they can fill those spots with substitutes, but when it reaches a point where there are no substitutes available, then I think that's what's happening in organized crime. It's become more difficult, and therefore it becomes less attractive for people to be recruited into those spots.[7]

A by-product of all this activity was a new sophistication about the structure and function of the organized underworld. By most reckonings, the core of organized crime, U.S. style, consisted of 5,000 members, broken down into twenty-four "families," operating as criminal cartels in the country's major cities (New York, New Jersey, Florida, Louisiana, Nevada, Michigan, Pennsylvania and Rhode Island claimed the wealthiest and most influential). Each family consisting of anywhere from twenty to 700 members, has a hierarchical structure closely paralleling that of the Mafia groups of Sicily. At the top is a "boss" charged with maintaining law, profits and order. Under the boss is an "underboss" who relays messages to the boss and passes on his instructions to underlings. On the same level as the underboss is the *"consigliere,"* generally an elder member valued for his advice and wisdom. Below are the *"caporegime,"* who serve as chiefs of the operating units and/or insulate the top men from the *"soldati,"* or "button" men. Thus, as the President's Crime Report points out, "All commands, information, complaints and money flow back and forth through" buffers.

In addition to enabling the crime-fighters to zero in on targets with new precision, the unfolding picture of how the organized underworld worked suggested the convenience that electronic surveillance might provide those whose duty was to combat it. Actually, court-ordered wiretaps constituted the major source of information for the

Kefauver Committee's investigation in New York City. The Committee said: ". . . the wiretaps in particular gave a vivid picture of Frank Costello as a political boss and an underworld emperor." Since Costello and his confreres could not be expected to cooperate, such information was thought otherwise impossible to come by.

On the surface the related theses that Robert Kennedy ran the FBI and that he was able to do so only because he had a brother in the White House exuded a certain logic. Under Robert Kennedy's prodding and with Jack Kennedy's backing, the FBI for the first time effectively entered the fights for civil rights and against organized crime. And immediately upon President Kennedy's assassination, the FBI unilaterally halted the bulk of its diplomatic relations with the Attorney General's office. Among other disruptions, the Bureau stopped sending a car to pick up the Attorney General as he traveled around the country; it started communicating directly with the new President rather than via the Attorney General, as protocol (and the practice of the Kennedy Administration) indicated; it bypassed the Deputy Attorney General in undertaking to clear potential judicial nominees; it excluded the Attorney General from its investigations for the Warren Commission (and then prematurely released their findings to the press, in violation of Chief Justice Warren's orders);[8] and it generally behaved in what Ed Guthman, Robert Kennedy's press secretary, characterizes as "an unmanly fashion." Indeed, the very afternoon of the assassination Jack Miller, the Assistant Attorney General in charge of the Criminal Division, flew to Dallas to take charge, only to be blatantly, rudely and improperly ignored by the FBI.

Without disputing the facts, another interpretation—and quite the reverse—is possible. During President Kennedy's life Robert never *attempted* to control either the Director or the FBI. He accepted the Bureau as another country which he was content to influence rather than capture, and he tempered his efforts to influence the FBI so as not to embarrass his brother. In practical terms, this meant that he had unwittingly ceded half of his power to Hoover and the FBI, and missed the chance to force Hoover's resignation.

After President Kennedy's assassination, Attorney General Kennedy no longer felt under the constraints of brotherly obligation. He no longer feared that confrontation with the FBI might undermine the larger goals of the Administration. And having accumulated three years' worth of expertise at FBI-managing (not to mention the advice of such neo-Hooverologists as Burke Marshall), he exerted new and important influence on the FBI's activities—especially in the civil rights area, which by then had come to preoccupy him. But always he made the basic concession: he assumed the FBI's right to control its own destiny, its own systems, people and information. He ceded to it the ultimate bureaucratic stake—the right to protect its own secrets and the right to run its own affairs on its own terms.

On the surface the Bureau had a reasonable argument for its unwillingness to share information or place its agents under anyone else's direction. The FBI argued that its security procedures would be compromised if it shared its top-secret intelligence with non-FBI personnel. It argued that its informant system would be jeopardized if it revealed informants' identities. And in general it insisted that the FBI's rigidly high standards would be contaminated and agent morale irreparably undermined if other agencies—even the Justice Department's own Organized Crime Section—were permitted to interfere with its chain of command.

"It was frustrating as hell," complains Silberling. "We'd get these reports and want to go back and follow up leads, but they would always tell us that the informants—whom we only knew as T-1 or T-2—were 'unavailable.'" At the time it looked like bureaucratic eccentricity. And frustrating though it may have been, the Kennedy men were prepared to humor the Bureau—to forgo interagency sharing where the FBI was concerned, in exchange for the FBI's parallel participation in the anti-crime drive, which it had withheld until the Kennedys came along. The compromise seemed unimportant, an irritating concession to the FBI's vanity. Silberling recalls, "I once got hold of a cover sheet. We were never supposed to see them because they had a legend which told who all the T-1s and T-2s were. It turns out that over half of them were credit reports and industry newsletters!" The revelation confirmed his suspicion—correct as far as it went—that the FBI was as concerned to promote its mystique as it was to protect its informants.

What nobody understood at the time, however, is that the FBI was *not* merely responding in its own peculiar parallel way to the aggressive insistence of a brash young man with a brother in the White House that they join the anti-crime crusade. To the contrary. As a high Justice Department official put it, "The FBI has things it tries out on every Attorney General and when it finds one that looks like he won't object, they go ahead and do it."

In retrospect nothing is clearer or more natural than the affinity of the FBI for electronic surveillance, commonly known as bugging, which involves a hidden microphone that (a) needn't be connected to telephone wires like a tap, and (b) can pick up much more than a tap, which only invades the privacy of a telephone conversation; a bug picks up anything in the room. For one thing, it multiplies the secret society's capability to acquire secrets. For another, it satisfies the secret society's appetite for participating in the magic rituals of the new technology. In more mundane terms, it would enable the FBI, following the model of its internal-security successes, to close the vast intelligence gap in the organized-crime area, incurred during the years when the Bureau had convinced itself that the Mafia didn't exist because the Bureau didn't have jurisdiction to go after it.

The FBI had experimented with bugs in organized-crime cases as early as 1954, and after the 1957 Apalachin meeting the Bureau had increased its bugging—although it had never made a massive campaign of it, partly because there had been no pressure on the Bureau to perform, partly because it was unaware of the dimensions of the organized-crime problem, but partly because the Bureau knew it might encounter resistance at the top. Attorneys General Brownell and Rogers were both lawyers in the Wall Street tradition—careful and cautious, not given to tolerating procedural departures except in internal-security cases, where, especially in Brownell's case, he saw red or at least saw no constitutional problems.

And then along came Kennedy. From the outside it looked as if, in the words of one Kennedy aide, "Bob was pressing the FBI to put up or shut up and they were doing neither. They claimed they were the greatest investigative agency in the world and therefore refused to work in tandem with what they regarded as inferior agencies. Yet—in '61 and '62—they weren't really producing." In fact, the FBI *was* producing—not results, but intelligence; not public exposés, but private secrets; not evidence for cases, but evidence that the FBI knew what was going on. It was following the highly successful model it had employed in the internal-security area. First, you bug and tap and find out what's going on. Then you infiltrate and/or establish your network of informants. The Communist Party cases, it will be recalled, surfaced *not* with electronic devices but with informants like Herbert (*I Led Three Lives*) Philbrick. The FBI's calculation was that as soon as it caught up in organized crime, as soon as it had an effective network of spies and informants, it would close off the bugs and nobody would be any the wiser. The FBI's miscalculation was twofold: First, it misread the law, making the dubious assumption that it had the same authority to tap and bug in the organized-crime area as it had in the internal-security area; second, it overestimated its own secret-keeping capacity. It is ironic that once the secret got out, once it was revealed that the FBI had engaged in illegal bugging, Hoover turned from secret-keeping to secret-managing and deftly began the selective release of top-secret information—an expenditure of resources to which he has resorted only in extremis—in an effort aimed at embarrassing and discrediting Robert Kennedy.

The public exchange between Robert Kennedy and J. Edgar Hoover in early December 1966, two years after Kennedy had departed the Justice Department, was brief, sensational, cryptic, ugly, disingenuous and incomplete. Hoover, embarrassed by rumors that in the early Sixties the FBI had tapped and bugged without authorization from the Attorney General, answered the rumors via a letter to Congressman H. R. Gross (who had conveniently raised the question in the letter to Hoover), assuring him that the FBI never bugged or tapped without authorization from the Attorney General and that "[Robert Kennedy] was briefed frequently by an FBI official regarding such matters. FBI usage of such devices, while always handled in a sparing, carefully controlled manner and as indicated, only with the specific authority of the Attorney General, was obviously increased at Mr. Kennedy's insistence while he was in office." Hoover documented his contention with two pieces of paper. One was presumably "evidence" that Kennedy knew of specific bugging in New York and the other "evidence" that the Justice Department generally knew the precise number of bugs in operation at any given time.

Kennedy denied the charge and produced a piece of paper of his own from Courtney Evans, the FBI agent who was supposed to have briefed him. At Kennedy's request after he left the Justice Department, Evans had written him:

> This letter is being sent to you, in line with your request and in confirmation of our conversation. It relates to information furnished to you during your tenure as Attorney General by me as an official of the FBI about the use of telephone taps and microphone surveillances.
>
> As you know, I was the FBI's liaison officer with the Department of Justice during this period.
>
> On January 10, 1961, while you were Attorney General-designate, a memorandum was delivered to you furnishing a summary on the use of wiretapping by the FBI in serious national security cases.
>
> Thereafter, individual requests in these serious national security cases for wiretap authorization were sent to you by the FBI for approval. These were the only wiretap authorizations which were ever submitted to you.
>
> Since prior Attorneys General had informed the FBI that the use of microphones as contrasted to telephone taps need not be specifically approved by the Attorney General, I did not discuss the use of these

devices with you in national security or other cases, nor do I know of any written material that was sent to you at any time concerning the use, specific location or other details as to installation of any such devices in Las Vegas, Nevada, or anywhere else.

When I asked him about bugging, Kennedy denied that he had any knowledge of FBI bugging practices, as he had about taps. "It all depends on who you believe, me or Hoover," he said. "Look, if you don't believe me, talk to Byron, talk to Nick, talk to Burke, talk to anybody whose word you respect. I worked with most of these men for three and one half years, sometimes twenty-four hours at a stretch. We were very close and had many intimate conversations about every subject you could imagine. You would think that if I knew about the Bureau's bugging practices, once in all of that time I would have had one conversation with one of them about it. But the fact is that I didn't. The first I heard about it was in connection with Las Vegas. Ask Nick about that."

On inquiry, Katzenbach says that aside from Las Vegas,* he never talked with Kennedy about bugging because he thought it was the Attorney General's business, not his, and the Attorney General never brought it up. William Hundley of the Organized Crime Section says, "I've known about it ever since Accardo, but if I asked the Bureau they'd flat out and lie to me. I thought Bob knew too, but when the [bugging story] began to break, I went trotting up to his Senate office and he asked me did I know, and when I said yes, he was hopping mad and said, 'Why the hell didn't you tell me?' Unless he's the greatest actor in the world, he didn't know." Ed Silberling says *he* himself knew and he assumed the Attorney General knew (because electronic equipment was discussed in his presence, although whether its use was legal or illegal was never discussed) but he never discussed it with Kennedy. Burke Marshall says he simply assumed and so did the Attorney General that the FBI would clear any questionable bugs with the Attorney General. In fact, virtually everybody interviewed on this subject tells the same story—whether they knew or didn't know or suspected, none of them had taken it up with the Attorney General.

It is difficult to recapture the atmosphere—and the naïve assumptions —of the day. More significant was the attitude of lower-echelon attorneys. While Thurgood Marshall, who was Solicitor General in 1966 when the government first confessed the bugging to the U.S. Supreme Court, is reported to have said, "Hell, he *had* to know,"

* See pp. 79–82.

Marshall's is a retrospective view. G. Robert Blakey, then a young attorney in the Organized Crime Section, recalls, "Once an agent I knew told me he was going to Army language school in Monterey to learn Sicilian. I asked him, 'What's the matter? Don't your informants speak English?' It didn't dawn on me until two years later why he had to learn Sicilian."

Henry Peterson, Hundley's assistant in the Organized Crime Section, says, "You could go out and talk to the agents in the field. They'd never say, 'We have an electronic listening device on the phone.' But the agents would say, 'We've got him covered like a glove' and now I know what that means. But if I were to ask officially about how they got a piece of information, they'd say, 'It's a highly placed informant whose identity cannot be disclosed.' "

Talks with all of these men and an effort, unsuccessful, to talk with Mr. Hoover have led to the following conclusions:

(1) That Robert Kennedy did not "know" about the FBI's illegal bugging practices in either the specific or the general;

(2) That he did not particularly want to know about the FBI's bugging practices, an uncharacteristic lack of curiosity on his part;

(3) That the FBI put the Department (and by extension the Attorney General) on technical but not actual notice of its activities;

(4) That the FBI believed it had technical authority to do what it was doing;

(5) That the headline charges back and forth between Kennedy and Hoover in December 1966 were one part semantic confusion and one part FBI deception, but essentially irrelevant;

(6) That the bugging was in part a response to the Kennedy-created environment of urgency (the war on crime had been generated by his puritanism, propelled by his expertise, accelerated by his non-stop energy, implemented by his muscle and if he was not exactly the sore loser portrayed in the anti-Kennedy biographies of Victor Lasky and Ralph De Toledano, he made it clear that he preferred to win);

(7) But that essentially the FBI made the decision to accelerate the electronic war on its own and used the war on crime as an excuse to do so;

(8) That much of the ambiguity and confusion surrounding the issue is traceable to the role of Courtney Evans, the FBI's liaison to the Attorney General, who ended up as more or less of a double agent attempting to act like a Kennedy but write like an agent. Thus he did what Kennedy wanted done and put on paper what Hoover wanted recorded. Since Kennedy was a man of action with too little regard for

the future and Hoover was a man of paper, of anticipatory records, with too little regard for the present, both were content—at the time— with the procedure;

(9) That Hoover *believed* Kennedy knew and *believed* the FBI had the Attorney General's authorization systematically and continuously to break the law not because of anything Robert Kennedy or any other Attorney General said or did, but because Hoover was eventually able to cite—within the private councils of the Department—a piece of paper going back to 1954 which he interpreted to give him that authorization; in addition, the FBI had, it must be conceded on the basis of the correspondence and memos Mr. Hoover released via Representative Gross, a paper record, albeit a thin one, against Kennedy. And in the secret society of the FBI the record, as far as the Director was concerned, was the reality.

Whether these calculated surmises about who knew what are right is less important than an understanding of why what happened happened. The FBI never really did anything that Hoover didn't want it to do— or at least it never did anything quietly and effectively that he didn't want it to do. From the revelation that the FBI was bugging en masse we can presume that whether or not Robert Kennedy knew about it, whether or not it was an "authorized" activity, it was something Hoover wanted done.

The suggestion here is that Kennedy's general attitude toward wiretapping encouraged Mr. Hoover in his will—and that to the extent that Kennedy was ignorant of the FBI's bugging practices, it was an administrative failure so flagrant that Kennedy is morally chargeable with the consequences of his ignorance. The pages that follow first document Robert Kennedy's general attitude toward electronic eavesdropping and then show why he is chargeable with knowledge of the FBI's activities. But once the evidence establishes the mix—bureaucratic desire (Hoover) plus policy-maker permissiveness (Kennedy)— which yielded the wholesale electronic improprieties of the Kennedy era, it is then vastly enlightening to look at the FBI's own documents, not for what they tell us about who was to blame (surely a joint proprietorship of Messrs. Hoover and Kennedy), but rather for what they show us about the relationship between the FBI and the Department, for what they indicate about how the Bureau operates.

Robert Kennedy's attitude toward wiretapping is available for inspection because the subject was under continuous review and discussion throughout his Attorney Generalship. Since he never admitted that he knew about FBI bugging, and indeed never really discussed the problems raised by bugging,* we must infer his bugging attitude from his tapping attitude. Despite the contrary impression that he carefully conveyed in both his New York Senatorial campaign against Senator Kenneth Keating in 1964 and his Presidential campaign of 1968, Attorney General Robert Kennedy was, on balance, pro-wiretapping.

Given his total commitment to the destruction of the crime syndicates and a tendency to regard civil liberties as part luxury and part obstacle, it is not surprising that Robert Kennedy favored the deployment of wiretapping. "There are over 100 million phones in the United States and the organized criminal syndicates engaged in racketeering activities involving millions of illicit dollars do a major part of their business over this network of communication. . . . It is used in bribery, extortion, and kidnapping," Kennedy told Congress. In his view, the need for wiretapping legislation was urgent.

Like every Attorney General since 1934 except Ramsey Clark, Robert Kennedy asked Congress to authorize via new legislation the use of that ultimate weapon in the war on crime.

Like Jackson, Biddle, Clark, McGranery, McGrath, Brownell and Rogers before him, he was unsuccessful in obtaining such legislation.

Like all of them he nevertheless followed the practice of approving FBI wiretap requests (for intelligence rather than evidentiary purposes —since the courts won't accept illegally obtained evidence) in the national-security area, despite the fact that Section 605 of the Federal Communications Act of 1934 states that "no person" is permitted to "intercept and divulge" telephone conversations.

Like his immediate predecessors he accepted Attorney General Jackson as his authority for the premise that it was permissible to "intercept" telephone calls if one did not "divulge" them and that communications within the executive branch of the government did not constitute "divulgence." Jackson arrived at this opinion only after he received a May 21, 1940, memo from President Franklin D. Roosevelt in response to a recent Supreme Court decision declaring wiretapping illegal. "I am confident," wrote FDR as Hitler's Panzer divisions rumbled across Europe, "that the Supreme Court never intended any dictum in the particular case which it decided to apply to grave matters affecting the defense of this nation. . . . You are therefore authorized and directed in such cases as you may approve, after investigation of the need in each case, to authorize the necessary in-

* If we are to take him at his word, as I do.

vestigating agents that they are at liberty to secure the information by listening devices directed to the conversation or other communications of persons suspected of subversive activity against the Government of the United States, including suspected spies. You are requested furthermore to limit these investigations so conducted to a minimum and to limit them in so far as possible to aliens." *

Actually, Jackson, who had renounced the use of taps prior to the letter from FDR, was not particularly comfortable with his own legal ratiocination. Francis Biddle, who served as Jackson's Solicitor General before succeeding him as Attorney General, has written in his memoirs:

> The memorandum [from FDR] was evidently prepared in a hurry by the President personally, without consultation, probably after he had talked to Bob [Jackson]. It opened the door pretty wide to wiretapping of *anyone suspected of subversive activities.* Bob didn't like it, and not liking it, turned it over to Edgar Hoover without himself passing on each case. When it came my turn I studied the applications carefully, sometimes requesting more information, occasionally turning them down when I thought they were not warranted.[9]

Like his predecessors, Kennedy was conscious of the hypocrisy and illogic involved in a situation where the federal government, not to mention countless state and local governments, was systematically engaging in activity which Congress repeatedly had refused to legitimize. This unsatisfactory state of affairs was one of his principal arguments in favor of the new legislation. As he stated on March 29, 1962, in support of the Justice Department's bill, "The existing situation with respect to wiretapping is chaotic." He said Section 605 "is unsatisfactory to almost everyone. It does not meet the needs of either the federal government or the states for effective law enforcement and it has not adequately protected individuals from a good deal of indiscriminate wiretapping."

Unlike most of his predecessors, Robert Kennedy had an experience-anchored belief in the indispensability of taps and a sense of urgency about their employment. As counsel to the McClellan Committee he had worked with wiretap material—virtually all of his information on Johnny Dio came from District Attorney Hogan's wiretap investigations, then permitted under New York law. Kennedy knew how top gangsters insulated themselves from direct involvement in crimes. He

---

* The President, of course, has no authority to authorize unconstitutional or illegal acts. Both he and Jackson ignored the provision of Section 605 which states that "No person shall use the same or any information contained therein for his own benefit or for the benefit of another not entitled thereto."

believed that informants—when they surfaced—were often eliminated,* and he saw electronic surveillance as a substitute for the informant system. Kennedy used tapes derived from District Attorney Hogan's taps in his Rackets Committee interrogation of Jimmy Hoffa and caught Hoffa in a lie. Later he commented: "The kind of proof makes a difference. He can say very forcefully someone's a liar—that's easy. But here we had his own voice on the tapes. He couldn't deny it." As G. Robert Blakey, current counsel to the McClellan Committee, observes, "Faced with the hard choice of talk, perjury or contempt, knowing you have his voice to keep him straight, the witness most often decides to cooperate."

Based on his analysis of the structure of organized crime, Robert Kennedy agreed that "The need to be able to intercept or overhear these otherwise inaccessible communications, if criminal sanctions are to be brought into play, is clear, for the leaders perform no criminal overt acts that can be witnessed by the police or citizens, who are not involved themselves. Live insider testimony is rarely obtained and incriminating documents are either seldom kept or always kept inaccessible. Therefore, some substitute, such as the product of electronic surveillance, is crucial." [10]

The thrust of Robert Kennedy's attitude emerged at one discussion on his Hickory Hill patio in early spring 1961 as he deliberated with his staff about proposed wiretap legislation. Miller and White were strongly in favor of it and Solicitor General Cox thought it could be supported. While various staff members had reservations about this or that provision, he was surprised to discover that Bill Orrick, Ramsey Clark and Joe Dolan opposed wiretapping except in national-security cases. "Do you mean to tell me," he asked Bill Orrick incredulously, "that if your little girl were kidnapped and a tap might help her get home safely you still wouldn't approve?" Orrick, who thought tapping was an inherently uncontrollable invasion of privacy and wrong, said, "Hard cases make bad law." Today Orrick remembers, "I wanted to get off that but he stayed with it. He couldn't understand my attitude. . . . Byron said, 'You sure you've thought about it?' I said yes." Kennedy saw "the heart of the problem" as "a proper balance between the right of privacy and the needs of modern law enforcement," and he often stated, "I do not know of any law enforcement officer who does not believe that at least some authority to tap telephones is absolutely

---

* In 1965 Attorney General Katzenbach testified that "We must dismiss [organized-crime cases] because key witnesses or informants suffer 'accidents' and turn up . . . in a river wearing concrete boots. Such accidents are not unusual. We have lost more than twenty-five informants in this and similar ways in the past four years."

essential for the prevention and punishment of crime."

It was more than a counter-crime strategy. It was an expression of his social vision, his order of priorities, his victim-oriented compassion. By 1962 Kennedy was in constant conversation with proceduralists like Solicitor General Archibald Cox, Burke Marshall, Nicholas Katzenbach and Byron White on how to legitimize tapping and at the same time bring it under control. He had a growing sophistication about the possibilities of abuse, but it was tempered by the assumption that he was going to be in charge and he was no abuser. Moreover, he was still persuaded that "There is no question that the telephone is an important criminal asset. Here is an instantaneous, cheap, readily available and secure means of communication. It greatly simplifies the commission of espionage, sabotage, narcotics and other major crime." *

Thus, from the outset, Kennedy had no moral qualms about wiretapping and, to the contrary, he believed it an effective and necessary weapon in his war on crime. That, presumably, is why, starting in 1961, he urged the Congress to pass wiretapping legislation. His rhetorical position was not static. As the years passed, from 1961 to 1964, he moved from being pro-wiretapping to being pro-wiretapping "with proper safeguards," to being anti-wiretapping "except in a limited number of cases," but essentially at the end, as at the beginning, he saw wiretapping as a law enforcement necessity rather than as a threat to individual liberties or invasion of privacy. The milieu was reflected in a remark by Nick Katzenbach some years later which captured the enlightened yet prosecutorial attitude that prevailed: "There is a problem in each case [in which a tap, if legal, would prove incriminatory] where the result is to allow a *known* guilty person to go free. It is a problem, particularly if it's a crime of violence. People who don't see it as a problem frustrate me."

In 1961 Kennedy disingenuously supported a wiretap bill which purported to restrict federal wiretapping to a limited number of cases but which left state and local law enforcers free to tap as local law permitted. Since Kennedy's expertise and experience on the McClellan Committee had exposed him to the fact that state and local wiretaps were available to federal authorities, it was not fully honest of him to support the bill as "restricted" or "limited," which is what he and other Department officials called it at the time. Later, after the Justice De-

---

* More logically, the argument might be that if organized crime *taps* government phones, the government should have the right to retaliate. But in fact, that doesn't follow any more than would licensing the government to murder and maim because organized crime does it.

partment had developed its second—and more carefully drawn—proposed wiretapping legislation, Ed Guthman passed the word to the press that the 1961 edition had been "hastily conceived" although Kennedy had defended it as late as September 24, 1961, against James Reston's insistent questions on "Meet the Press."

In early 1962 the Justice Department came up with an improved bill about which *The New Republic* editorialized, "There is substantial agreement among professional observers that [it] is the best bill on wiretapping that has been put forth since Alexander Graham Bell invented the problem." This bill, whose enactment Kennedy urged throughout the remainder of his term, subjected states to the same rigorous requirements as the federal government: tapping on court order in a specified number of "limited" areas for forty-five-day periods. It permitted the judge to approve taps if he determined that "there is probably cause to believe that the offense has been, is being or is about to be committed; that pertinent facts may be obtained through wiretapping; that no other means are available for obtaining the information; and that facilities to be tapped are being used in connection with the offense or are leased to or 'commonly used by' the suspect."

So far so good. But there were at least two respects in which the Justice Department's representations in behalf of the 1962 bill were, at best, fudging; and Kennedy was dishonest either with himself or the American people on the implications of his proposal. First, the emphasis on the "limited" areas in which an Attorney General could tap. Actually, the areas were "limited" to "national security," kidnapping, "interstate racketeering" and narcotics including marijuana. The tapping of Dr. Martin Luther King (discussed in Chapter III) shows how the definition of "national security" can be expanded at the Attorney General's or the FBI's whim. Gambling falls under "interstate racketeering." And it takes no leap of the imagination to project what use a nervous chief law enforcement officer could make of the marijuana exception. Thus, what was presented as a restricted or "limited" wiretapping bill, a bill with "proper safeguards," actually had built-in loopholes which made it deceptive, permissive, potentially dangerous and subject to easy abuse.

Both the 1961 or 1962 bills, moreover, omit any reference to bugging or electronic eavesdropping. Whether or not Kennedy knew about the FBI's illegal bugging practices, the fact is that he should have known—not as some general principle taught in Public Administration 101, but because on a number of occasions described in the following pages the theory and practice of bugging were up for discussion and in each case it was out of character for the super-inquisitive and ultra-curious Robert Kennedy not to want to know more. This is not to suggest that in an "eye-winking" way he conspired not to know. Rather, his lack of follow-up on bugs was consistent with his casual approach to the *handling* of taps (as distinguished from his more rigorous approach—demanded by Congressional relations—to the matter of proper wiretap legislation). Ten days before he took office, when Courtney Evans briefed him on Departmental tapping procedures in the national-security area, he never bothered to ask for a list of the taps in progress. He never sat down with Hoover or Evans (or had one of his aides sit down) to establish explicit and rigid criteria for national-security wiretapping. He never kept a record of the taps he had approved so he never really knew, in any systematic way, who was being tapped and when. He did not have any forty-five-day cut-off review period, which he could have instituted with no new legislation. He did not have any system at all for reviewing the utility of taps once authorized. As far as can be determined, he never turned down a Bureau wiretap request in the national-security area. And it never occurred to him, in the absence of legislation, to require any of the safeguards that his bill would have made mandatory.

By contrast, nothing was casual about his push to legalize wiretapping. He did testify for his bill, publish articles urging its passage, dispatch his Deputy to debate men like Washington *Post* editorial writer and civil libertarian Alan Barth on the bill's merits and generally conduct a massive and subtle public-relations campaign on its behalf. He even changed the language of his Congressional testimony to make it more palatable to *New York Times* readers when he published the testimony verbatim as an article in *The New York Times Magazine.**
He tried unsuccessfully to get Francis Biddle, who testified for the bill, to write a letter to *Life* objecting to a critical editorial (Biddle felt the editorial was fair criticism) and eventually he unleashed Joe Valachi in the vain hope that his sensational revelations would electrify the country and mobilize it behind his bill. Libertarian objectors were instructed to read the bill and if that didn't convince them, they were dismissed as "knee jerk liberals"—the most devastating put-down in the Kennedy Justice vernacular.

Did Robert Kennedy know about the FBI's bugging practices? He

---

* The testimony stated: "I am convinced that we need legislation to permit the use of wiretapping by law enforcement officials." The otherwise verbatim magazine article read: "I am convinced we need legislation to permit the revision of the present and ineffective wiretapping statute."

says he didn't, but not counting the after-the-fact "evidence" released by Mr. Hoover (analyzed below), there are at least six reasons why he should have known.

First, his experience on the McClellan Committee alerted him to the possible uses and abuses of taps and bugs. And so, if he were at all concerned about abuse-potential of such technology, all he had to do was ask.

Second, as an elementary principle of administration, a Cabinet officer must be held responsible for the public testimony of his subordinates. In Robert Kennedy's case he was in constant touch with his Assistant Attorneys General, particularly so with Jack Miller, head of the Criminal Division, and especially on anything relating to the passage of his favored wiretap legislation. Thus, Kennedy must be charged with knowledge of Miller's testimony on May 11, 1961, when he was asked about whether the Department would support legislation which covered bugging and if not why not. Miller said:

> S. 1221 raises the very broad generalized problem of eavesdropping. It is the considered opinion of the Department of Justice that the problem, although properly of concern to the subcommittee and to the Department as well, should not be allowed to dilute the concentration of effort upon the problem of wiretapping. We in the Department are studying the problem of eavesdropping and would suggest that until this area with all its ramifications is carefully explored, legislation should not be enacted.

Either Miller was lying and the Department was not "studying" the matter, or he was telling the truth and the Department was studying it but Kennedy didn't know about it. Or he was speaking prospectively, as testifiers are wont to do, but never got around to it. In either event, the Attorney General can't be assigned credit for *any* of the accomplishments of his administration if he is excused from the obligations and notice placed on him by Miller's testimony.*

Third, because of his active interest in the affairs of IRS, already documented, he should have known about the February 24, 1961, IRS order which called for saturation treatment of racketeers' files

---

* I believe Miller was telling the truth when he wrote me in a letter dated May 20, 1971, "With respect to who was studying the problem, I have no specific recollection. I am sure that I was involved in attempting to ascertain what type of legislation should be introduced, if any, with respect to eavesdropping devices. I would not have considered that legislation was necessary to prohibit the use of eavesdropping devices placed by trespass for the simple reason that it is already against the law. My recollection is that our consideration was directed primarily toward the utilization of mini-phones, briefcase recorders, voice automated recorders, and things of that nature."

and "full use" of "available electronic equipment." When Drew Pearson unveiled this order years later, in 1966, Kennedy denied knowledge. He said: "One, until this column was read to me I never even heard of the memorandum described. Two, I never knew of, let alone approved or instructed, the use of the kind of equipment described as being used by the IRS. Three, I think that although mistakes were made, the IRS has made a major contribution to the fight against organized crime in the U.S. for which all of us should be grateful." Robert Kennedy's comment is not good enough. He was responsible for the environment which encouraged the IRS to undertake such marginal measures. And therefore, it was incumbent upon him to anticipate the consequences of the sense of urgency which he had created. As a veteran tax lawyer points out: "Special agents are policemen to begin with. So it's not good enough to say you didn't know about it. They require lots of supervision. They are zealots and you have to watch them."

Fourth, the Attorney General is responsible for his *own* testimony—not only the correctness of his message but the understanding of the underlying issues which it implies. And on March 29, 1962, appearing before the Committee on the Judiciary in support of S. 2813, the Administration's wiretap bill, he admitted that the bills didn't treat eavesdropping (bugging) and explained why, thereby implicitly imposing on himself the obligation of familiarity with the FBI's bugging procedures. He said:

Both S. 1495 and S. 2813 do not treat eavesdropping. We recognize that eavesdropping may present serious threats to privacy. But, while Congress has a clear constitutional basis to legislate with respect to wiretapping or an interstate communications network, the powers of Congress to deal effectively with eavesdropping are far more limited. We believe we should concentrate our efforts on a wiretapping bill which Congress clearly has the power to enact and which is urgently needed.

Whether or not his analysis of Congressional powers was correct is secondary to the fact that such a proposition implies a level of sophistication and knowledgeability about bugging practices in general that is inconsistent with Kennedy's failure to find out more about the FBI's bugging practices in the specific.

Fifth, there is the fact that in May of 1963 when the FBI turned over to the Justice Department a two-volume document called "The Skimming Report," which detailed the illegal siphoning off of gambling profits by Las Vegas casinos to avoid taxes, it was obvious from the report that the FBI had gained much of its information from bugging devices, though bugging was explicitly outlawed by Nevada statute. According to William Hundley, three days after turning over the report the FBI learned that the racketeers under surveillance had gotten a verbatim copy and they accused the Department of careless security policy. "But," recalls Hundley, "there was only one copy and it went straight from my assistant, Henry Peterson, to me and I gave it to Jack Miller, who took it home over the weekend. We couldn't have leaked it. My personal suspicion has always been that the Bureau knew their bugs had been discovered and they turned the report over to us so that we would be the fall guys."

The report caused a great flap within the Department and three days after receipt Katzenbach brought the matter to Kennedy's attention; Kennedy instructed him to "Make sure they're not doing any more of this." "That was the first and only time I found out about FBI bugging when I was Attorney General," Kennedy told me five years later, "and I had the FBI stop right away. Ask Nick about it." Katzenbach recalls that on Kennedy's instructions "I asked Courtney [Evans], 'Am I absolutely assured that this is stopped?' and Courtney said, 'Yes, it's been stopped.' Neither Bob nor I ever viewed this as anything but a Las Vegas problem. They did stop it but only in Las Vegas. Bob never put it in a broader context to me and I never said it. I rather assumed it [the Las Vegas bugging] must have had some kind of authorization and must have been the Attorney General's business. It's incredible, but neither of us knew. Now in hindsight that was stupid on my part and his. But we got exactly what we asked for."

Katzenbach may have made a reasonable if erroneous assumption, but the Las Vegas situation should have triggered an Attorney General-ordered review of the FBI's over-all bugging practices. Or, at the minimum, the kind of open, frank, informal conversation with Courtney Evans and others which was the hallmark of Robert Kennedy's style in every other area of the Department's dealings. Because as Katzenbach points out, at the Attorney General's level, "Once you ask they tell. They don't lie. If you ask Mr. Hoover, he'll tell you."

This judgment is of course more easily made in retrospect and it is by no means inconceivable that while some, like Ed Silberling and Bill Hundley, had no doubt that the FBI was bugging and/or tapping in the organized-crime areas, it never occurred to others, equally shrewd about these matters. Hundley says, "After Apalachin, certain things were said by agents that led me to believe they were using devices on a selective basis. Now I honestly thought that all of this was being handled topside. I thought that every time the old man wanted to put one of those things in he'd trot over to the Attorney General's office and get his John Henry. Later on, I found out it wasn't that way at all.

"The FBI position always was, you tell us what you want done and if we agree we'll do it. Don't tell us how to do it. Stay out of our field. If they're interested—like the Smith Act—you'd have the whole FBI at your disposal. They'd go to Timbuctoo. If not, not. Bobby got them interested in organized crime."

Not till Edward Bennett Williams, acting on behalf of Las Vegas clients, brought an invasion-of-privacy suit a year later was it revealed to the public that the FBI had leased twenty-five telephone lines directly from the telephone company in Las Vegas, Nevada, to monitor telephone lines at the Desert Inn and other Las Vegas hotels. The lines were leased to the Henderson Novelty Company, a front with the same address as the Las Vegas FBI office. The monitoring had lasted eighteen months.

The point is less that Robert Kennedy should have known than that he should have instituted procedures to find out. And it is a mark against him that those of his lieutenants who thought they *knew* about FBI bugging *assumed* with Hundley "that it was being handled topside." He had contributed to an environment which discouraged questions about this sort of secret surveillance. In his own behalf, Kennedy asked me, "While I was Attorney General, why didn't Mr. Hoover ever discuss the matter of bugs with me? If they wanted me to know, why didn't they brief me? If somebody had written a memo . . . but there was none." His self-justifying answer was that Mr. Hoover never particularly wanted to get him into it and Courtney Evans wanted to keep him out of it. "The fact was that I didn't know. Maybe I should have known. Somebody somewhere should have known. But I didn't." On January 10, 1961, Courtney Evans briefed Kennedy on the FBI's wiretap procedures. Why, Kennedy asked, after the issue was in the headlines, was he never briefed on the Bureau's bugging practices? But Robert Kennedy was an asker. Robert Kennedy was on notice that there was such a thing as bugging, that it could be abused, that the FBI in at least one nest of organized crime— Las Vegas—had engaged in illegal bugging, and he didn't ask, he didn't investigate, he didn't issue any of the kind of serious, sweeping orders against bugging that Ramsey Clark did as part of the Lyndon Johnson Administration. Whether or not one faults Robert Kennedy for his social view—that tapping and bugging may be necessary as a counterforce to the Mafia conspiracy—is secondary to the point that as Attorney General he had an *obligation* to know, and that there he was technically, morally, administratively and in every other way responsible for the FBI's illegal acts. Kennedy makes the point that "the bugging intensified under me but it didn't begin under me." Fair enough. But *because* he created an environment of urgency he had a special obligation to check the excesses which urgency begets. His unsystematic handling of national-security taps undoubtedly contributed to the FBI's apparent assumption that it was bugging with his approval—spoken or unspoken—and that its bugging practices were consistent with Kennedy standards. Kennedy got no feedbacks on taps, and as Katzenbach, his deputy for much of the period, retrospectively concedes, "These procedures were just awful when you really come right down to it because the authorization had no time limit on it. You never knew whether it was disconnected or still going on, and you never knew what was developed out of it, whether it was fruitful or not. So at no given time did any Attorney General know how many wiretaps there were and who they were on."

Nor are hypothetical conjectures in order as to what would have happened had Kennedy found out. Perhaps he would have reached the sort of accommodation achieved by his successor, Nicholas Katzenbach, whom many believe to have been "sandbagged" by Mr. Hoover. After Katzenbach became Attorney General and discovered the wholesale illegal buggings in which the FBI was engaged, he had a series of meetings with Hoover in which he asked the Director to turn them off. But Hoover pointed out that 99 percent of the FBI's organized-crime program involved microphone surveillance and that if he precipitately turned the microphones off, that was the end of the anti-organized-crime program. "I was trying hard in that period to create a relationship with the Bureau without destroying it right at the outset," recalls Katzenbach, who was under the additional disadvantage of not having Courtney Evans to work with. Instead, the FBI had assigned Cartha DeLoach, much more of a rigid FBI traditionalist than Evans. Katzenbach agreed to let the FBI phase out the bugs over a six-month period, provided that during this period all bugs would be handled on the same basis as taps—that is, Katzenbach would approve (with his signature) all the bugs already in existence and if the FBI wanted to put in any more, it had to get the explicit approval of the Attorney General.

It is interesting to note that in the course of Katzenbach's discussions with Hoover about these matters, on two occasions Hoover told

Katzenbach that Kennedy did not know about the bugs, although Katzenbach says, "To be scrupulously fair, what he could have been referring to was specific approval on a bug-by-bug basis."

And so Katzenbach found himself in the peculiar position of ostensibly exercising "control" over the FBI—certainly more control than Kennedy did in this area—by collaborating with it in violating the law and thereby laying himself open to bureaucratic blackmail, since he was knowingly and on record authorizing a practice of dubious legality. Would Robert Kennedy have fallen into the same trap? Is it better for an Attorney General *not* to know about illegal activities which he considers essential if the alternative is to condone them?

That Robert Kennedy should have known but did not, that he should have asked but did not, that he is therefore chargeable with responsibility for the FBI's illegal privacy invasions—these charges are not to deny that the Director was the enthusiastic initiator and orchestrator of the FBI's illegal electronic surveillance program and, on its behalf, the effective manipulator of the General and his Department. All of the "evidence"—mostly self-serving documents released (or held at the ready) by the FBI at its convenience—is consistent with the hypothesis that in important respects the Director, J. Edgar Hoover, was the puppeteer and the Generals who passed in parade were the puppets.

But it is worth looking at this evidence closely not because it can reconcile Mr. Hoover's public charge that Kennedy knew precisely what the FBI was up to with his private statement to Katzenbach that Kennedy didn't know, but for what it tells us about the Bureau's style, its methods, its *modus operandi*. As far as is known, what follows is the first attempt at a systematic explication of Bureau-speak on record. Scholars of the future may wish to confirm or disconfirm this explication with new documentary evidence as it becomes available.

The FBI is a paper organization, so perhaps the most accurate way of scrutinizing its views is to analyze the paper Mr. Hoover has produced in support of his contention that Kennedy knew about the bugging. It is less interesting to consider what these pieces of paper "prove" about what Robert Kennedy did or didn't know than what they demonstrate about the organization which produced them. They are treated here roughly in the order of their public appearance (i.e., the order in which Mr. Hoover chose to leak them) rather than chronologically (the order in which they are dated), since the function of FBI memoranda paper is to serve rather than to reflect, to protect and argue rather than to record transactions, to anticipate the future rather than to preserve the past. Hoover has thus far released six documents and withheld countless others, two of which are directly on point.

Only a close textual explication of Bureau-speak as seen in these documents can get at the Bureau's purposeful and expert exploitation of ambiguity and can clarify the way in which the FBI has put its own bureaucratic and organizational interests ahead of the policies of the Attorney General.

First, some background. In May 1966, Solicitor General Thurgood Marshall told the Supreme Court in connection with a tax-evasion case involving Bobby Baker's associate Fred L. Black, Jr., that, unknown to the Justice Department or Internal Revenue officials, the FBI had bugged the hospitality suite maintained in Washington at the Sheraton Carlton Hotel by Black. After Black was indicted, FBI agents overheard conversations between Black and his lawyers, and they passed this on to the Justice Department lawyers without revealing their source. The FBI said that the bugging was part of "a criminal investigation of various individuals" and wasn't connected with the tax-evasion case against Black.

The Supreme Court asked the Solicitor for a supplemental memo which would spell out on whose authority the FBI had engaged in this apparently illegal bugging. And in July the Department filed another memorandum telling the Court that "Under Departmental practice in effect for a period of years prior to 1963 and continuing into 1965, the Director of the FBI was given authority to approve the installation of [electronic] devices. . . ." Although it wasn't spelled out in the Justice Department's statement to the Supreme Court, the "authority" consisted of a somewhat cryptic 1954 memorandum to Hoover signed by then Attorney General Herbert Brownell and negotiated by his then deputy, William P. Rogers (see Appendix, p. 452), plus the fact that the FBI had been bugging on its own since the late Fifties and no Attorney General had done anything to stop it.

Robert Kennedy—by then Senator Robert Kennedy—was fearful that such an assertion, unaccompanied by an unequivocal Justice Department statement denying that he personally had known of or authorized the bugs (he insisted till the end that he didn't), would be seized on as yet another piece of evidence in his ongoing feud with President Johnson. Black was an associate of Bobby Baker, Baker was a protégé of LBJ and, despite the fact that Katzenbach had handled the Baker case from the outset, it could appear that he instigated the bugs to embarrass Johnson via Baker-Black. Kennedy's fears were misplaced.

Public attention focused instead on all the cases in which the Justice Department had yet to come forward and admit that the FBI had, through illegal bugging, perhaps fatally tainted otherwise valid convictions. Before it was all over, more than fifty instances of such bugging in organized-crime cases were disclosed to the Supreme Court, and time and again the disclosures gave the lie to the general belief that during the Kennedy era, at least, the FBI had cooperated with other intelligence agencies on a full information exchange. To take some examples of eavesdropping on alleged racketeers:

In the Peter Balistrieri case the government told the Court that the investigative work of the IRS was not tainted by the FBI's bugging of Balistrieri's attorney, because neither the fact of nor the information from the bug was ever made available to the IRS.

In the Lewis, Michael and Frank DeNiro case (for which Kennedy had complimented the IRS at the time) the government said that the FBI hadn't informed the Justice Department of the bugging until after the government brief was filed.

In the Angelo A. Marino case when the defendant moved for a grand-jury transcript alleging IRS electronic surveillance, IRS and the Justice Department both denied it. But thereafter on February 24, 1967, the FBI advised the Tax Division that conversations of the defendant had been monitored by electronic surveillance. The Department said, "Information gained by this electronic surveillance was communicated to the Internal Revenue Service but the Revenue Service was not advised of the source of the information."

Kennedy himself encouraged the idea that the FBI had been acting on its own—at least to the extent that he hadn't authorized its illegal activities—both in private conversations and in public appearances. Thus in the spring of 1966, when he made a guest appearance on ABC Television's "Issues and Answers" (July 26, 1966), the following exchange took place:

Q. Senator, there have been recent disclosures indicating that a lot more wiretapping was done by the FBI in recent years than any of us knew about, some of it during the period when you were Attorney General. Did you authorize the FBI wiretaps of gamblers' telephones in Las Vegas in '62 and '63?

K. No, I did not.

Q. Did you ever authorize any wiretaps as Attorney General, except in national-security cases?

K. I did not.

Q. Well, as Attorney General weren't you supposed to have supreme authority to approve any wiretaps that were made by the Justice Department?

K. Yes.

Q. Would this mean that wiretaps were made by someone at the Justice Department without your knowledge?

K. Well, if there were any wiretaps that took place outside of national-security cases, then they were.

Q. Do you think this might mean the FBI was doing some wiretapping that you didn't know about?

K. Well, I expect that maybe some of those facts are going to be developed. The only time I authorized or was ever requested to authorize wiretapping was in connection with national-security cases under an arrangement that originally had been made by President Roosevelt and Attorney General Biddle.

Hoover got increasingly agitated, leaked a July 11, 1966, story to *U.S. News & World Report*, which suggested RFK was responsible for the FBI's bugging, and finally took the occasion of a December 5, 1966, inquiry from Congressman Gross about whether the FBI had engaged in "eavesdropping" without the authority of the Attorney General to unleash his charges against Robert Kennedy.

In the days which followed, Hoover published some prime samples of Bureau-speak. He (1) sent a letter to Representative Gross charging Robert Kennedy with full knowledge of the FBI's bugging practices, which he said were authorized; (2) released a letter Assistant Attorney Jack Miller had written on May 25, 1961, to Senator Sam Ervin in which he told the Senator how many bugs the FBI had on at that time (although there was no indication in the letter that any of the bugs were illegally installed*); (3) released, without going through normal declassification procedures, a "Top Secret" communication from the FBI signed by Robert Kennedy dated August 17, 1961, which asked his approval to lease telephone lines for microphone surveillance in New York. Kennedy's first response was to release his own letter from Evans which directly contradicted the pieces of paper Hoover put out since Evans said he never discussed the use of bugging devices with Kennedy, "Nor do I know of any written material that was sent to you at any time concerning this procedure or concerning the use, specific location or other details as to installation of any devices."

Hoover's reply: "Official records of the FBI not only reflect discussions between former Attorney General Kennedy and Mr. Evans concerning the FBI's use of microphone surveillances, but also contain documents—including some bearing Mr. Kennedy's signature or initials —showing that the FBI's use of microphone and wiretap surveillances

---

* At the time bugging that didn't involve a trespass was thought to be legal in many jurisdictions.

was known to and approved by Mr. Kennedy," after which he (4) released two memoranda from Courtney Evans to Alan H. Belmont, assistant to J. Edgar Hoover. One dated July 7, 1961, said that Kennedy had been contacted "relative to his observation as to the possibility of utilizing 'electronic devices' in organized crime investigations." It described Kennedy as "pleased we had been using microphone surveillances . . . wherever possible in organized crime matters." The other reported that Kennedy had "approved the proposed procedure" requested in the "Top Secret" communication.

Kennedy's counter-reply (December 11, 1966):

> It may seem "inconceivable" to Mr. Hoover that I was not aware of the "bugging" practices of the FBI during my term as Attorney General, but it is nonetheless true.
>
> Perhaps I should have known, and since I was the Attorney General I certainly take the responsibility for it, but the plain fact of the matter is that I did not know.
>
> Since Mr. Hoover is selectively making documents public, I suggest that he make his entire file available, and indicate under which Attorney General this practice began, whether any prior Attorneys General authorized it, and whether or not they were as uninformed as I was.

Obviously, Courtney Evans is the only man around who knows the truth, and he is not talking. When asked to shed light on the conflict, he replies: "Different people interpret the same words differently. . . . Mr. Hoover released a classified document. I said at the time and I say now, I can't comment on classified material." *

Whatever Mr. Evans' inner feelings, one suspects he reflexively met the FBI's Bureau-speak standards in his reports. As one agent puts it, "If anyone was ever careful, painstaking, thorough, completely conservative, it was Courtney Evans. And also completely and thoroughly loyal to the Bureau and to Hoover. If I had to make a bet I'd bet that anything he did or got involved in was correctly done from the Bureau standpoint. The problem is the Bureau demands total loyalty. Therefore if you get too close to the Attorney General you're a threat to the hierarchical structure. But that didn't mean Courtney stopped writing and thinking like an FBI man."

Katzenbach, explaining why Evans was such an effective liaison between Hoover and Kennedy, reinforces the point when he says, "Courtney would explain something to Bob one way and explain

---

* My own sense of the matter is that Evans told Kennedy little enough to keep him out of trouble. And he wrote up for Hoover enough to cover the FBI on paper; in other words, he told each what he wanted to hear.

something to Hoover another way. And I don't think anybody could have done the job any other way. And when he was trying to sell something to Bobby that Hoover wanted, it was explained one way that would make it palatable to Bobby and vice versa, and I think in part the whole wiretapping and bugging issue was that."

So much for background. As to the evidence itself, the first piece of evidence is non-existent. Whatever Robert Kennedy's delinquency in not carrying out a search-and-destroy mission aimed at illegal bugging, the fact is, as Katzenbach notes, "they make this elaborate presentation on wiretapping and they didn't say a word about the other." Surely if Kennedy was guilty of dereliction, the FBI was guilty of deception.

It should also be observed that, with two exceptions, all of the pieces of paper Hoover released were secondary sources—agents reporting on what they told somebody or what somebody said to them. As has been suggested earlier, FBI memoranda are written primarily to entertain and reassure J. Edgar Hoover and to protect the FBI against future damage. They simply are not reliable evidence of what happened in the real world.

The first of the two exceptions to the Hoover-supplied evidence against Kennedy's protest of ignorance was the letter from Jack Miller to Senator Ervin. It reads in full:

May 25, 1961

Honorable Sam J. Ervin, Jr.
United States Senate
Washington 25, D.C.
Dear Senator:

Thank you for your letter of May 19, 1961.

I have been advised that as of February 8, 1960, the Federal Bureau of Investigation maintained 78 wiretaps.

You also request information "relative to the nature and extent of the use of electronic eavesdropping apparatus by agents of the Department of Justice." I have checked with the Federal Bureau of Investigation and, as in the case of wiretapping, the technique of electronic listening devices is used on a highly restricted basis. The Federal Bureau of Investigation has 67 of these devices in operation. The majority are in the field of internal security with a few used to obtain intelligence information with regard to organized crime.

The Department feels the information in the third paragraph should remain confidential. However, whether the information should be made public is left with your discretion.

Sincerely,
Herbert J. Miller, Jr.
Assistant Attorney General

Of course the letter doesn't prove anything about what Robert Kennedy knew, although it is further confirmation that he should have known. There are, nevertheless, three peculiar things about the letter. First, as anyone who has followed Departmental typewriters would see, it was probably typed on a Bureau typewriter. It is not a full facsimile since it lacks the initials which under Departmental practice would tell who really dictated it,* but Miller thinks it is probably a verbatim incorporation of an FBI draft. Second, the final paragraph raises the question of why the Department felt that the number of bugs should remain "confidential" and not the number of taps—unless the FBI considered its bugging on shakier legal grounds than its Attorney General-approved tapping or unless it was trying to get away with something. Miller says, "With respect to the question of whether I was aware of the FBI bugging practices at the time the letter was sent, the answer is absolutely not. At the time I sent the letter I assumed, incorrectly, as I subsequently ascertained, that the devices referred to in the letter were legally placed and used. While I did not inquire (although hindsight certainly suggests that I should have) I merely assumed that the devices were placed in a public place, e.g., adjacent to a public telephone booth, in an automobile, or in similar situations. I had no knowledge then, and am firmly convinced that no one in the non-FBI section of the Department of Justice had knowledge that the FBI was in fact trespassing to place such devices. Had this been known to the Department, I am convinced that immediate steps would have been taken to stop the practice."

Finally, it will be recalled that in Mr. Miller's May 11, 1961, testimony he told the Judiciary Committee that he called the FBI the day before and they told him they had 85 wiretaps. Why should he now—two weeks later—quote Senator Ervin the wiretap figure "as of February 8, 1960 . . . 78 wiretaps?" It is one of those unresolved mysteries that casts yet further doubt on the significance of the document. The probability is that it was prepared by the FBI partly to get the Department on record; they knew, in the crush of business, it would be signed but not read carefully by Miller.

By far the most important document, though, is the one ostensibly signed by Robert Kennedy which requests authority to lease telephone lines in New York. The Kennedy response to this document was to publicly challenge Hoover to release his full file, and privately suggest

* Under Department of Justice policy, all letters are assigned by the Assistant Attorney General in charge. Thus if Ron Goldfarb, an attorney in the Criminal Division, dictated a letter to his secretary, Mary Jones, the letter would be signed by Assistant Attorney General Herbert J. Miller, but the initials would read as follows: "HJM: RG: MJ."

it would show additional language from Courtney Evans saying that he didn't think Kennedy understood what he had signed.

The August 17, 1961, document is critical because it is the only piece of paper that the FBI was able to come up with throughout the whole episode that actually bore the Attorney General's signature:

UNITED STATES DEPARTMENT OF JUSTICE
Federal Bureau of Investigation
Washington 25, D.C.
August 17, 1961

In connection with the use of microphone surveillance it is frequently necessary to lease a special telephone line in order to monitor such a surveillance. These situations occur when it is impossible to locate a secure monitoring point in the immediate vicinity of the premises covered by the microphone. Even though a special telephone line is utilized, this activity in no way involves any interception of telephonic communications and is not a telephone tap.

In the New York City area the telephone company has over the years insisted that a letter be furnished to the telephone company on each occasion when a special telephone line is leased by the FBI. It is required that such a lease arrangement be with the approval of the Attorney General. In the past we have restricted the utilization of leased lines in New York City to situations involving telephone taps, all of which have been approved by the Attorney General.

We have not previously used leased lines in connection with microphone surveillances because of certain technical difficulties existing in New York City. These technical difficulties have, however, been overcome. If we are permitted to use leased telephone lines as an adjunct to our microphone surveillances, this type of coverage can be materially extended both in security and major criminal cases. Accordingly, your approval of our utilizing this leased line arrangement is requested. A sample of the letter which it is proposed will be sent to the telephone company if a leased line is secured in connection with microphone surveillances is attached."

Approved: ROBERT KENNEDY (s)
Date:

At the time Hoover released this "top secret" document it ignited a national uproar over whether Robert Kennedy had known what he was signing. Hoover said yes and had Courtney Evans' memoranda to prove it. Kennedy, who didn't remember signing it, and his supporters said no and had Courtney Evans' later letter to prove it. And Courtney Evans said nothing. Nobody thought to do or say anything about the fact that Hoover had released a classified document without going through proper declassification procedures. When subsequently asked whether he had given any thought to prosecuting Hoover for this dereliction, Nicholas Katzenbach (who was Attorney General at the time) said not really and, besides, "If he *had* gone through the proper procedures he would have been able to declassify it himself." A final point for Kennedy—the memo said nothing of the Bureau's illegal trespassory practices.

Looking back at this memorandum more dispassionately now, one is struck by a curious bit of Bureau-speak buried in the second paragraph. The topic sentence says, "In the New York City area the telephone company has . . . insisted that a letter be furnished . . ." But then the memo moves into the passive tense and cryptically asserts, "It is required that such a lease arrangement be with the approval of the Attorney General." At the time most people following the controversy assumed—syntactically—that the telephone company was doing the requiring. But familiarity with the language of Bureau-speak leads one to attempt a closer explication of the text. One could see why the New York telephone company might "insist" that a letter be furnished, but why "require" authorization from the Attorney General himself? Wouldn't they accept the word of an Assistant Attorney General? Or of J. Edgar Hoover? "Of course we would," said William Mullane of New York Telephone when I put the question to him over the phone. But just to make sure, he went back to the records, checked it out with the telephone-company attorneys, "our security people," and those in charge at the time, and in a letter to me dated September 9, 1969, two months after the inquiry, he advised me that the telephone company had not set up any procedures for the furnishing of such lines, "whether by letter request or any other means," because the leasing in question never took place. And "Inasmuch as there is no lease arrangement, we have no requirement that the Attorney General or other Department of Justice employee sign a non-existent agreement."

In other words, the FBI's purpose in having the Attorney General sign the August 17, 1961, "authorization" was apparently not to lease a telephone line but to get the Attorney General's participation on record. Whether or not Robert Kennedy realized the implications of what he was signing is something we will never know with certainty. But Hoover's motives for having him sign it are open to the clear interpretation that he sought to implicate the Attorney General in the FBI's illegal activities. One of the conveniences of Bureau-speak is that at the time a document is to be signed, it has all of the advantages of poetic ambiguity—thereby obfuscating its real purpose. But when evidence must be adduced, Hoover can explicate the language with the simple authority of a teacher interpreting a McGuffey's reader.

Why, one is driven to ask, with an Attorney General so obviously open-minded about electronic investigations, so preoccupied with anti-crime goals, so intent on involving the FBI in the fight against the mob—a man whose program, priorities, predispositions, style and character all suggest the probability that he would have approved limited electronic eavesdropping—if only the FBI had put the issue squarely to him, did Mr. Hoover or his emissary refrain from doing so? First, because in any situation of choice, the secret society will always choose to preserve its secrets—and, in this case, enhance its mystique by its ability to listen in on the underworld. Second, because there was always the off chance that Kennedy—whose working contact with and growing respect for his Ivy League intellectual colleagues and friends was having its impact—might say no. Third, because he might say yes but with safeguards, or worse, yes, but you have to share this information with other investigative agencies, or with the Organized Crime Section. He might actually want to know just who was being bugged and why! Fourth, because it was the FBI's style to operate in this in-between world where they told you but they didn't tell you. And last, because they had pre-existing paper authority to do what they were doing and why risk it by bringing it to the new Attorney General's attention before they had closed their intelligence gap on organized crime?

As a matter of fact, the "authority" referred to so definitively in the supplemental memorandum requested by the Supreme Court in the Black case had never been publicly exhibited. All the Solicitor had told the Court was:

> Under Departmental practice in effect for a period of years prior to 1963 and continuing into 1965, the Director of the FBI was given authority to approve the installation of [electronic] devices . . . for intelligence [and not evidentiary] purposes when required in the interest of internal security or national safety including organized crime, kidnappings and matters wherein human life might be at stake. Acting on the basis of the aforementioned Departmental authorization, the Director approved the installation of the device involved in the instant case. . . .

Yet it was the basis of every FBI eavesdrop from 1954 until bugging was legalized under the anti-crime bill of 1969. I have seen this "authority" and now understand why the FBI has kept it quiet. It consists of the "Confidential" memorandum signed by Attorney General Herbert Brownell dated May 20, 1954, and was written in answer to a request from the FBI, which wanted to know how a recent decision of the U.S. Supreme Court (*Irvine* v. *California,* 347 U.S. 128) denouncing the use of microphone surveillances by city police in a gambling case would affect the FBI's use of microphone surveillance "in connection with matters relating to the internal security of the country." *Nothing* in the memorandum * gives the Director the authority to use microphones in organized-crime cases. As a matter of fact the memo states that in the Irvine case the Justices of the Supreme Court were outraged by what they regarded as the indecency of installing a microphone in a bedroom. They denounced the utilization of such methods in a gambling case as shocking. But they allowed that different considerations might apply in cases involving the national security. The memorandum then goes on to discuss the question of whether a trespass is actually involved and says each case must be resolved on its own merits, with the Department doing the resolving. The two references which might be interpreted in the utmost reaches of Bureau-think as going beyond national security are the last two sentences of the memo, coming immediately after the assertion that "The Department" will resolve any problems which might arise in connection with the use of microphone surveillance. The memo says: "It is my opinion that the Department should adopt that interpretation which will permit microphone coverage by the FBI in a manner most conducive to our national interest. I recognize that for the FBI to fulfill its important intelligence function, considerations of internal security and the national safety are paramount, and therefore, may compel the unrestricted use of the technique in the national interest."

It would, of course, be inconceivable that any organization other than the FBI would leap on phrases like "national interest" or "national safety," wrench them out of context, and then use them as an excuse to listen in on a bookie joint in Miami. And it is still a trifle difficult to accept that, when you get down to it, the FBI would rely on a memorandum that explicitly condemns the trespassory installation of a microphone in a gambler's bedroom and, acting on it, install through trespass a microphone in the bedroom of Las Vegas casino manager Carl Cohen.† As Justice Jackson, for the Court, stated in the Irvine case, which prompted the Brownell memo in the first place:

> That officers of the law would break and enter a house, secrete such a device, even in a bedroom, and listen to the conversation of the occupants for over a month would be almost incredible if it were not admitted. Few police measures have come to our attention that more flagrantly, deliberately, and persistently violated the fundamental principle declared by the Fourth Amendment as a restriction on the federal government. . . .

---

* See p. 451.
† His wife, when she found out about it, suffered a nervous breakdown.

Finally, since not even Mr. Hoover has claimed (although his rhetoric has given the impression that he was so claiming) that the FBI informed the Department on a bug-by-bug basis in each and every case, how could the Department "review the circumstances of each case in the light of the practical necessities of the investigation and of the national interest" as the Brownell memo required? Not only did the memorandum not give the FBI discretionary bugging authority, but Hoover and the Bureau were probably violating the literal terms of the 1954 memorandum, which if anything implies that the Bureau should be following the same procedures with trespassory bugs as it had followed with taps.

One could make other, more legalistic arguments—such as that a 1962 revision in the FBI manual which forbade "unethical practices" superseded the 1954 Brownell memo. It is perhaps diverting to make such arguments since a paper organization should be held accountable for all relevant pieces of paper, but the fact is that the 1962 revision, as Katzenbach describes it, was "a golden rule, without content." The point is not to win a *post hoc* argument but to suggest what the secret society was doing at the time and how it affected the ability of an Attorney General to uphold the traditions of his office.

There is a final piece of paper to consider, unreleased until now. It is a memorandum dated May 4, 1961, addressed to Byron White, Deputy Attorney General, from the Director, Federal Bureau of Investigation, "Subject: Technical and Microphone Surveillance."* Ostensibly written as a comment on the Attorney General's contemplated appearance before Congress to testify on wiretapping legislation, it clearly spells out the illegal nature of trespassory bugging ("In the interests of national safety, microphone surveillances are also utilized on a restrictive basis even though trespass is necessary, in our covering major criminal activities").

The memorandum is, on its surface, a devastating blow to the Kennedy case that he didn't know, since he was in daily touch with Byron White; although investigation establishes that White did not see it himself, no less talk to the Attorney General about it. (White did not remember the document when obscure references to it were made in the Kennedy-Hoover dispute of 1966, nor did it refresh his recollection when I quoted portions of it to him in the spring of 1971.) It arrived along with a few thousand other memoranda, but unlike hundreds of others it was not marked "urgent" or important, which suggests that it was designed to be written rather than read, and so is not evidence of much of anything other than the fact that the FBI wrote it.

* See Appendix, p. 448.

But why, then, did the Bureau not unleash this devastating document against Robert Kennedy at a time when Hoover went so far as to violate existing Departmental regulations and release classified material (the August 17, 1961, memo) without declassifying it? Was it merely that Byron White was now Justice White and Hoover, with his spectacular instinct for survival, decided to leave well enough alone? Was it that White hadn't even initialed the document, which meant that it was probably routinely processed by career civil servant James T. Devine, who handled such matters in the Deputy's office at the time? Not at all. The Bureau's problem was that the May 7, 1961, memo to White cited as "authority" for its illegal practices Brownell's 1954 memo to Hoover, and by way of documentation it quoted from Brownell's original memo. But the quote was so misleading, so clearly wrenched from a 1954 internal security context and dropped, without warning or elaboration into a 1961 organized crime context, that not even the Bureau could have convincingly argued that they had not purposely set out to mislead the Deputy—*if he chanced to see it.*

What we are left with then is the need to redefine our image of the way things worked. For we started with the picture of a brash, energetic, powerful Attorney General who rammed the heads of twenty-seven intelligence agencies together and for the first time got them to collaborate in the fight against the conspiracy of evil. Most particularly, for the first time he got the FBI into the fray. So far the picture is true. But now we must alter it ever so slightly. Despite the public-relations message about the New Cooperation and the New Responsiveness of the FBI, it is retrospectively apparent that what the Bureau was doing was expanding its prerogatives by carrying on parallel but autonomous activities.

And the Attorney General, whether he knew it or not, was a minority partner, a collaborator, in the FBI's own electronic war, in its attempt to accumulate and safeguard its own information stockpile. It was a classic case of not asking and not telling, but when the non-asker is the General and the non-teller is the Director, the non-gainer is the public. For, as Courtney Evans put it in the Bureau-speak which still lingers, "Any law enforcement officer will tell you it is an accepted principle of law enforcement to do what has to be done in the best interests of law enforcement at the time you are doing it." In other words, the law enforcers are, by FBI precept, above the law.

CHAPTER THREE

Civil Rights:
The Movement and the General

IN CIVIL RIGHTS, as in organized crime, the popular impression is that the brothers Kennedy, parlaying the power of the Presidency and the power of the prosecutor, gently but firmly ordered and edged the FBI into the war against discrimination.

The fact is that not only did the Kennedys not volunteer the FBI for arduous civil rights duty, but Robert Kennedy, who was ahead of his brother in these things, himself required a few years of on-the-job sensitivity training before he caught up with the NAACP. Until that happened—in mid-1963—he had no incentive to put the pressure on the FBI, and any escalation of the FBI's civil rights involvement must be credited primarily to the maneuvers of the Civil Rights Division attorneys themselves, led by Burke Marshall and guided in the field by John Doar.

This is not to suggest that Robert Kennedy did not relate to the problems of individual Negroes. He did. And he wanted action. As John Doar, first assistant in the Civil Rights Division, recalls, "He was always wanting to move, get something done, accomplish something, and when I first went up to see him—probably April 1961—he was for filing seventy-five cases by Thanksgiving." When asked to graph Kennedy's civil rights consciousness, Burke Marshall shot his right arm up to the sky. "The more he saw," says Marshall, "and this was true of me as well, the more he understood. The more you learned about how Negroes were treated in the South, the more you saw of that, the madder you became. You know he always talked about the hypocrisy. That's what got him. By the end of a year he was so mad about that kind of thing it overrode everything else."

But emotional involvement and good intentions are one thing and program priorities are another. From 1961 to 1963 Robert Kennedy had no civil rights program in the sense that he had an organized-crime program. Civil rights was in the rear ranks of the Kennedy Administration's early priorities. "I did not lie awake at night worrying about the problems of Negroes," Robert Kennedy freely conceded in later reminiscing. And as each crisis surfaced, the General confidently approached it on the assumption that it was a temporary eruption which he and his remarkable team could cool. The bus-burning at Anniston, the rock-throwing at the University of Mississippi, the church, motel and school bombings were all viewed more or less as the random, discontinuous by-products of a society evolving painfully toward racial integration. The trick was to encourage the inevitable integration but never at the cost of disturbing the social equilibrium. His most visible and most significant civil rights activities were responsive, reactive, crisis-managing, violence-avoiding. He and his people were cool, creative, imaginative, effective and risk-taking reactors, and they should be credited with converting the freedom rides into an ICC order desegregating interstate bus travel; with calling out the troops to back up court orders integrating Ole Miss (in response to James Meredith's initiative) and the University of Alabama (Governor Wallace in the doorway notwithstanding); with not calling out the troops and nevertheless preventing a racially explosive Birmingham from exploding into a bloody race war.

But the civil rights program of the new Administration was more limited than John Kennedy's campaign rhetoric would have suggested or than civil rights activists hoped. Candidate Kennedy had promised that an active President "could integrate all federally assisted housing with a stroke of the Presidential pen." After he was elected, supporters had to wait over a year and a half and mount an "Ink for Jack" campaign as the White House was drowned in ink bottles before JFK finally signed a watered-down, non-retroactive order. Candidate Kennedy had promised innovative litigation to speed school desegregation, but President Kennedy ignored the counsel of men like Harvard's Paul Freund and Mark De Wolfe Howe, Philip Elman of the Solicitor

General's office and William Taylor (eventually Director of the Civil Rights Commission under LBJ), who advised, according to a confidential memo prepared by civil rights aide Harris Wofford, that the government could sue to desegregate schools with no new legislation. And, of course, candidate Kennedy had hinted at a more vigorous use of the FBI, thereby endorsing the findings of the U.S. Commission on Civil Rights, some of which were critical of the Bureau. But President Kennedy did nothing to implement Wofford's private preinauguration memorandum which, among other things, called for more flexible deployment of the Bureau and gave as an example the handling of incipient violence in connection with school desegregation in New Orleans. Wofford had noted:

> Active FBI investigation of the persons engaged in the conspiracy of intimidation might itself have broken up the resistance—and might still do so. The present assistant Attorney General for Civil Rights, Ace Tyler, tells me that it is very difficult to get the FBI to move energetically in civil rights cases. I am sure our new Attorney General will be able to convince Mr. Hoover that our new Attorney General is just as serious about conspiracies against civil rights as about the Communist conspiracy.
>
> . . . if it turns out, as alleged, that prostitutes, small time underworld characters, and others with criminal records are in the forefront of the mob, it would be good for the public to know this. Many of these people would probably melt away under *any* serious FBI investigation of them.
>
> It is essential that Federal authority be tough at the early stages of such situations before any need for troops arises. The FBI plus US Marshals should be enough to prevent any overt campus intimidation.

Although it was retrospectively insufficient, the Kennedys must be credited with an arguably intelligent, initial civil rights strategy: forgo legislation (which would get bogged down in an unsympathetic Congress), forgo executive orders (which might alienate key Southern committee chairmen) and concentrate on litigation specifically aimed at winning Southern Negroes the vote. With the franchise, went the reasoning, the Southern Negro would hold the balance of political power and all other rights and privileges would follow. To this day, Marshall's First Assistant, John Doar, maintains, "The litigation strategy was the only approach which had a chance and it did in fact save the country. The program was to break the caste system. And the best handle you had was the vote." There was no "campaign" to involve the FBI in civil rights the way there was a campaign to involve it in the fight against organized crime. For the Attorney General himself became deeply involved in civil rights through events rather than planning, through necessity rather than philosophy, through emergency rather than deliberation. And by the time the quantity of events had changed the quality of his involvement, the pattern of FBI "cooperation" had already been set.

Not until the late spring of 1963, reacting in part to the natural outrage over Bull Connor's brutal confrontation with Martin Luther King's child demonstrators in Birmingham, and in the aftermath of Burke Marshall's heroic mediation of hostilities in that racial tinderbox, did the Kennedys sponsor civil rights legislation which matched JFK's campaign rhetoric. Burke Marshall recalls, "When President Kennedy sent up that [civil rights] bill every single person who spoke about it in the White House—every one of them—was against President Kennedy sending up that bill; against his speech in June; against making it a moral issue; against the March on Washington. The conclusive voice within the government at that time, there's no question about it at all, that Robert Kennedy was the one. He urged it, he felt it, he understood it. And he prevailed. I don't think there was anybody in the Cabinet—except the President himself—who felt that way on these issues, and the President got it from his brother."

But Robert Kennedy's commitment came too late to change the fundamental pattern of the relationship between the Justice Department and the FBI, and to that extent the commitment was seriously, if not fatally, diminished.

Robert Kennedy's civil rights "record" is of less significance here for the moment than the way his relationship with the FBI deflected that record, the way in which the tension between the Department and the Bureau limited the Administration's civil rights commitments. Of course Robert Kennedy's Justice Department got the FBI to do things it hadn't done before and thereby achieved some of the short-range, immediate-action objectives of the Kennedys. Also the inability of the FBI to end-run the Attorney General and go straight to the White House during the Kennedy years cannot be discounted in assessing the Civil Rights Division's confidence that the FBI would not go over its head. But the hypothesis offered here is that the cost of these short-range victories was the long-range increase in J. Edgar Hoover's and the FBI's domain of power.

Less than a month after Kennedy took office, John Doar, Burke Marshall, Robert D. Owen and other Civil Rights Division attorneys trooped up to the Attorney General's fifth-floor office, by appointment, to present the new Attorney General with the blueprint for the Justice

Department's right-to-vote litigation drive. In a sense, the meeting was a metaphor for the relationship with the FBI which followed. As soon as they arrived, the Attorney General instructed his secretary, Angie Novello, to "Ask Mr. Hoover to come over" (from his fifth-floor office down the corridor). It shortly developed that Mr. Hoover was "out of the building" but Courtney Evans would be over. Without the FBI's cooperation (which Evans assured the Attorney General they had) the right-to-vote litigation, at least as projected, would be impossible. Each case depended on painstaking investigation—analysis of voting rolls, compilation of demographic statistics, comparison of handwritings, careful interviews with registrars and with a statistically significant sample of black and white failed registrants, successful registrants and others.

There was nothing extraordinary about Mr. Hoover's assigning an emissary. The practice was standard for the FBI, although old-timers like James Bennett at the Bureau of Prisons remarked on the lack of social amenities between Kennedy and Hoover: "I noticed that Hoover did not show up at the staff luncheons of Attorney General Kennedy. He did not attend a single luncheon at which I was present throughout Kennedy's tour of office at the Justice Department. . . ." [1] But nobody thought odd the fact that the ambassador, the go-between, came from Hoover's court rather than Kennedy's.

The General accepted the arrangement not because he found it easier to talk to an intermediary (which he did) than to the fili- bustering Director, not because he was fond of Evans (which he indeed was and grew to be more so), not because he *wanted* a liaison, but because in dealing with the FBI his basic effort was to avoid upsetting it, to avoid confrontation over anything but great issues of policy. What he failed to appreciate was that by yielding to the FBI on matters of form, he had yielded to them on the only issue of policy which counted—Hoover's right to run the FBI without interference from "outside." In addition, of course, the alchemists of the secret society had long ago broken down the barriers between form and substance. And its capacity to confuse the components of form with those of content was one of the Bureau's sources of power.

So on one level the Attorney General and his Ivy League intellectuals beat the FBI at their own game. In a rather random, *ad hoc* way they developed a variety of effective bureaucratic strategies, each aimed at getting the FBI to do something which earlier it had either been un- willing or unable to do. In this sense only did Robert Kennedy exercise more influence over the FBI than his predecessor Attorneys General.

But on another, more profound level, the level of assumptions, ground rules, power distribution, it was *nolo contendere.* The General had yielded to the Director on the one thing that counted: control. Mr. Hoover's price for reluctantly going along in civil rights was that he have control of his own troops, that the FBI oversee its own men, use its own systems, follow its own rules, provide parallel rather than integrated services. This seemed a reasonable enough bargain at the time and Kennedy cavalierly traded control (which he never exercised anyway) for cooperation. The operational result was that "You could not say to the FBI 'Infiltrate the Klan,' " recalls Burke Marshall. "But you could ask for a 'preliminary,' 'limited,' or 'full' investigation of particular Klan activities. These were terms of art." The long-range results of Kennedy's enlisting the FBI in civil rights were (a) to enlarge the Justice Department's law enforcement capability, but (b) at the same time to give the FBI effective veto power over each and every civil rights activity in which it was a participant.

The difficulty was that Kennedy and his free-lance pragmatists were so adept, imaginative and brilliant at manipulating the FBI and so aware of their mini-triumphs that they never understood that as in the area of organized crime, Mr. Hoover had won by losing, since every new activity the FBI consented to undertake increased its power. Talk to Burke Marshall today and he is justifiably proud of the fact that under Kennedy the number of agents in Mississippi was increased by a factor of fifty (from three to over 150). When the Kennedy team arrived, the FBI was ignorant of KKK activities; when they left, FBI infiltration of the Klan paralleled its infiltration of the Communist Party. As Hoover himself boasted late in 1964, "We have been able to penetrate the Klan. There are 480 Klansmen in Mississippi. . . . I had our agents in Mississippi interview every member of the Klan there just to let those individuals know the FBI knew who they were and had an eye on them. . . ."[2] When they arrived, the FBI had no field office in Mississippi; by the time they left, J. Edgar Hoover had personally opened a major FBI office in Jackson, Mississippi.

These achievements weren't accidental. Nor may they be attributed primarily to the one-two punch possessed by the brothers Kennedy. Rather they signify the adroitness of Kennedy's pragmatists and their evolving expertise at the business of FBI-managing. It is instructive to look at four such successful techniques for Bureau-influencing developed and perfected during the Kennedy years, always keeping in mind that, added together, they amounted to *ad hoc* influence rather than control or power. We may term them Interrogative Overkill,

Investigation by Demonstration, Territorial Invasion and the Pennsylvania Avenue End Run.

Interrogative Overkill: It did not take the Civil Rights Division long to discover that in dealing with the FBI the first rule is to take nothing for granted. The Bureau's conditioned reflex to requests it did not particularly wish to fulfill was to interpret those requests literally. So the Department's counter-response was to give ridiculously literal requests, sometimes running to fifty pages. Thus John Doar didn't simply ask the FBI to investigate charges of discrimination by registrars in Walthall County, Mississippi. He first had his own lawyers—through local contacts—compile a list of persons who had attempted to register. Then he devised a long, detailed questionnaire which left nothing, including middle initial, race, creed, color or previous condition of servitude, to the individual agent's imagination. By breaking down investigative requests in this manner, he did more than guarantee that the Department would get the information it needed. He deprived the FBI (whose job it was to get these questions answered) of its excuse for not asking. A typical question list included the following entries:

In addition to obtaining full background and information from these individuals including education, business or farming experience, property ownership, military record, arrest record, obtain the following information from the interviewee:

A. Each time he has attempted to register.
1. Date or dates.
2. Where he attempted to register.
3. What other Negroes were there when he attempted to register.
4. The name of the person or persons to whom he applied for registration (circuit clerk or his deputy).
5. Full details of conversation with the clerk.
6. Full details of any conversation with any other white persons or officials when he attempted to register, such as the sheriff or deputy sheriff.
7. Full details as to what was required of him when he applied for registration such as filling out the application form, copy and interpreting provisions of the Constitution. If he was required to copy and interpret the Constitution, ascertain what provision or what it was about and its length.
8. Whether he passed or failed. Include any details of the conversation with the clerk.
9. Whether any white person for the county has talked to him about registration. If so, who, when, and full details of the conversation.
10. Whether he had paid his poll tax regularly. If so, obtain all original poll tax receipts he had in his possession. Include details, if he has had difficulty in attempting to pay poll tax.

Ascertain for each person interviewed the names of other Negroes who have attempted to register and interview them to obtain the above information.

Ascertain for each person interviewed the names of other Negroes in the county who are reluctant to attempt to register because of a conversation with white person.

There followed some specific instructions about questions to ask named individuals and finally, to guard against the Bureau not getting around to it for months, the closing sentence read: "Kindly conduct this investigation on an expedited basis."

Investigation by Demonstration: "It was unbelievable," recalls one civil rights lawyer. "They would interrogate a black and scare him out of his pants. They'd interrogate a white sheriff and then report his version straight-faced without 'evaluating' it." It was not that the FBI was *trying* to sabotage the civil rights program so much as the fact that they were simply carrying out the traditional routines. True, the FBI didn't want to jeopardize its relationship with local enforcers whose cooperation they needed in non-civil rights areas, but usually it was simply a matter of habit. The first thing an agent does when he arrives in a new community is to check in with the local law enforcement people. It says so in the manual. The fact that the local law enforcement people in the South were often part of the discriminatory system was not, in many cases, sufficient to shake the FBI's confidence in its pre-existing routines. Instead, they would conclude that there was no case to be made.

To remedy this condition, John Doar's genius was employed not to try to explain to or convince the Bureau but to show them. Thus when the FBI came back from Fayette, Tennessee, with insufficient information to make a voter intimidation case (economic reprisals against new vote registrants), Doar went down himself with a couple of lawyers and in a few weeks gathered enough evidence to make two cases. Although this step had the immediate unfortunate side effect of getting the FBI mad at Doar, the technique proved enormously effective in future, more complicated situations.

By creating such a model, he did more than give the FBI something to copy, more than "develop ways where we could help the journeyman investigator do the best job." In addition, he raised the specter of intruding on FBI jurisdiction, a guarantor that the FBI would fill the investigative vacuum.

Territorial Invasion: This was a less subtle but no less effective lever for edging the Bureau into the civil rights fray. Says Doar, "We'd go down South and make a tour of several counties, and we ourselves would interview Negroes that had made some effort to register. We'd get *their* experiences and ask the names of anyone they knew of who had tried to register. Then we'd come back and . . . ask the Bureau to interview. It was like a pyramid club. Out of that would come 250 interviews. We were self-starting—we didn't wait for complaints. And we used the expanding or ballooning interview. That resulted in a lot more shoe leather by the Bureau." After Walter Sheridan and his "Terrible Twenty" had convicted Hoffa of jury tampering in Chattanooga and made the case against the Teamster Pension Fund fraud in Chicago, he went to Kennedy and asked for his next assignment. Kennedy sent him to Mississippi, where Sheridan's men were named special deputies and given permission to carry guns. It was not too many days thereafter that Hoover agreed to open a Mississippi office.

The Pennsylvania Avenue End Run: The conventional wisdom— subscribers include most of the Justice Department Kennedyites and virtually all of the commentators—is that with the assassination of President Kennedy, Robert Kennedy lost all leverage with J. Edgar Hoover and he and the FBI reverted to their old, autonomous ways.

The litany is familiar: Hoover stopped reporting to the Attorney General and started reporting directly to the White House. Courtney Evans, who had been serving as *de facto* liaison with the Attorney General *and* the White House, was removed from the latter job and replaced by Cartha DeLoach, a friend of Walter Jenkins. Joe Dolan recalls asking for an FBI report on a prospective judicial candidate and being told, "We already did one for the White House." A staffman says, "Starting at 1:10 on November 22 they began pissing on the Attorney General." As Hoover himself boasted on November 16, 1970— the day he celebrated the publication of Ramsey Clark's book, *Crime in America,* by calling him "a jellyfish"—he didn't speak to Robert Kennedy during his last six months as Attorney General.

What the conventional wisdom ignores, however, is that while the Attorney General lost leverage with the death of his brother he gained maneuverability. And his ability to move Hoover had always depended as much on bureaucratic sensitivity as on relative power. Thus, following the ostensible murder of three civil rights workers in Mississippi in 1964, when it was apparent to all except the FBI that an FBI office was urgently needed in Mississippi, the General didn't confront the Director with the demand that he open a regional office in Mississippi. They didn't go behind Hoover's back or to the press and try to embarrass him into opening an office by leaking stories—of which there were many—of FBI inefficiency and investigative shortcomings in Mississippi. They didn't sit down with him and try to reason or argue him into opening an office in Mississippi. They didn't send him a memo. Rather, understanding that Hoover relates to power, they chose to make their approach through the power pinnacle of the President, and so they sent their memo to Pennsylvania Avenue. Understanding equally that Hoover is allergic to criticism, they camouflaged their critique in terms of praise and amicability. Understanding also Hoover's principle of jurisdictional monopoly, they preceded their request by dispatching Walter Sheridan and his unit to do some preliminary investigating, thus silently telling the Director that if he said no, the Department would do it on its own. And finally and foremost, they didn't attempt to tell the FBI how to go about its work once there— again, deferring to the Bureau on the key point. As Marshall put it in a cover note to the Attorney General: "The problem is rather to describe what is happening in such a way as to permit the Bureau to develop its own procedures for the collection of intelligence."

The memo, originally prepared by Marshall for Kennedy the first week in June 1964, was forwarded under Kennedy's name to President Johnson. It read as follows:

This week at my request Burke Marshall spent some time in Southwestern Mississippi and Jackson to get some first-hand impressions of the possibilities for this summer and the future. He has reported the following general conclusions to me:

1. There has unquestionably been, as you know, an increase in acts of terrorism in this part of Mississippi. As a result the tensions are very great not only between whites and Negroes, but among whites. This is not as true in Jackson as in the outgoing areas.

2. Law enforcement officials, at least outside Jackson, are widely believed to be linked to extremist anti-Negro activity, or at the very least to tolerate it. . . . For example, groups have been formed under the auspices of the Americans for the Preservation of the White Race to act as deputized law enforcement officials in some counties. . . . These groups appear to include individuals of the type associated with Klan activities. . . .

3. The area is characterized by fear based upon rumor. In Jackson, rumors of organized Negro attacks on whites appear to be deliberately planted to spread in organized fashion through pamphlets, leaflets and word of mouth. . . .

It seems to me that this situation presents new and quite unprecedented problems of law enforcement.

As one step I am directing some of the personnel here in the Department who have had organized crime experience to make a more detailed survey of the area to try to substantiate the details concerning acts of terrorism which are at least generally believed to have taken place in the last few weeks.

In addition, it seems to me that consideration should be given by the Federal Bureau of Investigation to new procedures for identification of the individuals who may be or have been involved in acts of terrorism, and to the possible participation in such acts by law enforcement officials or at least their toleration of terrorist activity. In the past the procedures used by the Bureau for gaining information on known, local Klan groups have been successful in many places, and the information gathering techniques used by the Bureau on Communist or Communist related organizations have of course been spectacularly efficient.

The unique difficulty that seems to me to be presented by the situation in Mississippi (which is duplicated in parts of Alabama and Louisiana at least) is in gathering information on fundamentally lawless activities which have the sanction of local law enforcement agencies, political officials and a substantial segment of the white population. The techniques followed in the use of specially trained, special assignment agents in the infiltration of Communist groups should be of value. If you approve, it might be desirable to take up with the Bureau the possibility of developing a similar effort to meet this new problem.

In July of 1964, the FBI opened its Mississippi office.* This move would not have been possible while President Kennedy lived—or rather would have been improbable—since Robert Kennedy was essentially reluctant to do anything which would risk confrontation with Hoover and thereby embarrass his brother, jeopardize other programs, anger Hoover and cause him to use his influence on the Hill against other programs, or generally leak his unhappiness to the press before the upcoming Presidential election of 1964. During President Kennedy's life, Robert never *attempted* to control either the Director or the FBI. He tempered his efforts to influence the FBI so as not to embarrass his brother. No longer was a clash between the Director and the General by interpretation a clash between the Director (with his vast constituency) and the President.

Yet it was symbolic that when Hoover journeyed to Jackson to open the new office, he conferred with Governor Paul Johnson, Mayor Allen C. Tompason, the head of the State Highway Patrol and the local chief of police—the very people that the civil rights workers felt they had to be protected *against*. He then proceeded to march across the street from the

* Allen Dulles had also made a trip south for the President and recommended the opening of such an office.

Governor's mansion to the post office, where he held a press conference, asserted in no uncertain terms that the responsibility for protection rested with local Mississippi police, and disavowed any intent to protect civil rights workers. Police Chief Collins of Clarksdale, Mississippi, a man cited in many SNCC worker affidavits charging brutality and intimidation, took the occasion to remark: "The FBI comes in here every day and we have coffee every day. We're good friends."

It subtracts no credit from Kennedy, Marshall, *et al.*, however, to recognize that brilliant and original as were such independent initiatives as the incursion into Mississippi—no previous Attorneys General had encouraged their ranking officers to thus crowd the Bureau—in fact they were improvised countermeasures whose purpose was less to control the FBI than to utilize it. Because these counterstrategies were so successful, it never occurred to the Kennedy team that they were the ones who were being used, that they had lost the larger power war with the Bureau, which kept getting larger budgets and more manpower without giving up any control over their own destiny in return. As the Kennedy team learned what you could and couldn't ask, as they developed sophistication in translating common sense to Bureau-speak, as they developed informal ways of working with the FBI, they concluded that the Bureau seemed to be more responsive. They believed, as Katzenbach put it: "It got better with the Bureau the whole time we were there. They got more cooperative, as is true of the federal government generally." They may have regarded the FBI as wrongheaded, irritating, rigid, quaint and eccentric, but at worst they saw the Bureau as a slower-downer, not as a power rival. As long as the Kennedy camp believed these things, there was no incentive to think in terms of a radical shift in the underlying power relationship. It does not diminish the shrewdness nor belittle the specific victories of Kennedy stratagems to recognize that by indulging the illusion that they possessed power over the FBI they undermined the possibility of achieving it. For in truth, random victories such as getting the FBI to gather registration statistics or expedite an investigation or even open a field office are the sort that committed staffmen boast of having inflicted on their more cautious superiors. They do not bespeak the power relationship one expects between Cabinet officer and one of his subordinates.

To the extent that he had one, Kennedy's strategy for dealing with the FBI in civil rights, like his strategy for dealing with the Southern white power structure, was to avoid confrontation. The Attorney General did not press the FBI to make arrests under existing civil rights laws—Section 241 or 242. He did not press the FBI to make *ad hoc* arrests of law-breaking Southern police (with minor exceptions like the Ita Bena, Mississippi, case in June 1963). He did not insist that the FBI rotate Southern-oriented agents out of the South. He did not dramatically increase the number of black agents (although he put pressure on Hoover to do something about the lack of Negro Special Agents).* He did not redistribute Departmental housekeeping chores to give the FBI an appropriate share of the civil rights burden. He did not attempt to regulate the nature of contacts between the FBI and local law enforcement officers of the South.

But these were issues brought to the Department's attention by the civil rights movement, deliberated and disposed of. The General or his staff had focused on them and either acted or *decided* not to. More important than the joined issues were the unexamined ones. Almost by definition, confrontation avoidance meant that despite Kennedy's talents at infighting, the Department's bureaucratic struggle with the FBI would be fought on the Bureau's own terms and territory. For the secret society has mastered the arts of unconfrontation: the strategic delay, the constrictive interpretation, the ambiguous but argumentative memorandum (which requires a request-for-clarification reply), the purposeful misunderstanding, rumor-spreading, information-hoarding, jurisdictional humility, underdeployment of resources and vagueness, to mention only the most frequent.

Thus while the Department was preoccupied with countering bureaucratic trivia, the FBI was defining and reinforcing the environment within which the Department made its decisions—therefore some of the critical assumptions about how a Department "not of Prosecution but of Justice," as Kennedy used to say, ought to conduct its business were subconscious, invisible. That is to say they were regarded, if at all, much in the way a tenant regards his lease. Occasionally he will complain to the landlord and he will try to exploit his lease (although he doesn't want to risk having his water turned off) but essentially he *assumes* the terms of his lease in his dealings. The assumptions Robert Kennedy and the Justice Department made about the FBI were of this quality, and as such they limited, distorted and otherwise determined Justice Department policy in ways that were often not apparent to those immediately involved. For the Kennedy stratagems were invariably aimed at solving specific problems. But the network of

---

* No official figures were ever released, but the joke was that there were two. "One took your coat and the other drove Mr. Hoover's car." By 1964 there were said to be twenty-eight.

often unexamined assumptions by and about the Bureau—which were never challenged by the Kennedys—are what gave rise to the problems in the first place. These assumptions defined the system; they, rather than Robert Kennedy's occasional departures from past precedent, mandated the relationship between the Director and the General. A look at some of these assumptions is a useful first step toward a cost accounting.

Assumption Number One: The FBI had the right to determine which secrets should be sacred.

This assumption exacerbated interagency tensions, as the case of the Department's relations with the U.S. Commission on Civil Rights amply demonstrates. When the New Frontiersmen came to power, a major question lingered over the role of the Civil Rights Commission, whose traditional function had been to act as gadfly to the government but which was staffed largely by men who were contemporaries of, and had gone to school with, Civil Rights Division lawyers. Berl Bernhard, the young Yale lawyer whom JFK named as staff director of the commission, was prepared to go out of his way to cooperate with the new President and still fulfill the commission's mandate, yet the result was bitterness and backbiting between the commission and its natural ally, the Civil Rights Division. Arthur Schlesinger, Jr., has observed that the difficulties between them arose essentially from the fact that "one was an agency of recommendation and the other of action." Undoubtedly this was true and yet whatever chance there was for real cooperation was undermined partly because the Attorney General never thought to challenge the FBI's policy of information-hoarding.

Career civil rights attorneys in the Justice Department tend to be scornful of the commission because it has investigative but no enforcement powers, yet its budget was larger than that of the division, and as one white attorney put it, "It's easy to play Jesus and it's fun to get in bed with the civil rights movement, but all of the noise they make doesn't do as much good as one case." This endemic tension perhaps blinded the Justice Department to the FBI's obstruction of a possible avenue of cooperation. Berl Bernhard recalls: "One difficulty was the fundamental question: What was the jurisdiction of the commission in terms of investigating denials of voting? Our view was that Congress gave us a mandate to investigate all *prime facie* denials of civil rights, including voting. The Department's view was that people were complaining to both agencies. This was causing conflict and duplication. Therefore once the Department of Justice had determined to look at a particular county the commission should stay out. In point of fact it was difficult for the commission to fulfill its responsibility without firsthand knowledge. This meant we should have had access to FBI reports. We didn't.

"When we'd get complaints my inclination was to defer to the Department because they could take remedial action. But then we'd want to get the factual basis from the Department and they wouldn't let us see the Bureau reports. The Attorney General acceded to the Bureau's policy.

"I requested through Burke [Marshall] that we straighten out these problems. They seemed to me to be unnecessary antagonisms. We had a meeting with the Attorney General and went over the whole thing. Basically, we didn't get anywhere. The Attorney General took the view that when it came to fulfilling his responsibilities he had to file law suits and that the commission's hearings and investigations— carried on simultaneously—would just confuse the people in the state. This was all very well, but then how could the commission carry out *its* responsibilities?

"This was a continuing problem. It became more difficult as Justice became more effective in the voting area where I think they did a terrific job. . . . In many counties we were there first. We had already started investigations. Justice would come in and we'd have a big meeting with Seigenthaler, Doar, Bob, Burke and me. There'd be lots of give and take. But in the end, we'd lose out because the Attorney General wasn't willing to take on the Bureau."

Here then was a case where the Justice Department protected the FBI's information-withholding policy (which perhaps was justified in other areas as a security precaution) at the cost of hours of haggling, intergovernmental duplication and non-cooperation with a sympathetic agency. Yet if you ask any attorney in the Civil Rights Division the cause of the problem, he will *assume* the FBI policy as a fact of life and blame the commission for its intransigent attitude.

Assumption Number Two: The FBI had the right to determine its own availability—and was generally unavailable.

This assumption cut down on the Justice Department's capacity for flexible response. Such was the situation at the University of Mississippi and again at the University of Alabama. When James Meredith integrated Ole Miss, the Kennedys were faced with a policy decision: Should they call out the troops, go in and directly confront the segregationists, as the NAACP Legal Defense Fund urged, or should they try to do it quietly, behind the scenes, in collaboration with Governor Barnett, the chief and most vocal public obstructionist to James

Meredith's rights? They tried the latter course—but each time Meredith arrived on campus, accompanied by John Doar, Chief Marshal James McShane and a handful of others, Barnett had arranged it so that Meredith was denied admission. Finally, a group of 432 white-helmeted marshals got him on campus, but a riotous crowd forced the marshals to fire tear-gas cannisters and eventually the troops were called in. Nicholas Katzenbach, who directed the Ole Miss operation on the spot, offers the tactical observation, "The bad part of the Ole Miss operation was that the marshal force was not large enough to keep order but it was large enough to provoke the crowds. If I could have gotten rid of the marshals—despite the state police attitude—I could have done it, I think."

Whether Katzenbach "could have done it" is less significant than that even in retrospect he doesn't consider what might have happened had he had available a responsive, reflexive, cooperative FBI contingent to call upon. That he didn't suggests how the inflexibility and unavailability of the FBI limited the perspective and options of the Attorney General.

Anxious not to repeat the mistakes made at Ole Miss, the Justice Department dispatched an Air Force plane to take photographs of the University of Alabama campus (in the spring of 1963), in advance of anticipated trouble with integration only weeks away. Again, the unavailability of the FBI was assumed rather than examined, this time with results directly embarrassing to the Administration, for the discovery of the flight caused a flap that reached to the White House. "Despite the abilities of everybody at Ole Miss," Katzenbach explains, "we still didn't know that surrounding the Lyceum [the main building] was the most offensive thing we could have done. It was like surrounding the tomb of Robert E. Lee. And we didn't know that construction was under way within brick-throwing distance. I knew we didn't know the Alabama campus and I thought if we were going to have a similar problem in Alabama, we ought to know what we were up against. So I called [Cyrus] Vance or [Roswell] Gilpatrick [of the Defense Department] so at least we'd know what we were doing. There was the matter of an infirmary—where was it? Most important— bricks. Were any new buildings going up? Bricks were the problem at Ole Miss. The Pentagon gave the assignment to the Alabama National Guard. It was sheer stupidity. By the time it got down to some colonel he assigned it to the Air National Guard."

When President Kennedy heard about it he called the Justice Department and asked Ed Guthman—everybody else was out—"Who pulled that rock?" "It wasn't your brother," said Guthman. "Did Nick do it?" asked JFK. When Guthman said yes, the President observed, "Well, he's a good fellow. What's he doing about it?" The fact, of course, was that Katzenbach was merely reflecting Robert Kennedy's and the Department's thinking when he didn't think first of the FBI. It was not that the FBI wasn't competent to do the job. It was not even that the FBI's self-image ruled such information-gathering off limits. It was probably not that Katzenbach feared sympathetic FBI agents would leak their mission to the local constabulary. It was simply that given all of the obstacles to dealing with the FBI, given the opportunity to call either an Ivy League compatriot at the Pentagon or a possibly reluctant agent, and given the interagency presumption that calls on behalf of Robert Kennedy would be as quickly honored as calls from the President, Katzenbach did what he did.

Not an unreasonable reflex, given the FBI's general posture: No, the FBI would not tell civil rights attorneys whether agents would be present at a publicly announced voter-registration demonstration. No, the FBI would not reveal the sources of its information on the Klan to Civil Rights Division attorneys involved in relevant litigation. No, the FBI would not permit its civil rights reports to go beyond the Department—to the Civil Rights Commission or anyone else. No, the FBI would not say how many Negro agents it employed.

Assumption Number Three: The lack of FBI *initiatives* on behalf of civil rights neither helped nor hindered the civil rights movement.

In fact, the absence of FBI initiatives strengthened and codified the segregationist *status quo*. For instance, in their investigations of judicial appointees, which Burke Marshall calls "worthless," they rarely looked for or turned up evidence of racial prejudice or segregationist history. Obviously, one reason they took no unilateral initiatives on this issue was that the Kennedys, especially in the first two years, when most of the appointments were made, were not particularly interested in alienating the Southern power bloc in the Senate, and so there was no pressure on the FBI to perform the way they did in the internal-security area. Had the FBI been as aggressive in developing background information on the racial views of Southern judicial candidates as they were in the area of internal security, the history of litigation in the Fifth Circuit might have taken a radically different turn. Appointments such as Judges Robert Elliott and Harold Cox (see Chapter V) might have been stymied.

Assumption Number Four: The FBI's "raw, unevaluated files"— especially when they included patent gossip, irrelevancies and untruths—didn't affect the perspective of the high-minded and sophisticated Kennedy intellectuals who knew very well that the data was sometimes loaded.

In fact, the FBI's reflexive use of its files helped characterize and sometimes dominate the tone and milieu within which the Attorney General had to operate. The Attorney General's much maligned meeting with a group of Negro intellectuals and friends of James Baldwin on May 24, 1963, was a case in point. All concerned—Kennedy, Burke Marshall, Ed Guthman and the Baldwin delegation (including Baldwin, his brother, Lorraine Hansberry, Kenneth B. Clark, Jerome Smith, a twenty-five-year-old CORE official who had been bludgeoned in a civil rights demonstration, and others) agreed that the meeting was a disaster. When one of the Negroes remarked that he wouldn't fight for the U.S. if we went to war with Cuba, Kennedy was shocked. When another asked why he had not gone to Ole Miss and walked in with Meredith, Kennedy laughed. When Burke Marshall told of his mediation in Birmingham, they wanted to know why the government hadn't used troops. Dr. Clark says, "We were shocked that he was shocked and that he seemed unable to understand what Smith was trying to say." (Smith had said it made him "nauseous" to have to beg his government for protection when he was fighting for the American dream of equal rights.)

Kennedy, for his part, had convened the meeting ostensibly to find out "What is it you want me to do?" Since they were telling him he didn't have any understanding of the problem, his calls for a solution seemed misplaced.

The meeting was initiated when Dick Gregory told Marshall that the Attorney General ought to meet Baldwin, who had recently published his searing essay "The Fire Next Time," on the imminent escalation of the race crisis. So Marshall set up a breakfast and drove Baldwin out to Hickory Hill, where the three men had a good conversation as Baldwin spoke about black people in the cities of the North and Kennedy kept saying he wanted to *do* something and asked what could he do. "Baldwin hadn't the foggiest idea," recalls Marshall, "and so he said he would collect some experts to meet with Bob and they would tell him what the Administration should do."

At this time the Justice Department was writing the revised civil rights bill, which eventually became the Civil Rights Act of 1964. The President was having hundreds of people called to the White House, most of whom Bobby was called upon to address, and one afternoon Kennedy and Marshall had a secret meeting in New York at the

Waldorf-Astoria with a group of businessmen about opening chain-store lunch counters to Negroes and employing them. "Then we went to this meeting where we expected Negro experts on urban problems who would have a program they could explain to the Attorney General so he could fit it into legislation."

The Attorney General and Marshall left the Waldorf and walked to Kennedy's apartment only to discover on arrival that of the group Baldwin had gathered, only two or three, June Shagaloff, Kenneth Clark and Theodore Barry, were "the kind of people who could help with a program. Otherwise there were artists, friends of Baldwin and actors. They were all worked up," Marshall recalls. "They were asking things like 'Why don't you send the army into Birmingham?' If we did that, the Army would declare martial law, so all the demonstrators would be arrested. I asked the Army what they'd do and that is what they told me. I went to a critical white businessman's meeting in Birmingham and their first proposition was the same thing. I told them that would ruin their business, and they agreed."

So Kennedy sat there as Harry Belafonte, Lena Horne, Clarence Jones (a New York attorney) and others either chewed him out or said nothing. Later some of them privately apologized, which upset him even more since he believed they should have spoken up in front of their friends or not at all.

It would of course have been too much to expect the FBI to respond to such a meeting by, say, investigating the charges of a man like Jerome Smith. Students of the Bureau also know it would have been too much to expect them to remain silent. Shortly after the papers reported the Attorney General's unhappy experience, the FBI's reflex action was to forward dossiers on all of those present, including such random information as the fact that one had been a member of the Labor Youth League (a late 1940s organization which had found its way onto the Attorney General's list) and a six-page report on James Baldwin which included the following presumably essential data:

> The New York *Herald Tribune* of June 17, 1961 in its "Letters to the Editor" section carried a letter by James Baldwin and William Styron which advocated the abolishment of capital punishment. This letter stated in part that "If there were a shred of proof that the death penalty actually served to inhibit crime, that would be sufficient reason—even from the point of view of 'misguided do-gooders' as J. Edgar Hoover calls its opponents—to maintain it." It goes on to state that Mr. Hoover "is not a lawgiver, nor is there any reason to suppose him to be a particularly profound student of human nature. He is a law enforcement officer. It is appalling that in this capacity he

not only opposes the trend of history among civilized nations, but uses his enormous power and prestige to corroborate the blindest and basest instincts of the retaliatory mob. . . ."

Confronted with unexpected militance, rudeness and hostility, the better part of Kennedy (Jules Feiffer's Good Bobby, Jack Newfield's existential Bobby) [3] would have wanted to know what made them feel this way. Were they representative or aberrational? What could be done about it? But the President's brother, the Attorney General of the United States, was, of course, irritated at the time-waste and the misplaced expectations. He felt he had been had, since he had come ostensibly to hear pragmatic program suggestions. Actually, that claim was a bit of an overstatement since the meetings were as much PR-motivated as they were information-retrieval nets, under the implicit and shrewd theory that involvement was the critical threshold for minority-group cooperation. The FBI's Pavlovian response, however, inevitably reinforced the tendency to suspect and to rationalize that these were not constructive people anyway and therefore could be discounted.

The foregoing is not to imply that the Attorney General took the FBI's "raw, unevaluated data" seriously; in fact, he passed it on to Marshall with one of those wry penned notes that were his hallmark: "What nice friends you have.—Bob." Nor is it to say that the Bureau should have investigated Smith's allegations instead of sending over a file on him, although that would not have been a bad idea. Rather, it is to note that the fact of the FBI responding in this way was part of the atmosphere of the United States Department of Justice. The Attorney General *did* read the FBI dossiers and so did Guthman, Marshall, *et al.*, and while they might privately dismiss, joke about and scorn much of the trivia, irrelevance and unsubstantiated rumors these files contained, the dossiers made it that much easier not to take seriously the militant disaffection expressed by a group of show-biz types, some of whom had, after all, belonged to "subversive" or suspect organizations.

Assumption Number Five: You don't use the FBI in cases, such as those alleging police brutality, which might embarrass their local relationships.

The result of this assumption (more conscious than many, and sometimes honored in the breach) was to intrude on the Civil Rights Division's manpower pool and to encourage police brutality, since violations were only rarely prosecuted. As Burke Marshall now concedes (although it was denied at the time), "FBI investigations in police brutality cases were *pro forma.* They were worth nothing. Therefore if you wanted to have a good case I had to devote two or three lawyers to the investigation. Now if you're going to accomplish anything, you want a chance with the jury. So we closed investigations which I just knew if we had the time and the resources we might have developed into cases—even though the chances of getting a conviction were slight. Only a certain number of lawyers can handle this type of case. So if you have sixteen lawyers of that caliber you have to conserve their energy."

An indication of the Department's attitude in these matters may be inferred from what happened when the Civil Rights Commission Report of 1961 observed that the FBI was sometimes reluctant to pursue investigations into police brutality. Hoover sent an angry letter of denial to Commission Chairman John Hannah and wrote: "I strongly resent any implication that there is any reluctance or lack of enthusiasm in fulfilling our investigative responsibilities in this most important area." He demanded, with names, the facts on which the commission based its report and asked to meet with Hannah. But, according to Foster Rhea Dulles, who wrote an authorized history of the Civil Rights Commission, the commission dropped the matter on the advice of Burke Marshall, who counseled its staff director that "poison pen correspondence never leads to satisfactory results" and the commission should drop the matter allowing time for Mr. Hoover to cool it.

Assumption Number Six: The FBI and the Justice Department spoke the same language; that FBI language (Bureau-speak) was descriptive and that it could be used by non-FBI personnel with impunity.

Not long after taking office, the Attorney General and his staff took to speaking the FBI's language, which was, of course, a vocabulary of convenience rather than description. The result was that Robert Kennedy misstated and underestimated his power. He repeated the FBI formulations so many times that he came to believe them. Asked on "Meet the Press" why the Department had not given protection to slain NAACP leader Medgar Evers, Attorney General Kennedy said, "We do not have the authority or manpower to provide it. That would have to be done by local authorities." When James Farmer called John Doar's assistant, St. John Barrett, from Plaquemine Parish, Louisiana, to describe how he had to be smuggled out of a church in a hearse for fear that an angry mob would lynch him, Barrett explained that "We have no authority" to send anyone in, although the

FBI could investigate the allegations of police mistreatment.

At the time such denials of "authority" seemed a harmless enough case of confused semantics. And to most, it still does. Marshall himself takes the blame: "When Robert Kennedy used terms like 'authority' he picked that up from me. When he used that rather than 'policy' it was my fault, although I never thought it was terrible. The Bureau was always talking in terms of what 'authority' it did and didn't have. I never paid much attention to that technical stuff. Robert Kennedy may have used words like 'authority' because his instincts were with the movement. He would always come back and say, 'Can't we do something?' "

Whether or not Marshall gave it much thought, and whether Kennedy picked the language up from the FBI or from Marshall who picked it up from the FBI, next to the lack of protection itself nothing alienated the civil rights movement more than the Justice Department's rhetoric, which they regarded as misrepresentation by understatement and as the cynical and conscious camouflaging of policy decisions against the movement.

In fact, to the extent that the rhetoric of federalism (discussed in the next chapter) was empty, the Justice Department had not so much decided against the civil rights movement as it had adapted itself to the requirements of not antagonizing the FBI.

Assumption Number Seven: The FBI's image was irrelevant to the day-to-day work of the Justice Department—and that because the FBI was independent of the Attorney General, he wouldn't be blamed for its inactivities.

Of course the FBI's style, its public face, its regional prejudices all helped give the Justice Department its image in the eyes of the idealistic young civil rights workers who, unsophisticated in the ways of the Justice Department, assumed that if the Attorney General would only pass the word, the FBI would respond. Thus, FBI intransigence tarnished the Justice Department itself, impeded the ability of the Attorney General to appeal to the civil rights community and the constituency they represented on moral grounds, and dissipated much of the extraordinary reservoir of credit the Kennedys had built up through rhetoric, through appointments (of Negroes and civil rights enthusiasts), through response to crises (such as the willingness to put troops on the side of the Negro, no matter how belatedly), and so forth. The occasions were many. As Harold Fleming of the Potomac Institute, one of the most articulate and levelheaded white civil rights administrators, notes: "Not protecting the kids was a moral shock, more than a cold-blooded, calculated reckoning. It was bruising and deeply emotional. To have the FBI looking out of the courthouse windows while you were being chased down the street by brick throwers deeply offends the sensibilities. So people wept and cursed Robert Kennedy and Burke Marshall more than the FBI, whom they never had any confidence in to begin with."

Fleming's point is an important one because it helps explain the bitter turn that the civil rights movement—or an important part of it —ultimately took. Some five years after the fact and in the comfort of the Potomac Institute's Washington quarters, Fleming elaborated: "Project yourself back to '61 or '62. There was a totally unjustified euphoria. The climate of expectation was created not by the Kennedys with an intention to deceive, but by the ethos of the moment. The feeling was: After Ike, at least we'll have an activist Administration. We were all unsophisticated about power. We thought it was there to be used. This was exciting. We didn't know about the inhibitions of power. There was a feeling of executive potential.

"SNCC *et al.* thought Justice's bargain was protection in exchange for a shift from direct action protest to a voter registration drive. Because of the Kennedys' own view of reality they encouraged this belief. So SNCC & Co. weren't given pledges. But they assumed—everybody overestimated the capacity of the Administration to intervene in an unlimited way. And everybody underestimated the prospective need for intervention.

"The sense of betrayal which came later was the inevitable hangover from the binge. Nobody would ever forgive the Kennedys for playing politics because they weren't supposed to on this front. The very fact that there was a sense of partnership had much to do with it. We all thought we were *part* of the Administration—which is absurd. We were not on the payroll. We were not forced to grapple with the Administration's priorities.

"It was *not* true that Kennedy or Burke created or caused to be created VEP [the foundation-financed Voter Education Project]. That was one of the fictions. Kennedy was not Svengali and the civil rights movement collective Trilbys. There was discussion and interaction. The initiatives—dickering with IRS, etc. for tax-deduction status [for the VEP project]—were all independent of Kennedy.

"The Justice Department was a floating brain trust around Robert Kennedy which encouraged directions and ideas. [Stephen] Currier [President of the Taconic Foundation, principal backer of VEP] already was a supporter of SRC [the Southern Regional Council] and sympathetic to VEP-type stuff. The idea's time had come. It hadn't come sooner because there was no indication of federal action sufficient to make the game worth the candle.

"I never heard anybody from the Justice Department say, 'Sure, you fellows go out there and we'll give you all the protection you need.' That may have been understood. But Burke was scarcely one to over-state these things. . . .

"Everybody knew so little. It wouldn't be like following the LBJ Administration. What the hell could you learn from the Eisenhower Administration except that doing nothing had bad consequences?"

Assumption Number Eight: The FBI had the right to determine its own legal boundaries.

The result was unofficial but *de facto* endorsement for the Bureau's policy of jurisdictional humility in civil rights cases. In fact, the under-lying principle which was reinforced every time the FBI refused juris-diction in a particular case was the FBI's right to self-determination in all cases. There is no better example of the phenomenon than an FBI press release issued on September 18, 1962:

> Attorney General Robert F. Kennedy announced that the FBI has turned over a summary of facts and evidence to local authorities following the burning of the I Hope Baptist Church near Dawson, Ga., early today.
> FBI Director J. Edgar Hoover stated this action followed the ques-tioning by FBI agents of four Terrell County residents observed in a car near the church after the fire was discovered. The FBI launched an intensive investigation into the burning of the church early this morning. This burning was the most recent of a series of church burn-ings under investigation by the FBI. The evidence in this case was given to local authorities because the FBI investigation established that the persons responsible did not burn the church specifically to intimidate Negroes from registering to vote, Attorney General Kennedy said.
> Mr. Hoover said the FBI investigation of the other burnings is con-tinuing. All services of the FBI Lab and the Fingerprint Identification Division are fully available to Georgia authorities in the event addi-tional assistance is needed for prosecution of state violations. . . .
> The Attorney General personally called Mr. Hoover and com-mended the quick, decisive action by FBI agents involved in the investigation of this case.

First, we may observe that Ed Guthman had early established the principle (which he prided himself on) that the lead paragraphs of all FBI press releases would feature Attorney General Kennedy as the senior officer of the Department. Thus, an apparent bureaucratic victory. But a symbolic rather than a real one, feeding the internal illusion—and the external one, too—that the Attorney General indeed was in charge of, and in control of, the Director. The price for this first paragraph was, of course, that the Attorney General implicitly always gave his blessing to everything that followed. To this day Ed Guthman believes that since all FBI press releases were cleared with him before being issued, he spared the Attorney General any embarrassment. But again, one suspects that knowingly or not, the problems caused whenever Guthman attempted to edit were such that he used his blue pencil sparingly. And so, once again, the FBI had contributed to the illusion of cooperation when in fact the Bureau had won the Attorney General's presumptive endorsements for their minimal activities and dubious policies.

With regard to the substance of the release itself, one might observe that until the accused is caught, one does not know what his "specific intent" is. Since the church burners had not yet been caught, the FBI may have ducked out of the case prematurely. (The careful reader will note that the finding of specific intent is put in the mouth of the Attorney General, thereby exonerating the FBI from its long-distance judgment.)

Also, according to its own testimony, the FBI doesn't evaluate, it only collects information. How, then, can it make a judgment of "intent" which surely involves some evaluation? Finally, one might ask why this was an occasion for the Attorney General to congratulate the FBI for its decisive action when that action consisted entirely in removing itself from the case (and turning it over to a presumptively unsympathetic local law enforcer).

The answer to these questions is less important than the situation which gave rise to them. Probably the FBI turned the case over to local authorities to avoid a bad statistic (since they assumed, correctly, that even if they found the guilty party, the odds were against conviction), and/or because of pre-existing relations with the local law enforcement establishment. And probably the Attorney General (or Guthman in his name) went along with the congratulations as a public-relations gesture which in addition to making the Bureau happy gave the aura of decisive action to the Kennedy Administration. But the fact is that the FBI managed in this wholly typical maneuver to avoid jurisdiction in a case it didn't want; not only got away with it, but won a commendation from the Attorney General in the process and camouflaged a shrinkage of federal responsibility in a claim of decisive federal action.

Assumption Number Nine: The FBI dispatched agents in response to the needs of any specific investigation.

In actuality the FBI reflected the quality of its enthusiasm with the quantity of its agents. To the casual observer, there is no relationship between the failure to prosecute (because a grand jury wouldn't return an indictment) the sheriff who caned C. B. King, the militant black attorney in Albany, Georgia, and the decision to prosecute the nine Albany civil rights workers accused of perjury or obstructing justice (by picketing the store of a white juror who had voted "wrong" on a civil rights case). Not so to those who were on the scene.

At the time, the Justice Department said that the case against C. B. King was dropped because the FBI had not developed enough evidence to convince the Justice Department that it could prove a federal case against the sheriff who caned King. But not long thereafter, on receiving complaints of "an organized Negro boycott against a grocery store owned by a white man who sat in a jury which [exonerated a sheriff who had shot a Negro prisoner]," the Justice Department decided to go ahead. The FBI had provided enough information to convince the U.S. attorney that he should proceed on the theory that the boycott was a retaliation for the man's jury vote, technically known as "obstruction of justice." The decision was made despite the claimed innocence of the civil rights workers, who assert they picketed solely because of the grocery store's racist hiring policies and of Joni Rabinowitz, the New Yorker accused of perjury, for insisting—as she does to this day—that she wasn't there.

The connection to the locals was more than apparent. As C. B. King told it on a dusty spring day in Albany: "The sheriff of Baker County, L. Warren Johnson, had from the evidence gone to the home of a Negro by the name of Charley Ware, got him out of bed, manacled him, bludgeoned him around in advance of putting him in a car, taken him to the front of the jail, fired on him at front range while he sat manacled in the front seat of the car. Three bullets went into the cervicle area of his neck. Miraculously none struck the cord and he lived. Carl Smith is a white man who operated a store in an all-Negro section of Albany and who was a juror serving on the trial of that case. There was picketing of his store. It was a simple question of fact: Was the picketing pursuant to the jury verdict? The Justice Department sent eighty-six FBI agents in here to investigate that case. They were thick as hogs. By way of contrast there were multiple instances of Negroes abused—my own sister-in-law savagely kicked while pregnant, my own bludgeoning while on client business. And the FBI was never heard from except for the local agent, who melts right in with the total whiteness of the community."

Now the Albany case was a complicated one. C. B. King thinks it was politically inspired. "They prosecuted Anderson, the head of the Albany movement, and others for perjury. It was left to RFK to decide this." On the other hand, Robert Owen, an attorney in the Civil Rights Division, who had joined the Justice Department under Eisenhower, says: "In terms of any simple decision to me as a young lawyer my estimate of the man [Kennedy] shot way up because he called the Albany Nine case as a lawyer. I don't know what went into his judgment. I do know that the prosecution was authorized by Robert Kennedy. It's tough to call a case against the good guys." Another complicating factor was that the case came up through Jack Miller's Criminal Division, which wasn't that opposed to bringing it, rather than Burke Marshall's Civil Rights Division, which would have been (and was) more sensitive to its implications vis-a-vis the civil rights movement. Miller recalls "there was some argument in the Criminal Division itself because of sympathy for the defendants, [but] . . . even those who were most sympathetic felt that there had been a violation and the case should be proceeded with. . . . I can remember that the U.S. Attorney felt quite strongly there had in fact been a blatant violation. . . ."

The issue here is not whether the case should have been brought. It is (a) that the FBI employed its energies in the area of its own enthusiasms and retrenched in the area of its reluctancies, and (b) that this message was not lost on black civil rights workers. The show of outside agents would have been less impressive had the resident agent been more effective. But as C. B. King noted, "When you complain about the FBI, you are talking about local people. A local redneck with an FBI tag. Not outsiders. The resident agent here is a Virginia boy who has only been in Albany for seven years. But he has psychological needs, he wants social approbation. He wants his wife to be accepted as the wife of a regular fellow in this community. He wants her to have friends to be invited to dinner. And the only people who are relevant to him are white people."

C. B. King's point echoes Martin Luther King's contemporary charge that Southern-based FBI agents didn't follow through on civil rights cases. Either way, white agents seemed to black civil rights workers to fit into the white establishment like pieces in a jigsaw puzzle. Little thought was apparently given to systematic rotation to prevent this phenomenon. And in any event, the FBI attracted a conservative breed, whose innate instincts were reinforced by a milieu which honored the Director's politics and made them the implicit ideology of the Bureau.

The impact of the Albany prosecution, one of many indirect consequences of the FBI's allocation of its resources, is dramatically spelled out in a private letter a group of six distinguished law professors (Paul Freund, Mark De Wolfe Howe and Donald Turner of Harvard, Alexander Bickel, Charles L. Black, Jr., and Fleming James, Jr., of Yale) sent urging the Attorney General to counterbalance the Albany prosecution with some action on the other side of the ledger. They eloquently argued that the prosecution of the Albany Nine had come to symbolize more than it signified and that

> . . . These young people . . . are, we believe, a national asset, and their morale, their sense of mission and their consciousness of support for their efforts in the country at large are properly matters of national concern. They face enormous difficulties and severe hardship and danger; most have been harassed, some have been abused and beaten, a few—as currently in Americus, Ga.—have been subjected to blatant persecution in local courts. They must have the sense that the country at large sustains them and that the federal government is sympathetic to their efforts and will support and protect them when it can lawfully do so. . . . We are greatly worried that these young people now face a crisis of morale, that a feeling of abandonment is taking the place of their consciousness of support. . . . We believe that many of them have come to feel that the government does not intend to use the federal criminal process or any other means to protect them. . . . This feeling is not unnaturally brought to a climax by government's impending prosecution of members of the Albany movement.

Whether the Albany Nine case should have been brought is of less matter than the fact that as disillusioning encounter piled upon disillusioning encounter—usually the result of FBI inaction, or insensitivity, or, more rarely overreaction—the civil rights movement became increasingly alienated from government itself. The movement's ally became its enemy.

Assumption Number Ten: The FBI in civil rights was a local law enforcement assister rather than national law enforcement enforcer.

In Chapter I it was suggested how, at the time of the freedom rides, the Justice Department assumed the FBI's unavailability and called in special deputized federal marshals while FBI agents looked through windows and took notes. But consider the account of William Orrick, then head of the Civil Division, who was an eyewitness to the proceedings.

On Saturday, May 20, at 8:30 A.M. the bus left Birmingham for Montgomery. FBI agent Robb told acting chief Stanley of the Montgomery Police at 9:30 A.M. that the bus had left Birmingham at 8:30 A.M. Detective Shows of the Montgomery Police Department told a reporter of the Montgomery *Advertiser* that morning that the Montgomery Police "would not lift a finger to protect this group."

At 10:00 A.M. Saturday morning, Police Commissioner Sullivan of Montgomery was advised by Floyd Mann, Director of the Alabama Department of Public Safety, that the bus had reached a point 14 miles beyond the city limits of Montgomery. The bus had been convoyed from Birmingham by 16 highway patrol cars and one airplane.

At the Montgomery bus depot a mob—which could have been readily controlled by proper police work—rioted and attacked the group of riders, beating them with pipes, sticks, clubs and their fists. At least four out-of-town reporters and photographers were beaten and an ambulance which arrived on the scene was chased away. People with no apparent connection to the trip were beaten, a boy's leg was broken and another boy had inflammable liquid poured over him and set on fire. Mr. Seigenthaler, who attempted to help a girl escape from the mob, was struck from behind and lay on the sidewalk for 25 minutes before police took him to a hospital. Police Commissioner Sullivan, when asked why an ambulance was not called for Mr. Seigenthaler, stated that "every white ambulance in town reports their vehicles have broken down."

A sheriff's posse of deputies assigned to control riots did not arrive on the scene until an hour and 15 minutes after the first wave of violence, thereafter 10 more police cars arrived to restore order.

Subsequently, a federal court found that the Montgomery police department "willfully and deliberately failed to take measures to ensure the safety of the students and to prevent unlawful acts of violence upon their persons." Because of the gross malfeasance of the Montgomery police, nobody thought to observe the nonfeasance of the FBI agents standing by (confirmed in their own eyewitness accounts of the proceedings) and the Bureau's misfeasance in supplying local police with information while not relaying back to Justice—if indeed it had secured—information about the illegal intentions of the Montgomery police. In addition to not obtaining (or relaying) information and not moving to protect the riders as did Seigenthaler, the FBI also did not apparently even consider—nor was it suggested that they should—making on-the-spot arrests of visible outlaws.* As a result, the FBI early established its reluctance to antagonize local law enforcers, and the Ad-

---

* Agents are authorized to make arrests without a warrant when a misdemeanor or a felony is committed in their presence or when they have grounds for believing a felony has been committed; yet they refrained from such actions in civil rights cases.

ministration early learned to assume that it was without what might have been its most valuable race-relations asset: a manpower pool permitting flexible response in crisis situations.

Assumption Number Eleven: Continuation of the *status quo* was neutral—and that letting the FBI alone made things neither better nor worse.

The fact was that the FBI prevailed not by lobbying for its view but by carrying on business as usual. The civil rights revolution raced by while the FBI stood still. John Doar believes, "Until December of 1963 Mississippi decided they didn't have to intimidate via violence because the legal structure was impervious. That was the Maginot line. Now the Maginot line began to crack. . . . Then Mississippi turned to violence. As the curve started up Bob Moses and his guys decided the way to confront that curve was to bring a lot of white kids down and get some white kids hurt and the country would be up in arms." Whatever the dynamics of the situation, the FBI wasn't keeping up. As late as 1964 the FBI continued to participate in segregated activities, such as graduation ceremonies at the high school in Iuka, Mississippi, which featured a resident Special Agent as principal speaker. Technically, this was known as keeping up one's local contacts. As SNCC head John Lewis pointed out at the time (again, helping determine the unhappy perspective of black civil rights workers) in a letter to Robert Kennedy:

> It is intolerable that the U. S. government should allow one of its official agents to appear before such a [segregated] audience. It is especially appalling when one considers the record—by now a matter of common knowledge—of FBI agents in the deep South who have established themselves in the minds of millions of Negroes as often working in collusion with racist officials. Time after time FBI agents have stood by and watched while the constitutional rights of Negro citizens were openly violated. FBI agents have frequently refused to make even the most cursory investigations of violations of First Ammendment rights of Negroes.[4]

Assumption Number Twelve: Where the FBI was uncooperative, it made sense for the Civil Rights Division to step in.

Where it was unenthusiastic, the FBI made it expensive, inefficient and unpleasant for the Justice Department to use its services. Thus often the Civil Rights Division found it easier to carry on its own investigations than to play games with the FBI. J. Harold Flannery, a young lawyer in the Division, says, "We always had to disguise it as interviewing potential witnesses; otherwise it was usurping the Bureau's function. We spent 50 to 75 percent of our time in the field to come to grips with the problem." But in addition to depleting resources, such activities led to other intermural complications. Sal Andretta, the Justice Department's career administrative officer, would complain to the Attorney General about the Civil Rights Division's overuse of marshals, U.S. attorneys, automobiles and telephones and its subpoenaing more witnesses than were needed. To such charges Assistant Attorney General Marshall would have to draft lengthy rebuttals, pointing out that

> . . . we prove our cases in large part from cumulative facts about schooling, comprehension, etc., of hostile witnesses. We have found that the best way to get truthful testimony from witnesses is to subpoena them on the basis of their handwriting, their appearance or the appearance of their homes rather than on the basis of an extensive, and I might add, an expensive, FBI interview. . . .[5]

The accumulation of such diversions took their toll.

Assumption Number Thirteen: Federal protection for civil rights workers would inevitably lead to a national police force.

This was one of Hoover's favorite *ex cathedra* assertions repeated so often on social occasions that Kennedy himself came to find the formulation convenient and used it with indifferent success when appearing on television programs and before students. Had he considered the numbers—6,000 agents as compared with, say, New York City's police force of over 30,000—the folly of the argument, without underestimating the dangers of either a national police force or an unbridled FBI, might have been apparent.

But the assumption was consistent with Hoover's long-term strategy for dealing with the Justice Department, which was to supplement bureaucratic infighting with a national publicity campaign mobilizing the American people against a series of poltergeists. The rising crime rate was his domestic poltergeist,* international Communism was his overseas poltergeist, and the specter of a national police force *cum* Gestapo was his civil rights poltergeist. The fear, as interpreted by Burke Marshall, was not irrational: "Once you accept the notion that some federal authority is going to arrest anyone who interferes with demonstrations or protest movements, then they could legitimately request federal protection in hundreds of places all over the South where we would have had to provide force, and we didn't have the resources. I never discussed this with Robert Kennedy, but he understood the realities." Arguable, but worth debate. The Kennedy crew, ultra-reason-

---

* W. H. Ferry, then of the Fund for the Republic, first invoked the image of a "red poltergeist" to account for Mr. Hoover's staying power in 1962. The elaboration is, of course, my own.

able men in so many other enterprises, could conceivably have come up with criteria to distinguish among the projected requests, but the point, as Marshall's observation confirms, is that the issue never surfaced to the level of discussion.

Kennedy, furthermore, bought Hoover's favorite bromide—that too much FBI involvement in anything the FBI didn't want to become involved in would inevitably lead to a national police force—yet ironically, by permitting Hoover dictatorial control over the FBI's ranks, rules and systems while enlarging its numbers, budget and paper jurisdiction, Kennedy was perpetuating and enlarging whatever danger there was that the FBI might function as a national police force. It is, of course, a tribute to Hoover's bureaucratic genius that Kennedy never even thought to question, no less discuss, the national police force bogeyman, preferring to wear it as armor against the intellectual onslaughts of his spiritual allies as he found himself more and more deeply enmeshed in the aspirations and programs of the civil rights community. "We *want* to provide the protection," he could say in effect, "but not at the cost of creating a national police force."

Assumption Number Fourteen, a corollary to Thirteen: If you used the FBI in one place, you would have to use it in all places. As Marshall put it when asked what he thought of the proposal by Howard Zinn, Boston University professor of politics and chronicler of SNCC's history, that there be a force of E (for Emergency) Men who would police trouble spots: "People like Zinn basically wanted us to use the Army as a police force. Actually there are only six hundred deputy marshals in the U.S. Take Mississippi. It has eighty-six counties. In Nashoba there is a sheriff and four deputies, and the sheriff is a son of a bitch. What Zinn really wants is for the federal government to provide sufficient personal protection for any student who wants to go anywhere. Our position was that fundamentally that's not possible. Even though we did it sometimes. We used marshals and FBI agents. But to accept Zinn's theory would have been impossible and deceptive. You encourage people to get killed. Zinn would say now you have the power to do it. We would say we didn't have the power and we didn't want the power. The best people we had were the Border Patrol. And who knows how many people got across the Border when we were using [the Patrol] at Ole Miss? I don't."

One can argue that the FBI's inflexibility contributed to Burke Marshall's rather rigid assumption that if you use a federal presence anywhere, you have to use it everywhere. That is the way the FBI thinks, the way it talks and the way it operates. But such thinking ran counter to the improvisatory pragmatism the Kennedy intellectuals exhibited in other aspects of their work. The fact that Marshall saw the issue as whether or not to use the Army (rather than the FBI) is simply further evidence that the premise of Kennedy–Marshall thinking on these matters was that the FBI had effectively removed itself from consideration as an organizational participator.

The result was a souring of the most idealistic of the civil rights activists. As Cleghorn and Watters concluded, after hundreds of interviews with civil rights activists:

> The failure of federal protection in the early 1960's was a bitter pill. From the radio gangbuster days to kidnappings and espionage cases, the FBI in war and peace seemed to be enforcing other laws, with arrests as well as investigations. In those cases, of course . . . it hadn't had to police the local police. . . .
>
> Failure to provide federal protection was especially bitter for the voter workers, for in the early VEP planning they had been led to expect full federal protection of rights and safety. In the context of the debate over voter registration versus direct action, this assurance seemed to mean that voter registration had a clear-cut advantage over direct action as a movement strategy. When the kind of protection expected was not forthcoming, disillusionment was doubly strong.[6]

A particularly stark example occurred on Freedom Day (October 7, 1963) in Selma, Alabama. Had the government ordered the FBI to act, perhaps there never would have been a need for Dr. King's famous Selma march two years later to *force* the government to act. The facts are not in dispute. Three Negroes, who had lined up at the Selma courthouse to register, were arrested by Al Lingo's state troopers and Sheriff Jim Clark (others were harassed and had their pictures taken— an intimidating gesture) as four FBI agents and two Justice Department attorneys stood by and watched this patent violation of federal statutes. The Justice Department had adapted to the FBI code and went along with it to preserve a modicum of consistency, to keep peace with the Bureau, to advance a theory of federalism (which in turn was born partly out of the non-cooperation of the FBI). It would surely be claiming too much to say that this complicity is what caused the civil rights movement to turn to militance, yet one cannot help but agree with Watters' and Cleghorn's conclusion:

> They had started out believing the best that America said of itself; they had acted on this and came to believe the worst, out of experiencing it. The important thing was that more and more Negroes who already shared their disappointment and disillusionment might come to share their unfortunate ways of expressing it.[7]

Assumption Number Fifteen: Despite its eccentric and abstemious ways, the FBI was a functional ally in the fight against illegal discrimination.

Not necessarily so. As a genre, the diaries of civil rights workers suffer from paranoia. And for every anti-FBI story there is a counterbalancing story which shows how the FBI assisted somebody to save his life, limb, his sense of self. As Hoover pointed out on his own behalf, when the FBI was on the defensive for not doing enough in the fall of 1963, "FBI investigations have enabled the Department of Justice to file more than four suits in five states to end racial discrimination in voting. FBI agents solved the case involving the burning of a Greyhound bus transporting freedom riders through Alabama in 1961. . . . An FBI investigation in September 1962 led to the arrest and conviction in state court of four persons for burning a Negro church in Terrell County, Georgia. FBI agents also arrested Byron De La Beckwith, the man charged with the murder of Medgar Evers, the Mississippi leader of the NAACP. . . ."

Nevertheless, in going through the files of the pro-civil rights-crusading, student-founded paper *The Mississippi Courier,* the Southern Regional Council and the VEP, and in reading original affidavits, one is struck by the recurring patterns of experiences by workers scattered all over the South. Five cases are cited here not to "prove" that the FBI was out to undermine the movement but, to the contrary, that in its personnel, its style, its normal conduct of business, the FBI could do much damage without willing it:

Exhibit A

When the movement came to Clarksdale, we encouraged the local people to talk to the FBI. We discovered that everything we told the FBI was told to the local police the next day. Our local people would be picked up by the police after they had spoken to the FBI, and the police would tell them everything they had said. . . .

At best the FBI is cold and unsympathetic, and worst, downright hostile. Let's face it, they just ain't with us. We don't expect them to hold our hands. We do expect cooperation. There is such a marked contrast between the way they deal with the local officials and our people. It is doubly disillusioning when we find the agent is from the North and holds the same view as the Mississippians.

—a SNCC field worker [8]

Exhibit B

I was arrested in Belzoni on criminal syndicalism on October 15. Criminal syndicalism means we were distributing leaflets on the street. Three days later the FBI came to the jail in Belzoni and questioned us. They asked us mostly about our behavior in jail (we had written Freedom Now on the walls, and then we were further charged with destruction of public property). They wanted to know why we were writing on the walls. We said they had taken away our toothbrushes and toothpaste and had beaten us up. We said, wasn't the FBI interested in that. They said no, they could do nothing about that. We told the FBI specifically that we were beaten in the Belzoni jail and then in the Oxford jail (where our case was removed to) and by the Oxford sheriff himself. The FBI people weren't interested in the story of our beatings. They were interested in questioning us about our activities.

—Robert Bass, twenty-one, a Negro civil rights worker from Belzoni

Exhibit C

[Special Agent Savage from Clarksdale] drove up in his car to the COFO office and asked that we come outside. He wouldn't come up. I asked him for identification. He said "I don't want to show it to you." He finally flashed it and I caught his last name. I told him that I knew the names of the people who had beat up Klondike (Abbott) and I had descriptions that two cars full of whites were circling the office and we knew who they are. He said "You know what you're telling me won't stand up in a court of law."

A few days later the local Marks police entered the COFO office and arrested me for gambling. We were playing cards but we had no money for gambling. There was no money on the table. Down at the police station, the cops said to me, 'We know you've been talking to the FBI. The FBI told us you told them a pack of lies, nigger. What did you want to do a thing like that for?"

—Alan Goodner, nineteen, from Ann Arbor, Michigan

Exhibit D

Last spring there was a series of bombings, cross burnings, and shootings throughout southwest Mississippi. There was a lot of shooting on the Tougaloo campus. Cars would ride by and shoot into faculty homes—nothing serious, unless you happened to be standing in the wrong spot. People were run off the road near campus by speeding cars. These incidents were dutifully reported to the FBI.

In April, a big cross was burned on campus. It was part of a co-ordinated series of cross burnings held at that time. Several students on campus saw two vehicles leave the scene, and that night they saw a dirty, greasy can of kerosene with fingerprints clearly visible in the grease near the cross. They brought it to me and I called the FBI. Nothing happened.

Three weeks later we took the burned cross to Pittsburgh, Pa., where we had a big fund-raising meeting. The cross was pictured on the front page of *The New York Times*. The can was sitting in my bedroom all that time.

Then, after the cross was on the front page of the *Times*, and the *Times* carried the story of the can, the FBI called (this was in May)

and said, "We understand you have some information and evidence we want." They came out to Tougaloo, spoke to me and interviewed all the students who had witnessed the burning. They really did a thorough search—three weeks later. They tracked down every student. They came back to me and said, "Your students don't have the story straight. Some say it was a gray car and some say it was a truck." Of course, there had been a car and a truck. They also asked me for the cross. I told them we had left it in Pittsburgh. They were indignant. Oh, yes, there was a further follow-up. My family in Tennessee started getting visits from the FBI.

I won't talk to an FBI agent again. To talk to the FBI is to endanger yourself. I still have family in the South. They have no comprehension of what civil rights and civil liberties are.

—Reverend Ed King, Tougaloo College
Chaplain and Assistant Dean of Men

Exhibit E

Mrs. Mattie Dennis (wife):

In February of 1962, after the Jimmy Travis shooting, my car was fired into three times while I was driving through the city of Jackson. I called the Jackson FBI. They refused to even consider an investigation. They said, "We don't have any proof that the shots were fired."

Mr. Dave Dennis:

In Shreveport in 1961, we began our demonstrations in October. During a banquet which we held at a church two molotov cocktails were thrown inside through the window. We called the police and the Shreveport FBI. The FBI didn't come out until the next day. We gave them the remains of the molotov cocktails. No arrests were ever made, but the next night the local police arrested most of our CORE people on the arson charge.

Also in Shreveport in 1961, one night a group of night riders were circling around my house. I called the FBI. The guy said, "Look, I'm asleep now. I won't drive down. Let me know if anything happens."

In Baton Rouge in December of 1961, a lot of us were put in jail. I was beaten very severely. I gave the FBI the name, badge number, and description of the police officer who had done the beating. I gave a general physical description—height and weight, the markings on his hands. His hands were the closest to me. The FBI asked me four or five times what the color of his eyes was. I wasn't concentrating on his eyes, I said. They led me to believe that the validity of my story depended on whether I could tell the color of his eyes. I had witnesses to the beating who also gave affidavits. Nothing ever happened to the police officer as far as I know. He was never arrested.

In the summer of 1962 in Hammond, La., after the ICC ruling concerning interstate travel (after the first freedom rides), the Hammond police threw a group of us out of the bus station. We gave badge numbers and names to the Jackson FBI. Nothing happened.

In Greenwood, Miss., in March of 1963 when we first began our demonstrations we had a lot of FBI people around. They witnessed how our people were treated at the courthouse by the local police. They took pictures; they made notes. We gave them badge numbers. Nothing happened. Whenever we held a Freedom Day in the South, we always call the FBI. They always come and take notes and pictures and nothing ever happens. They stand and watch people getting beat up by the police and by the mobs. As far as I know, no policeman has ever been arrested or removed from his position.

—Dave Dennis, CORE Program Secretary for the South,
and Mrs. Mattie Dennis, Assistant COFO Program Coordinator.

Quinn Tamm, the head of the International Association of Police Chiefs, who left the Bureau just as Kennedy was arriving, helps explain the hostile race-relations milieu of the FBI when he recalls, "The Bureau had a system of office-of-preference assignments. Eighty percent were that. So you usually pick your hometown or where your school was. Naturally, Southern agents would end up down South. When I was in the Bureau we didn't have any colored agents. The Identification Division had a staff of maybe 2,500 to 3,000 and didn't have a colored person in it when I was in charge."

And so there was an irony. During his years as Attorney General, Robert Kennedy's popularity with the civil rights movement was inversely proportional to his deepening involvement and commitment. Undoubtedly the passage through sadness after his brother's death lent new poignance to his understanding of the black man's plight, his willingness to identify with it and his renewed determination to do something about it. But it is doubtful that he underwent any magic transformation either. The irony was that even as his own inner consensus was emerging—as he became surer in his stance—his credit with the civil rights community was dissipating. For at the beginning, with the NAACP in the forefront, the Kennedys, come to office on a crest of inspiring campaign oratory, were given the benefit of every doubt. Now, with SNCC and CORE and SCLC and COFO—with the civil rights movement itself in the forefront—Robert Kennedy was increasingly perceived as the betrayer, was given the benefit of no doubt and was presumed to be responsible for the FBI.

Jack Newfield, the writer who believes that Kennedy was transformed after his brother's assassination from Hoffa-chasing wiretapper to existential hero, gives good and eloquent testimony of how he and other activists saw Kennedy in his last year as Attorney General. In his book *Robert Kennedy: A Memoir*, Newfield recalls the first time he saw Kennedy. It was in June of 1963. Medgar Evers had been assassinated a few days before, Birmingham's protesters had been water-hosed, police-dogged and brutalized, and about 3,000 black and white picketers assembled outside the Justice Department demanding that the Attorney General do something to protect the schoolchildren Martin Luther King had enlisted in the demonstrations who were arrested and now were overcrowding Birmingham's jails.

After about an hour, the slight, taut brother of the President emerged in shirt-sleeves from his fifth-floor office, stood framed in the doorway, and began to talk to us. I had, by then, been jailed twice in civil rights demonstrations, and with pure fury stared at Kennedy's crew-cut face. It was, I remember, a hard, Irish face; alert, but without much character, a little like the faces that used to follow me home from Hebrew school, taunting, "Christ killer."

"We haven't seen many Negroes come out of there," an angry voice shouted from the crowd, referring to the well-dressed white employees entering and leaving the building during the demonstration.

Kennedy tensed up even more. His skin seemed to draw tighter around his sharp features, and the hostility radiating from his blue eyes became even more intense.

"Individuals will be hired according to their ability, not their color," Kennedy shouted back into a hand-held bullhorn that made his voice sound both squeaky and strident. It was exactly the sort of impersonal legalistic response, blind to the larger moral implications of our protest, that we felt made Kennedy such an inadequate Attorney General.

As civil rights activists in 1963, we liked Kennedy as little as the Southern Governors did. We saw him recommend Harold Cox, James Eastland's college roommate, to be a judge in the Fifth District Court, where he was to call Negro defendants "chimpanzees" from the bench. We saw him indict nine civil rights workers in Albany, Ga., on conspiracy charges, while nine white men who burned down Negro churches, and shot at civil rights activists, went unpunished. We saw Negroes trying to register to vote in Greenwood, Mississippi, urinated upon by a white farmer, while lawyers from the Justice Department took notes destined to be filed and forgotten. We agreed with James Baldwin, who pronounced Kennedy, after their stormy confrontation, "insensitive and unresponsive to the Negro's torment." So when he bragged about his hiring policies, while our friends languished in Southern jails, we booed him in a hoarse, throaty roar that ricocheted off the white marble walls of the Department of Justice.

Had the FBI vigorously investigated Harold Cox's racist history before he was confirmed, had the FBI not vigorously investigated the activities of the Albany Nine, had the FBI made an on-the-spot arrest of Greenwood's eneuritic farmer, had the FBI investigated Baldwin's charges instead of Baldwin, would anything fundamental have changed? Probably not. And yet the accumulation of FBI attitudes and actions, as much as anything else, is what Newfield was reacting to and what lent young Robert Kennedy and his Justice Department their image. And that image—the image of official, lower-case justice—was not irrelevant. For that was the moment at which thousands of idealistic young men and women of both races who had made the journey south to work for the American dream had to choose whether or not to work within the system, had to decide whether the government was friend or foe, ally or enemy. And the FBI, through its actions and lack of them, affected that choice by misrepresenting the options.

Robert Kennedy was particularly vulnerable to invisible pressures in the civil rights area because the fact was that until the spring of 1963 —although he had instinctively responded to many civil rights crises on the side of the Negro—he had made no firm civil rights commitment. He was fast becoming the most militant member of the Cabinet, but he was highly subject to conflict between the requirements of Presidential politics and Presidential obligation on the one side and his increasing sensitivity to the profound requirements and demands of the Negro underclass on the other. The problem was compounded by the prevailing theory of federalism held by his advisers and the open reluctance of the FBI to get involved. As Kennedy became sensitized to the needs of the Negro, he also seemed to deepen rather than question his subconscious acceptance of the FBI's fundamental assumptions, thus obviating the need for any kind of showdown between the Bureau and the Department. He continued to believe that civil rights could be solved on a problem-by-problem basis within the framework of occasional executive orders and a voting drive, and he expressed his consciousness of the urgency of the race relations situation in a new commitment to the need for significant and immediate legislation.

The FBI, then, exerted its influence in a number of ways. It established the environment within which the Justice Department made its decisions. It was easy at the time and is more aesthetically convenient in retrospect to romanticize the Kennedy era and glamour, to portray Robert Kennedy's Attorney Generalship as one long party around the pool at Hickory Hill with the good guys taking time off to integrate schools and the not-so-good (but well-intentioned) guys tapping telephones to catch Mafiosi. But the FBI's style, its reflexes, language, people, paper and preferences set up a kind of counter-atmosphere to the Kennedy gaiety. It was like having someone in the room who made everyone else uncomfortable so that funny jokes weren't laughed at.

The FBI did not affect Kennedy's emotional involvement in the race issue, but without doubt it helped frame his perception of the way in which the federal system was supposed to respond to the race issue. By not using the FBI when he didn't have to, he diminished his actual, potential and psychological resources, his vision of the possible was contracted, his ability to maneuver was constricted. The possibility of an all-out, *total* 100 percent Justice Department anti-discrimination drive —the kind of thing Kennedy energy and imagination might otherwise have envisioned—was negated. Valuable time, energy and resources were diverted to bureaucratic infighting, credit with the civil rights community was expended defending the indefensible, the gap between the Justice Department and the civil rights movement widened and deepened, and the Justice Department boxed itself into a theory of federalism which—with a more flexible investigative arm—might have seemed unnecessarily limiting and rigid. All this because getting along with the FBI, although not perceived as an "issue" at the time, had as high an operational priority on the RFK–JFK list as solving the problem of the Negro.

No episode of Robert Kennedy's Attorney Generalship has been surrounded by more confusion, misinformation and misunderstanding than the tapping of Dr. Martin Luther King's telephone, yet no episode better illustrates the underlying relationship of the Attorney General and the FBI and the way in which that relationship affected the Attorney General's dealings with the civil rights movement. It deserves telling in detail.

The confusion comes from three sources. First, the general failure to distinguish tapping from bugging (see Chapter II), the complicated Constitutional, moral and legal issues involved, and the consequent veil of mystery that always cloaks anything to do with electronic surveillance. Even President Nixon contributed to public misunderstanding when he stated during his news conference on June 19, 1969, that he personally checked to see whether J. Edgar Hoover had acted "on his own or with proper authority" in ordering wiretaps on Dr. King and Elijah Muhammud, the Black Muslim leader.

"I find it [the wiretapping] had always been approved by the Attorney General, as Mr. Hoover testified in 1964 and 1965," Mr. Nixon said.

Perhaps. But most of the rumors about listening in on Dr. King related not to telephone taps but to transcripts of bugs, not mentioned by the President and a subtlety lost on the general population. This confusion is made without regard to ideology or party. The radical columnist I. F. Stone made the same error when he wrote in his News-letter of June 30, 1969:

> While the excuse for tapping King's phones was "internal security" its chief result was to permit the FBI to spread stories about King's sex life.

A second source of confusion was Robert Kennedy's ambiguous and inconclusive "denials" while alive. During his Presidential try of 1968, when Drew Pearson printed the charge that Kennedy had authorized a tap on Dr. King's phone, Kennedy answered indirectly. He said the only taps he authorized were in the national-security area, and he was forbidden by law to say who was and wasn't tapped. This was a dis-ingenuous statement since it sounded—to the uninitiated—like a de-nial. After all, to the layman "national security" conjures up images of Russian spy rings, the theft of an A-bomb sketch, the passing of papers to a Soviet attaché. In fact, Kennedy's elliptic assertion was consistent with the admission that he had authorized the tapping of King's phone for "national security" purposes, as he did. His campaign press spokesman at the time, Pierre Salinger, careful to make the distinction President Nixon later failed to make, nevertheless compounded the inaccurate implication (although technically telling no lie) when he announced in Portland, Oregon: "Senator Kennedy never authorized any eavesdropping [surveillance by hidden microphones] while Attor-ney General. He did authorize wiretaps in cases involving national security and on written request of the Federal Bureau of Investiga-tion."

Asked specifically whether Kennedy had authorized a wiretap of the late Dr. King, Salinger replied: "Senator Kennedy has not in the past and will not now discuss individual cases."

Candidate Kennedy, of course, had no trouble denying that he had bugged or tapped Jimmy Hoffa's phone—law or no law, individual case or not—since to the best of his knowledge he hadn't, and it was to his advantage to say so.

The third source of confusion was J. Edgar Hoover's misleading charges, in June 1969, after both Dr. King and Mr. Kennedy were dead, that Robert Kennedy while Attorney General proposed and ap-proved, over the FBI's objections, a tap on Dr. King's phone because he was "concerned about reports that Dr. King was a student of Marxism and that he was associating with known subversives—men with Com-munist connections." These claims echoed the earlier FBI-leaked charges leveled by Drew Pearson during the Oregon McCarthy–Kennedy primary in 1968 and were consistent with Hoover's general attitude about Dr. King. As one former agent (a ten-year veteran) acknowledges: "I think Mr. Hoover was convinced that Martin Luther King was a Communist. . . ."

Since Kennedy never fully and openly discussed the matter with outsiders, one can only attempt to reconstruct his position from what he admitted to when he was alive, what his informed colleagues, subordinates and supporters have conceded after he died, and from an analysis of those documents that have come to light since. Perhaps the clearest way to summarize this welter of information and supposition is through a sort of hypothetical question-and-answer exchange:

Q. Was Martin Luther King's phone tapped?
A. Yes.
Q. Did Bobby know about it?
A. Yes.
Q. At whose instigation was it tapped?
A. The FBI's.
Q. Why?
A. The FBI claimed that a so-called secret Communist who was also a close friend of Dr. King was trying to influence him on behalf of the U.S.S.R. They requested authorization to tap Martin Luther King's phone ostensibly to see if he was having any success. Robert Kennedy granted it in October of 1963, according to his intimates, (a) because the civil rights bill was coming up and if Dr. King were in any way tainted with Communist connections it could be used to defeat the bill; (b) to protect Dr. King—to prove to the FBI that he was *not* being influenced by Communist agents; (c) to make the FBI, which had wanted to tap Dr. King since 1961, happy.

Q. Did all the rumors about Dr. King's extracurricular sex-life arise from the wiretap which Kennedy authorized?
A. No. The authorized taps were restricted to the SCLC's Atlanta office, a New York office and Dr. King's home.* Those rumors arose from bugs installed either by local police forces or on the FBI's own initiative without the specific authorization or knowledge of Attorney General Kennedy or anybody on his staff. Alleged transcripts of these bugs of "goings on" in Dr. King's hotel rooms were shown by the FBI to selected reporters and leaked to Congressmen. Columnist Mike Royko

* The FBI has never conceded that it tapped Dr. King's home phone.

of the Chicago *Daily News* and Congressman Robert L. F. Sykes, Democrat of Florida and of the Appropriations Committee, for instance, both concede that they have been shown such transcripts (although Royko declined to use the "information"). Hence the confusions, rumors and half-truths.

Q. By what authority did Kennedy authorize the tap on Dr. King's phone?

A. Under Departmental practice dating back to Attorney General Jackson (based on a letter written by President Franklin D. Roosevelt in 1940 in anticipation of our entry into World War II), the Attorney General has felt free to authorize wiretaps in writing on a case-by-case basis where the national security is involved. Since the FBI claimed (and backed the claim with "hard" evidence) that a so-called secret Communist was attempting to influence Dr. King to the benefit of a foreign power, the Attorney General apparently believed—when he authorized the tap—that he was acting under the national security exception to Section 605 of the Federal Communications Act which prohibits the interception and divulgence of interstate messages.

Q. By what authority did the FBI bug Dr. King?

A. Prior to the passage of the Omnibus Crime Bill of 1968 which authorized bugs in certain cases (but after the Supreme Court handed down its opinion in the Silverman case in March of 1961, outlawing any bug whose installation entailed an illegal trespass), the FBI claimed—although it didn't overtly assert this claim until some years later—general authority to bug on its own initiative by virtue of a memo signed in 1954 by then Attorney General Herbert Brownell. According to the FBI, the Brownell memo gave them the right to bug in cases involving "internal security and the national safety" without getting the case-by-case approval of the Attorney General.

Q. Did Attorney General Robert Kennedy know of this memo when he was Attorney General?

A. No.

Q. Did Attorney General Robert Kennedy know of the FBI's illegal bugging practices when he was Attorney General?

A. No.

Q. Did Attorney General Robert Kennedy know of the specific bugs on Martin Luther King?

A. No.

Q. Did Attorney General Robert Kennedy know as a general proposition that the FBI was bugging anybody?

A. Probably, but he assumed it was confined to the organized-crime area and he assumed it was within the law.

Q. Did Attorney General Robert Kennedy know of *any* bugs on Dr. King?

A. Not specifically—although he may have suspected that local law enforcement officers were bugging Dr. King and that the FBI occasionally got access to their tapes.

Such, in outline, is the Kennedy version of the tapping of Dr. Martin Luther King's telephone. It is consistent only in part with J. Edgar Hoover's version, which he put out—with his infallible sense of timing —after the murders of Dr. King and Senator Robert Kennedy, respectively. On Hoover's behalf, it should be noted that he put out the FBI version only after the Bureau was embarrassed by the open court testimony of an agent in a June 1969 hearing on Muhammud Ali's (Cassius Clay) appeal in an otherwise unrelated case, that he overheard telephone calls between King and Clay when he was assigned to the FBI's Atlanta office, where his duties included monitoring a tap on Dr. King's phone. The agent said he had conducted the surveillance until May 1965, when he was transferred from his post, but he understood that the tap was continued by the FBI until a few days before King was assassinated. Since President Johnson had prohibited (in a declaration issued June 30, 1965) all wiretapping without the specific approval of the Attorney General, and since Ramsey Clark, in the Attorney General's office from October 3, 1966, through mid-January 1969, said he never authorized a tap or bug on King's telephone, either the agent was misinformed (as FBI agents are not supposed to be—at least not in public) or the FBI intentionally had broken the law and ignored a Presidential directive.* In either event, it meant bad publicity for the Bureau. Mr. Hoover's solution had the virtue of simplicity: He put out a bigger story—and the nation's attention immediately shifted from the FBI's blunder to the murdered Robert Kennedy and Mr. Hoover's revelatory memoranda involving him.

Set forth below, first is the FBI story of what happened; second, the points at which the FBI version and the Kennedy version conflict; and finally, my own understanding of what happened and its significance.

According to Hoover (as told to Jeremiah O'Leary of the Washington *Star*), Attorney General Kennedy first proposed tapping Dr. King's phone in June 1963. Hoover has a memorandum from Courtney Evans, the FBI's liaison to the Attorney General, to "prove" it.

---

* Unless, of course, Ramsey Clark is lying, which I don't believe. Surely Mr. Hoover would have come forth with "evidence" challenging Mr. Clark's claim if he had *any* basis to do so.

The Evans memorandum—unreleased at this writing—allegedly reports the substance of a conversation Evans had just had with Kennedy in which the Attorney General (a) expressed his concern about reports that King was a student of Marxism and that he was associating with a New York attorney with known Communist connections; and (b) wanted to know if it was technically feasible to use electronic devices to prove or disprove these allegations.

According to the memo, Evans pointed out that King traveled constantly and thus was a bad candidate for a tap; also that the FBI doubted the advisability of electronic surveillance because of possible political repercussions.

Nevertheless, on October 7, 1963, the FBI reported to Kennedy that it was technically feasible to apply wiretaps to King's telephones at the Southern Christian Leadership Conference (SCLC) headquarters in Atlanta and at an unnamed location in New York. Again, Mr. Hoover has a memo to "prove" it, this one the FBI's request to proceed with the tap "proposed" by Kennedy four months earlier. Kennedy approved the FBI request by signing the authorization on October 10, 1963, and the tap remained until April 30, 1965 (when Katzenbach was Attorney General). Thus, by Hooverian implication, did Robert Kennedy betray his friend and the civil rights movement with which the Administration was so closely identified.

Hoover's version was, of course, roundly attacked and discredited by the men who had been around Kennedy at the time, including Nicholas Katzenbach and Ramsey Clark, the respective successor Attorneys General. The pro-Kennedy version conflicts with the Hoover version in two essentials: (1) Kennedyites say the tap was Hoover's idea and installed at his urging; and (2) they deny that Kennedy ever entertained doubts about Dr. King's loyalty. "To say or imply that this tap was the original conception of Robert Kennedy—that he was the moving force in this situation—or that he had any doubts whatsoever as to Dr. King's integrity or loyalty is false," observes former Attorney General Katzenbach.

Ramsey Clark, who followed Katzenbach in the job, adds that it was "deceptive" for Hoover to portray the FBI as "a reluctant eavesdropper of Dr. King" because "Mr. Hoover repeatedly requested me to authorize FBI wiretaps on Dr. King while I was Attorney General. The last of these requests, none of which was granted, came two days before the murder of Dr. King."

Burke Marshall supported the charge that once again Mr. Hoover was engaging in the selective release of unrepresentative documents:

"It's outrageous for Mr. Hoover to give characterization of selected documents concerning principally two people now dead in order to deal with adverse publicity to the Bureau. The impression he gave when he did that was wrong."

My own inquiries have not been entirely satisfactory because (a) the FBI has given no cooperation, and (b) the men around Kennedy have given only limited cooperation, which they attribute entirely to their obligation not to divulge classified material, although the majority are also zealous protectors of the Kennedy reputation. But after literally hundreds of interviews, exposure to *some* unpublished memoranda to, from and about the FBI, and a careful reading of all published material concerning the King case, it is now possible to reconstruct much of what happened.

From the first days of Robert Kennedy's Attorney Generalship the FBI began forwarding memoranda reporting "information" that one Stanley Levison, a New York Lawyer and a close friend and confidant of Martin King, represented a danger to Dr. King. Whether they said he was a "known Communist," a "secret Communist," a "high official of the Communist Party," "engaged in espionage," an "associate of foreign nationals" or a "conduit of foreign monies," I have been unable to find out. Whatever they said, the allegations were serious.

They also charged that Jack O'Dell, a member of the SCLC staff, was either a "Communist" or a "secret Communist" and claimed he had been recommended to the SCLC staff by Levison. In informal conversation the FBI let it be known that they would like to tap Dr. King's telephone but they gathered that Kennedy was not receptive to the idea.

All of this data is, of course, technically "unevaluated"—to borrow Bureau terminology. But FBI memos build on each other, so that what is "an informant of unknown reliability" in one memo becomes "as referred to in our memo of (date)" in a second memo. And, according to one Kennedyite, "There were exceptions to the rule against evaluating data in the memos about Dr. King which have no parallel in other FBI memoranda. They would sort of summarize a lot of data in a way that I can only term a personal attack."

Kennedy asked, among others, Harris Wofford (JFK's civil rights man in the White House, whose idea it had been for candidate Kennedy to call Coretta King at the height of his Presidential campaign and express sympathy for her imprisoned husband, and who as Staff Director of the U.S. Commission on Civil Rights had known and worked with Dr. King) to approach King and underline the importance of his breaking off with Levison, who—according to FBI representations—might be "under Communist control," as one Justice Department alumnus put it.*

In the spring of 1963, the Administration was in the process of committing itself to a new, controversial and "strong" civil rights bill. The nation had been moved by the murder of Medgar Evers and the narrowly averted explosion in Birmingham against the background of Bull Connor's water hoses, cattle prods and bulldogs. Martin Luther King, having written his powerful "Letter from a Birmingham Jail," now personified the country's civil rights crisis, with all its tensions. That summer he gave his "I Have a Dream" speech at the March on Washington. That fall a Harris poll was to identify King as the black leader most liked by Negroes (88 percent of those polled voted for him, 95 percent of the black leadership was pro-King). As King gained more and more renown and respect, the FBI increased its flow of anti-King memoranda.

Today, rumors circulate that King's Washington hotel suite was "bugged" during the 1963 March on Washington and that the transcripts of this surveillance reflect sexual "goings on." If that is true, the bugging was without the authorization or knowledge of the Attorney General. And if King indeed was engaged in extracurricular interracial sex, as *Time* magazine has suggested, then one can further understand Hoover's sense of urgency about him. Hoover had made it clear on a number of occasions that he considered interracial sex a form of "moral degeneracy." †

On June 22, 1963, Martin Luther King visited successively with Burke Marshall, head of the Civil Rights Division, Attorney General Robert Kennedy and President John Kennedy. In a morning meeting Marshall told him explicitly about O'Dell, about whom King had been "warned" on previous occasions. Later that morning both the Attorney General and the President strongly urged King to sever O'Dell's connection with SCLC. And they warned him about Stanley Levison,

* When Wofford was cleared for the White House in 1961, the FBI found three "disturbing" items in his file. Unknown to the Bureau, Sargent Shriver showed him the file (which he got from the Attorney General) and Wofford was able to demonstrate that the FBI was factually wrong on each item. One had to do with his friendship with one Stanley Levison. The "evidence" was a series of telephone conversations between them—which suggests the FBI or local police were tapping or bugging Levison's phone before the Kennedys took office. In fact, Levison and Wofford did not know each other, but were in touch over the financing of a King trip to India. So when Wofford "alerted" King to Levison, he also let King know that the FBI had been triply wrong on Wofford, so there was no reason to believe they were any better informed on the matter under discussion.

† Former Special Agent Jack Levine reported another instance of Hoover's misplaced moralism. One of his co-trainees, Special Agent James Sturges, was warned that he could be fired for reading *Playboy* Magazine, because the Director looked upon *Playboy* readers as "moral degenerates."

although when Dr. King asked what evidence they had against Levison, they failed to provide any. I have seen internal Justice Department memoranda stating that "we thought it was not in the best interests of the United States" to divulge the nature of the "evidence" against Levison, so King was told—without evidence—that Levison was believed to be a "secret member of the Communist Party." Burke Marshall also warned the Reverend Andy Young and the Reverend Wyatt Tee Walker, both of SCLC, that since many people believed O'Dell, a member of SCLC's staff, to have Communist connections, his continued association with the organization "was not in their best interests." "The President," recalls a King lieutenant, "took Martin off into the Rose Garden and said there were reports that the Southern senatorial strategy was going to be to attack the civil rights bill and the whole movement as Communist-inspired and they were going to use Levison and O'Dell as scapegoats. He asked Dr. King to disassociate himself from them, not because he believed anything about them, but to protect the movement. Dr. King had the impression that even the President might be bugged and didn't want to talk in his office."

With the civil rights movement building in a crescendo, with a good civil rights bill in the wings, with King precariously straddling the increasingly militant younger activists identified with SNCC and the establishmentarian civil rights organizations like the NAACP, with his own reputation approaching its apex, and with a nation not yet fully recovered from the depredations of the McCarthy era when a red taint was fatal, Dr. Martin Luther King agreed to heed the warnings of his governmental friends—the President, the Attorney General and Burke Marshall. He said he would suspend O'Dell and break off relations with Levison. "None of us thought King was a Communist," recalls one of Kennedy's close advisers, "but none of us thought the Bureau was wrong on the point they raised."

On July 3, 1963, Dr. King sent the following letter to Jack O'Dell:

DEAR JACK:
   Several months ago you submitted your resignation pending an investigation of your alleged affiliation with the Communist Party, as was suggested by an article to this effect in the Birmingham and New Orleans newspapers. We accepted this temporary resignation because of SCLC's firm policy that no Communist or Communist sympathizer can be on our staff or in our membership. We felt that it was imperative to conduct an immediate investigation. As you know we conducted what we felt to be a thorough inquiry into these charges and were unable to discover any present connections with the Communist Party on your part.

The situation in our country is such, however, that any allusion to the left brings forth an emotional response which would seem to indicate that SCLC and the Southern Freedom Movement are Communist-inspired. In these critical times we cannot afford to risk any such impressions. We therefore have decided in our Administrative Committee, that we should request you to make your temporary resignation permanent.

We certainly appreciate the years of unselfish service which you have put into our New York office, and regret the necessity of your departure. Certainly, yours is a significant sacrifice commensurate with the sufferings in jail and through loss of jobs under racist intimidation. We all pray for the day when our nation may be truly the land of the free. May God bless you and continue to inspire you in the service of your fellow man.

(signed) MARTIN LUTHER KING

Levison was a different story. Although King had agreed to break with him, he couldn't believe that his close friend—who had been at his side long before King became the country's leading civil rights figure—would use him in this way. He told Levison of the Justice Department's and Kennedy's concern and Levison claimed innocence but agreed to go along for the good of the movement. Dr. King had known Mr. Levison since the days of the Montgomery bus boycott when they had been introduced by Bayard Rustin. Indeed, SCLC itself was conceived in the wake of the Montgomery bus boycott, in late-night conversations between Rustin, Ella Baker (its first Executive Director) and Levison, who became a friend in need and deed, managed the SCLC stock portfolio, did free legal work (along with Harry Wachtel and others), raised money, planned fund-raising concerts (like the one at Manhattan Center on December 5, 1956, for the Montgomery Improvement Association, to which he drew Harry Belafonte and Duke Ellington) and helped King with his copyright and other legal problems. After a Montgomery grand jury indicted King on a trumped-up charge of falsifying his Alabama state income tax returns for 1956 and 1958 and a deeply concerned Dr. King felt his credibility would be undermined, Coretta King recalls: "Our trusted friend Stanley Levison answered, 'Martin, it isn't your responsibility to defend yourself. You are in this trouble because of who you are and all you have done for the movement in this country. It is the country's duty to see that you are properly defended.' "[9] When King was stabbed by Mrs. Isola Corry, a black lady, with a Japanese letter opener, in Harlem in September 1958, it was Levison who met Mrs. King at the airport and took her to see the surgeon who had operated to remove the blade. And ten years later, at the time of King's murder, Coretta King recalls, Levison "came to offer assistance. . . . Always working in the background, his contribution has been indispensable."

In her memoir, *My Life with Martin Luther King, Jr.*, Mrs. King writes that of the thousands of tributes that had been paid to her husband since his death, "the one which best describes the meaning of my husband's life and death was written by two of his most devoted and trusted friends, Harry Belafonte and Stanley Levison." *

* "In a nation tenaciously racist, a black man sensitized its somnolent conscience; in a nation sick with violence, a black man preached non-violence; in a nation corrosive with alienation, a black man preached love; in a world embroiled in three wars in twenty years, a black man preached peace.

"When an assassin's bullet ended Martin Luther King's life it failed in its purpose. More people heard his message in four days than in the twelve years of his preaching. His voice was stilled but his message rang clamorously around the globe.

"He was stoned, stabbed, reviled, and spat upon when he lived, but in death there was a shattering sense that a man of ultimate goodness had lived among us.

"Martin Luther King died as he lived, fighting to his last breath for justice. In only twelve years of public life he evoked more respect for black people than the previous century had produced.

"We who knew him intimately cannot recall a single instance when he expressed a word of hatred for any man. Yet his indictment of segregation, discrimination, and poverty was a hurricane of fire that opened a new era of struggle for freedom.

"Martin Luther King was not a dreamer although he had a dream. His vision of a society of justice was derived from a stirring reality. Under his leadership millions of black Americans emerged from spiritual imprisonment, from fear, from apathy, and took to the streets to proclaim their freedom. The thunder of millions of marching feet preceded the dream. Without these deeds, inspired by his awesome personal courage, the words would merely have woven fantasy. Martin Luther King, the peaceful warrior, revealed to his people their latent power; non-violent mass protest, firmly disciplined, enabled them to move against their oppressors in effective and bloodless combat. With one stroke he organized his armies and disorganized his adversaries. In the luminescent glare of the open streets he gave a lesson to the nation revealing who was the oppressed and who was the oppressor.

"He was incontestably one of history's preeminent black leaders. Yet he was, as well, a leader to millions of white people who learned from him that in degrading black men, they diminished themselves.

"Few people know how humble this giant was. He had an inexhaustible faith in people, and multitudes felt it with their hearts and their minds, and went beyond respect almost to worship. And even fewer knew how troubled he was, and even tortured, because he doubted his own capacity to be unerring in the fateful decisions thrust upon him.

"He drained his closest friends for advice; he searched within himself for answers; he prayed intensely for guidance. He suspected himself of corruption continually, to ward it off. None of his detractors, and there were many, could be as ruthless in questioning his motives or his judgment as he was to himself.

"Today when millions of his portraits hang in simple cabins, in ordinary homes, and in stately halls, it is hard to recall that he forbade his own organization to reproduce his picture. He did not want to be idolized; he wanted only to be heard.

"He wrote his own obituary to define himself in the simple terms his heart

Levison had booked speaking engagements for King, he had worked on drafts of manuscripts and speeches, he had handled legal problems. And so, despite King's promise to break with Levison, he would call—from time to time—to find out a date or a location or to get some files. And, as Levison himself told me, "You don't sever a long relationship just like that." King had informed Levison of the Justice Department's warnings, and Levison like O'Dell—despite protestations of innocence—agreed, for the good of the movement, to step aside. But as King checked unfinished business, facts, dates and memories with Levison, they gradually resumed communication until Levison raised the issue with him: "Aren't we drifting back together? And aren't we giving the opposition something to muck around with?"

King's answer, after some deliberation, was "I have decided I am going to work completely in the open. There's nothing to hide. And if anybody wants to make something of it, let them try." And so they resumed their relationship as it had always been.

According to the Kennedyites, when the FBI saw that King hadn't really broken with Levison, this confirmed Mr. Hoover's worst suspicions—that King was either under Communist control or a conscious fellow traveler. "The FBI kept sending memoranda about contacts between the two men, advice that was given and taken, memos that [Levison] had prepared, speeches he wrote that King delivered," says a Kennedy intimate. As Katzenbach recalls, "It all culminated in a very long memorandum which was sent over to the White House and all around the damn place—to the Defense Department, the CIA, State—about King's alleged contacts. It was a really politically explosive document. Sending it over to the White House like that where nine people see it before it ever gets to the President is practically like sending it to the Washington *Post*. Bobby got furious and made them withdraw the memorandum . . . which they did. . . ." Shortly thereafter —in the fall of 1963—Robert Kennedy agreed to the FBI request for a tap on Dr. King's phones and the agreement was made final in an FBI-prepared request, which the Attorney General signed on October 10, 1963, where it said "Approved." The language was FBI-ese, but the ostensible purpose of the taps on Dr. King's phones was to see whether King was indeed the target of effective Communist influence. That the FBI had other motives for wanting to tap King's phones—

---

comprehended. 'Tell them I tried to feed the hungry. Tell them I tried to clothe the naked. Tell them I tried to help somebody.'

"And that is all he ever did. That is why, in the nobility of man, he is matchless, that is why, though stilled by death, he lives."

such as keeping track of the civil rights leader's strategy for its own intelligence purposes, so as to anticipate trouble, alert interested parties and trade information with other law enforcement agencies—is, of course, a probability, although such considerations were never openly discussed, and in fact it was a trade-off: You can have your tap if you will please stop circulating this damaging and unverified information.

One can accept the Kennedy version of what happened and yet reject the Kennedy interpretation and analysis, which can be broken into five parts.

First, the argument that the FBI instigated the tap and was the prime mover. This seems indisputable, although since the Attorney General as a matter of law and fact had veto power over all taps and was the *only* one who could authorize them, he is in no way absolved from responsibility merely because Hoover thought of it first.

Second, the argument that given the same facts Robert Kennedy was given, any other Attorney General would have made the same determination. As a former Kennedy aide told me at breakfast in the spring of 1968 before Hoover made his allegations: "Kennedy had hard evidence. It's classified. I can't describe it, but I can tell you this. If you believe at all that the Soviet Union has agents in the United States—unless you believe it's all a charade—you had to go along. It didn't involve somebody who was alleged to have associated with or been a member of the Communist Party in 1955. How do you ever know it's correct? You can't. You can know what kind of information it is and where it comes from and he did that and based on that there's not anybody who had the authority who would not have put a tap on the phone in that circumstance." Others have confirmed that the FBI stated their charges "flatly and positively" and add, "We didn't think King was influenceable but the problem is how do you pit your own judgment against the Bureau's?"

Of course, Katzenbach, who succeeded Kennedy as Attorney General, had the King tap turned off in May 1965—the first time it came up for review under his newly instituted procedures—because it hadn't revealed any subversion of Dr. King by Levison.* And when Ramsey Clark became Attorney General he denied repeated FBI requests for authorization to tap and/or bug Dr. King; the last one came, he has told us, two days before Dr. King's murder. Since Levison did not disappear from the scene we must assume that Clark, who approved other FBI "national security" wiretap requests on a selective basis, would have been

* The bugging of King's phone was authorized, however, for two- or three-day periods in hotels, in June, November and December of 1965.

an exception to the rule which Kennedy loyalists state with such certitude.

Then, too, it is important to distinguish the *allegations* against Levison and the *evidence* for the allegations against Levison.

Since we don't know precisely what these allegations were, it is difficult to make a judgment here. Nevertheless, having interviewed Levison and talked with countless members of the civil rights movement and the Justice Department, I have made one: I believe Stanley Levison when he says, "I can tell you I'm not a member of the Communist Party and I never was." Levison says his troubles stem from perjurious testimony about him by a vindictive former associate trying to clear *himself* of subversive-activity charges. I don't know whether this is the case, I don't know what Levison did or was technically accused of doing. Harry Wachtel, a New York lawyer and chain store executive who had worked with Kennedy to desegregate Birmingham's chain stores and did legal work for SCLC, at King's request met with Levison, listened to his story, asked a lot of questions, and "cleared" him. Another Levison intimate says of the charges against him, "It's something like when a husband and wife have a messy divorce and the husband knows the kind of crazy stories his wife has been telling his friends and there's nothing he can do about it since to deny them publicly just focuses attention on innocent parties." The most suspicious "fact" about him is that he took the Fifth Amendment in 1962 when testifying in executive session before the Senate Internal Security Committee. When I asked him about it he told me that although he had nothing to hide—his lawyers urged him to invoke the Fifth Amendment—he was reluctant to rehash sensational and misleading charges which could only end up in unfairly smearing Dr. King's reputation. (In addition to subversive activities, King smear-rumors related to his sex life and finances—one story gave him a secret bank account in Switzerland.) Others in the movement—Bayard Rustin, for one—suggest that, given the positions Stanley Levison has taken over the years both public and private, any Communists in the wings would recognize him as an enemy. I *do* know he has never been indicted under the espionage laws; he has never been indicted for failing to register as a member of the Communist Party or as an enemy agent; even the Senate Internal Security Committee was reluctant to make open charges against him.

Thus, however grave the allegations, one tends to doubt the "evidence" for them in the absence of further proof. Moreover, if the FBI had evidence against Levison (and if Kennedy examined it prior to authorizing the tap—there is no conclusive evidence that he did), then the Attorney General was subsequently derelict in not insisting on examining—perhaps on a daily or at least a weekly basis—the FBI logs on King's phones. Yet there is no record that the Attorney General *ever asked to look at*, or ever saw, the actual logs. Instead, business continued as usual. "We would receive scraps of information about King's travel plans or whatever," recalls Burke Marshall, "but you'd never know where they came from. The FBI would always identify its 'informants' only by number and letter."

As a Kennedy aide points out, "As far as I knew during the time it was on there was no evidence that supported the notion—the allegation or accusation—that Martin King was a secret Marxist or a profligate. And no evidence came out that the attorney involved had any sinister influence on King."

Third, the argument that actually the purpose of the tap was as much to protect Dr. King from false FBI charges (by proving his innocence) as anything. Katzenbach told me in late 1968, as he was preparing to leave his job as Under Secretary of State: "There was some reason to believe that known subversives were making efforts to influence Dr. King's movement and the question was how to deal with that, how to confirm whether they were or not, and under these circumstances, really as much for the protection of Dr. King as for any other reason, and not because of any suspicion or feeling that Dr. King himself was in any way subversive or disloyal, Mr. Kennedy authorized a tap." I am sure that Kennedy and the men around him convinced themselves that the tap on Dr. King was for his own good—although in retrospect it strains credulity (and is unforgivably patronizing) to suggest that it is permissible to invade the privacy of the spiritual leader of the civil rights revolution to protect him against himself. And it goes against everything Kennedy and Marshall and Katzenbach knew through personal experience with the obstinate, messianic, idealistic Dr. King to think that such a man could be persuaded over the telephone to do something he didn't want to do, something that was against his better instincts, no less sell out the civil rights cause and/or undermine the national security. He was, after all, the man who had resisted the pressures of the head of the Civil Rights Division, the Attorney General and the President himself to postpone civil rights demonstrations in Albany, Birmingham and Washington, D.C., among other places, when he thought they were right. He had chosen jail over bail, risked his life, hunger-struck, sat-in, marched, argued and listened and defied as a way of life. When I asked Burke Marshall if he had grounds for believing King so easily persuadable or so easily deceived, he said that he didn't.

One old hand at Justice has pointed out in addition: "If you really want to find out about A's attempt to influence B, you tap A, not B. That's the difference between 10 percent and 90 percent." There is no evidence that Levison's phone was tapped, a peculiarity. Andy Young, of SCLC, once observed that "All life is a recording studio for us" and, based on that assumption, all of the people around SCLC decided that since they were not a conspiracy and since they had nothing to hide and since they had little practical alternative, they would speak freely over the telephones. "We *knew*, for instance," says Young, "that there was a transmitter in our church. We found the bug and decided not to move it. The one time a field worker found one of those devices taped under a desk and destroyed it, Rev. Abernathy reprimanded him. Abernathy had a routine. He'd pick it up and call it a 'doohickey' and he'd preach to it. He'd say, 'Mr. President,' 'Mr. Hoover,' 'whoever you are,' and then he'd tell them what we were all about. It got to be a crowd-pleasing routine." Nevertheless, the fact was that if *protection* was the real aim, the Justice Department achieved that goal when they alerted Dr. King to the possibility that a secret Communist was out to subvert him. If they really believed—as they are unanimous in affirming they did—that Dr. King himself was above suspicion, then a tap on *him* was redundant.

Fourth, and the most common argument put forth by Kennedy loyalists *after* Hoover got out the official FBI version (although it hadn't been mentioned to me before), was that the *real* reason Kennedy went along was that the civil rights bill hung in the balance. Attacks on Dr. King, the symbolic leader of the civil rights revolution, would irreparably damage the bill's chances. Already the FBI or somebody had leaked information about Jack O'Dell, and Hoover was never particularly reticent about these matters. On January 24, 1962, he had told the Appropriations Subcommittee of the House:

> Since its inception the CPUSA has been alert to capitalize on every possible issue or event which could be used to exploit the American Negro in furtherance of Party aims. In its effort to influence the American Negro, the Party attempts to infiltrate the legitimate Negro organizations for the purpose of stirring up racial prejudice and hatred. . . .

And after the March on Washington of 1963 the FBI started circulating its latest memo. A number of Senators got word of the rumors and made official inquiry of the Justice Department. Some, like Senator Mike Monroney, Democrat of Oklahoma, were told informally about Levison. Others, like Senator Strom Thurmond of South Carolina, who would stop at nothing to defeat the incipient civil rights legislation, asked and the Attorney General answered as follows:

DEAR SENATOR:

This is in response to your inquiry of the FBI concerning the charges made in the hearings on S. 1732 that the racial problems in this country, particularly in the South, were created or are being exploited by the Communist Party.

Based on all available information from the FBI and other sources, we have no evidence that any of the top leaders of the major civil rights groups are Communists or Communist controlled. This is true as to Dr. Martin Luther King, Jr., to whom particular accusations were made, as well as other leaders.

It is natural and inevitable that Communists have made efforts to infiltrate the civil rights groups and to exploit the current racial situation. In view of the real injustices that exist and the resentment against them, these efforts have been remarkably unsuccessful.

Rather than risk the FBI's surfacing its damaging document through a disgruntled Senator, and thereby torpedoing the Kennedy civil rights bill, Kennedy decided to grant the FBI its wish and approve the tap. While there is a certain plausibility and appealing simplicity to a *post hoc* explanation, which portrays the tap on Dr. King as a kind of electronic insurance policy taken out on behalf of his civil rights program (with the nation's blacks as the beneficiaries), the fact is, of course, that it is unconstitutional, illegal and outrageously improper, not to mention an egregiously dangerous precedent, to tap a man's telephone, any man's, to help the passage of legislation, no matter how desirable that legislation may appear at the time.

Finally, there is the argument, a sort of afterthought in most serious discussions of the matter by Justice Department alumni, as to why he did agree to tap King's phone: "Because there would have been no living with the Bureau if he didn't." My own conclusion is that this afterthought is the *real* explanation of why Robert Kennedy went along—an explanation invisible to those too involved in the FBI environment to see what was happening to them.

The passage of the civil rights bill, the national security, the desire to protect their friend were all important considerations, but in the last analysis Robert Kennedy authorized the tap on Martin King's phone to avoid problems with the FBI! Not merely the problem of the FBI leaking the latest anti-King memo. Not merely the present problems of "living with the Bureau," having to face non-cooperation (in the guise of procedural regularity) in unrelated areas, risking an FBI torpedo aimed at the civil rights bill, inviting harassment from Congressmen, columnists and other legions of constituents who respond to Mr. Hoover's distress signals. Robert Kennedy's calculations had to project a future in which it was revealed, however improbable the hypothesis, that Dr. King had indeed been the target of an effective Communist conspiracy. It takes no leap of the imagination to project how Hoover might have used this fact to embarrass the Kennedy Administration (if not at the time, then perhaps later on).

The model for such a project was at hand in Hoover's handling of the Harry Dexter White case. During Harry Truman's Presidency, White, a high-ranking Treasury Department official, had been named as a member of a Soviet spy ring. Because the evidence against White was inconclusive, President Truman chose to keep him under surveillance rather than arrest him. After Harry Truman denied Attorney General Brownell's charge that he had recklessly promoted Harry Dexter White to the International Monetary Fund ("The FBI was to keep an eye on him," was Truman's somewhat vague explanation),[10] Hoover asked Congress for permission to testify and on November 17, 1953, told the Senate Internal Security Committee that White's promotion actually hampered the FBI. As if it were in any way conclusive, authorized FBI biographer Don Whitehead wrote, "Hoover spoke with a finality about his conversations . . . because after each discussion he had dictated a memorandum to his files."

Robert Kennedy's enemies while he was alive and his critics after he died have tried to use the King wiretap as evidence that the Attorney General was cynical, ruthless and hypocritical, embracing Dr. King in public, wiretapping him in private. The evidence suggests something quite different—the distribution of power between the Director, who resented the uppity Dr. King, whom he blamed for many of the country's and the FBI's problems down South, and the General, who trusted Dr. King to the point of privately alerting him to the FBI's worst suspicions.

The Director was permanent, the General was temporary. The General, when he cared enough to interrupt the FBI's rigid routines, could influence the present, but the Director had a lien on the future, especially when it came to reputations—reputations of individuals and, by extension, reputations of whole Administrations. A leaked file or a damaging rumor can, of course, ruin a career. When an Attorney General leaves office, his private files go with him and his official ones go to the archives, but the FBI files—drenched in "raw, unevaluated data" —remain. And so the Director, with the FBI files as his private library, is *de facto* caretaker to the nation's reputations.

This is not to suggest that an Attorney General with different predispositions might not have acted differently. Robert Kennedy did not share Hoover's assumption that Dr. King was a subversive (or subject to subversive control), nor Hoover's alarmist attitude toward the CPUSA.

But he also had no libertarian objection to wiretapping *per se*, and he conveniently failed to consult his libertarian advisor, Burke Marshall, prior to approving the King tap. (Although the loyal Marshall insists he himself would have concurred). It was characteristic rather than surprising that he never asked to examine the transcripts of the King tap, for he apparently never saw the transcripts of any other tap. It evidently never occurred to Robert Kennedy to ask that the tap be rejustified or turned off. (Nor, it might be added, did it occur to any of those who ran the Department in Robert Kennedy's emotional absence after his brother's assassination, which came just forty-two days after the King tap had been approved.) And so it stayed on through the remainder of his Attorney Generalship, even *after* the Civil Rights Bill of 1964 was passed, by which time he was moving beyond the shadow of his brother's murder.

Finally, if Kennedy and his top-level associates were insensitive to the dangers, the improprieties, the potential for abuse and erosion of the original purpose for tapping, they were not insensitive to the public-relations disaster they would suffer if word got out that King's phone was tapped—which goes back to the reason the tap was approved in the first place: the greater disaster to the Kennedy Administration's reputation if it failed to tap and Hoover, at some distant date, used it against the Kennedys. Hoover's tactic may have been to threaten historical reputations. Attorney General Kennedy's habit was to protect the particular reputation of his brother's Administration.

After Robert Kennedy resigned in November 1964, the Director— unable to contain his rage at this celebrated black man who had just won the Nobel Peace Prize, an honor which had eluded Hoover despite his years of service on behalf of public tranquility—exploded at a rare press briefing, and twice in the course of a three-hour meeting with a select group of women reporters he called Dr. King "the most notorious liar in the country." Later he told Katzenbach, "I don't know what everybody got so upset about. All I said was God's honest truth." He was ostensibly referring to Dr. King's suggestion that civil rights workers in Albany, Georgia, not bother reporting rights violations to the FBI because its agents were Southern-born and/or Southern-biased. But in fact Hoover bolstered his blanket charge with private circulation (to selected newsmen and Congressmen) of the bugging transcripts already discussed, which—by Hoover's lights—allegedly portrayed Dr.

King as "a moral degenerate." *

The Bureau, it has been learned from documents released in connection with the flap over organized-crime bugs, took the position that it did not need specific authorization to bug because it had a general authorization dating back to 1954, and, as one sardonic Kennedyite put it, "All subsequent Attorneys General would have known about this memorandum if only they took the trouble to read properly the five hundred pounds of paper which the FBI forwarded over the years."

So now it is generally conceded that at least during some of Robert Kennedy's Attorney Generalship, the FBI—*unknown* to the General—was bugging Dr. King as well as tapping him. "When I was in government I couldn't have believed what they did," says one who lost his innocence, "but I believe it now." And when the "evidence" of the bugs comes out—when a "transcript" is actually published (or leaked) —there will be a new flap. And again Hoover will claim he had authority and believe he is telling "God's honest truth" (since he possesses a memorandum written in 1954 which *he* interprets to have given him such authority). And the Kennedyites will rally around the standard and deny that he had any such authority or that Robert Kennedy or anybody else outside the Bureau knew anything about it. The public will be more confused than ever, and what will be lost in the charges and rebuttals and counter-rebuttals are the real lessons of the tapping of Dr. Martin King's telephone:

That you cannot ever protect a man's reputation by invading his privacy.

That no matter how noble the aim (passage of the civil rights bill included), wiretapping has a way of eroding original purpose, especially when conducted by an agency like the FBI, which has a vested interest in the accumulation of secret information.

That the underlying relationship of the FBI to passing Administrations—especially in the internal-security area—is in part the relationship of blackmailer to blackmailee.

That the cold war has fatally tainted the policy-making process in ways invisible to the public and the working press.

That the fact that in the vast majority of cases the Director has not chosen to exploit his advantage is testimony to his wisdom and our luck, not to the health of the system.

That the costs of involving a secret society like the FBI in the fight

---

* Cartha DeLoach, the Bureau's public-relations man at the time, showed transcripts to selected media representatives with the understanding that if they identified the source, he and the Bureau would deny it.

for an open society—an achievement widely hailed at the time—have yet to be computed.

The tapping of Dr. King was Constitutional but unconscionable. The bugging of the Mafiosi was righteous but unconstitutional. Robert Kennedy's values tolerated the former, about which he knew, and may have encouraged the latter, about which he was ignorant. Yet neither would have occurred were it not for the code of the FBI.

The code of the FBI, with its rigid hierarchy, its ideology, its insularity, its mystique of secrecy, its insistence on internal loyalty, was in a way a parody of the preoccupation with secrecy which Max Weber found to be an inherent characteristic of *all* administrative institutions. Agencies, he pointed out, keep secrets to maintain an edge over rival agencies. But such concerns tend to transform themselves into obsessions. Secrecy, which may begin as a means of protecting the privacy of others (hence the non-circulation of FBI files outside the agency) and as a means of advancing other organizational goals, tends to become an end in itself. In the case of the FBI, insularity from effective control became an obsession.

In the areas about which Robert Kennedy cared most—organized crime and civil rights—he made a Faustian bargain, trading policy for power. If the FBI would agree to join Kennedy's crusade against organized crime and his maneuvers for equal rights, then he would enlarge the Bureau's formal jurisdiction, increase its budget and leave it alone. By putting pressure on the FBI to produce, yet never questioning its right to be let alone, Kennedy inadvertently underwrote wholesale invasions of privacy, alienated the movement to which he was authentically drawn, diminished the Department's capacity for flexible action and encouraged the Bureau in a tendency which students of totalitarian societies have detected in all secret police—the accumulation of secret dossiers as a means of social control, of intimidating dissent. That was not what the Kennedys meant to do at all, and that was not all that they did, but the code of the FBI was a pressure in that direction.

PART TWO

The Code of the Ivy League Gentleman

CHAPTER FOUR

Federalism:
The Governor and the General

THE SCENE WAS Maxwell Air Force Base, Memphis, Tennessee. The time was late September 1962. The crisis had to do with the admission of James Meredith, a Negro, to the all-white University of Mississippi. General Creighton Abrams was on the telephone when an aide came running up with a note saying, "The Attorney General is on the phone and says it's urgent." Abrams nodded, but continued his telephone conversation. The aide, distraught, underlined the word "urgent," but the general was not to be interrupted. Again the aide retrieved his note, underlined the words "Attorney General" three times and "urgent" three times and returned it. The general paused, then said, "Excuse me, Mr. President, the Attorney General is on the other phone and says it's urgent." He put the leader of the free world on hold and took the call of the fourth-ranking Cabinet officer.

As the President's brother, Robert Kennedy had the opportunity to be the maximum Attorney General. When he spoke, he was assumed to hold the President's proxy. It was not *merely* the fraternal relationship. One doubts, for instance, that Lyndon Johnson's brother Sam, or Richard Nixon's brother Ed, or even Dwight Eisenhower's respected brother Milton, could or would have exploited the opportunity with Robert Kennedy's *élan*, his confidence, his energy. Partly, of course, this was because Robert Kennedy enjoyed and apparently merited the wholehearted confidence of his brother—a product of mingled blood, love, rapport, clan loyalty and plain friendship. Whatever the reasons, they imposed on his own actions some of the Presidential inhibitions. In one sense, he had more power than the President, since he had the Presidential clout without the formal constraints of office. Yet any list of RFK priorities would have to begin with his brother's reputation, the prestige and power of the Kennedy–Johnson Administration. In exploiting his power reservoir, Robert Kennedy was an adventurer. At protecting his brother's interests, he was a conservative, a husbander of the Presidential reputation. The tension between these two inclinations— the natural impulse to action and the familial pressures for restraint— helps explain the remarkable activity yet limited record in the civil rights area during the first two and a half years of the Kennedy Administration.

The Attorney General, along with the Secretary of State, has always been something of an anomaly in the President's Cabinet. Other Cabinet officers are expected, in part, to serve as lobbyists for the constituencies of their departments. Thus, the Secretary of Agriculture argues for the farmers, Labor for the unions, Commerce for business, Treasury for the financial community, etc. Even the State Department is the internal representative for the interests of client governments. Justice's job, however, is to represent the other agencies of government in the courts. Under the Kennedys—partly because Robert Kennedy had the dual role of lobbyist-at-the-White House and President's-ambassador-to-the-country—the Justice Department became quickly accepted, by all sides to the dispute, as the Administration's spokesman for and arbiter of the Constitutional claims of the Negro to be free from discrimination. Justice was the center of civil rights action.

It had not been planned that way. At the outset many assumed that Harris Wofford—who had directed JFK's campaign effort in civil rights, was named Presidential assistant for civil rights and organized a "sub-Cabinet group" of people from seventeen different agencies who met regularly in the White House to exchange ideas and report civil rights progress—would take charge and that the White House would be the center of civil rights action. In fact, Wofford's appointment was something of a fluke. He found out about it when he accompanied John Hannah, the chairman of the Civil Rights Commission under Eisenhower, to see President-elect Kennedy, who wanted Hannah to stay on. Hannah told JFK he would be willing to remain, "but only if you have someone in the White House responsible for civil rights." According to one present, "JFK said, 'But I have.' When Hannah asked who, Kennedy said, 'Why, Harris.' At which point Wofford, who was waiting outside planning to tell the President he couldn't serve in the White House if asked because he had already accepted a post with the Peace Corps, was told to raise his right hand, and sworn in." He ended up with both jobs, but left the White House in 1962 amid rumors of frustration. He later recalled, "My leaving the White House had nothing to do with difficulty in seeing the President or in my relations with him, which were good. The negative factor for me was simply that the center of civil rights power and decision-making in civil rights was in the Department of Justice. Fortunately, a very old and good friend, Burke Marshall, in whom I had the greatest confidence, was at the center of that decision-making. So this fact was not a criticism of the Administration's civil rights program."

Byron White, too, then Deputy Attorney General, was hoping that the White House would set up an organization to take the offensive in civil rights. That way, he felt, the Department could take the position: Look, we didn't make the law, but we have to enforce it. White says:

> There was an issue at this time in my own mind which I took up with the Attorney General and that was this: The Department is, among other things, a law enforcement agency and speaking for law and order is to speak for a very strong position but when you mix law enforcement with other things not necessarily related to it, you get law enforcement mixed up with other things. I had thought that the Administration ought to locate the primary leadership in the civil rights fight outside the Department of Justice. I thought it should be located either in the White House or a separate agency so that initiative, aggressive action, education, persuasion should emanate from a different source than the Department of Justice . . . mixing the two together made both less effective. In the long run, I suppose, it was inevitable that they would become mixed up. There seemed to me to be some desire at the White House to locate this matter somewhere else than Pennsylvania Avenue.

But the fact was that for whatever reasons, the President was unwilling to draw on the moral credit of his office to advance civil rights. And Robert Kennedy, who took on the symbolic leadership of the civil rights struggle, was—at the outset—content to delegate civil rights strategy planning and day-to-day operations to White and Marshall.

Legend has it that the job interview between the young Attorney General, who had no patience for small talk, and the reticent, frail-looking Burke Marshall, who had no ability at it, was a disaster—that neither man said a word for ten minutes, after which Marshall told his wife, "I blew it," and Kennedy confided to intimates, "I have nothing in common with that man." Looking back, Marshall concedes only that "It was not what you would call a paragon of communication."

Yet Robert Kennedy chose Burke Marshall, enlightened conservative,* brilliant Yale lawyer, successful partner in the distinguished Washington firm of Covington and Burling, young, dedicated, prototypical Ivy Leaguer, sophisticated anti-trust attorney, to head his Civil Rights Division and eventually to plan and oversee his civil rights policy. As Ed Guthman has put it, "They [Kennedy and White] decided that someone who had been in the forefront of any rights or racial cause might be handicapped by ideology or past associations in civil rights enforcement. Therefore, they began looking for an outstanding lawyer, someone no less sensitive than Wofford to the cause of equal rights but not identified with it."[1]

To the hard-core civil rights community, it looked like a dream deferred, like Negro rights delayed while this corporation lawyer got his on-the-job training. They would have preferred the job to go to a dedicated civil rights activist, like Harris Wofford. To Deputy Byron White it was a conscious decision: Instead of appointing a committed civil rights activist who was set on using law as a social instrument, "We thought it would be more interesting to get a first-class lawyer who would do the job in a technically proficient way that would be defensible in court—that Southerners would not think of as a vendetta, but as an even-handed application of the law."

Ironically, one suspects that had a Harris Wofford or a Joseph Rauh (onetime head of the ADA) served as Assistant Attorney General for Civil Rights, Robert Kennedy and the Department of Justice would have done less. It was Marshall's quiet style, his caution and precision that won the Attorney General's respect and total confidence in his judgment. A second irony was that Marshall, chosen for his technical, lawyerly competence, spent the bulk of his time and made his greatest contribution in a distinctly extra-legal capacity. For Marshall was the field general, the executive officer of the extraordinary Kennedy corps of problem-solvers, the free-lance pragmatists who were dispatched across the land on ad hoc assignments. Technical lawyering turned out to be only a small part of the job.

The importance of Marshall's appointment was not his theory of

---

* Not conservative in the partisan politics sense of the early Sixties, but in the Edmund Burke sense that he had an almost mystical faith in the system as an organic phenomenon that would work out its own destiny. Politically, he was a '60s-style "liberal."

federalism. That came later. "You can't understand the limitations of government without experiencing it," he says. Rather, it was the milieu from which Marshall emerged. Kennedy took Marshall on Byron White's say-so, even as he took Nick Katzenbach, the Rhodes Scholar who had known White at Yale Law School, and in turn recommended fellow Princetonian (as was John Doar) John Douglas—also a Rhodes Scholar and Yale lawyer, who became head of the Civil Division—and Louis Oberdorfer, the Alabama-born Yale lawyer who had clerked for Justice Black while White clerked for Justice Vinson. William Orrick, who headed first the Civil and then the Anti-Trust Division, had done his undergraduate work at Yale. Solicitor General Archibald Cox, who came to his job through John Kennedy, whom he had served as a consultant and in the campaign as research director, had been a distinguished professor specializing in labor law at the Harvard Law School.

The mix of these Ivy League intellectuals with Robert Kennedy's home-grown activists—men like Pulitzer Prize winner Ed Guthman and Nieman Fellow John Seigenthaler, Hoffa-chasing Walter Sheridan, Joe Dolan (near the top of his class at St. John's Law School) and John Nolan, who had clerked for Justice Tom Clark—yielded an unprecedented *élan* which in turn made the Justice Department a spirited place to be, with an aura of possibilities unlimited, rare in the annals of federal bureaucracies. But the intellectual boundaries, the political geography, the legal assumptions which underlay the various ingenious forms Kennedy's civil rights activities were to take, had, in a sense, been predetermined by the Ivy League mentality, the gentleman's assumptions about how things work.

Thus as crisis piled on crisis—the freedom rides of 1961, the integration of Ole Miss in 1962, Bull Connor in 1963—and Robert Kennedy himself assumed round-the-clock decision-making authority, got increasingly involved, committed and militant, the options he was presented, the judgment on which he came to rely, the perspective developed, very much reflected the Ivy League milieu from which much of his talented staff had emerged.

These men, who for the most part were graduated from the elite law academies of the Forties, brought with them the code of the Ivy League Gentleman, which involved, among other things, the assumption that negotiation and settlement are preferable to litigation; the idea that winning in a higher court is preferable—for precedential purposes—to winning in a lower court; the notion that reasonable men can always work things out; patience at the prospect of endlessly protracted litigation; the preference for defined structures, for order. They were oriented toward corporate enterprise. Anti-trust lawyers like Burke Marshall and Ramsey Clark (who had attended the University of Chicago Law School, "the Yale of the Middle West") had experience settling many a case with a plea of *nolo contendere* in exchange for a cease-and-desist order. Tax lawyers like Louis Oberdorfer were used to talking things over, working things out in advance, with the Internal Revenue Service. Despite their residence at Yale, which espoused the rhetoric of legal realism (a rebellion against the formalistic approach of Harvard) men like Katzenbach and White were products of the case method of instruction which is (a) preoccupied with matters of legal doctrine and formal analysis (even though Yale taught that such abstract formulations should be put in the service of social causes), and (b) focused on the development of law at the appeals level to the exclusion of the actual trial level. As one scholar has noted, "This method . . . tends to ignore the relationship of theory to fact." Without disputing the dynamism, good will, ingenuity or capacity of these men, without underestimating the unique benefits of an Ivy League education, without suggesting that they were genteel assembly-line products who thought and felt alike, one can still argue that the system by which they defined themselves predisposed them to peaceful co-existence with present injustice—especially where they could see light at the end of the appellate tunnel.

These Eastern establishment law schools—for the most part all white (or with token integration, as was the case at virtually all of the non-black law schools of that day)—had no courses yet on civil rights or poverty law or city problems. They prepared the nation's leaders to join the ruling class, to sit on boards of directors, to represent corporations, to deal with banks, to arrange mergers, to work out financing, to anticipate trouble-making possibilities—and to avoid them at all costs. Studies have documented that 70 percent of all partners in Wall Street law firms in the early Sixties were from one of three schools—Harvard, Yale and Columbia.[2]

As Ivy League products, these men dressed alike, talked the same language, spoke out of common experience and reference, had gone to the right private schools, belonged to the same clubs, *assumed* that the system which had floated them to the top was basically sound, that the main problem was to gain for the Negro admission to that system and that the way to achieve this goal was to think and behave like a lawyer, and a corporation lawyer at that.

Nowhere was this patience, this commitment to negotiation, this idea that reasonable men can work things out, this assumption that confrontation should always be avoided and that mediation rather than coercion is the proper way to achieve social change—nowhere were these attitudes more evident than in Robert Kennedy's incessant negotiations with Governor Ross Barnett of Mississippi in September 1962, when the Kennedys sought assurances from Barnett that he would protect James Meredith, the Negro applicant to the University of Mississippi, and maintain law and order.*

Monday, September 17, 1962. The Attorney General considers Governor Barnett's request that James Meredith register at Jackson instead of at Oxford like everybody else.

THE ATTORNEY GENERAL AND GOVERNOR ROSS BARNETT, 7:00 P.M.

Governor Barnett of Mississippi opened the conversation by saying that he was simply delighted to hear from me again. He asked if I was feeling well and said it was a great pleasure to have a chance to talk once more.

During the course of the conversation he made the point that he felt that Meredith should register at Jackson at the State House at 3 o'clock on Thursday. He said that this would be a most convenient hour and place for them. He said the Board of Trustees will be meeting at Jackson at 2:30 and he will have the registrar there and everything could be handled very nicely.

I raised the point as to whether this was an unusual procedure and he said some of the students registered at Jackson although the vast majority do register at Oxford. I said I would cooperate but this was not solely my decision but that Meredith would have to be consulted and that I thought it was very possible that he would want to register at Oxford rather than Jackson.

I asked him if the Board of Trustees had determined whether they would permit him to register. He said that decision had not been made but he suspected that that would be the result.

I asked him for the name of the individual with whom Mr. McShane, representing the Government and the Marshals, should be in contact. He gave me the name Dr. Jobe at the State House.

He said he was very anxious to avoid the kind of violence that they had in Alabama and felt that if he registered in Jackson there would be no "hissing" although he doubted they would have any trouble in either place.

I asked him why he preferred Jackson and he said it was to avoid the possibility of any difficulty. He indicated the Board of Trustees was meeting at that moment in another part of the building; that if I decide that Meredith should register at Oxford rather than Jackson, that he would get them back again tomorrow and tell them of our decision.

* What follows are verbatim transcripts and summaries of telephone conversations monitored by Justice Department stenographers at the time.

I told him I would see what the ramifications and the implications of this registering at Jackson might be and that I would consult with Meredith and would call him tomorrow and said I would try to make the call before noon.

He thanked me for my cooperation and I thanked him for his.

The conversation was courteous throughout.

[Later the same day.]

AG: *If he comes to Jackson will he be registered?*

Gov.:   *It is up to the Trustees whether or not they will permit him to register. We have a constitutional Board of Trustees. They have the right to control and direct all of the activities of the university. It may be the majority will not permit him to register. I couldn't promise they will register him. He will have the same opportunities in Jackson as up there. His whole transcript of grades are here.*

AG: *On the time, should we work that out?*

Gov.:   *Yes, send another telegram saying that he may present himself at 3 o'clock tomorrow—2:30 or 3. The Board, you see, has the authority to decide those things. That is the matter conclusively. It is bound on the discretion of the Board of Trustees. That's my judgment about it.*

They are going to make a mistake if they go to Oxford. The Board of Trustees has decided they want him to present himself in Jackson. If he doesn't do what the Board says, it won't be our fault.

AG: *If he goes to Oxford, you won't take responsibility for his safety?*

Gov.:   *It will be in violation of the orders of the Board. These people are very peaceful. This thing is serious to the people in the South and all over the world. This thing—it has the whole nation upset. We have telegrams from California to Maine. You would be surprised at the sentiment on this thing. He's been notified where to come.*

AG: *How many students have they told to come to Jackson? Have telegrams been sent to other students?*

Gov.:   *I couldn't answer that. I know of one.*

The Kennedy response to James Meredith's lonely fight to integrate Ole Miss was typical of its general civil rights posture in a number of respects. First, there was never any doubt that the Kennedy Administration would be on the side of Meredith, on the side of integration. Second, it should be noted that what Kennedy Justice did was react, respond to a situation somebody else had created, and the response was delayed at that. Third, there was the long-drawn-out attempt to achieve through negotiation and mediation what the courts had already made mandatory by their orders. Fourth, policies were articulated in terms of Burke Marshall's theory of federalism which highlighted court orders. Fifth, despite the rhetorical adhesion to orderly legal process, if preserving the peace required informal pseudo-legal arrangements, there was no hesitation to make them. And finally, there was the introduction of troops, of force, only as a last resort.

The theory of federalism—which posited an elaborate system of deferences to state and local authority—was attractive to Attorney General Robert Kennedy not because it accorded with his understanding of history or the Constitution (although he undoubtedly came to believe that it did), but because it neatly reconciled the three codes of conduct by which the Department of Justice was governed in the Kennedy era:

The code of the FBI, as we have already seen, posited the unavailability of the FBI and/or total self-determination over its development (and thereby limited the Justice Department's potential for flexible and creative response).

The code of the Kennedys, to be examined in later chapters, had principal relevance in the matter of priorities. Despite the lofty campaign promises, early Kennedy priorities put civil rights somewhere around the middle of the list—after organized crime, after Jimmy Hoffa, after anti-trust (although this soon fell to the back of the pack), after juvenile delinquency, but ahead of internal security, ahead of crime in the streets, ahead of such unglamorous fields as civil, lands and natural resources litigation.

And the code of the Ivy League Gentleman, which assumed that reasonable men can work everything out in due course.

"We came to see," Nicholas Katzenbach recalls, "that you could not on any level give the Southern Governors an excuse for not enforcing the law of the United States. It was our theory that if you take over the law enforcement from them, you won't be able to maintain it and they will abdicate. From this came the attempt to preserve the federal system until we could get through the idea that local officials have an obligation to enforce the law."

In other words, let George do it. George Wallace, that is, who vowed after an early electoral defeat to a segregationist opponent, "I'll never be outniggered again." Or Ross Barnett . . .

Tuesday, September 18, 1962. *The Attorney General agrees to ask Meredith to wait until the following Monday instead of registering on Thursday like everyone else.*
THE ATTORNEY GENERAL AND GOVERNOR ROSS BARNETT,
12:30 P.M.

RFK: *Governor, how are you?*
BARNETT: *Fine, General, how are you?*

RFK: Governor, I had a representative of the Department talk
           to this boy's lawyer and he in turn talked to Meredith and
           he feels strongly that he would like to register at Oxford
           and it's our judgment that it is the best judgment.

BARNETT: General, I think you're making a mistake there.

RFK: Well, I think it's up to the boy—

BARNETT: It's up to him, I know.

RFK: The vast majority of the students are registering in Oxford
           and he doesn't feel he should do anything unusual. But I
           think you can provide for his safety, can you not?

BARNETT: Of course, we will have to do that. We'll do that all right.
           What day now does he want to register?

RFK: Thursday.

BARNETT: He wouldn't want to wait until Monday?

RFK: Next Monday? He would rather do it Thursday.

BARNETT: They're going to have a lot of folks registering there
           Thursday. I'm trying to figure this thing out. From a
           psychological standpoint the atmosphere will be better,
           that's what I'm thinking about. They'll register all through
           next Monday.

RFK: Do you want me to take this up again? I will be glad to do
           that. If you want him to register Monday, I'll be glad—

BARNETT: We insist that he come then. It would just save us a lot of
           trouble and it would be easier. I don't understand why he
           won't come here.

RFK: The students are registering at Oxford and he wants to
           register at Oxford.

BARNETT: See if he will do this. See if—in other words, there are
           going to be a lot of them registering Thursday and most
           of them will go home Friday morning. Even if you try to
           have it that it could be Monday or even Saturday.

RFK: I'm going up to Massachusetts to vote, so I can give you
           a ring tomorrow morning. You would rather have him
           register Saturday or Monday? Let me go to work on that.
           I will try to do that later today.

BARNETT: Friday would be better than Thursday.

RFK: Any day but Thursday?

BARNETT: They're going to have such a gang up there at Ole Miss
           and a lot of them might resent it. General, some men here
           insist that he come to the Jackson State Office Building on
           the tenth floor where the Trustees meet. The registrar is
           here and he'll miss the whole crowd and it would be so
           much better for everybody. Frankly I think if you don't
           agree with me there is nothing—he'll just have to come up
           there.

RFK: I think he has considered it. Let me go over this again.
           First, we approached his lawyer and his lawyer said, "We
           want to go to Oxford." Then I told our attorney this is not

a decision for the lawyer, this should be taken up with the boy. I didn't talk to him myself.
BARNETT: *You'll call me tomorrow morning?*
RFK: *I will talk to you tomorrow morning and see if we can move it to another day. Thank you, Governor.*
BARNETT: *Thank you, General.*

Robert Kennedy captured the federal bureaucracy (except for the FBI) by ignoring the rules—by acting as if the quintuplicate carbons, the lines of authority, the organization charts, the budgetary and jurisdictional limitations, all of which were everywhere in evidence, didn't exist. But he was captured by state and local bureaucracies, *outmaneuvered* by the Southern Governors because he acted as if federalism, the federal system—a theoretical construct which didn't really exist—was everywhere in evidence.

As the theory emerged, federalism required drastic deference to state and local politicians in matters relating to the franchise, education and the administration of justice.

Since the Kennedy civil rights strategy focused on the franchise as the open-sesame to all other rights, it is instructive to recall that as Burke Marshall said, "Federal policy under Attorney General Kennedy was to try to make the federal system in the voting field work by itself through local action, without federal court compulsion." All very well. First, you try informal negotiation. And sometimes it works, as in the southwest Georgia county where, according to Marshall, "no Negro had been registered to vote for decades. Repeated visits by a Southern-born lawyer from the Department to the county board of registrars finally led to a policy decision by the board members that Negroes should be registered on the same basis as whites. More than three hundred Negro citizens were registered in the county in less than two weeks. State officials never became involved at all." There were countless other examples.

If negotiation didn't work, then and only then, under the strategy, you went to court. You didn't, however, protect civil rights workers who were involved in voter registration drives. You didn't, in advance, attempt to enjoin interference with voter registration activity, even where such interference was threatened, promised and delivered. You *never* used force except in extremis to counteract force. And you more or less looked the other way when scholars like William Van Alstyne made the common sense point that "Given state Governors who oppose Negro enfranchisement, given registrars who reflect that opposition, given employers, shopkeepers, bankers and private organizations who will act in conscious parallelism to protect the white ballot, the pervasiveness of control by the local, white-supremacist establishment cannot effectively be broken through piecemeal litigation in the federal courts."

Sometimes federalism was defended as a matter of Constitutional law. Thus, in his Gino Speranza lectures at Columbia in 1964, which came close to codifying the Kennedy–Marshall theory of federalism, Marshall defended the President's delayed action on behalf of the freedom riders entering Mississippi as follows:

> There was considerable evidence that there would be violence in Mississippi. Nevertheless, it was doubtful whether the President had any Constitutional choice about refusing in advance to accept the word of a governor of a state, and it was clearly necessary, in any event, to try immediately to reestablish the responsibility of states to use the constitutional police powers to maintain order. The federal decision was made on that basis.

Left out of this account: the fact that Senator Eastland had given his word—"as a gentleman"—to Robert Kennedy that there would be no violence in Mississippi if the freedom riders proceeded to Jackson (where they were promptly arrested). Such behind-the-scenes negotiations, quite common in corporate-law practice, are a better clue to the style and values of the Kennedy Justice Department than the federalism theory which its officers kept articulating.

On June 24, 1964, Attorney General Kennedy told an NAACP delegation that the federal government "lacked the power" to take preventive police action in Mississippi. And when he boarded a plane for West Berlin a few days thereafter, he added that the situation in Mississippi, where three civil rights workers were murdered, was "a local matter for law enforcement" and that federal authority there was "very limited."

Here it is sufficient to note that there was responsible *legal* opinion on *both* sides of the issue of federalism, which the Administration came to defend as dogma. It was therefore not sufficient to look to *legal* theory alone for the explanation for the Justice Department's activities or lack of them.

For instance, within a week of his West Berlin embarkation pronouncement, twenty prestigious law professors from six of the nation's best universities directly challenged the Attorney General in a joint statement. They cited Section 333 of Title 10 of the U.S. Code (which Kennedy himself had cited at the time troops were sent to assist James Meredith's entry to Ole Miss). Under that section the President is authorized to use the state militia and the armed forces of the nation "whenever he considers that unlawful obstructions, combinations of assemblages . . . make it impracticable to enforce the laws of the U.S. . . . by the ordinary course of judicial proceedings."

The professors cited an opinion by Supreme Court Justice Joseph P. Bradley in an 1879 electoral-laws case:

> We hold it to be an incontrovertible principle that the Government of the U. S. may, by means of physical force, exercised through its official agents, execute on every foot of American soil the powers and functions that belong to it. . . .

The statement suggested that Kennedy was couching policy in terms of legal authority and that this was misleading to the country, wrong as a matter of law and damaging to the civil rights cause.

On countless occasions the Justice Department denied it had legal power to do what one or another civil rights organization demanded, only to confound the civil rights community some months later by doing it (e.g., charging people on information rather than not proceeding without a grand-jury indictment—since white Southern grand juries were loathe to indict whites for civil rights violations).

When Kennedy wanted to do something specific he had no hesitation. William Taylor of the Civil Rights Commission remembers a meeting at which "we were talking about the executive order on housing as it related to the Federal Reserve Board and somebody raised the political science question about the independence of the Federal Reserve Board, which would preclude the President from telling it what to do. Bobby said bring me a list of Federal Reserve Board members and when their terms expire. He received the list, looked it over and said, 'I see they're only independent until June of 1963. Doesn't —— have a son who works for the federal government?' " But when they didn't want to do something, like promise protection, the theology of federalism was invoked.

On matters of policy, as of law, there were ample grounds to argue with the government's position. Selective protection was possible even with limited resources, ran one argument. Part of the idea of federalism, ran another argument, was that the federal government is supposed to act to secure the federal civil rights of individuals when the states do not. Simon Lazarus III developed this thesis in the *Yale Law Journal*, where he maintained: "The crowning glory of American federalism is not states' rights. It is the protection the U.S. Constitution gives to the private citizen against *all* wrongful governmental invasion of fundamental rights and freedoms." The federalism issue was constantly debated between the government and the civil rights community.

Thus Burke Marshall explained in a February 26, 1963, letter to Leslie
Dunbar of the Southern Regional Council why the President shouldn't
ask Congress for a mandatory school desegregation date: In addition to
the difficulties of passage, "I am afraid that the problems of enforcement in some places, before the free exercise of the franchise, are almost
insurmountable under the federal system. It would perhaps be constitutional to destroy the system for all practical purposes in some states until
school segregation has been ended. Obviously, this is no minor matter."
To which Dunbar replied, he was aware "of the question of the value
of the federal system" and believed "that the value was large but less
in these circumstances than that of the individual rights. . . ."

A third argument considered and rejected the tactic of negotiating
with the enemy. "History has borne out that Robert Kennedy's tactics
were wrong," argues William Taylor, who became Staff Director of the
Civil Rights Commission under President Johnson. "Everyone agrees
that the states have the first responsibility. But how do you get them to
exercise it? By telling them you don't have the power? Our theory is
you tell them, 'If you don't do it, we will.' The Mississippi State Highway Patrol didn't start doing its job until the Bureau sent a hundred
agents to Jackson in 1964. In that respect the Justice Department was
late."

Thursday, September 20, 1962 (*Registration Day*). *The Mississippi
legislature passes a bill aimed at making Meredith ineligible for admission to Ole Miss (because of a trumped-up criminal charge) and
another bill investing Governor Barnett with full power to act for the
University in all matters pertaining to Meredith. Chief Marshal James
P. McShane and John Doar, then First Assistant in the Civil Rights
Division, accompany Meredith to Oxford, where they confront hundreds of state troopers lined up shoulder to shoulder. Governor Barnett
reads a proclamation declaring Meredith ineligible for admission and
they leave. Robert Kennedy and Burke Marshall are on the phone with
Mississippi officials throughout the day.*

ATTORNEY GENERAL PATTERSON AND BURKE MARSHALL, 9:50 A.M.

GEN. P: *. . . over which I had nothing—I had no control. I will
not be able to assure you of the things I thought I could
yesterday when I spoke with you. I regret it with all my
heart, and I want you to know that it is a thing over
which I had no control at all. The only thing I could do
was frankly to call you and let you know what the situation
was.*

BM: *General Patterson, could you tell me more what that
means.*

GEN. P: *There is a warrant out for his arrest that I didn't know existed yesterday when I spoke with you. There may be an attempt to arrest him by local officials. I told you yesterday that he would have peaceable entry into Mississippi and to Oxford. I told you that I would be able to get him back to Memphis. I can't assure you of that this morning. I regret it with all my heart. All I can do is call you and tell that that is the situation.*

BM: *General Patterson, I appreciate that very much.*

GEN. P: *Colonel Birdsong was here in my office yesterday when we spoke and he is here now. This is something I regret but is just one of those things. In Mississippi the Attorney General doesn't have the direct control over local officers as they do in most states. Local prosecutors are autonomous. I have no control over that.*

BM: *Could you tell me this—do Colonel Birdsong's men—are they the people that would make such an arrest?*

GEN. P: *No, sir. I think it would be a sheriff or a deputy sheriff.*

BM: *Of a county?*

GEN. P: *Yes.*

BM: *General Patterson, will I be able to get in touch with you later?*

GEN. P: *I will be here in this office as far as I know. The way things are developing it may be necessary for me to go.*

BM: *General, if possible, I would appreciate it if you would leave word where you will be—the Attorney General or I may want to talk with you.*

GEN. P: *Allright, Mr. Marshall. I just wanted to get this word to you before these people leave Memphis.*

BM: *I appreciate that.*

GEN. P: *You will have time to make that contact in Memphis?*

BM: *Yes, I will. They may decide to come anyway.*

GEN. P: *I just wanted you to know of the changed circumstances.*

BM: *Yes, sir, we will be in touch with you.*

ATTORNEY GENERAL PATTERSON AND ROBERT KENNEDY, 3:15 P.M.

GEN. P: *General Kennedy, Judge Mize and Judge Cox have issued their order on any arrests of any kind. I have contacted the District Attorney of that district who is in the city of Oxford and told him that it had been done and for him to direct his sheriff to respect these orders of Judge Mize and Judge Cox, and to refrain from any effort to arrest him. I have been assured from the Governor's office that the same word has been sent out to other sheriffs. Here in Mississippi the Attorney General does not have direct control over law enforcement officers and all I can do is advise them so I am not in that position, otherwise I would direct. The Governor's office as I say have told the office the same thing. The chief of our highway patrol,*

Colonel Birdsong, with whom McShane has talked, is in the town of Batesville and they were going to come down from Memphis. They were going to contact the colonel at the patrol station. Birdsong is there now, so I will call him back and tell him when to expect them.

RFK: I just talked to Mr. McShane about three minutes ago, so what we thought we'd do . . . he is going to leave now and tell him to go right through and look for Colonel Birdsong. I suppose it will take . . .

GEN. P: It won't take . . . I'm not familiar with the highway . . . but even then it won't take more than an hour. They have a new interstate highway. It is only twenty-eight miles from Batesville to Oxford and there is a direct highway.

RFK: He will be down sometime over an hour.

GEN. P: I will call Birdsong . . . he is a fine fellow and a lifelong officer . . . and tell him that Mr. McShane and his deputies and Meredith will contact him at the highway.

RFK: That's fine. You will be keeping in touch with how it progresses and you will call me if there is any problem?

GEN. P: Yes, I will. Frankly, what I think they should do in this matter is, and I understand that is all they wanted to do, is to present Meredith to the registrar there and of course, whatever the registrar does . . . if he denies admission and denies registration, I assume they will have accomplished their mission.

RFK: That's correct. Will you make arrangements for them to leave and for someone to take them out?

GEN. P: I will tell Birdsong to escort them in and out. Will they take him to Memphis?

RFK: That I don't know. I'll find out.

GEN. P: I understand from Mr. McShane that they would want to go to Memphis and don't want to go to Jackson and go to the Board of Trustees there.

RFK: No, they don't want to do that.

GEN. P: It seems the logical thing would be to return to Memphis.

RFK: Maybe they could give them a ride to Batesville.

GEN. P: We will give them an escort not only to Batesville but back to the Mississippi line.

RFK: I really appreciate your help. It will make a helluva difference.

GEN. P: General, I hope we can get together to talk about this sometime.

ATTORNEY GENERAL PATTERSON AND ROBERT KENNEDY, 4:40 P.M.

RFK: General, how are you? We just got word from the Bureau down there that they talked to the sheriff of Oxford and he said he had orders to arrest Meredith.

GEN. P: Oh my gosh.

RFK:	*And that he was intending . . .*
GEN. P:	*My information is from the Governor's chief assistant here in his office that the Governor has directed them not to.*
RFK:	*We checked. We got that report and you said that to me. We called back to find out when they talked to the sheriff and he said he talked to the sheriff within the last thirty-five minutes. The gist of the conversation was that he got an earlier one . . . but he since got a different one. He said the Governor was in Oxford. He said, "The Governor's directing us and has instructed us to arrest Meredith when he comes to," is it the Lyceum Hall?*
GEN. P:	*I don't know but I will call Chief Birdsong and find out if that is correct.*
RFK:	*The best thing for both of us to recognize . . . if the court has said he can't be arrested and then could be arrested . . . arrest him in the company of a couple of marshals . . . put handcuffs on him and take him to jail . . . that's a direct problem for all of us and . . .*
GEN. P:	*I thought the whole thing had been cleared.*
RFK:	*I have had a lot of conversations with the Governor. Should I call him myself?*
GEN. P:	*I don't think it would hurt.*
RFK:	*I will call him and tell him. I wonder where I could locate him. Could I locate him through Jackson?*
GEN. P:	*That would be difficult. I would say direct your call to the University of Mississippi for the Governor.*
RFK:	*If you hear anything further, will you give me a ring? Thanks a lot.*

SUMMARY OF BURKE MARSHALL'S TELEPHONE CALLS TO TOM WATKINS,* SEPTEMBER 20, 1962

Following Patterson's call at 9:50 A.M., I discussed the situation with the Attorney General. Then sometime in the morning I called Tom Watkins and told him that we understood the Governor intended to have Meredith arrested. I pointed out that there was a court order forbidding his arrest.

Mr. Watkins said that he had not been consulted about the decision to arrest Meredith and that he disagreed with it. He said he believed that the Governor would change his mind about that and said that he would call me back.

Sometime in the early afternoon, Mr. Watkins called back and said that he had discussed the matter with the Governor and that Meredith would not be arrested.

At about 4:15 P.M., Al Rosen of the FBI reported to me that their agent had just learned from the sheriff in Oxford that the sheriff was

* Jackson, Mississippi, attorney and friend of Governor Barnett who had the confidence of Burke Marshall and played the role of an intermediary.

*going to arrest Meredith. It was for that reason that the Attorney
General made his additional telephone call to the Governor at about
4:50 P.M.*

GOVERNOR BARNETT AND ROBERT KENNEDY, 4:53 P.M.

RFK: *Hello, Governor, how are you?*
           *Governor, we spent a good part of the day working on this
           problem of the possibility of the arrest of Meredith, and
           the federal courts have issued an order signed by Judge
           Mize and Judge Cox prohibiting his arrest at this time.
           Now, I thought that that had been worked out reasonably
           yesterday and there would not be that difficulty.*
BARNETT: *Well, now here, I understand that Attorney General
           Patterson had agreed that if he did present himself he
           would not be arrested. We are going to abide by that. I
           understand he is coming here to the university and not to
           Jackson and present himself here.*
RFK: *That's correct.*
BARNETT: *I told the sheriff here that that's the understanding not to
           arrest him and they agreed not to do it. They will go away
           without any arrest. Everything will be peaceful. There
           won't be any violence here.*
RFK: *I appreciate that. You have been very cooperative. We
           received word within the last forty-five minutes that the
           sheriff was going to arrest him.*
BARNETT: *That's not right. We agreed that should not be done.*
RFK: *Thank you, Governor. Nice to talk to you.*
BARNETT: *Thank you, General.*

How, one might ask, could the dedicated, alert and brilliant band
of staffmen Kennedy attracted to the Justice Department, in conjunction
with an Attorney General who constitutionally abjured theory for
practice and whose impulse in every area other than civil rights was
activist, get bogged down in a philosophy of inaction, an ideology of
impotence?

How—especially when Kennedy surrounded himself with pragmatic
doers like John Seigenthaler, Walter Sheridan and Ed Guthman, who
looked on theory with suspicion, and energetic Yale lawyers like
Marshall, Katzenbach, White and Douglas, trained to be suspicious of
dogma in the Yale Law School of the Forties, the home of the legal
realists?

How—especially when Kennedy's system was, as Katzenbach recalls,
free-wheeling? "He was not a systematic administrator. He was inspirational. That was his quality. His method was to create a little bit
of a madhouse by picking people rather than organizing. He was in-

clined to trust people and give them broad authority until they proved they didn't merit it. His whole instinct was people."

How—especially when he was a compulsive activist? A part of Robert Kennedy, perhaps the most important part, was committed to movement *per se*, to action *qua* action. He wasn't result-oriented as the cliché had it. He was action-oriented. Slowness was more irritating than incompetence, goofing off a greater sin than failure. At one interdepartmental meeting John Dolan, representing the Justice Department, was told that a committee representative would depart on a key assignment in two weeks. "Two weeks?" Dolan asked incredulously. "Why can't he go tomorrow? You guys know what Department I come from. And you know it'll be my head if I go back and tell the Attorney General *anything* is going to take two weeks."

At least part of the attraction of federalism was that it functioned as a form of therapy, an *explanation* or rationalization for inaction in the face of injustice and brutality. The anthropologist Bronislaw Malinowski once observed that ". . . the function of myth is not to explain but to vouch for, not to satisfy curiosity but to give confidence in power . . . [to] enforce belief. . . ." [3] In that respect, federalism was a myth which served Robert Kennedy better than it served the country.

On one level the function of the theory was to answer criticisms from the left that the federal government wasn't doing enough and from the right that it was doing too much. "Blessed are the peacemakers," said the sign in Burke Marshall's office, "for they catch hell from both sides." But the point is that they *were* peacemakers more than they were justice-guarantors, and so on a second level the function of the official theory of federalism was not to instruct others but rather to convince themselves. It explained to Robert Kennedy (and Katzenbach and Marshall & Co. as well) why they should stand idly by when confronted with murder, brutality, violence, lawlessness, intimidation, hypocrisy—everything they abhorred, everything they stood against.

How else could Robert Kennedy possibly have answered, without a tinge of guilt, Ted Poston's sad query about why the Justice Department hadn't provided protection for the slain Medgar Evers? Having the authority and not choosing to use it would have been what the 1968 Robert Kennedy liked to call "unacceptable." He preferred to believe he didn't have the authority. Anything else would have gone against the Kennedy grain.

Monday, September 24, 1962. *Meredith was yet to be registered. The Fifth Circuit Court of Appeals has ordered the Ole Miss Board of*

Trustees to rescind the action relieving university officials of registra-tion duties and naming Governor Barnett substitute registrar. Barnett has issued another proclamation declaring that the federal government has usurped state powers. Robert Kennedy tells Governor Barnett that the courts have ordered the university trustees to register Meredith at 2:30 P.M. the next day.

ROBERT KENNEDY AND GOVERNOR ROSS BARNETT, 9:50 P.M.

RFK: *Governor?*

BARNETT: *General, how are you tonight?*

RFK: *I expect that you probably have heard the decision of the court and the agreement of the Board of Trustees to register Meredith down in New Orleans.*

BARNETT: *Did they agree to that?*

RFK: *Unanimously.*

BARNETT: *All of them? That's really shocking to me. I heard it a little while ago.*

RFK: *They agreed to do it by two o'clock tomorrow.*

BARNETT: *By two?*

RFK: *I think they have to report back to the court by four o'clock.*

BARNETT: *Did the trustees actually sign anything?*

RFK: *They all got up in court and agreed and then they polled the one who was absent and he agreed and the President announced it and they agreed to pass a resolution. . . .*

BARNETT: *They told the court that?*

RFK: *That's correct.*

BARNETT: *I'm surprised at that really. They were so firm about it two days ago. They changed their minds mighty quick.*

RFK: *The court's decision was unanimous that they should do this.*

BARNETT: *Did they do this under any threat that the court would fine them?*

RFK: *No, they asked the court what they wanted them to do and the court told them and they said they would do it. They met and agreed unanimously they would take this step.*

BARNETT: *I am surprised. I thought they were going to stand stead-fast.*

RFK: *I think there's a great problem here. If we don't follow the order of the federal court, we don't have anything in the United States. I understand how you feel and the feeling of the people down there. You are citizens of the state of Mississippi but you are also citizens of the United States.*

BARNETT: *I expect we got more than a thousand letters this morning.*

RFK: *That's not the problem. Whether the thousand people think so or whether I think so or whether you think so. The court has acted and there is nothing we can do. If you are working to avoid anarchy and disorder and tremendous distress, there is really not much choice on it. He is coming back again now.*

BARNETT: He is going to try to register tomorrow? I haven't heard from anyone down there. Not at Jackson but at the university?

RFK: I think it was left up in the air.

BARNETT: They didn't say whether—I didn't know that.

RFK: Well, it's supposed to be by two o'clock. Can I make some arrangements with you, Governor, as far as his safety there?

BARNETT: He's under two court injunctions.

RFK: The federal court has also taken that under consideration and is going to issue an order that anyone who arrests him is violating the federal law.

BARNETT: In contempt of court. They don't pay attention to the Mississippi courts. That's getting pretty rough, Mr. Kennedy. That's pretty low down. They're not paying no attention to what the chancery courts have to say. Without any hearing—strike it down. General, that won't work. It won't work in any court.

RFK: The court has taken that action and I don't want to get into a major conflict down there.

BARNETT: I tell you now I won't tell you what I am going to do. I don't know yet.

RFK: I've got to see he's protected.

BARNETT: I can't tell you what I'm going to do. I am honest with you. I don't appreciate such doings, you know. I got no respect for it. I don't think the American people have had as much of the federal courts. They can't strike down orders without hearings. The lawyers here are very disturbed and lawyers all over the nation. Our phone rings constantly getting calls from good lawyers all over the country. Kennedy, you ought to rescind this order. Really and truly, you ought to do something about this thing, General. I am frank.

RFK: I think what's going to happen—he is going to arrive in the state tomorrow and make an effort to register. I think the registrar is going to register him and the trustees have made this decision. The only problem is whether he is going to be protected by the state of Mississippi or left to us. That's what I want to decide with you this evening.

BARNETT: Of course I don't know what steps we will have to take. I will have to discuss it with several people here.

RFK: Will you call me, Governor?

BARNETT: General—

RFK: Would you call me?

BARNETT: I will have to find out more about this thing before I make a statement about what I am going to do.

RFK: *Will you call me then?*

BARNETT: *Tomorrow morning?*

RFK: *You will meet tonight?*

BARNETT: *I don't know whether I can call you back on this thing. I just hate to promise. I want to keep my word.*

RFK: *Yes, and you have.*

BARNETT: *I appreciate that. This is a serious matter down here and I don't know what to do. Frankly, I am just not in a position to make a statement.*

RFK: *I wonder how we can leave it between the two of us. It's a quarter of eight down there?*

BARNETT: *It's nearly eight o'clock here. What time is it there?*

RFK: *It's about ten o'clock. I wonder if I might call you in a couple of hours and see how you are coming and if it has to wait until tomorrow morning—*

BARNETT: *I would have to wait until tomorrow morning before I know. I will have to think about it and I might not know tomorrow.*

RFK: *I have the responsibility for his protection. I don't want to send in a lot of extra people with him. Do you think I should plan to do that?*

BARNETT: *I frankly don't know what to tell you. I am shocked. I really am. I just don't know what to tell you.*

RFK: *I will have to make plans to send people in to protect—*

BARNETT: *To send people in to protect him. I certainly haven't heard of anything—*

RFK: *I heard from down there. If you can guarantee his protection—you have always kept your word—I am certainly happy to put that in your hands. I know you are a man of your word, that's why I—*

BARNETT: *How can I assure you?*

RFK: *The same way you assured us the last time. If you can give me your word, then I won't have any difficulty. That responsibility is on my shoulders.*

BARNETT: *Just one second. [Pause] General, I can't think of any statement about anything. I don't know. I'm just not in a position—I can't make any commitments because we haven't decided.*

RFK: *When would we be able to talk about that? I would rather have this done by the local authorities, not by the federal government. The arrangements you made the other day were completely satisfactory. I would much rather have it in your hands. If I can get assurances we will stay out of it, but we have to have assurances from you. I can understand that you want to think about it but think about whether we can—*

BARNETT: *It's about ten o'clock there?*

RFK: *Yes, what time could I call you?*

BARNETT: *Well, I think about eight o'clock in the morning.*
RFK: *I'll plan to do that?*
BARNETT: *I don't know—I have several engagements in the morning. I have no idea. Wait just a minute. [Pause] General, I will either call you or I'll wire you before nine o'clock in the morning.*
RFK: *O. K. I appreciate that.*
BARNETT: *I'll either wire you or call you as to whether or not I can advise you as to what—*
RFK: *Can I run through this situation with you briefly—run through the legal ramifications of this? First, [we had the district court order] . . . then we have had the dispute over the period of the last week. Now it has gone before the Court of Appeals and they declared unanimously with one absentee that Meredith should be registered at the University of Mississippi. They said—the Board of Trustees and the President—announced that they would arrange for the registration of Mr. Meredith.*
BARNETT: *They said that?*
RFK: *The registrar got up in court and said he would register Meredith. You've got now that the federal courts have acted—*
BARNETT: *Ellis, the regular registrar?*
RFK: *I don't know. I imagine it was he. The federal courts have acted. This is a union of which Mississippi is a member as is Massachusetts. As I said before, as well as being a citizen of the state of Mississippi, you are also a citizen of the United States. The federal courts now have issued a ruling and to prolong this any further, we are all on the brink of a very dangerous situation. You say you have received a thousand telephone calls—*
BARNETT: *Letters.*
RFK: *Letters. I can understand the feeling of the people. The problem is that the federal courts have acted and our responsibility—you as an official of Mississippi and I as Attorney General—*
BARNETT: *I am in a big hurry now. I appreciate your calling. I will let you know tomorrow whether or not I can advise you of our proceedings and—*
RFK: *And work out his protection?*
BARNETT: *I will let you know what our proceedings will be.*
RFK: *Thank you, Governor.*
BARNETT: *It was nice to talk to you.*

Ivy league lawyers are trained to solve problems. The genius of the Kennedy system, which involved the *ad hoc* dispatch of an army of free-lance pragmatists, was that it took advantage of and extended the extraordinary array of talent Robert Kennedy had managed to attract to the Justice Department. "He got everybody to play above their heads," observes Joseph Kraft, the Washington columnist who kept close tabs on the Justice Department of the Kennedy era. Its defect was that as often as not the Kennedy men looked for trouble spots rather than injustice spots. The immediate mission and ultimate skill of men like Burke Marshall, John Doar, John Nolan, Bill Geoghegan, Nicholas Katzenbach, *et al.*, was to problem-solve, resolve, mediate, arbitrate, postpone, cool down, avoid, evade, lid-keep, volcano-cap, defuse, peace-make, negotiate, compromise.

Kennedy ran an intellectual open shop. His system was free-wheeling, demanding, flattering and fun-loving, with a maximum delegation of responsibility and minimum bureaucratic nit-picking. It was founded on the theory that the well-trained attorney, the paradigmatic Wall Street lawyer, whatever his specialty, is equipped to solve any problem. And so, little attention was paid to the organization charts as Kennedy created an interdisciplinary stew which institutionalized the casual and undermined the conventional.

He was always running fast and expected his people to do the same, whatever their primary task within the Department. He sent a tax man (Lou Oberdorfer) to desegregate schools, a Civil Division old-timer (Carl Eardley) to enjoin Alabama policemen from terrorizing freedom riders. He had his Civil Rights chief (Marshall) checking anti-trust cases. He commandeered an Immigration and Naturalization Service plane to fly junior Justice Department attorneys from the Solicitor General's office around Mississippi in an attempt to get the appropriate courts to issue orders to stop Governor Barnett from blocking the integration of Ole Miss. He sent his deputy (Katzenbach) to face down the Governor of Alabama at a schoolhouse door, used civil rights lawyers (Doar, *et al.*) to conduct FBI-type investigations into voter intimidation. He had his Get-Hoffa Squad investigate the KKK, and he assigned E. Barrett Prettyman, Jr., who had clerked for no fewer than three U.S. Supreme Court Justices, to negotiate playground facilities for ghetto children in the District of Columbia. He detached New York attorney William vanden Heuvel from Senator Jacob Javits' law firm long enough to set up a free school in Prince Edward County, Virginia, which ran until Prince Edward's own public schools reopened on an integrated basis.

He put the head of his Civil Division (John Douglas) in charge of liaison with the March on Washington. And although the Kennedy brothers had originally opposed the march as counter-productive and likely to derail delicate negotiations within the Congress to get what became the 1964 Civil Rights Bill through, the march's coordinator,

Bayard Rustin, recalled, "He almost smothered us. We had to keep raising our demands to keep him from getting ahead of us."

Once the Civil Rights Bill was passed, he put the head of his Tax Division (Oberdorfer), who already had held White House civil rights briefings for hundreds of business, religious and professional men, in charge of organizing compliance with it.

In the middle of the crisis at Birmingham he had the head of the Anti-Trust Division (Bill Orrick) circulate the names of 375 top officers of Alabama companies among the Kennedy Cabinet and arrange a one-to-one telephoning operation with each Cabinet member instructed to ask his contact to ask the Governor of Alabama not to precipitate a school crisis.

As Nicholas Katzenbach notes: "The big job a President has is to make the bureaucracy work for him. Most Presidents resist this. They don't have confidence in it. They create other mechanisms to short-cut it, to go around it. The one thing Robert Kennedy did was he *made* the Department of Justice work for him and President Kennedy, and if you can translate that into government you can make the whole government work. You can't bypass the bureaucracy. . . . without knowing, I doubt that any Department worked more effectively than the Justice Department worked for Bobby."

Moreover, the intellectual milieu reflected the special blend of excellence and unorthodoxy taught at the Yale Law School of the 1940s at which so many of these men had studied. It was a time when the law school emphasized the limitations of legislative formulas, the possibilities of law as a policy instrument. It reflected the legacy and approach of teachers such as Judge Jerome Frank, the ex-New Dealer who taught fact skepticism (as well as law skepticism) and believed that all judges should be psychoanalyzed; Thurmond Arnold, who, as head of the Anti-Trust Division under Biddle, brought so many trouble-making cases that the Attorney General instituted a policy (which holds to this day) requiring his personal signature on all anti-trust briefs; Fred Rodell—fishing companion of former Yale law professor Justice William O. Douglas—who had such contempt for conventional law that he never bothered to become a member of the bar and who vowed in the late Thirties never to write another footnote, an oath which for the most part he has kept; and Robert Hutchins, who had been Dean at twenty-eight, before moving on to radicalize the University of Chicago.

It was not surprising, then, that within the boundaries of Ivy League jurisprudence, these men were super-responders, often not content to stay within the limits of their assignment.

John Doar, who spent about 180 days a year on the dusty back roads of the hard-core South, was—in theory—supervising litigation: to gain the vote, to integrate schools, to underwrite the administration of Justice. Typically, his behind-the-scenes actions outstretched his mandates. When he went over the list of applicants to the schools of Tuskegee, Alabama, to be sure the board was fair, he acknowledged, in a memo:

> This puts the Department of Justice deep into the supervision of the school system prior to any objections by the Negroes and it takes the burden of policing the school board off the backs of the Negroes' attorney. [But] . . . The experience we gain here will be useful in counseling the board and the court on a feasible school desegregation plan. . . .

Ramsey Clark toured the South to report on trouble spots but ended up recommending a wholesale overhaul of the Kennedy Administration's case-by-case approach to school segregation.*

Yet all this insight, energy and commitment was contained by the geometry of federalism which, according to the official Kennedy map, declared great chunks of legal territory off limits. In broad contour, the federal government had charge of the economy and foreign affairs, and state and local government were in charge of law and order. The theology of federalism invoked the Founding Fathers, who were supposed to have (a) anticipated a balance of power between state and federal government, but (b) declared individual rights to all federal

---

* On August 28, 1963, he followed up an earlier memorandum to the Attorney General with a call for a radical revision in the Administration's anti-segregation litigation policy:

> My recent trips throughout the South on the school desegregation matters had led me to some general conclusions which I pass on for your consideration.
> 1. The national interest must be represented in the school desegregation cases. Private prosecution of school desegregation is ineffective, unfair and capricious. Baton Rouge, La., has had a desegregation case pending for seven years, while Shreveport, La., schools, which are comparable, have never been sued. The financial burden of the prosecution falls on the wrong people. The persons responsible for the prosecution of the suit have no direct responsibility to the public, and are largely in full control of the litigation without the needed checks and balances. The quality of the representation is not always as good as it should be. The institutional rights of school children should not depend upon the desire and ability of private interests to protect these rights. While the role of the NAACP has been essential heretofore in the prosecution of these cases, in the broader sense it is not desirable to have a private organization primarily responsible for the selection and prosecution of these cases. There is a great need for a coordinated, long-range planning for effective integration in depth in all areas where segregation exists whether under color of law, or de facto, and an apparent present lack in any such approach. I feel that something like the Equal Education Opportunity Act, outlined in my memo of May 15, 1963, to the Attorney General, is urgently needed. . . .
> If something on this order cannot be enacted then we should consider wholesale plans for intervening or the filing of amicus briefs.

citizens which the federal government had no way of protecting. The geometric theology was suspect because in organized crime, and many other areas, the federal government did not defer to local spheres of authority. Indeed, as already stated, one reason the FBI was reluctant to put the heat on Southern law enforcers was that it needed their cooperation in non-civil rights investigations. Also, the free-lance pragmatists were poking their noses under any number of non-federal tents *on behalf of* tranquillity. The theory didn't prevent Burke Marshall from *ex cathedra* conversations with sitting Justices on the Fifth Circuit. It didn't prevent John Doar from working with school records in Tuskegee. It didn't prevent high Justice officials from sneaking into McComb, Mississippi, under cover of darkness and pulling down the shades as they worked out strategy with white moderates to avoid the next confrontation.

Federalism was an enlightened apology for the existing social order. With Burke Marshall as its architect and Kennedy its popularizer, it seemed to accept the Edmund Burkean notion that the nation-state had some kind of organic reality over and above its parts and that to disrupt the fabric of the nation-state was a greater evil than not to protect the human rights that the federal system was supposed to guarantee in the first place. It was typical of an Ivy League intellectual to have elaborated such a theory with Marshall's relentless reason. Its ultimate logic, of course, was the preservation of existing social, economic and political arrangements for the black minority. To the extent that the free-lance pragmatists did their job, they patched the existing social framework and postponed radical reconstruction. This was done despite Burke Marshall's accurate reflection some years after the fact: "I was not for peace without change, I was for peaceful change."

Tuesday, September 25, 1962. *The Court of Appeals has entered a temporary restraining order against interfering with Meredith's registration. Governor Barnett and the Attorney General and others are on the phone throughout the day, but when John Doar, Chief Marshal McShane and Meredith, accompanied by three or four marshals' cars, arrive in Jackson at the state capitol, where the registration is to take place, they discover that the Governor has physically restrained the Trustees from complying with the court orders as they had agreed. He reads another proclamation (after asking, "Which one is Meredith?" —Though Meredith is the only Negro present). Meredith & Company go back to the airport and that night the Fifth Circuit Court of Appeals issues an order to show cause why the Governor should not be cited for civil contempt for preventing Meredith from registering. Barnett is ordered to appear on the twenty-eighth. Kennedy tells Barnett that Meredith will show up at Oxford the next morning to attend classes.*

ROBERT KENNEDY AND GOVERNOR ROSS BARNETT, 12:20 P.M.

RFK: *Hello.*
BARNETT: *Yes, General, how are you? I was meaning to call you. I
           sent you a telegram this morning. I told you last night
           I would wire you at nine o'clock. I sent you a telegram
           assuring you that we were exercising every diligence to
           prevent violence. I stated in the telegram we would take
           every precaution to prevent violence. We all agreed on
           that. We have been in session. What about yourself?*
RFK: *First, I have to find out what's going to happen. He is
           going to arrive down there and will let you know when he
           is coming.*
BARNETT: *What time is he expected?*
RFK: *I thought I would work it out with you.*
BARNETT: *Do it about two o'clock.*
RFK: *Let me first discuss this with you. He arrives and arrange-
           ments as I understand will be made for his personal
           protection. He will go to campus or Jackson, whatever we
           arrange with you. Will there be anything done by the state
           officials or the city officials to interfere physically?*
BARNETT: *I couldn't promise you that. Not physically.*
RFK: *Nobody will interfere physically?*
BARNETT: *I wouldn't answer that. About going on the campus or
           not. We are going to do it peacefully. We are not going to
           have any violence here.*
RFK: *The problem, Governor—I appreciate that and you have
           kept your word. But I thought we should have complete
           understanding and—*
BARNETT: *You anticipate any violence?*
RFK: *No, I don't anticipate violence. If you tell me there won't
           be any, there won't be any.*
BARNETT: *There won't be any as far as we're concerned.*
RFK: *He arrives and he goes to register. Is there going to be any
           effort to interfere with him?*
BARNETT: *Well, we're going through about the same thing as before.*
RFK: *But I mean, no one is going to try to stop him physically?*
BARNETT: *Nobody is going to try to hurt him. We are not anticipat-
           ing anything like that.*
RFK: *You have no information that anyone will attempt to
           arrest him?*
BARNETT: *No, they're not going to do that. Arrest? For what do you
           mean?*
RFK: *Arrest him for anything. You have no information or
           knowledge they are going to arrest Meredith?*
BARNETT: *There is a federal case pending against him. I don't an-
           ticipate anything like that happening.*

RFK:	He will arrive—and there won't be any interference with him—and he'll attempt to register—and nobody's going to try to arrest him?
BARNETT:	I say there won't be any physical force and I hope there won't be—I say that we won't try to block him, you know.
RFK:	You just say you won't try to keep him out?
BARNETT:	I don't mean that—all about not keeping him out.
RFK:	You are going to keep him out physically? He gets there and says, "I want to go in." Will someone stop him?
BARNETT:	He may be faced with that.
RFK:	That's quite different now. Is someone going to try to physically stop him?
BARNETT:	He'll probably be told.
RFK:	Who will tell him that?
BARNETT:	I am going to tell him that.
RFK:	You are going down there personally?
BARNETT:	Well, I don't know yet. First, I don't know where—Where will he present himself?
RFK:	I will try to work that out with you. Governor, he is under—
BARNETT:	The same procedures as we did the last time. Then we go to court again. There won't be any physical violence.
RFK:	But, Governor, he gets to the campus and wants to get in and from what I understood there would not be—
BARNETT:	I said he won't be blocked.
RFK:	What do you mean "blocked"? I think that's important. If there are people out there telling him not to pass and he has a U.S. Marshal with him, are they going to keep him out?
BARNETT:	It depends on what action he takes.
RFK:	Will they keep him out physically? That I think is terribly important.
BARNETT:	I don't think so. If he breaks through the line I don't know what will happen then. If he is confronted with a line.
RFK:	He is going through it.
BARNETT:	I won't tell you what is going to happen. He is going to have to listen to what we have to say.
RFK:	I understand he has a court order permitting him to register.
BARNETT:	We have an injunction saying he can't register. Mississippi ought to be recognized like any other courts.
RFK:	We recognize them.
BARNETT:	I don't believe you do. He has been enjoined from entering Ole Miss.
RFK:	What do you do if there is a federal court considering all these things? Do you consider you are a part of the Union?
BARNETT:	I consider the Mississippi courts as high as any other court

*and a lot more capable—ten times more capable—and
a lot more integrity and honesty than any federal courts
except maybe for the district court here in Mississippi—
just to be frank with you.*

RFK: *This discussion won't get us very far. Mr. Meredith arrives
and you are going to have police keep him physically
from going in—is that the plan?*

BARNETT: *Well, I don't—hold the line just a minute. General, the
only reason why we may have police officers there is to
keep the peace. That's the reason for that.*

RFK: *I appreciate that.*

BARNETT: *We are hearing you have ordered an army here.*

RFK: *Oh, no, Governor. I wouldn't do that—I wouldn't do
it without telling you about it. I will be glad to tell you
when I do that. I had not planned to send any more than
the last time.*

BARNETT: *I don't see any need for sending lots of folks.*

RFK: *This fellow, Meredith, gets out of the automobile and he
walks up the steps. Is someone going to physically keep
him from going in?*

BARNETT: *If it brings on a breach of the peace.*

RFK: *That's what is going to be the problem. It is such a
major step for us.*

BARNETT: *Does the state have a right to say about Ole Miss or Tuttle
and that court and the federal court in New Orleans
have a right to control it or the state of Mississippi?
That's the issue and I won't test it out.*

RFK: *I think you have had the test and I think it is quite clear
in the United States that the federal courts have the last
say. You might not like it. . . . These matters have been
resolved many years ago in the course of our history. I
said last night that you are not only a citizen of the state
of Mississippi but also a citizen of the United States.
For you to send your police out after the federal court—*

BARNETT: *Our courts have acted too and our legislature have acted
too. I am going to obey the laws of Mississippi.*

RFK: *Are you going to obey the laws of the United States?*

BARNETT: *I have taken the oath of the state of Mississippi and I
can't violate—*

RFK: *Haven't you taken the oath of the United States?*

BARNETT: *Yes, sir, and that is what we're trying to preserve and it's
being whittled away.*

RFK: *The courts have acted on it, Governor.*

BARNETT: *Yes, they are whittling it away piecemeal by piecemeal.*

RFK: *What about the Constitution?*

BARNETT: *The Constitution is the law of the land, but not what
some court says.*

RFK: *Governor, I think we have to try to resolve this point be-*

tween us. As Mr. Meredith arrives you are going to have police or others who are—

BARNETT: To . . . the people, that's all.

RFK: They are going to keep him out of there?

BARNETT: I will say they're only for the purpose of—

RFK: Have they received instructions not to allow him to come on the campus?

BARNETT: Well, I think so.

RFK: I will have to reconsider how many people we send in. I suppose then I will have to send more people in to get him on the campus? As I say, I thought this was resolved. Do you want to fight a pitched battle?

BARNETT: That's what it's going to boil down to—whether Mississippi can run its institutions or the federal government is going to run things. Why don't you bring him on and if we tell him no let him go back to court on this thing. You don't want any violence.

RFK: I don't understand, Governor. Where do you think this is going to take your own state?

BARNETT: A lot of states haven't had the guts to take a stand. We are going to fight this thing.

RFK: Are you going to fight it?

BARNETT: All the way as long as any courts will hear us. That's the trouble now.

RFK: What about Georgia?

BARNETT: They are weak-kneed.

RFK: In Georgia, Governor?

BARNETT: A lot of them are. This is like a dictatorship. Forcing him physically into Ole Miss. General, that might bring on a lot of trouble. You don't want to do that. You don't want to physically force him in.

RFK: You don't want to physically keep him out?

BARNETT: No, we don't want to use force. We will ask him to stay out. We will ask him very quietly to stay out and not enter it.

RFK: That will be in violation of the federal law.

BARNETT: If he enters, it will be in violation of the Mississippi laws. I have taken an oath to uphold the laws of this state. We have a statute taken a few days ago to have anyone barred from entering the institution of higher learning who has a criminal charge against him. We believe in high-class people going to higher schools, not people who commit perjury in courts. He admitted that. Do you want us who are honorable and upright, who are free from commiting crimes—

RFK: I think the problem is that the federal courts have acted and when there is a conflict between your state and the federal courts under arrangements made some years ago—

BARNETT: *The institution is supported by the taxpayers of this state and controlled solely by the Trustees.*

RFK: *Governor, you are a part of the United States.*

BARNETT: *We have been a part of the United States, but I don't know whether we are or not.*

RFK: *Are you getting out of the Union?*

BARNETT: *It looks like we're being kicked around—like we don't belong to it. General, this thing is serious.*

RFK: *It's serious here.*

BARNETT: *Must it be over one little boy—backed by Communist front—backed by the NAACP, which is a Communist front?*

RFK: *I don't think it is.*

BARNETT: *We know it is down here.*

RFK: *Governor, can I get back in touch with you and let you—*

BARNETT: *I will appreciate it. I will be right here. I am going to treat you with every courtesy, but I won't agree to let that boy to get to Ole Miss. I will never agree to that. I would rather spend the rest of my life in a penitentiary than do that.*

RFK: *I have a responsibility to enforce the laws of the United States.*

BARNETT: *I appreciate that. You have a responsibility. Why don't you let the NAACP run their own affairs and quit cooperating with that crowd? We would appreciate that a lot.*

RFK: *Governor, I am only in it because there is an order of the court. I believe in the federal courts, in the Constitution of the United States, I believe in the Union. That is why I took an oath of office and I intend to fulfill it. The orders of the court are going to be upheld. As I told you, you are a citizen not only of the state of Mississippi but also of the United States. Could I give you a ring?*

BARNETT: *You do that. At Fl 3–4938 or Fl 3–1585 or if both lines are busy, just call the Governor's office. You are going to let me know when and where he is going to appear. Do that before—*

RFK: *I will try to do that within the next half hour.*

BARNETT: *Good to hear from you.*

ROBERT KENNEDY AND GOVERNOR ROSS BARNETT, 3:25 P.M.

RFK: *Hello.*

BARNETT: *General, how are you?*

RFK: *Fine, Governor. Well now this Mr. Meredith will be leaving from New Orleans in another—I suppose within the next half hour or so.*

BARNETT: *All right.*

RFK: *What time do you have?*

BARNETT: *We have one twenty-five.*

RFK: *And he'll be coming to Jackson. I assume it takes about an hour.*

BARNETT: *That's right.*

RFK: *He should be there about two-thirty.*

BARNETT: *All right.*

RFK: *I will have an automobile to meet him there in Jackson—*

BARNETT: *You will have an automobile to meet him in Jackson at the airport. All right.*

RFK: *My present plan is that he will go to the U.S. attorney's office and then we will make our plans from there as to how he is going to go and what action we are going to take and—*

BARNETT: *He's going to the Federal Building? He's going to try to register there?*

RFK: *He's going to go there first.*

BARNETT: *You don't know where he is going to register.*

RFK: *I am not sure. I am going to work it out.*

BARNETT: *The court order orders him to register here.*

RFK: *I will study that and I will be in touch with you afterwards.*

BARNETT: *All right. Thanks.*

RFK: *There will be no interference and he will be protected there?*

BARNETT: *There will be no violence at all.*

RFK: *And no interference with him?*

BARNETT: *No physical violence, no. We never have had any violence here, you know. We are exercising every degree of diligence to prevent violence. We don't anticipate any. We certainly don't want it.*

RFK: *You and I will talk about it a little later.*

BARNETT: *I want to know where he is going.*

RFK: *We will talk after he gets there to the building.*

BARNETT: *All right.*

BURKE MARSHALL'S SUMMARY OF ADDITIONAL TELEPHONE CONVERSATIONS

Between the Attorney General's conversation with the Governor at 12:20 P.M., and the conversation at 3:25 P.M., I discussed this matter with the attorneys for the Board of Trustees, particularly Charles Clark. We agreed that Ellis would come to the Federal Building to register Meredith. At the time of the Attorney General's conversation at 3:25 with the Governor, that was the understanding.

Following the telephone conversation at 3:25, I was informed by Mr. Clark that Ellis was physically prevented from leaving the State House to go to the Federal Building. Mr. Clark said that Mr. Ellis was under subpoena to a legislative investigating committee, and that they would use police if necessary to prevent him from leaving the room where he was to be questioned.

I called Mr. Tubb, the president of the Board of Trustees. Mr. Tubb repeated what Mr. Clark had said. Mr. Tubb said that when they arrived at Jackson the Governor and his people had completely taken over the offices of the Board of Trustees.

Mr. Clark also told me that his clients intended to stick to the letter of the court's order, and that if Meredith did not appear to be registered by 2:00 P.M. Jackson time, he would have to appear to be registered during regular office hours at Oxford at some time in the future.

Following these conversations, I called Judge Tuttle. By order of the court the time during which the Registrar was required to be available to Meredith on that afternoon was extended. We then decided that Meredith should go to the State House to see what happened. . . .

Robert Kennedy's and Burke Marshall's charismatic ability to attract the elite men from the elite schools to a Department previously famous for its recruitment problems should not be underrated. And the Kennedy free-lancers were close to the vanguard of enlightened liberal thought. But fast as the Kennedy men moved, the civil rights movement moved faster. The Kennedys cannot be blamed for not anticipating what few if any white liberals anticipated as the future of the civil rights movement, the future of integration. Neither should they automatically be credited with any particular vision. Aside from the fact that anything after the Eisenhower era of bland consolidation would have been an improvement in the eyes of the civil rights movement, history itself dictated at least *some* of the direction of the movement.

In a way, the theory of federalism served merely to codify the preexisting assumptions of the top corporation lawyers and Ivy League professors who had recently joined the Department. Their vision was bounded on the left by the demands of Walter Reuther, Joseph Rauh, the Civil Rights Leadership Conference (NAACP Executive Secretary Roy Wilkins, *et al.*), the U.S. Civil Rights Commission—in other words by that group whom the Kennedys privately and contemptuously labeled knee-jerk liberals. There was no feeling that men like Bob Moses, the idealistic young civil rights worker who put his life on the line in grass-roots civil rights activities, Howard Zinn, the militant and radical historian, or even organizations like SNCC spoke for the future or even an important point of it. The furthest from the mainstream that the Kennedy imagination ventured was Martin Luther King, whom they couldn't very well ignore and to whom it would have been wise to keep lines open, in any event. Even James Farmer and his militant colleagues at CORE were not taken seriously.

The Kennedy pragmatists thought that *they* were the intellectual vanguard of the civil rights movement. The left-most saw themselves doing battle—on issues like the interpretation of the Fourteenth Amendment's equal-protection clause or on what constitutes "state action"—with less enlightened followers of the dicta of Justice Felix Frankfurter, who had a different view of the meaning of the Constitution and the role of the courts in the polity. But they didn't take the "knee-jerk" liberals seriously—those who were against all wiretapping (even Robert Kennedy's "responsible" bill of 1962), were anti-anti-Communists, soft on Chester Bowles, soft on Cuba, tough on J. Edgar Hoover (for all the wrong reasons) and in favor of doing whatever the NAACP or CORE or the early SNCC or Martin Luther King or the ADA asked them to do. And they didn't seriously *consider* that there might be brewing a cadre of *responsible* militants whose assumptions went beyond and challenged the "unrealistic" and "naïve" programs of the knee-jerk liberals as tokenism, irrelevant, inadequate. They were the leadership class, and whatever their rhetorical commitment to change and equality, they had been trained to accept the cultural norms which the Ivy League existed to perpetuate.

They assumed, like good Ivy League gentlemen, that they were dealing with the paradigmatic "reasonable man" who parades through the case books at the nation's better law schools; that white Southern law enforcers, like themselves, were decent human beings, men who didn't break their words, who didn't lie, who weren't rude—an attitude that Charles W. Morgan, Jr., the white liberal Alabama lawyer-in-exile (he now practices in Atlanta, where he runs the ACLU's regional operation for the South), calls "the philosophy of sweet reason." Persuasion was their medium, coercion their court of last resort—a philosophy neither alien to the American way nor at odds with the Ivy League lawyer's training as problem-solver, generalist, evidence-sorter and advocate. This was a serviceable philosophy, perhaps, but not when one was dealing with a Governor Wallace, a Governor Barnett or a Mayor Arthur Haynes of Birmingham, who stated, "I hope that every drop of blood that's spilled he [Robert Kennedy] tastes in his mouth, and I hope he chokes on it," or men like Mississippi's then Lieutenant Governor John Patterson, who called the Attorney General "a jackass braying at the American eagle," or even the carefree students of Ole Miss with whom John Kennedy pleaded non-violence over nationwide television even as they were rioting and rock-throwing in protest over the integration of Ole Miss ("2-4-1-3, we hate Ken-ne-dy!").

They were corporation lawyers. Not in the sense that they were gray-flannel men trained to do their clients' bidding. To the contrary. Burke Marshall, for instance, who had taught a seminar (with Harris Wofford) at all-black Howard University Law School, had a *private* citizen's affinity for civil rights and belonged to the ACLU (he resigned membership on assuming office). It was private citizen Marshall who came up in the late Fifties with the idea for federal registrars which percolated up to then Attorney General Rogers, who converted the suggestion to the tamer one of federal referees. He had, after all, turned down the anti-trust job for the civil rights job. But when all is said, the predominant fact is that Burke Marshall and his colleagues, by breeding, by class, by education, by life style, *thought* like a corporation lawyer.

Such thought processes highlight caution, moderation, respect for precedent, patience in the face of protracted litigation, commitment to the system as is and painstaking attention to detail. On a case-by-case basis—especially in the voting-rights area—such qualities may be virtues. But in the larger scheme of things, they may have limited the government's vision of the possible at an otherwise opportune moment in history.

An example of the corporate-lawyer mentality in action is found in the voter registration cases, which required careful analysis of voter registration records (you had to initiate a "records demand" process to get them). As Marshall has recalled it: "For instance, Alabama requires, among other things, that its applicants fill out correctly an application and a twenty-one-question form of four pages. To analyze the form of each of the thousands of applicants accepted and rejected is a formidable but fruitful task. Thus, in the Montgomery, Alabama, case,* the government filed a largely factual brief of 293 pages and eight attachment volumes of documents depicting graphically, statistically and otherwise every item of the many forms of discrimination that characterized registration there in recent years. . . .

"The trial took a week and required the testimony of over 160 witnesses for the government and the defense. Preparation for that single case—wholly apart from the time consumed in the investigation before the case was brought—required us to assign one lawyer—with two law clerks and two secretaries—to analyze 36,000 voter registration applications over a period of three months. We needed four, some-

* U.S. v. Penton, Md. Ala., No. 1741-N.

times five, lawyers doing intensive preparatory work in the interviewing days in the field immediately before the trial. After the trial, three, and at times four, lawyers spent over two weeks preparing the appeals."

It was symbolic that in the 1963 debate over whether to base the Civil Rights Bill (of 1964) on the commerce clause or the Fourteenth Amendment, former anti-trust lawyer Burke Marshall argued forcefully for the commerce clause, while Robert Kennedy—increasingly sensitive to human (as distinguished from procedural) values—argued for the Fourteenth Amendment on the ground that the civil rights community saw the issue as a moral one and the Fourteenth Amendment a more appropriate instrument to make the point. Ultimately, the Department rested on both grounds, and the commerce clause had the advantage of getting the bill considered in the Commerce Committee rather than Senator Eastland's Judiciary Committee. Marshall recalls: "The Attorney General was right and I was wrong when he foresaw that the public would debate the 'morality' of relying on the commerce clause rather than the Fourteenth Amendment in the 1964 civil rights bill. I couldn't see that at all. The Fourteenth Amendment had the obvious problem—the Civil Rights Cases.* It seemed silly, even recognizing that times and courts change, to base a statute on an erroneous legal theory when you didn't have to." (The Ivy League mentality again.) "The day the Supreme Court decided the case [testing the law] I received a telegram from the Attorney General saying, 'I'm delighted to see that my view of the Constitution has prevailed.' "

They orchestrated philosophical arguments about the nature of federalism, libertarian arguments about the dangers of a national police force, practical arguments about not being able to guarantee the safety of all rights workers, Constitutional and legal arguments about whether the federal government had to wait "until something happens" before it could act, about whether if rights were "individual," remedies could be group remedies. They didn't mention that Ivy League gentlemen abhor confrontation almost as much as they fear violence, a fear not without foundation since violence begets violence. Yet this passion for and expertise at confrontation-avoidance, buttressed by the FBI's unavailability, is a clue to much of what happened at Justice from 1961 to 1964.

It is human nature to do what one is good at, to exploit one's

* Popularly known as the Civil Rights Cases, the first round of public-accommodation suits under the 1875 Civil Rights Act construed the Fourteenth Amendment to apply only to state action, and not to the actions of innkeepers, railroads or other private persons or organizations.

talents, give scope to one's expertise, and the Ivy League gentlemen were skilled in the art of negotiation—of grouping together opposing sides and reaching a compromise. They knew how to reach out-of-court settlements. "You have to know what you can give away and what you can keep," Nicholas Katzenbach once remarked in a nice insight into the realities of the negotiating process. "The secret is not to be stuck on words. Words are the best thing to give away. If anybody objects, you want to know why they object. The grounds of the objection are often much narrower than the provision itself. If you know why, you can draft around it." Burke Marshall was a genius at getting adversaries to translate lofty slogans into five- or six-point demands which could be mediated, arbitrated, negotiated. They "understood" that litigation can be—always is—a protracted, complex process, and they were more than willing to put up with procedural delay, postponement, appeals and appeals from appeals so long as it seemed like an alternative to violence, to force, to coercion, so long as it looked as if the system was capable of problem-solving.

There was, therefore, a preference bordering on the obsessional against the introduction of troops into the civil rights context. Beyond the logical, tactical and historical arguments against troop use, except in extreme cases, armed force was the antithesis of Ivy League gentility and counter to the corporate-law style. Troops were the visible admission that reason, negotiation, good will, concession, *compromise* (where necessary) don't work. They were "the last resort." "Bobby had almost a thing about troops," recalls Katzenbach. He and his people regarded it as a victory when they avoided troop use, as in the freedom-rider crisis, even though buses were burned, heads cracked, tires slashed, marshals called out and Constitutional rights postponed; and they regarded it as a defeat where they used troops, as in the Meredith case, even though they achieved the stated objective— providing black James Meredith admission to all-white Ole Miss.

The federalism argument against troops was, of course, that these were not matters of national responsibility. Also as a practical matter, the federal government did not have the resources and so (a) it would endanger the youngsters, and (b) you couldn't get the troops out, and (c) in the long run you needed a local solution. Looking at the civil rights demonstrations that occurred during a week such as that from June 7 through June 13, 1963, one is impressed with the argument, although it does not take into account the possibility of selective protection—the likelihood that especially a man of Burke Marshall's precise judgment could be relied on to use troops judiciously. Here is a Justice Department report of the demonstrations for that seven-day period:

June 14, 1963
Demonstrations for period June 7 through 13

ALABAMA, *Gadsden*	300 demonstrators marched here on 6/12/63 protesting arrest of woman demonstrator.
CALIFORNIA, *Los Angeles*	On 6/7/63 CORE picketed the Beverly Hilton Hotel.
WASHINGTON, D.C.	On 6/14/63 demonstrations at White House, District building and Justice Department.
FLORIDA, *Bradenton*	Beach closed 6/8/63 after demonstrations and whites milling around.
FLORIDA, *Sarasota*	Negroes picketed downtown theaters on 6/7/63.
FLORIDA, *Tallahassee*	Negroes picketed theaters. Demonstrating for the last two weeks, 6/12/63. Demonstration at State Office Building cafeteria on 6/7/63.
GEORGIA, *Atlanta*	Demonstrations at cafeteria Saturday, 6/8/63. Fights started. 100 persons gathered to watch.
GEORGIA, *Savannah*	About 300 Negroes on 6/13/63 marched with placards into downtown area demanding for immediate desegregation. Shots fired at Negro home, no one was hit. Arrests in last 10 days passed the 500 mark. 3,000 demonstrated on 6/12/63.
MARYLAND, *Cambridge*	More than 300 shouting white persons demonstrated. Both Negroes and whites marched, 6/13/63. Mayor has asked Governor Tawes to declare martial law, 6/14/63.
MARYLAND, *Ocean City*	On 6/9/63 members of CORE conducted sit-in here. Re: restaurants.
MISSISSIPPI, *Jackson*	Demonstrations continue after shooting of Medgar Evers. Police arrested 90 persons on 6/13/63.
MISSOURI, *St. Louis*	30 Negro parents blocked transportation, demonstrations re: schools. 6/7/63.
NEW JERSEY, *Rahway*	Some 700 prisoners at the Rahway, N.J., prison farm reported on sick call in what officials declared was a demonstration stemming from racial tensions. 6/10/63.
NEW YORK, *New York*	Biracial demonstrators protesting al-

leged job discrimination fought with police 6/13/63 at the construction of Harlem Hospital.

NORTH CAROLINA, Greensboro	More than 1,000 Negroes demonstrated Friday night 6/7/63, conducted a street "sit-in." Demanded desegregation.
NORTH CAROLINA, Lexington	Mayor declared state of emergency Friday 6/7/63 as 500 whites battled about 50 Negroes who have been demonstrating.
OHIO, Columbus	Demonstrations at State Legislature for fair housing bill on 6/13/63.
RHODE ISLAND, Providence	250 Negroes and whites jammed House galleries 6/13/63 demonstrating for fair housing bill.
SOUTH CAROLINA, Beaufort	100 Negro demonstrators were arrested while attempting to get service at restaurant. More than 300 have been arrested in week-long drive. 6/10/63.
SOUTH CAROLINA, Charleston	Thirty-three Negroes were arrested on 6/13/63 for trespassing after seeking services at a hotel and drugstore lunch counter.
TENNESSEE, Nashville	Police arrested 12 demonstrators at grocery store, demonstrating for jobs. 6/7/63.
TEXAS, Texarkana	200 demonstrated against desegregation of Texarkana Junior College, paraded into downtown district. No arrests.
VIRGINIA, Danville	More than 250 Negro demonstrators jammed into the Municipal Building steps 6/13/63 and requested some to hear desegregation demands. Demonstrations occurred for past two weeks.

What it came down to was that the Justice Department under Robert Kennedy was in a war and it was the policy of his field general not to use troops. Harold Reis, First Assistant in the Office of Legal Counsel, recalls, "People like Burke and me were very concerned about the complex legal and political problems implied in the use of federal force. Section 333 *applies* to Mississippi, so we could have written an executive order permitting an occupation of Mississippi for five years. But as a practical matter it was impossible. As a policy matter it was undesirable. Suppose the FBI or marshals and state law officers started arresting each other. That creates more than a legal problem."

Katzenbach observes, "It's all very well to move troops in, but once there, how do you get them out?" The lack of options was the Ivy League lawyer's nightmare.

There was no ambiguity on the troop-use point. Alabama-born Lou Oberdorfer, the Assistant Attorney General in tax matters who double-timed as civil rights trouble-shooter, reflected in 1968: "When I was growing up, which is after World War One, federal troops were a dirty word. My grandfathers were confederate soldiers. My wife's father had been a prisoner and he had to eat rats. It's a hell of a thing to impose soldiers on a people. That's axiomatic. And there's always the danger of setting a precedent for some less civilized President to use in a tyrannical way. Civilian authority ought to avoid the use of troops like the plague. Look what the National Guard did in Newark and Detroit. Look at Czechoslovakia. It's an insult to the people." Had two years passed, he might have added Jackson State and Kent State.

Gentlemen live by the rules, the system, the law. Yet despite the high rhetorical priority given to procedural regularity when it came to confrontation-avoidance, the proprieties could be fudged. When Robert Kennedy told Lou Oberdorfer to move the deputy marshals to Oxford, Mississippi, in the Meredith case and "with no notice at all, just changed all the rules," Oberdorfer obeyed without second thought. This was precisely the kind of non-bureaucratic response that characterized the Kennedy entourage, who were programmed for responsiveness.

Says Oberdorfer: "I thought back about why I was so responsive to that. No argument at all. He wanted it done and we would do it. This wasn't a military relationship; this isn't a military organization. I have often thought that the relationships that he establishes in situations like that are—as I say, he gets people around him to play over their heads. I just knew that if I did all right, that would be fine, but that if it had been a disaster in some way or if my responsibility in it had not come off . . . I never had the feeling that somebody was going to point the finger at me and say, 'You messed it up.' I just know that if it went wrong, the Attorney General or the President would take the responsibility and not try to alibi it on to me.

"With these fellows behind you, you didn't have to worry about your back. That's important."

September 25, 1962. *Continued conversations.*
ROBERT KENNEDY AND GOVERNOR ROSS BARNETT, 6:10 P.M.

RFK: *Governor?*
BARNETT: *How are you, General?*

RFK: *Fine, Governor. Mr. Meredith is at the U.S. Attorney's office in—*

BARNETT: *In Jackson—*

RFK: *And I understand that there is a big crowd around the State House, where he is going to come and register. I wonder if you could arrange for some room for him—*

BARNETT: *We will have a room.*

RFK: *Can you clear the crowds so we don't make a big circus?*

BARNETT: *You would have a big space. They're not going to bother him.*

RFK: *It will make it difficult. We just want to make sure the way is clear.*

BARNETT: *Just make sure the way is clear.*

RFK: *What entrance is he going to come in?*

BARNETT: *He can come in—I would say the north side—well, it's the east side—*

RFK: *The east side?*

BARNETT: *Of the building.*

RFK: *What room number is this?*

BARNETT: *It's on the tenth floor.*

RFK: *Do you have a lot of people standing there right now?*

BARNETT: *Not so many.*

RFK: *Are you going to try to clear that—how many people do you have there?*

BARNETT: *Oh, I don't know. I can see about fifteen or eighteen right now. They're high-class people.*

RFK: *You will have that under control?*

BARNETT: *Oh, absolutely.*

RFK: *What room number?*

BARNETT: *He comes to the front office of the Board of Trustees of the Institute of Higher Learning and he won't be bothered. They are not going to try to hurt him.*

RFK: *You have got the registrar there?*

BARNETT: *It's room 1007. Oh, yes, he's here.*

RFK: *He'll come to the east entrance.*

BARNETT: *Immediately across the street from the new capitol.*

RFK: *Is it clear there?*

BARNETT: *Oh, yes.*

RFK: *Will you tell them he's on his way?*

BARNETT: *Oh, yes.*

RFK: *Will you have an elevator—*

BARNETT: *There will be an elevator—that will be clear for him. General, that's the last thing we want is violence.*

RFK: *I hope this is all conducted with the dignity of the United States and the Governor of Mississippi.*

BARNETT: *It will be.*

RFK: *They'll be over.*

BARNETT: *Thank you, General.*

ROBERT KENNEDY AND GOVERNOR ROSS BARNETT, 7:25 P.M.

RFK: *Hello.*

BARNETT: *All right.*

RFK: *Everything all right down there?*

BARNETT: *Why, certainly. Nobody even made any overt acts whatsoever. Just as smooth—they did a lot of cheering and booing.*

RFK: *Who were they cheering?*

BARNETT: *They were cheering our side and booing Meredith. Nobody tried to fight him.*

RFK: *And he didn't get registered.*

BARNETT: *No, I read the proclamation similar to the one I read the other day. I told Meredith and the others, the marshals, that when I took the oath of office as Governor I swore that I would uphold the laws of the state of Mississippi and our own constitution and the Constitution of the United States; that I was going to keep faith what I told the people I would do, and a few words to that effect. Nobody was discourteous and certainly none of our crowd was discourteous as far as I was able to learn.*

RFK: *He is going to show up at classes tomorrow.*

BARNETT: *At Ole Miss? How can you do that without registering?*

RFK: *If there is any problem—I don't think they will raise any problem about it. He made his effort to register—but he is going to show up for classes. I think they arranged it.*

BARNETT: *The chancellor arranged classes for him?*

RFK: *I don't know who—so he is going to show up and go to class then.*

BARNETT: *Tomorrow morning? And not make any effort to register?*

RFK: *I suppose if something else comes up but I think they will accept him. It is all understood.*

BARNETT: *I don't see how they can. They're going to give him special treatment? They can't do that, General.*

RFK: *He is going to go to classes. He is going to be there.*

BARNETT: *Well, I don't know what will happen now. I don't know what we'll do. I didn't dream of a thing like that. I appreciate your telling me that. Is he going up to Oxford tonight?*

RFK: *No. I am trying to find out whether he went back to New Orleans or to Memphis. But he will come in tomorrow morning.*

BARNETT: *All right, General. I am glad we didn't have any violence, you know. That always looks bad. There was no bloodshed today—tomorrow or any other day I can't guarantee it. I can't stay up at Ole Miss.*

RFK: *We will send someone to protect him.*

BARNETT: *I don't think—*

RFK: *You can't control bloodshed, why do you do it?*

BARNETT: *I said this. I don't anticipate any trouble but I say tomorrow I can't stay there all day and every day—*

RFK: *I don't think you have to do that. Just keep somebody up
there to keep him safe.*

BARNETT: *I will try to. I will encourage them not to have any violence, I sure will. I'll do it every time I talk to them.*

RFK: *That will be fine. He will show up there—*

BARNETT: *If you knew the feeling of about 99½ percent of the
people in this thing you would have this boy withdraw and
go somewhere else. I am sure though you don't appreciate,
you don't understand the situation down here. Why don't
you look into this? I would be glad to send a committee
to talk to you about it.*

RFK: *How about while the committee is here letting him get in
that university? Let's try it for six months and see how it
goes.*

BARNETT: *We can't do that—let him come in for six months. It's
best for him not to go to Ole Miss. It's so much better
for him.*

RFK: *But he likes Ole Miss.*

BARNETT: *I don't believe you know the background of all this. We
know pretty well what's going on. I think he's being paid
by some left-wing organization to do all this. He has two
great big Cadillacs, no income, riding around here. Who
is giving him all this money? You see, General, the
NAACP, I told you this morning, no doubt in my mind,
it's a front organization for the Communists and they
would do anything about bringing about hatred among
the races. We never have trouble with our people, but
the NAACP, they want to stir up trouble down here. I
wish you could talk to them about the South. Get them
to let us alone down here. We will be so grateful. We
don't want a lot of trouble.*

RFK: *I understand that, Governor. He will be there sometime
early tomorrow morning and you and I will keep in touch
with each other.*

BARNETT: *You call me any time and I will appreciate it. If I hear
anything you should know I will give you a ring. Thank
you very much now.*

ROBERT KENNEDY AND GOVERNOR ROSS BARNETT, 7:35 P.M.

RFK: *. . . Governor, this isn't a question of the boy going to
the University of Mississippi. It's the federal government.
If you were here as Attorney General you would have to
do the same thing. I never knew the name up until a week
ago and have no interest. Hell, it's my job and my responsibility and I took an oath to uphold the laws of the
United States and I have the responsibility to see the laws*

are upheld. I would not be here if I were not prepared to do that. Governor, I feel if you were here in my position that you would do the same damn thing. You have lots of judges on that court from Southern states and they were all unanimous, they were not weak-kneed. This is not a bunch of Northerners telling you this. They are all Southerners. I am just making sure the laws of the United States are being maintained. I can't understand that you cannot understand this principle. You and I don't want to get into an argument about that.

BARNETT: *We would argue all night about that. You can never convince me that the white and the Negro should go together.*

RFK: *That doesn't have anything to do with you or me.*

BARNETT: *One of the questions here is moral turpitude.*

RFK: *Are you against him because he is a Negro?*

BARNETT: *Oh, no—*

RFK: *Would you let another Negro into the University of Mississippi?*

BARNETT: *It depends on a lot of things—qualifications—I would have to uphold the laws.*

RFK: *What you said a little earlier—that you never could see the two races going to school together—this has nothing to do with moral turpitude. You just don't want a Negro going to the University of Mississippi.*

BARNETT: *If a white boy should be convicted of a crime he would never get to the university—he would not be eligible.*

RFK: *You can't tell me this was stirred up because he was convicted of a crime—it's because he's a Negro.*

BARNETT: *That's one of the reasons—*

RFK: *That's one of the reasons. We're talking man to man. That's the reason—you don't want a Negro going to the University. The problem is it has nothing to do with my personal feelings—this is the law. Wouldn't you be enforcing the law if you were here?*

BARNETT: *Not the laws you're trying to enforce. That's not the law. I think you owe it to the American people to tell the Supreme Court that the Brown vs. Topeka decision is not the law of the land.*

RFK: *What do we do about the judges of the circuit court—are they crazy?*

BARNETT: *I didn't say they were crazy.*

RFK: *Are they wrong?*

BARNETT: *. . . Oliver Wendell Holmes, Justice Cardozo, White . . .*

RFK: *Are you going to decide what decision—*

BARNETT: *When they don't follow the Constitution—it's so plain and unmistakable—and I consider the law of the land instead.*

RFK: *Can every citizen do that?*

BARNETT: *If enough people in America would do that the—will put
             their head to the ground and find out how people do that.*
RFK: *This is a circuit court in your own area. Judges from Geor-
             gia, Alabama and Texas. But anyway, Governor, they will
             be down there at ten o'clock.*
BARNETT: *Ten o'clock will be all right. I appreciate your telling me
             what time.*
RFK: *If they enter that airport they will arrive between nine-
             thirty and a quarter of ten.*
BARNETT: *You are not anticipating any violence?*
RFK: *I am not anticipating any violence.*
BARNETT: *No, sir, we don't want any violence on that campus.*
RFK: *So he will be there between nine-thirty and a quarter of
             ten. All right?*
BARNETT: *With the same people?*
RFK: *Yes.*
BARNETT: *Thank you, General. Come by to see us.*

Kennedy had adopted a cautious but aesthetically appealing strategy:
litigate the vote. Once blacks achieved political power, everything else
would follow, went the theory—school and restaurant doors would
swing open, jobs would pay better, Negroes would move from second-
class to first-class citizenship. By May 1963 the Kennedys had filed
thirty-seven voter registration suits under the 1957 and 1960 acts,
eleven in Mississippi and the rest in Georgia, Louisiana, Alabama and
Tennessee. They looked good in comparison with the Eisenhower
Administration, which had filed only six suits altogether. As a Southern
Regional Council field report at the time said: "The Justice Department is a magic phrase and in the deep South holds an unbelievable
position of confidence, presently, in the minds of the oppressed. . . ."

Yet ironically, as Burke Marshall got his on-the-job training and as
Robert Kennedy got his on-the-job involvement, as their commitment
to equal justice grew more personal, more profound, more real and
tangible, at the same time they found themselves so busy handling
day-to-day problems and month-to-month crises (like the admission of
Meredith to Ole Miss, the demonstrations at Birmingham, the integration of the University of Alabama over Wallace's doorway obstruction, the random bombings) that they virtually forgot about the grand
strategy and spent most of the time trying to cool it, to mediate,
negotiate, arbitrate. Whenever there was a choice, the Justice Department gave peace priority. ". . . The Civil Rights Division advises it
will see what it can do to prevent demonstrations," Oberdorfer wrote
in one of his weekly civil rights reports to the Attorney General. At the
time of the freedom rides, Reverend William Coffin admitted that

"People in high places in the Attorney General's office did ask us—most circumspectly—to reconsider our decision to make the trip." Even the proposed new civil rights legislation of July 1963 was designed to cool down trouble as much as to correct injustice. "The Administration's Civil Rights Bill (S. 1731)," Robert Kennedy wrote to Robert Knight of the Treasury Department for use in preparing a memo for members of a newly organized Business Council, "is designed to alleviate some of the principal causes of the serious and unsettling racial unrest now prevailing in many of the states. . . ."

What happened was that the itinerant problem-solvers of Robert Kennedy's Justice Department ended up sacrificing civil rights in favor of civic tranquility. As John Nolan, who single-handedly prevented a riot in Gadsden, Alabama, put it, "We weren't trying to solve the civil rights problems of the United States of America. We were just trying to keep people from getting hurt. We wanted to prevent bloodshed. They were lid-keeping operations."

But the cost of Justice's success as peace-keeper and cooler-downer was the preservation of the status quo for millions of Negroes and the progressive alienation of the civil rights movement. Although the movement was the Department's ally in the fight against Southern segregation, to the extent that Justice was willing to sacrifice present rights for present peace it was the strategy opponent of its policy ally. The strategy of the movement, after all, was to instigate confrontations, while the tactic of the Department was to avoid them. "Our philosophy was simple," recalls James Farmer, at the time National Director of CORE. "We put on pressure and create a crisis and then they react. I am absolutely certain that the ICC order wouldn't have been issued were it not for the freedom rides. I base my view, among other things, on the fact that the Morgan decision and the Boynton decision had been on the books for a long time but they were never enforced.* The issue had to be made." Justice was in the violence-prevention business at a time when, as Watters and Cleghorn have written, "the national conscience reacted not to injustice but to Bull Connors' cattle prods."

The mediatory posture of the Department where present peace was in conflict with ultimate justice was clear from the time of the freedom rides when it will be recalled the Attorney General called for "a cooling-off period" on both sides.

* *Morgan* v. *Virginia*, decided in 1946, held that states had no power to impose segregation affecting interstate passengers.

Boynton v. *Virginia*, decided in 1960, held that interstate bus terminals and facilities came within the desegregation policy stemming from the Interstate Commerce Act.

Ultimately, of course, the Department took the creative and unprecedented step of petitioning the ICC to do via administrative proceedings what the riders had tried to achieve through symbolic demonstration. But at the time a story by James Clayton in the Washington *Post* accurately reflected the message the Department put out. Incidentally, one might observe that while "You didn't have to swear undying fealty," as one reporter put it, Kennedy and Guthman favored a select band of reporters from elite publications whose sympathy, talent and responsibility they had come to trust. Clayton, along with men like Anthony Lewis of *The New York Times*, Peter Maas of the *Saturday Evening Post*, Joseph Kraft and a few others had unprecedented access. Thus Clayton's story must be read more as a release than a revelation:

> The overriding interest of the Attorney General has been to end violence and to assure that law and order is maintained. . . .
> Up to the moment that the marshals went south . . . no freedom riders other than the original group had appeared. Then, with police protection assured, there was an outburst of them.
> That did not sit well with the Justice Department. "It took a lot of guts for the first group to go," one man said, "but not much for the others." Those making the trip from Montgomery to Jackson on Thursday were the safest people in America, the Department thought.
> Throughout the week, Kennedy has tried to make two things clear to Negro leaders. One is that he agrees with their basic goal—full realization of their constitutional rights. The other is that the federal government will not help a movement which results in violence.
> Once violence begins to appear, Kennedy has taken the position that he only has one job—to maintain law and order. He does not feel that the Department of Justice can, at these times, side with one group or the other in disputes over constitutional rights.
> That was the reason Kennedy urged the freedom riders to put up bond in Jackson, Miss., after they were arrested. They had a court case; they could strike down segregation through legal means; their presence in jail did not help their legal fight but instead made good propaganda for America's enemies.[4]

The impulse was always honorable and a great leap forward over the passivity of the Eisenhower–Nixon Administration which had preceded it: to try to bring the leaders of both sides together and work out differences by mutual give and take. Legal action always came only after informal attempts at reconciliation. Attorney General Kennedy told Michael Dorman, author of *We Shall Overcome*:

> The reason we do it is that civil rights is a sensitive area and there is a good deal of misunderstanding, mistrust and ill-feeling. We would

not take legal steps until we had local officials to try to work out a solution to their racial problems. We have never brought suit without going to the local people, explaining our responsibility and giving them time to work something out. If we find a situation is going to get out of hand, we know a lot of Southern mayors and city and state officials, and we communicate with them. If we feel that the timing of protest demonstrations is bad, we communicate that to Negro leaders. We have communications with groups across the South. Frequently we're the only ones available who'll talk to both sides.[5]

It wasn't a case of peace at any price. But it was peace at various prices. In 1961 it was as cheap as the telegram Kennedy sent Albany, Georgia, police chief Pritchett congratulating him on keeping the peace (which he did by the simple expedient of jailing the non-law-breaking demonstrators). In 1962 it was as inexpensive as the $172 fine paid by "a mysterious stranger" who bailed Martin Luther King and the Reverend Ralph Abernathy out of a Georgia jail against their will (they were prepared to remain behind bars by way of symbolic and provocative protest). "It's the first time I've ever been railroaded out of jail," commented Abernathy. In 1963 it was as expensive as the FHA housing project Kennedy was reported to have promised the restless blacks of Cambridge, Maryland, in exchange for the promise of no more demonstrations after eight months of trouble in a community where 29 percent of the Negroes were unemployed.

And sometimes Justice got somebody else to pay the price. In the spring of 1961, in the aftermath of the freedom rides, Justice (represented by Burke Marshall) attended a series of meetings sponsored by the Taconic Foundation sounding out CORE, SNCC, SCLC, NAACP and others on whether they would be willing to cooperate on a voter registration project in place of the direct-action activities. This tied right in with Justice's over-all civil rights strategy and assumption: Litigate to enfranchise the Negro and all else will follow. If, and only if, all civil rights groups agreed to work together, the Taconic Foundation promised significant financial support. SNCC and others thought Justice's bargain was federal protection for civil rights workers in exchange for a shift from direct-action protest to a voter registration drive.

The point was that (a) nobody told SNCC & Co. "Sure, you fellows go out there and we'll give you all the protection you need"; but (b) Burke Marshall, representing the Department of Justice, the Attorney General and President's brother (and by implication the President himself) gave his implicit blessing to the activity and ultimately Taconic came across with $339,000.

Another time the Administration secured private support for its confrontation-avoidance activities in Birmingham during Bull Connor's reign of terror of 1963 when the arrest of Martin Luther King was followed by five weeks of protest marches, cattle prods, police dogs, water hoses and national headlines, at the end of which 3,000 people (one third children) had been arrested for everything from parading without a permit to disorderly conduct, trespass, loitering and resisting arrest.

Ronald Goldfarb, a former Criminal Division attorney, has reported in his book on the bail system, *Ransom*, that the one Negro bondsman in town—the only one who would bail them out—ran out of the necessary collateral to post bonds with 840 demonstrators still in jail. "It soon became apparent," writes Goldfarb, "that the organized Negro community would not be satisfied until all demonstrators were let out of jail. The negotiators called Attorney General Kennedy and asked what he could do. Kennedy called Walter Reuther, who in turn sought the advice of Joseph Rauh . . . and the following plan was proposed: The AFL-CIO, the United Steelworkers Union, the Auto Workers Union and the Industrial Union Department of the AFL-CIO each raised $40,000. . . ." The $160,000 was wired to Birmingham the next morning, and that night the 840 demonstrators were out on bail on bonds totaling over a quarter of a million dollars.

Here was a case where the Justice Department achieved peace by purchasing liberty. The Voter Education Project was a case where the Department thought it fostered tranquillity by encouraging the under-writing of voter registration. But the thrust of the Department's role was that of a peace-keeper, an arbitrator, a mediator, a compromiser, a free-lance pragmatist—in the crunch, a quieter-downer. And as Charles Black, Jr., of the Yale law faculty remarked to a *New York Times* executive at the time of the freedom rides: "With respect, I think the mistake the *Times* has made is the sort of thinking that must be abandoned if we as a people are—and I speak literally—to be saved. I refer to the idea that hope is to be found in the mere extrapolation of the gently sloping curve of 'progress' discernible in the past fifty years. I urge you strongly that it is too late to think about doing a little bit more each decade."

Wednesday, September 26, 1962. *McShane, Doar and Meredith flew to Oxford, where they were joined by a large force of unarmed marshals. At the university, Lieutenant Governor Paul Johnson, subbing for Governor Barnett and backed by eighty-two sheriffs, refused to let Meredith in even when former prize fighter McShane clenched his fists and tried to push his way through.*

Thursday, September 27, 1962. *Burke Marshall, Tom Watkins, Governor Barnett and Robert Kennedy have an extended round of conversations about what kind of show of force is appropriate at Meredith's next attempt. Meredith and Company were seventy miles on the road to Oxford when Attorney General Kennedy, based on his conversations with the Governor, ordered the car turned around and postponed the showdown.*

ROBERT KENNEDY AND GOVERNOR ROSS BARNETT, *September 27, 1962,* 2:50 P.M.

RFK: *Hello.*
BARNETT: *Hello, General, how are you?*
RFK: *Fine, Governor, how are you?*
BARNETT: *I need a little sleep.*
RFK: *I just talked to Mr. Watkins and we were going to make this effort at five o'clock this afternoon your time.*
BARNETT: *They will be here about five o'clock our time?*
RFK: *Is that satisfactory?*
BARNETT: *Yes, sir. That's all right.*
RFK: *I will send the marshals that I have available up there in Memphis and I expect there will be about twenty-five or thirty of them and they will come with Mr. Meredith and they will arrive wherever the gate is and I will have the head marshal pull a gun and I will have the rest of them have their hands on their guns and their holsters. And then as I understand it he will go through and get in and you will make sure that law and order is preserved and that no harm will be done to Mr. McShane and Mr. Meredith.*
BARNETT: *Oh, yes.*
RFK: *And then I think you will see that's accomplished?*
BARNETT: *Yes.—[Inaudible] Hold just a minute, will you? Hello, General, I was under the impression that they were all going to pull their guns. This could be very embarrassing. We got a big crowd here and if one pulls his gun and we all turn it would be very embarrassing. Isn't it possible to have them all pull their guns?*
RFK: *I hate to have them all draw their guns, as I think it could create harsh feelings. Isn't it sufficient if I have one man draw his gun and the others keep their hands on their holsters?*
BARNETT: *They must all draw their guns. Then they should point their guns at us and then we could step aside. This could be very embarrassing down here for us. It is necessary.*
RFK: *If they all pull their guns is that all?*
BARNETT: *[Inaudible] I will have them put their sticks down before that happens. [Inaudible] There will be no shooting.*
RFK: *There will be no problem?*
BARNETT: *[Inaudible] Everyone pull your guns and point them and we will stand aside and you will go right through.*

RFK: *You will make sure not the marshals but the state police will preserve law and order?*

BARNETT: *There won't be any violence.*

RFK: *Then we can get the other people out as soon as possible.*

BARNETT: *One second. General, we expect them all to draw their guns. Lieutenant Governor Johnson is sitting here with me [inaudible]. Will you talk to him?*

JOHNSON: *General—*

RFK: *How are you?*

JOHNSON: *It is absolutely necessary that they all draw their guns. There won't be any shooting.*

RFK: *Can you speak a little louder?*

JOHNSON: *We are telling them to lay their clubs aside and to leave their guns in their automobiles. But it is necessary to have all your people draw their guns, not just one. [Inaudible] . . . and anyone who shoots at all to leave. We appreciate what they have done so far and go back home and that there would be no shooting under any circumstances.*

RFK: *The one problem—when we come down there representing the federal government and draw guns it's going to disturb your people, understandably—*

JOHNSON: *As much as it would bother them if they just drew one gun and three hundred and fifty highway patrolmen—*

RFK: *If they all draw their guns and they go into the university, thereafter, law and order will be preserved by your people?*

JOHNSON: *We are going to attempt to preserve it.*

RFK: *They won't leave, will they? What I want to be sure is that it won't be left up to our people.*

JOHNSON: *We can possibly leave many people up here today. We will do that.*

RFK: *As I understand from Mr. Watkins and from the Governor, law and order will be preserved by the local people. I don't anticipate a great problem but I don't want an angry crowd descending on Oxford this evening. You'll be sure?*

JOHNSON: *Yes.*

RFK: *I don't care how you do it just as long as you take that responsibility.*

JOHNSON: *[Inaudible]—all be on this campus.*

RFK: *So I've got assurances from the Governor that no harm will come to Mr. Meredith and the marshals.*

JOHNSON: *Not as far as we're concerned.*

RFK: *We will do anything to preserve law and order.*

JOHNSON: *We will do everything to preserve law and order at all times.*

RFK: *As long as I have the Governor's assurance and yours.*

JOHNSON: *To the best of our ability. I believe that we have sufficient men to take care of it.*

RFK: *Let me talk to the Governor again.*

ROBERT KENNEDY AND GOVERNOR ROSS BARNETT, SEPTEMBER 27, 1962, 3:50 P.M.

BARNETT: *General, I felt like I ought to call you back. What we talked about, General, it is something that I think this thing ought to wait until you send him back here. Why can't you wait until Saturday morning? Here's the thing about it. We want the people to subside a little bit.*

RFK: *I think the problem for you, Governor, you will have that court case tomorrow and that's why your lawyers wanted it done today.*

BARNETT: *Can't you pass that case for a while?*

RFK: *They won't do that. You can't do that now.*

BARNETT: *I think this case ought to be put off. I am honest with you.*

RFK: *I will call them back and we won't do it.*

BARNETT: *We better postpone this thing and some of the others will be in touch with you about this thing. Let's not have any misunderstanding. We can't afford to have that. At five o'clock it's getting pretty dark down here.*

RFK: *I think you are making a mistake on it. I think the problem on Saturday is going to be much more difficult. I think it is going to be much more difficult and your situation before the courts will be more difficult. I think it is a great advantage to do it today as your lawyers—*

BARNETT: *The people probably will find it out.*

RFK: *There's not going to be any mention of it from here.*

BARNETT: *Certainly not here. Our conversations weren't taken down here.*

RFK: *You never had anything that's come out of this office and I never said I talked to you and I have never made one statement about you or anything to do with Mississippi, so I think—*

BARNETT: *One man said, "You will all compromise in this thing?"*

RFK: *You are not compromising—you are standing right up there. Your lawyers advised you on this—your lawyer and everybody else in order to remedy the situation for yourself and get through this case in the best possible fashion. Tomorrow by the time the case starts the situation changes completely. We're not going to make any statement on this. I am happy it gets resolved.*

BARNETT: *—one man said to me, "You compromising this thing?"*

RFK: *Governor, we're coming in at five o'clock and sending twenty-five marshals bringing their guns and, third, I am asking you whether you will take the responsibility for law and order. You said you would.*

BARNETT: *That's right. General, the Lieutenant Governor wants to speak to you.*

RFK: *Governor, as far as you're concerned, there is not going to be any statement out of here and for your own sake and the sake of your state, get it resolved today. I am happy to have all the marshals pull their guns and force their way in. It's better that way than troopers running around.*

BARNETT: *Of course, you and I are in agreement. They are going to point their guns—*

RFK: *I'm asking from you law and order to be preserved in Mississippi and you have no choice then.*

BARNETT: *The Lieutenant Governor wants to say something.*

JOHNSON: *General Kennedy, we are trying to be completely honest about this thing. We got a few intense citizens here, got a lot of men who are not directly under us who are involved to hold the fort such as sheriffs and deputies. We cannot assure anybody that those people or someone maybe hotheaded won't start shooting and didn't want to assure you of anything unless we knew it could be carried out.*

RFK: *If you are going to tell me now in contradiction what you told me a half hour ago that there won't be any shooting, I won't send in any marshals there that might be shot—*

JOHNSON: *That's what we are asking you for—time. We've got to have time in order to discreetly move these sheriffs out of here—*

RFK: *Lieutenant Governor, let me explain something to you. It's a quarter of two here, and your difficulty is that tomorrow you have got this court case and by then it's too late. If you and the Governor don't go to court they will issue a bench warrant and then they will have troopers arrest you and come in and also keep the university open and that situation will be worse. You've got a couple of hours to tell the sheriffs and others to go home and suddenly I will call at four o'clock your time and tell them he is coming in.*

JOHNSON: *I can't move these people out of there, General. Some won't leave.*

RFK: *Lieutenant Governor, it's completely up to you. If you say there might be shooting I will call it off.*

JOHNSON: *I am not telling you there will be any at all as far as we can control.*

RFK: *I can't take the chance.*

JOHNSON: *And we couldn't here. That's the reason why we called you. There are three hundred, four hundred or five hundred people and we can't shake these people in this length of time and get rid of people whom we don't have complete control over.*

RFK: *That's up to you. We will face it in court tomorrow.*

JOHNSON: *That's what I wanted to get over to you. We don't want anything to happen. We don't shoot Americans. We've got some hotheaded people in this state who are in this group and we've got to have sufficient time to move them.*

RFK: *You can't get this done today?*

JOHNSON: *No, certainly not.*

RFK: *May I speak to the Governor again?*

BARNETT: *General? Let me say this. One man had a gun and I said, "How many times does it shoot?" and he said, "Six times and if that doesn't get the job done I got a little one here for number seven." That's what we want to control. I am the last man in the world to want any trouble. We can't have it, you know. If half a dozen people got killed it would hurt me, you, the Lieutenant Governor, all of us. Why can't you do this—*

RFK: *I can't do that, Governor. I don't have any control over it—*

BARNETT: *I am talking about this afternoon. Pass it over for a few days. Let us know that these folks are cool-headed and no trouble. I will go all the way out. It might be, General, that they might make a statement to the press that you are going to have to use force and we could tell our men just walk back and do nothing. You need to think this thing out, General.*

RFK: *I was relying on what Mr. Watkins said and what others said but I think neither one of us want to do it unless there won't be any violence.*

BARNETT: *The Lieutenant Governor is thoroughly convinced we might be acting foolish here to do it this afternoon.*

RFK: *O.K., Governor. He won't come.*

BARNETT: *You have not broken your word to me. I told a lot of people—you have been kind. I have the legislature in session right now and it's rough on me. I'm driving 170 miles— it's rough. You think it best this Meredith matter—*

RFK: *I don't know. You're going to court tomorrow.*

BARNETT: *That's contempt against me. General, I am not committing wrongdoing here. I wish you'd tell them to pass for thirty days.*

RFK: *I can't do that now, Governor. They said I should have used force against you. They're mad at me and mad at you. I have seen in the papers that they think we should have answered the force you used. They are not very pleased with either one of us and are not going to compromise in my judgment. We're going to have a great problem tomorrow evening by this time and that's why I wanted to resolve it today.*

BARNETT: *Just a minute, General. You think this case is going out the window if this matter is not settled?*

RFK: *I talked to your lawyer about that. Went into it in some detail. I have no control over the court but I think it*

would be a major step forward if we could get Mr. Mere-
dith in the university before they hear that case tomorrow
morning.

BARNETT: *General, if they get me in jail I will have to sit up there. I*
hate to do that but I can do it.

RFK: *Sit up where?*

BARNETT: *Sit in jail. I'm trying to uphold the laws—*

RFK: *If you can get this fellow in the university this evening a*
lot of our problems would be resolved. Why does anyone
have to know this fellow is coming there until I should
call you—

BARNETT: *We have had several hundred men—*

RFK: *Can't he come in a gate and I call and say this conversa-*
tion has not taken place and he is coming through such
and such a gate?

BARNETT: *Yes—*

RFK: *Again there is a question of law enforcement but I would*
have to rely on you that law enforcement would be pre-
served. I can't do that with twenty-five men. I would have
to rely on you.

BARNETT: *General, this thing could be handled a lot better if we*
wait a few more days on the Meredith case. He is not
suffering. Just a few days until the case is settled.

RFK: *As your lawyer would tell you, they brought all these judges*
from all over the country. The whole circuit is coming to
hear the case. That's the difficulty.

BARNETT: *All nine judges.*

RFK: *They are there tonight in New Orleans. I can't tell them*
to go home. I have no control over this. This is the court.
They're mad at me but they're madder at you.

BARNETT: *Will they get an idea we compromised this thing? Will*
the judges think we settled this thing? They won't be
thinking we compromised this case?

RFK: *You mean—if he gets in, that's what they are primarily*
interested in.

BARNETT: *General, hold just a second here.*
General, I am sorry to have to keep you so long but we will
get busy here and do our dead-level best to keep people—
there are two or three I'm worried about and I'll see them
personally.

RFK: *I will have our people call . . . [Pause] Governor, how*
long would it take before you check with those people?

BARNETT: *About I would say forty minutes.*

RFK: *Call me then. I will hold these people from leaving. That*
will push it up to about five-thirty.

BARNETT: *That will be all right. I will call you right back in thirty*
or forty minutes.

RFK: *All right, Governor.*

ROBERT KENNEDY AND GOVERNOR ROSS BARNETT, SEPTEMBER 27, 1962, 4:20 P.M.

RFK: *Can I rely on you that there won't be any violence?*

BARNETT: *Yes, sir.*

RFK: *I am taking a helluva chance. I am relying on you.*

BARNETT: *There won't be any violence.*

RFK: *The Lieutenant Governor agrees on this too?*

BARNETT: *He agrees there won't be any violence. Of course we can't guarantee everything.*

RFK: *I understand that. Your people—*

BARNETT: *Our people are going to be law-abiding.*

RFK: *O.K., Governor. They will—*

BARNETT: *They will be there at five o'clock.*

RFK: *It will be a little later than that.*

BARNETT: *You understand we have had no agreement.*

RFK: *That's correct.*

BARNETT: *I am just telling you—everybody thinks we're compromising.*

RFK: *I am just telling you that we are arriving and we are arriving with force.*

ROBERT KENNEDY AND GOVERNOR ROSS BARNETT, SEPTEMBER 27, 1962, 5:35 P.M.

RFK: *The thing is we just received a report from the FBI regarding instructions to state police down there and that they have been told these marshals are coming and told that you want to preserve law and order and there is not to be any disorder, and that once this fellow gets into the university it is the responsibility of the marshals to preserve law and order. I didn't want a misunderstanding—*

BARNETT: *After he gets in you certainly don't expect us to guard him all the time.*

RFK: *I just want to make sure—*

BARNETT: *We will do our best, of course. The local law enforcement—*

RFK: *From our understanding and my agreement with you law and order would be preserved by the state of Mississippi.*

BARNETT: *You mean after he gets in—well, as far as we can.*

RFK: *I understand. I don't want to do anything but wanted to be sure—*

BARNETT: *You mean local authorities?*

RFK: *Whatever is necessary, Governor. Whatever is necessary to preserve law and order.*

BARNETT: *But, General, I declare I don't think I could agree to guarantee the man after he gets in. When he gets in he is one boy—*

RFK: *I had better call it off, Governor.*

BARNETT: *You want me to call the National Guard or anything like that?*

RFK: *I want to make sure law and order is preserved. From conversations with you the other times you said law and order would be preserved.*

BARNETT: *As far as it can.*

RFK: *That's all I ask.*

BARNETT: *As far as we can with reasonable diligence.*

RFK: *Governor, all I want from you is the same assurance that you will do what is necessary to preserve law and order.*

BARNETT: *General, wait a minute here. The Lieutenant Governor has an idea here.*

JOHNSON: *General, our local officers are here on the campus and in the county and in the city. They are the ones who would be responsible here.*

RFK: *My agreement and understanding, Lieutenant Governor, is with the Governor and you. I don't know them, and from the conversations with you, I have to look to you. I don't care what arrangements you make with the other people but I have to be sure order is preserved by the local officials or by whom I don't care. But I want to be sure with you.*

JOHNSON: *That is nothing we can afford to do. When I talked with you before I told you local law enforcement officials would be on hand to keep the peace if it goes out of hand. Then, of course, we would come in.*

RFK: *We had over a period of the last four or five days in conversations with the Governor, he always assured me law and order will be preserved. Can I have the same assurance?*

JOHNSON: *We do that everywhere in our state.*

RFK: *I don't say there's a problem. If you can give me your assurance I don't care how it's done.*

JOHNSON: *All right. We couldn't assure you that students will be friendly. You see what I mean.*

RFK: *I don't mind that, but I want to be sure someone will preserve law and order.*

JOHNSON: *We can't leave our officers here on the campus for the protection of the boy. The local officers will take over. If it looks like a riot or something of course our—will be immediately on the spot.*

RFK: *Are the local authorities willing to take that responsibility?*

JOHNSON: *Oh, yes.*

RFK: *That's all I want to make sure. I don't care who is doing it. All I want to do is to have assurances from you two gentlemen whose word I have confidence in and whose word I staked on—*

JOHNSON: *We are going to do the ultimate.*

BARNETT: *We'll give the same protection as anyone else.*

RFK: *This is a difficult situation and you understand you have to watch it more carefully. But you have given me now your word as an individual and as Governor of the state of Mississippi as far as humanly possible—not superhuman —that law and order will be preserved.*

BARNETT: *Yes, sir. This thing here—I don't propose to do anything out of the ordinary.*

RFK: *If it looks like you are going to have some difficulty there you are going to have to take some steps.*

BARNETT: *We always do that.*

RFK: *Governor, I don't know whether you are trying to tell me something without saying it. I am relying a good deal on your word and I don't want to be misled.*

BARNETT: *General, we will do what every reasonable and prudent official would do. Try to keep peace and order all over the state of Mississippi. . . .*

ROBERT KENNEDY AND GOVERNOR ROSS BARNETT, SEPTEMBER, 27, 1962, 6:35 P.M.

BARNETT: *General, I'm worried—I'm nervous, I tell you. You don't realize what's going on. There are several thousand people in here in cars, trucks. Several hundred are lined up on the streets where they are supposed to land. We don't know these people.*

RFK: *I had better send them back.*

BARNETT: *There is liable to be a hundred people killed here. It would ruin all of us. Please believe me. Talk to the Lieutenant Governor, he'll tell you.*

RFK: *I just have to hear from you, Governor.*

BARNETT: *There are dozens and dozens of trucks loaded with people. We can't control people like that. A lot of people are going to get killed. It would be embarrassing to me.*

RFK: *I don't know if it would be embarrassing—that would not be the feeling.*

BARNETT: *It would be bad all over the nation.*

RFK: *I'll send them back. . . .*

A good example of the Justice Department's role is found in the Greenwood, Mississippi, voter registration drive of 1963. Robert Moses and two fellow civil rights workers had almost been killed in February while conducting voter registration work in a county where only 250 Negroes (out of 13,547) were registered, as compared with 9,000 whites (out of 10,274). Things were so bad that the Justice Department did what they claimed in Albany, Georgia, in 1961 and 1962 they didn't have the power to do—they enjoined local interference with voter registration activities—only to agree, a few days later, not to press the suit if Greenwood authorities would agree to release from prison eight

Negro voter registration workers, who had become a rallying point contributing to community tension.

As crisis crowded crisis, one reason the Justice Department wanted to quiet down Greenwood was that Birmingham loomed on the horizon.

There had been lunch-counter sit-ins, followed by protest marches, followed by Easter Sunday kneel-ins. There had been court injunctions, police dogs, cattle prods and the arrest of Martin Luther King, Jr., and thousands of other forms of harassment. By the time Burke Marshall arrived, thousands of Negroes were in the streets (over half of them children). The hard-core whites were convinced it was all the work of King and "outside agitators." The Mayor, who was convinced that "Martin Luther King is a revolutionary," said that "The nigger King ought to be investigated by the Attorney General. This nigger has got the blessing of the White House."

Contemporary analysts identified the problem as communication. The whites, according to the theory, were so obsessed with the idea of "outside agitators" that they never listened to, or just forgot, the demonstrators' demands. Robert Kennedy patiently explained to a group of Alabama editors in a private, off-the-record White House meeting, called in the wake of the Birmingham crisis to get their cooperation in keeping things cool: "You have to understand this about Martin Luther King. If he loses his effort to keep the Negroes non-violent, the result could be disastrous not only in Birmingham but all over the country. Remember, it was King who went around the pool halls and door to door collecting knives, telling people to go home and to stay off the streets and to be non-violent. Compare that with Nashville, where they have pictures of a Negro chasing a white down the street carrying a knife. If King loses, worse leaders are going to take his place. Look at the black Muslims." [6]

Marshall arrived and his technique was appropriate. He talked and talked and talked and talked. He reminded the whites of the minimal demands of the blacks—the right to have a cup of coffee, the right to token jobs, amnesty for the demonstrators. He warned King against trying to provoke outside troops, arguing that the solution had to come from within. And he warned local business leaders that failure to arrive at a solution was, among other things, bad for business. David Vann, a white Birmingham lawyer, who had clerked for Justice Hugo Black, recalls that at a tense point in the negotiations "Burke took me in the kitchen—we were meeting in the home of John Drew [a leading black businessman]—and told me not to yield: King was happy with the terms, but Shuttlesworth wanted a more specific employment agreement. Burke said what we had wouldn't cause trouble. He was right, you know. I think Burke Marshall is one of the great public servants of this era. We were deeply influenced by him. You could trust him."

According to Joe Dolan, the situation in Birmingham turned around at a businessmen's luncheon where the head of something like one hundred trade associations got up and started baiting Marshall. "The real problem," he said, "is that the only way to solve this is for the President of the United States to come down to Alabama and take a little girl by the hand and he's afraid to do that. Isn't he afraid to do that? Isn't he? You tell me. Isn't that the real problem, Mr. Marshall?" It was all very tense. Nobody knew what Marshall would say. And then he said, "No, that's not the problem at all. The problem is for many years a substantial percentage of the people of this country have been deprived of their rights—rights they are entitled to under the Constitution and just as fellow human beings. That's the problem." Reason prevailed even though the Mayor subsequently denounced the negotiators as "a bunch of quisling, gutless traitors." "I don't know what would have happened if it hadn't been for Burke," says one who was on the scene. "King would have been killed and we would have had either a civil war or hundreds of thousands of troops down here. That could have happened."

Then, two days later, when two bombs exploded in the Negro section of Birmingham and brought 2,000 Negroes into the street, Reverend Fred Shuttlesworth, a key civil rights leader, convinced that the movement had been had, called a press conference to announce that the truce was off. But even as he was on his way to the podium, Joe Dolan grabbed him with his left arm (as he frantically dialed Washington with his right). "The Attorney General wants to speak with you," said Dolan and again a bloody and perhaps tragic confrontation was avoided.

Again, it is important to remember that while mediation and cooling down often placed peace over injustice, it also often achieved change for the better, and it often "worked"—at least in the government lawyers' own terms. No event is more symbolic of the way it worked than John Doar's famous stroll down the middle of North Capitol Street in Jackson, Mississippi, after Medgar Evers' funeral. The Negroes, after singing "We Shall Overcome," started chanting "We want the killer! We want the killer! We want equality! We want freedom! Freedom! Freedom! Freedom!" Out came the local police chief's bull horn, his police dogs and his patrol wagons. As pop bottles flew and TV cameras whirred, Claude Sitton of *The New York Times* was there to record John Doar's extraordinary feat. He "strode down the middle of the street, shifting slightly now and then to dodge bottles and brickbats. 'You're not going to win anything with bottles and bricks,' Mr. Doar called to the rioters. He could hardly be heard over the . . . crowd, which began to encircle him, the camera and crew and a reporter. 'Hold it!' shouted Mr. Doar. 'Is there someone here who can speak for you people?' A Negro youth emerged from amid the rioters and joined the federal official in the street. 'This man is right,' he said, pointing to Mr. Doar. The youth began berating hoodlums who had taken refuge behind a group of women and were throwing bottles into the street. 'My name is John Doar—D-O-A-R,' the official kept calling to the rioters. 'I'm from the Justice Department and anybody around here knows I stand for what is right.' Other Negroes began joining the effort to calm the mob. . . . Within a short time, the street was clear."

In keeping with its self-image, the characteristic intervention, especially at the outset, was one which minimized the likelihood of confrontation yet promoted progress. Hence the series of informal summer meetings in Dallas, Memphis, Chattanooga and New Orleans with local school boards in anticipation of fall desegregation. Hence the fulfillment of Atlanta, Georgia, Mayor William Hartsfield's request that Robert Kennedy's press secretary, Ed Guthman, urge national media not to disrupt prospectively quiet Atlanta desegregation with obtrusive cameras, reporters and general press overkill (Guthman called a meeting of network representatives, who agreed to cooperate). Hence Marshall's response in February 1961 when Howard B. Pickard of the Department of Agriculture's General Counsel's office called to ask if the Justice Department wanted to withhold Louisiana's $2,224,607 in school lunch program money for the year and $508,418 in school milk program money for the year, in view of the fact Louisiana, as part of its anti-desegregation program, was not passing on these funds to the Orleans Parish schools. Marshall said the Justice Department would rely on "the legal course of action presently sought through the civil contempt proceeding of compelling the payment of these funds to the Orleans Parish School Board, and that we did not wish, at present, to pursue the possible alternative of withholding funds from the entire state."

Hence the interminable long-distance telephone conversations with Southern officials. "Burke had it down to a science," recalls a frequent visitor to his office. "He'd get on the phone and begin by saying, 'Now, Governor, we just can't have those boys killed. . . .' " An actual transcript of the Marshall side of one such conversation with the Attorney General of Mississippi is typical of the genre:

There is something going to occur tomorrow that I didn't know whether or not you knew about it—but someone should know about it. It might raise some sort of law enforcement problems. The federal government doesn't have any responsibility for this, so I wanted to be sure you knew about it.

There is a Negro woman running for Congress in the Second District. . . . I am informed that her supporters, tomorrow, have planned . . . I guess she is going to be there—there will be a sort of political picnic rally to be held at the Recreation Center at Sardis Lake. . . . Now that lake is one that was created by a flood control project by the Corps of Engineers, so it is federal land, and that is why they told us about the picnic. We have no jurisdiction over it, however. It is operated under license to the state of Mississippi, so it is under state control. I am informed, but I don't know the accuracy of this, that in the past these facilities have been segregated and that Willows Cover is an area used only by whites. . . . Our view of course is that they have a right to be there. But that is not why I called you. The reason I called is that I was thinking back to Biloxi a few years ago. Someone in the state having to do with law enforcement should know about this, so I just wanted to tell you . . .

Well, that is, General, you and I may disagree over what they should do, but I think the responsibility and jurisdiction for law enforcement in the area is clear. I should also make this clear—and I have discussed this with the Corps of Engineers, and this is their position. You know the Wilmington Parking Lot case, decided in the Supreme Court in the spring of 1961 that the Constitution requires that these places be operated on an open basis—that is, without racial segregation. . . .

So despite the fact that White and Marshall and others felt, as a matter of principle, that Justice didn't belong in the role of mediator, that law enforcement was enough of a job, they took it on because, as Bill Geoghegan says, "There was nobody else in the Administration who was prepared to do it."

The sequence of preferences was clear: persuasion, negotiation, pressure, maneuver, litigation, court orders, enforcement of court orders via marshals and, only in extreme extremis, troops. The self-image was clear. Even as some civil rights groups felt at the outset "that we were partners with the Administration," Justice felt a kinship with the civil rights movement, especially its "responsible" element—the NAACP, the Urban League, the AFL-CIO, the Leadership Conference, etc.

Hence the hundreds of quiet interventions that nobody outside the Department (and the principals) was aware of, but that anticipated and "resolved" crises.

"You have made it possible for the federal government's interest to be expressed without irritating or provoking anyone and I believe that you have caused the school board in particular to realize the absolute necessity of proceeding in good faith with some token action," wrote a leading citizen of Mobile, Alabama, to Ramsey Clark in August 1963 after he returned from the South to his job as head of the Lands Division. Actually, Clark's 1963 Mobile meeting was an outgrowth of a 1962 Huntsville meeting led by Marshall. A memo to the Attorney General reveals that Marshall met with the president of the local bank, a local businessman and director of the bank, the owner of a large grocery business, the editor of a local paper and the superintendent of city schools. It is worth quoting the memo because it reveals Justice's "reasonable" approach and limited goals:

> The first four are collectively responsible for a realistic and sensible approach to the racial problems in Huntsville. The city has desegregated its golf course and lunch counters of the chain stores. They are committed to the hiring of Negro policemen. . . . They all recognize that a start has to be made by the Huntsville schools. They are all of the opinion that it cannot be done this September. The time is too short and they are all of the opinion that Governor Patterson would interfere in a massive way, even to the use of the National Guard as in Little Rock. They are all willing personally to make a commitment for a start of desegregation in the fall of 1963. I told them that we were interested more in having a start than in what specific steps were taken. We discussed the attitude of George Wallace. I pointed to his campaign. I expressed doubt that he would permit desegregation in Huntsville on a voluntary basis, although a court order would give him a retreat, as in the cases of Vandiver in Georgia, Davis in Louisiana, Almond in Virginia. They recognize this point. . . .
>
> Accordingly my guess is that we will have to file suit in Huntsville, if any step is to be taken even in the fall of 1963. It is also my guess that we could not get a court order effective before that.
>
> They also said it would be easier if other cities went at the same time. They pointed out that the Governor would be less apt to try closing schools if schools in more than one city were involved. They suggested Mobile . . . and Montgomery. I think we should consider two suits in Alabama.
>
> On the facts the Huntsville suit is a good one . . . [partly because of the military feature].

Never has there been more energetic, improvisatory short-run activity on behalf of the civil rights policies of the enlightened majority. In the long run, however, by serving as defuser, by giving an inadequate system the *appearance* of effective activity, their efforts may have been counter-productive.

Friday, September 28, 1962. The Governor failed to appear in court and was found guilty of contempt of the temporary restraining order.

He was ordered committed to the custody of the Attorney General and fined $10,000 a day unless by October 2 he had shown the court he was complying with the order. The same penalty was leveled against Lieutenant Governor Johnson. The Attorney General advised the Governor to come out for law and order and agreed not to use Negro Marshals.

ROBERT KENNEDY AND GOVERNOR ROSS BARNETT, 1:35 P.M.

BARNETT: *General, how are you?*

RFK: *Fine, Governor, how are you?*

BARNETT: *A little tired and sleepy. General, you have been very nice to let us know the dates in coming, you know, and the time, and we want you to know that we appreciate that very much, and the Lieutenant Governor appreciates it and the others. Now, we hate to just keep our force just day and night not knowing what might happen. I wonder if we could keep that good relation going? In other words, should we know if you are going to send him back? Will you—*

RFK: *Governor, it was so unsuccessful with you yesterday. I just want to find out what's going to happen. It seems to me just notifying you stirs up rather than helps the situation.*

BARNETT: *Here's the thing about it. When I talked to you yesterday I didn't dream there was so many people there. Some of them are pretty rough and rugged, you know. Honestly, I looked that crowd over and saw them growling and carrying on and after I went back and told you that it just wouldn't do to go. The Lieutenant Governor reported the same conclusion that it would be a tragedy.*

RFK: *Could I make a suggestion to see if we could work something out? What if you make a statement coming out for law and order, that you put the situation in Oxford in the hands of the state police and whatever the colonel's name is whom I understand is a fine officer—give him the responsibility of law and order and see, because of the near disorder yesterday, that no more than three or five people could get together. Send the sheriffs and assistant sheriffs back to their places and leave it in the hands of the colonel to have the responsibility for law and order. I think if something like that was done and you made it clear to the students—it doesn't have a thing to do with Meredith— you made it clear to the state and students not to get together in any one place and your state police will have the responsibility for law and order, then you would have the situation in such control that at an appropriate time we could then work out when this fellow could come in.*

BARNETT: *General, it wouldn't amount to a hill of beans. Those people down there would not pay a bit of attention. They*

> *wouldn't listen to that. I got up and told the student body, we all have a good name for peace and order in Mississippi. I said, let's be able to control our physical faculties and mental faculties and the people in the nation will admire you. It didn't amount to a row of beans. When they make up their minds about something they got to have a cooling-off period.*

RFK: What about making arrangements informally for the head of the state police and officers to talk to us about the problem down there? Would you want to send them up here?

BARNETT: I will have a committee—we might do that. I will get together with them tomorrow morning and see. General, you might not be familiar with this. Mississippi has a law that will pay this boy's school, his expenses—I wouldn't want to be quoted on this—but we have quite a number of colored people who are going to school in other colleges, preparing themselves for doctors and lawyers.

RFK: Governor, he is going to the University of Mississippi.

BARNETT: It looks to me, General, like such a foolish thing for him to keep his mind on that.

RFK: I think the courts have decided that.

BARNETT: If he decided to go somewhere else, wouldn't they agree to it?

RFK: They have already given their orders and it will be carried out. I would much rather have you have the responsibility for law and order. If you can't do it—

BARNETT: I couldn't have kept order yesterday.

RFK: If you applied yourself and gave proper authority to the local people like they have been able to do in other states, you could maintain law and order. If you can't maintain it in your state, obviously it would have to be taken by us.

BARNETT: General, do you know about this man's army record?

RFK: Yes. There's no purpose running through that again. Would you consider sending somebody up here and giving me a ring?

BARNETT: I will get a committee—

RFK: Professional people who know about law enforcement.

BARNETT: Oh, yes, I'll do that. I will talk to Birdsong and—

RFK: And then maybe talk to your lawyers.

BARNETT: Our lawyers, and will get in touch with you. I can't get together with them today since the lawyers are all in New Orleans now.

RFK: Where are you now?

BARNETT: I'm in Jackson—at the Governor's Mansion. It's Fleetwood 3–1811.

RFK: O.K. Have a good rest now.

BARNETT: I haven't had much sleep here lately. I'm just resting for an hour or so.

RFK: O.K., Governor.

BARNETT: *Can I tell these marshals not to be worrying me every
           minute about bringing more on until you and I agree on
           something?*

RFK: *I don't know what the court is going to do. I think every-
           body ought to do what is proper. They might tell us to go
           in right away. I think everybody better do what they think
           is proper.*

BARNETT: *Not today.*

RFK: *I haven't heard from down there. O.K., Governor.*

BARNETT: *Thanks a lot, General.*

ROBERT KENNEDY AND GOVERNOR ROSS BARNETT, 4:00 P.M.

BARNETT: *General, how are you?*

RFK: *How are you, Governor?*

BARNETT: *I am fine, fine. General, you cooperated wonderfully as I
           said to you before in letting us know the time and place
           in order to keep down riots, turmoil and strife. General,
           you are going to have to let us know something about
           when you are going to send the man up there. If you don't,
           anything can happen.*

RFK: *Governor, I just talked to Mr. Watkins, your attorney in
           New Orleans, and I talked to him about the whole matter,
           so why don't you talk to him and if you want to call me
           back and see if that's satisfactory, I will be here. If you
           want to talk to me again.*

BARNETT: *All right, all right. Just one second. I will call him and
           after I talk to him—just a second—General, let me give
           you my opinion. You send troops, marshals, don't send
           Negro marshals. They won't do.*

RFK: *I won't do that. You will—*

BARNETT: *It just wouldn't do to send Negroes.*

RFK: *I don't think there are Negro marshals in the ones we send.
           In any case, why don't you call—*

BARNETT: *Tom Watkins—*

RFK: *And if you have a problem—*

BARNETT: *Is he in the courtroom or do you know?*

RFK: *I am not sure—he's not in the courtroom. I am sure he
           will get in touch with you. Until he talks to you, then
           you can get in touch with me if there's a problem.*

BARNETT: *Until I have had a conversation with him. All right.
           Thank you a lot.*

RFK: *Call me if there is a problem.*

If exhibitions of anti-Negro violence, especially those recorded by
television cameras, rather than proclamations of injustice moved the
American people to outrage and *their representatives to action*—then
the Justice Department was more than the *strategic* opponent of its
policy ally, the civil rights movement. It was, objectively, a foot-dragger

in the effort to win the Negro equal justice.

This judgment is not to question Robert Kennedy's or Burke Marshall's or John Doar's or Nicholas Katzenbach's motives. Probably no higher-minded men ever inhabited their respective positions. But they were, in a way, fixers. Top-echelon fixers. Brilliant fixers. Humanitarian fixers. Compassionate and progressive fixers. Fixers not by trade or choice but by circumstance. Fixers nonetheless. Nor need this be an invidious label, but it is intended to suggest that expertise at behind-the-scenes manipulation may be a dubious talent when institutionalized, for no matter how pure the motives of the manipulators, the first priority ceases to be the cause (in this case Negro rights) and tends to become—as in the case of the FBI—the maintenance of the manipulative apparatus, of itself, of organization.

And when Administrations start playing such games and seeing themselves as directors, as puppeteers, as orchestrators of history, history itself may suffer. Or they trivialize their talent and waste energies. The Kennedy whiz kids were no exception. The March on Washington was a case in point.

A glorious occasion, 200,000 Negroes—the first mass demonstration of its kind—to pressure the nation's capital for Negro rights. And the Administration ended up lobbying to edit the speech of young John Lewis, a passionate and dedicated civil rights worker and then the head of SNCC, who had come to D.C. to speak from the heart. Lewis went along to a degree—at the urging primarily of A. Philip Randolph (who was urged by Walter Reuther, who was urged by Robert Kennedy). But what was gained by that? What would have been lost had Lewis spoken his mind? Indeed, might the future of SNCC been different had not hundreds of such decisions been tainted by governmental intervention?

After first opposing the March on Washington in the summer of 1963, the Kennedys accepted it when it became obvious that the march was going to take place. The committed and activist SNCC leader Lewis, arrested twenty-two times, agreed to drop from his speech the question "I want to know, which side is the federal government on?" Murray Kempton reported Malcolm X's observation that "Kennedy should win the Academy Award for direction." Kempton shrewdly observed:

> The White House knew that the ordinary Negro cherished the Kennedy brothers and that the larger the assemblage the better disposed it would be not to embarrass them. When [John Kennedy] finally mentioned the march in public, he issued something as close as possible to a social invitation. . . .

If the march was important, it was because it represented an acceptance of the Negro revolt as part of the American myth, and so an acceptance of the revolutionaries into the American establishment. That acceptance, of course, carries the hope that the Negro revolt will stop where it is. Yet that acceptance is also the most powerful incentive and assurance that the revolt will continue.[7]

Yet it was brilliantly managed. And it was Robert alone among the Kennedys who was urging the Administration to join the Negro march rather than oppose it or stand aside. And that night when it was over, Robert Kennedy, with grace, care and an administrator's sure instinct, called John Douglas—who, along with Bayard Rustin, coordinator of the march, shares historic credit for the orderliness and smoothness and joy of that day—to ask for a list of those who should be personally thanked. Mr. Douglas had not thought to have one at the ready. And so a few minutes later he returned the call and imparted the roster of honor. Within the hour, the Attorney General was on the phone to twenty-five, including the local police chief, to express his personal appreciation "for the fine job I hear you did."

Take James Meredith's courageous and successful one-man integration of Ole Miss. It demonstrated some of the strengths and weaknesses, tensions and opportunities of the Ivy League gentleman's approach.

First, it should be noted that it was not the federal government's idea to integrate Ole Miss. Despite the arguments by men like William Taylor (in *The George Washington Law Review*) that the government had the power to institute desegregation suits even in the absence of affirmative federal legislation, the government took the position—consistent with its theory of federalism—that it did not have such power. So the issue arose only because one stubborn black man decided to make it an issue. Typically, Meredith involved the NAACP Legal Defense Fund, Inc. (known in legal circles as "the Inc Fund"), which convinced the government to come in as *amicus curiae* ("friend of the court").

From the moment it became obvious that the university, the state, and the Governor of Mississippi were going to gang up to prevent *one* young Negro from entering their hallowed institution, Robert Kennedy had but one goal: to integrate Ole Miss, but to do it by court order, by arrangement, by negotiation, by telephone, by trade-off, by a testimonial from Ole Miss alumnus and pro-football hero Chuck Connerly (who refused to go along with Kennedy)—by anything other than force.

Before it was over, JFK sent 23,000 federal troops into Mississippi,

500 of whom were needed to protect Meredith while there, at a cost estimated to be $4,919,800. As far as the country at large—not to mention the underdeveloped countries of the world—was concerned, the Administration had "won": Ole Miss was integrated. But the integration of Ole Miss had, to their credit, never been an issue for Kennedy, Marshall & Co. They *assumed* it would end up integrated. The only question was *how*. And so *their* effort over the protracted period of negotiations was to integrate Ole Miss peacefully. By their own standard, they failed.

The Kennedys, buttressed by the Ivy League sensibilities of their advisers, were hardly alone in their reluctance to use force to obtain rights. One needs to go back no further for an example than to the preceding Administration of Dwight Eisenhower, who told a press conference well *before* Little Rock that "I can't imagine any set of circumstances that would ever induce me to send federal troops into any area to enforce the orders of a federal court, because I believe that the common sense of America will never require it."

Nor is it suggested that Kennedy was "wrong" in his strategy, although a strong argument could be made that Jack Greenberg of "the Inc Fund" was right in his analysis: "The issue was whether or not to assume that Mississippi was a sonofabitch and march in and bowl them over, or to negotiate. Barnett was out of his cotton-pickin' mind. Justice wanted room to maneuver and asked us to go slow. Since they had the army and we didn't, we acquiesced. We wanted Meredith to register on the first available day. Justice didn't. They were negotiating with Barnett. We wanted Meredith to register in Oxford like everybody else. They wanted him to register in Jackson. We wanted troops and they wanted to do it with a handful of marshals. We wanted a confrontation and a showdown. They wanted to avoid a confrontation."

Regardless of whose strategy was "right," the Kennedy pattern was consistent with the style of the elite, establishment lawyers who ran the Justice Department. Contrary to the white South's image of Bobby as "Little Brother," "Raoul" or "Bobby the Ruthless," he was cautious to the point of timidity when it came to risking any kind of confrontation with an escalation potential. Ramsey Clark cited another instance of Kennedy's caution, undoubtedly justified, to author Richard Harris when he compared the Justice Department's restrained response to the Ole Miss situation in 1963 with what happened in February 1968 when the Negro students at South Carolina State College in Orangeburg demonstrated for three days against a segregated bowling alley, and state troopers, panicking, fired into the crowd, killing three boys and wounding twenty-seven others. Said Clark:

The maximum number of students present . . . was four hundred.
. . . Well, there were fifty state and local police and two companies of the National Guard standing not more than two hundred yards away. If the kids were breaking the law, why weren't they arrested? Surely there was enough armed force there to [round] up the whole bunch and lock them up without firing a shot. Compare the situation to the one at the University of Mississippi when James Meredith enrolled there as the first Negro student. Our force was made up largely of U.S. marshals. They were mostly old men, they were inexperienced in law enforcement techniques, they were in alien surroundings at night, they were confronted by a huge howling mob that had already killed three people and was spraying bullets all over the place, and they were scared out of their wits. They called the Department and asked if they could fire back when fired on, and Bob Kennedy said no. Then they called back a little later and asked if they could at least take their pistols out of their holsters as a show of force, and Bob said no. Well, these men didn't fire a single shot. If they had, there would have been a real blood bath, because the other side was just spoiling for a fight. Scores of people would have been killed, and nobody down there would have forgotten it.[8]

While Burke Marshall coordinated the integration of Ole Miss from Washington, Nicholas Katzenbach, the Deputy Attorney General, was dispatched to Mississippi to run operations on the firing line. Katzenbach, who excelled at projecting confrontation-avoidance scenarios, once recalled that "One of the most pleasing moments of my life was an argument at the White House. I advised against the advice of Bob McNamara, Robert Kennedy, Theodore Sorensen, Buz Wheeler and Burke [who doesn't remember the scene], 'Don't send troops into Birmingham [at the height of tension].' And he didn't and my advice was 'right' because there was no riot. If there had been a riot, I'd have been 'wrong.' I felt the movement of troops would be provocative, that sending them in would be more likely to cause a riot than prevent it. John Kennedy said, 'I think Nick is right about this.' It was a difficult decision. It looks right now but you can never be sure it was the right one."

In Walter Lord's authoritative account of the integration of Ole Miss, he reports on the marathon Kennedy–Barnett negotiations and the simultaneous movement and massing of FAA planes, FCC monitoring cars, nine navy buses and others from the Bureau of Prisons (none from the FBI), five border-patrol transports and a convoy of forty-nine trucks and jeeps from Fort Campbell, Kentucky. It was the day Meredith moved in. Lord, who had access to the files, reports:

At 10:00 a heavy-hearted Nick Katzenbach called the White House; he was afraid they'd have to have troops. Technically, of course, the actual decision was the President's, but it was really not that clear-cut. They had been working toward this step for an hour; now they simply agreed together that the time had come. For Katzenbach believing almost till the end that he would do the job without troops . . . it was a moment of the bitterest disappointment.

Till the end, nobody wanted to admit that Barnett was not going to keep order. Norbert Schlei, of the Office of Legal Counsel, recalls, "I was drafting the Executive Order and proclamation that the President would have to sign in order to call out the troops, and about seven o'clock Burke Marshall came in and said, 'We've got a deal with Barnett, you can forget about that and go home because he's going to let Meredith register.' But somehow I had listened to some of these telephone conversations, and I just didn't believe that any deal was going to stick. So I kept my secretary there and I finished the documents. I got home maybe ten-thirty or eleven o'clock.

"I made myself a drink and got maybe halfway through it, and Burke Marshall called up and said, 'The deal is off. The President wants to sign those documents. Go on down and see him.'"

Bill Geoghegan, on the other hand, a Harvard-educated Kennedy campaigner whose sister had roomed with Jean Kennedy at Manhattanville and who served as an assistant in the Deputy's office where he was on the margins of the inner circle, has a different notion: "I'm sure that Bob Kennedy and the President and Burke Marshall wanted to do everything possible to avoid sending troops into the South. This was how we concocted this idea of getting a force of our own. Looking back, I think it was a mistake on our part.

"I think we were over-reacting to what occurred in Little Rock during the Eisenhower Administration. I think we felt that President Eisenhower had made a great political mistake and one which seriously hindered the advancement of the integration effort by sending troops into the South. I think subsequently it turned out that the Southerners reacted more favorably to troops than they did to marshals because the marshals were identified with, as they like to call us, the federal government. I don't think it made a whole lot of difference really; we thought it made a great deal of difference whether we had men in uniform there or men not in uniform. In my own opinion I think we'd have been better off if we had just used troops every time we had a problem."

The differences were tactical. And the rhetoric had to do with federal-state relations. But in the integration of Ole Miss, as in the freedom rides which came before and the crisis at Birmingham and the integration of the University of Alabama which came after, the constant goal of the Justice Department was to keep the lid on.

Saturday, September 29, and Sunday, September 30, 1962. On Saturday, President Kennedy and Governor Barnett agreed that Barnett and Lieutenant Governor Johnson would go to Oxford, while Meredith slipped into Jackson to register. Later in the day, after the football game in Jackson, Governor Barnett called off the agreement, and at last the President did what civil rights groups had been calling for all along. He federalized the National Guard.

By this time Barnett had promised the people of his state, "We will not surrender to the evil and illegal forces of tyranny." He had ordered jail for federal officials who arrested law-defying state officials. At the Saturday football game he had announced, "I love Mississippi" to thunderous applause and as one student remarked, "It was like a Nazi rally." [9] *And of course Governor Barnett was celebrated by the local press, whose editorial position was summed up in the Fayette* Chronicle *as: "Any yellow-livered appeasers . . . get out of Mississippi." "The courageous stand of Governor Barnett has electrified the nation," said the Clarion* Ledger. *"Thousands stand ready to Fight for Mississippi," wrote the Jackson* Daily News.

On Sunday, September 30, the Attorney General and the Governor got on the telephone again. What follows is taken from an affidavit prepared by Burke Marshall in connection with Governor Barnett's contempt case but not filed, at the President's request, because it could encourage divisiveness at a time when national unity seemed required by the Cuban missile crisis.

Governor Barnett called Attorney General Kennedy at approximately 12:45 P.M., Washington time. He stated that he and Mr. Watkins were there by themselves. He suggested that we should postpone the admission of Mr. Meredith to the university as a student. The Attorney General replied that we could not.

The Governor then stated that we should have enough troops to preserve law and order. He said he would do everything in his power to preserve peace. He then said that he would have about 175 or 180 patrolmen come unarmed to form a first line; 75 to 100 sheriffs and deputy sheriffs for a second line, also unarmed; and 200 to 300 "soldiers" behind the sheriffs, unarmed. He said that he would be in the first line and that when Meredith presented himself he would read a proclamation denying him entrance. He would say that he wanted peace and that there should be no violence. Then he suggested that the forces of the United States should draw guns and that he would then step aside.

The Attorney General replied that this would be a mistake; that it would not help the people of Mississippi or the people of the United States. The Attorney General stated that he thought it was silly and dangerous to go through a farce of federal officials drawing guns followed by the Governor stepping aside. He said that he thought the matter had gone beyond the stage of politics, that the Governor had a responsibility to the people of Mississippi and to the people of the United States, and that what the Governor proposed was a real disservice.

The Governor replied that he had said so many times that there couldn't be any integration, that he couldn't back down.

The Attorney General suggested that the Governor could say that the National Guard had been called up; that the Governor didn't want Mississippi people responsible for putting Mr. Meredith in the institution; and that the Governor therefore was stepping aside. The Governor repeated that he had to be confronted with troops.

The Attorney General suggested that federal marshals might come down and take over the campus on Sunday. There was discussion of this suggestion. The Governor stated that the men would have to be armed, and suggested that it should be done on Monday rather than Sunday. The Attorney General pointed out there would then be a large crowd and that if the federal officials came with guns it would be a difficult situation. The Governor said that he didn't think so if people from other states would stay away.

The Attorney General then said that the President was going on television that night; that the President would have to explain why he had federalized the National Guard as he had done around midnight of September 29; that the President would have to say that the Governor had made an agreement with the President on Saturday, September 29, for the registration of Mr. Meredith; and that the Governor had broken his word to the President late in the evening of that day.

The Governor asked that the President not say anything about any prior agreement. The Attorney General said that the President would have to do so; that the Governor now suggested that the United States send troops to fight their way through a barricade. He repeated that the Governor and his representative, Mr. Watkins, broke their word to the President.

The Governor then responded with the suggestion that Mr. Meredith should be flown in that afternoon. He asked that what had been said be treated as confidential. The Attorney General suggested that the Governor discuss it with Mr. Watkins and call back with a specific plan. The Attorney General said that he wanted to maintain law and order.

Governor Barnett then put Mr. Watkins on the telephone. The Attorney General repeated to Mr. Watkins that an agreement made with the President of the United States had been broken, and that the President would discuss that when he spoke to the nation on television. Mr. Watkins objected on the grounds that there had also been an agreement that the discussion with the President would be in confidence. The Attorney General said that the conversations were confidential on the understanding that the agreement would be carried out. He said that the Governor was now calling on the United States to bring out troops, and that the Governor was suggesting that he would *have his own army there for political reasons.*

At this juncture the Attorney General said that there was no further point in his talking with Mr. Watkins. He said that I would talk to Mr. Watkins.

Mr. Watkins told me that the Governor realized he could not avoid the physical forces of the United States, and that the Governor would be willing for Mr. Meredith to be flown into the university that afternoon. I said that he would not have Mr. Meredith taken to the university until the situation was physically under control and law and order was being maintained.

Mr. Watkins said that the Governor had understood from the Attorney General that Mr. Meredith would be brought in by helicopter that afternoon. I replied that we could not do that unless the situation was under control. I said that the Governor would have to say that the state had yielded to the physical force of the government. I also said that the state police would have to help to keep order. Mr. Watkins said that would be done and that the chief of the state police would be sent immediately to Oxford.

Mr. Watkins further said that he would never have had any conversations if they had not been in confidence. I replied that the discussion had been with the President of the United States about a great national problem; that the President had been willing to suffer criticism if that would permit the Governor to get himself and the state out of its situation without violence; but that no one could reach that kind of agreement with the President of the United States and then call it off.

After further discussion of this point, Mr. Watkins said that the Governor agreed to recognize the authority of the federal officers and to maintain peace and order. He said that the highway patrolmen would give every assistance. . . .

This was agreed. Mr. Watkins said that he hoped the Attorney General would apologize to the President for him and ask the President not to say anything about the previous talks. The Attorney General said it would be helpful if the Governor could make his statement before the President went on television.

The Governor then returned to the phone and talked to the Attorney General. In response to questions from the Governor, the Attorney General said that there was no objection to the Governor's saying that he was surprised, or to his saying that he would continue a legal fight. . . .

At approximately 8:35 EDT (6:35 Jackson time) the Attorney General called Governor Barnett and told him that Mr. Meredith had arrived at the university and was in fact in his dormitory. To this point, everything had proceeded in accordance with the arrangements discussed in the prior conversations.

The Attorney General informed Governor Barnett that Mr. Meredith had not been put on the university campus by helicopter, as discussed, but had landed at the airport and had proceeded by car and under escort to the campus. Accordingly, the Attorney General men-

tioned that the opening part of the Governor's proposed statement would therefore be factually inaccurate. The Governor replied that he could not change his statement at that point because he had no typist.

In October 1963 Burke Marshall recommended to the Attorney General that a desegregation suit be brought in Bay County, Florida. It was not merely that the school district was in violation of the law, which it was—there was something else. The school district had not lived up to its agreement with the Justice Department. As Marshall's memo stated:

> *This is an impact-area school with which we conducted negotiations last spring. After obtaining agreements for desegregation from neighboring counties, we finally obtained a commitment from Bay City that they would accept Negroes into the white school under the Florida Pupil Placement Statute. The neighboring counties did this this fall. Bay County has rejected two qualified Negro students and has refused even to discuss the matter with us. In addition, I am informed that the office of the Florida Attorney General, which has been very cooperative in the past, has been unable to get any satisfaction from housing authorities.*
>
> *Since this involves a broken commitment, I have concluded that we have to file suit in the county. This is particularly necessary in view of the fact that two neighboring counties made similar commitments and lived up to them.*

In other words, the school district had broken its word, and gentlemen don't break their words. Reasonable expectations had been violated, and the Justice Department would take appropriate action.

Burke Marshall had a tightly reasoned speech he would give to civil rights workers, students and other interested parties about why it was okay for the government to send troops to Ole Miss or the University of Alabama and not to Albany, Georgia, or wherever the petitioners' particular interests lay. It came down to the fact that at Ole Miss (and at the University of Alabama) the government was acting persuant to a federal court order.

The history of the Ole Miss litigation, Marshall pointed out, was on the books for all to see. Meredith had applied for admission to Ole Miss in January 1961. But the Justice Department didn't get formally involved until August 31, 1962, in response to a request from the U.S. Supreme Court, and on September 10, 1962—arguing that admitting Meredith wouldn't work great hardship on the university, but keeping him out could cause Meredith injury—Justice Black issued an order which in effect enjoined interference with Meredith's admission.

Burke Marshall told a gathering of the Washington Chapter of the Yale Law School Association: "Once this order of the Supreme Court of the United States was issued, it became the plain duty of every citizen—and beyond question the duty of every lawyer and every state and federal official to uphold the law—to accept the order as the law. The responsibility of the President and the Attorney General, if they were to fulfill their oaths of office, also became inescapable—to see that the order was enforced but they also had the duty to make every effort consistent with that obligation to enforce it with the least possible damage to the relations between the federal government and one of the states, and above all to avoid by any possible means the use of military force against American citizens in the enforcement of this order."

On September 13, 1962, Governor Barnett, in a televised speech, proclaimed defiance of the federal law, invoking the doctrine of interposition, although as Judge Minor Wisdom, an Eisenhower appointee to the Fifth Circuit, later pointed out, "the supremacy clause makes hash of the so-called Doctrine of Interposition," which he called "political poppycock."

Without going into the complexities, the legal upshot of Barnett's activities was that the Fifth Circuit, on its own, cited Governor Barnett for criminal contempt, the penalty for which is a jail sentence. The extra-legal upshot was the night of violence at Ole Miss for which Barnett must bear heavy responsibility. A TV cameraman from Atlanta was pummeled. An Agence France-Press newsman was murdered. A local jukebox repairman was killed by a stray .38 bullet. A U.S. marshal was shot in the throat—twenty-eight marshals shot in all, 160 injured. The other wounded figures were never released. At midnight, with pop bottles, bricks, buckshot, acid and flaming gas bombs still in the air, Governor Barnett had gone on the radio and after halfhearted appeals for order he now announced, "We will never surrender." Had Burke Marshall's rhetoric about upholding court orders been a true forecast and description of the way in which the federal government made its decisions, Governor Ross Barnett of Mississippi,* would have gone to jail.

But the fact was, of course, that under no circumstances did Kennedy or Marshall want Governor Barnett in jail. They didn't even want him cited in pleadings.

Louis Claiborne, a young Southern-born attorney in the Justice Department who was sent down to work on the case, recalls, "My

* And probably Lieutenant Governor Paul Johnson.

instructions were that I had a free hand except that I shouldn't cite Barnett in any pleadings."

Here was a situation where the Governor of Mississippi had stood up to the President, the Attorney General, the Court of Appeals, the District Court and the Supreme Court of the United States, yet the Justice Department asked the court for a restraining order that required the registrars to ignore the Governor. "The government was enjoining the other guys from paying attention to Barnett instead of enjoining Barnett from doing what he was doing," says Claiborne.

Clearly, the Attorney General and Burke Marshall and the President hoped to avoid a confrontation. Robert Kennedy, especially, "understood" the politics of the situation and was willing to let Barnett posture out front as long as a reasonable settlement could be worked out behind the scenes.

But if on stage Barnett was behaving like a boor, backstage he was anything but a gentleman and in fact Kennedy felt he had gone back on his word. He reneged on his agreement with the President that Meredith would be registered. He told the Attorney General one thing and his local law officers another. He promised that the State Highway Patrol would "give every assistance" and then gave the head of the State Highway Patrol a sealed proclamation authorizing him to withdraw the highway patrol on his own discretion (which he did).

On September 25, after Barnett had systematically inflamed rather than cooled down local passions, the government decided it could no longer ignore him in its court orders and finally initiated civil contempt proceedings against him. "But it was all part of the deception," says Claiborne. "For it was still Robert Kennedy's assumption that if he and the Governor could work things out over the telephone, court orders could be patched up later. This showed a lack of respect for orderly process—and a lack of realism. He dealt with Barnett as though he were dealing with the Secretary of the Interior on how to get around a budget limitation and still remedy a pollution problem on the Potomac."

Again, the issue is not whether the impassioned young Claiborne— who was not privy to any of the hundreds of considerations which affected the Attorney General's decision—was right or wrong. The lesson of the Meredith case is that while Justice Department officials were always careful to act pursuant to court orders, they did not necessarily act *because* of court orders. They got court orders because they wanted to act. And Southern justice was at a sufficiently low ebb to guarantee that legal occasions for the requisite court orders would rarely be lacking. When Justice didn't want to act, it found an out.

The government was not interested in putting Barnett in jail. Meredith, after all, was in school. The Governor, after all, had collapsed before the show of federal force. The underdeveloped world, after all, had been told in unforgettable terms that JFK was willing to call out tens of thousands of troops to guarantee one lonely Negro's entrance to school. And besides, the Kennedy view of the federal system argued against confrontation. As Burke Marshall looks back he recalls that "Although technically in criminal contempt, Barnett was representing a piece of the United States—a piece of society. And I didn't really believe in using criminal process as a proper or effective way of dealing with this."

The White House agreed with Marshall, and the Attorney General agreed with both. A White House memorandum at the time made the argument:

January 12, 1963

Those who are willing to look at all the practical aspects of the situation will remember that in 1923, former Governor Theo G. Bilbo was sentenced to serve thirty days in the Oxford, Mississippi, jail for contempt of the United States District Court, presided over by Judge E. R. Holmes. This was for failing to obey a witness subpoena. No racial question was involved. Bilbo announced for Governor from the jailhouse steps upon the completion of his sentence, and came very near being elected that time. He was elected Governor in the next race and thereafter was elected three times to the U.S. Senate. When those who wish to promote the prestige and dignity of the courts deal with a fellow like [Lieutenant Governor] Johnson on the kind of case they have against him, they are defeating the very purposes they are hoping to achieve. The charges against him should be dismissed and he should be relegated as beneath the notice of the U.S. Court of Appeals unless, indeed, they are going to hail up every person who galloped to the Ole Miss campus and participated in everything that went on there.

As to Barnett, it is true that he, being the Governor, acting as Governor, did intentionally defy and frustrate certain orders of the Court of Appeals, it is hard to see how he would have any legal defense to charges of contempt of court, in so far as that is concerned. However, he is Governor of one of the fifty states. His term will expire within the year. If he is to be tried on the merits of the case, the Court of Appeals should defer that trial until Barnett goes out of office. The court will then not be interfering with the state of Mississippi but will only be trying an individual. And then, if he is convicted, the court should not assess any imprisonment. For the court to put Governor Barnett in jail simply will be to imitate the example of the federal government which imprisoned Jefferson Davis for two years at Fortress Monroe. It is true that the facts are much different. But the general public will look at it the same way. Barnett will be made a hero when, as a matter of fact, at the beginning of the Oxford episode he was on the lowest limb of any Governor in seventy-five years. Putting him in jail will not add to the ability of the federal courts to deal with the racial question in a successful way.

If the trial is deferred as to Barnett, it will not only give the people time to settle down from the hysteria that has been running rampant for four months, but it will also negate the idea that the tyrannical federal government is simply rushing in to satisfy a thirst for blood and using any kind of pretext to humble and humiliate a portion of the Union.

The trial was deferred and eventually, after a side issue went up to the Supreme Court, the whole issue was dropped in 1965 when the Fifth Circuit Court of Appeals said, in effect, that it didn't matter any more.

It did matter. On October 24, 1962, one month after Barnett's defiance, Burke Marshall—at the Fifth Circuit Court of Appeals' request—was about to file an affidavit (excerpted on pp. 231–234) setting out his version of the Attorney General's conversations with Barnett. But the Attorney General was the President's brother, and the Kennedys had another crisis to contend with—the Cuban missile crisis. It wouldn't do to have the sovereign of a sovereign state thrown in jail (and suppose he wouldn't go?) at a time when JFK needed national unity. So Marshall didn't file the affidavit and instead, says Marshall, "I was asked by the Attorney General and I guess by the President— he called me during the crisis weekend and asked me to see to it that the courts didn't do something that would require troops and I did. I called the court—Judge Tuttle."

Others in the Department—especially in the Solicitor General's office—were distressed that the Kennedy code and the corporation lawyers' propensity for off-stage settlements took precedence over the legal code. Louis Claiborne argues to this day that "The fact that Governor Barnett defied the court and the Attorney General and the President and got away with it made inevitable Governor Wallace's stand in the schoolhouse door. No [Southern] Governor worth his salt could do less."

Clearly, the Attorney General was not interested in pressing the case —yet he couldn't quite bring himself to quash it or moot it. In November of 1962 when he received a memo stating the Department's position that Barnett and Johnson were not entitled to a jury trial (because it was a contempt case) he scratched in the margin, "Can't we remain silent on this unless asked by the court?"

The following month at one of the Attorney General's beer-and-pretzels meetings for young lawyers where he would go around the room asking each man what he was working on, Kennedy stopped when he came to Claiborne, the attorney working on Barnett, and said, "That's a very difficult case." The young attorney expressed surprise, since he said Barnett had clearly violated the court order, and asked the Attorney General if he was referring to Barnett's contention that he was entitled to a jury trial. "Not only that," said Kennedy, "but the whole issue of prosecuting a Governor."

Shortly thereafter Solicitor General Cox approached Claiborne and said the Attorney General had told him he was offering a prize to anyone who could find a way of mooting the Barnett case. Cox said, "I thought I should mention this to you, but I'm not interested in that prize." "Neither am I," said the young lawyer.

Cox argued the jury-trial issue eloquently, and the government prevailed in the Supreme Court. But as the months dragged on, it became apparent that time had dimmed the issues; the Civil Rights Act of 1964 was passed, Barnett was succeeded by Johnson, Kennedy resigned, ran for and was elected to the Senate from New York, and the Fifth Circuit Court in its discretion decided that the public interest would not be served by continued prosecution of the case.

Obviously Kennedy learned something from the experience. And in 1963, when Governor Wallace threatened defiance—after *taping* a "private" meeting with Kennedy (the Southern Governors had learned something too)—Kennedy had the troops at the ready (even though Judge Seymour H. Lynne of the Federal District Court had told Wallace's attorneys in chambers that if Wallace displayed more than token defiance, he'd get more than a token sentence for contempt—and since Lynne was no integrationist judge, Wallace's attorneys had no choice but to believe him).

Kennedy, Marshall & Co. seized on court orders as a way of explaining to civil rights militants why they couldn't do more and to Southern segregationists why they couldn't do less. The federal court order was the rhetorical solution to the limitations of federalism. But the Barnett case illustrates that court orders, like the official theory of federalism, were not the critical variable.

Had Robert Kennedy assumed the availability of the FBI, the unreasonableness of Governor Barnett and/or the primacy of the contempt-of-court orders against Barnett over the immediate needs of the Kennedy Administration, perhaps he would have had a different view of the federal system, one closer to that of Judge Minor Wisdom, who lectured (in a dissent) his brethren for dropping the Barnett case as no longer relevant:

> State officials must know that they cannot with impunity flout federal law.
>
> In fact, Meredith was admitted not by reason of Barnett's substantial compliance with the court's decree, but by the superior force of military arms. Therefore it was the government's obligation, under law, to put Barnett in jail. But the government had this technical notion of the federal system and this fear of public confrontation of the South, so it didn't do it.
>
> The offense occurred at a time calling for moral leadership of the highest order. No great clairvoyance was needed to foresee death and disorder resulting from the confrontation of two armed forces. No one can say that the rioting and insurrection that took place September 30, 1962, in Oxford, Mississippi, and the death and disorder that have occurred in many other places in the South since that insurrection were not due, at least in part, to the imprimatur the Governor of Mississippi placed on lawless defiance of the federal courts.
>
> Although Barnett was technically in contempt of the court, he was actually in contempt against the nation—against American federalism, as established in the Constitution and as defined by the federal courts. The serious threat Governor Barnett posed was to the Constitutional relationship of the states to the federal government. A public wrong of such enormity carries with it a corresponding and unshirkable duty on the federal court to vindicate the rights of the nation by bringing the alleged contemnor to trial.
>
> The Governor of Mississippi, trained in the law, knew or should have known that the supremacy clause makes hash of the so-called Doctrine of Interposition. All informed persons know that this political poppycock has never been recognized in a court of law. . . .
>
> What cannot be overestimated . . . is the importance of federal courts standing fast in protecting federally guaranteed rights of individuals. To avoid further violence and bloodshed, all state officials, including the governor, must know that they cannot with impunity flout federal law.

Throughout the Ole Miss crisis, Robert Kennedy, who was getting on-the-spot reports from Katzenbach, was ten or fifteen minutes ahead of the President, who was getting his information from the Pentagon.

When it was all over, one of the generals, flying back to Washington, asked Katzenbach how he had one-upped the Signal Corps. To the consternation and fury of the top Pentagon people in Washington, the Deputy Attorney General reached into his pocket and pulled out a dime. On arrival at Ole Miss he had placed two collect calls, one to the Justice Department and one to the White House, from local pay phones and kept the lines open throughout the night.

James Symington, an assistant to the Attorney General, recalls arriving on the scene where Katzenbach was surrounded by broken glass, baseball bats and bricks. "In the midst of that chaos and desolation," says Symington, "he went outside to give an interview to a Canadian television guy. He stood in the sunlight and gently, graciously and without imputation of evil designs to anybody, he described what was happening on TV in French. He had the *sang-froid* to do this. That's impressive."

One cannot overestimate the resourcefulness, imagination, determination and cool displayed by the Kennedys and their people in the successful effort to support the heroic James Meredith's integration of Ole Miss. Yet as Harold Fleming, a close student of civil rights, has observed in *Daedalus*, "It can be persuasively argued that much of the violence might have been prevented if the Governor's assurances (which were not fulfilled) had been given less credence, or if it had not been for an unaccountable delay in the arrival of troops." [10]

The textbooks on organization theory tend to assume that when a policy fails the search for alternatives is intensified. But as the sociologist Harold Wilensky has written, "This assumption underestimates man's capacity for clinging to prophecies already proven wrong. The failure of a prediction lays waste actions taken in preparation for its fulfillment. Thus, men use a variety of ingenious defenses to protect cherished convictions under the onslaught of devastating attack. The believers may convince themselves that only the date of the promised millennium is wrong . . . when the deliverance does not come according to schedule, they set new dates." [11]

In the end the Ivy League preference for non-confrontation with the caste system of the South backfired, but the idea that equal justice could be postponed by *ad hoc* negotiation and peace-keeping lived on. Eight months later, there was Katzenbach in the schoolhouse door, his baldish head gleaming in the Tuscaloosa sun, confronting Governor George Wallace and integrating the University of Alabama. To the nation, Kennedy's representative appeared as courageous egghead, committed activist, an intellectual who put principle ahead of expediency, public good before personal safety. There was truth in the perception, but the real significance of his "confrontation" with Wallace was not that the Kennedy–Ivy League had learned the lesson that confrontation-postponement can be frought with perils; rather, they had become more adept at confrontation-avoidance. For while the cameras recorded Katzenbach's eyeball-to-eyeball charade with the Alabama Governor, the two Negro students (in accordance with

Katzenbach's scenario) were quietly escorted to their rooms out of the range of popping flash bulbs. Later in the day they registered without difficulty.

William James once divided people into tender-minded and tough-minded. The former, said James, seek refuge in systems, in which reasoned articulation and intellectual symmetry is the essence. The latter, on the other hand, are empiricists, usually willing to take experience for what it is. Although the Ivy League lawyers were "tough" in the Kennedy sense of that word, by the James test they were tender-minded insofar as their conduct came to be dictated by the theory of federalism which they had articulated, if not invented. Kennedy, tough-minded by Jamesian and non-Jamesian standards as well, had little use for theory, and in civil rights especially was genuinely moved by iniquity, angered by the hypocrisy and shocked to a new awareness of the Negro's condition by the prevalence of injustice. John Doar spoke for the whole Civil Rights Division when he said, "With Robert that situation was unacceptable. That's why we worked so hard. It was the best place in government, the greatest corner on earth to work in. . . . The line of authority in the biggest corporation in the world was short and straight." Nevertheless, till the end of his days as Attorney General he allowed the theory of federalism to circumscribe whatever radical impulses he may have been cultivating.

CHAPTER FIVE

Southern Justice:
The Judges and the General

WHEN ROBERT KENNEDY retired as Attorney General in September 1964, in the principal Southern states there were no Negro circuit court judges (twelve white ones), no Negro district court judges (sixty-five white ones), no Negro U.S. commissioners (253 whites ones), no Negro jury commissioners (109 white ones) and no Negro U.S. marshals (twenty-nine white ones). As a study of the Southern Regional Council concluded, "A Negro involved in a federal court action in the South could go from the beginning of the case to the end without seeing any black faces unless they were in the court audience, or he happens to notice the man sweeping the floor."

In the non-violent America of the early Sixties, nobody expected John Kennedy to appoint or Robert Kennedy to recommend Negro judges south of the Mason-Dixon line. The white *and* Negro liberal establishment were encouraged by the Kennedys' appointment of ten Negro judges up north, including Thurgood Marshall,* who had come to fame as Director-Counsel of the NAACP Legal Defense Fund, countless Negro ancillary law officers, and an increase of Negro at-

---

* On September 26, 1961, Marshall was nominated to the Second Circuit Court of Appeals. One year later, less two weeks, Senator Eastland's Judiciary Committee reported the name out, and he was confirmed.

torneys in the Justice Department by over 500 percent (from six to sixty). But because to every Negro who walked into a Southern courtroom it *looked* like enemy territory, because the Kennedys were committed to civil rights progress, because the Justice Department lawyers involved in the nitty gritty of judicial selection were (correctly or incorrectly) thought to be—in the terminology of the day— "liberals," and because the Kennedy civil rights strategy was to litigate rather than legislate, integrationists believed Deputy Attorney General Katzenbach when he said, "We do not expect to find or to be able to obtain confirmation for militant civil rights advocates in the South. What we seek is to assure ourselves that nominees will follow the law of the land. We are satisfied with that much."

That is not what happened. The Kennedys named no fewer than 25 percent non-law-of-the-land followers (five out of twenty appointments) to lifetime judgeships in the Fifth Circuit, the district which encompasses Florida, Texas, Georgia, Alabama, Louisiana and Mississippi, the heart of the deep South. William Harold Cox of Mississippi, E. Gordon West of Louisiana, Robert Elliott of Georgia and Clarence Allgood and Walter Gewin of Alabama have all been singled out by students of judicial decision-making in the South as anti-civil rights, racist, segregationist and/or obstructionist. While there can be legitimate debate about their motives and fine distinctions may be made among them—and in individual cases it can be said that they have mellowed with time—there can be no denying that during the turbulent Kennedy years these men, along with others whose records are spottier, consistently decided civil rights cases against Negroes (and white civil rights proponents) who had clear law on their side, as evidenced by the fact that their rulings were invariably overturned in the upper courts.

No aspect of Robert Kennedy's Attorney Generalship is more vulnerable to criticism than these appointments. For it was a blatant contradiction for the Kennedys to forego civil rights legislation and executive action in favor of litigation and at the same time to appoint as lifetime litigation-overseers men dedicated to frustrating that litigation. It was also a comedown from the characteristically lofty JFK oratory of May 20, 1961, the day he signed the Omnibus Judgeship Bill and commented: "I want for our courts individuals with respected professional skill, incorruptible character, firm judicial temperament, the rare inner quality to know when to temper justice with mercy, and the intellectual capacity to protect and illuminate the Constitution and our historic values. . . ."

Yet at a period in our history when men, money and time were in short supply, when the Civil Rights Division's 1961 budget was one of the Department's smallest, when *ad hoc* crises requiring the government's legal attention were erupting daily, the Kennedy Justice Department was forced to devote thousands of man hours, hundreds of thousands of dollars, untold energy, imagination and brilliance, all to counter the obstructionist tactics of its own appointees, five of whom decided over one hundred cases against the Negro, the Civil Rights Division and the Constitution while Robert Kennedy was Attorney General. In the process they contributed—to what degree we can never know—to the alienation of the black American from law as an effective problem-solving instrument. They solidified Southern resistance to desegregation at a time when it had a chance of cracking. They undermined the effective administration of justice. They undermined respect for law. They appeared to make a mockery of the Kennedys' pledge of equal justice for all.

Judge W. Harold Cox of Jackson, Mississippi, appointed in June of 1961, perhaps the most famous of the segregationist judges, was also perhaps the most outrageous. From the bench he referred to Negro litigants as "niggers" and asked such searching questions as "Who is telling these people they can get in line [to register] and push people around, acting like a bunch of chimpanzees?" He ordered the U.S. attorney in Mississippi to jail for refusing to prepare perjury indictments against two Negro witnesses whose "perjury" consisted of a technical memory lapse connected with their attempt to register to vote. He issued an injunction against CORE, restraining it from encouraging Negroes to use the McComb, Mississippi, interstate bus terminal after the ICC had declared it desegregated. He refused to stop a Mississippi prosecution of an unlawfully arrested Negro during a voting drive in a county where no Negroes were registered though there were 2,490 Negroes of voting age (he attributed the lack of Negro registrations to "the fact that Negroes have not been interested to vote. . . ."). He refused to find a "pattern or practice of discrimination" in Clarke County, despite the fact that only one Negro—the principal of the local high school—had registered in thirty years, and even he had to show up seven times and interpret a clause of the Mississippi constitution which had stumped the Mississippi State Supreme Court. The list goes on. In all of these cases Cox was reversed on appeal.

Judge E. Gordon West of Louisiana, who was appointed in September of 1961, has been called by one leading civil rights attorney "The worst judge I ever appeared before." [1] If other judges quarreled with precedent, Judge West's tactic was to ignore it. For instance, Judge West, who called the U.S. Supreme Court's 1954 *Brown* decision out-lawing public school segregation "One of the truly regrettable decisions of all time" and said, "The trouble resulting therefrom has been brought about by outsiders," once cited a 1907 Supreme Court decision to back up his 1964 ruling that a Negro denied admission to a Louisiana college could not sue the Board of Education because state agencies are immune from suit. In the process, he conveniently failed to take into account no less than five more recent decisions which held that a state agency can be sued. He was reversed on appeal.

A second West tactic: delay ruling in a case until it can't be avoided and then decide only a procedural issue. He waited six months after a Negro tenant farmer filed a damage suit claiming he was beaten for attempting to register to vote, and then Judge West ruled that the court lacked jurisdiction. The farmer appealed and got bogged down in the courts for two years until the *procedural* issue was settled. (Judge West was reversed.)

As Yale law professor Alexander Bickel wrote in *Politics and the Warren Court:*

> In the summer of 1964, Judge West of Baton Rouge, La., had to be directly ordered by his superiors on the Court of Appeals for the 5th Circuit to issue a decree in a school desegregation case. The Negro plaintiffs were forced to institute a mandamus proceeding against Judge West, which is about as rare a thing as is known to law and which can succeed only if the appellate court is convinced that the judge has been guilty of what in any other officer of government would be called, bluntly and simply, dereliction of duty. Against Judge West it succeeded. But at what cost!
>
> The case involved the school system of St. Helena Parish, La. Suit was begun over 11 years ago. By February '62, all possible issues of any substance had been litigated and the Supreme Court denied a second appeal. At this time, Judge West was asked to issue a decree. He did not even set the case down for a hearing. Plaintiffs went back to Judge West a year later. Now he set the case down for a hearing, but he never held one. A year later, the plaintiffs were back again, and Judge West did hold a hearing, in March, 1964. But then he neither did anything nor expressed any intention to do anything, not even after the petition for mandamus had been filed. Pretty clearly if the schools of the Parish were going to be desegregated, Judge West was not going to be the one to do it, no matter what the Supreme Court might say. [2]

Eisenhower-appointee Judge Elbert Tuttle of the circuit Court decried Judge West's "startling, if not shocking, lack of appreciation of the clear pronouncements of the Supreme Court and the [lower courts] . . . which make it perfectly plain [after eleven years] that time has run out. . . ."

Judge Robert Elliott of Georgia, appointed in January of 1962, found against Negroes in over 90 percent of the civil rights cases that came before his court during Kennedy's tenure as Attorney General. Ten years after the *Brown* case he refused to enjoin the operation of segregated schools in Muscogee and Colquitt counties in Georgia and was reversed both times; he issued restraining orders against Negro demonstrators in Albany, Georgia, where he had no jurisdiction, but he voted against intervention when the state of Georgia held four Americus, Georgia, civil rights workers without bail on capital charges of insurrection. A three-judge court was convened and he lost, 2–1.

Documentation of the discriminatory decisions of Judges Allgood and Gewin as well as those of Cox, West and Elliott abounds. It can be found scattered through such books as *Southern Justice* edited by Leon Friedman, *Climbing Jacob's Ladder* by Watters and Cleghorn, *Politics and the Warren Court* by Bickel, in a 1963 study published in the *Yale Law Journal*, in the writings of Columbia law professor Louis Lusky, in numerous unpublished doctoral dissertations (including especially that of Mary Curzan *), in the accumulated experience of countless civil rights lawyers and organizations such as the NAACP Legal Defense Fund, Inc.

The demonstrable damage these judges inflicted was threefold. First, they cruelly postponed justice—thus further delaying the enforcement of Constitutional rights already one hundred years overdue. Second, they dealt a severe blow to the civil rights movement, which became increasingly frustrated, fragmented and radicalized as a direct result of the open injustice exhibited by the official, federal justice-dispensing instrument. No more eloquent testimony of the dynamics of disillusionment is available than the diary of a young civil rights worker who tells what he felt as he watched a Kennedy judge free a white policeman charged with shooting a voter registration applicant:

> I personally didn't understand myself the day of the trial. . . . The case had been presented to the jury and it seemed they were just begging for somebody to give them an excuse to acquit the man. The judge did. . . . The sap sucker did it and nobody in the darn court thought otherwise. The judge more than anyone else, even the poor [defense attorney] who didn't have a case and knew it. [The defendant] got up in the chair and lied his tail off and nobody said a mumbling word.

* Who was kind enough to show me her concluding chapter, although the bulk of her study is "classified" because information was procured on a restricted-use basis.

I looked at the jury and then at [the defendant] and then at the judge sitting up there in his robe and I was disturbed within me. All within me twisted and turned. My guts bubbled. I hated that man, not the system that produced him, not [the defendant] or the jury, but that man in his black robe of shame.

I said it over and over. If I were violent I would have tried to do harm to that man's physical body. I left that room and walked the streets . . . for half an hour, and every white face I saw I said to myself, "I hate it."

Man, I was afraid of myself; I did not understand what was happening, and supposed that it was only happening to me. We were all in bad shape, I later found out when I told this to the group. I called a special meeting and spilled the beans. I felt much better and understood what was happening much better after we all got in there and struggled with these issues.

This had been a development of continued frustration at the throne of justice all over Mississippi, in Louisiana, the school case in Virginia . . . and all the Albany cases, the most immediate ones on voter registration and the hundreds on civil liberties and civil rights. Here was the skunk sitting on them. I saw him sitting in that room representing the stench of death across the South which must take somebody with it before it goes. He represented all that I hate about the system of segregation, and it is men like him who rob us all, black and white, of the living we have fought for, and die and live to fight again for. As you can sense, I have not quite gotten over it as yet; I'm trying hard. . . .[3]

Third, through deceit, delay and direct, extra-legal challenges to federal authority, they undermined the Justice Department's fundamental strategy of litigate-rather-than-legislate. Perhaps the most blatant offender was Judge Cox of Mississippi, Senator Eastland's old roommate and the Kennedys' first appointment under the new Omnibus Judgeship Bill of 1961. While Judge Cox's courtroom derelictions have been widely reported in the press, his behind-the-scenes outbursts and maneuvers—not generally available for inspection to the public—provide a better barometer of the depths of local opposition to the changes which the Constitution, and ostensibly the Kennedys as its enforcers, demanded. There follows a letter from Judge Cox to John Doar in response to a detailed inquiry from Doar as to when a long-delayed critical voter registration case might get action.

October 16, 1963   US v. State of Mississippi
                                            Civil Action No. 3312

DEAR MR. DOAR:

I have a copy of your letter of October 12 regarding the above case and thought I had made it clear to you one time in Hattiesburg that I was not in the least impressed with your impudence in reciting the chronology of the case before me with which I am completely familiar. If you need to build such transcripts for your boss man, you had better do that by interoffice memoranda because I am not favorably impressed with you or your tactics in undertaking to push one of your cases before me. I spend most of my time in fooling with lousy cases brought before me by your Department in the Civil Rights field and I do not intend to turn my docket over to your department for your political advancement. You have been given every consideration and every courtesy in my court and I don't think that you have any sense of gratitude or appreciation therefor. You are completely stupid if you do not fully realize that each of the judges in this court understand the importance of this case to all of the litigants. I do not intend to be hurried or harassed by you or any of your underlings in this or any court where I sit and the sooner you get that through your head the better you will get along with me, if that is of any interest to you. I do not think that the very important actions in this case should be shelved just because you are in a hurry to make some kind of showing in your docket and I shall not vote for any such irregular and completely improper procedure simply for the advancement of your political goals.

> Yours very truly,
>
> Harold Cox
> cc: Ben F. Cameron, Hon. John R. Brown

The letter provoked a chain reaction of conferences, calls and memoranda within the Department. A Civil Rights Division attorney drafted a five-page research memo on the possible disqualification of Cox from the case. This memo prompted Harold Greene (then head of the Civil Rights Division Appeals Section, now a judge in the District of Columbia) to conclude in a memo of his own that the government could probably get Cox disqualified, but on balance he thought it best not to do so. Burke Marshall, head of the Civil Rights Division, brought the matter to the attention of Deputy Attorney General Katzenbach, and eventually it was discussed with the Attorney General himself. On November 17, 1963, Robert Kennedy wrote to Judge Cox:

> . . . I was quite frankly shocked by the language and tone of your letter which was addressed to one of the finest trial lawyers in the Department of Justice. After careful consideration I have decided to call the matter to the attention of the Standing Committee on Federal Judiciary of the ABA. I am also sending copies to the former chairman and to the former member of the 5th circuit of that Committee both because they were responsible for investigating and reporting to me on the qualifications of all potential judicial appoint-

ments in the circuit, including your own, and because they are, respectively, past President and President-elect of the American College of Trial Lawyers.

Very truly yours,
Robert F. Kennedy /s/
Attorney General

Whatever inclination there might have been to pursue the matter further dissolved four days later when President Kennedy was assassinated.

The need for Doar's letter and the aftermath of Cox's are merely minor examples of the frittering away of top talent on problems which would never have existed were it not for the dubious activities of Kennedy-appointed judges.

If the Cox appointment stood alone, it might be explainable if not defendable. As a practical matter, Joe Dolan points out, "He was Senator Eastland's boy and the ABA rated him Extremely Well Qualified. What did you expect us to do?" Burke Marshall adds, "I checked with the NAACP and others and what they came up with was what we already knew: He was Eastland's roommate at college. That was enough for a reasonable presumption to look further but it wasn't a reason to turn him down. White Citizens Councils were all over the state and he was unique in not being a part of it, although looking back I'll bet Senator Eastland told him not to join." Moreover, in addition to the normal FBI and ABA investigations, the Attorney General himself (with Byron White present) conducted a half-hour interview with Cox prior to his nomination. As Marshall wrote some years later in a private letter to Yale law professor Bickel (with reference to a Bickel book review that criticized the appointment in *The New Republic*):

> Judge Cox's appointment was approved after a long personal interview with the Attorney General in which Cox stated his intentions of fully complying with the decisions of the Supreme Court and the Fifth Circuit in civil rights matters. He was rated Extremely Well Qualified by the American Bar Association Committee and had no public record at all on racial matters. If his appointment were to have been turned down, it would have had to have been almost solely on the basis that he was suggested by Senator Eastland and had been Eastland's personal friend for many years.

When I asked Robert Kennedy what he and Cox had talked about, he said, "Cox wanted to give me his word that upholding the Constitution would never be a problem."

The Kennedy version of the Kennedy–Cox interview is undoubtedly true. But as Judge Tuttle is reported to have remarked, "The trouble with that interview is that they were talking different languages. When Bobby asked him if he would uphold the law of the land, he was thinking about *Brown* v. *Board of Education.* But when Cox said yes, he was thinking about lynching. When Cox said he believed Negroes should have the vote he meant two Negroes." Byron White, who was present at the interview, has a more charitable interpretation. "Cox was willing to enforce the Constitution but he was unwilling to interpret it your way. The Fourteenth Amendment was in flux and its frontiers were being explored and exploited." To which a civil rights official and informal consultant to the Justice Department during those years retorts, "They [the Kennedy Justice Department] wanted to believe that every redneck who came down the pike was another Hugo Black." Perhaps the most prophetic observation was that of Roy Wilkins, Executive Secretary of the NAACP, who warned, "For 986,-ooo Negro Mississippians, Judge Cox will be another strand in their barbed-wire fence, another cross over their weary shoulders and another rock in the road up which their young people must struggle." At his confirmation hearing, Senator Norris Cotton, Republican, New Hampshire, asked with a smile, "You have no Yankee blood whatever, do you, Judge?" Cox replied, "None at all."

Bill Geoghegan has speculated that the Cox appointment was the price Kennedy paid for the passage of the anti-crime bills. Bill Taylor, later Staff Director of the Civil Rights Commission, notes, "Don't forget, Cox was seeking the job and I am sure he was discreet in his interview. If you want to convince yourself that a segregationist can be fair, you can do so. But can he be fair? What is fair?" A harsh interpretation of the episode is advanced by Bickel in his reply to Marshall's letter. He responded:

> I don't know why the fact a man is the choice of Senator Eastland should not be held against him. It certainly is a red flag. Of course I can't know how deeply such a conversation as you describe between the Attorney General and Cox can have probed, or indeed how deeply such a conversation can ever probe, but the Attorney General made a judgment based on that conversation, the judgment turned out to be wrong or insufficiently perceptive, and it seems to me it is perfectly proper to assess responsibility for the action that resulted. How could such a mistake have been avoided? By making a more perceptive judgment. Or by declining, in Mississippi, of all places, to take such a risk.

Robert Sherrill has charged in *The Nation* that the appointment came about in a Senate corridor where Eastland spotted the Attorney

General and accosted him with this quasi-threat: "Tell your brother that if he will give me Harold Cox I will give him the nigger" [meaning Thurgood Marshall]. A less conspiratorial explanation: In addition to gratitude for favors done, the Kennedys were reluctant to antagonize needlessly the powerful chairman of the Senate Judiciary Committee so early in the game.

Whichever version one believes, the critical fact is that the Cox appointment did not stand alone. It was part of a pattern, though certainly not a pattern cynically aimed at settling for segregationist judges. Indeed, the Ivy League attorneys whose assumptions and expectations reinforced the pattern were, if anything, personally anti-racist and institutionally on the lookout to keep the bench free of hard-core segregationists. Nevertheless, the Kennedy approach to judicial selection as realized through the work of first Byron White and then Nicholas Katzenbach (both Yale), assisted by Joe Dolan (St. John's) and secondarily Bill Geoghegan (Harvard), guaranteed that a limited but significant number of obstructionist judges would seep through. To understand how this worked, a look at the judicial selection system is in order.

According to the U.S. Constitution, the President "shall nominate and by and with the advice and consent of the Senate, shall appoint . . . Judges of the Supreme Court, and all other officers of the U.S. whose appointments are not herein provided for." (Article 2, Section 2)

According to most contemporary students of American government Alexander Hamilton had it wrong when he prophesied, consistent with the Constitution, that "there will of course be no exercise of choice on the part of the Senators. . . . They can only ratify or reject the choice of the President." The sophisticated assumption today is quite to the contrary: that the Senators from the President's own party nominate the federal judges who sit in the states which these Senators represent. Or, as Katzenbach puts it, "The President can't appoint over a Senator's no, but he has veto power."

Whatever the Kennedys' attitude and assumptions about judge-picking, they would have to deal in the realities of Senatorial power and prerogatives. If they did not already know this, they learned through encounters such as the one that occurred when powerful Senator Robert Kerr of Oklahoma submitted the name of Luther Bohannon as a potential judge. Byron White, who was then Deputy Attorney General, and Bill Geoghegan, one of White's assistants, paid the Senator a visit to inform him that the FBI report, the ABA committee's informal report and their own "spotters" (informal judicial talent scouts with political ties to the Kennedys) had all found Bohannon unqualified. Senator Kerr's response was short and to the point: "Young men," he said, "I was here a long time before you came. I'm going to be here a long time after you go. I stand by my recommendation."

White took the matter to the Attorney General and the Attorney General took it to the President, who needed Kerr's cooperation on a variety of legislative proposals before the Congress. "It was decided," recalls Geoghegan, "that an independent investigation would be made in addition to that which the FBI and the ABA had already undertaken. John Seigenthaler and I were selected to do that. We spent about a week in Oklahoma and interviewed about ninety to one hundred lawyers. We came back and recommended against his appointment. Our recommendations were supported by lengthy memoranda from both of us recounting our interviews with these lawyers that we had contacted during our visit to Oklahoma. The upshot of it was that he was appointed—but we gained some concessions; we got a much better U.S. attorney in Tulsa and we gained some concessions in terms of the marshals' appointments." *

Judicial selection can be viewed as a bargaining process between the Administration, which is charged with upholding the independence and quality of the judiciary, and the Senators, jealous to preserve and expand their patronage prerogatives—a perspective reflected in Dolan's reference to judges as "ours" (qualified judges preferred by the Justice Department) and "theirs" (unqualified judges preferred by the Senators). Or it can be interpreted as a negotiation between the Administration, anxious to pass out patronage plums to the party faithful, and the Senators, watchdogs for the public interest—a viewpoint underlined by the Senate's role in defeating the Nixon nominations of Judges Haynsworth and Carswell to the U.S. Supreme Court. Actually, whichever way one looks at it, the process is complicated by the ever-increasing role of the American Bar Association, self-appointed overseer of judge-picking. The ABA, which sees itself as impartial arbiter of the legal profession, rates prospective nominees as "Qualified," "Well Qualified," "Extremely Well Qualified" or "Not Qualified." And the other participants—the President's men and the Senators—act partly in response to or anticipation of the ABA's ratings.†

The Kennedys are, of course, morally, politically and tactically responsible for the judges they picked. Nevertheless, had it been up to

---

* As it happened, Bohannon turned out to be a strong pro-civil rights judge.

† The rating system is in flux. These were the ratings during the Kennedy years.

them alone, undoubtedly no segregationists would have been appointed to the Southern bench. Thus to understand how what happened happened, one must look at the interaction between the three interested parties—the Kennedy Administration, which tended to downgrade the importance of the judiciary; the hard-core Southern Senators, who tended to upgrade the importance of "not letting any more Skelly Wrights * slip through"; and the real bureaucrats of judicial selection, the ABA, which was officially committed to professionalizing and upgrading the bar, but on occasion was more interested in preserving its role in the process than in protecting the public interest. Taking the Administration first:

By style Robert Kennedy was a delegator, which meant that in light of his involvement with the Kennedy Administration's struggle for anti-crime legislation, foreign-aid legislation, a space program, Comsat, a test-ban treaty, tax reform, recouping the good will dissipated by the Bay of Pigs, capitalizing on the good will generated by the Cuban missile crisis, and so many other issues, he let Byron White (and later Katzenbach) handle routine judge-picking while he served as the President's trouble-shooter, took trips around the world and deliberated on national security. In judge-picking as in most everything except organized crime, Hoffa and, later, civil rights, Kennedy got involved only where there was a problem, a top policy decision to be made. White, who was actually running the day-to-day business of the entire Justice Department (and early on suffered a duodenal ulcer), himself delegated the initial nominee-screening to Joseph Dolan, which meant that Dolan, whose background, like the Kennedys', was legislative-political (he had worked for two Senate committees, served as a JFK aide and served a term in the Colorado legislature), was the working judge-picker. He had worked briefly for JFK in the Senate and had his confidence. And he had worked with White in the Citizens for Kennedy campaign, and so it was natural that they imparted political attitudes and perspectives into the judicial-selection arena. The Kennedy–White–Dolan improvisatory style was in marked contrast to the more routinized approach of their Republican predecessors, who had themselves delegated more of the judicial-selection process to the ABA.

By temperament Robert Kennedy was an activist who tended to regard the bench as a sort of premature retirement. He simply *assumed* that top talent would be most interested in the active life of the execu-

* See pp. 272–273.

tive branch. It never occurred to him to have Byron White and his deputies mount a talent hunt for judges the way he got Sargent Shriver, assisted by Harris Wofford and the well-connected and tough-minded Adam Yarmolinsky, to mount a talent hunt for New Frontiersmen. Judge-picking was more of a processing than a searching operation. When White himself was mentioned as a possible Supreme Court replacement for Justice Whittaker, Robert Kennedy asked Dolan, "Do you really think Byron wants to go on the court?" It was not quite believable to Kennedy that White would prefer a job on the U.S. Supreme Court to the number-two job in the Justice Department, where, to the Attorney General's way of thinking, the real action was. Katzenbach, then head of the Office of Legal Counsel, volunteered, "I can understand why you don't want to let Byron go." Today Katzenbach says, "I knew this would offend Bobby but I think it was fairly instrumental in helping to persuade him."

By background Kennedy was a Congressional committee lawyer and by experience he was a politician (as were White and Dolan). He was less sensitive to the power of a judge than that of a boss. His environment was not the courtroom but the back room. He had neither political respect for the conservative politics of the ABA nor professional respect for such classic ABA criteria as "professional reputation" and "courtroom experience." Native ability and less tangible qualities of character counted more with the Kennedys. If the Kennedy predecessors, Rogers and Deputy Attorney General Lawrence Walsh (who resigned a federal judgeship to take the judge-picking job because he thought it that important and is now head of the ABA's judicial selection committee), were on a first-name basis with local bar leaders throughout the country, Kennedy, White and Dolan were on a nickname basis with the political district leaders, ward heelers and bosses.

By perspective the Kennedys were legislative branch men rather than judicial men. John Kennedy had spent his public life in both houses of the national legislature. Robert Kennedy had worked first for the McCarthy Committee and then for the McClellan Committee. They tended to assume the Senate framework—that judicial nominations would be cleared through the Senate Committee on the Judiciary, headed up by Senator James Eastland. That to antagonize a Senator on a judgeship was to risk losing a vote on foreign aid or the test-ban treaty. They paid more respect to the institution of Senatorial courtesy than to the ideal of an independent judiciary.

Judge-picking for the Kennedys was an extension of politics in the sense that they saw nothing wrong with searching for the best man from among the party faithful as well as in the sense that there was little illusion or rhetoric in the Kennedy camp about the judiciary being a thing apart from, or above, politics. Byron White told the ABA House of Delegates (who thought, along with 1960 Presidential candidate Richard M. Nixon, that judges should be picked on a bi-partisan basis), "There is nothing odious about the preference for Democrats. Picking judges is a political process in the best sense of those words." The theory was that there was no contradiction between respecting Senatorial prerogatives yet discouraging the abuse of those prerogatives.

Asked to describe the process, Nicholas Katzenbach says, "Basically, the policy on judgeships was play ball with the ABA, play ball with the Senator, do the best you can, don't let anyone through who has personally attacked the President. The Senators could understand that." It was less a problem, then, than an opportunity for trading that Judge Cox was sponsored by the powerful Senator Eastland, that Judge West was a protégé of Senator Russell Long, that Judge Robert Elliott's whole political career had been involved with Georgia's first political family, the Talmadges.

Liberal dogma had it that Kennedy cynically or shrewdly, depending on how you saw it, traded Coxes to the South for Thurgood Marshalls up north. That, however, is not at all how it generally worked. For the most part, the bad Southern choices were the products of the pre-exist-ing judicial selection system which the Kennedys inherited and more or less perpetuated without much question, at least during the first half of the Kennedys' tenure. The appointment of Robert Elliott of Georgia is evidence the system easily accommodated a built-in anti-civil rights bias.

Elliott was appointed in January 1962 after the antics of Judge Cox had alerted the Administration to the perils of judicial recalcitrance and after hard evidence of Elliott's racist outlook had come to its atten-tion. On June 26, 1961, Burke Marshall forwarded to Byron White a memorandum attaching some news clips relating to the white primary bill which was proposed in 1947 by the segregationist leaders in Georgia. Mr. Elliott had been a chief strategist in support of the bill along with Roy Harris, still a leader of the extreme segregationists. Elliott at the time was floor leader of the House for Governor Herman Talmadge. The purpose of the bill was to make it impossible for any Negroes to vote in the Democratic primary in Georgia.

In Georgia's 1952 election Elliott went on record as stating, "I don't want these pinks, radicals and black voters to outvote those who are trying to preserve our own segregation laws and other traditions." [4] In 1960, he was again elected to the House, this time as floor leader for Governor Eugene Talmadge. C. B. King, a black attorney in south Georgia, remarks: "The legacy of Talmadge is predicated on the word 'nigger.' And the appointment of Elliott, I assume, was his reward."

In his correspondence with Bickel, Marshall had advanced the only possible defense of the Elliott nomination:

> Judge Elliott was appointed after much soul-searching after consultation with Judge Tuttle.* Judge Tuttle gave Mr. Kennedy his view, based upon his consultation with Judge Bootle,* among others, that Judge Elliott would be fair. That appointment would not otherwise have been made. Elliott was, incidentally, also supported by some of the principal Negro political figures in Georgia.

And Bickel responded with the only possible reply:

> . . . the operative word seems to be the word "fair" . . . I really don't know what this means, and the assurances that were obtained may therefore have been insufficient because the wrong question was asked. West and Elliott have both talked in demonstration cases about being fair both to Negroes and to the communities involved, and I am sure they thought they were being fair. But what is in question is a judge's attitude in these matters and his conception of a federal judge's function in the South in this day and age. They have, after all, law to make as well as to apply, and fairness in some elemental sense of evenhandedness in the application of existing rules is scarcely all that is desired. I suppose it could be said of Tuttle, Rives and Johnson that they are unfair.
>
> As to Elliott, should not his public record have been an absolute disqualification?

When asked why Elliott wasn't disqualified, Burke Marshall pointed out that Colonel Austin T. Walden (the head of Georgia's Negro establishment) was supporting him. Elliott had the backing of the local NAACP! "Without that backing," says Marshall, "we might have been able to block him." In other words, the Kennedys *assumed* that Senatorial prerogatives were fixed and that the way to challenge a nominee was not to challenge the prerogative but to expose it to a countervailing power. And when the occasion arose legitimately to challenge the abuse of those prerogatives, they looked for their evidence to a man already deeply implicated in the existing power structure. Whether or not this was done cynically, the fact was that it did not occur to the genteel lawyers of the Justice Department to check out Elliott's reputation with and acceptability to men like the impolite and militant C. B.

---

* Liberal Eisenhower appointees in the Fifth Circuit.

King, with the far-out representatives of SNCC and with men like Andy Young of SCLC. In this important sense the Elliott appointment is evidence less of the Kennedys' willingness to abandon business-as-usual in favor of catering to Southern prejudice than of their commitment to the pre-existing establishment and its methods.

This is not to deny the good faith of the Kennedys and their willingness to use the judge-picking system against itself when the occasion presented itself. For instance, when the Justice Department discovered that a Georgia attorney named Hall, a Talmadge-backed nominee for the Northern District of Georgia, was a white supremacist, they withdrew his name from consideration and supported Lewis R. Morgan, another Talmadge man, but without visible prejudice, who was nominated and confirmed in the summer of 1961.

If the Kennedys underrated the importance of lower-court judges, the power structure of the South, if anything, exaggerated it. They had seen what men like Skelly Wright, who had ordered the integration of the schools in New Orleans Parish, could do. And because of existing Senatorial rules involving seniority, committee chairmanships and majority control, when the Democrats had a majority—as they did under John Kennedy—Dixiecrats controlled the machinery of judicial selection, as well as other areas critical to programs the Kennedys valued more highly. Mississippi's Senator James Eastland, after all, ran the Judiciary Committee—open sesame to all Justice Department-sponsored legislation. Georgia's Senator Richard Russell was chairman of the Armed Services Committee, critical to JFK's foreign policy— which JFK gave priority over domestic policy—and a prime mover on the Appropriations Committee, without whose authorizations government could come to a standstill. Virginia's Harry F. Byrd was chairman of the Finance Committee, and only slightly further west Senator Robert Kerr had replaced Lyndon B. Johnson as the most powerful figure in the Senate.

Whatever power these wily gentlemen possessed individually and through their committees was magnified because they possessed it in concert. It was power, moreover, underwritten by the age-old, self-serving rule of "Senatorial courtesy" whereby the Senate perpetuates its role in the judicial selection process by unanimously rejecting any nominee not acceptable ("personally obnoxious") to the relevant Senator from the state involved (Senators from the President's party generally take turns in nominating judicial appointees).

So even an Administration alert to the critical role of the judiciary and intent on seeking out moderates would have had no easy time of it. But the bureaucrats of judicial selection had yet another edge on the Kennedys—a stick presented in the guise of a carrot. On May 19, 1961, four months after John Kennedy took office, Congress passed an omnibus judgeship act which created seventy-one new judgeships. The act had been drafted and cleared in the fall of 1960, but despite lame-duck President Eisenhower's assurance that he would distribute judicial appointments evenly between the two parties, consulting and heeding Democratic Senators on Democratic appointments, Congress (with a two-thirds Democratic majority in the Senate) refused to pass the new judgeship bill until after Kennedy had taken office. Ike had argued that the judiciary was about evenly divided and if Congress would only pass the new bill, he would keep it that way. He was strongly seconded by the ABA, which stood to multiply its influence in an evenly split judiciary. Vice President Richard Nixon told the ABA House of Delegates in 1959: "I believe it is essential . . . that the number of judges in our federal courts from each of the two major political parties should be approximately equal." Of course the reason the bench was politically balanced in 1960 was that for the past eight years Eisenhower had appointed 92.5 percent Republicans, thus evening the imbalance created by twenty years of Roosevelt and Truman, who had appointed 95 percent and 91 percent Democrats respectively and who were themselves merely following in the tradition of Harding, Coolidge and Hoover—95 percent, 92 percent and 82.7 percent partisan, respectively.

Judicial selection under the Kennedys was without precedent in American history. President Kennedy filled more vacancies in sixteen months than Presidents Hoover, Coolidge and Harding collectively filled during their entire terms. Including vacancies, he had nominated 128 people to the federal bench, 113 of them to lifetime judgeships, which meant that during the year following the new bill, the months when he appointed the five malefactors, he had been nominating federal judges at the rate of almost ten a month. Except for Truman and Eisenhower this was more vacancies than any President of the United States had filled in two entire terms of office. In keeping with the tradition, the Kennedys ended up appointing 91.2 percent Democrats.

The administrative burden of processing such an extraordinary volume of judgeships took its toll in a failure to focus on the damage these men might do, a prospect which the Southern Senators viewed with quiet glee.

As Professor Mary Curzan has concluded in her unpublished doctoral
dissertation comparing the performance of Kennedy and Eisenhower
judges in the Fifth Circuit (over-all she didn't find much difference):

> A Democratic President like JFK is always one step behind in the
> bargaining process. The original suggestion begins with the Senator;
> the administration must accept or reject it. The Department of Justice
> when it runs its investigations of the candidate must often consult
> with the very forces in the state that support the Senator—the political
> party, the local bar, the elected state officials. Furthermore, a Demo-
> cratic President knows that his legislative program may suffer from
> disgruntled southerners who decide to take revenge for the rejection
> of a favored nominee for the federal bench.

This is not to say that the Senate system was totally immune to influence or takeover. In fact, on rare occasions the Kennedy people
were able to use the contradictions of the system against itself. One
such was the time they secured the selection of the able and moderate
William A. McRae in the Southern District of Florida despite the fact
that neither of the Florida Senators—George Smathers and Spessard
Holland, both Democrats—had nominated him in the first place.

Senators Smathers and Holland had recommended to the Justice
Department the name of a Jewish attorney from Miami who got bad
marks from both the ABA and the Kennedy "spotter" in Florida. While
the Senators searched in vain for a "Qualified" alternate with the same
ethnic payoff, the Kennedys turned to former Governor Leroy Collins
and asked him to recommend a compromise candidate. He came up
with the name of McRae, a Rhodes Scholar with a BA in Jurisprudence
from Oxford, a B.Litt. and an MA. He had won the Legion of Merit
while serving in the Air Force during World War II, had a successful
practice in Jacksonville, was a consultant to the UN and a law professor
at the University of Florida. When the ABA gave him an "Extremely
Well Qualified" rating, it was difficult if not impossible as a public-
relations matter for the Senators to turn him down—and they didn't.

That the Kennedys were able to outmaneuver the Florida Senators
on this nomination is a tribute to their ingenuity and occasional expertise at dealing with the bureaucrats of judicial selection—deploying,
as they did, the Senators and the ABA to the ultimate benefit of the
judiciary. But then one must ask why they didn't use such tactics to
thwart the nominations of the more obvious segregationists. The
answer is partly that they did not care enough in terms of other
Presidential priorities to risk the political consequences, but mostly it
is to be found in the role played by the third major participant in the
judicial selection process—the American Bar Association.

In comparison with the Republicans, who dominate its committees, membership and leadership, the elite Ivy Leaguers and the tough-minded Democratic and liberal lawyers whom Kennedy attracted to the Justice Department were hostile to the ABA. Nevertheless, they included the ABA in their world view as the predominant extra-governmental institution to be reckoned with in the judicial selection process. When the Kennedys went beyond their own talent scouts in checking someone out, their universe was bounded by the NAACP Inc. Fund on the left and the ABA on the right. Or when they talked to blacks in the South, it was to Georgia's Colonel Walden, not to Bob Moses. Bernard Segal, chairman of the ABA Judicial Selection Committee, worked out a system whereby the ABA would render "informal" ratings in advance of formal ones so that Kennedy could, presumably, refrain from nominating men whom the ABA found to be unqualified. And a judicial candidate who had attended Harvard, Yale or Columbia had the best chance of an "Extremely Well Qualified" rating.

Thus even though the net impact of the Kennedys was to *lessen* the ABA's influence on the judicial selection process from what it had been under the Republicans, in the larger scheme of things the Kennedys were eminently comfortable dealing with the ABA. As Bernard Segal says, "There was not a day that I was not on the phone to Dolan or Katzenbach or White or, in rarer cases, to Bob. My time sheets show I put in forty to forty-five hours a week on it." The ABA was a *de facto*, albeit informal, part of the judicial selection process. A number of consequences flowed from the ABA's role.

First, despite the Kennedys' quarrel with ABA criteria, they named only eight judges whom the ABA found "Not Qualified." Ignoring the political values which permeate the ABA rating system, *The New York Times*, on March 9, 1962, editorialized, "It is shocking that President Kennedy should have named to the federal bench anyone whom the Bar Association found unqualified to serve." While the ABA may have striven to purge political values from its professional judgments, a list of the ABA's political stands from 1937 to 1960 leaves little room for doubt as to that organization's bias.* In fact, most of the Kennedy "unqualifieds" had to do with "qualifications" that the Kennedys felt

* Professor Harold Chase of the University of Wisconsin cites the ABA's opposition to the Child Labor Amendment, to the Wagner-Murray-Dingell National Health Insurance Bill, to the Genocide Convention and the Covenant on Human Rights, and to having an ABA observer with the United States delegation to the UN. They supported the Tidelands Oil Bill, the Mundt-Nixon Internal Security Bill, and the Bricker Amendment, and they commended the House Un-American Activities Committee, the Senate Internal Security Committee, even the old McCarthy Committee.

arbitrary or at least debatable. An example was the ABA position on age, articulated by Segal in March 1961, before he had had much experience with the Kennedys.

> . . . It is only three years since it has become *firmly established* that no lawyer 60 years or over should be appointed to a lifetime judgeship for the first time, unless he is regarded by professional opinion as "Well Qualified" or "Exceptionally Well Qualified," and is in excellent health. This rule has not been applied to a Federal judge under consideration for elevation to an appellate court, but the rule has been that in no event, should anyone, even a judge being elevated to an appellate court, be appointed if he has passed his sixty-fourth birthday. Congress itself has decreed that a Federal judge, with the requisite years of service, may retire at age 65 with full pay for life. Surely, this is not the age at which a person should be tendered a new appointment.

The issue arose when, after months of wrangling, Attorney General Kennedy named Ramsey Clark, then head of the Lands Division, as unofficial Ambassador to his native state of Texas to see if he could reconcile the conflicting patronage claims of Democratic Senator Ralph Yarborough (a Kennedy friend) and an already sensitive Vice President Lyndon B. Johnson, whom the Kennedys didn't want to antagonize needlessly. Clark, with deep Texas bonds and happy relations with all factions, worked out a package deal of four nominees, including Judge Sarah T. Hughes, then over the ABA's age limit of sixty-four. The ABA let it be known that they considered Judge Hughes unqualified by reason of age (despite her robust health and the fact that in twenty-six years as a state circuit judge she had an almost perfect attendance record, much popular support and a flourishing legal reputation). Kennedy, not wishing to buck the ABA unnecessarily, said to Clark, "I'll give you three minutes to tell me why we should take Judge Hughes."

The thirty-three-year-old Assistant Attorney General replied: "There are three reasons. First, we need women judges. She has served twenty-six years on the bench and has been a good judge. Second, women live longer than men, so if you want to be scientific about it, give her the benefit of the doubt. Third, a gentleman never asks a lady her age."

Whether it was Clark's little speech that did it or Lyndon Johnson's continued pressure on her behalf or the reported intervention of House Speaker Sam Rayburn (another Hughes fan), who when he heard that the Attorney General was hesitating over the age issue was reported to have said, "Sonny, in your eyes everybody seems too old," Kennedy got the message. He went ahead with the carefully arbitrated package recommendation, and three years later on a tragic November day in 1963, Judge Hughes swore in Lyndon B. Johnson as President of the United States. Ten years later she was still very much alive and had earned a reputation as one of the best judges on the circuit.

Although the ABA views itself as an elevator of judicial standards, its effect under the Kennedys in the South—primarily because of its fear of being excluded from the mechanics of the judicial selection process—was on too many occasions to lower standards. Or at least to alter them to meet passing contingencies or policy needs. An ironic example, because it was one of the few times the ABA lowered its standards to *combat* racism, was the Kennedys' first judicial appointment in Texas.

When the Kennedys decided on political policy grounds that the post should go to a Mexican American, they frankly told the ABA that they had set out to find not the best lawyer in south Texas but "the best Mexican American lawyer in south Texas." The names of Garcia, Garza and Salinas were submitted, and the ABA initially found none of them qualified. Eventually Joseph Dolan convinced Bernard Segal, whose self-image (despite his co-chairmanship of the National Nixon for President Committee in 1960) was considerably to the left of the ABA mainstream on civil rights matters, that it would be in the best interests of the federal judiciary to have the Mexican Americans represented. Segal convinced the ABA committee, and Reynaldo B. Garza, BA, LL.B, University of Texas, was rated "Qualified."

The Kennedy men could have openly disregarded the ABA's ratings. Instead, the Ivy League instinct, and the Kennedys' political instinct as well, were to seek ABA approval. The Kennedy Administration's political interest coincided with the ABA's bureaucratic interest, and the result was cases like Garza where, from the highest of motives, the ABA compromised its function as independent arbiter.

Professor Harold W. Chase, of the University of Wisconsin, who did an exhaustive study of judicial selection during this period for the Brookings Institution, concluded:

> In a two-year period in the Kennedy Administration, by my reckoning, almost 29 percent or 29 of 101 informal ratings differed from the formal rating. Seventy-two ratings [by the ABA] showed no change; 7 which looked not qualified on the informal were qualified on the formal; 1 went from qualified to not qualified; 17 went from qualified to well-qualified; 1 from well qualified to qualified; 3 from well qualified to qualified; 3 from well qualified to exceptionally well qualified. Perhaps, of even more significance is the fact that of 9 qualifieds which I counted in the 72 as unchanged, there was indica-

tion (in the informal rating) that the Committee had some reservations about the candidate being qualified. In short, in the "give and
take" of discussion something happened in nearly 30 percent of the
cases, usually resulting in up-grading.

These figures are not intended to suggest that the ABA was unwilling to fight for its principles but merely that on occasion its pragmatic
approach tended to undermine them. On other occasions, of course,
where the ABA thought it might prevail, it rigidly fought for its credo.
The nomination of Irving Ben Cooper of New York, declared by the
ABA "unqualified" because they felt he lacked "judicial temperament,"
is a case in point. The merits aside (nobody questioned Cooper's integrity or ability), the Kennedys nominated him because Congressman
Emanuel Celler, who as chairman of the Judiciary Committee was
Eastland's counterpart in the House, wanted him. Bill Geoghegan
recalls, "We had eight New York appointments and no Democratic
Senators there. So it's natural then that a senior member of the
House delegation would have something to say about an appointment,
at least one of those appointments. Celler was never a very demanding person in terms of political patronage but this was something that
he really wanted and he had, of course, a great deal of our legislation—
most of it would go through the Judiciary Committee." The Kennedys
appointed Cooper while Congress was in recess, and then got him confirmed over the ABA's objections—a device which they were reluctant
to employ in the case of nominations to the Southern bench.

Often, although not in the vast majority of cases, the ABA compromised its standards to preserve its role, about which it was quite in-
secure. Two weeks before the Kennedys took office Bernard Segal and
ABA President Whitney North Seymour met with Robert Kennedy
and Byron White. Segal thought "we obtained an unequivocal commitment that they would appoint only those who were pronounced clearly
qualified by the Committee." White and Kennedy, though, believed
that they agreed only to the policy of submitting names to the ABA
Committee. They felt free to act contrary to the ABA's recommendations. A dramatic example of the way the system worked was the appointment of Byron White, then Deputy Attorney General, to the U.S.
Supreme Court. When Bernard Segal was told that among those being
considered was Harvard's Paul Freund, the Negro judge William Hastie
and Abraham Ribicoff, an early Kennedy supporter then serving as
Secretary of HEW, and that Kennedy was leaning toward the appointment of someone connected with his Administration, the ABA let
it be known that Ribicoff lacked sufficient courtroom "experience." But

when Segal was *told*, after the fact, that the President had decided on and was going to announce Byron White's appointment without consulting the ABA (although Segal was actually among those who suggested White in the first place), he virtually guaranteed an "Extremely Well Qualified" rating if the President would hold up the announcement until the committee had a chance to convene. The ABA had not yet established with the Kennedys its interest in passing on nominations to the highest court in the land, and here was an occasion to do so. The President agreed to delay the announcement a few hours. Segal held a two-hour conference call "meeting" of his committee, which ended up designating White "Extremely Well Qualified" despite the fact that he was—by dint of his youth—a year short of meeting the entry requirements of the American College of Trial Lawyers, a presumption against him under the ABA's rigid "experience" requirement.

In dealings with the ABA over their Southern nominees, the Kennedys were at a double disadvantage. Although they dealt with the ABA as an institution and accepted without too much fuss its role in the judicial selection area, they were not as familiar as the Republican establishment with the politics of the local bar. At the same time, the "spotters"—Kennedy men on the scene who were supposed to render informal assessments—were tied in with the very Democratic political machines that were doing the nominating and may well have been advising the ABA in the first place. By luck or design the assistant attorneys general represented a geographical cross section— Oberdorfer from Alabama, Orrick from California, Clark from Texas, Miller from Minnesota, et al.—and so whenever appropriate, the relevant assistant attorney general sounded out his own contacts as an additional check. Nevertheless, the result was that Kennedy intelligence in this area was often circular and left much to be desired. For instance, the Kennedys didn't know in 1961 what the Republicans apparently knew in 1955 when a vacancy opened up on the Fifth Circuit Court of Appeals and the Eisenhower Administration decided to take advantage of the occasion to improve relations with the chairman of the Judiciary Committee, Senator Eastland. William Rogers, now Secretary of State but then Deputy Attorney General, was dispatched to ask the Senator for suggested nominees. When Eastland recommended the names of Judge Mize (a diehard segregationist judge of the Southern District of Mississippi) and W. Harold Cox, Rogers literally laughed at the suggestions. In fact, Rogers considered the idea so implausible because of what he understood to be Cox's segregationist reputation that he neither ordered a preliminary investigation within the Justice Department nor

asked the Bar Association Committee to check him out. He told Eastland that what he wanted were *reasonable* suggestions, not impossible
ones. Two weeks later, Eastland came back with the name of Benjamin C. Cameron. Rogers had him checked out, recommended and appointed. That Cameron turned out to be a confirmed segregationist
shows that Rogers was not all *that* circumspect about his own recommendations, but the episode further underlines Cox's notoriety and also
suggests the intelligence difficulties the Kennedys were up against.

The same intelligence gap presumably accounts for the good report
that the tough-minded, Alabama-born, Ivy-educated Lou Oberdorfer—
in charge of the Tax Division—turned in on Clarence Allgood and
Walter Gewin, who went on to become judicial obstructionists.

Clarence Allgood, whose chief experience was as sometimes bankruptcy referee, had an undistinguished record. By reason of little legal
ability and even less legal experience (in or out of court), the ABA's
informal report found him "unqualified," a perfect occasion for the
Kennedys to find an alternate nominee as they did in the case of ex-
Rhodes Scholar McRae in Florida. But instead of commencing negotiations with Alabama's Senator Sparkman (who had originally suggested
him) or Senator Hill (a Kennedy loyalist), they assumed the Senatorial
prerogative and began negotiations instead with the ABA to get Allgood's rating enhanced. Hence Oberdorfer was dispatched to his
native Alabama and shortly returned with the report that Allgood
would be an adequate judge, that he was an honorable man and that
he had the backing of local civil rights leaders. Based on this "new"
information, Bernard Segal got the ABA committee to call him "qualified."

In addition to suggesting the flawed nature of the Administration's
sources—Lou Oberdorfer still says, "Based on the information I got,
I'd make the same recommendation again today"—the Allgood nomination reflects the erroneous Kennedy assumption that the South had
a monolithic political structure and that it was impossible to play off
Senators against each other. The fact was that Senator Lister Hill had
agreed to back Allgood only because Senator Sparkman agreed to back
another segregationist—Walter Gewin—for the Fifth Circuit Court of
Appeals. The Kennedys then put up a token fight against Gewin
not because they thought he might be a segregationist but because they
didn't think seats on the Court of Appeals (which covered more than
one state) should be apportioned on the same state-by-state basis as
district court judgeships.

Even here, had the ABA functioned merely as impartial rater, the

Allgood appointment might have been avoided. But three factors put it across. First, the ABA's willingness to go along if that would help solidify its role. Second, the feeling of the Kennedy judge-pickers—confronted with over 100 judgeships to fill and a judicial selection bureaucracy wired with political traps—that merely getting a nominee through was something of a victory. And third, the assumption of the Ivy League lawyers, even home-grown ones like Alabama-born Oberdorfer, that if the old-boy network didn't veto a man he could be counted on to uphold the law—that professional values would prevail over regional ones.

If the Cox appointment reflects the shrewdness of the Senatorial bureaucrats of judicial selection, if the Elliott appointment reflects the Kennedys' placing political values—in the narrow sense—over judicial ones, and if the Allgood and Gewin appointments reflect the limitations of a judicial talent scouting system relying essentially on a network of law school and old political ties, the appointment of E. Gordon West reflects the ultimate danger of a presumably independent auditor—the ABA—placing its bureaucratic stake ahead of its professional obligation. Had the Kennedy judge-pickers and the ABA not shared so much in the way of assumptions, background and rhetoric, *no matter their differences, which were substantial,* the appointment of a West—as distinguished from a Cox and a Gewin, men whose technical legalistic qualifications were in order—might well have been impossible. But the informal establishment jurisprudence, of which both the Kennedy men and the ABA partook, provided a common frame of reference. They were comfortable in each other's milieu; they could, they thought, do business together.

And that's what they did in the case of Judge West, who, although a graduate of Louisiana State University, was born in Massachusetts and had no record whatsoever on the race issue. The establishment lawyers therefore assumed he had establishment values. The trouble with West as a prospective judge was that he didn't have much of a record on anything else either, except errand-running for, and loyalty to, Senator Russell Long. His most impressive job was as a Louisiana inheritance tax collector. The ABA's committee informally let Byron White know that they didn't think they could give West a "Qualified" rating. Again, instead of pressuring Senator Long into accepting another judge—actually West's was one of thirteen names submitted by *both* Louisiana Senators as "acceptable" for three Louisiana vacancies —the Department successfully convinced the ABA that it should rate E. Gordon West "Qualified." Ironically, their main argument was that it would be useful to have a man of West's Northern background on the Southern bench.

Incidentally, a retrospective case might be made for the appointment of West on the ground that it facilitated the simultaneous appointment of Robert Ainsworth, a liberal Louisiana lawyer and law professor at LSU, who had served as president pro tem of the state senate and chairman of the board of managers of the Council of State Governments. After turning in a list of thirteen acceptable candidates, Senator Ellender let the Department know that although he had placed Ainsworth's name on it, Ainsworth was really his last choice. He argued that unless he saw evidence disqualifying the others, he would veto Ainsworth, who was the Department's first choice, all of which caused a delay. Upset at the wait, Ainsworth asked the Department to withdraw his name on the ground that the on-again, off-again rumors surrounding his potential judgeship were injuring his reputation. Dolan persuaded Ainsworth to withhold his withdrawal, and Robert Kennedy guaranteed the appointment of West (thus securing Senator Long's support for Ainsworth) and convinced Ellender that it would be bad politics to oppose a man he himself had nominated. On September 21, 1961, Ainsworth was confirmed, with the quiet support of both Louisiana Senators—a half credit to Kennedy Justice but no vindication of the ABA's role. Although Ainsworth has turned out to be a moderate, John Nelson, one of the few activist, integrationist white lawyers in New Orleans, notes: "Ainsworth was a leader of the Louisiana Senate when *all* the segregationist bills were passed. He is a loyal, patriotic American—a man who helped me personally. But he is a man of his time. When segregationists were strong and powerful, he was a segregationist. He got a federal judgship and now he calls them like he sees them."

Here, then, was a case where the Kennedys, the ABA, the Senators and the high-minded Justice Department lawyers, each trying their best to advance their own cause, unwittingly collaborated to undermine the judiciary and respect for law.

The West case is consistent with the style of horse-trading at which the Kennedys, working in tandem with the ABA, were so adept. That such a system yielded so unfortunate a by-product is attributable to the interaction of the system, the South, and such variables as the local passion for resisting the changes decreed by the Supreme Court, Southern dominance of the national legislature, the tradition of a judiciary arising from the community in which it sits, the lack of penetrating FBI intelligence or civil rights organization ammunition to counter the sometimes shallow and insulated dossiers prepared by the ABA and the mostly establishment Kennedy contacts, and the absence of any deep, abiding and overriding Kennedy commitment to the integrity and quality of the Southern judiciary itself.

This situation was reinforced by the Kennedys' reliance on the ABA—even though it was less than Eisenhower's before and Nixon's after—and by the ABA's reliance on local bar representatives, who reflected the prejudices of their milieu, principal among them Charles J. Bloch, the Fifth Circuit's representative on the ABA's judicial selection committee, whose conservative approach to civil rights was evident to all who dealt with him. Most important, though, was the Kennedys' general deference to the ABA ratings themselves, whose criteria gave rigid primacy to litigation and courtroom experience, thereby automatically eliminating as candidates for judgeships those Southerners most likely to take a liberal, cosmopolitan, more sensitive approach to race relations—government lawyers, large-firm metropolitan lawyers with research capabilities or drafting specialties, and law professors.

How good a job did the Kennedys do of appointing judges, all things considered? Even in the South the Kennedys named more decent judges than dishonest, incompetent or racist ones. And prevailing clichés to the contrary, the Republicans have not done that much better. One scholar, Dr. Mary Curzan, classified the judges selected in the Fifth Circuit between 1953 and 1963 as segregationists, moderates and integrationists, and she found modest difference between the Eisenhower and Kennedy Administrations: *

	Eisenhower Appointees	Kennedy Appointees
Segregationists	5	5
Moderates	8	3
Integrationists	2	8

Dr. Curzan attributed the cliché that Eisenhower's appointments were more liberal than Kennedy's to three factors: First, two of the most prominent integrationists, Elbert P. Tuttle and John M. Wisdom, were named by the Republicans. Second, Kennedy's segregationists attracted the most publicity. Third, the ABA publicly had favored Eisenhower. But she added:

* Some scholars might quarrel with her rating system, which measures judges by case-results without factoring in delay and other obstructionist tactics along the way to these results. Nevertheless, the criteria are clearly identified and the study is therefore useful.

Finally, there is one empirical basis upon which the Eisenhower appointees do appear to be more liberal than the Kennedy appointees to the courts of the Fifth Circuit. If one takes the total number of civil rights cases decided by all the Eisenhower and Kennedy judges in each year and determines the percentage of those cases that favored the Negro plaintiff, the Eisenhower judges have a more liberal record than do the Kennedy judges.

Professor Harold Chase puts it more modestly:

In sum, despite the attitudes of both Presidents on civil rights and for whatever reasons, the Eisenhower-appointed judges, patently, have at least as good a record as the Kennedy judges with respect to vindicating the Negroes' civil rights.

By the time Robert Kennedy himself was Democratic Senator from New York, his successful fight for reform Democratic candidate Sam Silverman for a local surrogate court judgeship to dramatize the unsatisfactory nature of machine-controlled judicial politics, as well as his nominations of such highly qualified and politically disinterested judicial candidates as Judges Jack Weinstein and Marvin Frankel, reflected a genuine concern for the judiciary. Moreover, as Attorney General after early 1962 he nominated no more judicial disasters, although his slowness in spotting the terrible impact of his mistakes in this area is evidenced by a press conference he gave at the Atlanta, Georgia, post office on April 23, 1963, when he told those present:

I'm very proud of the judges that have been appointed. We looked into all of them for questions of integrity and whether they would uphold the law of the land. They didn't decide for the government in every matter, and I wouldn't expect that they would. That does not mean that I question their integrity, their ability or their willingness to follow the law and meet their oath of office.

If the system is the villain, if judgeships have been regarded as legitimate patronage since the time of Andrew Jackson, if the Kennedys didn't *knowingly* or willingly appoint any diehard racists—with the possible exception of Judge Robert Elliott—to the Southern bench, what might they have done differently or better? First, it should be observed that while the judge-picking system may define the limits within which any Administration may operate, it need not determine the inevitability of any particular judicial candidate nor the philosophical coloration of the bench, especially in an Administration with the one-two punch of the brothers Kennedy. Critics have advanced a variety of options which retrospectively seem to have been available, among them appointing racial moderates while Congress was in recess, playing off the ABA against the Senators or outflanking the Senators (as they successfully did in the cases of McRae in Florida and Ainsworth in Louisiana), switching judges from Northern circuits to serve in the South, bargaining pork-barrel legislation for judgeships, or simply vetoing unacceptable candidates. As Katzenbach points out, a judicial vacancy is more of an embarrassment to a Senator than to the Administration since it says to his constituency that the Senator doesn't have the clout to get his boy through. The effectiveness of these tactics is debatable. That they were not systematically attempted in the South of the Sixties, however, is beyond debate. But whatever the Kennedys might have tried, they could not have abolished by fiat the tradition and fact of Senatorial prerogatives.

Nor can the Kennedys be blamed for the FBI, which carried on as usual. Nevertheless, had the FBI done its job, the probability of segregationists on the Southern bench would have been significantly diminished. Hard evidence of racism would have made mandatory Departmental objection to some nominees, provided the Department with an arguing point about others, and incidentally deprived the Kennedys of the possibility of what might be called "convenient ignorance," as in the case of Cox. Had the FBI undertaken inquiries into the race views of Southern judicial nominees with the same diligence they displayed in investigating the political views of potential classified-information handlers, it takes no great imagination to project the Bureau's impact on the judge-appointing process. Katzenbach says the FBI was told to include evidence of racism in its reports, but Burke Marshall recalls that from a civil rights viewpoint, "The FBI reports were worthless." He adds, "We didn't rely on the Bureau. There wasn't an appointment in the South that the Attorney General didn't discuss with me." The difficulty, of course, was that the Civil Rights Division had neither the time nor the contacts to develop a fool-proof information-gathering net. Although it is significant that the worst appointments were made in the first year and a half before either the Kennedys or the country had been fully alerted to the perils of an obstructionist judiciary.*

* The procedure by which the Department transmitted FBI report information to the Senate Judiciary Committee is worth noting since it illustrates the close links between the Bureau and Senator Eastland—a relationship which might have inhibited Eastland's political dependents from speaking freely. According to Harold Chase, "An officer of the Department . . . calls on the Chairman of the Senate Judiciary Committee with the FBI file of a nominee which the Committee is to consider. The officer gives an oral résumé of anything in the file which might possibly be considered derogatory and answers any questions the Chairman may ask by way of clarification. If the Chairman wishes to look at the file, he will do so

Had the ABA, moreover, been less interested in creating the *appearance* of ABA-ratification of judicial nominees and more interested in the actual quality of the appointees, had the liberal Bernard Segal *avoided* rather than played politics, the ABA's total influence might have appeared less but its real influence in the South might have been critical. For instance, had the ABA stuck to its original preliminary "Not Qualified" assessments of West and Allgood, their candidacies might well have been defeated.

Had civil rights not been a stepchild in the initial constellation of Kennedy priorities and had Robert Kennedy appreciated the possibilities of judicial activism and the danger of obstructionism, even without the assistance of the FBI he might have avoided these appointments. As it was, the same tunnel vision which kept him ignorant of the FBI's illegal bugging practices perhaps assisted his ignorance of potential judges' unconstitutional theories. Here, too, it was an insensitivity to the relevance of procedures that did him in—a district judge can dismiss a suit for, among other reasons, failing to state a federal cause of action, for failing to defer to the state courts, or for not exhausting administrative remedies. And so here, too, although he did not consciously set out to undermine the law, Kennedy was responsible in more than a technical sense for what happened.

It was not that Robert Kennedy was soft on segregationists. It was that Robert Kennedy was soft on the proprieties of judicial selection. Sometimes this attitude was irrelevant, as when he *told* Joe Dolan he was going to appoint Griffin Bell to fill the vacancy on the Fifth Circuit Court of Appeals. No inquiry was made into Bell's race record because he was being rewarded as a Kennedy loyalist. As it happened, Bell has turned out to be a moderate judge on racial issues, and so the sloppiness of the selection procedure has not come under liberal scrutiny. The case of Frank Ellis, too outrageous to be typical, nevertheless illustrates the perils of the Kennedy orientation. It would have been impossible under an Attorney General with either a higher regard for the bench, a more lawyerly view of the bench as capstone to the legal career, or a more distant relationship with the President.

When a vacancy opened up on the Fifth Circuit Court of Appeals in late 1961, Judge J. Skelly Wright, who had courageously and imaginatively enforced the mandates of the U.S. Supreme Court in the Southern District of Louisiana, was the logical appointee. Judges Tuttle

---

but only in the presence of the officer. . . . As a practical matter, therefore, the members of the Judiciary Committee only know what the Chairman wishes to tell them."

and Wisdom told Burke Marshall that Wright would be an excellent choice and if he were passed over, it would be regarded as a punishment for his liberal decisions. But Senator Russell Long told the President that he couldn't be re-elected to the Senate in 1962 if he did not veto Wright's promotion to the Fifth Circuit Court of Appeals. In a concession to Senator Long, President Kennedy appointed Wright to the Court of Appeals for the District of Columbia, thus making the merited promotion, but again going out of his way not to antagonize the powerful South (and incidentally depriving the South of Judge Wright's accumulated wisdom). But the Kennedys didn't take advantage of the situation to bargain with Long in terms of a progressive replacement for Wright.

Instead, President Kennedy submitted the name of Frank Ellis, who upon confirmation immediately set about overruling Judge Wright, including his decision in the *Busch* case, first brought in 1956, where he enjoined an Orleans Parish from operating segregated schools. Since that time every legal artifice known to Southern man had been invoked to frustrate Wright's order. The case was appealed up to the U.S. Supreme Court. The local school board sought to have Judge Wright's action appealed, vacated and mooted by action of the legislature. Louisiana's Attorney General went into the state courts to prevent the school board from following Wright's plans. The superintendent of schools declared a school holiday to prevent Wright's plans from being followed. The Governor of Louisiana took over the schools to prevent them from following Wright's plans. The Louisiana legislature passed no less than twenty-three laws (all declared unconstitutional by a three-judge district court) to avoid following Wright's plans. By 1962, when it looked as if all conceivable avenues of obstruction had at last been exhausted, Judge Wright ordered the first six grades integrated (originally he had called for a grade-a-year integration) and departed for the District of Columbia's Court of Appeals to which the Kennedys had appointed him. One of Judge Ellis's first acts was to stay Wright's order and to grant the school board a new trial.*

Here our concern is less with the impact of such devastatingly demoralizing decisions than with the process by which Judge Ellis came to sit. Ellis, who served as Kennedy's Louisiana campaign manager and Democratic State Chairman in 1960, had expected a Cabinet post but instead was appointed Director of the Office of Civil Defense

---

* I have not included Ellis among the hard-core segregationist appointments because after the first year, he started conforming some of his decisions to the rulings of the higher courts.

Mobilization. A prime pusher of the fallout-shelter program, he turned out to be inadequate as an administrator and an irritant to the President. Ellis had, for instance, publicly appealed for more funds than Kennedy had approved for him and generally sought ways to alert the public to the paramount importance of civil defense. In his memoir *Kennedy*, Theodore Sorensen, Special Counsel to JFK, recalls "Upon learning that Ellis planned to fly to Rome to seek a testimonial from the Pope in behalf of the Ellis plan to install a fallout shelter in every church basement, the President gently suggested that it would be a mistake to bother the Pope at that time."

"It was during one of the periodic emergency evacuation tests," claims one who was there, "that the President began to wonder what it would be like sealed in with Ellis, as evacuation procedures specified, in the event of a genuine emergency. Not long thereafter he began to consider the possibility of changing Ellis's job." Although it strains credulity that the President would so cavalierly undermine the integrity of the judiciary, the fact remains that he was unhappy with Ellis's performance in Washington but nevertheless felt that he owed Ellis a debt as one of his earliest and most effective Southern supporters. In one of the few direct Presidential interventions in the district court judge-picking process, JFK decided to use the impending Wright vacuum to solve the problem of the Ellis presence. He instructed Joe Dolan that Ellis was his choice and therefore the conventional inquiries would not be necessary.

Sorensen sheds additional light on the President's motives in his account of JFK's May 25 address to Congress calling for shelters as a form of "survival insurance" and announcing the transfer of jurisdiction over civil defense from the Office of Civil Defense Mobilization (Ellis) to the Defense Department (McNamara). Sorensen writes:

> . . . A long and difficult negotiation between the two men on the terms of the transfer, mediated by the Budget Bureau with my help, had not yet been completed by the time of the President's speech. Ellis was willing to have only the shelter program transferred to Defense, McNamara wanted full responsibility or none. To obtain the agreement of both men to the language in Kennedy's announcement, I carefully worded that portion of the President's message to read somewhat ambiguously: "I am assigning responsibility for this program to . . . the Secretary of Defense." Each man assumed this meant I had decided he was right. But shortly thereafter all civil defense functions were moved to Defense, the OCDM was reorganized into the Office of Emergency Planning, and Ellis resigned to accept a judgeship.[5]

The President rarely gave Dolan such directives, but when he did, Dolan respected them. Senator Long had no objection, since Ellis was an old friend. Senator Ellender, however, had recently defeated Ellis in a hard-fought primary fight and at first strongly opposed the nomination, claiming that Ellis was not qualified. JFK personally contacted Ellender and Ellis personally contacted Ellender, but Ellender was adamant. In his view Ellis was not qualified.

Despite Ellender's opposition the Justice Department gave Ellis's name to the ABA committee, which, after a talk with the Attorney General, found him qualified. JFK's theory was that Ellender couldn't afford to oppose Ellis. It would look as if he was retaliating for Ellis's primary challenge. This kind of bluff poker—which the Department was unwilling to play against Senators with their segregationist or otherwise dubious nominees—worked. Ellender unenthusiastically forwarded to the Judiciary Committee a batch of telegrams allowing as how Ellis would be better than Skelly Wright. In a one-man Subcommittee hearing, Senator Eastland asked Ellis, as he had asked Ainsworth and West, "Now if we approve you, you are not going to be another Skelly Wright, are you?" He also asked Ellis a lot of other questions about his earlier testimony before the Subcommittee on Armed Services which had indicated a potential conflict of interest between his civilian defense job and his private obligations. Eastland seemed to have some reservations about Ellis.

Before the Judiciary Committee acted on the Subcommittee's favorable recommendation, Bernard Segal came upon and turned over to Senator Hruska of Nebraska evidence—received subsequent to the ABA's "Qualified" recommendation—that Ellis had perjured himself. He had not received one of the degrees he claimed on his résumé and there were other, minor discrepancies. More damaging, Segal told Hruska he had evidence that Ellis allegedly was receiving drugs on the prescription of a New York physician. Segal and the Committee found this new evidence shocking if true and urged Hruska to reopen the Eastland Subcommittee hearings to see if the drug charge had any basis in fact. (There was no question but that he had perjured himself.) Hruska, however, declined to do so, saying it was out of his hands. Byron White, then Deputy Attorney General, said that nothing could be done about it. And the ABA Committee, despite its strong disapproval, decided since Ellis was going to be appointed anyway, no useful purpose could be served by damaging his reputation. They decided not to fight.

The Senate hearing was over, the President and the ABA were on record, and it would be embarrassing to all concerned if word got out.

So Eastland swallowed his qualms. Hruska swallowed his qualms. Byron White swallowed his qualms. Bernard Segal most reluctantly swallowed his qualms, and Frank Ellis was appointed U.S. Federal District Court judge in Skelly Wright's old Louisiana seat. The Kennedys got their man and in the process compromised the future president of the ABA, the chairman of the Senate Judiciary Committee, the Senator from Nebraska, the President of the United States, the U.S. Attorney General, his Deputy, his Deputy's Assistant—and how many others, no one knows.

The vice of the Ellis appointment, in addition to its lack of serious concern for the damage such a man might do to the civil rights cause,* was prospective. How could the Attorney General or his agents ever again expect to appeal to Senator Ellender or Long, for that matter, on grounds of principle or morality in opposition to a segregationist nominee? They couldn't—and didn't. "It was the worst appointment we made," concedes Dolan, who considered his job to upgrade the quality of the judiciary throughout the country, and despite a politically permissive orientation, took these things personally.

Had Ivy League values—which honor the judiciary—prevailed, Ellis and some of his brethren might not have gotten through. But in the case of these appointments to the Fifth Circuit, the Ivy League milieu —which honors the ABA, itself beholden to the Southern legal establishment—conspired with Kennedy priorities to undermine the integrity of the judiciary and thereby to compromise the quality of justice thousands of litigants would receive in the years to follow.

* In fact, as the circuit got more militant, Ellis started obeying most of the circuit court's orders and eventually resigned due to ill health.

CHAPTER SIX

Lawyering:
The Solicitor and the General

"IT WAS A TOUGH TICKET. Everybody in town wanted to see Bobby Kennedy get his teeth knocked out," recalls Bruce Terris, the young Harvard lawyer from the Solicitor General's office who briefed the Attorney General on the occasion of his first and only courtroom appearance—oral argument before the U.S. Supreme Court.

It was January 17, 1963, and Robert Kennedy, decked out in a morning coat and striped trousers, "looked like a nervous and uncomfortable bridegroom," said the Washington *Post's* James Clayton. The tradition is that each Attorney General argues one case before his term is over and Kennedy had chosen to argue *Gray* v. *Sanders,* a case testing the constitutionality of Georgia's county unit system of primary elections, in which the U.S. was appearing as a friend of the court.* Under that system it was possible to win the Democratic nomination for Governor by getting half the votes in counties representing only 22.2 percent of the population. The state of Georgia candidly admitted that its county unit system was specifically designed to achieve a special balance between urban and rural voting power. The

* Archibald Cox cites chapter and verse proving that it is not really a "tradition" for the Attorney General to argue at least one case. But so many modern Attorneys General have acted as if it were a tradition that the point is academic.

case had originally been brought by Morris Abram, a leading Georgia attorney, since gone on to the presidency of Brandeis and a law partnership with New York's prestigious firm of Paul, Weiss, Goldberg, Rifkind, Wharton and Garrison, following four earlier unsuccessful suits challenging the system. By 1963, however, the Supreme Court had ruled that courts could pass on state apportionment and the case seemed strong. Kennedy, with characteristic bravado, had let the Justices know in advance that he would be happy to answer questions from the court—an ordeal which most Attorneys General forgo. When his predecessor, William Rogers, had argued *his* case, he didn't ask the court for questions but the irrepressible Frankfurter asked one anyway —about a page citation in the brief—and the frustrated Rogers gave the wrong answer.

Attorney General Kennedy conducted his argument with courage and talent, and his side prevailed as the court decided that once districts are chosen, individual votes cannot be weighted. The oral argument he gave was his own. Solicitor General Archibald Cox, Burke Marshall and others had all written drafts which he declined to use. Mr. Katzenbach recalls: "He spent a helluva long time preparing it— unconscionably long, but understandably so." He wrote it, had it checked out and then memorized it, using his own political experiences to emphasize his points. He closed by quoting "that old Massachusetts saying, 'Vote early and vote often.' With Georgia's county unit system," Kennedy told the court, "all you have to do is vote early."

Bruce Terris, who spent four to six hours a day with the Attorney General in the days preceding the oral argument, recalls, "Cox wrote a script, but Bobby junked it. He had no particular legal experience, but I tell you he was acute. I also know, despite *Time* magazine's statement to the contrary,* that he did not read his argument. I've argued fifteen or sixteen cases up there, and I wouldn't dare get up without a note."

Terris has the day more firmly fixed in his mind than most. He had asked Kennedy's secretary, Angie Novello, if his wife could get a ticket, and she was skeptical. All of the Kennedys were going and so, it seemed, was half of the New Frontier. Then around seven or eight o'clock the night before, the phone in the Terris house rang. It was for Mrs. Terris. Ethel Kennedy, who was on the line, wanted to know whether Mrs. Terris, whom she had never met, could sit with the Kennedy family as their guest. And that is what happened. "After it

---

* In its issue of January 25, 1963, *Time* wrote, "At first he seemed nervous, even while reading from a brief prepared by Solicitor General Archibald Cox and Assistant Attorney General Burke Marshall."

was all over," remembers Terris, "my wife came back to my office and someone came running down to the office and said the Attorney General wants to see you. On the way down we saw Archie and the three of us were waiting to see him but somebody said the AG wants to see you and your wife. So we left Archie out there and went inside. He wanted to talk about the argument, to hear what he'd done wrong. He was tired, drawn out. I was a grade twelve or thirteen and Archie was waiting down the hall to see him. I couldn't have been less important to him, so this whole thing was extraordinary."

The press focused less on the significance of the argument than on how Bobby had done—not bad, by most standards—and who was on hand to cheer him on: Ethel, Rose, Jean, Eunice, four of his then seven children, Dorothy (Mrs. Arthur) Goldberg, Marian (Mrs. Byron) White, Teddy, Jackie and others. Morris Abram complained that with all the attention paid the thirteen Kennedys in attendance, nobody said anything about the fourteen Abrams—and he had brought the case in the first place.

Aside from a few journalists like Anthony Lewis of *The New York Times* and James Clayton of the Washington *Post*, the media paid little attention to the substantive significance of the case in terms of reapportionment law. (Although the case was directly relevant to legislative reapportionment, technically it was distinct since it dealt with vote-weighting in the selection of a state's chief executive rather than its legislative districts.) And *nobody* outside the Department commented on the real implications of the fact that Kennedy had argued the county unit case rather than a civil rights case, an organized-crime case, an anti-trust case or any other kind of case.

The most interesting aspect of Robert Kennedy's argument in *Gray* v. *Sanders* went totally unremarked—namely, the fact that Solicitor General Cox had permitted him to make it. To understand why this should be significant, one must look at the traditional role of the Solicitor General, the relationship between Archibald Cox and Robert Kennedy, and the special sense of proprietorship Solicitor General Cox exercised over any and all matters pertaining to reapportionment, even those as indirectly related as *Gray* v. *Sanders*.

The Solicitor General is the third-ranking officer in the Justice Department, but he is traditionally autonomous and the nine lawyers in his office—most of whom have clerked for a Supreme Court Justice— regard themselves as the elite, the *crème de la crème* of the legal profession. "When you enter the Solicitor's office, you join one of the most exclusive clubs in America" is the way one alumnus puts it.

Archibald Cox was the thirty-second in a list of Solicitors General which includes such distinguished predecessors as William Howard Taft, Charles Evans Hughes, Robert Jackson, Stanley Reed, Francis Biddle, John Davis, William Mitchell, Charles Fahy. The Solicitor General can conduct and argue any case in which the government has an interest. No appeal is taken by the government in any appellate court or to the Supreme Court without his authority. The Solicitor General's office argues over 60 percent of the cases the U.S. Supreme Court hears. He is in fact what the Attorney General is in name—the chief *legal* officer of the U.S. government as far as the courts are concerned. One of the recurring jokes which Robert Kennedy told on himself had to do with the time his brother called and asked for a legal opinion on an issue which was troubling the White House. "I'll get on it right away," Bob answered, to which the President replied, "I said I wanted a *legal* opinion. Don't you get on it. Get Archie Cox on it."

If Robert Kennedy was the Attorney General who had never practiced law, sometimes it seemed to the younger men in the Department that Archibald Cox, by general agreement among the most distinguished Solicitors General in the history of the office, was the Solicitor who couldn't see beyond the law. Nowhere is the tension, the institutional pull between law and policy, greater than that between the Solicitor General's office and the Attorney General's office, just around the corridor from each other on the Justice Department's fifth floor.

It is in the nature of things that the Attorney General, *any* Attorney General, is adviser to the President, and the Solicitor General, *any* Solicitor General, is adviser to the U.S. Supreme Court. It is in the nature of things that the thrust of the Attorney General's attention is on broad policy questions, and the thrust of the Solicitor General's attention is on narrower legal ones. It is in the nature of things that the Attorney General focuses on short-range political results and the Solicitor General focuses on long-range constitutional-law implications. Robert Kennedy and Archibald Cox, by an accident of history, caricatured these tendencies already inherent in their respective offices.

Robert Kennedy had never practiced law, never argued a case in a courtroom, was in the middle of his class at the solid but second-rung University of Virginia Law School, was uninformed about legal technicality, irritated by procedural obstacles and had no particular commitment to jurisdictional regularity. His strength was an instinctive ability to cut through the legal lacunae and deal with the policy issue at the core.

Archibald Cox's life was the law. He had served on the *Harvard Law Review*, clerked for that quintessential figure of American jurisprudence, Judge Learned Hand, worked as an assistant in the Solicitor General's office itself, and was the leading labor-law authority at the nation's number-one bastion of orthodox legal education, the Harvard Law School. His genius had to do with anticipating the long-range consequences to the Supreme Court of what appeared to be short-term technical decisions. "My whole life and career had trained me to look upon the Solicitor's office as second only to God," says Cox.

The contrast between the two men's approach to law could not have been greater. Edwyn Silberling of the Organized Crime Section recalls sitting in on a conference between Deputy Byron White and Kennedy. After White had started to outline the technical grounds of an issue that could go either way, Kennedy waved his hand after a couple of minutes and said, "Give me a yes or a no." Nicholas Katzenbach, who replaced White as Deputy, recalls, "He never went through what the law was. You'd come to him and say here's a real close one and he'd decide—but not on legal grounds." He used the Office of Legal Counsel more than most Attorneys General, mainly because the Deputy had enough to do running the Department in Kennedy's frequent absence. Camaraderie rather than rivalry was the hallmark of this group of Yale lawyers, and the Office of Legal Counsel was the logical clearinghouse for law points.

One old-timer in the Solicitor's office, Oscar Davis, now a judge, speculates, "I really think that when Robert Kennedy came into the Department he had great feelings of inferiority toward people he thought to be good lawyers and he had a great deal of defensiveness and lack of confidence in his own feelings as a lawyer and I don't doubt that it reflected itself in his dealings with Archie Cox."

Kennedy's uninterest in legal doctrine was a fact rather than a weakness. But as Burke Marshall wrote in the *Georgetown Law Journal* after Kennedy's murder, the tendency to attribute RFK's achievements as Attorney General to his administrative capabilities, his staff and/or his having a brother in the White House "ignores the fact that the Attorney General is called upon to decide extremely difficult, complex and important legal issues, and to do so himself. Robert Kennedy did so often.

"His technique of self-education on the issues he had to decide was the one used by most lawyers I know . . . as any busy lawyer should in dealing with a significant new problem, he steeped himself with information through reading what was suggested to him and through briefings, and then tested whatever tentative conclusions he reached against the best minds available to him."

Among other examples, Marshall cites the moment in May 1961 when Kennedy "had to find a constitutionally acceptable basis for the deployment of federal physical power to protect the freedom riders and other citizens of Montgomery. The use of specially deputized marshals . . . was unprecedented as matters stood and required a prior federal court order in a government lawsuit involving many novel features.* The timing was very tight, the situation extremely dangerous. . . . The legal issues to be decided involved the most difficult of the relationships between the states and the federal government—the administration of justice and the preservation of law and order—and were the object of disagreement and debate among the most experienced lawyers in the Department. Robert Kennedy moved through this maze as surely as the best of trial lawyers at a critical moment in court; his telegram to Governor Patterson, dictated by him in the midst of crisis, is a model of a concise brief of the essential points of the government position."

There is, however, a difference between sound judgment, which Kennedy exemplified, and thinking like a lawyer, which Cox epitomized. Since Kennedy came more and more to delegate his law-making judgments to Yale lawyers like Katzenbach and Marshall—and despite the fact that Robert Kennedy himself studied law at the University of Virginia—it was the difference between law as taught at Yale and at Harvard, or rather between the symbolic Yale and the symbolic Harvard.

The Harvard that produced Archie Cox is symbolized by the late Felix Frankfurter, noted for his philosophy of judicial self-restraint, his commitment to procedural and jurisdictional regularity, a respect for the passive virtues, for judicial neutralism, a strong sense of institutional boundaries, an idea that the court should where possible avoid "the political thicket." Not coincidentally, Cox preferred to staff his office with Harvard men—like Richard J. Medalie, Nathan Lewin, Bruce Terris, Philip Heyman (now a Harvard law professor)—men who had studied with Cox and/or clerked for someone like Frankfurter or Justice John Marshall Harlan, although their philosophies of law varied quite widely. Once when a young man from Tulane Law came highly recommended for a job by Judge Skelly Wright and Judge John Minor Wisdom of the Fifth Circuit, for whom he had clerked, it

* *United States* v. *U.S. Klans, Knights of Ku Klux Klan, Inc.,* 194 F. supp. 897 (Md. Ala., 1961).

took the intervention of Frankfurter for Cox to put the talented young man on his staff. In the view of one contemporary, it was not the boy's academic record or that he had failed to impress in his personal interview; it was primarily that the boy had had the misfortune not to have attended Harvard, and in the chosen circle of the Solicitor's office there just did not seem to be a place for a Tulane boy.

The Yale that produced Byron White, Nicholas Katzenbach, Lou Oberdorfer, Burke Marshall, John Douglas, *et al.*—the men whose cautious, policy-oriented legal philosophy Robert Kennedy instinctively found so congenial—was symbolized by a man like the late, incautious Judge Jerome Frank, who believed that the dominant minds at Harvard were seeking an unrealizable "platonic" certainty in the law because, as he put it in the psychological jargon of his day, they "have not yet relinquished the childish need for an authoritarian father and consciously have tried to find in the law a substitute for those attributes of firmness and infallibility ascribed in childhood to father."

According to the compound of cliché, caricature and quarter-truth which was part of the prevailing mythology when most of those running Kennedy Justice had attended their respective law schools— although it has had ever less correspondence to reality as the two schools moved into the second half of the century, each responding to the pressures of the age and each copying the other's innovations— the elite 500-man Yale and the peerless 1,500-man Harvard law schools were easily differentiated: Yale trains judges, Harvard trains lawyers; Yale doesn't teach you any law, Harvard teaches nothing but; Yale turns out socially conscious policy-makers, Harvard turns out narrow legal technicians; Yale thinks that judges invent the law, Harvard thinks that judges discover the law; Yale is preoccupied with social values, Harvard is preoccupied with abstract concepts; Yale is imaginative, Harvard is precise; Yale is interested in personalities, Harvard is interested in cases; Yale thinks most legal doctrine is ritual mumbo-jumbo, Harvard thinks it comprises a self-contained logical system; Yale cares about results, Harvard cares about precedents; Yale thinks the law is what the judge had for breakfast, Harvard thinks it is a brooding omnipresence in the sky.

If such stereotypes ever captured the complexities of either institution, they were quite dated by the early Sixties. And, of course, the lawyers from law schools like Harvard, Yale, the University of Chicago had the common denominator of their elite education, which overrode any institutional distinctions. Yet the men to whom Robert Kennedy delegated much of his legal thinking adopted in broad contour the styles and assumptions of the Harvard and Yale models suggested above.

Kennedy, who was shirt-sleeves informal, had a casual approach to his office, which had the accidental impact of opening it up, of making more things possible, of minimizing bureaucratic impedimentia, of exciting imaginations. Cox, who was morning-coat formal, with a mind as clear and sharp as his crew-cut, was on stiffer, more regular terms with the Attorney General than were the network of Assistant Attorneys General who had been recruited by White from the tables down at Mory's. Cox joined the Justice Department at the personal request of JFK, at whose side he had sat through the long hours of debate over the 1959 labor reform bill and whose Presidential campaign he served as Research Director, although he once almost quit because he felt that the research operation was not being properly utilized. According to contemporary rumor, he told JFK, "I'll take any job you think I'm right for, so long as I don't have to work with Ted Sorensen" (who had not followed many of Cox's recommendations during the campaign). Thoroughness, precision and rigorous application were his hallmark, were what he looked for and for the most part got in the way of assistance. He derived his approach from traditionalists like Judge Learned Hand and Justice Frankfurter.

At the outset, relations between the Solicitor and the General—which eventually grew from toleration to fondness and respect—were complicated by a number of factors.

First, at forty-nine, Archibald Cox was Robert Kennedy's senior in every respect—age, experience, expertise, professional standing. He must be forgiven if he embarked on his job suspicious that his superior was under- if not unqualified. Cox, moreover, was the only member of the Justice Department's top echelon who had a pre-existing consultant's relationship with JFK. White had served candidate JFK in an administrative capacity, where he worked primarily with Robert and others had worked *for* JFK, but Cox had worked *with* him intimately and, having been recruited neither via the Byron White–Yale axis nor by Robert Kennedy, he entered the Department believing that he had a direct line to the White House. A proud man, he could not have been totally oblivious to the fact that he was second choice for the job. Initially, JFK had offered it to Cox's Harvard colleague, Paul Freund, the man who, after Learned Hand, has been most nominated to the Supreme Court by people other than the President. When Freund turned the job down despite a concerted effort to win him over, JFK reportedly remarked, "I thought you would rather make history than write it"—and perhaps subconsciously crossed Freund off the list of candidates for the U.S. Supreme Court. "Did he or did he not want to get into the fray? That was the question," says one of Freund's colleagues.

Second, unlike White, Marshall, Oberdorfer, Katzenbach, *et al.*, "Archie wasn't a utility infielder," as one of the Attorney General's assistants puts it, meaning that he wasn't available for odd jobs. This was partly because at first he didn't partake in the general camaraderie, although when he wanted guidance on a point of law he would readily consult White or Katzenbach or Marshall; and the President didn't hesitate to call Cox about the education bill, about what to say after the Supreme Court handed down its decision banning prayers from public schools, about the steel price increase. Partly it was because he was reluctant to delegate. Other Solicitors General—before and after—would rely on their assistants to write briefs, articles and speeches. "With Cox," recalls a young man who served three Solicitors, "you'd give him a memorandum and *he* would write the brief. He didn't want your stuff. He had an original and creative mind and nothing went by in that office without the impress of his personality and mind." Rick Medalie, one of the young Harvard lawyers on Cox's staff, remembers, "He put everybody else to shame. His family wasn't with him for the first six months, so he'd stay until midnight and argue two or three cases—the cream of the crop—every month. Rankin had argued about one case a month."

As a result, Cox, who was brilliant, dedicated, stuffy, rigorous, thorough, pompous, professorial, shy, decent, proud and formal, was also more ego-involved in the work of his office than might have been the case had he been a delegator. He took his job as seriously as a Harvard freshman takes his law exams. That, combined with his natural vanity and formidable erudition and sense of propriety, made him a poor prospect for any impulse the Attorney General may have had to cut procedural corners on behalf of passing political expediency.

A third complicating factor in relations between Cox and Kennedy were their widely disparate styles. One young attorney recalls, "Archie Cox accompanied him on his rounds of our office, and Archie always looked a little pained. Kennedy would ask you your law school, your rank in class and whether or not you were on the Review. It struck us as funny that he, who had gone to a second-rate law school, was not in the top third of his class and didn't come close to the Review was always impressed." Cox introduced one man and said, presumably by way of small talk, "He got the top mark in my class." Actually, the young man had done brilliant work at Harvard *except* for Cox's labor-law class. Were these trips then a waste, counter-productive to the restrained atmosphere the Solicitor encouraged? Not at all. "You did get a feeling of excitement simply because Kennedy was there," observes one hold-over from Eisenhower days who had never met Rogers and never *seen* Brownell. "He had a desire for excellence, he gave you the feeling of accessibility, and he gave the place an electricity."

Cox's contrasting style was partly an expression of his shyness, partly a result of his years at Harvard, partly a result of his image of what a Solicitor was supposed to be. His Supreme Court performances were marvels to behold—polished, thorough, impeccable, although one former clerk objected to them on the grounds that "My judgment is you don't put on a polished performance when you argue a case. You should make them forget it's a performance, make them listen to what you have to say. Archie's intellectuality meant that psychologically the court had its guard up. When you are confronted with someone as articulate as Archie you always want to know, 'Am I being beguiled?' "

If Kennedy was the student, Cox was the professor. He was pedantic both in private conversation and in court, a lecturer. "After he had made his case," recalls one admiring but amused associate, "he found it difficult to believe that anybody could remain unconvinced—largely because he never made a case unless a part of him was convinced that it was the only logical conclusion." His oral arguments before the Supreme Court reminded some former students of his Harvard classes. When a Justice would interrupt, he might say, "If you'll wait a minute, Mr. Justice, I'm coming to that in due course. . . ."

Early in his tenure, Cox was confessing error in a narcotics case. As Robert Stern, who put in many years in the Solicitor's office, once remarked, "Whether or not error should be confessed . . . usually does not present a simple problem. The Solicitor General is aware that to confess error will not only infuriate the attorneys who have handled the case for the government below, but also the [lower court] judges who were persuaded [by the government] to decide in the government's favor. . . ." In this particular case the issue was whether or not there had been a sale when some narcotics had been passed on. No money had changed hands and Cox, who had lectured on the law of sales at Harvard, wanted the court to know that he wasn't confessing error lightly. By way of example he cited a hypothetical case, beginning: "Now let us suppose that I, *Professor* Cox . . ." He brought down the house and the court gave him an extra half hour for argument, so that the U.S. Supreme Court could hear Professor Cox's full lecture on the law of sales.

Fourth, there was Cox's quasi-judicial notion of the job. Undoubtedly he would have agreed with Judge Simon Sobeloff, one of his predecessors, who articulated the notion of the Solicitor as more than the executive's litigator. He said: "The Solicitor General is not neutral, he is an advocate; but an advocate whose business is not merely to prevail in the instant case. My client's chief business is not to achieve victory but to establish justice." As Cox saw it, a critical part of the Solicitor's job is to protect the court as much as to convince it. His duties as an officer of the court distinguished him, he felt, from the other sub-Cabinet rank Presidential appointees.

In the abstract, few could quarrel with the philosophy. But what happens when the Solicitor's idea of his obligation to the court conflicts with the Attorney General's idea of his obligation to carry out Presidential policy? The civil rights community believed that to be the situation in a number of sit-in and housing discrimination cases in the early Sixties and, probably because they disagreed with the Solicitor on the merits, argued that Presidential policy should prevail over legal theory.

Joseph Rauh, long-time civil rights advocate, onetime ADA president, who applauded Robert Kennedy's nomination as Attorney General on the theory "What the job needs is an administrator and wise politician, not a Harvard A student," remarked: "The independence of the Solicitor is crap. The Attorney General is the top legal officer. If the Solicitor General doesn't agree he has every legal right not to argue it, but the Attorney General and the President have to make the decision. The Deerfield case is a good example.* It isn't even a problem today. We'd win in a walk. Now even Cox holds my views. But I asked Archie to come in as an *amicus* [friend of the court.] It was of gigantic importance to the cause of integrated housing. We had a perfect cert.† But a private cert petition without the government's support is a tough thing to get the Supreme Court to grant, so I asked Archie. He was on the fence. Burke Marshall recommended it and the Civil Rights Division sent a brief over to be filed. But Cox kept saying

* When Morris Milgram's Progress Development Corporation let be known its intention to build an integrated housing development in Deerfield, Illinois, the Deerfield Park District condemned the land the developers had planned to use, the Illinois Supreme Court upheld the condemnation, and the U.S. Supreme Court denied certiorari. The Solicitor General declined to intervene as *amicus* in the petition for rehearing.

† When the U.S. Supreme Court denies "cert" (certiorari), as it did in the Deerfield case, the court doesn't pass on the merits of the issue. It simply decides not to decide the case.

he'd have to rewrite the whole thing and he didn't have the time and besides, he was not sure we were right.

"I kept asking Bobby to act as a judge between us but he would never get us together. He'd listen to my ideas separately, but he didn't have enough confidence to make the decision as between us. So here my idea that the Attorney General didn't have to be a lawyer came back and smacked me in the face."

When the decision against the Deerfield housing project came down, costing the integrationists their $200,000 investment, Rauh said bitterly, "Bobby Kennedy sold out to white suburbia and he bears that on his shoulders. The principle that was lost was the principle that people have a right to live where they choose—to live next door."

The fact was that the decision not to file an *amicus* brief probably had nothing to do with selling out to white suburbia and everything to do with the Solicitor General's idea about a technical point of law, his conservative approach to the question of whether it was permissible to disqualify an otherwise unexceptionable state action on the grounds that the *motive* behind it was discriminatory; it also had to do with Robert Kennedy's reluctance to tell his Solicitor what to do. As Cox recalls it, "I don't think anybody even knew of the case until after the cert petition had been filed and denied—or if we did know about it, nobody was focusing on it. Then Joe Rauh made his big effort to get the Department in on it. Bob was in on it. Burke was in on it. There was lots of pressure from various people. I was convinced we ought not go in at that late stage on a petition for rehearing because (a) I thought the court wouldn't change its mind and would affirm the court below and I didn't want to draw on my bank account for no good purpose; (b) I thought the government would look silly. If we hadn't thought the case important enough to go into in the first place, why were we screaming for a rehearing? Another point—Burke Marshall and I were both convinced that the court was not yet ready to hold an otherwise constitutional action invalid because of the discriminatory motives of the people who were for it."

Today Joe Rauh says, "I now believe that if Bobby had had more confidence in himself as a lawyer, he would have granted my request to let me meet with him and Cox at the same time and hear me put my case against Cox's, and he would have been persuaded." What Rauh doesn't know is that Kennedy probably *was* persuaded. He agreed with the Rauh position. But he wasn't interested in overruling his Solicitor, and certainly not in front of as garrulous a man about town as Joe Rauh.

The issue rose again in connection with a series of sit-in cases. The government had entered so many cases as *amicus* during the Kennedy years that for it to stay out began to create a negative pregnant, the presumption that there was something wrong with the case and maybe the court should stay out, too. This time, the issue revolved around the question of what was "state action" under the Fourteenth Amendment. Ever since the landmark case of *Shelley* v. *Kramer* in 1948, which seemed to some scholars to say that the courts could never enforce any kind of segregation, even "legal" private segregation, because the courts were an agency of the state and the states were prohibited from enforcing discrimination under the equal protection clause of the Fourteenth Amendment, liberals and judicial activists were engaged in an effort to expand and crystalize the categories of discriminatory actions which the Supreme Court might declare unconstitutional and/or unenforceable. The Solicitor General came to the Department with a generally Frankfurterian approach to the matter, believing that "state action" was roughly coterminus with official action, that it wasn't the court's job to legislate morality and that it wasn't the Department's job to push the court further than its own words had already taken it.

The liberal view, put forth by men like Jack Greenberg, the Columbia-trained chief counsel of the NAACP Inc. Fund who took over after Thurgood Marshall went on the bench, was that in today's complex world it made little sense to talk about "state action" in the narrow meaning of that term which the Solicitor seemed to favor. "What you ought to look for," Greenberg would argue, "is what's public and what's private. What's public ought to be non-racist." But his main point was that regardless of what one believed to be the better theoretical position, the law was in flux and therefore the Solicitor should not decide such an issue on the basis of legal theory but rather on the basis of Departmental policy. Greenberg, who had been invited to the Justice Department to air his opinions on the state-action issue, once told Cox, "If you believe your position, write it up for the *Harvard Law Review*. But now you're the Solicitor General of the United States, and it is the policy of the Kennedy Administration to oppose discrimination wherever it can."

Cox's position wasn't static. Shortly after he arrived at the Justice Department, he was presented with a case involving the discriminatory activities of the Wilmington Parking Authority. Cox filed an *amicus* brief, but as one young attorney who had served under Solicitor General J. Lee Rankin, Cox's immediate predecessor, recalls, "Cox had to work his way through laboriously to a position Rankin and these other guys took instinctively."

In September of 1962 Burke Marshall and Jack Greenberg visited with Cox to discuss the *Glen Echo Amusement Park* case, one of a number of cases which were to come before the court with increasing frequency involving allegations that civil rights workers had trespassed in the course of a sit-in. The issue was whether the state could punish the sit-inners. Marshall and Greenberg wanted Cox to take a hard line arguing that refusal to allow Negroes entry into this otherwise open-to-the-public amusement park was "state action" which the courts were forbidden by the Fourteenth Amendment from enforcing. After the visit Cox sent the Attorney General a memo saying he was "undetermined" what to do in the case. On November 7, 1962, he characteristically told the Supreme Court that it needn't reach the basic question because the convictions (of the sit-inners) violated the Fourteenth Amendment anyway since the owner of the property had as an employee a specially deputized sheriff, and therefore the expulsion of the protesters constituted state action.

In the *Griffin* case, Joe Rauh recalls, "We didn't ask the government to take our extreme position—that not only could a sit-inner not be arrested but also that he had a positive right to be served. Ultimately, Goldberg, Douglas and Warren took that position. We only wanted the government to take the more moderate position that even though a sit-inner might not have a right to be served, he couldn't be arrested. This is what we wanted Cox to say, but he filed the worst possible brief. It was stinky."

Greenberg says of the debate: "The question was whether a state officer in a state court can enforce a discriminatory rule which originates with a private person. We argued that private action has to be seen as part of the laws of the South. We made a philosophic argument that everything public is state action.

"Cox had a narrow view of state action—that it equals official action. In the next to last sit-in case, which arose in early '64, he refused to file any brief, which was his way of saying he disagreed with us. The Civil Rights Act of 1964 eventually made it moot, although the court had voted 5–4 to require him to file a brief. This was important to us because the votes on the court were getting closer and closer and for the government to be implicitly against us was no good. I remember Burke brought us to see Cox in a private elevator. Cox did finally file a brief on our side—although it took the most conservative position. Even so, his heart wasn't in it."

The government's *amicus* brief was a model of caution, indulging such locutions as:

. . . while we stress the presence of the state in the arrests and prosecution, we do not urge that such state action in support of private discrimination is alone enough to constitute a state denial of equal protection of the laws. . . .

And a footnote pointed out:

There is considerable ground for arguing that the 14th Amendment imposes upon the states a duty to provide equality of treatment under the law for all members of the public without regard to race in establishments which the proprietor voluntarily throws open to the general public to such an extent that legal protection of the public is a normal part of the legal system. Although there is little direct evidence, the history of the Reconstruction period furnishes no little support to that thesis. . . .

In view of the elements of affirmative state involvement present in these cases we mention but do not pursue the foregoing line of analysis.

At the time of the murder of Medgar Evers, the bark and bite of Bull Connor's police dogs and countless other extra-legal and repressive measures against idealistic civil rights workers of all colors who were hauled off to dirty jails and often mistreated, the response of men like Greenberg and Rauh, quite moderate in terms of both today's and yesterday's political spectrum, was understandably one of irritation, impatience and occasional outrage at the Kennedy Administration's failure to recognize the elemental.

Thus, such men tended to underrate or overlook the evolution and significance of the Solicitor's grudging, inch-by-inch shift on the state-action issue, which may have sounded to the layman like legal nitpicking but which could have vastly significant consequences for the civil rights movement and the country, for it had to do with the black man's right to private as well as public dignity in the fight to guarantee equal treatment for all. And the battles were fought over the terrain of conventional and conflicting jurisprudential theory. Who would prevail—the traditionalists, represented by Cox, or the "realists," represented by the more militant of the civil rights contingent, who seemed to have won the Attorney General's heart but not convinced him to override his learned Solicitor?

Burke Marshall understood that Cox always thought of the Solicitor General as being an officer of the court. "He was determined to understand and be persuaded that these pro-civil rights positions were the right positions to take because they were Constitutionally and legally sound. He'd come in and talk to me about reapportionment and sit-in cases for months. His concern was 'Don't mislead the court into doing something that might look right now, but wrong a hundred years from now.' "

Marshall points out that the question of whether the Solicitor General was an advocate for Departmental policy or an adviser to the court was one on which there could be legitimate disagreement.

"I always thought that we *could* not, that it would be wrong for us— even weighing and accepting the role of the court—that it would be wrong for the U.S. government to take the position in the U.S. Supreme Court that it was opposed to the civil rights movement.

"You could get technical but I always thought that arguing that any sit-in conviction should be upheld was wrong. Therefore our function was to find a way of not doing it. That was the issue. There were serious questions. The Solicitor General had grave doubts about the legality—justified doubts—of some of the sit-in actions that resulted in some of those cases.

"From my point of view our purpose was to support the sit-in movement. From his point of view our purpose was to protect the court. I was interested in protecting the court too. I understand all that. But if I had to decide whether to take a position that the court should take as an institution versus supporting the overturning of convictions, I'd take the latter and I think the Attorney General agreed with me. The Solicitor General would take the former."

Subsequently the Civil Rights Act of 1964 passed—partly no doubt due to pressures generated by the actions of the sit-inners. Although civil rights activists outside the Department had not entirely gotten their way, nobody had any question about which side the government was on. It takes a Mitchell–Kleindienst regime to underline the importance of such institutional sympathy.

Looking back, Archibald Cox now says, "The whole point in the sit-in cases was to keep the court deciding Constitutional cases on the side of civil rights and yet never decide the gut question of whether *any* sit-in conviction was a violation of the Fourteenth Amendment, as the civil rights people wanted the court to do. We wanted to avoid that for three reasons. First, it could foul up prospective legislation [which dealt with public accommodations]. Second, if they ever decided it, our judgment was that it would be decided against the civil rights view. At one point the gossip was that they stood four and one fourth to four and three fourths, since one Justice was three fourths against expanding the state-action concept. Third, if the court had done this by judicial decree rather than our getting a bill through, it would have been tougher to gain acceptance."

Cox didn't enter the sit-in cases willingly, but he entered. Ralph Spritzer of his office, now a law professor at the University of Pennsylvania, recalls that "in the last round of sit-in cases the government filed the brief on the narrowest of grounds, so narrow that Cox felt impelled, as was his scrupulous wont, to add a sentence saying that although you don't have to reach the broader issues, if you want us to deal with them we can file an additional brief. Somebody picked it up at the oral argument and asked me about it and I said yes, if the court requested it, we would. Then the court came out with a remarkable order—four dissents to that order—directing the government to file a brief on the issues."

It was not a case of good guys versus bad guys. The assumption of Burke Marshall and the Civil Rights Division was that you don't under any circumstances let down the civil rights movement. The assumption of Cox and the Solicitor's office was that you don't under any circumstances let down the court. It was when these assumptions came into conflict that the Ivy League reservoir of common assumptions and expertise came into play to minimize that conflict. Thus two weeks after JFK's assassination, when Robert Kennedy was effectively immobilized, and the views of his lieutenants would prevail, Burke Marshall accurately reflected the consensus in his weekly report to the Attorney General:

2 December 63:
The Supreme Court has instructed the Solicitor General to file a brief on the broad constitutional issues involved, which is whether the owner of a facility otherwise open to the public may constitutionally refuse to serve Negroes and call upon the police to eject any Negro who refuses to leave the premises. The difficulties of the constitutional question, and other consequences of the case, are such that we have been attempting to avoid briefing this basic constitutional issue. Among the factors are the following:
a) If the Court decides in favor of the petitioners [Negroes] the most that would be decided is that the police cannot be called upon by the owner of the facility. Such a decision could, and undoubtedly would, in many places, invite the owner of the premises or mob —to take it upon themselves to deal with any Negroes demanding service. . . .
b) On the other hand, a brief by the Department of Justice rejecting the claims of the Negroes would lead to a very serious breach between Negro groups and the Administration, as well as to a general loss of faith in the ability of whites to understand and to take action dealing with Negro grievances.

c) . . . These factors emphasize, of course, the importance of the public accommodations portion of the legislation.

Every Attorney General has an understanding with his Solicitor and tends to leave him alone, since to precipitate an open disagreement can produce negative fallout for the Administration. When James Mc-Granery became President Truman's Attorney General and reportedly asked his Solicitor General, Philip B. Perlman, to settle the politically explosive Dollar Line steamship case, which scuttlebutt said he had promised Nevada's Senator Pat McCarran would be settled as a condition precedent to his Attorney Generalship, Perlman resigned. When President Eisenhower's first Solicitor General, Simon E. Sobeloff, was confronted with the case of *Peters* v. *Hobby* in which the government took the position that an accused man could lose his job without having the right to confront his accuser, Sobeloff refused to argue the case or sign the brief—and perhaps cost himself a Supreme Court nomination. Instead, the man who did sign was head of the Civil Division, a young attorney named Warren Burger. Lee Rankin, who succeeded Sobeloff, never went to court on the issue of off-shore oil litigation without first checking at the White House, since Ike had made some campaign commitments in Texas that seemed at odds with the Justice Department's traditional position that off-shore oil belonged to the federal government. Nor did Rankin balk when Ike personally suggested changes in the government's *amicus* briefs that went with *Brown* v. *Board of Education*, the school desegregation cases, although Rankin stated orally to the court what the Eisenhower-edited brief left unsaid—that segregation is unconstitutional.*

Robert Kennedy's strategy vis-à-vis the strong-willed, autonomous, prestigious Archibald Cox was quite simple: never directly to try to convince him of anything. Rather, on the key issues, the strategy was to make it easy for the Solicitor to convince himself. In many ways the story of Robert Kennedy's impact on the law, as distinguished from his impact on the Justice Department or on particular social pathologies like organized crime, is the story of Archibald Cox changing his mind.

---

* When the *Brown* case first arose in the Truman Administration, Solicitor General Perlman told a member of his staff, despite the Department's position that segregation is unconstitutional, "The country isn't ready, that's going too far." So the government had intended to stay out, but after Perlman resigned in the middle of the Eisenhower–Stevenson campaign of 1952, McGranery, at the instigation of Philip Elman and Robert Stern of the Solicitor's office, gave the green light and in effect overruled Perlman. Because the country was in the midst of an election campaign, the government postponed filing its brief until after the election and thereby kept the issue out of partisan politics.

And Kennedy's achievement—a tribute to his skill and perception as an administrator—was to assist that process through the subtle combination of democratic meetings, subliminal signals, delicate deference and strategic non-intervention.

Kennedy had never really thought about the meaning of the Fourteenth Amendment's guarantee of equal protection of the laws against arbitrary "state action." He had never grappled with the great issue of its reach: Could it, for instance, be extended to strike down the malapportioned state legislatures which certainly seemed to deny urban voters across the country "equal" representation vis-a-vis their rural counterparts? On such issues he seems to have instinctively had the "knee-jerk liberal" response that he regularly mocked in other contexts. Yet he was not about to argue with his Solicitor General, who although a specialist in labor law, was presumably learned in the constitution as well.

It was not merely that Cox had done his thinking in the musty corridors of the Harvard Law School where the legacy and spirit of Felix Frankfurter stalked the halls and that he probably would be deeply troubled at the thought of entering the "political thickets" which the young Attorney General found almost magnetically attractive. It was Cox's style to agonize, test, introspect, weigh—not to be convinced in the sort of face-to-face exchange the Attorney General favored.

Solicitor Cox's oral argument in the *St. Regis Paper* case is a good guide to the mentality the Attorney General was up against. The FTC was investigating the St. Regis paper company, in connection with possible anti-trust proceedings, and had subpoenaed its records, including duplicate copies of its census reports, which St. Regis kept in its own files. St. Regis resisted and the matter came before the Supreme Court with the FTC, supported by the populistic Anti-Trust Division, insisting that the reports could be subpoenaed ("If you can subpoena duplicates of the corporate tax forms, which are also private information, why not census reports?" asks one Anti-Trust Division lawyer). The privacy-protecting Census Bureau, backed by the Bureau of the Budget, argued that the material should be privileged.

In such a situation it is the Solicitor's job to determine which side has the more consistent position and support it. Cox's solution, however, was singular. He chose to go before the U.S. Supreme Court, and as the nine robed men sat there slightly awe-struck he commenced to argue both sides of the case as fully and honestly and persuasively as he knew how. Then, since the government was so badly divided, according to the Washington *Post's* reporter James Clayton, "he thought that as Solicitor General he had an obligation to tell the Justices his personal views about the issue, which were contrary to those of the Anti-Trust Division," whose position had been upheld in a lower court. At this Justice Frankfurter erupted: "How do you expect us to decide this matter if you can't even get an agreement inside the Justice Department?"

Cox replied with a self-confident grin: "Oh, Mr. Justice. If the dispute were only inside the Justice Department, I'm sure I could settle it." As things worked out, he presented the other side of the issue so well that, in the words of a colleague, "he knocked himself out of the box, and the Anti-Trust Division's view prevailed. It takes a lot of *chutzpah* to think you can argue both sides. Some people might even say it goes against the theory of the adversary system."

It was not that Cox was unbending or rigid. It was that he was a man with a heavy conscience and severe sense of propriety, a man who had resigned as chairman of the Wage Stabilization Board in 1952 to protest Harry Truman's approval of a pay increase for coal miners beyond that recommended by top defense officials. He was a man of stiff principle, pride and toughness, but in the crunch not unreasonable or unpragmatic. Not wishing to provoke unnecessary confrontation, the Attorney General would dispatch Katzenbach to feel Cox out in the belief that no good could come of direct disagreement between himself and his Solicitor since—among other things—the issue would always be framed in legal terms and regardless of who had the merits, press critics could have a field day reporting on how Little Brother had questioned the judgment of the learned Harvard law professor. And because he conserved his credit, Kennedy succeeded the few times he gingerly tried to cash in on it. When Congressman Emanuel Celler, for example, who made few demands on the Kennedys, insisted that the Department ask for certiorari in a case involving the New York Port Authority that on its merits did not seem to Cox or anyone else in the Department to warrant the government's pressing, Katzenbach was dispatched for an advance talk with Cox. If Cox seemed sympathetic, Robert Kennedy would call him; if not, not. In this particular case, Kennedy told Cox, "There's going to be a hell of a political problem if you can't even ask for cert." He did not order Cox to ask for cert. And he did not ask Cox to ask for cert. He did not even tell Katzenbach he *wanted* Cox to ask for cert. But he gently let Cox know what would happen if he did not ask for cert. And in fact had Cox *not* asked for cert the Kennedys might well have had to face up to the thorny political problem of an antagonistic chairman of the House Judiciary Committee. Cox's reply: "I can do this twice a year and the court will understand. But you're using up one of your options." As Katzenbach says, there was substance to this minuet.

Archibald Cox was more than just another Assistant Attorney General, more than just another in a distinguished line of Solicitor Generals. Lee Loevinger, head of the Anti-Trust Division, was, like Cox, intellectual, senior, self-admiring—and also a recruit from outside the Byron White–RFK talent search (Sargent Shriver had sent him over and Hubert Humphrey had given him a good reference). But when it turned out that the loquacious Loevinger could not function effectively in the free-wheeling Kennedy orbit, he was quietly appointed to the FCC and replaced by William Orrick, who had done an efficient job as head of the Civil Division.

Had Robert Kennedy wanted to (the thought never occurred, as far as anyone knows), he could not have given Cox the Loevinger treatment. For Archibald Cox was, by common consent, "the best Solicitor of our time." Cox worked too hard, argued cases too well, administered his office too efficiently, saw his job too clearly to be replaceable against his will without a major political ruckus. Only a change of Administrations or a desire on Cox's part to move on and/or up could have dislodged him from the job he did so well. Cox knew too much law and Kennedy too little for the Attorney General ever to risk a public disagreement with his Solicitor on a question of legal policy.

And yet, in the summer of 1963 the Attorney General and the Solicitor General appeared to some to be headed on a collision course. Six cases—involving New York, Maryland, Virginia, Alabama, Delaware and Colorado—were coming up before the U.S. Supreme Court. In each case the petitioners claimed malapportionment and argued that the state legislature should be reapportioned on a one-man, one-vote principle. As Morris Abram had argued in the Georgia county unit case, "A vote is a vote is a vote." Robert Kennedy was sympathetic to the argument, although he was preoccupied with civil rights. Bull Connor's police dogs had surfaced in Birmingham, which itself had exploded. Medgar Evers had been murdered. Martin Luther King had written his moving letter from a Birmingham jail. A radically revised civil rights bill had been submitted to Congress in July. A national March on Washington was scheduled for August. He favored the one-man, one-vote position, out of the same impulse that increasingly engaged him in the Negro's struggle for the franchise. But he did not evidence any real awareness of the national stakes involved. Other things being equal, he would probably follow the advice of Burke Marshall, under whose jurisdiction reapportionment originally fell on the organization chart.

The Solicitor, while he had no unalterably firm position on the matter, was skeptical if not alarmed by the one-man, one-vote standard. The arguments against it were many: It was too simplistic, too difficult to enforce—what would you do if the states didn't obey?—and it didn't take care of the problem of gerrymandering. It confronted the court, furthermore, with an all-or-nothing choice; it was too revolutionary (Cox estimated that forty-six out of the fifty sitting state legislatures as then composed would be judged unconstitutional by its standards), and it failed to take into account other legitimate interests —for instance, geographic representation. And as a matter of tactics, since the plaintiffs were already arguing the one-man, one-vote position, if the government came into these cases it was the only logical arguer for a less radical position. And in any event, it seemed clear to Cox that the standard should not be applied to *both* houses of a bicameral legislature. (In Colorado, one house had already been reapportioned on an equal population basis, and the voters had approved by referendum a rurally weighted apportionment for the second house.)

No better example of Robert Kennedy's success at getting the Solicitor to change—or make up—his mind or to move in the direction of Presidential policy exists than that of these landmark reapportionment cases. Even after the procedural giant step of *Baker* v. *Carr*, where—with Cox's cautious approval—the Supreme Court took jurisdiction of the malapportionment issue, the Solicitor remained unconvinced that anything resembling a one-man, one-vote standard should be urged on the court. The trend in the law was clearly in the *direction* of one man, one vote. But the Solicitor was not interested in contemporary trends. He was concerned about his obligation to the court, to history, to the future, to the course of Constitutional law.

It is of course impossible for anyone with only limited access to files, memories and documents to reconstruct the entire institutional decision-making process of those cases. But based on an extensive canvass of those involved, my conclusion is that here was a moment when history was in the balance. It could have gone either way. Unlike the civil rights movement, a social development that had its own momentum to which the courts responded, however late and tentatively, the reapportionment issue had no momentum and no real constituency, since it had no dramatic impact on individuals and it was in the "Catch-22" nature of the beast that there could be no constituency to lobby for it until reapportionment was first mandated by the court. Thus if the court had decided the other way, the issue would probably have been dead for the foreseeable future. In that sense the reapportionment cases involved the most important, discrete legal event of Kennedy's Attorney Generalship. Chief Justice Earl Warren himself said, after his retirement, that "all things considered, the case of Baker against Carr is about the most basic case that has been decided in our time." [1]

Moreover, it seems clear from internal Justice Department memoranda and off-the-record comment that the government's support as *amicus* in *Baker* v. *Carr,* the landmark case, was crucial in persuading at least two members of the U.S. Supreme Court—Justices Potter Stewart and Tom Clark. Without their vote the decision below would have been reaffirmed and there probably wouldn't have been any reapportionment cases. After Cox became Solicitor, Potter Stewart inquired through an intermediary whether Lee Rankin, the Solicitor at the end of the Eisenhower Administration, had decided to come in as *amicus* for the petitioners in *Baker.* Rankin had, and it was clear that Stewart cared. Government support mattered in a broad psychological way. It made the cases more respectable, indicating that an idea's time had come. Some of the earlier cases had been filed by cranks, and even the *Baker* case itself, in the opinion of courtroom observers, was messily argued by Charles Rhyne, who made high-sounding speeches but wasn't able to answer the Justices' hard questions. Men like Justice Brennan needed all the help they could get in the way of respectable answers to the questions that Frankfurter was sure to ask in conference. That Archie Cox, whose juridical posture was not that far from Frankfurter, took such a far-out position may well be what made the difference. Cox himself was to acknowledge the critical role of the government in *Baker* v. *Carr* in an internal memorandum he sent to the Attorney General the following year on the subject of standards in the upcoming reapportionment cases, which came to be known as *Reynolds* v. *Sims.* He said, in passing: "It is no exaggeration to recognize among ourselves that we played the most important role in *Baker* v. *Carr,* and our brief and argument may even have determined the result. We have a somewhat similar opportunity in the present case."

It is conceivable that even in the absence of the collective coaxing to which he was so artfully subjected, the self-demanding and introspective Solicitor would have arrived at the identical reapportionment position which he ended up taking. Today he maintains he knew where he was going to come out all along, that ultimately the government did what *he* wanted to do, that all along his only real resistance was to the one-man-one-vote formula, not to the main thrust of the cases. But the evidence suggests otherwise. Without automatically attributing Frankfurter's views to Cox, we can recognize that Cox was not uninfluenced by Frankfurter's opinion in the landmark case of *Colegrove* v. *Green*, where he had observed that the drawing of Congressional district lines by a state is a matter "of a peculiar political nature and therefore not meet for judicial determination."

Cox's milieu was probably close to that of his Harvard colleague Paul Freund, who had warned in 1962 that the government should beware of embracing any reapportionment formula which exceeded the requirements of the specific case. Freund had written:

> . . . It is sometimes said that when legislatures and executives cannot be moved to advance the cause of liberalism, the opportunity and responsibility devolve on the courts. Stated thus baldly, the counsel is surely a dangerous invitation, dangerous to the standing of the Court and false to the liberalism in whose name it is propounded. But in the context of the Tennessee apportionment case the default in the law-making machinery had special relevance, for the very structure and processes that are presupposed in representative government had become distorted.
>
> The future will test the Court's resourcefulness in defining the rational bounds of representation without resorting to a simplistic criterion of one man, one vote—a criterion meaningful in an election for a single state-wide office or for a particular representative but question-begging in the case of a collegial body to be chosen with a view to balanced representation. . . .[2]

What Cox might have done solo we can never know. What we do know is that on the Attorney General's part there was a delicate and sensitively managed bit of patience which took account of the Solicitor's integrity, his ego, his inclinations—an act of faith that paid off. But it paid off at least partly because Robert Kennedy had created an environment where the younger men—like thirty-year-old Bruce Terris, a Harvard lawyer in the Solicitor's office, Harold Greene, head of the Civil Rights Appeals Section, and others—felt free to stretch the boundaries of their assignment and believed that "if you could only get the Attorney General's ear, you could convince him." They were not content to be safe bureaucrats.

A brief history of the key reapportionment cases under Kennedy–Cox explains how the process of accommodation worked.

Colegrove v. *Greene*, decided in 1946, was the landmark case and seemed to stand for the principle, as Frankfurter said, that "courts ought not to enter this political thicket. The remedy for unfairness in districting is to secure state legislatures that will apportion properly, or to invoke the ample powers of Congress."

But in 1960 Eisenhower's Solicitor, Lee Rankin, decided that the government ought to file as *amicus curiae* in the Tennessee case of *Baker* v. *Carr*. Nothing illustrated the illusory quality of the Frankfurterian remedy proposed in *Colegrove* better than the situation in Tennessee giving rise to *Baker* v. *Carr*. The Tennessee constitution, which made legislative representation contingent on the number of qualified voters in each county, called for decennial reapportionment in accordance with the population standard. Yet for sixty years, from 1901 to 1961, during which time the population had quadrupled and shifted to the cities, the legislature had taken no action. The result: voters in the lower-house districts varied from 42,298 to 2,340. Counties with just over a third of the population could elect almost two thirds of the members of the senate. In addition to situations where state legislatures violated state constitutions, two thirds of the state constitutions turned out to impose significant restrictions on equitable apportionment; and uniformly, rural voters had, through natural population shifts, ended up with disproportionate influence.

For twenty years judges avoided confronting the issue by citing Frankfurter and either denying their power to hear "political questions" or reaffirming the undesirability of venturing into the "political thicket." They ignored the obvious pitfall of the Frankfurter doctrine—malapportioned legislatures would never reapportion themselves, so another branch of government had to do it. Nobody paid much attention to the epigrammatic common sense of Professor John Roche of Brandeis, who pointed out in the mid-Fifties with respect to the "political question" doctrine that "A juridical definition of the term is impossible, for at root the logic that supports it is circular: political questions are matters not soluble by the judicial process; matters not soluble by the judicial process are political questions. As an early dictionary explained, violins are small cellos, and cellos are large violins."

But now Solicitor Rankin had notified the court of the Justice Department's intention to come in as *amicus,* and Archibald Cox inherited the case. As a former member of the Solicitor's office, now on the bench, recalls, "Archie was very lukewarm and leery about its correctness. He was a Frankfurterian. He was leery as a matter of Constitutional law. He hadn't made the decision to go in and at first he wasn't going to argue it." He talked with Byron White about it, who thought the government couldn't get out. And in casual conversation with Oscar Davis and Bruce Terris, a former student of Cox's who had served under Rankin and stayed on at Cox's request, both told him he should argue it. At one point he suggested that Davis argue it but as a colleague notes, "That would have been a dead give-away and undermined the government's case. The issue was too important for anyone else [other than Cox] to argue."

The pressure was on. On February 28, 1961, Burke Marshall forwarded his weekly "Monday Report" to the Attorney General. Item D read:

> We have prepared and sent to the Solicitor General an *amicus* brief on the reapportionment case from Tennessee in which the Supreme Court has granted certiorari. The draft brief asks the Supreme Court to overturn the decision in *Colegrove* v. *Green* in which the court held that the federal courts had no power to order reapportionment of Congressional seats. The Tennessee case arises under the 14th Amendment and involves the failure of the Tennessee legislature to reapportion the legislative districts since 1901. The case is of considerable legal and political significance since there have been similar failures by the state legislature in a number of other states. . . .

Since Kennedy and his entourage had been in office only a few weeks, there was no knowing what an open disagreement within the Justice Department might bring and a real desire on everyone's part to avoid it.

Another source of pressure was Anthony Lewis, who was covering the Justice Department and the U.S. Supreme Court for *The New York Times* but in effect was doubling as a lobbyist for reapportionment. He had written the definitive analysis of reapportionment for the *Harvard Law Review* while on a Neiman Fellowship in 1958. And he did not hesitate to let either the Solicitor or the Attorney General or their aides know how he felt about the matter, although he did his best not to overstep the boundaries of propriety.

So, although Cox now doesn't remember it this way, in the beginning, according to his staff, "Cox didn't want to go into the reapportionment cases at all. He felt it was a political question, impossible for courts to enforce if states choose not to obey." Another observer adds that "It is correct that Archie had to be brought around, slowly and tortuously, to the true-blue view on reapportionment . . . the first time around [*Baker* v. *Carr*] was relatively easy because he could and did adopt a sophisticated lawyer's position on the 'political question' doctrine without expressing any view—perhaps not even to himself—on the ultimate substantive question of what the standard of apportionment should be. He was also encouraged by the fact that his Republican predecessor had already started the machinery for intervention on behalf of the petitioners."

If Cox was instinctively reluctant to enter the thicket, Robert Kennedy was instinctively ready to conduct an extensive safari. As a Senator, John F. Kennedy had written a pro-reapportionment article. And as Burke Marshall recalls, "Robert Kennedy thought Congress wasn't working right and state legislatures weren't working right. It was a political—not partisan—judgment. He wanted, instinctively, to see the democratic process work right. It is the same instinctive reaction he had about the Negro vote. If you set up a political structure dependent on the vote and rig it so that the vote doesn't count, that's no good.

"The Attorney General understood the point about the Supreme Court. We had meetings on it. It was a matter of convincing Archie that he should support the position the Department finally took—the straight position of equal representation.

"Archie didn't disagree on what was the right result. He did have difficult and proper doubts about the proper role for the court. . . ."

How Robert Kennedy, Burke Marshall, Bruce Terris, Anthony Lewis, *et al.*, got Archibald Cox to take the action he took is characteristic of Justice under Kennedy. Terris sent memoranda. Marshall pointed out the pitfalls of not taking it. Kennedy asked "dumb" questions about the merits. All agreed on the strategy of taking the court along one step at a time—of postponing the question of what the ultimate standard should be and arguing only that the court had the right to pass on such cases.

Whatever kibbitzing Anthony Lewis did was probably less important than the contribution he had already made in the pages of the *Harvard Law Review*, where he made such pertinent points as the one that "The political thicket of malapportionment has not, as a rule, scared off the courts of the states. They have granted relief in a large number of lawsuits brought by private citizens against state officials to challenge apportionments. Districts have been held in violation of state constitutional requirements that they be of approximately equal population, be compact in shape, be made up of contiguous territory, or follow town boundaries. . . . There is virtually no discussion of justiciability in the state cases." Cox made the same point in his brief *amicus* in *Baker*, calling attention to decisions from a number of state courts in which jurisdiction was accepted and effective remedies were fashioned.

Had Robert Kennedy called in Cox and "laid down the law," as a

Joe Rauh might have urged him to do, the vain, easily offended and highly principled Solicitor would either have resigned, appealed to JFK or refused to sign the briefs and argue the cases—a course of action which subsequent events have made clear might have killed reapportionment. But Kennedy, abetted, assisted and directed by his colleagues within and without the Justice Department, had the antennae and the intelligence to let the Solicitor arrive at his own decision.

When he left the courtroom, after a brilliant performance in his oral argument in the *Baker* case, Cox turned to his assistant, Bruce Terris, and murmured, "Frankfurter was right!" although even Frankfurter conceded in his dissent from the *Baker* case that the *Colegrove* case was not precedent for denying jurisdiction on the grounds of "want of power." What Frankfurter objected to was that the court was going against the "uniform course of decision over the years" and that it was violating the precept of self-restraint in political matters.

Next came *Gray* v. *Sanders*, the Georgia county unit case, which Kennedy himself argued and won. On paper Burke Marshall recommended to the Solicitor that the Department participate in the case because "In Georgia it heralds the possible end of a system of rural domination in which a candidate in a statewide primary election could win a majority of the popular vote but lose the election. Winning the Democratic primary in Georgia is, of course, tantamount to being elected." Marshall's memo argued:

> Nationally . . . the standards set forth by the three-judge court for determining whether a county unit system is in violation of the equal protection clause . . . are quite relevant to the question of the proper standards for determining whether the apportionment of seats in a state legislature is consistent with that clause.
> On the merits, we think the county unit system . . . is invidiously discriminatory. . . .

Marshall added that it was

> not necessary to decide whether a county unit system per se contravenes the equal protection clause, although an argument to that effect might be persuasively advanced.

The Georgia county unit case, in addition to its Constitutional significance, was noteworthy as a case study in the engineering of Solicitor General Cox. The co-conspirators in the deed were Nicholas Katzenbach, Deputy Attorney General, and Burke Marshall, who, as head of the Civil Rights Division, had jurisdiction over reapportionment. It was Marshall's idea that Robert Kennedy should make an appearance in court and it was Katzenbach who said to Marshall that Kennedy shouldn't argue civil rights and he shouldn't argue crime. "We wanted to get him in one important enough for the Attorney General to argue," Katzenbach recalls, "but not so technical that you'd have to go through 9,000 pages of record. What was or became perfectly clear was that he should argue reapportionment."

Cox, however, didn't trust his own *office* on reapportionment, no less the legally inexperienced Attorney General. He had a clear idea of where he wanted the law to go on reapportionment and was reluctant to delegate to anybody—least of all a young man who had never appeared in a courtroom before—what might turn out to be the critical case in the field. "Then we had a great and subtle negotiation," recalls Katzenbach. He and Marshall met with Cox and "innocently" went down a list of possible cases which they proposed, encouraging the Solicitor to find reasons against Kennedy arguing each and every one of them until, as Katzenbach says with a Cheshire grin, "We got him to the point where he eliminated everything but this case and finally Archie said, 'I guess this is the case.'" Kennedy, who had been clued in on the proceedings from the beginning, was then publicly told the Solicitor's decision and he said, "It sounds like a good idea."

"Archie was a prince of a fellow," says Katzenbach. "We pushed the lobster into the trap but he did everything possible to help."

Of course once the case was selected, the Solicitor made sure that the Attorney General took a conservative line, which he did.

Although the Attorney General told the court that the U.S. was intervening "to restore some confidence in representative government" and he argued that the Georgia system was "a gross and arbitrary discrimination" that violated the equal-protection clause of the Constitution's Fourteenth Amendment," he also said: "We are not against a county unit system as such but against one which discriminates against urban voters. . . . We are not saying that under all circumstances every vote must be given the same weight."

When Chief Justice Warren asked if Kennedy could think of a Constitutional system of weighting voters, the young Attorney General admitted it was difficult. Then there occurred an exchange with Arthur Goldberg on whether county unit systems are bad *per se*:

JUSTICE GOLDBERG: Isn't the logic of your position that all county unit systems are bad? Why doesn't the government have the courage of its convictions?

RFK: We have the courage, Mr. Justice. I just don't think it's necessary to say it now. It might be that there are states where legislatures would come up with a system making some sense.

GOLDBERG: But you can't conceive of that.

RFK: But I can't conceive of that.

Anthony Lewis summarized Robert Kennedy's oral argument as saying "Departures from absolute equality would be justified . . . only if not too severe and if designed 'to further the elective process.' For example, he said legislative districts could recognize historical and geographical factors to some extent."

Baker v. *Carr* had given the court jurisdiction, *Gray* v. *Sanders* had said you can't weight votes once districts are chosen, but now it was the spring of 1963 and the Solicitor had to face the question which until then he had artfully avoided: By what standards should states be reapportioning, by what standards should existing districts be declared constitutional or unconstitutional? The liberals, with whom Kennedy was instinctively allied on this issue, were essentially for a one-man, one-vote standard; the Frankfurterians were more cautious in arriving at a formula.

It is, of course, a gross oversimplification to call Archibald Cox, whose views were on the march with history, however painful the process might have been, a Frankfurterian. But it seems fair to say that he entered the reapportionment field somewhat reluctantly, that he approached it conservatively, that he instinctively rejected arithmetic or pat conclusions, and that he predicted the court would not buy such a radical formula as one man, one vote. The result, to jump ahead a moment, was that the Justice Department under Robert Kennedy never actually embraced the one-man, one-vote formula that the court ultimately adopted. Yet as Cox himself says today, "I was wrong in my fears. But I think I am right when I say that if we hadn't moved the court step by step they might never have taken the great leap forward. . . ."

It may also be said that were it not for the free play the Kennedy environment at Justice gave some of the younger men and the fluidity it encouraged in relations with "outsiders" like Anthony Lewis, who had been in Robert Kennedy's class at Harvard (although they hadn't known each other well), and who, during his days as a Neiman Fellow, had forged a close friendship with Cox, Cox himself might not have urged the court to move step by step. This is not a judgment, to be sure, on which he himself would concur. And part of his style was to put his associates and subordinates on their mettle by taking more doctrinaire positions in early argument and debate than his instincts told him were ultimately necessary. Nevertheless, the virtually unanimous opinion of those with whom he did business was that it took some quiet and subtle convincing on the part of others before Cox had convinced himself of the correctness of the reapportionment position which the Justice Department ultimately took.

Bruce Terris, the attorney with operating responsibility for the reapportionment cases, exercised an important influence on the Solicitor whom he served and with whom he argued. If the hypothesis offered above is incorrect and the Solicitor would have arrived at his relative radicalism on the reapportionment issue on his own, then it is *still* significant that men like Terris felt free and encouraged to disagree out loud, at length, in meetings and on paper.

Like many other young attorneys in the Justice Department in 1960, Terris was at first deeply distressed and bitterly disappointed when he heard that Robert Kennedy was to be the new Attorney General. He considered Kennedy "unqualified, illiberal and a beneficiary of nepotism." But as he saw the caliber of the men Kennedy recruited and watched the new young Attorney General in action, his bitterness converted to hopeful respect. And his experience working with Kennedy in connection with the Georgia county unit case, where Terris found "He asked all the right questions and he had good answers," had convinced him that Kennedy was an able and serious man. He knew from his briefings in the *Gray* case that Kennedy was more daring if less informed on the one-man, one-vote issue than the Solicitor, whose sarcastic aside about Frankfurter's being right Terris remembered. He conferred with contemporaries in the Civil Rights Division Appeals Section and others and decided on a strategy.

When the string of cases which came to travel under the name of *Reynolds* v. *Sims* presented themselves, Terris believed, as Jack Greenberg had believed in the sit-in cases, as Joe Rauh believed in the *Deerfield* housing integration case, that the Solicitor General was about to decide a policy issue on legal criteria. He knew it was impossible to outargue the Solicitor General of the United States—although often he observed Cox listen and the next day come back with a variation of an opponent's argument, call it his own, say, "What do you think of this?" and without ever admitting to anyone, even himself, that he had followed the logic of an argument rather than the prejudice of a pre-existing conviction, changed his mind.

Terris sent one-page summary memos on each of the cases coming up before the court—Alabama, Maryland, Virginia, New York, Delaware and Colorado (which was briefed separately)—and in each case showed how the existing apportionment departed from the one-man, one-vote standard and was in any event so outrageously unbalanced as to be unconstitutional.

But the critical memorandum sent by Terris was dated July 3, 1963. It ran eleven pages and dealt with "The Substantive Standards under the Fourteenth Amendment for Apportioning State Legislatures." In the memorandum Terris set forth the case for government support of a strict population standard, but he did more than that. First, he argued the importance of reapportionment. He wrote:

> I doubt whether even the sit-in cases are of equal significance as the state apportionment cases. I say this because the Negro civil rights movement will almost surely continue regardless how the sit-in cases are decided. . . . In contrast, the issue of apportionment depends almost entirely on what the courts and particularly the Supreme Court decide.

Second, he pointed out what was common knowledge in the Solicitor's office, but not generally known outside the most intimate legal circles of the government—the importance of the Solicitor's role in this particular line of cases:

> . . . the position taken by the government is probably of considerably greater influence in these cases than in almost any others in which the government appears as an *amicus curiae*. It is generally accepted, and I am sure the Court agrees, that we carried the brunt of persuading the Court to decide *Baker* v. *Carr* as it did. I think that it is unlikely that the Court will impose a stricter standard on the states than we suggest. However, I think that there is probably a majority for deciding as strict a standard as we are willing to support.

He argued that the proper standard under the equal-protection clause was that both houses must be apportioned on the basis of population. He added that "I think it is plain that it would significantly benefit the country if our state legislatures were reapportioned on the basis of population," and then said, ". . . It would be a tragedy if the great victory in *Baker* v. *Carr* were thrown away by our persuading the Supreme Court to accept a weak substantive standard." He argued that ". . . it will be easier for the Court to say that equal protection means complete equality in representation than it was to hold that equal protection did not allow segregation even when the facilities provided were equal." He pointed out that the court "went beyond our argument [in *Gray* v. *Sanders*] . . . and cited the trend toward political equality in this country which it stated means 'one person, one vote.'" He said that "the intrusion of the courts can best be minimized by their laying down a clear, unambiguous standard. . . ."

But Terris saved the critical point for the conclusion. After arguing that the equal-protection clause requires that both houses be apportioned on the basis of population, he wrote:

> Nonetheless, I recognize that the choice between the various standards largely depends on questions of policy. I have therefore gone on to suggest that the population standard is, as a matter of policy, best for the country because it is most consistent with contemporary concepts of democracy and with a strong federal system. However, despite my views on the correct policy, I recognize that this vital issue is largely outside my province. *It seems to me to be a political decision properly made at the highest levels of government. Until that decision is made, I do not believe that our legal position can be formulated.* [Italics added.]

What he had done was to shift the issue—not to who is right, the Solicitor or a subordinate, but rather to who should decide it, the Solicitor or the Attorney General or possibly the President. By asserting that it was *not* a legal issue, he had opened the way for the Solicitor to rationalize a retreat from his opposition to the one-man, one-vote principle.

Terris was not fighting a lonely battle. A week and a half after he had raised the issue with Cox, two young attorneys in the Civil Rights Division, David Rubin and Howard Glickstein, ostensibly on their own initiative but actually after extended consultation with Terris and others (including the ubiquitous Anthony Lewis), fired off a memorandum dated July 15, 1963, to Harold Greene, chief of the Appeals Research Section of the Civil Rights Division. Terris had no idea what, if anything, Cox would do with his memo. Rubin and Glickstein knew that Greene would forward it to Marshall (since Marshall was Greene's superior as head of the Civil Rights Division), and Marshall in all probability would bring it to the attention of both Cox and the Attorney General. They directed their memo to the questions raised most insistently by the case in Colorado, where one house was apportioned by the population and the other not, and said, "We wish to express our strong agreement with [the view that both houses of a state legislature must be apportioned on the basis of population]." They argued, among other things, that

> 1 . . . Absent such a standard the unrepresentative house will retain veto power over legislation proposed by the house which is fairly represented.
> 2 . . . we do not see why such inanimate factors as land or cows

should be represented in a legislature. . . . Minorities are protected
by bills of rights. . . .

6. It is extremely important for the court to formulate a standard
which is clear and forthright. . . .

7. The reapportionment issue cannot be divorced from the problem
of securing Negro rights. Large numbers of Negro citizens live in urban
areas, and the looser the representation of these areas in the state
legislature conforms to a population standard the more likely it is
that state laws will respect the rights of the Negro and remedy his
condition. . . .

Ten days later the expected memorandum went from Greene to
Marshall. Dated July 19, 1963, Greene's three-page memo attached the
memoranda from Terris (who had sent him a carbon) and from
Rubin and Glickstein. He said he found them persuasive and added
three pages of his own.

Greene judiciously divided his memo into two parts—the "legal
arguments" and the "practical arguments." To the legal arguments
already covered he added the thought that "The federal analogy is not
apt because, unlike the United States, no state is operating internally
on the basis of a federal system." And he said, "Modern transportation
and communications have diminished geography as an important
factor."

His practical arguments, however, indicated a less ambitious and
rigorous standard than Terris or Rubin and Glickstein had called for.
Greene argued:

1. Failure to apply a population standard will have the effect of
leaving rural interests in control in most of the big states.

Nevertheless, he said:

I do not believe the Department should argue . . . the strict population principle. . . . As I read Mr. Terris' memorandum, while it
argues for the principle of a strict population standard, it concedes that
a deviation from the standard up to a 10–20% spread between the
largest and smallest districts . . . would be appropriate.

I agree with that qualified approach. . . . We should argue that
[population] should be the exclusive factor in one of the houses of the
legislature. . . . In the other house, too, population should be given
controlling weight, but there perhaps somewhat greater variations,
based on geography or districting, might be allowed. In my judgment
we should suggest, however, that it is unnecessary in these cases to decide the extent of the allowable variations since in the four cases which
present the upper house problem (NY, Va, Md and Ala) the variations from the population standard are too great in any event. . . .

It should be noted that Terris, Rubin, Glickstein and Greene were all arguing *for* the population standard and in varying degrees that it be applied to both houses of a bicameral legislature. None openly admitted that the Solicitor had been considering not only not supporting the population standard but actively opposing it. One might assume, however, that a closing paragraph by Greene was aimed at influencing the Solicitor's position. Greene wrote:

> I am doubtful that an absolute population standard for both houses can be justified, either now or in the future. History and the federal example too strongly militate against such a result. But in any event, that issue may safely be left for another day and, in view of the enormity of the problem of legislative apportionment, it is wise to do just that.

Archibald Cox's response to the paper war was characteristic. He gathered together all of the various memoranda, arguments, documents, papers and cases and proceeded to draft a thirty-three-page memorandum to the Attorney General, dated August 21, 1963, in which he concisely set forth his views on the matter. But what was of special interest about the Cox memorandum was that it precisely reflected his state of mind—a kind of tortured but clear, painful thinking aloud, brilliantly setting forth alternatives, preferences, tactics, law, policy, philosophy and jurisprudence. And, in a repeat of his St. Regis performance, he did his scrupulous best to give the opposition its due. A few examples of his style and method of reasoning demonstrate the dimensions of the mind contending with an Attorney General who had himself determined a course favoring a one-man, one-vote standard.

The first question Cox raised—one which everyone else assumed to be settled—was "Should the United States file a brief *amicus curiae* in the legislative apportionment cases?" Though he recommended that briefs be filed, one of his arguments against is a clue to his stance:

> . . . almost any brief that we might file would stimulate considerable criticism. If the position advocated in this memorandum is adopted the criticism in some quarters may be rather vociferous because the doctrinaire liberals and ardent proponents of reapportionment will be dissatisfied with anything less than advocacy of "one man-one vote"; and they always make the most noise.

The critical question was whether the United States should support the one-man, one-vote standard. As Cox put the question, it was:

> . . . whether the United States should espouse the view that the guarantee of equal protection of the law requires the apportionment

of seats in each house of the legislature in substantially the same ratio
as the population of the districts, thus giving effect to the principle
"one man, one vote." The plaintiffs in all four cases are presenting this
view. . . . Furthermore, it is doubtful whether the plaintiffs in the
New York case can prevail unless the Court espouses this view or something very close to it.

As Cox saw it, most political scientists were in favor of one man,
one vote, and most Constitutional lawyers were against the court laying down so rigid a rule. He then went on:

> In my view each is right within its sphere. Legislatures *ought* to be
> apportioned, in both houses, in proportion to population; to this ex-
> tent the political scientists are right. But to impose that one rule upon
> the fifty states through a Supreme Court decision purporting to inter-
> pret the Constitution would be exceedingly bad, I think, for the
> country as well as the courts; hence to this extent the teachers of con-
> stitutional law seem correct.
>
> I shall try first to present as effectively as I can the arguments in
> support of the view that the Equal Protection clause of the 14th
> Amendment requires the apportionment of seats in both houses of a
> state legislature substantially in accordance with population. Against
> the chance that I fail to do them justice, I attach two Staff memoranda
> arguments for that view. I shall then state the reasoning in support of
> the opposing view, which, in my case at least, stems largely from per-
> sonal conviction concerning the nature of our federal system, the
> proper role of the Supreme Court in our national life, and the obliga-
> tion of the Solicitor General to the Court.

So he attached the Terris and another memorandum to his memo
and quite frankly asserted the motivation behind his concern about
the course of action which the Civil Rights Division so wholeheartedly
seemed to favor. And he did more than that. He said, in effect, that as
a matter of what one might call political policy, he would favor reapportionment by population but as a matter of what we might call
legal policy he did not favor the government saying so. As he put it:

> In a state constitutional convention my vote would go to apportion
> both houses of a bicameral legislature in accordance with population,
> but I cannot agree that the Supreme Court should be advised to im-
> pose that rule upon all 50 states by judicial decree. In my opinion any
> such decree would be too revolutionary to be a proper exercise of the
> judicial function and too rigid to comport with the principle of fed-
> eralism.

Cox was practical but scrupulously fair. On the politics of the thing
as far as the court was concerned, he pointed out:

Many men believe that the present Court has already gone too far too fast in imposing its ideals upon the states. Some are segregationists but many are not. Some are Birchers . . . but many are men of moderation. I do not share their view, but my appraisal of sentiment within the legal profession—and probably outside—is that while the invalidation of the egregiously malapportioned legislatures would command a consensus of opinion, a "one man, one vote" decision would precipitate a major constitutional crisis causing an enormous drop in public support for the Court. Indeed, I doubt whether the decision could be made to stick. . . .

He gave his philosophy of the court:

The court's ability to make the system work depends upon exercising enough self-restraint not to get too far ahead of the country on too many fronts.

And he expressed his sense of obligation to the court:

. . . in *Baker* v. *Carr* we repeatedly asserted that the government did *not* contend that the test was one man, one vote. Having persuaded the court to accept jurisdiction on one basis, we would engage in double-dealing now to seek to have jurisdiction exercised in accordance with the rule we disavowed.

Ultimately, then, Cox made two general recommendations and then applied them to the specific cases. First, he recommended that the government, having induced the court to accept jurisdiction in *Baker* v. *Carr*, should not withhold its assistance in facing the more difficult question concerning the applicable standards. Second, he recommended that the government intervene on behalf of the reformers in cases in Delaware, Virginia, Alabama and Maryland based on the following philosophy:

I recommend that the United States should espouse standards that would have the practical effect of requiring representation according to population in one house of the legislature while allowing substantial deviation in the other where the deviation is not extreme and is justified by such historic policies as giving each town or county one representative or representing countries equally in the State Senate; but that we should not argue that both houses must be apportioned on the basis of the principle—one man, one vote.

His attempt to apply this standard to the case of *WMCA* v. *Simon*, challenging the apportionment of the New York legislature, gave him the most trouble. Terris had pointed out in his memorandum on the *WMCA* case that 35 to 38 percent of the people can elect a majority of the Assembly. But Cox found that while minorities can control both houses in New York, "Neither is small when compared to the situation in other states." He also was moved by the fact that the district court had upheld the existing apportionment. His conclusion:

> I am inclined to think that its decision will, and probably should, be affirmed. Advocating affirmance would have some technical advantages in handling the other cases. However, it seems undesirable to argue against those who are seeking more representative apportionment and, consequently, I recommend that we be authorized to file a brief seeking reversal if we can develop respectable arguments for that position, but that our presentation make it plain that the New York case is much closer than the others and that the Virginia, Alabama and Maryland apportionments should be invalidated even if that of New York is affirmed.

Meanwhile, over in the Attorney General's office, Kennedy had received Cox's memorandum, spoken with Marshall and Katzenbach and called a meeting. But this was an informal best-minds-in-the-Department and whoever-else-happened-to-be-in-the-vicinity meeting. It consisted of, among others, Robert Kennedy, brother-in-law Sargent Shriver from the Peace Corps and Stephen Smith, who had no official government responsibilities whatsoever, but whose political savvy the Kennedys had come to know and trust, Theodore Sorensen, Kenneth O'Donnell and Lawrence O'Brien from the White House, Burke Marshall, Archibald Cox and Bruce Terris. Everybody present had read both the Cox and Terris memoranda.

As usual in that kind of situation, the confident Solicitor thought he wasn't going to have any trouble. Kennedy asked him to set the stage for the discussion. So the Solicitor started to talk and gradually it became apparent that he was giving his reapportionment lecture. It went on for what seemed to two of those present like twenty minutes, when the Attorney General began to get fidgety. He got up and poured himself some orange juice and sat down again. He drummed his hands on his desk and played with his tie. Finally, in the politest way possible he interrupted his Solicitor and said, "Archie—isn't the real issue should some people's vote count more than other people's vote?" According to one who was present: "Cox agreed and shut up." O'Brien then picked up and started on the politics of the issue by saying he was not sure that the Democrats would gain anything by it. In fact, if one man, one vote went into effect, it might cost the Democrats some seats. He said the suburbs would gain more representation but it was far from clear whether the suburbanites would vote Democratic. And he ran down, state by state, the probable political impact of the decision. Again, Kennedy cut him off and said he did not want any more political discussion. Cox then made what sounded to one lawyer present like an *interrorum* argument. He said, in effect, that no matter what's right or wrong, I'm telling you that the United States Supreme Court won't accept it and if we don't state a decent position the whole ball game might be lost. The discussion continued—with Cox saying he *personally* was for one man, one vote, but as a matter of law, you couldn't ask the Court to be that rigid, and others asking for alternative standards that were more reasonable. Finally, it was apparent to all that the meeting was not going to get any further, and Kennedy said to Cox, "Archie, I know you can put this issue in a way that will convince the Supreme Court. I have full confidence." Nothing had really been decided. But that is precisely what Cox did. He did not quite argue the one-man, one-vote theory but stopped just short of it. But he did help convince the court.

On the way out of the Attorney General's office Cox turned to his assistant—as though young Bruce Terris, whose memo had precipitated the thing, was on his side, the *lawyerly* side, and said, "You know these guys don't really understand what this is all about." Cox felt he could communicate with Terris on a professional level, and as a matter of law he was probably right. He and Terris (and Marshall and Katzenbach, too) were the only ones involved who appreciated all of the nuances of the thing. But the irony of it was that in human terms Cox was probably the only man in the room who didn't know what it was all about. For the purpose of the meeting was not to arrive at a decision—Kennedy already knew what he wanted. The purpose of the meeting was to make the Solicitor General of the United States feel good, to let him know that his own reservations were not being taken lightly, to let him know by implication that it would be unthinkable to come out *against* one man, one vote—to reaffirm his right to make up his own mind to assure him that it was *his* decision to make. And the Department's brief came out midway between asking the court to knock down specific apportionments without giving them a precise standard and citing a strict one-man, one-vote rule.

Just in case the Solicitor had not received the message, the ever-vigilant Anthony Lewis had arranged to get a set of the *Reynolds* brief galley proofs straight from the printer before they had been officially ratified by Cox. Lewis had been an active kibbitzer from the outset, and Terris attributes to him a key role in persuading the Solicitor against his original inclination explicitly to oppose the one-man, one-vote standard. Lewis doesn't claim any such influence, but his own recollections are suggestive.

"At an early point in the briefing period," Lewis recalls, "I talked to Bobby, telling him that I knew Archie was personally unconvinced of the one-man, one-vote standard, and I thought it would be a tragedy to have the Department of Justice take an antagonistic position; at worst the brief should avoid the ultimate question but find the particular apportionment in each of the cases at issue invalid on some ground. Bobby, as usual, was quite silent in this first talk on the subject, not giving me any real feeling about the degree of his interest or sympathy. But fairly soon thereafter, as I remember, he brought the subject up in another conversation and made it very clear that he was completely convinced of (a) the Constitutional rightness of one man, one vote, and (b) its urgent importance, politically and socially, for the country. I remember very clearly my happy—that puts it too shallowly—feeling that he understood and would do what had to be done. But he also told me that time that it would be a very delicate problem working with Archie. He, Bobby, was not in a position to order Archie to say something he did not believe; to have a fight with his Solicitor General, moreover, would not help the case because the court would know it and might see any brief filed over Archie's head as a political, not a legal, document. Again later, after what must have been much arguing that was beyond my knowledge, he made some remark to me on the delicate nature of the persuading process.

"I talked with Archie from time to time, during and indeed before the time he and others were working on the *Reynolds* brief. But I always felt it would be improper to try to push views on him; maybe I was a little too respectful. What happened, as I remember, is that I explored the state of his thinking; I avoided making direct suggestions but tried to nudge him a little farther by making a point here or there at the edges. Archie is a strong-minded man, and a proud one, and I thought it would be both improper and self-defeating to act as if I were on a level to argue with him. But I did talk often with Bruce Terris and the other assistants, I knew what was going on, and I guess Archie understood where I hoped he would go in the end. . . .

"There is no doubt that Archie was basically worried about the whole thing, that he was a Frankfurter man at heart, but he largely got over that intellectually, if not emotionally; because putting the burden on the other fellow to justify what he does is nine-tenths of the ball game in Constitutional law and was, indeed, all I had ever dreamt of achieving in the apportionment field. I remember one specific example of Archie's thinking. He told me that he thought a state would have a valid justification for giving a whole seat in one house to an island or other separate, geographically cut-off area, even though its population was much less than other districts'—because a mainland legislator whose district included the island would not really represent the special island interests at all and so it would be deprived of any effective representation. (I think he briefly mentioned this island theory in the brief.) He cited Martha's Vineyard and Nantucket to me as examples; I agreed with him and still do. But you see that his mind had reached the point where he had to find some very concrete reason to allow any departure from population representation. That was a long way from the extremely cautious view I know Archie took at the time of *Baker*. When he told the court then that all he urged was jurisdiction, with no real view of the ultimate Constitutional standards, he meant it."

One weekend Lewis returned home, found the *Reynolds* galleys and was disturbed on reading them to discover a number of places where he felt "Archie was giving too many hostages. There were phrases, that is, that seemed to disavow ever arriving at a strict one-man, one-vote rule." The tricky line of the Solicitor's argument was that it was possible, without facing the ultimate question of the strict one-man, one-vote rule, for the court to strike down each of the six challenged apportionments—an intellectually responsible but exceedingly difficult argument to make and not one particularly calculated to convince a wavering court. "On reading the proofs," Lewis recalled six years later, "it seemed to me that Archie—his conscience and his doubts too strong to be suppressed altogether—had let it slip in a dozen places or so that he really did not believe in the one-man, one-vote theory. I pondered what to do."

What Lewis did was to phone Bruce Terris, from whom he learned that it was too late for any more staff arguments and that it would take the aggressive intervention of an "outsider" if any more pressure was to be put. Lewis, anticipating the new journalism, shed any pretense at objectivity and drove out to see the Solicitor, who lived on a farm farther out in Virginia than Lewis's own home in McLean. "I went out, feeling very nervy for doing so," Lewis remembers, "and told him of my objections to those passages. I know I was deferential, but it was certainly the most direct plea I had made. He argued back on the merits of each point, not telling me just to go away. Finally I left, not sure what he could or would do—and of course I don't remember what he did!"

Some of the passages that worried Lewis *were* changed, though others may have brought the same points to the Solicitor's attention, or he may have rethought them himself. But more important than whether Anthony Lewis had a specific impact was the fact that the Kennedy Justice Department's environment was such that *The New York Times*'s very proper lawman, coming on these highly technical points as an outsider and recognizing their relevance to national policy, felt it not totally inappropriate to go beyond the boundaries of conventional journalistic propriety and add his own thoughts to the policy-deciding mix at the highest operational level.

Finally, there was the Colorado case, which was not briefed until after completion of the arguments in the other five reapportionment cases and which gave the Solicitor more problems than any of the others. The voters in every single county of Colorado (including Denver, the most populous), had rejected, in a statewide referendum, a proposal that both houses of the legislature be apportioned on the basis of population; and they had chosen a plan whereby the lower house would be selected on a one-man, one-vote basis, but the upper house would involve both population and area factors in its apportionment.

Essentially Cox felt that there was nothing Constitutionally improper with what Colorado had done. Yet, as he points out, "How would we look coming out against reapportionment?" His solution: Have the government refrain from filing an *amicus* brief in the case. Terris, as expected, argued that the government *had* to take a position:

> Since we have taken such an important part in the reapportionment cases—in the Supreme Court probably the leading part—our absence will surely not be merely ignored. The court will probably guess that the government's absence results from grave doubts that the plaintiffs are correct since we have supported the plaintiffs in other cases.

He added, in a lawyerly ploy, that it would be better to support the state (which he knew Cox knew would go against the Attorney General's grain) than do nothing, since in that way the government could make clear the narrow grounds of its action.

The Solicitor was not convinced. On February 4, 1964, he forwarded a memo to the Attorney General recommending "that the United States refrain from supporting the plaintiffs in the Colorado reapportionment case now before the Supreme Court" and proposing that the U.S. file a brief urging dismissal of the bill on technical grounds. His recommendation—which would have permitted the *status quo* in Colorado—was based on five grounds:

> 1. The position is at variance with our entire Constitutional history.

2. The position is contrary to our basic federal philosophy in that it would ask the Supreme Court to fasten upon the people of every state a doctrinaire system of representation regardless of their wishes.

3. For the Supreme Court to accept the government's invitation to impose its will upon the states regardless of their wishes would risk a severe Constitutional crisis.

4. The government would be going back on the position which it urged when it argued, in *Baker* v. *Carr*, that the Supreme Court has jurisdiction over apportionment cases.

5. To present the argument would endanger the ground that we hope we have gained in the five reapportionment cases last autumn.

He attached a memo from Burke Marshall which made no recommendations, but it did point out with compelling logic the illogic of interpreting the Fourteenth Amendment one way for one house and another way for the other house; it found the federal analogy—which involved a compromise with the prerogatives of pre-existing sovereign states—totally irrelevant; and it also argued the irrelevance of Colorado's referendum: "While unquestionably this fact presents a psychological obstacle, it would seem that whether or not a man's neighbors vote to settle for less than per capita representation has little bearing upon the rights involved. . . ."

Again there was a meeting. Again there were some outsiders, including Sorensen. In advance of the meeting it was known that Cox was dug in, that he wasn't going to support one man, one vote, and the Attorney General felt that he couldn't not support the liberal view in the Colorado case. Again, the conference was supposed to resolve the impasse. Again, Cox was the man who had to be convinced. Marshall, Katzenbach and John Douglas, Assistant Attorneys General whose legal judgment Cox respected most, had all told him they had no quarrel with his view of the *law*. The question was one of practicality. In fact what happened was that on the way to the meeting Burke Marshall said to Cox, "Look, this is an impossible situation. Bob won't file a brief that you won't sign. On the other hand, Bob can't turn around and take the state side in the Colorado case. You've got to find a way out both to satisfy your conscience and still say Colorado is bad under past standards, and if the court didn't agree they should exercise their discretion and not decide."

Typically, it was Katzenbach (after a secret meeting with Terris and Joe Dolan, who had been a member of the Colorado legislature and had some strong ideas on the subject) who came up with the solution —an imaginative compromise suggestion that violated nobody's principles but solved what threatened to be an unpleasant impasse. On

February 11, 1964, he got off *his* memorandum to the Attorney General in which he suggested that the government need not decide between one man, one vote and leaving the thing alone. "It seems to me possible," he wrote, "that we can support the plaintiffs on a more narrow ground which would leave to the future whether both houses of the state legislatures must be based on population."

Katzenbach pointed out that "We argued that a small minority controls the legislature where 37 percent of the people elected a majority of the Assembly and 38 percent a majority of the Senate (of New York). In Colorado, under the 1960 census only 33 percent of the people elect a majority of the Senate. . . . Consequently, if we could fairly say that a small minority controlled both houses of the New York legislature, *a fortiori*, a small minority controls the Colorado Senate."

As Cox is the first to admit, he proved a poor prophet. Professor Robert McKay, writing about the reapportionment cases some years later, observes:

> Probably the single most significant aspect of the Supreme Court disposition of the states legislative apportionment cases is the literalistic, no-compromise reading given to the equal protection clause of the fourteenth amendment as a command for nearly absolute equality, showing judicial respect for the right of franchise in terms nearly as absolute as those formulated by the Court in the area of racial discrimination. . . . That the Court should have settled on this principle is particularly revealing in view of the fact that the Solicitor General of the United States, as *amicus curiae*, although urging invalidation of the state apportionment plan in each of the six cases before the Court, had in each case supported the voter plaintiffs on grounds narrower than those settled by the Courts.[3]

Cox had offered the court an invitation to test, experiment and postpone, but no member of the court took it. The court went beyond his "halfway house" argument, which included an invitation to the court to dismiss the case if he hadn't persuaded it that Colorado's apportionment was unconstitutional. The court got around the popular-approval issue by saying: "An individual's constitutionally protected right to cast an equally weighted vote cannot be denied even by a vote of a majority of a State's electorate."

So this was the progression. With *Baker*, the Solicitor convinced himself and the court that the court had jurisdiction. *Gray* said you can't Constitutionally classify voters within a state based on where they lived. And on two Mondays in June 1964 the U.S. Supreme Court held unconstitutional the apportionment formulas for nearly one third of all state legislatures and said that the equal-protection clause required that "The seats in both houses of a bicameral legislature must be apportioned on a population basis."

On June 15, the day *Reynolds* v. *Sims* was decided, Anthony Lewis, seated at a little desk just below the bench and next to the table where the Solicitor General and his assistants sat, wrote a brief note while the Chief Justice was reading his opinion and passed it to Cox. It said: "How does it feel to be present at the second American Constitutional Convention?" Cox passed a note back: "It feels awful."

As Nicholas Katzenbach puts it, "Basically Archie got his way on our apportionment presentation and basically the court saw to it that it went much faster than he wanted it to go." But not faster than the Attorney General wanted it to go. After he left the Department, Professor Archibald Cox has been heard on more than one occasion to tell his students and other visitors at Harvard that his proudest achievements as Solicitor General were the reapportionment cases. He had moved from a presumption against entering the political thicket to a presumption against one man, one vote; from a presumption against one man, one vote in both houses of a state's legislature to a rebuttable presumption in favor of one man, one vote in both houses. Ultimately, he entered all of the key reapportionment cases on the side of the reformers and made it possible for the U.S. Supreme Court to go beyond where he was willing to ask it to go. Having gotten there, he is now inclined to rejoice in the destination.

A respectable band of libertarian scholars, like Alexander Bickel at Yale, the late Robert McCloskey at Harvard and others, have entertained serious reservations about the wisdom of the reapportionment decisions. Some of these reservations were anticipated by Archibald Cox himself and by his Harvard colleague Paul Freund. The formula, they say, is too mechanical and misses such gross evils as gerrymandering. Professor Cox is unfazed. "I regard the reapportionment cases as great cases and important steps," he says. "There is a good deal to be said about the tendency of the court to run the reapportionment cases into the ground in extreme cases, and Alex Bickel and others are right in saying the Supreme Court can't do the whole job. But the answer is that if the Supreme Court can't do everything, it can do something. And this is one way of getting around the Constitution that the Supreme Court has scotched; gerrymandering it still hasn't reached, but malapportionment was the biggest problem." *

How much of the change in the Solicitor and in the law of the

* One benefit of the court having gone beyond the intermediate position Cox advocated, seems to be that the one-man, one-vote standard has avoided the morass of litigation a *less* mechanical standard might have precipitated.

land happened because the shirt-sleeved, casual, unlearned Robert Kennedy sat in the Attorney General's big red leather chair, it is difficult to say. This much, however, is known. The young reapportionment Turks, like Terris, Rubin, Glickstein, Greene & Co., were generally and specifically encouraged by the atmosphere of possibility, unorthodoxy and openness to change that Kennedy had helped generate. The young Attorney General understood and utilized to the utmost the ambassadorial potential of men like Katzenbach and Marshall. *Because* he refrained from attempting directly to persuade his Solicitor of anything, he may have helped guide the Justice Department and thereby the court and the country into a more representative democracy. And *because* he was conscious of, if not self-conscious about, his own lack of technical legal skills, law problems were not decided by a man from the middle of his University of Virginia Law School class, but they were worked out in a dialectical way as the values of Harvard and Yale struggled to assert themselves through some of the best men either of these elite institutions had to offer.

In the area of litigation, especially U.S. Supreme Court litigation, Kennedy's Ivy League gentlemen and corporate lawyers served the country and the Kennedys well. That, after all, is what these elite attorneys, a number of them former Supreme Court law clerks, had been trained to do.

In the area of informal negotiation this same cadre of lawyers served the Kennedy Administration effectively as they defused crisis after crisis although they occasionally misjudged their adversary, as in the case of Governor Barnett, with tragic results. Whether the long-range interests of the country were served by the corporation lawyers' preference for the artful compromise is, of course, a more difficult question.

In the area of judicial selection in the South, the corporation lawyers served the Kennedys and the country least well. Creatures of the corporate milieu, they did not focus on the damage a district-court judge in Jackson, Mississippi, could do, until it was too late. They were joined in their dereliction by their professional brethren, the ABA, which too often forfeited its role as independent auditor in favor of consolidating its role as participant.

The *bona fides* of Yale lawyers like Marshall, Katzenbach, White, Oberdorfer and Douglas were above reproach. Yet when they spoke about "the South" they meant the white South. When they talked about not splitting the country in half, they ignored the fact that the Negro underclass was already split. When they spoke of upholding the law, they were talking about upholding the integrity of the legal process rather than protecting the integrity of individual rights.

One can speculate that the failure to protect civil rights workers ultimately meant that the civil rights movement would move totally outside the system. But who can say whether an alternative civil rights policy would have yielded an alternative intellectual development. One can argue that if, instead of three Negro attorneys in the lower echelons of the Civil Rights Division, it had been staffed with a dozen early-Sixties-style militants, many of the things Burke Marshall took for granted would have been opened for inspection and discussion. But who can say whether the government would have taken an expanded view of its role, or what the impact of such a decision would have been?

It is, nevertheless, important to recognize that John Kennedy had raised the country's civil rights expectations during the Presidential campaign of 1960—a factor that no doubt helped attract so many Ivy League intellectuals to the Justice Department. But once enlisted, they functioned to contain these escalating expectations by devising a philosophy that made the federal government responsible for only a small part of them.

PART THREE

The Code of the Kennedys

CHAPTER SEVEN

Charisma:
The Family and the General

ACCORDING TO a State Department backgrounder, the ransoming of the Bay of Pigs prisoners in December of 1962 was strictly a private operation. Those who asked were told that:

1. The release of the prisoners was being arranged by a group called the Cuban Families Committee, incorporated in Florida as a tax-exempt charitable institution. The committee was a private group composed of the parents, relatives and friends of the Bay of Pigs prisoners which came into existence in July of 1961 following the collapse of the tractors-for-freedom committee headed by Eleanor Roosevelt.

2. In April 1962 after the prisoners had been tried and sentenced to thirty years of hard labor or fines of over $50 million, representatives of the committee (all Cubans) went to Havana to discuss with Fidel Castro the possible release of the prisoners and gained the impression that Castro would accept commodities instead of cash for the fines and that the release of the prisoners was negotiable. At the same time Castro agreed to the release of sixty of the more seriously wounded prisoners against the committee's personal pledge to raise funds equal to their fines ($2.9 million).

3. Because of the emotional involvement of the committee's representatives they hired outside counsel to assist them, one being James B.

Donovan, former OSS officer who had represented and negotiated the exchange of Colonel Rudolph Abel with the Soviet Union. In August and September Mr. Donovan went to Cuba, confirmed the earlier impression and began contacting pharmaceutical houses to see if it would be possible to put together a ransom package. In October he received from Castro a detailed list of the items Cuba would require for the release of the prisoners, and now he was actively seeking sources for the items in order to conclude the negotiations. When it was rumored that Robert Kennedy's Justice Department had run the show, Donovan denied it and on December 27, 1962, he told the Washington *Post*, "We did have the cooperation of the authorities. We could never have succeeded without them. But it was not the government or the Attorney General who was responsible for dealing with the drug companies. . . . I was purely responsible for this."

After it was over, the word quickly spread that it had not been a private operation at all. In fact, it had been a Justice Department operation, stimulated by the Attorney General and overseen by Louis Oberdorfer, Assistant Attorney General in charge of the Tax Division, and intergovernmentally coordinated by Katzenbach. As bits and pieces of information were leaked the following configuration of events emerged: Between November 30, 1962—barely a month after the Cuban missile crisis—and Christmas Day, Robert Kennedy's Justice Department, building on the valuable preliminary negotiations of James Donovan, arranged in exchange for $53 million in food and drug ransom the release of 1,113 Cuban prisoners. Working in concert with private attorneys, a number of whom later went on the Justice Department payroll (John Douglas, E. Barrett Prettyman, Jr., John E. Nolan, Jr.), the Justice-directed team convinced drug and pharmaceutical companies to pledge $23 million, surgical, dental and veterinary instrumental companies to pledge $7 million and baby-food companies to pledge $14 million. And they arranged for $9 million in powdered milk through the Department of Agriculture. Working out IRS tax rulings that made such contributions advantageous yet kept them consistent with prior tax law, they set up systems for determining the tax status of contributors in hours rather than months. They involved President Eisenhower in a scheme to reassure reluctant and Republican donors that partisan politics was not involved. They enlisted the International Red Cross to supervise the collection and shipment of goods within the United States. They obtained critical rulings from the ICC and CAB making it possible for railroads and airlines to donate equipment for transport. They stilled manufacturers' fears of anti-trust and trading-with-the-enemy prosecutions. They co-ordinated State Department, Immigration and Public

Health officials, all of whom were involved in receiving prisoners on arrival. They assembled 20 percent of the goods in Florida and shipped them to Cuba by the Christmas-eve deadline as down payment. And they arranged a complicated financial guarantee to Castro that if the rest of the ransom didn't arrive, he would get the remainder of the $53 million in cash—a transaction which involved, among others, the Red Cross, the Royal Bank of Canada, the Morgan Guaranty Trust Company and the Bank of America. At the last hour, "as a token of good faith," they raised the $2.9 million cash which had been promised Castro in April for the release of the sixty wounded prisoners. At 11 P.M. on Christmas eve, Deputy Attorney General Nicholas Katzenbach was able to call Robert Kennedy at his home in Hickory Hill and tell him that the transaction was a success—the down payment had been delivered and the prisoners were on their way to America.

It was, by common consent, a spectacular display of efficiency, organization, mobilization, judgment, *élan*, speed, negotiation, tough-mindedness and purposeful administration. Oberdorfer had operating responsibility, Katzenbach had served as a kind of roving ambassador, and the Attorney General, who kept in touch throughout, put in his personal appearances when and as needed. The operation was, of course, transgovernmental, involving not only the Justice Department, but State, Public Health, ICC, CAB, Agriculture and even the White House.

In fact, then, the Bay of Pigs prisoner ransom, which one columnist dubbed Operation Habeas Corpus, was one part private—the Cuban Families Committee; one part public—the Justice Department; but it was also one part Kennedy, without which it could not have happened.

It would be silly to deny that Robert Kennedy had more clout than the average Attorney General, partly because he also had a brother in the White House. But it would be misleading not to emphasize that Robert Kennedy's ability to make things happen was more than the arithmetic sum of JFK-power plus RFK-power, an equation that doesn't account for the Kennedy network, the Kennedy style, the Kennedy values. If J. Edgar Hoover's actions reflected the code of the FBI and Burke Marshall's actions reflected the code of the Ivy League lawyer, the Attorney General's conduct reflected the code of the Kennedys, which consisted of three principal elements, none unrelated to his blood tie to the President, but each going beyond it.

First and foremost it should be recognized that Robert Kennedy did not define himself in terms of his status as President's brother, but rather Robert and John alike drew their sense of identity from membership in the Kennedy family. As a *Saturday Evening Post* writer observed as early as 1957, "Each Kennedy takes pride in the achievements of the others. Each, instinctively, had rather win the approval of the family than of outsiders. And when an outsider threatens to thwart the ambitions of any of them, the whole family forms a close-packed ring, horns lowered, like a herd of bisons beset by wolves." [1] There was a presumption in favor of Kennedys—in favor of their innocence when accused of wrongdoing, in favor of their competence when up for job consideration, in favor of their judgment when engaged in deliberation with non-Kennedys. Loyalty ranked high in the family value system. What was good for JFK was good for the country.

What distinguished the Kennedy family from other first families was that, contrary to contemporary cliché, they were not merely a tightly knit group, a closed circle, a clan, a clique for the privileged few. They were more like an extended family, an informal organization, a network. Membership was relatively open. There was, of course, the hard-core blood Kennedy family. But there were Kennedys by marriage like Sargent Shriver and Stephen Smith and Ethel Kennedy; there were Kennedys by political alliance ("before Wisconsin") like Byron White and Joe Dolan; Kennedys by having dated one of the Kennedy girls, like White's Deputy, Bill Geoghegan, who had dated Jean; Kennedys by having served on the Rackets Committee, like Walter Sheridan and James J. P. McShane and Carmine Bellino; Kennedys by having gone to school with Bobby, like Dean Markham and David Hackett; Kennedys by ordeal, like Burke Marshall and Nicholas Katzenbach, who passed the test of early Justice Department crises. The list is long, which made the Kennedy family phenomenon that much more pervasive. For in addition to enjoying the special rights and privileges that went with membership, they were all on notice, like members of that other family which Luigi Barzini wrote about in *The Italians*—the Mafia—that being a Kennedy was "a state of mind, a philosophy of life, a conception of society, a moral code, a particular susceptibility prevailing among all members of the family. They are taught in the cradle or are born already knowing that they must aid each other, side with their friends and fight common enemies even when the friends are wrong and the enemies are right."

It was one of Robert Kennedy's major achievements as an administrator that he found ways of converting selected bureaucrats into on-the-job Kennedys. In effect, he deputized honorary Kennedys. He was in an optimal position to do this because the Justice Department was the *de facto* alternate White House, a second center of government —and unhampered by White House protocol, it was where the action was.

Second, there was the government-on-the-run Kennedy style. The cliché was that the Kennedys were all style and no substance. In fact, Kennedy style undermined the wall of separation between style and substance in the sense that Robert Kennedy's style had substantive consequences (his disrespect for organization-chart boundaries, for instance, made possible the war on crime), and the Kennedy substance took on meaning only as the Kennedy style translated it into policies and programs (a personal sense of responsibility for the Bay of Pigs prisoners was translated into the crash program for the prisoners release). The Kennedy style was informal consultation, anti-bureaucratic, round-the-clock vigils, the crash program, the hasty decision, the quick telephone call. Kennedy valued action, energy, motion and speed almost as much as direction. "Think it over, take as long as you want," Kennedy told Bill Orrick, who had flown to Washington in early 1961 to decide between job offers in the Pentagon and the Justice Department, "just so long as you let us know by tomorrow morning."

At first glance this sort of decision-making à go-go seems to run counter to the requirements of serious deliberation—the systematic search for information, the sober weighing of alternatives, the consultation with relevant experts, the attempt to purge oneself of preconceptions. Yet as one student of the decision-making process has pointed out in another connection, it is equally plausible to argue that "when the decision is urgent, the distortions of hierarchy, specialization, centralization and doctrine are minimized. Ironically, the hasty decision made under pressure may on average be better than a less urgent one." [2] By way of example one might compare the careful deliberation, spanning two Administrations, which preceded the Bay of Pigs fiasco, and the thirteen days "when the world stood still" (Robert Kennedy's words) as the President, the Attorney General and a handful of others met on an emergency, round-the-clock basis and successfully resolved the Cuban missile crisis, with its threat of nuclear destruction.

The third element in the code of the Kennedys was the Kennedy value system itself, which reads a little like a list of homilies but had an important role in the way in which Robert Kennedy exercised his prosecutors' discretion. Barren of any dogma, any ideological doctrine, it ranked loyalty right up there with excellence; put results slightly ahead of process; thought that achievement outranked pedigree; assumed integrity; reserved compassion for the courageous, the victims, the pure in heart, and contempt for the corrupt, the wheeler-dealers, the conspirators of evil. Each of the Kennedys related to this constellation of values in his own way, and while it is doubtful that Joseph P. Kennedy, Sr., ever actually said, "He [Bobby] resembles me much more than any of the other children and he's a great kid. He hates the same way I do," as *Newsweek* reported in 1963 and as Robert Kennedy's critics have gleefully repeated ever since, the fact was that hatred was not too strong a word to characterize the puritanical Attorney General's attitude toward men like Hoffa and the vice lords of organized crime whose evil activities he felt were a clear and present danger to the Republic.

The sociologist Max Weber identified three types of legitimate authority. The first and most impersonal, which he called "legal authority," is rational in character, based on the belief in a rationally established system of laws, of rules and routines. We may analogize it in that respect to the code of the FBI. The second might be called "traditional authority" and is based on belief in the sanctity of traditions and the legitimacy of those called upon to exercise power. Especially in their approach to the federal system, we may analogize it to the code of the Ivy League Gentleman. The third, which Weber called "charismatic authority," is based on people's willingness to abandon themselves to a heroic or exemplary individual. As it happened, the Kennedy network, the Kennedy style and the Kennedy values combined to create a charismatic authority system to reinforce any inherent charisma (in the popular sense of possession of the gift of grace or star quality) that Robert Kennedy might have possessed on his own. Family relationships enabled Robert Kennedy to borrow some of his brother's institutional charisma and circulate it throughout the network of honorary Kennedys. And the Kennedy salvationist style of mobilizing the troops to deliver us from evil (organized crime, Hoffa, Castro's dungeons) was in the classic mould of charismatic leadership.

One manifestation of the code of the Kennedys, then, was to channel Robert Kennedy's efforts to promote justice into a struggle between the charismatic authority of the honorary Kennedys who roamed the land and the traditional and bureaucratic authority which they were trying to circumvent.*

A look behind the scenes at the Justice Department's role in the Cuban prisoners' ransom helps explain how Robert Kennedy's personal

---

* It is fashionable to dismiss "charisma" as too vague a concept for useful analysis. Weber's notion of a "charismatic authority system," however, seems to me relatively helpful, and directly relevant to the Kennedys.

leadership potential and his blood link to the Presidency interreacted with his role as the Kennedy family's representative at the Justice Department. It also establishes him as a shrewd and effective administrator.

The day before he committed the Justice Department to the ransom operation, he had Lou Oberdorfer and Ramsey Clark out to his Hickory Hill home to talk about it and probably to make up his mind about who to put in charge. He decided on the Yale-trained Oberdorfer, who turned out to be a shrewd choice if only because of the fact that Lloyd Cutler, the senior partner from Oberdorfer's old firm of Wilmer, Cutler and Pickering, numbered among his clients the Pharmaceutical Manufacturers of America. And in a preliminary session with Oberdorfer he correctly anticipated the two dominant concerns of potential pharmaceutical contributors: the tax consequences of their charitable contributions and their fear that working with each other might make them liable to anti-trust prosecution.

The critical meeting with the pharmaceutical manufacturers came seven days later. In advance of the meeting they had secured an Anti-Trust opinion that no anti-trust prosecutions would result from the operation; they were able to assure the manufacturers that the transaction didn't come under the Trading with the Enemy Act; and they had secured a tax ruling from IRS that a manufacturer who made a charitable contribution was entitled to claim as a deduction his selling price in the lowest usual market. In industries where there is a proximate relation between production cost and sales price, such a ruling—originally handed down in 1958—made sense. But as Senator Kefauver's hearings had recently revealed, sales price to pharmacies (the lowest usual market) so greatly exceeded the cost of production that it would be possible for a drug manufacturer actually to make money on charitable contributions. The ruling had an additional advantage for the drug manufacturers. Cutler had made it clear to Oberdorfer that the drug companies "would have to be assured that they would not be required to disclose their cost and mark-up data in order to secure tax deduction," and the formula decided upon guaranteed that assurance.

Morton Mintz, who covers the pharmaceutical front for the Washington *Post*, has explained how the tax ruling worked to the advantage of the drug companies:

> Let us take a hypothetical example. You donate $100 to a group of medical missionaries working among an Indian tribe in South Dakota. When you claim this as a charitable deduction you will reduce your tax liability by, say, $20. You have nonetheless given a net of $80 to charity. Now suppose that a drug company donates to the missionaries

a quantity of a drug that cost it $10 to produce but which it sells to the pharmacist for $100. Allowed to claim the selling price of $100 as the value of the gift, the company would, unlike you, be ahead. The $100 would be deducted from the company's income. This would reduce the corporate income tax otherwise payable by the company by about $50, and this, minus the cost of $10, would result in the company's actually being better off by $40 than it would be without the donation.

There was, then, considerable incentive for the pharmaceuticals people and others to contribute. Nevertheless, the drug companies were unsympathetic to the Administration, the previous tractors-for-freedom committee * had been a bust and gotten some bad publicity, they feared charges would inevitably be made that they were currying favor with the Administration trying to ward off anti-trust prosecutions on other fronts—and besides, why were they doing business with that bearded, cigar-smoking Communist, anyway?

"No one could so fire others with their plans, no one could so impose his will and conquer by the force of his personality as this seemingly ordinary . . . man . . ." wrote a contributor to a *Daedalus* symposium, arguing that such a capability, in the case of Nicolai Lenin, qualified him as a charismatic leader. Lou Oberdorfer recalls that at the meeting "Robert Kennedy convinced people by the sheer force of his personality, his belief in himself and the rightness of his cause."

It was a difficult assignment because the Attorney General couldn't commit himself, by word or gesture or inflection, to any policy of special favor or reward for participation in this project; nor could he hint that there would be retribution—that he would "get" Senator Kefauver to go after them, if they *didn't* participate. As Oberdorfer put it, "There couldn't be any eye-winking. Yet Robert Kennedy, according to one who was there, overwhelmed them. He told them about the physical condition of these men in prison, about the courage of those who came back from Cuba in an open boat, about the wounded

* An abortive, ostensibly private organization, but actually formed at the request of President Kennedy, headed by Dr. Milton Eisenhower, Mrs. Franklin Delano Roosevelt and Walter Reuther. Its purpose was to raise money ($28 million) to buy tractors which would be used to ransom the Brigade prisoners. The committee got embroiled in partisan politics, was attacked by citizen Richard Milhous Nixon, among others, who said the deal was wrong because it aided Castro and also because "Human lives are not something to be bartered." The committee was disbanded June 25, 1961. Out of these activities came the Cuban Families Committee for the Liberty of the Prisoners of War, which became one of the parties to the later drug deal. The most complete account of the prisoners may be found in *The Bay of Pigs: The Leaders' Story of Brigade 2506*, by Haynes Johnson (Norton, 1964).

prisoners brought out during the summer for promises of cash reward, about attorney Donovan's crucial role in getting Castro to agree to a deal in the first place. He explained why the U.S. government couldn't write a Treasury check for this money (Congressional leaders had vetoed any such action) and that the items on Castro's "wish list" were things that people who were supposed to know had determined were not of strategic value and wouldn't increase the Cuban war potential because such goods were for sick people. He emphasized the humanitarian aspect and pointed out the need to get it done by Christmas because of immediate health hazards to the prisoners, but also underlined the public-relations advantages, thus anticipating the picture in the morning papers on Christmas day of families being united. He acknowledged that political risks were involved, but he couldn't imagine that either the business risk or the political risk would survive those pictures. He made it as clear as he could that they would get nothing in return.

It was a moving experience. The Attorney General's office runs east to west and because of the strong wind, Oberdorfer recalls, the flag waving outside his window "looked like a picture, and it was an extremely dramatic experience to see and hear him talking about the responsibility of both the U. S. and the people of the United States for the rescue of these prisoners who had risked their lives in what was, of course, they thought to their interests, but also in an effort to protect and safeguard us all." Says Oberdorfer:

> There was nothing more than a straightforward declaration by a man who was obviously a man of massive integrity. The later press accounts that suggested that there was some looseness in the government's stance in the sense that there were unreasonable or under-the-table concessions made either in the tax field or the anti-trust field or some other field were so offensive to me, having been at the meeting, as to appear almost obscene. Such accounts, besides their factual errors, are also based on a complete misapprehension of the character of the Attorney General. The meeting was a very dignified affair and it had a tremendous impact on those businessmen. They came back to my office with red eyes, and they went back to their offices and they really got busy. They were on the phone with me the next afternoon talking about inventory that they were stacking up, and getting ready to move. This meeting really launched the project.

Robert Kennedy was a compassionate man, and he had the capacity to convey that compassion. He was an honest man, and he had the capacity to convey his integrity. He was a humanitarian, and he had the ability to transmit his humanitarianism to others. Moreover, he had that extra fire, the personal magnetism that won him the loyalty of men like Oberdorfer and, in situations like this, enabled him to convey the absolute justness of his cause. "*L'état, c'est moi,*" said Louis XIV. With equal assurance, the Attorney General, who devoutly believed that what was good for the Kennedys was good for the country, could have said, "Kennedy, *c'est moi.*" For indeed, part of his power of persuasion, part of his charisma flowed from a case of mistaken identity—he looked like his brother, he talked like his brother, he had the absolute confidence of and unparalleled rapport with his brother, he acted as an agent for his brother, he was next in line according to the well-advertised Kennedy order of succession, and so in a symbolic sense those who dealt with him felt they were talking to his brother.

By setting the Christmas-day deadline in the ransom episode, the Attorney General had created something of a crisis, and the charismatic leader thrives in times of crisis. He is, according to the literature, "one in whom, by virtue of unusual personal qualities, the promise or hope of salvation—deliverance from distress—appears to be embodied." [8] There were good reasons for getting the job done by Christmas Eve—good compassionate human reasons in terms of the prisoners and good public-relations reasons in terms of the Christmas spirit and the American people. But it was Robert Kennedy's personal and administrative style to come into crises and help solve them. And when there wasn't a crisis—such as the freedom-rider bus burning, the admission of Meredith to Ole Miss, the near explosion in Birmingham—perhaps subconsciously he created a crisis atmosphere which generated an intensity of effort, of round-the-clock work, of emotional response. Having previously created the crisis psychology, Robert Kennedy arrived at his meeting and he spoke for the Administration, he spoke for the Kennedys. There was nothing for anyone to worry about. And undoubtedly, as Oberdorfer suggests, it was the force of his personality which carried the day.

It is not necessarily cynical to recognize the self-interest benefits that accrued to the drug industry once the decision to participate was made; the *fact* of Robert Kennedy's magnetism and the salvationist style of the save-the-Cuban-prisoners operation is not diminished simply because the skills of the Ivy League lawyers like Oberdorfer satisfied the goals of both the Kennedys and the potential contributors. Thus to protect the drug companies against the inevitable charges that they were doing it for the tax windfall, the government suggested that they give any "profit" to charity. Merck & Co., for instance, gave its net to the Merck Foundation (whose own good works gave them the public-relations benefits, of course). Haynes Johnson, who wrote the Kennedy-authorized account of the Bay of Pigs prisoners, which did not really dwell on the Justice Department's role at all, defends the actions of companies like Merck in his eloquent account. He says:

> Despite these advantages to the drug manufacturers, their motives concerning the ransom operation were humanitarian as well as personal, and the reaction of one drug industry spokesman to criticism of the tax write-offs was understandable. "It's a little like helping a traffic victim into the ambulance," he said, "and then meeting a guy rushing around the corner to accuse you of picking the victim's pockets." [4]

Morton Mintz, perhaps the country's leading expert on the pharmaceutical industry, counter-argues that while the overriding consideration was, and should have been, the humanitarian one of getting these 1,200 courageous and suffering men out of prison, and it was of secondary importance that Merck was reported to have netted an estimated $300,000 after taxes on its wholesale-value donation of $2.5 million, or that Pfizer, according to Ben Weberman in the New York *Herald Tribune* in January 1963, netted $120,000 on its contribution, which had an ascribed net worth of $1.5 million, the fact was that

> On January 19, 1963—only a few weeks after the prisoners were released—Merck's president, John T. Connor, addressed the Texas Medical Association. Connor, who had participated in the project almost from the start, called it an "incredible success," and "a dramatic example of what free men can do in cooperation with officials of their own government to bring about results beneficial to the public interest and the interests of the participants." He described how the operation had "made possible the release of the prisoners and joyful family reunions for Christmas that we all saw on TV." Then he got down to the "tax rulings which made the whole transaction possible." Finally, Connor spoke these brutally frank words to his audience in Austin: "Without the tax rulings, absolutely nothing would have happened. The men would still be in prison." [5]

Equally unromantic motives for giving existed on the anti-trust front. It takes nothing away from Robert Kennedy's sincerity, his integrity, his powers of persuasion, the honesty with which he proceeded or his motives in going to the drug and other companies to recognize that despite his stern warnings about no favoritism, these companies had extracurricular motives to give. In fact, Kennedy and Oberdorfer gave *de facto* recognition to the situation when they recruited private attorneys like John E. Nolan, Jr., who officially was working for the Cuban Families Committee but had an office in the Justice Department. Nolan recalls, "There was a sense of urgency and commitment about the whole operation." Oberdorfer had called him on Thursday, Friday he was in New York making arrangements, and Sunday he met with the baby-food people in the conference room in the Tax Division, from where they proceeded to Robert Kennedy's office. The Attorney General, dressed in casual muffler, sweater and jacket, gave his pitch. Says Nolan, "By the end of the day we had $2.3 to $2.6 million pledged. We could see that the method worked—that it was administratively and legally feasible. I'd call people, they'd come in and get on-the-spot *ad hoc* rulings on tax and other matters and then somebody would give them the pitch. But we saw we'd need more people like me—private—to carry on negotiations with the companies. It was a matter of propriety. If the Anti-Trust Division calls you and says, 'Don't you want to make a contribution?' it's bad. Therefore, we recruited other private attorneys, and we could all use Justice facilities, but Justice couldn't solicit."

After it was over, Anthony Lewis wrote a wrap-up story for *The New York Times* in which he stated—presumably on the basis of the authoritative sources to which he, more than any other reporter in Washington, was privy—"But no list of the contributors has been put together and it is not certain that any will ever be published." [6]

Unbeknownst to Lewis, a list had indeed been put together by John Duffner, a career attorney, at the request of the Justice Department's Public Information Office. But it was not published for the simple reason that it showed that of more than sixty contributing firms in the Cuban prisoner exchange, almost every one was at least under anti-trust or FTC investigation. At the time thirteen were actually defendants in anti-trust actions, twelve in FTC actions and seven in both, for a total of eighteen different companies as defendants.* As Jack Rosenthal, then an assistant in the Public Information Office, put it in a memo to Ed Guthman, press secretary: "Nothing to crow about here. I suppose a quiet death is the best answer."

Were it only a case of Robert Kennedy's personal charisma operating in tandem with the drug contributors' self-interest, the Cuban prisoner ransom story would have only marginal interest. But had it not been for the Kennedys as a family there would have been no prisoner ransom. A Kennedy had gotten them into prison, and so another Kennedy would get them out. It was a debt of honor, and the code of the Kennedys dictated that it be repaid.

---

* See Appendix to Chapter Seven, pp. 453–457.

The style was pure Kennedy. John Kennedy had relied on the CIA in getting us in, but Robert Kennedy did not think to use *his* intelligence apparatus—the FBI—to get the prisoners out. Rather, he called upon a Kennedy potpourri, a public-private mix of family, friends, *ad hoc* committees, free-lance lawyers, sympathizers, bankers and power brokers within, without and throughout the government, the network, the charismatic authority structure, the honorary Kennedys.

The deputizing of honorary Kennedys was not all calculated. And even those who weren't part of the circle benefited from it. As John Duffner, a mild-mannered Justice Department veteran, remarked, "For fifteen years, I'd call and want to talk to somebody in another government agency, and they might call back the next day or week. But you could see the difference with the Kennedy brothers. They'd call right back. This was like an arm of the White House."

William Orrick, head of the Civil Division, recalls that one of the first problems he dealt with concerned whether the government ought to continue to subsidize the New Haven Railroad or move in court on the matter. "It was a lawyer's decision to advise the client. Somebody in the White House, maybe Mike Feldman, called us up and said it looks like we'll pour more money in. I said, 'Look, Mike, that's my decision.' He said, 'Well, the President has decided and that's what he wants to do. . . .' So I went up to Byron and said I don't think this is the wise thing. He says have you looked at it? I said yeah. He said we better go over and see him. I said do *what?* See the President? He said you don't believe Feldman, do you? So he called Mike and fixed up an appointment. We went over, saw the President, and he said what do you recommend? And we told him, and he looked at Mike and said that's [Orrick's recommendation] the way it will have to be. And thereafter they stopped 'The President says' business. It enables you to run the division because you don't have to tell guys that. Everybody knew we had made a recommendation and the President backed it."

Partly because Robert Kennedy was adept at manipulating the symbols of being a Kennedy to provide satisfaction for others, minor Justice Department functionaries were, for the first time in their lives, invited to White House events. Meetings were held around the Kennedy pool at Hickory Hill. Nick Katzenbach recalls going out to Bob Kennedy's house one Saturday night to discuss an executive order on equal employment opportunity which he had redrafted (Lyndon Johnson had submitted an earlier draft, which had been worked on by Bill Moyers and Abe Fortas) only to discover the President of the United States on hand. The President started asking Katzenbach about the order. "I answered his questions, but I felt embarrassed," recalls Katzenbach. "A good staff man would have briefed his boss and let his boss do the answering, but Bob couldn't have cared less."

It was not merely that the Attorney General included select Justice Department lawyers in Kennedy activities—such as the famed Hickory Hill seminars which helped give the New Frontier its image of intellectuality, gaiety and fun—but that he included the Kennedys in the activities of the Justice Department. As Patricia Collins, a lawyer in the Solicitor's office who had joined the Justice Department when Robert Kennedy was nine years old and who was married to the late Salvatore Andretta, the career Assistant Attorney General for Administration, remembers it:

> He'd do wonderful things but he'd expect a lot. He'd say [to Sal] goddam it you do it or I'll find someone who will. Then he'd be disarming. The tone of the Department reflected Bob's personality—sunshine and rain. We felt as if we were in the family in a way. He'd say to Angie [his secretary], "Have we got a lunch in the office today?" She'd say yes and he'd say tell them to come out to the house at noon. We'd get there and there would be an elaborate spread with chocolate cake, ice cream in chocolate sauce and we'd sit around the pool. This reflected a good mood.
>
> Sal had never had wives moving in and advising on decorations. Ethel wanted all the walls painted off-white. We got the impression that whatever Jackie did Ethel was quick as a flash to do the same thing. When the papers said Jackie was buying new china for the White House, Ethel selected a pattern of Lenox china with the seal of the Justice Department on it. Sal said, "Where in hell am I going to get unauthorized money to buy unauthorized china for an unauthorized dining room?" Sal had to find a way to pay all of Bobby's friends and special assistants and consultants. Nobody knew what they were doing. Ethel was the Kilroy of the Justice Department. Whenever anyone saw an off-white wall it was a joke: "Ethel was here!" She'd write Sal the cutest notes saying, "Dear Sal: You don't really mind if we do such and such. It will make it so much nicer." She'd put Steuben glass and flowers in the dining room and then tell Sal to buy it. Sal asked Bob, "Where are we going to get the money for this?" Bob would say just listen to her but don't pay any attention. They put a little snack bar in the courtyard with flowers, parasol and had music piped in until the lawyers on the first floor complained. They couldn't get any work done. It was known as Sal's pizza palace until the music drove lawyers on the courtyard crazy. After Ethel's infiltration a number of wives felt they had to get into the act. Lydia really gave us a psychedelic set-up with orange chairs, shocking pink carpets, the works. Bob always had lots of friends and assistants wandering in and out. God knows what they were doing. Not to mention his kids, his sisters and his dogs.

Often when he worked late, his children dined in his office. They were ripping around chasing each other at top speed to the annoyance of TV cameramen while Katzenbach was down in Tuscaloosa integrating the University of Alabama over the ostensible protests of Governor George Wallace.

It was Robert Kennedy's style to move around the Department and the country meeting Justice Department lawyers, asking about their problems, shaking hands, making small talk, but also asking informed, up-to-the-minute questions. He understood the national appetite to participate in the aura of the Kennedys and he, more than any other Kennedy, did his utmost, consciously or otherwise, to satisfy that appetite. I sent a questionnaire to more than ninety U.S. attorneys, the nation's federal prosecutors who, although nominally under the control of the U.S. Department of Justice, for the most part run their own shops with only occasional interference from Washington. Of the thirty percent who answered, each one mentioned as one of the outstanding features of Robert Kennedy's Attorney Generalship the fact that he had actually taken the trouble to visit with them, to tour the office, to meet the younger attorneys and generally to pepper them with informed questions. "Ramsey Clark tells me you are about to settle a major lands case for X dollars—cahn't we do bettah?"

William E. Scent, U.S. attorney for the Western District of Kentucky, for instance, was not particularly close to the Attorney General, but remembers, "He made it a point to personally visit as many U.S. attorney offices and hold as many meetings with the U.S. attorney staffs as was possible, and in those cases where it was not possible the U.S. attorneys and at least one or two assistants out of the offices were invited to regional meetings at which Kennedy presided." Scent recalls that fifteen minutes after the jury returned a verdict of conviction in the first criminal case under the Gambling Paraphernalia Act, "Kennedy telephoned me to congratulate our office on the successful prosecution of the case."

Moreover, it was interest without intervention. Scent cites the case that his office instituted against the Great Lakes Carbon Corporation involving several hundred acres of land for the Barkley Dam and Lake project. "It is my understanding that Mrs. Ethel Kennedy's family was the largest stockholder in that corporation. The case was fought out in court and the property owner received an award of $100,000 compared to a deposit made in court of $75,000, and our offer to settle for $90,000. No mention was ever made to me by anyone in the Department of Justice that the Attorney General or his family in any way was concerned with that matter."

On those occasions when it was important to do so, he did not, of course, hesitate to involve the President—a fact not lost on either those with whom the Justice Department did business or the honorary Kennedys themselves, who like their boss had all rolled up their sleeves, unloosened their collars, hung crayoned pieces of paper prepared by their kids on their office wall, and tried their best to be pragmatic. One such occasion arose during the prisoner ransom operation in connection with the use of government surplus milk.

"Because of the low mark-up on milk," Katzenbach wrote in a memo to McGeorge Bundy on January 4, 1963, "the tax law did not make it advantageous for the companies to contribute milk and their offered gifts were composed largely of dietary foods of the Metrecal type. For similar reasons the baby-food manufacturers were not able to provide more than about three million of the fourteen and one half million dollars of baby foods requested.

"Thus in putting together a $53,000,000 list of goods which Mr. Castro would accept, it was necessary to include a substantial amount of milk. In the quantities required here, the natural, if not only, source was government surplus, which is in the form of powdered skim milk. . . ."

Cuba, which had initially rejected the offer since it was not whole milk, reversed itself after a lot of skirmishing and said it would accept twenty million pounds if it could be moved immediately. Of the two statutory routes open, one permitted AID to make surplus commodities available to private agencies for emergency relief of "friendly" peoples. And AID furnished an informal opinion saying that "there were no insuperable obstacles" to making the milk available. Despite the opinion, the judgment was that it might be bad public relations if it got out, so they took the other statutory route—Section 1431 of Title 7 of the U.S. Code—which deals with the disposition of commodities to prevent waste. A conference was held on December 15, 1962, with representatives of the Department of Agriculture, Red Cross, Justice Department and Mr. Donovan's committee. The result: an exchange of letters between the Red Cross and Secretary of Agriculture Orville Freeman granting a Red Cross request for a gift of up to fifty million pounds of milk to be used in the exchange program.

Despite the exchange of letters a slight problem remained: the declaration of policy prefixed to the Agricultural Act of 1961, which said that

> . . . it is hereby declared to be the policy of Congress to . . . expand foreign trade in agricultural commodities with friendly nations,

as defined in Section 107 of Public Law 480, 83d Congress, as amended (7 USC 1707), and *in no manner either subsidize the export, sell or make available any subsidized agricultural commodity to any nations other than such friendly nations* and thus make full use of our agricultural abundance. . . . [italics added].

This would be the only shipment to Cuba where it could be said that the direct cost was borne by the government. Because of this fact Freeman, who signed the exchange of letters with the Red Cross after he got the approval of his General Counsel, nevertheless asked that the use of Commodity Credit Corporation milk be specifically approved by the President before the letter was released. "Later the same evening," according to Katzenbach's January 4 memo, "the Attorney General [who was on his way to South America] reported that he had discussed the matter with the President and that the President approved of the CCC milk being used."

On January 9, 1963, the Department of Agriculture transferred five million pounds of non-fat dry milk solids to the American Red Cross for the benefit of the Cuban Families Committee and put out an official statement which said:

> Transfer was made in response to a request by the American Red Cross pursuant to Section 1431 of Title 7 of the U.S. Code. Under this section, the Department is authorized to donate surplus commodities such as milk for distribution to needy persons in foreign countries. However, the Red Cross has indicated that the Cuban Families Committee expects to raise funds to reimburse the Department. . . .

The Secretary of Agriculture had made a request that the President of the United States specifically approve a legally marginal transaction. His response was not a piece of paper with the President's approval—the traditional bureaucratic safeguard in such a circumstance—but rather the Attorney General's word that "he had discussed the matter with the President and that the President approved." Nobody thought to ask the Attorney General what was said, nobody dared question whether the President really understood the provisions involved, and most important, even if the Attorney General had not spoken with the President, his personal assurance that he had was all anybody needed.

Such direct resort to brotherly intervention, however, was the exception. A much more normal example of the Kennedy system at work came at a critical moment when Louis Oberdorfer wanted the first planeload of drugs destined for Cuba repacked with high-quality items since that is what Castro's men would be inspecting. The Air Force colonel in charge of the "volunteer" Air Force loading crew objected, saying he had neither the manpower nor the time. Haynes Johnson, who chronicled the loading operation, wrote that Oberdorfer quietly said, "Colonel, do you want to order these men to reload the plane, or do you want the Secretary of the Air Force to order it?" What other head of a Tax Division in what Administration could have made that statement?

Even more spectacular was the effectiveness of those honorary Kennedys who had *no* government status at the time. E. Barrett Prettyman, Jr., who had clerked for three Supreme Court Justices, attended the University of Virginia Law School with RFK and was in private practice, is an exemplary case. Eventually he became a special assistant to the Attorney General, with primary duties to untangle the District of Columbia playground bureaucracy in keeping with the various promises the Attorney General had made to ghetto kids as he visited them at play. But during the prisoner ransom activities he was conscripted as a volunteer, working with Don Coppock, Acting Commissioner of Enforcement in the Immigration Service, to oversee and obtain free transportation for $11 million worth of goods in about ten days and see that all of the goods reached Cuba in time for Christmas. Prettyman was called December 10 and went to work December 11. Given the Christmas crush on transportation anyway, it looked like an impossible task. As Prettyman put it in a private memorandum setting down his experiences after the fact:

> . . . it was a short, not-so-happy course in the problems of transportation, complicated by the fact that experts in the field told us flatly that this operation was impossible—$11 million worth of goods could not be solicited from all over the country, prepared for shipment, transported by rail, air and truck, reloaded at a common point for transporting by sea and air and unloaded in Cuba, all within less than two weeks.

Nobody told Prettyman he was an on-the-job Kennedy or that he could pull any kind of rank. But Prettyman *was* told that the job had to be done. It is instructive to run down his "solutions" to some of the minor problems he faced:

1. *The problem:* There was no possible way to ship the supplies by air. The baby food alone (300 tons) would have required fifteen planeloads. *The solution:* Prettyman enlisted two staff members of the Maritime Administration to contact all available shipping groups, and eventually they came up with a ship that could do the job.

2. *The problem:* Railroads can carry goods free for charitable purposes under Section 22 of the Interstate Common Carrier Act, but no comparable provision for airlines existed, and the Air Transport Association said it would take *weeks* to obtain an exemption from the CAB.

The solution: Two hours after Prettyman called, the chairman of the CAB had a meeting and issued a blanket exemption permitting *all* airlines to participate.

3. The Red Cross sent all information about the nature of each shipment to the Commerce Department several times a day and also to a member of the Immigration Service (stationed at the Justice Department), who kept a running account of pledges and shipments, so that Oberdorfer's office could know how close it was coming to meeting the promised quota of goods. On Tuesday, December 18, for the second time, *the problem:* "We again ran out of planes. After a number of calls I discovered one plane that had been chartered by the Navy," says Prettyman. How to get it? *The solution:* "I called Paul Fay, Under Secretary of the Navy [and long-time chum of the President] and in a very short time the plane was released by the Navy and put at our disposal."

4. Every water carrier must file with the Department of Commerce an Application for Export License and a Shipper's Export Declaration. These documents must list in detail the precise nature of the goods to be shipped, including basic ingredients, composition, size, weight in pounds, type, gauge, grade, processing code, group number, unit price, etc. Because shippers were rushing goods to Miami in split shipments, with delayed paper work and, in some cases, with unmarked boxes, it was impossible to determine the precise nature of all the goods in advance of loading. The situation was further complicated by the fact that different types of material required separate licenses. *The problem:* If either the shippers or the Red Cross filled out the required paper, the exchange would be delayed months. *The solution:* Coppock and Prettyman met with a number of Commerce Department officials to try to get them to agree to have the Red Cross fill out a single Application for Export license. Commerce could attach it to all invoices as received by the Red Cross. When the Commerce officials balked, Prettyman left the room, called Nicholas Katzenbach and asked that an immediate appointment be set up with Secretary of Commerce Luther H. Hodges. Prettyman and Coppock went straight to Hodges' office. In minutes, Robert Giles, Commerce's General Counsel, approved the plan.

5. There was a serious narcotics snafu, whose resolution is depicted in a memo from Prettyman to Oberdorfer, dated December 19, just before Prettyman left for Miami:

> *The problem* in regard to narcotics is not one of exporting, but rather of importing. Under international conventions, a country must give its approval before narcotics may be imported into that country.

The Narcotics Bureau is concerned because Cuba has not yet specifically given its permission for the importation of narcotics which
have already been earmarked for shipment as part of the first twenty
percent and which, in some cases, have actually been moved to Miami. . . .

The solution: Prettyman worked out an arrangement with the Commissioner of Narcotics and with the transportation coordinators at Red
Cross so that every shipment of narcotics was labeled for special
clearance and eventually Dr. Leonard A. Scheele, a former Surgeon
General, who was in Cuba with James Donovan on another phase of
the operation, returned with the appropriate documents signed.

6. *The problem:* The Post Office was unwilling to displace Christmas mail and packages to make room for supplies on regular air
flights. Without such special treatment, the supplies would probably be
delayed days and perhaps weeks. *The solution:* Prettyman called Post-
master J. Edward Day, explained the situation, and he passed the word
that if unavoidable, the displacement should be made.

In May 1961, when Castro had first proposed the ransom of the
prisoners of Brigade 2506 for $28 million in tractors, skeptics and
political foes like Richard Nixon said it couldn't be done and it
shouldn't be done. But confidence builds on confidence, and it was
after the Kennedys had emerged from the successful showdown of the
Cuban missile crisis, in which Robert Kennedy played such a decisive
role for peace, that he resolved to get the prisoners home by Christmas.
In addition to dispatching his troops, the General got on the phone
himself and, with the deadline dangling, successfully prevailed on
family friend Richard Cardinal Cushing to contribute an imperative
$1 million which he immediately procured from church sources; and
utilized General Lucius Clay—with Katzenbach dispatched to Canada
to handle the delicate negotiations—to convince Roland Harriman,
president of the Red Cross, to commit his organization over a weekend,
to a $53 million letter of credit.

He was willing to expend Kennedy moral and political credit in order
to obtain financial credit. That willingness, plus his extraordinary system of honorary Kennedys, was an ingenious if unconscious device
for the circulation and distribution of charisma throughout the *ad hoc*
Kennedy organization, and guaranteed ultimate success. On December
21 Donovan and Castro signed a memorandum of agreement. On December 23 the first prisoners arrived in Florida. And after a weary
Nicholas Katzenbach called the Attorney General on Christmas eve
at home to tell him that the transaction was a success and that he and

the rest of the Justice Department team were going home, there was a pause, and then the Attorney General said—his voice had been put on the intercom so that everybody could hear what he had to say at this propitious time—"Now let's get Hoffa!"

On December 29 JFK inspected Brigade 2506 at the Orange Bowl in Miami and made a moving speech about the bravery of the Brigade and the aims of the *Alianza para progresso.* Then, as if to tell the world, in case anyone hadn't noticed, that the ransoming of the prisoners had been a Kennedy family affair, the President turned the microphone over to his wife, who spoke in Spanish and "expressed pride that young John had met the officers of the Brigade." She said: "He is still too young to realize what has happened here, but I will make it my business to tell him the story of your courage as he grows up. It is my wish and my hope that some day he may be a man at least half as brave as the members of Brigade 2506." [7]

The Cuban prisoner ransom operation, then, was a case study in the exercise of charismatic authority and, at the same time, showed the Kennedy capability. It also captured the Kennedy style. And on inspection it contains some of the secret of Robert Kennedy's success as an administrator—not the least of which was his ability as a delegator and backer-upper. Louis Oberdorfer attributes his own confidence as director of the drive to his belief that no matter what happened, Kennedy would back him up. Says Oberdorfer: "I just never had the feeling that if it had collapsed that I would have been pilloried or that anybody else would have been left out on a limb. . . . I suppose . . . my recollection of the speech the President made after the Bay of Pigs invasion may have affected my feeling and my judgment. We watched that on television in the Attorney General's conference room. I was watching the President with one eye and the Attorney General with the other. I recall now quite vividly, and I am sure it affected, shall I say, my confidence in the operation. I remember the President saying 'the responsibility is mine'—whatever he said. I remember the look on the Attorney General's face when he said it. It seemed to express the thought, 'That is the way to stand up for your people. . . .'

"I am sure he brought out the very best in everybody that participated in this. Everybody was playing over their heads and that is a function of leadership."

What is perhaps most striking about the Cuban prisoner ransom operation is that it was ideologically contentless. Not that the Kennedys were out of sympathy with the anti-Castro politics of the Brigade. But it was more to the point that the men were being honored for their bravery, not their program; they were celebrated for their courage, not their doctrine; the Kennedys got them out because the Kennedys got them in, not as pawns in the great struggle between the Marxist Castro and American-style capitalism.

In this respect as much as any other, the ransom was typical Kennedy. For the Kennedys were governed by situations, not theories. They moved from problem to problem, not doctrine to doctrine. The cliché was that the Kennedys were pragmatists—a shorthand term for toughness, practicality and an intolerance for those they called "knee-jerk liberals," which meant, roughly, people who were unalterably opposed to things like wiretapping. Pragmatists they were, but the definition of the word as applied to the Kennedys was wrong. They were not all that tough. Compassion, for instance, was a real motivating factor in the Cuban prisoner situation. But they were pragmatists in the sense that they were non-doctrinaire problem-solvers. They were, in many respects, John Dewey's instrumentalists, people whose goals arose from the crises that confronted them, reactors who mixed means and ends in the process of trying to do a job. They were propelled, as often as not, by the possibility of a solution as much as by the need for one. Robert Kennedy had a restlessness and a work ethic that combined to make him more irritated at a lawyer caught reading a novel on company time than at one who worked round the clock and then lost a winnable case. He once sent an aide down to the bus stop on Constitution Avenue outside his office because from his fifth-floor window he saw some lawyerly-looking men lined up at 4:30 P.M. and wanted to make sure they weren't from the Justice Department. And on George Washington's birthday he had another aide copy down the license plates of those cars parked in the Justice Department garage and he sent the owners letters of commendation for working on a holiday. ("I cannot tell a lie," responded one recipient, "I was in town for the 1¢ sale and I needed a parking space.")

Robert Kennedy's real impact on the Justice Department had to do with the *fact* that problems were tackled at all, the standards that were expected of the tacklers, the skill with which these problems were approached, and the square assumption of the code of the Kennedys that with energy, intellect, judgment and imagination these problems could all be solved. That, rather than the ideological coloration of the solutions, the "accomplishments" Robert Kennedy reeled off, suggests his real contribution. One consequence of this lack of a formal ideology, however, was the tendency of other value systems to assert themselves where the Kennedy values were neutral. For instance, corporate-lawyer values surfaced in and helped dispose of the long-standing General Aniline case. And FBI values and style were the key to the public relations disaster Robert Kennedy suffered when newsmen received 2 A.M. knocks on the door in the midst of the steel price-rise crisis of 1962.

Take the case of General Aniline and Film. The official position of the Justice Department when Kennedy arrived was that General Aniline and Film, which had originally been seized in 1942 as enemy (German) property, belonged to the U.S. And that Interhandel, the Swiss holding company which claimed title to most of its stock, was in reality a cloak for I. G. Farben, a Nazi cartel which had used slave labor at Auschwitz. Under Kennedy, the case was settled out of court with William Orrick and Nicholas Katzenbach handling the negotiations with the Swiss.

The case presented factual issues, moral issues, public-relations issues and legal issues.

The factual issue came down to whether Interhandel was now or had ever been a cloak for I. G. Farben. It is beyond dispute that in 1925 I. G. Farben, the German concern, incorporated in Switzerland a company known as I. G. Chemie, which became Interhandel in December 1945; that early in World War II, I. G. Farben sent a memo to the German Ministry of Economy outlining a plan to switch shares so that I. G. Chemie would appear to be free of German influence; and that a Nazi government directive had already stated that "it will be necessary that companies and enterprises abroad which are subject to German foreign control, be cloaked. . . . In many cases it will therefore be advisable to abandon pre-existing, formalized, legal ties with their German parent companies if the parent's actual control, insured by other means, remains strong enough to safeguard its interests." The question, then, wasn't whether Interhandel was ever a Nazi front; the question was what could be proved about Interhandel's present and past owners (all of its old records had by then been destroyed).

The moral issue, predicated on the assumption that there was some Nazi connection with Interhandel, was whether that connection precluded our government's negotiating a reasonable deal. Conventional Wall Street lawyer values posed no problem here since you do what will earn your client (in this case, the U.S. government) the most money.

The legal issues were quite complicated, and it was Katzenbach's judgment that the case would drag on in the courts for another ten years. Nevertheless, Justice Department lawyers felt that the United States would ultimately prevail.

The public-relations issues were two-fold: First, the appearance, however erroneous, that we were doing business with Nazis could not help the Kennedy Administration. And second, as Drew Pearson pointed out in some columns at the time, the Kennedys had appointed a number of family friends to various positions in and around the company. Carmine Bellino was a consulting accountant. Family friend K. Le Moyne Billings, a Vice President of Lennen and Newell advertising, was signed on. Harold E. Clancy, a former editor of the *Boston Traveler* and friend of the family, was made a director. William Payton Marin, listed in Who's Who as "legal counsel for Joseph P. Kennedy and family," was vice-chairman, and there were others.

Typically, a Kennedy in-law, Prince Stanislas "Stash" Radziwill, made the first contact. A Swiss resident, he put Dr. Alfred Schaefer, a leading Swiss banker (and operating head of Interhandel) in touch with RFK, who referred him first to Orrick and ultimately to Katzenbach. Victor Lasky has charged that Radziwill was on the payroll of the Swiss but when asked about this, Radziwill stated: "I have never been on anybody's payroll." It was strictly a friendly gesture that he made at a White House reception.

Here then was a case that an ideologically oriented Attorney General might have seen as involving the great moral issue of our time—indeed, Jack Wolfe of the trial staff felt the government was selling out by not trying it—but Kennedy was content to have it handled like a Wall Street negotiation, although not quite. William Orrick recalls, "The case had been on file for fourteen years, had been to the World Court, the Supreme Court of the United States twice and nothing was happening. I determined to treat it as a law suit. . . . I decided to get two teams of lawyers—one preparing it for trial, the other working on a settlement." Orrick got what he thought was a fair settlement, but there was still great pressure to bring it. "The easy thing to do," Orrick says, "was . . . try the case. [Bob] knew for a certainty that he would be in big trouble with the Jews. If you try it, nobody can fault you. But that wasn't in the public interest. He knew it and did it." But not till he had satisfied those Justice Department attorneys who felt that the American case was good enough so that we should settle for nothing less than a 2–1 split in our favor. The Swiss, on the other hand, who had won the most recent round in court, had instructed their local counsel, a Washington lawyer named John Wilson, who had worked on the case for twenty-five years, to settle for nothing less than 50–50. Nicholas Katzenbach ultimately solved the problem with an ingenious proposal, which both sides ultimately accepted: If Interhandel would agree to pay $24 million in disputed government tax claims plus about $16 million in penalties from its share of the proceeds of the sale, Justice would agree to a 50–50 split. That way, although the official settlement met Interhandel's technical demand, Kennedy could claim, in announcing the settlement, that "although the exact amount each side would receive cannot be known until the sales price is known," the split would probably be about 2 to 1. As he put it, "If the sales price, as an example, is $200 million, the government would receive about $140 million and Interhandel about $60 million. If the price were $250 million the government's share would be about $170 million and Interhandel's about $85 million." In addition, Interhandel representatives gave assurances that payments to the Swiss would be accomplished in a manner which would not adversely affect the United States balance-of-payments position—a major concern at the time.

Characteristically, the deal was sealed in a Saturday meeting in Robert Kennedy's office. As John Wilson recalls, the rather stiff-necked and formal Swiss banker, Dr. Alfred Schaefer, came over to sign a memo of intent written by Katzenbach. "Being a hell of a good Swiss banker, he naturally expressed his unhappiness with the deal. Nick said if you want to take an appeal to the Attorney General you can see him tomorrow. Schaefer said yes—he'd see him. At dinner Schaefer expressed the classical Swiss point of view—that he had been short-changed.

"The next day we went to the Attorney General's office in the forenoon. Bobby, two Swiss, Nick and I were there. Schaefer started off by complaining that they were being short-changed. He remarked he had two million people watching this transaction, the most important international event in Switzerland. The Attorney General said, 'I have one hundred and ninety million people watching me.'"

RFK: "My boys tell me we could lick you."

Wilson: "General, why don't we leave the merits out of this. I have been in this case for many years, and I can't tell you to a moral certainty that I can beat you but you can't tell me to a moral certainty that you can beat me. So let's get on with the negotiation."

They were in the big room for twenty minutes with Katzenbach at one corner of the Attorney General's huge desk, Wilson at another and the two Swiss facing Kennedy. "Here was a confrontation between cold-bloodedness and stiff-neckedness," says Wilson. "Throughout the conversation there were 'whams' on the door. The Swiss would nervously look at it, and Nick would wink at me. Finally I said, 'General, why don't you let him out?' The Attorney General said, 'I believe I will,' at which point his dog Brumus leaped in and lay down beside me, probably smelling my terriers."

Jack Rosenthal, who worked for Ed Guthman under Kennedy and became press secretary when Katzenbach was named Attorney General, compares the style of Katzenbach with Kennedy and observes that "Robert tended to polarize an issue. He'd get everybody in a room, listen to the arguments on each side, decide which was right and then run like hell. I think he liked to see the bodies as they fell. Nick would always try to find a solution that would reconcile the different viewpoints. To deny that the problem really existed." The General Aniline episode was a case where Kennedy's non-ideological inclination to problem-solve, reinforced by his staff's legal establishmentarian preference for and expertise at negotiation, overcame his stylistic preference for polarization. The result: A problem that had dogged the Department for twenty-five years—and promised to hang around for another ten—was eliminated.

Part of the problem-solving impulse undoubtedly arose from the simple fact that the Kennedy Justice Department had an unparalleled problem-solving capability—a problem-solver surplus, as it were—what with the Ivy League corporation lawyer expertise at its disposal.*

The Justice Department's response to U.S. Steel president Roger Blough's announcement (Arthur Goldberg called it a "double-cross") on the afternoon of April 10, 1962, of a $6-a-ton price increase, four times the cost of the new labor settlement which adhered to the President's guidelines, is an example of what happened when Kennedy problem-solving deferred to FBI styles and values. Earlier in the day President Edward Martin of Bethlehem Steel was reported as having told his annual meeting, "We should be trying to reduce the price of steel, if at all possible." Yet after Blough's announcement, Bethlehem was the first to join U.S. Steel in the increase. The whole thing smacked of deceit on the part of the steel industry and perhaps a conspiracy or violation of the anti-trust law. FBI agents were dispatched to interview President Martin and also three reporters who had attended Bethlehem Steel's annual meeting. That night one of the reporters was called and another visited by the FBI at 2 A.M. (a third was called and refused to let them in) and the nation was soon up in arms over the "Gestapo tactics" of "Little Brother," who apparently had no compunctions about intimidating the press with 2 A.M visits if it served his brother's vendetta against big steel. Years later, when Robert Kennedy

* The Washington firm of Wilmer, Cutler and Pickering were brought in as special counsel in connection with the General Aniline settlement.

announced for the Presidency, everybody, including Robert Kennedy himself, denied that he had anything to do with the episode. "Nobody is going to believe it," Kennedy said, "but I did not know about it until after it happened. Everyone in the Department of Justice knows that and people within the government know it. But it is accepted as an established fact that I did it. My saying now that I did not know anything about it will not convince people that I didn't do it." Ed Guthman takes the blame for not specifically instructing Courtney Evans to tell the agents *not* to wake the reporters up: "As a reporter I had been rung up in the middle of the night many times, so it never occurred to me. The difference was that this was an FBI interrogation." But the consensus is that it happened, as one man on the scene puts it, "because of Nick Katzenbach's unfamiliarity in coordinating the FBI and the Anti-Trust Division." Byron White had been nominated to the Supreme Court, and Katzenbach was the new Deputy. "We didn't want to involve Byron," says Katzenbach, "because it might come up in court and we didn't want him disqualified." Katzenbach told Courtney Evans around 6 P.M. that he needed the newsmen's story for a 7 A.M. White House meeting the next morning. And even today he says, "I still can't figure out what the FBI was doing for eight hours." What they were doing was waiting to interview one of the steel company presidents first, and he hadn't gotten home till midnight; at which point they called Evans, who rolled over in bed and told them yes, to go on and interview the newsmen. So Evans takes the blame, Guthman takes the blame, and Katzenbach takes the blame for not having given more specific, literal instructions, which is what one soon learns to do when dealing with the FBI.

Thus the proximate cause of the flap was not Robert Kennedy's ruthlessness but rather the inconsistent and/or unfamiliar-to-each-other styles of the FBI and the Rhodes Scholar newly named Deputy Attorney General.

But the *reason* the FBI moved in the middle of the night, rather than the next day, the reason Katzenbach wanted information for the next morning's meeting, was that Katzenbach, like Burke Marshall, Lou Oberdorfer, Ramsey Clark and Lee Loevinger, were all familiar enough with anti-trust litigation to know that goliath corporations are not above destroying or removing relevant records when a subpoena threatens. By moving fast, Justice officials hoped to forestall such shenanigans. That, plus the environment of urgency, the Kennedy aura of crisis, made the need for speed so apparent that even the insulated FBI got the message. Blough's action in hitting JFK with the price rise without any prior warning was more than a threat to the President's anti-inflation wage-price policies; it was a direct insult to the number-one Kennedy. And the rest of the family was anxious to do something about it. So what was presented as an issue of national economic policy was at the same time a family problem. It is not without symbolic significance that although JFK won the immediate battle to roll back steel prices, a year later the industry raised prices on 75 percent of its products. And the Kennedys, having acquired an anti-business image, spent the rest of their days trying to live it down, to the detriment of the Kennedy Administration's anti-trust program.

Machiavelli counseled that it is best to be both loved and feared, but if you can only be one or the other it is better to be feared. The brothers Kennedy had solved this problem, as far as the outside world went, by letting JFK be loved and RFK, who presided over the political campaigns, the civil rights struggle and the other volatile issues of the day, be feared. It was an effective formula as far as the country was concerned, but it does not of course account for the esteem in which Robert Kennedy was held by those with whom he had sustained contact, especially his colleagues in the Justice Department.

Dorothy Junghans, a secretary and fifteen-year veteran in Justice's Office of Public Information, recalled, "When you dealt with the Kennedys, you dealt with the whole family. They were all in and out of here. It was a mess. But I wouldn't trade those days for anything."

And a career attorney in the upper echelons of the Department makes a point when he says, "Bob had the failings of a prince. It might be you who had to schlep Brumus [the Kennedys' dog] out of the office. If you worked for him he regarded you as working for *all* of him. So if Ethel lost her bags, you might have to track them down through the airport. But you knew he would listen, so if you got his attention—it was rewarding."

Robert Kennedy's impact, then, was not so much on the policies and programs—the product of the Justice Department—as it was on the institution itself, its people, patterns and practices.

His style as a delegator worked. It gave people a sense of pride in their work, raised their sights, imbued them with the Kennedy work ethic. Katzenbach remarks, "A great deal of our relationship was as it was on the immigration bill. He gave me a blank check and said go to it. And I had a kind of personal pride, maybe it was foolish, I don't know, in getting it done myself. It took a long time getting off the ground. Everybody said we were nuts. But it worked."

His way of dealing with people worked, as illustrated by an incident involving Henry Peterson of the Organized Crime Section. "You could disagree with him forcefully," recalls Peterson. "Once I took a letter up on a piece of legislation. He turned around and said, 'This sentence sounds like a lot of shit to me.' I said that's beside the point, it's right. We talked for fifteen minutes, and finally he said, 'I'll tell you what. You take this letter and think about it for twenty-four hours and if you still think you're right, you can sign my name to it.' " Peterson doesn't remember whether or not he signed the letter, but he never forgot the gesture.

His style as a question-asker worked. In the middle of an Organized Crime Section meeting in his office, Kennedy asked one of the men around the table how a case in Iowa was going (he had an encyclopedic memory for racketeer case names). The young lawyer reported that he had turned the case over to the local prosecutor, who so far hadn't moved. "So while everybody is sitting there," recalls the young lawyer, "Kennedy calls the poor bastard in Iowa from out of nowhere and says, 'Hello, this is Bob Kennedy. I just want you to know I'm very interested in that ———— case.' "

It was not just his own access to the President, which never failed to impress, but the fact that he himself was accessible and visible around the Justice Department, and his accessibility set the tone for his colleagues. Civil rights leaders and lawyers from the deep South still talk affectionately of the days when they could call Burke Marshall collect at the Justice Department, and he personally would take the calls.

Robert Kennedy operated on the simple theory that standards were contagious, that excellence was catching and within the reach of the Justice Department. He expected it at every level and looked for it everywhere. He assumed it and asked for it. A needling memo to all Assistant Attorneys General in September 1962 was typical:

> Once again I want to remind all of you of my continued interest in knowing who in your Division has done well so that I may call or write a note. I have been forced to reach the conclusion that everyone is doing only mediocre work as I hardly ever hear from you regarding outstanding contributions.

He believed in the significant gesture—the note, the telephone call, the merit award—although he recognized it for what it was. At the merit-awards ceremony which came shortly after Robert Soblen, convicted Communist spy and bail jumper, had succeeded in stabbing himself while on a transatlantic flight back to the States in the custody of Chief U.S. Marshal and Kennedy crony James J. P. McShane, Kennedy passed McShane on the way to the podium and said out of the corner of his mouth, "You're not getting one."

Nicholas Katzenbach says, "Robert Kennedy was the most successful bureaucrat in Washington because he made his Department responsive to the President's will." The Kennedy system constituted a rare capability. That the values it served were unspectacular, that this capability often went unrealized, does not detract from the astonishing fact that its mere existence helped transform the bureaucracy.

CHAPTER EIGHT

Ethics:
The Politicians and the General

IN THE SPRING OF 1966, Senator Robert F. Kennedy received a telephone call from his successor, protégé and friend, Nicholas de-Belleville Katzenbach, the new Attorney General. It was a courtesy call but a painful one. The Justice Department had discovered—and Solicitor General Thurgood Marshall was going to confess to the U.S. Supreme Court—in connection with the Fred Black case that the FBI had engaged in illegal eavesdropping back in 1963. Since the bugging had taken place while Kennedy was Attorney General, Katzenbach was calling to alert him—as he had called former Attorneys General Herbert Brownell and William Rogers—to the forthcoming revelation, in which Justice would say that bugging took place "under Departmental practice in effect for a period of years prior to 1963. . . ." Katzenbach did this "Because I didn't want a former Attorney General saying it's not true. When you make a representation to the Supreme Court," says Katzenbach, "you want to be sure it's accurate."

Kennedy asked Katzenbach to put in the Department's brief that he had no knowledge of the FBI's bugging practices in this case or in general. Katzenbach, who believed Kennedy was telling the truth, nevertheless declined on the grounds that it was irrelevant. "Bobby got very angry with me," Katzenbach recalls, "and he sent me a nasty note. He thought I was trying to save myself problems with the Bureau. Well, I was, but that's not why I didn't do it. I really thought it was irrelevant and didn't belong in there. But I also told Bobby that it would cause problems with the Bureau and he could never win a public fight with Hoover. I believed Bobby when he told me he didn't know, but when you get in a public fight with the Bureau, then you have to worry about the evidence, and they had too many pieces of paper which looked bad." Another influence on Katzenbach was Solicitor General Thurgood Marshall, who just said he couldn't sign a brief that stated it Kennedy's way. He took the position that "Looking over all the documents—not being a party to this—I can't say that these were unauthorized."

In fact, events proved Katzenbach a good prophet. When the government's brief was filed, scant attention was paid to what Kennedy had or hadn't authorized, and he sent his old friend Katzenbach a note of apology. But when Mr. Hoover brought the issue into the headlines in December 1966—in his famous correspondence with Representative H. R. Gross—there followed a confusing and damaging barrage of charge and counter-charge and when all the memos and correspondence and leaked files had settled, it was generally conceded that Hoover had won the public-relations war, although those who read the small print deduced that his charges were misleading.

That Katzenbach was right, however, did not change the underlying cause of Kennedy's initial upset. The Kennedys had given Katzenbach his first break in politics. The Kennedys had promoted him to the number-two spot at the Justice Department. The Kennedys had taken him into the inner-family circle after he passed such trials-by-ordeal as his all-night vigil at Ole Miss. And when Robert Kennedy retired as Attorney General, he had tried to make Katzenbach's appointment as his successor a virtual condition of his resignation.

Katzenbach rationalized his resolution of the conflict between loyalty to law and loyalty to friend by arguing—to himself and to RFK—that there was no conflict, that by leaving out the requested language he was acting in Robert Kennedy's best interest as well as the Justice Department's. Nevertheless, he had violated one of the unspoken tenets of the Kennedy code—that when there is a disagreement between a hard-core Kennedy and an honorary Kennedy such as Katzenbach, the former prevails, even when a non-Kennedy like Lyndon Johnson happens to be President—and the relationship was never quite the same thereafter.

The story is important less for what it shows about Katzenbach's

decision than for what it suggests about Kennedy's assumption in dealings with other members of the extended Kennedy family: that where
the formal requirements of the legal system and the informal requirements of politics or personal obligation conflict, the code of the Kennedys should prevail, or at least be given great weight.

This is not to say that as Attorney General Robert Kennedy exercised his prosecutor's discretion by asking only is this or that course of
action good or bad for the Kennedys. But in reconciling the tension
between law and politics which is built into the Attorney General's
office, Robert Kennedy's task differed from that of his predecessors and
successors to the extent that the code of the Kennedys, with its
strengths and weaknesses, asserted itself in the decision-making process.

Every Attorney General in the history of the Republic, one could
correctly argue, has the same problem. On the one hand he has an obligation to law, and on the other he is a human being who comes to
office with a grab bag of other loyalties—to family, to party, to ideology,
to constituents, to friends. And when the other loyalties conflict with
the official ones, the Attorney General reconciles them as best he can.

But what distinguished Robert Kennedy's extra-legal loyalties from
those of every prior and subsequent Attorney General was, quite simply,
that they were not random. They came as part of a package, linked in a
network of people, values and politics reaching right up to the Presidency. They had an adhesive quality that served to polarize his options,
to dramatize the conflict between law and politics inherent in the
Attorney General's job.

There are two radically different images of the job of Attorney General. One emphasizes the legal and procedural obligations of the job.
Abraham Lincoln's Attorney General, Edward Bates, described it when
he observed, "The office I hold is not properly *political*, but strictly *legal*;
and it is my duty, above all other ministers of state, to uphold the law
and resist all encroachments, from whatever quarter, of mere will and
power." [1]

The other frankly recognizes that the Attorney General is the President's chief political officer and his main job is to execute the President's will. Attorney General Robert Jackson was acting in that
tradition when he supported FDR's 1941 seizure of the North American
Aviation Corporation. A decade later, when he was sitting as a Justice
on the U.S. Supreme Court considering the Constitutionality of President Truman's 1952 seizure of the steel mills, and government counsel
attempted to cite his earlier position as authority for its action, Justice
Jackson said: "I do not regard it as precedent for this, but even if I did,

I should not bind present judicial judgment by earlier partisan advocacy" [2]

Midway in Robert Kennedy's Attorney Generalship, political analyst Joseph Kraft, a close Justice Department observer and Kennedy intimate who had served in the Pacific with Burke Marshall, borrowed Walter Bagehot's distinction between the "dignified" and the "effective" to describe these two opposing ideas of the Attorney General's role. Kraft traced the "dignified" concept from the Anglo-Saxon tradition that the sovereign as well as the citizen is subject to the law of the land. "By that tradition," he wrote, "the ideal Attorney General is an upright man, learned in the law, and with the most delicate sense of fairness, who acts less as a player on the government team than as an umpire exerting a legal check on arbitrary action of the executive." [3] The "dignified" tradition finds its expression in the inscriptions and mottoes which embellish the Justice Department building on 9th and Pennsylvania, among them: "Where law ends tyranny begins" and "The U.S. wins its point whenever justice is done its citizens in the Courts." The "effective" tradition, on the other hand, finds expression in the tendency of so many Presidents to name their political managers Attorney General.

Kraft found that Robert Kennedy fused the two traditions. Perhaps. But the point is that *because* of the code of the Kennedys Robert Kennedy never found himself in the position of President Jackson's Attorney General, who was told, apropos some reservations he had about an action Old Hickory wanted to take over the establishment of a national bank: "Sir, you must find a law authorizing the act or I will appoint an Attorney General who will."

Nor would it be adequate to accept the view, popular in both the South and certain intellectual quarters of the North, that because Robert Kennedy was no law man, and because his primary self-definition was as a member of the Kennedy family, that ruthless Robert was Jack the Giant Killer's hatchet man. Again, as suggested below, the code of the Kennedys had a momentum of its own that in some respects went beyond the individual will of the President or his chief prosecutor. For the General had imbued his troops with the ideals of Kennedyism, a fact which ironically circumscribed Robert Kennedy's options in a number of his most agonizing decisions. Thus even if Robert Kennedy had been lacking in personal integrity (he wasn't), or if he had not appointed a brilliant second layer of proceduralists and libertarians (he did), the fact that no major policy decision was taken without reference to the Kennedy values would have served as a private system of checks and balances against the outrageous exercise of Presidential whim.

On the eve of Robert Kennedy's Attorney Generalship, Alex Bickel of the Yale Law School argued "The Case Against Kennedy for Attorney General" in the influential pages of *The New Republic* (January 9, 1961). It was a devastating piece, citing and documenting Robert Kennedy's witness-badgering tactics as chief counsel for the McClellan Committee against him. Bickel did not question Robert Kennedy's motives or his capacity. But he made two telling points: (1) That the law and the canons of professional ethics provide minimum standards only, that the Attorney General must place means above ends, process above results, that he is "keeper of the executive conscience." (2) That as Staff Director of the Rackets Committee, the righteous and moralistic Mr. Kennedy seemed to place ends before means and to be insufficiently sensitive to the requirements of procedural due process.

By 1968 Professor Bickel was an active partisan of Robert Kennedy and campaigned for him in the California Presidential primaries. After Kennedy's murder, Bickel delivered a touching address in which he spoke eloquently of Kennedy's contributions to civil liberties.

Bickel was not really wrong about the character traits he had originally identified: Robert Kennedy *did* tend to have a rather starkly etched moral universe, he *did* tend to value results over process, he *did* have an agenda of evils that he intended to do something about, he *did* emphasize the "effective" over the "dignified." But what Bickel's original argument failed to take into account, in addition to Kennedy's capacity for growth—his "educability," as the ACLU called it—and his ability to detect, attract and hold top intellects, was the impact of Kennedyism on the decision-making process.

It is seen most starkly in cases involving members of the extended Kennedy family, cases where Robert Kennedy's duties as the nation's chief law enforcement officer seemed to conflict with his duties as a Kennedy. At first glance this observation appears to be contradicted by events in the public record of the Kennedy Administration. Thus the brothers Kennedy refrained from recommending family friend Frank X. Morrisey for a federal district judgeship despite much in-family pressure to do so. They prosecuted and convicted Judge J. Vincent Keogh, the brother of New York Congressman Eugene Keogh, credited with rounding up about one third of the 114-vote New York delegation for JFK in Los Angeles in 1960. They prosecuted Mayor George "Cha Cha" Chacharis of Gary, Indiana, who helped deliver 70 percent of Gary to JFK, visited the White House and was prominently mentioned as a candidate for Ambassador to Greece. And they prosecuted family friend, confidant and White House Special Assistant James Landis, formerly Dean of the Harvard Law School, on charges of tax fraud. He was convicted and sentenced to a humiliating thirty days in jail.

The contradictions are superficial. The non-appointment of Morrisey, despite the appointment in other districts of eight judges declared "unqualified" by the American Bar Association, was accompanied by the non-appointment of anyone else to the vacancy—an attempt to reconcile Kennedy obligations with official obligations. The indictments of Keogh, Chacharis and Landis happened the way they did *because* of the Kennedy code rather than despite it. A look at these cases in conjunction with the Hoffa cases, described in the next chapter, helps one to understand how the code asserted itself in the interstices of justice and Justice. Part of the Kennedy style had to do with the interruption of Justice Department routines, and since routines institutionalize regularity and regularity is a hand maiden of the even-handed distribution of justice, to the extent that the Kennedyites succeeded in undermining business-as-usual, Robert Kennedy was rendered extravulnerable to the temptations of selective justice. Finally, there was the complicating factor that Robert Kennedy personally had two codes of justice—one for the corrupters, another for the victims. Both were within the law. Neither was inconsistent with the more lofty, abstract values of Kennedyism. To understand his double-barreled jurisprudence is to begin to account for the otherwise oxymoronic image of him as a "ruthless"-"compassionate" man.

Early in the spring of 1961 Robert was explaining to the President why an appointment their father wanted for a friend was impossible. The President said, "What shall I tell Dad?" Robert said, "Tell him he's not the President."

The conversation was not about Boston Municipal Court Judge Frank X. Morrisey but it might as well have been. For Morrisey was, as Richard Whalen recorded, part of the "tight, protective circle of retainers, agents and hangers on" who always surrounded Joseph Kennedy. During John Kennedy's first Congressional campaign, Morrisey was regarded by the young campaign workers as "the Ambassador's spy." He had served JFK as secretary in charge of his home office and already in 1961 he was shepherding Edward Kennedy to political meetings across the state in what Bostonians regarded as Teddy's preparation for a political career. Joseph Kennedy wanted Morrisey to get a federal district court judgeship.

The rumors of Judge Morrisey's nomination to a district court judgeship in Massachusetts began to circulate in June of 1961, shortly after the omnibus judgeship bill had passed, creating seventy-one new vacancies. On July 3, Anthony Lewis elaborated in *The New York Times*: "Though many lawyers have made critical statements privately, they have so far been unwilling to go on the record against Judge Morrisey for fear of damaging themselves. However, it is believed that one or more bar association officials will make public statements against the nomination if it is made."

Lewis went on to report that both Byron White and Robert Kennedy were "worried about the nomination" but that the President wanted to make it. "Looking back," Nicholas Katzenbach, who succeeded White, says, "Morrisey was a very nice guy. It was awfully difficult for Robert and John. It was for papa Joe. Bob knew what the problems were with Morrisey [who was totally unqualified for the job]. He tried to talk to me about it. It was difficult because the father did not impose himself on them and this was one of the few minor things which would have made a great difference to him."

Shortly after Lewis's story appeared, he went to see the Attorney General for one of the private background sessions that Kennedy occasionally granted selected reporters. Lewis remembers, "I raised the question of the objections to Morrisey and asked whether in fact the appointment was likely to be made. Kennedy did not shout or anything, but he made it very clear that he was angry. He rose, indicated that the interview was over, walked me to the door of his room and said as we walked, 'I'm going to see that Frank Morrisey is appointed just to make it clear that *The New York Times* is not making the judicial nominations around here.'"

But Robert Kennedy didn't submit Morrisey's name—even though the question was reraised after Joseph Kennedy's heart attack in 1964 and was reraised every time the late Cardinal Cushing, Kennedy family friend and prelate at the Presidential inauguration, who had pledged a million dollars at a critical point in the Bay of Pigs prisoner-ransom episode, got within whispering distance. Of course Morrisey's name was ultimately sent to the Senate by President Johnson when Katzenbach was Attorney General, at the request of Senator Edward M. Kennedy, and his scandalously unqualified background (he hadn't really gone to law school) caused such a controversy that the nomination was withdrawn.*

---

* Ted Kennedy sent the name over to the Justice Department and Katzenbach forwarded it to the White House on a day when Ramsey Clark, then Deputy Attorney General with operating responsibility for passing on the qualifications of judicial nominees, and his Assistant, Ernest Freisen, were both out of town on a speech-making tour. The President announced the nomination from Texas.

Years later, when Robert Kennedy was in the Senate and Tony Lewis had become a personal friend, the newsman asked Bob why President Kennedy had not nominated Morrisey. "He explained that he had to resist a great many judicial appointments pressed by Senators by arguing that their men were not qualified, and it would greatly have complicated that function for him if he himself had picked someone so widely deemed unqualified. I thought at the time, and I still think, that that answer was less than wholly truthful. I think that Bobby portrayed himself as somewhat more cynical than he really was; I believe one reason for what happened was that Bobby had himself come to consider Morrisey unqualified. Kenny O'Donnell once indicated as much to me, saying that Bobby was resisting pressure for the appointment."

One need not agree with Lewis's analysis of RFK's motives to recognize that here was a case where Jack-Kennedyism conflicted with Joe-Kennedyism in the sense that it was in the President's interest (regardless of his preferences in the matter) not to be chargeable with cronyism in the matter of judicial appointments, and it was in old Joe's credo that loyalty and friendship should not go unrewarded. Robert chose not to embarrass the President. But he also did not want to embarrass or insult his father or his father's intimates.

The result: For four years, with court congestion at its peak and the jails jammed with men awaiting trial unable to afford bail—an issue of which RFK was keenly aware—the people of the federal district of Massachusetts went without a district court judge. When I asked Joe Dolan, Byron White's Deputy who had operating responsibilities for judicial selection, whether he had made any recommendations for the vacancy, he looked at me as if I were cockeyed and said, somewhat incredulously, "With a President from Massachusetts and an Attorney General from Massachusetts and a Democratic Senator from Massachusetts, who happen to be brothers, you assume that they will work that one out among themselves."

Congressman Eugene Keogh was, according to one member of the Kennedy circle, "as responsible as any man for John Kennedy's winning the Democratic nomination for President in Los Angeles in 1960." The claim may be inflated but a case can be made. Theodore White credits Keogh, along with Joseph P. Kennedy and Charles Buckley, with lining up the critical New York delegation votes behind JFK. JFK needed a first-ballot victory to win, since many of his delegate commitments did not go beyond the first ballot. Without the actual and psychological support of those votes he might not have made it on the first ballot, and if not, he might not have made it at all. Congressman Keogh was close to old Joe, a friend of JFK and an Administration loyalist on the House Ways and Means Committee. He was, in other words, a member of the extended Kennedy family. "If Bob had his druthers," says Katzenbach, "he wouldn't have brought the Keogh case. Yet he didn't kill it. Bobby had very, very strong feelings about not letting politics interfere with the Department's operations." Yet it is part of the Kennedy legend and was part of the Kennedy environment that politics would not be permitted to distort the processes of justice. It was typical, for instance, that when Arthur Garrity, the U.S. attorney in Massachusetts after consultation with John Douglas, Assistant Attorney General in charge of the Civil Division, brought suit alleging breach of contract and other improprieties in the construction of a VA hospital in the Boston area against Matt McCloskey, a key Democratic fund-raiser from Philadelphia and former Ambassador to Ireland, there wasn't the slightest hesitation about proceeding. When Garrity told Kennedy about it after the fact, all he said was "Well, thanks a lot, Arthur, for that suit."

Of course politics inevitably intrudes on law, and the issue is how the prosecutor handles it. Thus when a Baltimore grand jury had heard the evidence against Democratic Congressman Thomas Johnson on an obstruction-of-justice charge, Katzenbach remembers, "There was no question that if we recommended prosecution, the grand jury would indict. And there was no question that if we indicted, he'd lose the election. We did, and he did. My feeling is that if he'd have been a Republican, we'd have waited till after the election." On the other side, Henry Ruth of the Organized Crime Section, a great admirer of Attorney General Kennedy, recalls that in the fall of 1963 Kennedy concluded a briefing saying he thought we ought to do more in Philadelphia. "So we started to look into public officials with the idea of tax investigations. We started to look at files. Somebody called Congressman [William] Green. He called Bobby and said what are you doing in Philadelphia. It's October and you have an election coming, and I hear you're looking into tax returns—*my* tax return! Kennedy called [us] and said, 'What the hell are you doing to me? There are times to start an investigation and times not to start. Can't you wait till December?' " Ruth waited, but by then LBJ was President and "without any visible communication from anybody everybody lost heart."

Yet William Shannon was correct when he wrote in his dispassionate analysis, *The Heir Apparent*, "Where political wrongdoing was concerned Robert Kennedy was sternly incorruptible. During his three years in office, the Justice Department prosecuted numerous Democratic politicians including two Congressmen, three State Supreme Court justices, five mayors, two chiefs of police, and three sheriffs. One of those convicted was New York State Supreme Court Justice Vincent Keogh, the brother of Congressman Eugene Keogh. . . ." [4] Four days before the indictment, JFK and Congressman Keogh attended the Army–Navy game together.

On the surface the Keogh bribery case seemed clear-cut. As the *Wall Street Journal* told it, the FBI in a routine investigation into a Maryland jukebox racket stumbled on the rumor that a New York Justice had taken a bribe to fix the sentence of Sanford Moore, the operator of a jukebox company who had been convicted of bankruptcy fraud. After an investigation disclosed the foundations to the rumor, a grand jury was convened and Keogh and his co-defendants—including an assistant U.S. attorney named Elliott Kahaner and Tony "Ducks" Corallo, a Teamster and Mafioso whose nickname stemmed from his reputation for "ducking" convictions after arrest—were indicted and convicted. The chief witness against them was co-defendant Dr. Robert M. Erdman, a Bronx orthopedist who had once been associated with Moore in a Maryland jukebox operation; and whose case was to be tried separately; he testified that he had served as bag man (middle man) for the money. According to the government, Assistant U.S. Attorney Kahaner and Judge Keogh had entered into an agreement to help Moore and his co-defendants get a light sentence in the bankruptcy case in return for $35,000. Both Kahaner and Keogh were to speak with Judge Leo F. Rayfiel, the sentencing judge. Corallo paid Erdman, who passed the money on to Keogh and Kahaner.

Keogh was sentenced to two years in prison and declared that he had been victimized by "international criminals, racketeers and perjurers" who had been "coddled at taxpayers' expense protected by the U.S. government through the Attorney General." He began a long fight for vindication in the courts which met with no success and eventually he served eighteen months in prison with time off for good behavior.

From the beginning there were rumors that the fix was in. As Jack Miller, head of the Criminal Division, recalls, "First, there were rumors that we were not going to convene a grand jury. Then there were rumors that we were going to throw the case in the grand jury. Then that we were going to blow it at the trial. Then that we were going to recommend overnight probation. Then that we had built error into the record and were going to fold on appeal. Then that we were going to take a dive on the petition for cert. But none of those things was true, and Keogh went to jail."

When it was all over the public had to concede, as William Shannon reported, that Robert Kennedy was incorruptible, that he had ignored the Kennedy bond and without interference let justice take its course.

It is impossible to reconstruct all of the delicate behind-the-scenes maneuvers relating to a sensitive prosecution like the Keogh case. Much of the information is confidential, and nobody knows what Robert and John Kennedy said to each other. But this much can be stated with certainty and not necessarily to the discredit of an Attorney General doing his best to reconcile irreconcilable pressures: nothing about the Keogh case was routine.

First, although the *Wall Street Journal* reported that an FBI investigation into a Maryland jukebox racket contributed some evidence to the Keogh case, *The New York Times* reported that "Judge Rayfiel, through a friend, heard that Moore was saying he 'had the judge in his pocket.' The judge notified the FBI and an investigation was started." Both stories could have been true, but the fix was actually uncovered by John Lally, an attorney from Ed Silberling's Organized Crime Section at the Justice Department. "Keogh was a 'smell case,' " recalls Silberling. "I was interested in Sandy Moore, who had pleaded guilty [on March 30, 1961] and thrown himself on the mercy of the court and then on sentencing day tried to withdraw his guilty plea. You don't plead guilty like that unless it's arranged. He obviously expected a suspended sentence, and he got three years. His lawyer had told him if he didn't plead he would have only gotten six months. He was kicking and screaming. It was cockeyed and I thought something was fishy, so I sent in Lally to investigate."

John Lally had interviewed Moore twice without success, trying to pin him down on his relationship with Tony Corallo. The interviews were conducted in the detention station of the Eastern District. He was on his third try when who should come ambling through, on one of those informal visits which were his hallmark, but the Attorney General of the United States, Robert Kennedy. Walking with his arm slung around the Attorney General's shoulder was Assistant U.S. Attorney Elliott Kahaner, a holdover from the previous Administration then rumored to be bucking for appointment as U.S. attorney from the Eastern District. When Moore saw Kahaner with his arm around the Attorney General's shoulder, recalls Charles Shaffer, another lawyer who worked on the case, "something snapped" and Moore turned to Lally and said, "I won't tell you about Tony Ducks but I'll tell you a story you won't believe," and he proceeded to spin out the bizarre story of payment to Kahaner and Keogh, in return for which they were supposed to speak to the sentencing judge.

Had it not been for the Kennedy–Silberling system of centrally based prosecutors invading local U.S. attorneys' turf and in some cases replacing FBI men as investigators, Lally might never have interrogated Moore. Had it not been for Robert Kennedy's free-wheeling habit of touring local jails, FBI offices, U.S. attorney offices and detention facilities, Moore would not have seen him with Kahaner "and I'm telling you," says Charles Shaffer, who worked with Lally on the case, "that's what broke him."

Shaffer had been in New York at the time with Walter Sheridan, head of the Get-Hoffa Squad, looking into Teamster matters involving Tony "Ducks" Corallo, investigating an old stock-manipulating case (United Dye) and generally running afoul of the strait-laced and highly independent U.S. attorney in the Southern District, Robert Morgenthau, who felt both Shaffer and Sheridan were poaching on his territory. Morgenthau succeeded in expelling Sheridan from the District but Shaffer had developed some information on Erdman and so he was transferred to the Keogh case. Shaffer, a former U.S. attorney, was a flamboyant, aggressive young *Fordham Law Review* alumnus who had been personally interviewed and hired by Robert Kennedy for the Get-Hoffa Squad. He recalls: "As soon as Moore tells us the name of the doctor [Erdman]—the bag man—we subpoena him right out of the operating room. We don't want him to call his lawyer. We don't want him to start trying to bullshit his way out of it. Down comes Erdman and under clever interrogation he admits everything."

Once the case was developed, there was the matter of convening a grand jury.

"I was not eager to have anybody in the area know about the case until after a grand jury had been convened," recalls Silberling. "I wanted the Bureau to follow up our initial investigation with a thorough investigation. Suddenly there was a holdup of four to six weeks and no investigation by the Bureau. Congressman Keogh was informed and the local U.S. attorney in the Eastern District was informed. I didn't know what was happening."

Silberling recalls a late-night scene in the spacious, red-carpeted Attorney General's office. Present were Robert Kennedy, Byron White and Silberling, who had just finished his presentation insisting that the case be brought. "You've *got* to prosecute this," says Byron White. The Attorney General, who had been pacing, put his head face down on the big desk, wrapped his elbows around it and said, "Goddam it, I told my brother I didn't want this job."

Had Kennedy not sought and attracted as his Deputy a man of White's iron integrity and rigid probity and had he not personally recruited a gangbusting zealot like Silberling to head up his organized-crime drive, such a meeting probably would never have taken place.

For the next five months the careful Lally and the firebrand Shaffer presented their case to the grand jury, and Shaffer recalls that throughout the period, there were rumors around town that the fix was in. And throughout the presentation, he and Lally kept being called back to Washington, where Jack Miller, head of the Criminal Division and Silberling's boss, wanted to know what was happening. Finally, remembers Shaffer, they had not yet completed the presentation but were summoned to the Attorney General's home in McLean. "This is very disturbing news. Byron White is there waiting for us and he is very concerned. Why? Because the Attorney General is concerned. Why? Because the President is concerned." Shaffer recalls, "So Kennedy asks me, 'You think you have a case?' 'A damned good one,' I tell him and I show him a postcard that Erdman received from [Judge] Keogh thanking him for 'the package' and I tell him Erdman told the grand jury that the 'package' meant the money.

"I told the Attorney General it was a strong case. I knew it was a *weak* case because the only witnesses we have are the bag man and the con. But I also know he knows it could be a runaway grand jury and I want to bring the case, so I tell him, 'Look, if you want to fix it, fix the case. I don't give a shit.' "

Soon after, in August, Shaffer was recalled and assigned to other duties. "To show you how crazy Shaffer was," says one Assistant Attorney General, "when I asked how the case was going, he said, 'It's a little weak on the Judge.' It turned out he was talking about Judge Rayfiel, the guy Keogh was supposed to *talk* to. We had *nothing* on Judge Rayfiel!" To replace Shaffer, Kennedy sent William Hundley, a Republican holdover. As counsel for the McClellan Committee, Kennedy had criticized Hundley, who headed up the Organized Crime Section under Eisenhower. Kennedy felt he could be bringing better and quicker cases. But as Attorney General, he had used the knowledgeable Republican holdover for odd jobs to insulate the Department against charges of partisanship. For instance, he had dispatched Hundley to work out the intricacies of Bernard Goldfine's tax situation.

Before Hundley left for New York, Kennedy told him, "It's a judge and a United States attorney. Their entire careers are at stake. Give them a fair shake." But when Hundley arrived in New York he found a suspicious grand jury, fired up by Shaffer, who had told him, "As long as I'm here, you don't have to worry about a fix. If they get rid of *me, then* you have to worry!" "When I first put in an appearance before the grand jury," says Hundley, "they were ready to indict me!"

On October 9, Kennedy had a meeting to hear the evidence—as it had been presented to the grand jury—against Judge Keogh. White, Katzenbach, Marshall, Guthman, Seigenthaler and Oberdorfer joined the Criminal Division attorneys for the occasion. Unquestionably Judge Keogh had taken gifts from Dr. Erdman, and as Kennedy went around the room, the overwhelming sentiment was to ask the grand jury to indict.

But Kennedy still had doubts and pointed out that if the judge were indicted—regardless of what followed, he would be finished. He said, "I'd hate to have that on my conscience."

One of the fringe benefits for Justice Department lawyers of lower rank during the Kennedy years was an invitation to the annual White House judicial reception. A fringe by-product of that occasion was the opportunity to overhear such conversations as that between Ken O'Donnell, Byron White, the Attorney General, Miller and Hundley. There were, recalls an eavesdropper, raised voices. "They were talking about the Keogh case," he says. "O'Donnell was in favor of having Judge Keogh resign and dropping the whole thing. Then Byron said something. I think it was a joke about Bob's dragging his feet—and Bob's face lost color. 'How could you say that?' he asked. He was really upset. He thought Byron was accusing him. I think Byron was just wisecracking. Anyway, Bob walked away shaking."

By mid-October Kennedy asked Hundley—over the FBI's objections —to have the Bureau administer a lie-detector test. Judge Keogh agreed but the results were inconclusive.

Then there were rumors—hotly denied—that Congressman Keogh himself was involved. On December 5, morale in the Criminal Division sinking, Kennedy gave the green light. The grand-jury indictment came down on December 7, 1961—nine months after Moore was sentenced, and the case went to trial in May of 1962. Hundley was in charge assisted by Lally and a young member of the Organized Crime Section, Henry Ruth, now on the staff of New York Mayor John Lindsay. The scuttlebutt is that Kennedy privately told Hundley to keep the judge's brother—Congressman Keogh—out of the case by name at whatever cost.

At the trial Judge Keogh conceded that he took a new Dodge, storm windows and free medical care from Dr. Erdman, but denied he was ever bribed to do anything. There was testimony by both Erdman and Moore that Congressman Keogh also had tried to get Judge Rayfiel to go easy on Moore. As Hundley recalls, "The trouble was that every time a government witness got a chance they stuck a knife in the Congressman." * Ruth remembers that every time Eugene Keogh's name was mentioned, the phone rang and it was the Attorney General. "The lid nearly blew off," he says, "when Congressman Keogh was called as the surprise witness for the defense. He denied that he had ever tried to intercede in behalf of Moore. But I don't think Hundley was prepared for his cross. . . ." That night there was a message in writing for Hundley at the St. George Hotel: "URGENT—Call the Attorney General immediately." When he returned from the phone call, Ruth recalls that Hundley was shaking. But when asked all he said was "Bob said, 'Don't worry about the Congressman. Carry on as usual.' "

If Hundley's instructions were in any way to play down Congressman Keogh's role—he denies that they were—this, of course, would run counter to what a prosecutor is supposed to do with a witness for the other side. Kennedy loyalty to a member of the extended family then may thus have asserted itself at this late point in the proceedings, although it didn't, as far as one can judge, affect the outcome of the case. On the night of the verdict, Nicholas Katzenbach arrived at Hickory Hill, and it fell to him to inform Robert Kennedy that Keogh had been found guilty. Because rumors that the government was throwing the case were still in the air, "It would have been the worst conceivable thing if he had lost this one," says Katzenbach. "Nothing could have been worse. But when I told him the verdict, he said, 'Thanks.' It was very sardonic. He got absolutely no pleasure. It was very painful to him."

Traditionally, when assistants win a case like the Keogh case they get letters of congratulations from the Attorney General. This time there were no letters. "I am sure the letters were drafted and sent over for his signature," says one who worked on the case, "but I guess he didn't have the heart to sign them. Yet he really wanted to win it— he was interested every step of the way."

"You've got to give Kennedy a lot of credit for this one," says young Henry Ruth. "There were people in the White House who did not

* Under cross-examination Moore conceded that he had not implicated Congressman Keogh when he testified before the grand jury, but said "I've had plenty of time to think things over and reconstruct them in my mind the last few months."

want the Keogh case brought, and it was an easy case to say it's not strong enough. The only one who affirmed Moore's story was the fixer. So you could have turned it down as to Keogh because it's common practice for judges to call one another about sentences. The whole issue in the case was—do you believe Dr. Erdman? And he was not a particularly credible witness. If that had been a tax case, they never would have brought it since they want 100 percent assurance. But it was only 50–50 on Keogh and when you indict a prominent person like that you'd better be damned sure you're going to convict him."

Would Kennedy have brought the case if tigers like Silberling hadn't been pushing, if Shaffer hadn't fired up the grand jury? Did he tell Hundley not to implicate Congressman Keogh even at the risk of losing the case? Given the White House inclination to drop it, might not an Attorney General with a *less* secure link to and stake in the Presidency have gone along? *Was* Congressman Keogh himself involved and spared the ultimate embarrassment of implication? Was the case brought—despite the disreputable nature of the government's chief witness—*because* Robert Kennedy wanted to demonstrate the incorruptibility of the Kennedy Administration?

The answers to these questions are not, for the most part, knowable. It seems like a reasonable hypothesis, however, to suggest that in a sense Kennedy values—what the Kennedys came to stand for at their best—triumphed over Kennedy luggage, the debts which encumbered them when they came to office. At the same time the agents of this victory were in part the young prosecutors imbued with the Kennedy message of fearlessly rooting out corruption wherever they might find it. Kennedyism triumphed over the Kennedys.

The Chacharis case, like the Keogh case, looked from the outside like a clear-cut case of Kennedy virtuously prosecuting an old political crony without fear or favor. As *Time* magazine reported at the time:

> For a while, the dream of chubby George Chacharis to return to his native Greece as U.S. Ambassador did not seem so impossible.
> But it was not to be—partly because of that Kennedy called Bobby. As chief counsel for a Senate Committee investigating corruption in Lake County in 1959, Bobby Kennedy scraped up enough dirt to inspire the formation of the privately financed Northwest Indiana Crime Commission. The investigations of Commission Director Francis Lynch unearthed evidence that Chacharis and his cronies had regularly accepted payoffs from construction companies that wanted city contracts and licenses. When he could not interest the county prosecutor in his evidence, Lynch went to see Bobby Kennedy, who set up a federal grand jury.

Not quite. It was true that Robert Kennedy's work on the McClellan Committee had inspired the formation of the Northwest Indiana Crime Commission, and it was true that Robert Kennedy himself had uncovered suspicious evidence about Lake County's prosecuting attorney, Metro Holovachka, which led him to recommend in *The Enemy Within* that "the Bar Association of Indiana might look into the situation regarding Holovachka. . . ." But it was Organized Crime Section Chief Edwyn Silberling who dispatched Jay Goldberg, a fast-talking, hard-driving graduate of the Brooklyn Law School and alumnus of New York District Attorney Frank Hogan's office, to Gary. And it was Silberling and Goldberg who ultimately had to pressure Robert Kennedy into bringing the case.

Lake County was a natural for the anti-crime drive. In 1961 Indiana professional gamblers rated first in the nation in the amount paid for federal wagering taxes—which meant that they were willing to comply with the federal law (ultimately to be declared unconstitutional on Fifth Amendment grounds) because they had no fear of state prosecution. It was prototypical corruption in that local officials were so tied in with the mob that only an outside agency could hope to clean things up. As young Goldberg told a citizens' testimonial dinner in his honor after all the shouting, the indictment and the trial had passed, the corruption was so pervasive that during his many months of work in the area "Not a single person came forward to testify in court."

When Goldberg arrived in Gary in September of 1961, the FBI told him that it had no evidence of corruption and advised him to head downstate "where the big-time operators are." He was ready to take their advice until he conferred with IRS, and the resident agent [Oral Cole] told him, "My God, this area is filthy with corruption." By the time Cole finished talking and showed Goldberg his "evidence"—a collection of check stubs which indicated a complicated system of payoffs—and shared his suppositions about how that system worked, Goldberg was convinced that he had stumbled onto something big and that what was needed was "a grand jury to force these people to talk."

In the months that followed, Goldberg was directed by the Attorney General to interview Mayor Chacharis: "The Mayor wants to offer his cooperation. Call him and set up a meeting." When Goldberg refused the Mayor's request to show the "evidence" he had, Goldberg was summoned back to Washington—on the eve of the grand-jury investigation, which he had to cancel—for a confrontation in the Justice Department with Chacharis and his newly hired attorney, Alex Campbell, the Democratic National Committeeman from Indiana and former head of the Justice Department's Criminal Division. (Goldberg was accused of having threatened to "lock Chacharis up as soon as the grand jury convenes," but by the time he arrived at the Justice Department, Chacharis had tearfully retracted his allegations and the meeting was called off.) IRS internal memoranda accused the Justice Department of leaking evidence to the accused. Goldberg was besieged with telephone calls from Criminal Division chief Jack Miller, relaying complaints from Chacharis about Goldberg's conduct. And in the midst of his grand-jury investigation he was again summoned back to Washington, this time by Edwyn Silberling's assistant ("I didn't have the heart to call," says Silberling), where he was told that a member of the Indiana Congressional delegation had threatened to withhold critical Administration support within the House Rules Committee unless Goldberg was recalled.

Meanwhile the Indiana papers had predicted "U.S. JURY WILL PROBE/GARY MAYOR'S INCOME TO BE INCLUDED IN INVESTIGATION"; they had reported rumors that Gary tax evaders had settled with IRS "quietly paying their bills." And now the headline was "BOB KENNEDY KEY MAN IN FATE OF BIGSHOT POLITICIANS IN GARY." Gary citizens sent coconuts to the White House painted with the word "help" calling for Goldberg's return. Whether these public manifestations were the result of Goldberg's machinations, a penchant to "try his cases in the papers" as some in the Justice Department believed, or the result of alert reporters and concerned citizens, is in dispute. Probably a little bit of each.

What is not in dispute is that Goldberg, like Shaffer in the Keogh case, was a no-holds-barred, brash, flamboyant prosecutor. Were the phone calls constantly directed at him from Washington a tribute to Chacharis' pull or the result of his own indiscretions? Probably both. His technique for interrogation was to sit in a high-backed rotating chair with back to door so that he would be totally hidden. When the "witness" would come in, Goldberg would stick out an arm and point to a chair (from which the witness still could not see Goldberg's face) and say: "Look. You're standing in 150-degree water. It's in your power to cool that water off to about 50 degrees, or make it much hotter until it gets up to 250 degrees and you can't stand it. Which are you going to do?"

Goldberg wanted Chacharis' chauffeur to testify against the Mayor and one day told him so directly. Goldberg recalls: "To get across the fact that the federal investigation had great momentum and the witness would have to choose whether to be an unharmed observer or whether he was going to get caught up in the investigation, I stated that there was, in effect, a ten-ton truck bearing the markings 'Federal

Government' coming down the street. I indicated that I could give this witness an opportunity to stand on the sidewalk and watch this truck go by without getting hurt by it. To effect this result, the witness was told he would have to be cooperative. However, I continued, 'If you lie, it will be as though you placed yourself in the path of this oncoming truck, this truck which is destined to reach its objective.' Well—the next morning I received a telephone call from an excited official in Washington who was assigned to check out the latest allegation. Did I, he wanted to know, threaten to run this witness over with a ten-ton truck?"

Finally Goldberg was told to present the indictments, and on February 21 the grand jury publicly charged George Chacharis with receiving $226,686 in payoffs that he failed to report on his tax returns. Having indicted the Mayor and a host of other public officials, Goldberg returned to Washington only to discover that a new team from the Tax Division would handle the trial. Such a procedure went contrary to the ideal of Silberling's section—that the same man would investigate, prepare and prosecute the case. The new men presented seventy-five witnesses and four hundred items of evidence, and after the government had completed its case, Chacharis changed his mind and pleaded guilty. The day of the conviction Francis Lynch, of the Citizens Crime Commission of Northwest Indiana, said: "From our point of view, the citizens of Lake County owe an extremely large debt of gratitude to Mr. Goldberg. Unquestionably it was his aggressive and persistent action through the grand jury which resulted in the indictment and the strong case against the political personages and resulted in the plea of guilty of George Chacharis this week. . . ."

But not long thereafter Jay Goldberg, the hero of Gary reformers, recipient of press accolades and a Crime Committee testimonial dinner, resigned from the U.S. Department of Justice and returned to New York and the private practice of law. "I advised Jay to leave," says Silberling. "He was dead. So there was no point in his staying."

James Misselbach, Silberling's assistant, adds: "The usual attacks are made on Goldberg for his lack of balance. He certainly was energetic and willing to try any technique. But if it hadn't been for Goldberg and Silberling who kept it alive and ultimately brought it to prosecution and conviction, it would have died. There were enormous pressures in the Chacharis case."

In the aftermath of the Keogh and Chacharis cases, Silberling left and Misselbach also left the Department. "From Keogh on," says Silberling, "it was a losing fight. Every invasion caused resentment. For instance, in Kansas City I sent two guys out and the local U.S. attorney successfully opposed some of the prosecutions I insisted upon." "Probably the worst call Bobby ever made," says Harry Subin, a young attorney who was recruited for the Organized Crime Section by Silberling, but stayed on under Hundley, "was putting Miller over Silberling and then getting rid of Silberling. Hundley was excellent, but Bobby should never have let Ed go." Byron White saw it principally as a conflict of styles between Silberling, who was not interested in mending any political fences, and Miller, much more sensitive to the requirements of politics.

Whatever the truth, the case *was* brought and it would be wrong-headed to deny Robert Kennedy the credit for bringing it regardless of his motives. The sour aftermath was at least partly a function of Goldberg's ultra-aggressive personality and the nature of the work. As Tom McBride, also an attorney in the Organized Crime Section and alumnus of D.A. Hogan's office, said, "The work burns you out. You put all of your energy and guts in it, and inevitably you're going to rub people on your own side the wrong way." McBride himself retired from crime fighting in favor of a tour of duty as a Peace Corps representative followed by a staff position with the Urban Coalition.

Robert Kennedy's commitment was not to let politics interfere with his anti-organized-crime activities. But as Katzenbach says, "Politics *were* involved. It was painful, but he recognized what he had to do. He took the political situation into account. But he did it."

The Chacharis case, as much as any other, should shatter the stereotype of a single-minded, puritanical Attorney General prosecuting friend and foe alike without regard to the consequences. At the same time, not too many implications should be attached to his device of referring Chacharis to Jack Miller "to work things out." Once, at columnist George Sokolsky's suggestion, he referred Roy Cohn to Robert Morgenthau and suggested they get together "to work things out." * It was his real assumption that if there were *honest* misconceptions, they *would* be worked out. Again, it might be observed that had it not been for the men Kennedy had recruited, imbued with the Kennedy spirit and in a direct way carrying forward the work he had personally begun on the McClellan Committee—which led to the Crime Commission, which in turn fed information to IRS Special Agent Oral Cole, who

---

* Cohn saw Morgenthau, mentioned his high-placed friends in the press and suggested that he was the victim of a vendetta carried on by Robert Kennedy. Later, when Kennedy had resigned but Cohn's troubles with the law continued, he publicly and incessantly insisted he was the victim of a vendetta carried on by Robert Morgenthau.

was in touch with special prosecutor Jay Goldberg only because the Kennedy communications network got investigative agencies to cut across Departmental lines—the case against Chacharis would probably never have been brought. This is not to deny that there comes a point in any controversial prosecution where the embarrassment of bringing it is countervailed by the greater embarrassment of not bringing it. As career attorney and former FBI agent Nathaniel E. Kossack, then head of the Criminal Frauds Section, observes in a more general context, "The Justice Department is a set of files in a goldfish bowl. When you have one of these cases and it involves agents, an assistant U.S. attorney, some lawyers from the Organized Crime Section, the head of the Organized Crime Section, an Assistant Attorney General and the Deputy Attorney General, not to mention subpoena servers, marshals, secretaries, etc., do you think the Attorney General can just say 'Shshsh' . . . and it will go away?"

It should be noted, finally, that whatever Robert Kennedy's motives for subjecting Jay Goldberg to delay and then ultimately authorizing full speed ahead, the Chacharis case distressed him personally—and not merely because Chacharis was a political ally whom the Kennedys owed. What bothered him as much was that Chacharis had not been pocketing any of the money for himself. Unlike Teamsters head Dave Beck, for example, who had been put behind bars as the result of RFK's McClellan Committee investigations, George Chacharis had not built himself an estate with a swimming pool. He lived modestly and used all of the graft money to keep his political machine going and growing. By Chacharis' *own* code he had not really been doing anything wrong.

Kennedy's very real distress in the Chacharis case is well illustrated by some of the ancillary corruption cases in Gary. Katzenbach, who by then had become Deputy, recalls, "There were four councilmen in Gary—two Republicans and two Democrats. They tried the first one, I think, in 1962. The jury didn't believe our chief witness and acquitted. Basically it was because he was lying. He was *not* lying about the case. He *was* lying about his own involvement. We had the same witness in the three other cases. Query: Do you try the three other cases? Bob dismissed the indictments over the opposition of Silberling, who said I can get convictions on the other three because they have worse records. Bob said, 'You don't play roulette like that with people's lives.' "

As Silberling recalled the same case, the question was which councilman to prosecute first. He wanted to go after the most vulnerable one first and suggested that the councilman who doubled as a bartender would be a good place to start. "What's wrong with being a bartender?" asked Kennedy. "My grandfather was a bartender."

The code of the Kennedys, with its emphasis on loyalty, which had served Kennedy the Administrator so well, complicated the life of Kennedy the Prosecutor. For the same network of rights, privileges, duties, debts, loves, hates and obligations that made the extended Kennedy family possible rendered the impartial exercise of prosecutor's discretion—where the family was concerned—more difficult, if not impossible. In the Keogh case Robert Kennedy had prosecuted a political ally who broke the law for money. In the Chacharis case he had prosecuted a political ally who broke the law for power. The major test of Kennedy's incorruptibility was to come in the Landis case, where Kennedy was to prosecute a member of the innermost family circle who apparently had broken the law out of perversity, if not inadvertence.

On the surface the Landis case was clear-cut. Landis, an intimate of the Kennedys, had failed to pay his taxes for five years. The Internal Revenue Service found out about it, he was indicted, pleaded guilty and was sentenced to thirty days in jail. In addition, according to public accounts at the time, the Attorney General properly disqualified himself from playing any role in the case.

"Bobby had nothing to do with it," says Nicholas Katzenbach. "I wouldn't let him. Landis was so close to the family. I said, 'You cannot make a decision not to prosecute Landis. If you can't make that decision, don't make any.' I said I wouldn't discuss it with him. I told the President that Bob was out of this and so should he be, and when it came to a conclusion I would let him know what we were doing and how. It was the most unpleasant thing I had to do in the Department."

Robert Kennedy may have disqualified himself but that did not mean the code of the Kennedys would not assert itself in the course of the proceedings. In fact, were it not for Landis' relationship to the Kennedys and an IRS bureaucrat's image of how the Kennedys did business, in all probability James Landis would have been spared the humiliating sequence of events which ended with his death by drowning in 1964. The Landis situation deserves recounting in some detail because it is in many ways a metaphor for the political and ethical obstacles which get in the way of any prosecutor who would temper justice with mercy. That the prosecutor was the Attorney General of the U.S., the President's brother and a Kennedy, that the justice he wanted to temper had both a large and a small "j" and that the defendant was a member of the innermost family circles meant merely that the attempt to reconcile personal obligations and official ones would be complicated by the glare of publicity.

The life of James Landis and the life of the Kennedys had been intermingled since the early Thirties. In 1934 it was Landis who cast the deciding vote, at FDR's request, in favor of making Joseph Kennedy SEC chairman.* In 1937 it was Joe Kennedy's politicking, over the objections of Felix Frankfurter, that won Landis (who had succeeded Kennedy as SEC chairman) the deanship of Harvard Law School. Landis and Joe Kennedy had remained friends down through the years. In 1948, when Landis learned that Harry Truman was not going to reappoint him to another term on the Civil Aeronautics Board, it was Joe Kennedy who invited him to Palm Beach and advised him to beat Truman to the punch by announcing that he wouldn't *accept* the reappointment because he would be managing Joe Kennedy's financial interests. In 1950 Joe Kennedy and Landis collaborated on a privately published pamphlet defending the decision of Belgium's King Leopold II to surrender his army to the Germans in late May 1940.

In the late Forties Landis came up with and sold to Congress and the Revenue Commissioner—arguing in terms of the public good—an amendment to the Revenue Codes whose purpose was (a) to close a loophole in the tax laws on the sale and leaseback of charitable institutions; and (b) not incidentally to save the Kennedys millions of dollars in taxes on the Merchandise Mart, the huge Chicago office building they were acquiring from Marshall Field and Company; it was the only building in the country which qualified under the new provision.

Landis did financial and legal work for the Kennedys without billing them for it. And only on the prodding of his law partners did he occasionally bill for cash disbursements. He was involved in all of JFK's political campaigns, writing speeches and drafting legislation. When Kennedy went to Berlin it was Landis who came up with that line from Robert Frost about "something there is that doesn't like a wall." He personally recommended both Robert and Edward Kennedy to the University of Virginia Law School. He was the Kennedys' house intellectual. The President-elect's first announced appointments were J. Edgar Hoover to continue running the FBI, Allen Dulles to continue running the CIA and Dean James Landis to prepare a study of the regulatory agencies. Eventually, JFK made Landis a Special Assistant

* By law the SEC Commissioners were empowered to elect one of their number as chairman. By naming Kennedy to the longest term (five years) Roosevelt had indicated his preference.

to the President and the chatter around town was that Landis might be appointed to the Supreme Court.

Justice Frankfurter, who heard a rumor that Robert Kennedy took Justice Douglas to lunch after JFK was elected and offered him the Ambassadorship to India as a means of getting one friend off the court to make room for another—Jim Landis—sent word to Joe Kennedy that *he* was preparing to get off the court for health reasons anyway, and if he had anything to say about his successor he no longer had any objections to Landis. At the time Landis remarked somewhat cryptically to a colleague that he was not interested in a Supreme Court appointment because he didn't want to subject himself to a confirmation hearing.

In other words, by the spring of 1961 Dean James Landis, who incidentally was a trustee of the fund Joe Kennedy had set up for the Kennedy children, was a virtual member of the immediate family. His relationship to the Kennedys could not have been closer.

In addition to heading the regulatory agencies' task force, Landis was deputized to work out and negotiate an airline agreement with the Russians at about the time when another White House aide, Frank Reeves, the Negro National Committeeman from the District of Columbia, was discovered to be in arrears on his taxes. It was a great embarrassment for the President, who then ordered routine *post hoc* FBI checks on all White House staffers, regardless of status or rank, including Special Assistant James Landis.

Shortly thereafter, Justin Feldman, a partner in the firm of Landis, Feldman and Reilly, received a call from old Joe Kennedy. Feldman was a young, liberal New York politician who had been the middle man in getting Franklin D. Roosevelt, Jr., to campaign in the Virginia primary for JFK. He knew Joseph Kennedy but remembers being somewhat taken aback by the peremptory nature of the conversation which ensued. It went more or less as follows:

KENNEDY: Who does your law firm's tax returns?

FELDMAN: We have an accountant.

KENNEDY: Yeah, but who is he?

FELDMAN: If you must know he's been recommended to us by Tom Walsh [the in-house accountant for the Kennedy interests].

KENNEDY: Who prepares the partners' tax returns?

FELDMAN: Some of us do our own. He does some.

KENNEDY: Who prepared Jim's?

FELDMAN: He does his own.

KENNEDY: Are you sure?

FELDMAN: I'm reasonably sure because one night he took home a bunch of papers and said he was working on taxes.

KENNEDY: Is it conceivable that Jim hasn't filed any tax returns for five years?

FELDMAN: Hardly.

KENNEDY: I picked up a rumor. Would his secretary know? Would she have copies?

FELDMAN: I'll check.

KENNEDY: Do you know where Jim is? I tried to reach him in D.C. and he's not at the White House. I'll try to reach him and you try to find his tax returns.

A half hour later Joe Kennedy called Justin Feldman and said, "Tell the secretary to stop looking. He hasn't filed them. I got him off a platform in Pittsburgh, told him to go see Bobby and then to get his ass back to New York. I told him I want those goddam tax returns filed and those taxes paid as soon as possible. You get his secretary and records and him."

Landis came back to New York the next day, and the Kennedy accountant was inundated with documents. It took several weeks to prepare the returns, in the course of which Landis' strange story came out. It explained, among other things, a discrepancy Feldman thought he had noticed earlier in the year when one of Landis' bank statements crossed his desk and showed a balance of close to $80,000 in his checking account. When Feldman asked about it and suggested that he not keep such large amounts in a checking account, Landis had said, "Oh, no. I need it for something." It now turned out that what he needed it for was taxes—which he hadn't paid, but intended to pay any day, perversely postponing it in the crush of other work, but every year for the past five years setting aside the additional tax monies.

The story: In the mid-Fifties James Landis' daughter and her husband both contracted paralytic polio. He brought them to New York and put them in the Rusk Institute for rehabilitation. He needed money, so he sold some stock which he had inherited from his mother in the 1920s. The total value of the stock was $3,700. When he went to file his return he found he didn't know the cost basis of the stock, so instead of making up a number or putting zero, he obtained a ninety-day extension and wrote to the Boston attorney who had represented his mother and who told him *she* had inherited it from his father—so Landis applied for a second extension.

He got jammed up that summer and just didn't apply for the next extension. The following year he prepared a new return, but one of the questions on the return form is always: Did you file a return for last year? He wasn't going to say yes and he was afraid to say no. So he put the return aside and repeated the procedure every year through 1960, always computing how much it was going to be and putting the money aside in his checking account.

Apparently, the way Joseph Kennedy found out was that in the course of the security check started after the Frank Reeves incident, the FBI asked IRS for Landis' tax records. IRS couldn't find them, and Kenneth Moe, the district director in charge of the New York office, instead of going through channels and informing the Assistant IRS Regional Commissioner for Intelligence, who would then have informed the Regional Commissioner, who would then have informed Washington, called a friend in the office of Joseph P. Kennedy. Thinking this a way to do the Kennedys a favor and maybe do himself a favor at the same time, Mr. Moe, who had been with the IRS office in New York since 1923 and knew everybody in town, capitalized on his contacts and got word to Joe Kennedy's tax expert and adviser, Tom Walsh, who in turn got word to Joe Kennedy.

Landis, as instructed by old Joe, saw the Attorney General, who already knew about the story from his father. The Attorney General called Mortimer Caplin, the Commissioner of Internal Revenue, told Caplin that Landis had a problem and said he didn't know if anything could be done, but would Caplin see Landis? Caplin saw Landis, told him to get his returns filed as soon as possible and "we'll see what happens."

Landis had the money to pay the back taxes and interest, which he had figured on, but not the penalties, which he hadn't. He liquidated every asset he had, and Joseph Kennedy lent him the additional money. Since Landis had been performing legal services for the Kennedys for years without billing them, the "loan" might even have been construed as payment for services rendered. In any event, on June 9, 1961, Landis filed a delinquent return for each of the years in question and paid $48,347.02.*

The returns were filed directly with Mr. Moe, at his request, rather than with a clerk. On his own, Mr. Moe accepted the return as a "voluntary" late filing. He didn't flag it in any way for Washington, although following their previous conversation Landis told Caplin it was filed. Whether or not the filing was "voluntary" was, of course, the key legal issue. As Howard T. Taylor, Regional Commissioner of IRS

* And on September 10, 1962, he filed further amended returns for the years involved and paid an additional sum of $46,145.23.

at the time, explains government policy, "Disclosure would be voluntary if it were made before the IRS began any investigation, and that would forestall prosecution. However, if the IRS has already begun an investigation and you then file delinquent returns, it is not thought to be voluntary."

The files on the Landis case are not open for public inspection, and nobody who was in government at the time is willing to talk, so what happened next is difficult to uncover. But shortly thereafter, IRS began an internal inquiry of Moe as to whether the return had been voluntarily filed, when it had been filed and how it was filed. Whether this inquiry was on the initiative of Commissioner Caplin or as the result of IRS's "routine cooperation with New York state officials," who also were unable to come up with Landis' tax forms and had referred this fact to IRS's Intelligence Division, is unknown. Probably both agencies were involved, since once New York State got into the act with Rockefeller as Governor and potential Republican Presidential candidate, the assumption of a national Democratic Administration had to be that he would have access to and could expose any cover-up.

For whatever reason, the inquiry got under way. Landis submitted his resignation but President Kennedy wouldn't accept it. (According to one theory the President agreed to accept it in September 1961 only because Landis was named as corespondent in divorce proceedings by his secretary's husband. At the time, nobody was in a position to say that actually he had resigned three months earlier.) Moe was asked about why and whether he handled the Landis filing outside of channels. As far as can be determined, no disciplinary action was ever taken against him nor did he ever receive any award. He died at the age of sixty-five a few months later.

Meanwhile a special agent in the Intelligence Division of IRS was put on the case, and as Justin Feldman recalls, "Those returns were gone over in the most unbelievable way. Every check he had or received was examined. Clients received questionnaires. It got to such refinements as to whether he had paid fair market value for a Cadillac." During the course of the investigation, Landis was called down to the Regional Counsel's office where IRS officials were supposed to make the determination as to whether the delinquent return had indeed been filed voluntarily. Landis went down to testify, and on his return he said to his law partner Feldman, "I think I've done a very stupid thing." To the question of why did he file when he filed, Landis, incapable of taking the Fifth Amendment, incapable of fudging, incapable of lying, had said: "Joe Kennedy told me to get my ass back to New York and get those returns filed immediately."

Asked what he did after he was notified about the Landis case, Regional Commissioner Howard Taylor says, "I immediately called the Regional Commissioner in Washington . . . and then the case was turned over to Intelligence, and the regular procedures for such a case went into operation."

Instead of making a finding on the "voluntary" issue one way or the other, Commissioner Caplin is said to have sent a memorandum to the Justice Department declining to make a determination. Technically, this is known as a criminal reference report, a copy of which went to Robert Morgenthau's office as the U.S. Attorney under whose jurisdiction the case fell. But in view of the involvement of the President's father and the peculiar position he occupied vis-à-vis the government and the taxpayer, and in view of Mr. Moe's involvement, Caplin wanted the Justice Department to make the determination. He must have had *some* conversations with the Attorney General about it because he concedes that "When I told Bob it looks like we're going to recommend prosecution, he was really disturbed." Today, neither Caplin nor his aides will say *what* he formally recommended, but one associate of Kennedy says, "I think Bob would have been less angry with Caplin had he found it to be *in*voluntary and referred it to the Department for prosecution. He probably hoped Caplin would find that it was voluntary —although he was never going to ask him to or tell him to."

Kennedy raved and ranted about Landis' stupidity in going down to the Regional Counsel's office without a lawyer but what was done was done. Once in the Justice Department, the case was automatically referred to the Tax Division, where Lou Oberdorfer, the Tax Chief, disqualified *him*self on the ground that when he was appointed Robert Kennedy had sent him to Landis for advice in advance of his confirmation hearing on how to avoid and handle a potential conflict-of-interest situation. Oberdorfer said that since Landis never charged him a fee, it could be said that Oberdorfer owed a debt to Landis, who had acted as his personal attorney; ergo, a conflict of interest.

So the Attorney General had disqualified himself, the Commissioner of Internal Revenue had declined to make a recommendation, and the head of the Tax Division had disqualified himself. And the disqualifications were real. "I wouldn't have accepted Bob's comment [on Landis] and he wouldn't have given it to me—I wanted a *real* record showing that he didn't have anything to do with it," says Nicholas Katzenbach, then Deputy Attorney General, who made the decision to go ahead and prosecute. But first, with Oberdorfer's permission, he got a bright young attorney in the Tax Division—a man who subsequently joined the Harvard Law faculty—and asked him to write a memo with the best possible arguments "that we should *not* prosecute." Says Katzenbach, "That's not the only case in which we did something like that, but I felt in conscience that I had to do it. Then we read the memo and we just couldn't buy his arguments."

Justin Feldman, loyal to Landis till the end, thought the decision to prosecute arose in part because "It was already 1963 and the Kennedys were very uptight about the 1964 election. They were very embarrassed by the Caplin memo. They were concerned that Senator John Williams [Republican, Delaware] would get hold of it and that it would become a campaign issue in 1964—if there was no prosecution Williams would charge that Justice killed it." After the fact, Kennedy told Feldman, "That sonofabitch Caplin left us no alternative."

By this time it was the summer of 1963, and Landis, who had retained Dean William C. Warren of the Columbia Law School as defense counsel, had started to fall apart. He underwent treatment his friends thought was neurological at the Columbia Presbyterian Hospital. The case was forwarded to Morgenthau for prosecution. Feldman, who had served as Morgenthau's campaign manager in his abortive try for the Governorship the previous year, approached Morgenthau even as Dean Warren approached Mortimer Caplin, each with the same argument. Landis was a psychological wreck, and they didn't see how he could survive a prosecution, mentally or physically. They added that in view of new evidence as to his mental condition, perhaps the question of "voluntariness' could be reviewed. Then it turned out that Dean Landis had been undergoing psychiatric treatment intermittently since 1945.

As Katzenbach suggests, "Obviously it was psychological. He wasn't trying to cheat, he just didn't pay. It's always true that the guys that cheat pay. They are the crooks; it's just that they try to cover up what they really owe. The guys that don't pay at all are the psychological cases." But the government took the position, as Morgenthau puts it, that "The courts rather than the prosecutor determine the relevance of psychiatric problems to committed crimes. The government can't make a decision on a psychiatrist's report which you can't cross-examine." In addition, as Morgenthau's office saw it, the early irregularity in the handling of the case deprived his office of any pre-existing discretion they might have had not to proceed. "But we would have gone ahead anyway," he adds. The fiercely independent Morgenthau, U.S. attorney from the traditionally autonomous Southern

District, was perhaps the country's leading prosecutor of white-collar crime. He was to indict, among others, J. Truman Bidwell, chairman of the Board of Governors of the New York Stock Exchange, Carmine De Sapio, former Tammany Hall chief, and James Marcus, Water Commissioner in the Lindsay administration. He was engaged in a campaign to clean up and rout out corruption in the IRS, and anything that smelled at all like a fix would, he felt, undermine these efforts. In fact IRS investigations accounted for 64 percent (1,214) of the Justice Department's convictions in Kennedy's organized-crime program.

When the government's firm intention to prosecute seemed clear, Feldman raised the possibility of Landis pleading not guilty on the question of "willfulness." Feldman's argument anticipated a point raised by the judge at the trial when he said: "Now if [Landis] at all times intended to file his returns and if because of incidents that occurred in his life, due to human weaknesses . . . he omitted to file the returns, he is not guilty of a crime. He is charged here with willfully and knowingly failing to file these returns for those years . . . to say that he at all times intended to file the return is substantially telling me that this defendant has pleaded guilty to a charge of which he is entirely innocent." In other words, if he had intended to file (as his separate bank account and already-made-out returns suggested he did) but did not because of psychological or other problems, then he was not guilty. Katzenbach came to New York in July to discuss the issue with Dean Warren in Morgenthau's office and subsequently with Feldman in the Feldman–Landis office. When Feldman advanced this theory, Katzenbach argued strongly that Landis should plead guilty. Feldman felt that Landis had a good chance of getting off. When Katzenbach saw he wasn't making headway with Feldman he said, "You ask Jim whether he is prepared to go to trial on this basis—and thereby prove in open court that the fellow who was on the President's staff, the fellow on whose recommendation the President has reorganized eight administrative agencies, is psychiatrically incompetent."

Feldman said, "Nick, that's unfair." Katzenbach said, "That's where it's at," and added, "I think you're talking to yourself, Justin. I don't think you're talking to Jim. I don't think you're entitled to make this decision for him." Feldman tried again suggesting another alternative. Since what Landis was charged with was a misdemeanor, the U.S. attorney had the option of charging Landis on a prosecutor's information, as he planned to do, or he could bring the matter before a grand jury. Said Feldman, "If you take the grand-jury route, I can send him and a psychiatrist in there [the grand jury] and if they recommend *no* indictment, then we're all off the hook." Katzenbach said no because "It would *have* to come out that one of the considerations is psychiatric." Katzenbach then outlined what the government proposed to do. Suggesting that the whole thing could be done with a minimum of publicity, he said the government had control of the timing—and thereby of the calendar and of what judge it went before. He said if Landis pleaded guilty in early August, then the case could be brought on August 30, the Friday before Labor Day, perhaps before an ambitious Kennedy-appointed judge looking to go on the Court of Appeals. Judge Wilfred Feinberg, who had been Feldman's college classmate, was one obvious candidate. He said the government would take the position that the money is paid, Landis is obviously a dedicated servant with a distinguished career, and it would end up in a suspended sentence and a fine.

At this point, Feldman brought in Dean Landis, who had been waiting in his own office. Landis listened to the arguments and said, "I've embarrassed the Administration enough. Nick's quite right. One thing [Landis' reorganization plan] has nothing to do with the other [Landis' mental health] but the press won't buy that. I think the reorganization plan * is sound and I don't want to jeopardize it. So I put myself in Nick's hands." Feldman recalls: "We agreed on the timetable, the sentencing and the judge, Wilfred Feinberg." He was indicted on information and pleaded guilty on August 2, 1963.

On Friday, August 30, nothing went quite as planned. First, the story was *not* buried in Labor Day holiday statistics but became and stayed front-page news. Second, a number of potentially sympathetic judges became unavailable, including Judge Feinberg, who went to Chief Judge Sylvester Ryan, said that he and Feldman had been classmates and friends and thought *he* should be disqualified. Judge Ryan said, "Well, you're a young judge with a career ahead. I'm senior judge and ready to retire. Let me take the sentencing." Third, a technicality, but it turned out, according to IRS, that Landis owed more than he had paid. Finally, Judge Ryan, instead of handing down the expected fine and suspended sentence, suspended only part of the sentence, put Landis on a year's parole, but also sentenced him to a term of thirty days' confinement. "My purpose," he said, "would be to give you a time for reflection, not so much by way of punishment, so that you may perhaps appraise yourself in quietness and perhaps make some

---

* "Report on Regulatory Agencies to the President-Elect," printed for use of the Senate Committee on the Judiciary, 86th Congress, 2nd Session, 1960.

resolutions that would strengthen your will to carry you on in the future to a useful life."

Morgenthau, whose office, in accordance with practice dating back to 1953, had made no sentencing recommendation, was livid. He called Feldman with the bad news and both agreed that the unexpected sentence "made no sense in terms of rehabilitation, punitive justice, deterrence, tax law or any theory you can think of. This was not a fraud case—it was not a wheeling-and-dealing case."

On inquiry, Morgenthau told Feldman that on a thirty-day sentence Landis would be sent to the West Street jail for processing and "on this short a sentence they'll probably have him serve it out at West Street." Feldman asked Morgenthau to please hold him in the Marshal's office while he and Edward Costikyan, a fellow lawyer who was in the office, former County Leader of the New York Democratic Party and a partner in the leading New York law firm of Paul, Weiss, Rifkind, Wharton & Garrison, researched the law to see what could be done. Costikyan found a provision in the code which stated that with prior medical certification, on a finding of the Attorney General the Director of the Bureau of Prisons could rule that if prison facilities were inadequate to a convict's medical needs, he could be moved to a private hospital. Landis' doctor said he was prepared to make the appropriate medical representations—that Landis needed the neurological treatment facilities he had been enjoying at the Columbia Presbyterian Hospital. After much telephoning back and forth, during which Feldman traced the Attorney General to a fishing boat off the coast of Maine, Robert Kennedy sent word making the appropriate finding, but the Director of the Bureau of Prisons, James V. Bennett, felt that Columbia Presbyterian was a bit much and instead he ordered Landis to the Public Health Service Center on Staten Island.

Because of the medical certification, Landis was treated as a potential suicide. A weekend on Staten Island drove his wife Dorothy to distraction. "You've got to get Jim out of there," she told anyone who would care to listen. "He's got to get to Columbia Presbyterian, where his doctor can treat him. They took his belt and tie away and wouldn't let him have cigarettes—he's a chain smoker. He is in a public ward. They won't give him a razor, and he isn't getting any medical care."

Kennedy was due back from his fishing trip on Tuesday morning and Landis' law partner, Justin Feldman, arranged with Kennedy's secretary, Angie Novello, to be first on his appointment list. "By that time," recalls Feldman, "I had a legal memo in support of the Attorney

General's authority to send Landis to Columbia Presbyterian. The Bureau of Prisons would provide guards and since it's at our request, we'd pay the excess per diem over what the law provided." Feldman arrived at 8:30 A.M. and told Kennedy, who had not been fully briefed, the whole story.

He explained to Kennedy that he had researched the statute and was persuaded that the Attorney General had the *legal* authority to do what Feldman was asking him to do. "Have you talked to Nick?" Kennedy asked. "Yes," Feldman replied, "and he doesn't want to do it." "On legal grounds?" asked Kennedy. "He didn't mention legal grounds," said Feldman. "Have you talked to Morgenthau?" asked Kennedy. "He says it's up to you," said Feldman.

The Attorney General pushed a button and got his Deputy on the line and said, "Justin's in my office and he tells me, among other things, that Dorothy is going crazy, that we have the authority to transfer Jim to Columbia Presbyterian to serve his sentence up there under guard, that he's got the appropriate documents and that you've turned him down."

"That's right," said Katzenbach.

"On legal grounds?" asked the Attorney General.

"No," said Katzenbach, "I think you do have the authority. I think Justin's right."

"Then why didn't we do it?"

Katzenbach: "Because I think it would look terrible for you to intervene so that a close friend of the Kennedy family serves his prison sentence in the Harkness Pavilion, which is a plush, luxury—"

"Is that all you're concerned with," Kennedy interrupted, "the way the press will handle it?"

Katzenbach: "Yes."

Kennedy: "Well, as far as I'm concerned if the press wants to say that after prosecuting, in what I consider questionable circumstances, the best friend the Kennedys ever had, that the Administration has now shown a little humanity, I'm prepared to take that and I think the President will be, too. I'm sending Justin downstairs. You make the arrangements with Morgenthau for the transfer."

The code of the Kennedys was profoundly entangled with James Landis' fate. His tax delinquency was discovered because he was on the Kennedy White House staff. It was brought to old Joe's attention because the District Director of the IRS shared the nation's image of the clannish, behind-the-scenes way the Kennedys do business. The case proceeded through channels partly because the Kennedys had officially disqualified themselves, partly because it was *not* part of the Kennedy way of doing business for Robert to tell his old University of Virginia tax professor, Mortimer Caplin, to get him off the hook at the expense of the integrity of the tax code, partly because Kennedy loyalists didn't want the Kennedy Administration vulnerable to charges of fix. Landis pleaded guilty so as not to embarrass the Kennedys, despite evidence that a not-guilty plea might have been sustained. He was sentenced to confinement, seldom the case in failure-to-file convictions, undoubtedly in part as a tribute to his importance as a member of the Kennedy family.

Obviously this was not simply a case of personal loyalties in conflict with official obligations. The Kennedy factor aside, an impartial Administration might have decided to prosecute for the reasons Nicholas Katzenbach spelled out in a letter on Landis' behalf to the judge presiding at the Landis disbarment proceedings in January 1964 (Landis was disbarred for a year and drowned before it was out):

> The decision whether to prosecute was a difficult one. The tax burden borne voluntarily by the overwhelming majority of citizens is a heavy one. And Congress has specified that any willful failure to file a tax return is a misdemeanor, even in the absence of an intent to evade taxes. Any indication that people of prominence are somehow subjected to lesser duties would completely undermine the self-assessment system. At the same time, the isolated nature of the infraction, its unique origin, and Mr. Landis' complete cooperation and candor with the Government officials are the kind of factors which must always be weighed in a decision to institute criminal prosecution. Here perhaps Mr. Landis' public contribution weighed against him. If it were decided not to prosecute and his failure to file came to the public eye (as it certainly would), he would face not only the obloquy of income tax delinquency but also the charge, albeit completely unjustified, that he had somehow used his position and connections to escape prosecution. Thus it was only after intensive consideration that the Department decided that prosecution would have to be undertaken.

Or an impartial Administration might have concluded that neither the immediate goals of the tax code (revenue collection, uniformity of the law, voluntary compliance) nor the long-range integrity of the system would be furthered by the prosecution of a former Dean of the Harvard Law School with apparent psychological problems, who had avoided rather than evaded his taxes, already suffered a cruel and unusual amount of punishment-by-publicity, paid his taxes, interest and penalties and was a true penitent.

Robert Kennedy's administration of the Justice Department, however, was not impartial. He did what he had to do, trying to take account of, rather than ignore, some painful and conflicting obligations. He too sent a letter to the judge in January of 1964 asking that James Landis be allowed "to continue in the practice of his profession" and restating his friendship with, respect for and belief in Landis, his integrity and legal ability. And then, in one of those handwritten pen squiggles that were his hallmark, he added, "I hope you will be kind to him. Bob Kennedy."

A prosecutor's discretion is one of the great uncharted areas of the law. Of Robert Kennedy it can be said that with the possible exception of Hoffa and the Teamsters, discussed in the next chapter, he did not abuse that discretion by using the law as a weapon to punish political enemies. In the marginal cases, however, the code of the Kennedys asserted itself. Katzenbach recalls how Kennedy vacillated before authorizing the indictment of Ralph Ginzburg, publisher of *Eros*, "a magazine devoted to the joys of love and sex," and other publications judged to be obscene before the current wave of hard-core pornography invaded the market. "Bob felt, 'I ought to prosecute him but it will hurt politically. They will blame it on my Catholicism.'" Then Ginzburg came along with an issue portraying interracial love and sex, which he promoted all over the South at the height of the country's racial tension in the aftermath of the integration of Ole Miss. Katzenbach says, "He was terribly offended but terribly reluctant. I said I think it's a clear-cut case and you ought to do it. Ginzburg was saying if you don't prosecute me this time I'll force you to prosecute me next time. But he wasn't vindictive. He was always distressed when the verdict came down." Ultimately Kennedy puritanism triumphed over Kennedy politics, and Ginzburg was indicted.

A common denominator of the Keogh, Chacharis and Landis cases, which all involved friends and allies, is that once the decision was made to prosecute, in each case the tendency was to act in a way that would be least embarrassing to the President. You don't lose cases against close and important friends of the Administration. You don't prosecute and perhaps convict the Republican City Council members in Gary after the Democrats have been let off. You don't plead insanity on behalf of a man whose report recommending the overhaul of the regulatory agencies has been accepted by the President, although you may show a little mercy after the punishment has been meted out. Also, one must not forget that Kennedy had attracted to Justice a host of young men imbued with the Kennedy ethic. The followers may have guaranteed the conscience of their leader.

CHAPTER NINE

Civil Liberties:
Hoffa and the General

IN JUNE OF 1942 four German saboteurs, clad in Marine fatigues, landed on Amagansett Beach, Long Island, in a rubber boat dropped under cover of night by U-boat No. 202, the *Innsbruck*. Four days later four more saboteurs were deposited on a beach twenty-five miles south of Jacksonville, Florida. Ten days after the landing J. Edgar Hoover interrupted Attorney General and Mrs. Francis Biddle's dinner with the Yugoslav Ambassador and his wife to report that the last of the saboteurs had been caught.*

Three days thereafter, President Roosevelt dispatched a confidential memorandum to the Attorney General which stated, in part:

> I have not had an opportunity to talk with you about the prosecution of the eight saboteurs . . . nor have I recently read all the statutes which apply.
> It is my thought, however:
> 1. That the two American citizens † are guilty of high treason. This being war-time, it is my inclination to try them by court martial. I do not see how they can offer any adequate defense. Surely they are as

---

* Although the FBI got great and deserved credit, what actually happened was that one of the saboteurs had turned himself and the others in.
† Two of the eight saboteurs were American citizens.

guilty as it is possible to be and it seems to me that the death penalty is almost obligatory.

2. In the case of the other six who, I take it, are German citizens, I understand that they came over in submarines wearing seamen's clothes—in all probability German Naval clothes—and that some of them at least landed on our shores wearing these German Naval clothes. I think it can be proved that they formed a part of the German Military or Naval Service. They were apprehended in civilian clothes. This is an absolute parallel of the case of Major Andre in the Revolution and of Nathan Hale. Both of them were hanged. Here again it is my inclination that they be tried by court martial as were Andre and Hale. Without splitting hairs I can see no difference. . . .

Roosevelt followed up this memorandum with a private conversation in which he told the Attorney General (according to Biddle's memoirs, *In Brief Authority*), "I want one thing clearly understood, Francis: I won't give them up. . . . I won't hand them over to any United States marshal armed with a writ of *habeas corpus*. Understand?"

Biddle understood well. For although it had not been mentioned, between the President's desire and its execution stood the troublesome precedent of *Ex Parte Milligan*, decided by the Supreme Court in 1866, after Lincoln had approved the arrest of thousands of civilians without warrant on suspicion of disloyalty during the Civil War. Reacting against such dubious procedures, in 1863 Congress provided that if these people were not indicted by grand juries, they should be discharged.

Milligan had been arrested by the military in Indiana, found guilty of aiding the rebels and inciting insurrection and had been sentenced by the military—with the approval of President Lincoln—to death. Since the grand jury had not indicted him (in accordance with the 1863 statute) Milligan petitioned the court for his discharge. The U.S. Supreme Court decided unanimously that Milligan should have been released, and five Justices went further, stating that no civilian could ever be tried by a military commission as long as civil courts were open and properly functioning.

Biddle understood that the Attorney General was under "a very special obligation to obey the law" but, like President Roosevelt, he wanted to have the saboteurs executed. "I urged the President," he wrote, "to appoint me prosecuting official before the military commission. . . . 'We have to win in the Supreme Court, or there will be a hell of a mess,' I said. 'You're damned right there will be, Mr. Attorney General,' replied FDR, grinning back at me, and told me to see Stimson. The Secretary of War did not like it, it was most irregular, it had never been done before—a civilian prosecuting for the Army. But he knew how eager I was to try the case myself and smiled and said, 'Talk to Cramer [the Judge Advocate].' As it turned out the Judge Advocate . . . was relieved not to have to take charge . . . and we sat most amicably together in trial and argument. He was unwilling to take any active part in either."

Biddle rationalized away *Milligan* primarily on the grounds that even the American citizen-saboteurs were not civilians but soldiers. Except for two who turned state's evidence, the saboteurs were convicted and executed within a month.

Twenty years later, Professor Arthur Miller of the George Washington Law Center expressed some retrospective reservations. The case was not that easy, he said. "It has disturbing aftertones. One of them . . . [concerns] the relationship of the Attorney General to the President. The President was determined to have the would-be saboteurs executed. . . . [Biddle] was equally determined to find a way to accomplish that end. . . . Granted, there are certain actions which must be taken by any head of government during time of war. . . . But should these actions be clothed in the familiar garb of legality to which we are accustomed during time of peace? Does this not put law and the legal process, including the federal courts, deeply into politics and thus tend to negate the very idea of law?"

Professor Miller's vocabulary is perhaps unfortunate, since the issue is not that "politics" inevitably subverts law and that therefore the two should go their separate ways. Obviously, politics is on occasion indispensable to making law effective. What concerned Miller is that in time of war, law may be put in the service of politics, results may determine process, law may be used as a political weapon—especially where the Attorney General enjoys a "relationship to the President" that eliminates the sort of checks and balances within the executive branch that function to restrain executive exuberance.

Under the Kennedys, who enjoyed precisely that sort of relationship, the U.S. government considered itself at war with Jimmy Hoffa and the Teamsters. They regarded him as a potential saboteur who had the power, at any moment, to bring the nation to a halt. All of the conditions for the abuse of process identified by Professor Miller were present. Hoffa and the Teamsters, of course, claim that the Attorney General was guilty of such abuse—mobilizing the law to carry on a personal vendetta, persecuting through prosecuting.

Professor Monroe Freedman, in a discussion of "Prosecutorial Ethics" in the *Georgetown Law Journal*, articulated the argument when he wrote:

From the day that James Hoffa told Robert Kennedy that he was nothing but a rich man's kid who never had to earn a nickel in his life, Hoffa was a marked man. When Kennedy became Attorney General, satisfying this grudge became the public policy of the United States, and Hoffa, along with Roy Cohn and perhaps other enemies from Kennedy's past, was singled out for special attention by United States Attorneys. This is, of course, the very antithesis of the rule of law, and serves to bring into sharp focus the ethical obligation of the prosecutor to refrain from abusing his power by prosecutions that are directed at individuals rather than at crimes.[1]

Kennedy's defenders stoutly deny the charge. As Jacob Tanzer, a young member of the Organized Crime Section during the Kennedy years, wrote to *The New Republic* criticizing Gerald W. Johnson for referring to "the use of highly questionable means to secure the conviction of James Hoffa":

> Hoffa was furnished millions of dollars by his union with which he hired the most capable lawyers and investigators available to him. Through their efforts, every facet of the case against Hoffa has been fully reviewed in the courts. In the age of Escobedo, Miranda and Wade, the courts are sufficiently sensitive to governmental impropriety in criminal investigation, yet they found that the only wrongdoing was on the part of Hoffa, the perpetrator of corrupt crimes, rather than Kennedy.[2]

Or, as Adam Yarmolinsky put it in *The New York Review of Books* when answering Hans Morgenthau's reference to Kennedy's alleged persecution: ". . . his prosecution of Hoffa was vigorous, as it needed to be, but also fair, as is demonstrated by two affirmations of Hoffa's conviction in the U.S. Supreme Court." [3]

What Kennedy and the Justice Department under him did and didn't do vis-à-vis Hoffa is worth looking at in some detail, if only because it is the primary source of so much of the Kennedy-as-ruthless-prosecutor legend which has partly clung to him in death as it dogged him in life. But also because the Get-Hoffa drive is a clue to his moral universe, it illuminates the relationship of morality to policy and policy to action, it was intimately involved with the code of the Kennedys, it tells us something about his image of justice, and, along with the ransom of the Cuban Bay of Pigs prisoners and the passage of the 1964 Civil Rights Bill, it was among his most successful undertakings as Attorney General. When the Hoffa unit Kennedy founded was dispersed after four years, it had accounted for the conviction of Hoffa in two major trials—jury fixing in Chattanooga, Tennessee, and conviction in Chicago for fraud in connection with Teamster Pension Fund loans totaling more than $20 million. In addition there were federal indictments returned against 100 Teamster Union officials and 90 persons identified as close business or personal associates of the Teamsters. Of these 190 indictments the Justice Department had obtained 115 convictions by the time Kennedy left. By any standard Kennedy's anti-Hoffa campaign, if that's what it was, represented an extraordinary administrative accomplishment. Finally, and most important, it touched on the profoundest questions of prosecutor's discretion. For every citizen is the potential victim of an Attorney General's arbitrary discretion. Thus the question of his standards for its exercise becomes critical. The risk to the nation in such situations was well defined by Attorney General Robert Jackson in April 1940 when he told the Second Annual Conference of U.S. Attorneys:

> [The most dangerous power of the prosecutor is] that he will pick people he thinks he should get rather than pick cases that need to be prosecuted. With the law books filled with a great assortment of crimes, a prosecutor stands a fair chance of pinning at least a technical violation of some act on the part of almost anyone. In such a case it is not a question of discovering the commission of a crime and then looking for the man who has committed it, it is a question of picking the man and then searching the law books or putting investigators to work, to pin some offense on him. . . . It is here that law enforcement becomes personal, and the real crime becomes that of being unpopular with the predominant or governing group, being attached to the wrong political views, or being personally obnoxious to or in the way of the prosecutor himself.

Let us first look, then, for background in the pre-1961 history of Kennedy–Hoffa, with an eye toward identifying the "subjective" (if any) and the "objective" (if any) reasons for the various anti-Hoffa lawsuits and other activities; second, let us look at the nature of Kennedy's anti-Hoffa campaign, the establishment of Walter Sheridan's "Get-Hoffa" Squad, its *modus operandi* vis-à-vis Hoffa and the Teamsters, vis-à-vis Kennedy, vis-à-vis the Justice Department and vis-à-vis the FBI. Only then can we begin to identify the excesses of which Kennedy & Co. may have been guilty and to make some judgments about Kennedy's motives, the actions of the Justice Department under his direction and the impact of the Hoffa drive on law enforcement.

The history of the RFK–Hoffa relationship is available, among other places, in Kennedy's book *The Enemy Within*, in Hoffa's book *The Trials of Jimmy Hoffa*, in Clark Mollenhoff's book *The Tentacles of Power*, and in a seven-part 1959 *Saturday Evening Post* series by John

Bartlow Martin; it needs no retelling here except insofar as it is relevant to what came later.

First, and probably foremost, is the fact that as a result of the McClellan Committee investigation he ran (1957–59), Robert Kennedy came to regard Hoffa and the Teamsters as a conspiracy of evil and to believe that they had engaged in law-breaking, corruption, extortion, thuggery and murder, yet somehow managed to undermine the judicial process and elude effective prosecution. He heard testimony and came to believe that Hoffa associated with the gangster element. Among his associates: Paul (Red) Dorfman, formerly of the Capone mob, who assumed control of a Chicago waste-handlers local after the murder of its former president; Johnny Dioguardi, New York labor racketeer, who arranged for Bernard Spindell to wire the Teamster building so that Hoffa could listen in on private conversations; Tony "Ducks" Corallo, who joined with Dioguardi and Hoffa to set up seven "paper" Teamster locals in New York that enabled them to gain control of the Teamsters Joint Council, which had jurisdiction over the trucking industry in the New York area; Jerry Connelly, convicted of extortion and dynamiting, whom Hoffa helped raise $54,000 for lawyers' fees; Joey Glimco, friend of the Capone mob, who operated as trustee of Chicago Teamsters' Taxi Local 777; Sam (Shorty) Feldman, convicted safecracker, robber and burglar, whom Hoffa helped get a charter in the Hotel and Restaurant Workers Union, and later served as business agent for Philadelphia Teamsters Local 929; Frank and Herman Kierdorf, cousins whom Hoffa hired as business agents (Frank eventually suffered a flaming death while committing arson); Frank Matula, convicted perjurer and treasurer of Los Angeles Teamster Local 386, and many others.

He heard testimony and came to believe that Hoffa personally profited from and misused union funds through a variety of deceptive devices, the most common of which was borrowing from people who secured Teamster loans which Hoffa had the most to say about approving. He borrowed $25,000 from a former Teamster business agent who was promoting the Sun Valley Project in Florida, which was financed with the help of the Teamster treasury; he borrowed $4,000 from a Teamster accountant who had borrowed $75,000 in Teamster funds to finance a construction company; he borrowed $25,000 from a man in May of 1956, exactly one week after Hoffa's own Local 299 had loaned the man $25,000. He arranged for the transfer of $300,000 in Teamster funds from a Detroit bank to a Florida bank, which then loaned money for development of the same Sun Valley Project in which Hoffa had an interest. He took in at least $10,000 cash a year, which he listed on his tax form as "collections"—he said it was money he had won on the horses; Kennedy believed it was money received from employers who got favorable treatment on their contracts.

Kennedy heard testimony and came to believe that Ed Chevlin, fifty-year-old former vice president of Teamster Local 838, was telling the truth when he identified Hoffa as one of four men who "beat me up with chains" when he was organizing for the CIO in Detroit. "He was hired by somebody to do a job on me and he did it," testified Chevlin. He came to believe that Hoffa intimidated and/or paid off political figures to pass on evidence given in supposedly secret grand jury hearings; that Hoffa was involved in threatening the lives of witnesses who testified or might testify against him; that when Hoffa was not fixing judges or coercing witnesses he was buying the jury.

In other words, Kennedy believed that bombings, shootings, beatings, bribery, violence and financial manipulation were an integral part of Hoffa's way of doing business. What troubled him even more was that this criminality had infected an institution of unprecedented power— the Teamsters. As he wrote in *The Enemy Within,* essentially a summary of his findings on the McClellan Committee:

> The Teamsters Union is the most powerful institution in this coun-
> try—aside from the United States Government itself. In many major
> metropolitan areas the Teamsters control all transportation. It is a
> Teamster who drives the mother to the hospital at birth. It is the
> Teamster who drives the hearse at death. And between birth and
> burial, the Teamsters drive the trucks that clothe and feed us and
> provide the vital necessities of life. They control the pickup and de-
> liveries of milk, frozen meat, fresh fruit, department store merchan-
> dise, newspapers, railroad express, air freight, and of cargo to and from
> the sea docks.
> Quite literally, your life—the life of every person in the United
> States—is in the hands of Hoffa and his Teamsters.
> But though the great majority of Teamster officials and Teamster
> members are honest, the Teamsters Union under Hoffa is often not
> run as a bona fide union. As Mr. Hoffa operates it, this is a conspiracy
> of evil.[4]

Robert Kennedy was not content to make his case against Hoffa in the report of the McClellan Committee. He took his show on the road, and inevitably it became entangled in Presidential politics. John Kennedy, who had, of course, served on the McClellan Committee and, with Archie Cox at his side, played a major role in crafting the anti-corruption Landrum–Griffin labor reform bill, had himself made public his unhappiness at Hoffa's activities. This resulted in exchanges such as the one which took place when Robert appeared on "Meet the Press" the week before the 1960 election:

Q. Senator Kennedy has been criticized for something he said in one of the debates with reference to Jimmy Hoffa, and that is, he is unhappy because he is still free. I know you directed that investigation and I wonder if you feel the same way about Hoffa?

RFK: I think it is an extremely dangerous situation at the present time, this man who has a background of corruption and dishonesty, has misused hundreds of thousands of dollars of union funds, betrayed the union membership, sold out the membership, put gangsters and racketeers in positions of power, and still heads the Teamsters Union.

Robert Kennedy saw Hoffa not merely as a man who stole from those he was supposed to serve and got away with it, but—and this became critical to the nature of the anti-Hoffa campaign he ultimately mounted —he saw Hoffa and the Teamsters as engaged in a conspiracy against the legal process itself. Kennedy chose the Jack Paar Show to educate the American people to this aspect of the threat when he told Paar:

Oh, I think that they seem to feel, and I think that if you watched the hearings you can see that they feel that they are above the law and the government of the United States—he and his colleagues. There's no question about that. They feel that—that nobody can touch them, that they can fix juries, that they can fix judges, that they can fix members of the legislature. They don't have to worry about this. They have enough money. They have—Mr. Hoffa has said in the past, every man has his price! So they don't worry. . . .

By the time Kennedy became Attorney General his "feud" with Hoffa had become something of a spectator sport. He was Ahab, and Hoffa was his whale. And both Kennedy and Hoffa had contributed to the spectacle. There were, of course, the confrontations in the committee itself, where each tried to outstare the other, where Hoffa confounded Kennedy by refusing to take the Fifth Amendment and consequently provoked exchanges such as the famous colloquy over the Teamster purchase of some pocket-sized miniature tape recorders called Minifons, which Kennedy believed Hoffa had used to bug Teamsters testifying before grand juries to keep them from revealing family secrets:

HOFFA: What did I do with them? Well, what did I do with them?

KENNEDY: What did you do with them?

HOFFA: I am trying to recall.
KENNEDY: You could remember that.
HOFFA: When were they delivered? Do you know? That must
            have been quite a while.
KENNEDY: You know what you did with the Minifons and don't
            ask me.
HOFFA: What did I do with them?
KENNEDY: What did you do with them?
HOFFA: Mr. Kennedy, I bought some Minifons and there is no
            question about it, but I cannot recall what became of
            them. I have to stand on the answers that I have made
            in regards to my recollection and I cannot answer unless
            you give me some recollection other than I have an-
            swered.

Then there was the 1957 Cheasty trial. Hoffa was indicted and tried
for attempting to plant John Cye Cheasty, a New York lawyer, on the
staff of the McClellan Committee, where he would pass on confidential
documents for money. FBI cameras actually recorded the transaction
(with Cheasty's secret cooperation) as Hoffa handed Cheasty $2,000
and Cheasty gave Hoffa a Committee memorandum, and FBI agents
arrested Hoffa the next day with Committee reports on his person.
J. Edgar Hoover, along with twenty-eight special agents, personally
took part in the operation. "If Hoffa isn't convicted," promised
Kennedy, "I'll jump off the Capitol dome." Hoffa was acquitted (see
below), and Edward Bennett Williams, his lawyer, publicly offered to
send Kennedy a parachute.

This was followed by two unsuccessful wiretapping trials in 1958,
where Hoffa and Bernard Spindell, an electronic eavesdropping
specialist, were charged with tapping the wires of his fellow Teamsters.
(Ironically, the government used evidence from its own wiretaps, then
legal in New York, where the cases were tried, to make its case.) The
first trial ended in a hung jury (11 to 1); in the second trial Spindell
and Hoffa were found not guilty.

In addition, Kennedy made it his personal business and that of the
McClellan Committee to do more than "expose" Hoffa. After Dave
Beck was jailed, Kennedy attempted to intervene in the Teamster
elections to Hoffa's disadvantage, and when Hoffa won, Kennedy
succeeded in influencing the Temporary Board of Monitors, which
the court appointed to oversee Teamster affairs.* As labor expert Paul

* A three-man board, appointed by the court but paid for out of union funds.
Its job was to supervise Teamster affairs while the courts decided whether Hoffa's
election as Teamster president had been rigged, as charged.

Jacobs concluded in a damaging-to-Kennedy law-review article on "The Extra Curricular Activities of the McClellan Committee," in both the fight against Hoffa within the Teamsters and in assisting anti-Hoffa representatives on the court-appointed Board of Monitors in their attempt to oust Hoffa, Kennedy went beyond the bounds of propriety. He wrote:

> . . . it seems clear to me that the McClellan Committee's direct involvement in the *Cunningham* vs *English* (361 US 965, 909–10) (1959) law suit, and in the ensuing affairs of the Board of Monitors, went far beyond the committee's specific mandate and the general mandate of congressional committees. The evidence demonstrates to me that the committee and its staff, under Robert Kennedy's direction, trespassed heavily on the rights of Hoffa and the union.[5]

A piece of Washington folklore goes that Kennedy, driving home at midnight after his usual eighteen-hour day, spied the light on in Hoffa's Teamsters office and turned his own car around and went back to work. Kennedy had held two sets of exposing Hoffa hearings, and still Hoffa was elected Teamster president. Now it was the summer of 1958, and Kennedy was planning to call Hoffa back again. He commented at the time: "A lot of people felt we shouldn't have Hoffa back the third time. The members of the committee get tired of Hoffa. Newspapermen, too. But I'm not harrassing him. This is an important thing. The only way to get people to do the job—the courts, the Justice Department, the Congress—is to keep the pressure on. And to keep it on *him*. This is not maybe the purpose of the Congressional committee. But I think he's a very evil influence in the U.S. A tremendous power, and I just think that something has got to be done about it. If no one else is going to do it, we will. And I want Jimmy Hoffa to know we're still in the ball game." [6]

On the brink of the JFK–Nixon Presidential campaign, the public image of the RFK–Hoffa clash was informed and reflected by John Bartlow Martin's conclusion to his seven-part *Post* series. He wrote (August 8, 1959):

> For two and a half years Hoffa and Kennedy have been locked in combat. There is no reconciling their views of each other. Kennedy considers Hoffa wholly "evil," the means by which gangsters will in a few years take over the economy of the U.S. Hoffa says Kennedy is "a spoiled kid," a "parasite" who lives off government and wouldn't know how to run a business. Kennedy earnestly says he intends to make his whole career in government and so long as he does, "I won't be through with Jimmy Hoffa." Hoffa says with no show of concern whatsoever, "If this kid don't get away from this, he'll crack up. . . ."

Kennedy's preoccupation with Hoffa was good copy and even made the Washington women's pages as Maxine Cheshire, the Washington *Post*'s entertaining gossip columnist, wrote about the time Ethel was riding with her children near the capitol and stopped for a red light. She pointed to a building on the hill.

"What's up there?"

"The Teamsters Union," responded four or more little Kennedy voices.

"And what do they do?"

"Work overtime to keep Jimmy Hoffa out of jail!"

"And?" Ethel prompted.

"Which is where he belongs!" was the happy response.

Kennedy and Hoffa had literally argued about who could do more push-ups * and those American people who cared about this sort of thing couldn't wait to find out.

There was the unhappy and unmistakable fact that three times the U.S. government, based on the Rackets Committee hearings, had taken Hoffa to court, and the government record was 0 for 3. It rankled Kennedy, who in 1958 had charged foot-dragging by the Justice Department, which he said had failed to take action on "perjury evidence" before the committee. Malcolm Anderson, Assistant Attorney General in charge of the Criminal Division, countered in a letter which said that over half the cases that Kennedy's committee had referred (eight out of fourteen) had been dropped for "insufficient evidence" and the rest were pending. In his book, Kennedy made further charges:

1) In the Cheasty bribery case, the Justice Department didn't investigate the jurors and therefore didn't learn until after Hoffa's acquittal that several had police records; also, they didn't expect Hoffa to take the stand and thus were unprepared to cross-examine him when he did.

2) At the Hoffa wiretapping trial in New York, the government's case disintegrated when its chief witness testified he met Hoffa in Detroit on a day that Hoffa was able to prove he had been in Seattle. Three weeks before the trial, Kennedy wrote, his staff gave prosecutors details of Hoffa's whereabouts every day for three months—including that day in Seattle. After the trial, said Kennedy, the government attorney "made the astounding admission that he had not read the memo."

As Attorney General, Kennedy meant to "do bettah."

---

* The argument took place in 1957 just before the Cheasty trial. Hoffa said he could do twenty-seven, Kennedy claimed fifty.

Finally, Kennedy lived with the knowledge that he, more than any man in the country, was responsible for Hoffa's being where he was— in the sense that his revelations had toppled Dave Beck, making it possible for Hoffa, whom he considered the greater evil, to take over. When asked how he felt about the fact that if he hadn't gone after Beck first, Hoffa might never have ascended to the Teamster presidency, Kennedy said with a smile, "I feel I have a debt to society."

According to the Organization Chart, the labor and racketeering unit is a subdivision of the Organized Crime Section of the Criminal Division of the U.S. Department of Justice. From 1961–1964 that section was, again according to the Organization Chart, inhabited by a cadre of specially recruited attorneys, like John Cassidy, who had done legal work with Jack Miller for the court-appointed Teamster Monitors. According to normal procedures Cassidy should have reported to his section chief, who should have reported to the head of the Organized Crime Section (Silberling and then Hundley), who should have reported to the head of the Criminal Division (Miller), who should have reported to the Deputy Attorney General (White and then Katzenbach), who in turn reported to the Attorney General.

In fact, John Cassidy, who recalls "It was all very informal. We all did what we had to do and consulted with Walter or Jack," reported to a non-lawyer named Walter Sheridan, who bypassed everybody and reported directly to the Attorney General, although he coordinated with Jack Miller, whom he had known when he worked as an investigator for the McClellan Committee and Miller was lawyer for the anti-Teamster Monitors. Walter Sheridan, a Fordham graduate, had briefly attended Albany Law, served four-years with the FBI, subsequently worked as Chief of the Counterintelligence Section, Special Operations Division, Office of Security, National Security Agency, an intelligence arm of the Defense Department, and then as Assistant Chief of NSA's Clearance Division. A church friend then put him in touch with the Rackets Committee, and "Bob hired me walking up the stairs—which is where we had most of our conversations." In *The Enemy Within* Kennedy says of Sheridan (who worked as Pennsylvania coordinator in the JFK Presidential campaign) that "His almost angelic appearance hides a core of toughness, and he takes great pride in his work. In any kind of fight, I would always want him on my side." Sheridan's unit, also known as "The Hoffa Squad," "The Get-Hoffa Squad" and "The Terrible Twenty," was, as one might deduce, primarily concerned with Teamster matters. Walter Sheridan was on the Attorney General's payroll as a $19,000-a-year Confidential Assistant, and although he was in regular touch with Jack Miller, he was also on the phone with the Attorney General "two or three times a day every day since the day after Bob took office," so that lines of authority didn't mean much.

Viewed as a subdivision of the U.S. Department of Justice, the Sheridan unit was a curiosity. It was headed by a non-lawyer. It was staffed by men whose experience for the most part was investigative rather than legal. It was paid out of the budget of the Organized Crime Section, yet as Organized Crime section chief Ed Silberling admitted, "It burned my ass. I had to justify my budget requests by work produced, but half of the jobs were Hoffa Squad jobs. They used up a lot of the top grades, which interfered with my hiring and, besides, I didn't have control over them." Its men were on twenty-four hour call. It had constant access to, and the interest and wholehearted support of, the Attorney General. It had free access to the files of the McClellan Committee. It was in touch with grand juries throughout the country. It had an undercover air of mystery about it. Its *modus operandi* was cloak and dagger. Sheridan was never available when you called him and nobody knew where he was, but somehow if it was important, he would always get back to you in fifteen minutes. And unlike every other unit of the Justice Department, which is organized around subject areas of responsibility, the Sheridan unit's *raison d'être* seemed to be not a subject area but a target: Jimmy Hoffa. Its relations with the FBI were highly irregular in that it received little or no cooperation from the top, yet Sheridan, an ex-FBI man, had a degree of line cooperation in the field that was, in some respects, unparalleled. He actually coordinated FBI agents with his own men—told them where to go when, and they went. Courtney Evans, who served as FBI liaison with the Sheridan unit in matters involving the Attorney General, had worked as the FBI man with the McClellan Committee. Since Sheridan was, in a sense, intruding on FBI turf, the situation was highly irregular.

But it is insufficient to regard the Sheridan unit as a subdivision of the executive. The Sheridan unit was, primarily, a carry-over from the legislature. A McClellan Committee investigator served as its chief; the McClellan Committee files were available to and used by it; the McClellan Committee findings were the basis of many of the major lawsuits that Robert Kennedy brought against Hoffa and the Teamsters; McClellan Committee insights into Teamster life styles dictated the Sheridan squad's strategy; and it was the business of the Sheridan unit to finish the anti-Hoffa job that the McClellan Committee had started.

The staff, appropriately, had an investigative flavor. Sheridan had been chosen to head the unit over Kennedy family accountant Carmine Bellino, another Rackets Committee stalwart and former FBI agent whom Kennedy had called "the best investigative accountant in the business." Bellino, who was a cousin to RFK's secretary Angie Novello (who herself had worked for the FBI before she joined Kennedy on the Rackets Committee), had an office in the White House, where his title was Special Consultant to the President, and another one in the Justice Department, where he assisted the Sheridan operation in an *ad hoc* way. At first, it was unclear whether Sheridan or Bellino was to be in charge. Bellino's way of catching Hoffa was "on the accounting sheets"; Sheridan's way was "in the alley." Sheridan told Kennedy it was Bellino or he, that "you can't have both of us running the thing." Bellino's painstaking and imaginative reconstructions from long columns of dull numbers had already been accomplished but, as one member of the Hoffa squad put it, "If they fix a jury or bribe a judge or intimidate a witness you can lose in the alley what you win in the courtroom." So Kennedy chose Sheridan and gave him a free hand in hiring lawyers or shifting career Justice Department lawyers onto the Hoffa squad. Among those he chose were Thomas J. McTiernan and James Canavan, from the Internal Security Section, who also were former FBI agents; William Ryan, a former Marine colonel; Robert Peloquin, who had done investigative legal work for the FCC; Charles Smith, a black assistant U.S. attorney from Seattle, who had worked on the Beck case and was talent-scouted by Ed Guthman, the Seattle-based reporter specializing in Teamster corruption.

In addition to Sheridan's twenty-odd lawyers, in the background were men like Courtney Evans, Chief Marshal James J. P. McShane, Pierre Salinger and Kenneth O'Donnell in the White House, Guthman and Seigenthaler * in the Attorney General's office, each of whom played a role in connection with the Rackets Committee hearings and, like the President himself, each of whom retained an interest in seeing James Hoffa behind bars. As Robert Kennedy made his Justice Department rounds and had new attorneys in his office for beer, pretzels and conversation, any time he spotted a live one, the surprised young man might be invited to join. "Anyone who doesn't feel he has enough to keep him busy," Kennedy would tell the young lawyers of the Department, "come see me." So when Bill French, a bright young Notre Dame graduate from the Lands Division took him up on it, he soon found himself on the Get-Hoffa Squad. Charles Shaffer had been

---

* A Nieman Fellow who exposed Teamster corruption in Tennessee as a reporter for *The Nashville Tennessean*, which he now edits.

working in the U.S. attorney's office in the Southern District of New York and had won some major cases, had been *Law Review* at Fordham, and, like Sheridan, he had a church friend who recommended him to RFK. He recalls being interviewed by Sheridan and then by Kennedy himself: "Some people say Kennedy was out to get Hoffa. Well let me tell you, they are 100 percent right. When I was hired I knew I wasn't going to prosecute draft dodgers. And Bobby couldn't wait. He asked me when was the earliest I could start. I said two calendar months. He said be here Monday. I said I couldn't possibly. I had cases to clean up, work, obligations, family. . . . He said a week from Monday and that was that." At the suggestion of his good friend from the University of Virginia Law School, John Hooker, Jr., Kennedy hired James Neal, a bright young Nashville lawyer who came to Washington expecting to head up the Tax Division, won a major case against Hoffa associate Benjamin Dranow and went on to argue the two major Hoffa cases in Tennessee, and subsequently to become U.S. Attorney in the area. And of course Jack Miller, Sheridan's technical superior, like the Attorney General, was a psychological member of the Get-Hoffa Squad. Miller had served as embattled attorney for the anti-Teamster faction of the Board of Monitors, which was where he and Kennedy had come to know each other. It is not without significance that this Republican, who had never engaged in criminal law practice, was put in charge of the Criminal Division. He had proved his bona fides in the Get-Hoffa arena, and that seemed to be good enough—a tip-off to the Attorney General's priorities.

When asked how intimately involved Robert Kennedy was in the minute-by-minute decisions of the group, Sheridan says, with his "angelic smile," "Why don't you say he was 'interested'? He was very interested. He kept close tabs." *Thirteen Days* is Robert Kennedy's vivid and moving diary of his deep involvement in the events leading up to and resolving the Cuban missile crisis. What he omits from that account, but what is confirmed in Walter Sheridan's log, is the fact that simultaneously he was engaged in daily long-distance strategy discussions with Walter Sheridan, who was in the midst of the Test Fleet case, the first Hoffa trial under Kennedy, in Tennessee. If nothing else, he had the capacity to keep these things in equilibrium, a capability which William Shannon identified when he wrote in another context:

> Robert Kennedy's claim to be qualified for the Presidency rests objectively on his record as Attorney General. Politics, sentiment and glamour aside, he proved in those three and one-half years that he is

capable of directing a major department of government and performing effectively. He showed that he could recruit and hold able subordinates, delegate authority, stay reasonable and unshaken in times of crisis, make clear-cut decisions when decisions were necessary, and has the intelligence and energy to keep a dozen different lines of policy in mind and under control. His residual moralism and his keen political pragmatism were always in unstable equilibrium. "From one day to the next," a friend has said, "you never knew which Bobby Kennedy you're going to meet." But this proved to be a creative, not a destructive tension. He could be rude, restless, impatient, but he was also brilliant, inspiring, forceful.[7]

The point is that the Get-Hoffa Squad was irregular only from the perspective of the Justice Department bureaucracy. As far as the Attorney General was concerned, it was a creative and flexible instrument to deal with Hoffa and the Teamsters on their own terms. Its excesses were Kennedy's excesses. Its accomplishments were his accomplishments. It was an acting out of Robert Kennedy's will and capability. The Get-Hoffa Squad did what the Attorney General of the United States would have done himself had he had the time. It was a definition of where he was at.

As the Keogh, Chacharis and Landis cases demonstrate, where Robert Kennedy's goal-values were in conflict, where his loyalty to law conflicted with his personal morality, the decision-making process was determined largely by bureaucratic momentum. The bureaucracy under RFK had internalized the values of Kennedyism, which prevailed over the traditional career bureaucrat commitment to regularity.

But in the case of Hoffa, Kennedy's goals were not in conflict at all. Personally he felt Hoffa was involved in a conspiracy of evil, and where evil men were concerned, Kennedy's image of justice, of the role of law, had elements of a morality play. Although he had no systematic jurisprudence, his public and private observations showed him sympathetic to St. Thomas Aquinas' idea of a natural law, which meted out justice in accordance with Aristotelian principles of retribution and reciprocity—a jurisprudence ideally suited to accommodate a Get-Hoffa Squad. That Robert Kennedy simultaneously entertained other conceptions of justice, which emphasized protection of the personality, freedom and equality, proved no barrier at the time, since in a rather naïve way he felt that these were the prerogative of the pure, the young, the poor, the disadvantaged. Robert Kennedy in the early Sixties had little difficulty accommodating the notion that there were two kinds of justice; one for society's enemies, another for its victims.

The Get-Hoffa Squad embodied the jurisprudence of retribution;

the Civil Rights Division embodied the jurisprudence of equal protection. Kennedy had subconsciously segregated the doers from the
thinkers. He put the doers in the Hoffa-chasing business and the
thinkers in the rights-protecting business. But of course "doers" like
Seigenthaler and White were proceduralists, and "thinkers" like Burke
Marshall and Nicholas Katzenbach and Lou Oberdorfer turned out to
be superb administrators, tough organizers and pragmatists. So there
was enough cross-fertilization to contaminate any overly neat hypothesis
of separation. Ramsey Clark and Archibald Cox took part along with
everybody else in debates over whether to bring which Hoffa cases how.
Nevertheless Sheridan had operating responsibility for Getting Hoffa
and the psychological involvement and support of the brothers
Kennedy, so that in the end the Hoffa drive was liberated to a significant degree from conventional Departmental procedures and at the
same time from those pressures and bureaucratic restraints that sometimes conspire, almost accidentally, to preserve democratic values, to
protect fundamental civil liberties and human rights.

It was, as David Halberstam, Jack Newfield and others have demonstrated, a trait of Robert Kennedy to mix social, business and political
friends. And it was a Kennedy family trait to personalize political relations, hence the overriding importance of loyalty. Kennedy's relationship to the men he worked with on the Rackets Committee is
reflected in the late James J. P. McShane's recollection that "It's
common procedure when an investigation closes for the chief counsel
to call you in and say you did a hell of a job and the Senator wants
to shake your hand, but as of Friday you're off the payrolls and good
luck. We had thirty-four investigators on that committee and Bob did
not leave until the last investigator had been placed. I know, because
I was the last investigator. . . ."

The loyalties forged in Rackets Committee days endured in the
Justice Department but not without unmixed results. Once, according
to a member of the Organized Crime Section, Sheridan came in with
"What I would characterize as a latrine rumor—as a matter of fact, it
was a latrine rumor. Sheridan wanted to use it in connection with a
federal prosecution. Jim Misselbach, who was working as an assistant
to the head of the Organized Crime Section, objected and said he
thought different ground rules apply in the federal courtroom than in
Senate hearings. Jim said you don't ask questions to which there are no
answers, only headlines. Jim said the federal prosecutor has a duty to
the accused and that a philosophical issue was involved. Walt [Sheridan]
stormed out of the session, and Henry Peterson, a career attorney in

the Organized Crime Section, was aghast. The next thing that happened was that the AG called Silberling over the weekend and asked for Misselbach's carcass. The following week Ed talked him out of it and it all simmered down. Misselbach was never happy after that, and eventually he left, too."

The purpose of the Sheridan unit was to investigate, coordinate other investigations (FBI, local, Congressional, other agencies of government, like the Labor Department), assist in preparing presentments to grand juries, serve as special prosecutors, conduct whatever guerrilla warfare and counter-guerrilla warfare were necessary *within the law* to "Get Hoffa," as Shaffer put it, or, more accurately, to convict him of crimes and clean up the Teamsters Union.

The grand strategy was (a) to go after Hoffa adding to the information developed in the McClellan Committee and (b) simultaneously to get lower-rank Teamsters and others who were covering for Teamsters by destroying records, serving as front men, middle men, bag men and the like. By knocking off lower-rank Teamsters, went the theory, by going after the perjurers, shaker-downers, justice obstructers, the legend of the invincible Hoffa would go down with them, his hold on his men would be weakened, and some informants would come forward to testify against the man himself; others would choose to cooperate with the government rather than risk prosecution for perjury.

So shortly after Kennedy took office, no less than fifteen grand juries, scattered across the country, were investigating Teamsters affairs, and the fruits of his Rackets Committee labors were soon visible. Frank Collins, secretary-treasurer of Hoffa's Detroit Local 299, was convicted of perjury and sentenced to three years. William "Big Bill" Presser, chairman of the Ohio Conference of Teamsters, was convicted of contempt of Congress. Mrs. Sally Hucks, the hapless telephone operator at the Woodner Hotel where Hoffa and the Teamsters held court, was given twenty months to five years for destroying telephone-call records that were under subpoena. Barney Baker, a Hoffa Central States organizer, got two years for taking money from an employer in violation of the Taft-Hartley law. Anthony Provenzano was convicted of extortion and sentenced to seven years in prison. Four officers in Local 224, Teamsters Line Drivers' Union, were convicted of embezzlement and fined and two were sentenced to three years in prison. The list was long and impressive.

Concurrently, Walter Sheridan personally kept track of the round-the-clock movements of Hoffa. "I knew where he was twenty-four hours a day," Sheridan recalls. And the surveillance took its toll. As

Esther and Robert James report in their not unsympathetic study of Hoffa during the Kennedy years:

> Between 1957 and 1964, Hoffa's life was dominated by his fear of "that little monster," Robert Kennedy. Under Kennedy's direction, Hoffa believes, FBI agents followed him wherever he went, tapped his phone, opened his mail, and beamed electronic listening devices on him from half a mile away, aided by invisible powder they had rubbed onto his clothes. During the Miami Convention in 1961 Hoffa warned the delegates that Kennedy had sent female spies to pry secrets out of them and ordered them to avoid strangers. He was also certain that Kennedy would try to block the convention, a move which never occurred. He claims that dozens of FBI agents—disguised as bellhops, desk clerks, doormen, maids and waiters—swarmed about the hotel where his Executive Board met and negotiations were held. He is convinced that officials of his own organization, including at least two Vice Presidents, reported to the FBI. . . .
>
> In addition he believes that Kennedy used pressure tactics to force others to move against him; that with this purpose in mind, the IRS combed the tax returns of Teamster officials and key employers; that the FBI stole Teamster records and then accused the union leaders of destroying them; and that Pension Fund borrowers were indicted on a variety of charges. In each case, he claims, the Justice Department threatened prosecution unless the individual broke with Hoffa or testified against him or his associates.[8]

The rationale for the Sheridan group was not hard to come by. "On the other side, you had a group of criminal defendants prepared to do total and unreserved battle," says Nathan Lewin, who became the Get-Hoffa Squad's intellectual-in-residence. "That included jury-tampering, bribery, you name it. They had limitless funds and used them, and they didn't play by the rules. Hoffa didn't care about lower courts because he could go to a higher court. They were not ordinary criminal defendants. During the Nashville case Hoffa had six high-priced lawyers sitting in a hotel room to consult with the four other lawyers they had in the courtroom. That's more than the government had working on the trial. He probably spent as much money defending himself as the government spent bringing him to justice. You had to meet that with similar resources and flexibility from the government side."

The Sheridan squad's utility was demonstrated in the midst of the first case Kennedy brought against Hoffa, when Edward Grady Partin, an informant in the Hoffa camp, brought evidence of possible jury-tampering to the government's attention. "What *do* you do," asks one of the government lawyers on the case, "when in the middle of a trial you are told by someone the FBI considers 'unreliable' [which is how they viewed Partin] that one of the jurors is going to be fixed on a lonely country road that Saturday night? Normally, the FBI says we're not interested—you forget it. Or you make an appointment with the U.S. Attorney. He makes an appointment with the Criminal Division in Washington. They make an appointment with the Deputy. He makes an appointment with the Attorney General and by that time the fix is in. Just being able to follow up investigative *leads* made all the difference. For that you need authority, and Walter had lots. He didn't need meetings or signed authorizations. He could do what had to be done."

Aside from some court-approved tapping, discussed below, there is no evidence of any bugging or tapping of Jimmy Hoffa and the Teamsters while Robert Kennedy was Attorney General. Sheridan asserts, "We never under any circumstances in any way bugged or wiretapped Jimmy Hoffa."

The day after he defeated Eugene McCarthy in the Nebraska Presidential primary in April 1968, I talked with Senator Robert Kennedy as he flew from Omaha, Nebraska, to Detroit, Michigan. I thought he would want to savor his victory but instead he wanted to talk about this book. When I expressed some skepticism about his professed ignorance of the FBI's bugging practices, he asserted his innocence, and then added as the clincher, "And you would think if I knew about the bugging the one person who would have been bugged was the person I was supposed to want to 'get'—the person against whom everybody says I was carrying on a vendetta—Jimmy Hoffa."

When I ventured, half in jest, "You were too smart to bug Hoffa," the corners of his mouth turned down, and I got one of those cold, steely, blue-eyed looks that one reads about but can't quite believe without experiencing it. The click was almost audible. "If you think that," he said, "there's no point in talking with you." *

---

* Incidentally, Kennedy's disarming ability to make jokes at his own expense was frequently suspended where Hoffa was concerned. William Orrick recalls, "He was always worried about Hoffa. 'How are we going to get to Hoffa?' One day at a lunch meeting I said, 'You can take his deposition.' He said, 'You can't get to him.' I said, 'Eventually you can.' He said, 'How would you get to him?' I said, "All right, you be Hoffa and I'll be the lawyer.' So I said, 'State your name,' and he could hardly gag out, 'James R. Hoffa.' "

One wants to assume that Kennedy—like Sheridan—was telling the truth. This is not to say that the campaign Kennedy and Sheridan did mount against Hoffa and the Teamsters was not the moral equivalent of bugging and tapping, but simply that such blatant violations of the law did not occur.* Partly, this was because Kennedy *would* have gone out of his way to avoid giving Hoffa the opportunity to invoke valid Constitutional or legal objections to any government case against him. Partly it was because of the FBI's peculiar approach to its job: Although the FBI had little compunction during the Kennedy years about bugging for *intelligence* (i.e., background) purposes, despite the fact that every illegal trespass connected with the installation of these bugs was a violation of the Fourth Amendment's guarantee against unreasonable searches and seizure, they rarely ever bugged for *investigative* purposes (i.e., when a man was under investigation in connection with a potential case). The ostensible reason was that such bugging could taint the evidence in a case, get it thrown out of court and embarrass the FBI. Since Jimmy Hoffa and the Teamsters were, from the day Robert Kennedy became Attorney General and before, under *perpetual* investigation rather than an occasion for the gathering of background intelligence, the FBI would not, as a matter of general policy, have bugged or tapped Hoffa. As one attorney remarks, "In other words, in the schizo world of the FBI they had absolutely no compunctions whatsoever about violating the Fourth Amendment, which they did every time they trespassed and put in an illegal bug; but they were reluctant to violate the Sixth Amendment [a man's right to counsel and speedy trial]—which might happen if they had listened in on a man whose case came to trial."

The third reason the FBI refrained from bugging or tapping Hoffa and the Teamsters is the most ironic and, one suspects, the most compelling; it involves relations between the Sheridan unit and the FBI.

"The FBI hated Walter," recalls the Get-Hoffa Squad's Charles Shaffer. "It looked like we were going to do things historically reserved to the Bureau. This violated the unwritten rule—that nobody ever competed with the FBI. Hoover didn't want that. In addition, Walter had quit the Bureau and Hoover hated that because this showed independence. As a result, the Bureau would never help us. We'd request

---

* In subsequent litigation it was revealed that shortly before Ewing King, Hoffa's co-defendant in the jury-tampering case, was indicted, he had a conversation with Edward Partin in Partin's car, which the FBI had bugged with Partin's permission. King claimed that this violated his rights under the Fourth Amendment, but the courts denied the claim.

stuff and it wouldn't come."

Katzenbach confirms Shaffer's analysis but from a different perspective. "What Bob was trying to put together," he says, "was cooperation." "The great problem was the Bureau. They don't like to work in tandem with other people. They've been burned before and they're better than most investigative agencies so they end up picking up somebody else's piece of work. They didn't want to lend themselves to something they couldn't control. Investigative responsibility belongs to the FBI, not Mr. Sheridan. I could understand that."

In other words, it was *because* of the extra anti-Hoffa group that the FBI could be counted upon *not* to violate Hoffa's right to privacy as it had trespassed on the rights of organized crime figures. At first the FBI worked with Sheridan and in fact—on the line level—Sheridan had FBI cooperation throughout all of the major Hoffa trials. But as Sheridan himself concedes, "Hoover hates my guts. I used to get Christmas cards from 'J. Edgar Hoover and Associates.' After Chattanooga he took my name off the list. I heard that a Bureau letter went out saying agents in their contact with me should be 'extremely circumspect' which is their way of saying, 'Don't work with Sheridan.' "

Chattanooga had been the scene of Hoffa's conviction on charges of jury-tampering in an earlier trial in Nashville. In connection with the Chattanooga trial Sheridan had asked the FBI to survey five men who he had reason to believe might try to repeat the Nashville jury-rigging or otherwise interfere with the orderly course of the trial. Sheridan says he gave strict instructions that "under no circumstances were they to survey Hoffa or his attorneys" for fear that the government could be accused of interfering with Hoffa's Sixth Amendment right to counsel. But naturally, in following Hoffa's close associates, whenever one of them happened to be traveling with Hoffa or his attorneys, the FBI was also following Hoffa.

Unknown to the FBI, the late Bernard Spindell, Hoffa's wiretap expert and one of the five subjects of the FBI surveillance, had tuned in to the FBI radio car network. Here is a sample of the transcript Spindell made of his interception:

"Say, Bill, the two occupants were the man [Hoffa] and the ex-boxer [Chuck O'Brien, a Teamster business agent]."

"That's 10–4 correct. [10–4 means, "Do you understand?"] Is the car parked on the Eleventh Street side?"

"That's affirmed. The light-beige Chevrolet right there in front of the hotel, is that 10–4?"

"That's 10–4, Bill, Nashville tag."

There were lots of references to "the man" and where he went when, and at one point Bernard Spindell even picked up the following:

> "Twenty-three, are you trying to transmit me?"
> "Not me, Chief."
> "What's all that noise?"
> "I think we're tuned in."
> "That's probably Bernard."
> "Hi-ya Boinie . . ."
> "Ha, ha, maybe there is a hanky-panky, huh?"
> "Could be."
> "Hi-ya, Boin. Doing fine, making lots of money working for Mr. H? He's a good boy."
> "Go home, Bernard." . . .
> "There is a damn good chance that if this fellow is listening to all you said, there is another good chance he is recording it, so you might consider that, 10–4."
> "Seven, I presume he knows if he is that that's a violation of federal statutes over which we have jurisdiction."

And so forth. The publicity from these intercepts, some of which found their way into the Chattanooga trial record, made the FBI look both improper, since it sounded as if they had gone beyond the Sheridan mandate and followed Hoffa and O'Brien, and silly, since they got caught. To top it off, when Hoffa was finally convicted, in March 1964 after seven years and five trials at which the jury had either acquitted or been hung, *Life* did a story which gave the Sheridan squad all the credit and showed a picture of some fat FBI men playing touch football with the Hoffa Squad's William French. When Robert Kennedy gave a victory party at Hickory Hill he told Sheridan to invite Bill Sheets and Ed Steel, the FBI agents who had done the most on the case. They politely declined the invitation and when Sheridan asked why, they said they would never be able to explain it to the Director, who would take it as a sign of disloyalty.

In addition to the Get-Hoffa Squad there was something known as the Interdivisional or Interdisciplinary—depending on whom you ask—Hoffa Task Force, which would meet once a month in a conference room on the Justice Department's second floor. Richard Stern, a bright young Yale law graduate in the Anti-Trust Division, was a member, along with Nathaniel Kossack, of the Fraud Section of the Criminal Division, and other representatives of other divisions. Stern recalls, "Kennedy and White were usually there. The idea was to use the interdisciplinary approach to bring to bear the specialized knowledge of all of us, we were told, to see what laws had been violated. It was a task force aimed at Hoffa. I thought my time was being wasted. It was unsuccessful, minor, silly, a dumb kind of thing. It didn't work out, and I stopped going—and I think after White went to the court, it stopped meeting."

Kossack puts it in a different light. From his perspective: "We [the Fraud Section of the Criminal Division] were working on a mail fraud case against Hoffa before Robert Kennedy got there. Kennedy felt you should not forgo the talent of the rest of the people in the Department simply because they are categorized as Civil Division or Anti-Trust or Tax Division. So a group of people sat around and discussed the law of mail frauds, the law of evidence, what kinds of proof we had and what kinds we needed. It was a utilization of various legal minds to apply different theories to a set of facts. In any problem he'd have no hesitation about cross-fertilization, and so the Hoffa group was no different from others."

If the Get-Hoffa Squad was an objectification of Robert Kennedy's will, his fantasy life, a mirror of the inner Kennedy, it is important to see what it did and did not do and to ask whether ultimately this furthered or undermined the processes of law enforcement which Kennedy, as Attorney General and "keeper of the executive conscience," was charged with upholding.

Although some of what the Get-Hoffa Squad and the Department at large did is on the record, much is not. The issue has been confused first by the hit-and-miss Hoffa charges of across-the-board rights violations and his unconvincing protestations of innocence, as well as by the late Teamster lobbyist Sid Zagri's effective anti-Kennedy lobbying on the hill; by the willingness of Kennedy critics to accept all of the Teamster allegations as true, especially when they involved allegations of rights denied or intruded upon; and finally by the irrelevance of the Kennedy response. As Frank Mankiewicz put it in a memorial tribute to Kennedy on television:

> The stuff about Jimmy Hoffa bothered him. He wondered why it was that so many people who really are rather decent people, on so many other questions, were so sore at him for having prosecuted Jimmy Hoffa as vigorously as he did. And he finally concluded that there is a certain kind of person who sort of automatically assumes that if somebody is a loser they must have something good about them. I don't know if he ever came any closer to the reasons about Hoffa, but every time another appeal of Hoffa's would be denied, he would say, "Well, do you think anyone will believe now that one of those terrible things happened?" And then I would say, "No, I don't think so. Any-

one who believes it will go on believing it." And he said, "Yes, I guess you're right." [9]

The issue, of course, was not the abuse of law; it was the abuse of discretion. Everybody knows the Justice Department's procedures held up in court; the question is whether they hold up out of court. For the law deals in limiting cases, telling us what is legal and illegal, nothing more.

The three cases Robert Kennedy's Justice Department, aided and abetted by the Get-Hoffa Squad, brought against "the man"—in Nashville, Chattanooga and Chicago—prompt us to ask, first, whether they would have been reasonable cases to have brought had Hoffa not been involved, and then what questions, if any, of prosecutorial ethics they raise.

Nashville: The government charged that Hoffa and another Teamster official, now deceased, had in 1949 established a truck-leasing business ("Test Fleet") under the names of their wives (for tax purposes, Hoffa said) which did business with employers (Commercial Carriers, a Detroit trucking firm)—a conflict of interest in violation of the Taft-Hartley law. The indictment charged that they had grossed $242,000 between them from the deal over the years. If the charge was true, they had committed a misdemeanor, with a maximum penalty of one year in prison. Hoffa, who had made no attempt to cover up what he had been doing, did not consider the arrangement illegal or unethical. As he describes it:

> Since Test Fleet didn't do its own trucking business or in any other way become involved with the Teamsters, I just couldn't see where there was a conflict of interest. Leasing trucking equipment to truckers was no more ominous, to me, than, say, selling gasoline to truckers or selling cigarettes to truck drivers.
>
> Can an executive in General Motors invest his savings in a gas station? I know several pharmacists and doctors who own stocks in drug-manufacturing companies, and no one complains. I even know of a doctor who owns an interest in an undertaking establishment, and it is likely that some of his patients have ultimately become patrons of the funeral parlor, but no one has ever suggested that he has deliberately created business for the latter.

Within the Department, Byron White, Nicholas Katzenbach, Burke Marshall (who flew down in the middle of the trial with Howard Willens, First Assistant in the Criminal Division), former labor law professor Archibald Cox and Ramsey Clark were among those consulted on the case, and with the exception of Clark—whose experience as a private attorney with the trucking industry convinced him that the evidence was insufficient to show a significant departure from the practices of the trucking industry—they all felt a legitimate case might be made. In addition to these high-powered consultants, James Neal, a native Tennessean who had recently won a major conviction against Teamster Pension Fund manipulator Benjamin Dranow and had the added advantage of a Tennessee accent, was flown in to help try the case. Walter Sheridan and his unit were on hand—in touch with a respectable complement of FBI agents—to guard against, document and report, interference with the orderly processes of justice. The government had an informant—Edward Partin—in the middle of the Hoffa camp. A daily transcript of the trial was made available—over the protests of Charles Shaffer, co-counsel on the case, who resented the interference—to Carmine Bellino, formerly investigative accountant for the McClellan Committee, now a White House Special Assistant. Sheridan was personally on the telephone with the Attorney General, despite the overlap of the trial with the Cuban missile crisis, at least once a day. Nathan Lewin, a brilliant young Harvard Law graduate, who had recently clerked for Supreme Court Justice John Marshall Harlan, was specially flown down with his wife to join the government team and produced so many memoranda in such a short period that Hoffa stopped calling him "that Jew" (an identifying characteristic in the Get-Hoffa Squad, which was mostly Catholic) and started referring to him as "instant law." Never in history had the government devoted so much money, manpower and top level brainpower to a misdemeanor case.* The trial lasted two months, and the jury vote was 7 to 5 for acquittal when, on December 23, 1962, the judge declared a mistrial because of the jury's inability to reach a verdict.

The government was criticized for bringing the case in Nashville, where Kennedy aide John Seigenthaler had recently been named editor-in-chief of the influential *Nashville Tennessean*, rather than in Detroit, Hoffa's home town. Test Fleet had been incorporated in Detroit, but operated out of Nashville, so "Given total neutrality, you'd bring it in Detroit," as one of the government lawyers on the case conceded, "but these kinds of choices are made all the time. The Hoffa case wasn't anything special in that regard."

The New York Times asked at the time, since it was charged that employer-payoffs were involved, why the employers weren't indicted

---

* The Teamsters countered, inside and outside the courtroom, with their own unprecedented battery of high-priced, prestigious legal counsel.

as well as Hoffa and the unionists. In fact, Commercial Carriers, Inc. *was* indicted, and fined, pleading *nolo contendere* (no contest), which Hoffa never offered to do, so the government can't really be faulted on that score.

Finally, there was the criticism that the government had raked up a ten-year-old minor charge, to which the government responded that maybe the charge was old but the Test Fleet arrangement continued through 1960, new witnesses had shown up and the purpose of the grand jury—with James Neal and Charles Shaffer presenting the new evidence—was to rethink the seriousness and validity of the charges.

While the Test Fleet case was no *per se* example of a vendetta, it seems more than fair to conclude that had the defendant not been Hoffa and had the Attorney General not been Kennedy, the case would not have been brought. The *bringing* of the Test Fleet case, then, is a piece of objective evidence that Hoffa was, in part, the victim of selective justice.

Chattanooga: Not long after the Test Fleet mistrial, another grand jury was convened. This time witnesses testified that Hoffa and his associates had been trying to bribe jurors in connection with the Test Fleet case, to pressure the families of jurors and to participate in a conspiracy to subvert the administration of justice. The trial was moved to Chattanooga because Hoffa claimed that newspaper publicity—in connection with disbarment proceedings against one of his attorneys, Z. T. Osborn (see below)—had prejudiced his chances of a fair trial in Nashville. On March 4, 1964, Hoffa and his associates were found guilty and Hoffa was sentenced to eight years in federal prison and fined $10,000. As Edward Bennett Williams is reported to have remarked, only Jimmy Hoffa could escalate a misdemeanor into a felony.

The evidence of jury-tampering was considerable, and although many witnesses changed their stories more than once in the course of the proceedings, much of it held up in court. Among the key charges:

(1) In October of 1962, on the first day of the Test Fleet litigation, the best government jury prospects—those thought most likely to convict Hoffa—were called by telephone and asked about the case by someone who erroneously identified himself as "Allen from the Banner [the Nashville *Banner*]" and had to be disqualified. Three men were indicted and acquitted on obstruction of justice charges in connection with these calls.

(2) On October 24, 1962, James C. Tippens, a prospective juror,

asked to see Judge Miller and said he had been contacted by a neighbor and offered $10,000 in easy money if he'd vote for Hoffa. Lawrence (Red) Medlin, the neighbor, was found guilty of attempted bribery, but nothing was proved against Hoffa in connection with the attempt. (It was tried separately from the Chattanooga case.)

(3) On November 17, 1962, Ewing King, boss of the Nashville Teamsters, was observed by FBI men at a lonely spring off River Road on a rainy night, contacting a Tennessee highway patrolman (James Morris Paschal), who later testified that King offered to get him a promotion if he would influence his juror-wife, Mrs. Betty Paschal, on Hoffa's behalf.

(4) According to testimony at the trial, a Teamster business agent in Detroit (Larry Campbell, a Negro) had contacted an uncle (Thomas Ewing Parks), who in turn had contacted the family of Gratin Fields, a Negro juror in the Nashville case. Two of the juror's children eventually admitted to a $10,000 bribe offer by Parks, and one of them admitted to taking a $100 downpayment. Parks took the Fifth Amendment when Hoffa gave him the five-finger signal in the courtroom.

(5) It was charged but never proved to the satisfaction of the jury that a West Virginia businessman, Nicholas Tweel, conspiring with Hoffa and his Chicago insurance associate, Allen Dorfman, was also working on a method "to get the jury."

At the time, the Judge excused Tippens, Paschal and Fields from jury service, and in retrospect there seems little question that the Test Fleet jury was the target of a number of rigging attempts on Hoffa's behalf. Given the evidence they had accumulated, Kennedy Justice would probably have been derelict had they not brought one or another jury-fixing case.

Yet a lot of soul-searching went on at the Justice Department before the jury tampering case was brought and a number of very troublesome questions of prosecutorial ethics were raised by the case that eventually put Hoffa behind bars, most of them surrounding the role of the government's informant in the Hoffa camp, Edward Grady Partin, who acted as sergeant-at-arms at the door of Hoffa's Nashville hotel suite throughout the Test Fleet trial, and without whose cooperation Hoffa could not have been convicted.

Partin had a twenty-year criminal history, which included conviction of breaking and entering, a bad conduct discharge from the Marines, indictments for rape, embezzlement and falsifying records, forgery and first-degree manslaughter. He was under federal indictment for misuse of union funds when he contacted the Justice Department from his cell in a Baton Rouge, Louisiana, jail.

The local prosecutor immediately contacted A. Frank Grimsley of the Get-Hoffa Squad, who listened to Partin's strange tale—that Hoffa had asked him to throw a plastic bomb at Robert Kennedy's house—and contacted Sheridan, who contacted Kennedy, and shortly thereafter Partin was out of jail and Kennedy had FBI protection. A few days later—on October 8, 1962—Partin called Hoffa, recorded the conversation, and arranged to see him in Nashville on October 20, just about the time the Test Fleet trial was scheduled to start. "Just keep your eyes and ears open for any evidence of jury fixing," Grimsley said. Partin was given Sheridan's telephone number in Nashville as his only government contact.

"He was a perfect informant," says Walter Sheridan. "The FBI wouldn't work with him—they didn't trust him—but I worked with him, and every time he told me something I had the FBI check it out, and it always checked out just like he said."

Partin told Sheridan about the attempt to bribe prospective juror Tippens before it happened. He told Sheridan about the late night meeting with state patrolman Paschal—it was called off the first time, which Partin also reported, but took place the following Saturday night—before it happened. Partin reported Hoffa's comment that he had a Negro juror—Gratin Fields, as it turned out—in "his hip pocket," which prompted the Hoffa Squad, working in tandem with the FBI, to conduct an elaborate investigation. Hoffa Squad lawyers McKeon and French worked with the Detroit FBI. Hoffa Squad lawyer Paul Allred worked with the Louisville FBI, and together they traced—by going through thousands of toll calls—the chain of contacts whereby Hoffa's Detroit business agent (Larry Campbell) tried to get at juror Fields.

Sheridan recalls: "The Bureau didn't want anything to do with Partin. They were afraid of him. They tried to be cautious. The Bureau's inclination was to leave him alone because he might be a double agent. So I had all the contacts with him. The Bureau didn't 'refuse' to work with him, but the reality of the situation was that if I didn't they weren't going to do it." Sheridan's view of Partin's reliability was subsequently ratified all the way up to the U.S. Supreme Court, with only Chief Justice Warren dissenting. Since the credibility of an informant is a matter traditionally left for juries to decide, Warren explained his minority-of-one reasoning:

> Here the Government reaches into the jailhouse to employ a man who was himself facing indictments far more serious (and later includ-

ing one for perjury) than the one confronting the man against whom he offered to inform. It employed him not for the purpose of testifying to something that had already happened, but, rather, for the purpose of infiltration, to see if crimes would in the future be committed. The government in its zeal even assisted him in gaining a position from which he could be a witness to the confidential relationship of attorney and client engaged in the preparation of a criminal defense. And, for the dubious evidence thus obtained, the Government paid an enormous price. Certainly if a criminal defendant insinuated his informer into the prosecution's camp in this manner he would be guilty of obstructing justice. [Incidentally, this was just what the Government accused Hoffa of trying to do in the Cheasty case.] I cannot agree that what happened in this case is in keeping with the standards of justice in our federal system and I must, therefore, dissent.

Hoffa argued and still argues that Partin's presence in the Hoffa camp was the human equivalent of an electronic bug, that Partin was perjuring himself, that Partin had a deal with Sheridan—if Partin would "cooperate" in the case against Hoffa, the government would go lightly against Partin. The court rejected these and Hoffa's other claims as a matter of law, but did not, of course, dispose of anything as a matter of propriety.

A first question relates to the extent to which Partin interfered with the confidentiality of Hoffa's relationship with his lawyers. How much did Partin actually hear, how much did he tell Sheridan about defense strategy, and what did Sheridan do with the information? On cross-examination at the trial, it was developed that Partin had told Sheridan that Hoffa witnesses were flown in and given written questions and answers before they testified. Sheridan had passed this information on to prosecutor James Neal, who used it to embarrass a witness by asking whether he had received written assistance in his testimony. Arguably, preparing questions and answers for witnesses is itself enough of an impropriety to justify Partin's passing it on to Sheridan as another instance of obstruction of justice. And in any event the courts did not find it a ground for disqualifying Partin's testimony. But it does suggest that while the letter of the Sixth Amendment's guarantee of right to counsel (with its concurrent lawyer-client privilege) may not have been violated, the spirit was not respected.

A second question relates to the Government's good faith in the Test Fleet case itself. Had there not been jury-tampering and a follow-up case, what assurance do we have that the Government would ever have revealed Partin's presence as an informant in the enemy camp? Not till evidence of jury-tampering came in did the Government file a sealed envelope with the court which told of Partin's presence. Until that time, he was a closely guarded secret. Only Sheridan, the Attorney General and one or two others knew of his double-agent role. This is an important question, because it was unknown in advance whether the Courts would consider Partin's presence a ground for declaring the whole case tainted. When Cecil Branstetter, the lawyer for one of Hoffa's co-defendants in the jury-tampering case, argued that Partin was no different from the electronic eavesdropping in the Judith Coplon case (dismissed back in the Forties because it had violated the confidentiality of the attorney-client privilege), U.S. attorney James Neal countered with the argument that, had Hoffa been convicted in the Test Fleet case, the verdict might have been tainted because of the government informant, but that this had nothing to do with the Chattanooga case. It was a fall-back debating point, but nevertheless a reasonable one, since the legality of Partin's role in Test Fleet has never been litigated. (The Test Fleet case was never retried.)

A third question relates to Sheridan's instructions to Partin before he, still posing as a legitimate member of the Hoffa entourage, was summoned along with other of Hoffa's associates to appear before the Nashville grand jury investigating jury-tampering in connection with the Test Fleet case. Clark Mollenhoff, the muckraking reporter who had put Kennedy onto Teamster corruption in the first place and was, if anything, as involved as Robert Kennedy in these proceedings, was on the scene and in regular touch with Sheridan. In *Tentacles of Power*, which approvingly chronicles some of the creative counter-guerrilla tactics employed by Sheridan and his men (raising too many questions to be explored here), Mollenhoff reports: ". . . it was on Sheridan's advice that Partin went along with the suggestion [by Hoffa's camp] that he use the Fifth Amendment when questioned by the Nashville grand jury.

"Sheridan knew that certain of Hoffa's associates had arranged 'leaks' from grand juries in the Detroit area in earlier years. If there had been a 'leak' from the Nashville grand jury [it] would have indicated that Ed Partin was true to the Teamsters' code and was following a conspiracy of silence." [10] Had Partin testified that he was a double agent, the risk was that word would get out.

Intelligent counter-espionage, yes, but also dubious prosecutorial practice. For, after all, Sheridan's advice had the result of misleading and preventing the grand jury from getting the full story. To an unsympathetic prosecutor Sheridan's advice might even have looked like obstruction of justice, especially when one considers the hold that the federal government had over Partin, which was such that its "advice" could not be lightly disregarded.

Then there was the related question of Partin's compensation. Shortly before the Nashville trial Partin had contacted the government from a Baton Rouge cell where he was being held on charges of embezzling $1,600 of Teamster funds. After Frank Grimsley of the Get-Hoffa Squad interviewed him, administered the lie-detector test and became convinced that Partin was telling the truth, his bail was reduced, the federal case against him in Louisiana was not brought, and his wife was paid $1,200.

Again, the point here is not the strict legality of it. Hoffa's lawyers argued unsuccessfully that the $1,200—paid out of a confidential fund —was a witness fee in violation of federal law. The government successfully argued that it was only expenses; the fact that the money, paid in $300 monthly installments to Partin's wife, was the same amount he owed his wife under their separation agreement did not change the court's finding. In private conversation Hoffa Squad lawyers maintain that Partin's real expenses, which he itemized, were greater than $1,200, but he only asked that his wife's monthly payments be met. Whatever the payment represented, a confidential memo in the government files reflected the undercover nature of the operation. Dated July 3, 1963, from Walter Sheridan to S. A. Andretta, Administrative Assistant Attorney General, it read:

> Subject: Confidential Fund Item
> In connection with the forthcoming trials in Nashville, Tenn., it is requested that a check in the amount of $300 be drawn against the confidential fund beginning July 8th, made payable to A. Frank Grimsley, Jr., Attorney in the Criminal Division. . . . He will cash the check and give the money to a confidential source.
> It is also requested that a check be drawn each month through November, 1963, made payable to Mr. Grimsley and mailed as above.

The court established that the payments were "legal." But the payments, plus the reduction of bail, plus the dropping of recent charges against Partin, plus settlement on an income-tax claim of $5,000 against Partin, were in the background against which this man was given "advice" by Sheridan.

The major question raised by the government's decision to bring the jury-tampering trial, however, goes beyond Partin. The evidence of jury-tampering was, one gathers, compelling. Much *less* compelling was Hoffa's link to all this, which was strictly circumstantial without the testimony of Partin. While it was true that Partin's information

about those other than Hoffa checked out, all of his information about
Hoffa was uncheckable. There is no easy answer to what the government ought to do in such a circumstance. Ramsey Clark—alone among
the Assistant Attorneys General who were consulted—took the position
that "you don't stake a jury-fixing case on the word of a man like
Partin, who has a twenty-year criminal history." * The counter-
argument, which won the day, was that to omit Hoffa would be the
grossest impropriety of all. "He was in the middle of all this," says
Nathan Lewin, the Get-Hoffa Squad's intellectual-in-residence, now in
private practice. "He *had* to be behind it. Everybody knew that. So
how can you let him get away while a poor shmuck like Parks helps
out his nephew [Teamster business agent Larry Campbell] and goes
to jail?"

Had the decision to indict Hoffa for jury-tampering been born of
such nice questions of theory, then it would probably not have
raised so many sticky issues of dubious precedent. The deliberations,
however, were conducted in the Get-Hoffa environment that per-
vaded the Justice Department, and as such are correctly suspect.

Chicago: The Chicago case, which was brought on April 27, 1964
(it had been postponed so that jury-tampering might be tried first—
a strategic decision designed to warn off potential Chicago jury-
riggers), involved thousands of documents, three months' worth of
witnesses, and charges that Hoffa, along with Benjamin Dranow and
others, had personally benefited from Teamster Central States South-
east Southwest Pension Fund loans. The jury found Hoffa and his
associates guilty of fraud in the handling of millions of dollars which
were being held in trust for pensions, life insurance and disability of
over 200,000 rank-and-file Teamsters. Hoffa was found guilty on four
of twenty-eight counts, sentenced to serve five years in jail on each
count, terms to be served concurrently.

The trial, which involved fourteen loans granted by the Teamster
Pension Fund, is too complex to reconstruct here. There was evidence
that Hoffa used Pension Fund bank deposits to secure a loan for a ven-
ture in which he had a 45 percent interest, that he and his friend Benjamin Dranow got a 10 percent kickback on a $4,300,000 loan for the
expansion of a luxury hotel in Miami, and that he was involved in a
morass of financial deception, manipulation and/or fiscal irresponsi-
bility.

---

* As this book goes to press another challenge to Partin's credibility has been
mounted in the form of an unsigned affidavit printed in the Manchester *Union
Leader*, alleged to have been written by Partin, asserting that his testimony was
given under duress.

The Pension Fund case was like the Test Fleet case in that it was based partly on materials originally uncovered by the McClellan Committee; and like the jury-tampering case in that most of the evidence didn't directly implicate Hoffa. (An added fillip was the government's summation to the jury. William Bittman, a latecomer to the Hoffa Squad, he replaced Abe Poretz after the trial started—perhaps too late to have known of Edward Partin—spent some hours describing how Hoffa had conspired to defraud the rank and file, and then concluded: "Who are you going to believe—Benjamin Dranow or all of these witnesses?" Of the government's 114 witnesses, Bittman couldn't recall one with a criminal record. Dranow, on the other hand, pointed out Bittman with contempt, "[he] has been convicted of mail fraud, bankruptcy fraud, income tax evasion and bail jumping.")

Again, one assumes with the jury that Hoffa was guilty, although it might be noted that the Pension Fund was thriving, that he was only one of sixteen trustees (albeit the government convinced the jury that he was the key member) and that whatever he did with the money he was supposed to have manipulated (Walter Sheridan believes to a certainty that Hoffa used these moneys to pay off Congressmen) he didn't really use it for personal enrichment or high living.

The findings of the Pension Fund jury belie charges of vendetta; yet the method of accumulating the evidence raises yet another beyond-the-law issue of prosecutorial ethics to which there is no simplistic answer. The case against that method was eloquently advanced by Sidney Lens, the Chicago labor leader and historian in *The Progressive* magazine prior to the bringing of the Pension Fund case, but the question he raises survives the guilty verdict:

> Does the Justice Department have the right to go fishing into every area of a person's activities, *looking* for possible crime? Or should the Department investigate only specific charges where it has reasonable assurance that a crime has been committed? The government has a right to subpoena a particular businessman if it has reasonable grounds to believe that he made a payoff to Hoffa to get a loan from the Teamster Pension Fund. But it has no right to subpoena a hundred businessmen or even to send FBI agents to interrogate them, just on the chance that one of them did make such a payoff. Yet, the Justice Department is following the latter course, hitting in all directions in the hope that something will be uncovered which can be used to "get Hoffa."

The Get-Hoffa people counter Lens's argument by pointing out that here you had substantial amounts of money being siphoned off from the Teamster Pension Fund. No individual Teamster was strong

enough or knew enough to do anything about it. "In one sense," says
a member of the Sheridan unit, "it was a victimless crime. So investigating a pension fund is *not* the same thing as saying, let's see
what we can get on these guys. The Pension Fund was famous for
being played around with, and the rank and file were powerless to do
anything about it. To that extent it was legitimate to investigate
those who did business with it." This argument sounds eminently
sensible when applied to the Teamster Pension Fund. If a George
Wallace, however, charging the NAACP with champerty, barratry and
financial chicanery, should seize the occasion to interview every
person who did business with them, then the potential for abuse inherent in such across-the-board interrogations might be more apparent.

In other words, under the Kennedy code as long as you operated
within the law—which meant no wiretapping, no bugging that had not
been cleared in court, no interfering with a man's right to counsel,
and the like—*anything* you did that helped send Jimmy Hoffa to jail
promoted the ends of justice. As Murray Kempton once put it:

> Bob, who had an underlying distaste for the kind of people his father
> used to buy, recognized the devil in Hoffa . . . something absolutely
> insatiable and wildly vindictive. With the older guys, like Dave Beck
> and Frank Brewster, I think Bob felt that they were just self-indulgent
> and rather weak men. . . . But he recognized in Hoffa a general
> fanaticism for evil that could be thought of as the opposite side of his
> own fanaticism for good . . . and, therefore, involved direct combat.
> Hoffa and Kennedy had feelings about each other of an intensity that
> can scarcely be described. . . . There was in both of them a passion
> for the other's discomfort.[11]

Thus, when Senator Robert F. Kennedy was retrospectively accused of
having planted an article in *Life* by disaffected Teamster Sam Baron
entitled "I Was Near the Top of Jimmy's Drop-Dead List," an outraged
Kennedy showed up at Senator Edward Long's committee, which had
made the charge, and displayed great indignation (a) at the way the
charge was made, (b) at the imprecision of the charge and (c) at the
erroneous implication that he gave *Life* a specific article aimed at a
specific trial. What passed him by was the impropriety of the U.S. Department of Justice putting anybody in touch with a national magazine
to facilitate a negative story about a man already under indictment by
the U.S. Department of Justice.

The memoranda, claims and counterclaims connected with this
episode are revealing enough to warrant reprinting here:

To: E. K. Thompson [Managing Editor]
From: Suydam, Washington [Editorial writer]
Date: March 6, 1961

Last Saturday I got a phone call from Bob Kennedy asking if I could drop whatever I was doing and come to his office. I did, and when I got there he closed the door and told me the following: in a back room was a high official of the Teamsters, a man who had been privy to the inner workings of the organization since 1953. He was particularly knowledgeable about Hoffa. This official is honest, said Kennedy, and also quite an idealist. The man had been working directly with Kennedy and in secret for the last two years. He was now so disillusioned and disgusted with the corruption he saw all around him, particularly as concerns Hoffa, that he has just about decided to make a public break with the union. Kennedy said he had suggested to this man that he make his break via an article in *Life* in the form of a personal word that for the moment only you and I would know of this matter. Kennedy feels, perhaps melodramatically, perhaps not, that the man's life would be in danger if word leaks out of his intentions. I told the Attorney General that if you were interested in this man's story, and if we did go ahead, more and more people at *Life* would have to become involved. Kennedy understood this, but pointed out that if we are not interested, then only two people, as he put it, that he personally knows and trusts, will have to know about it. I gave my word. He also asked that if we do want to go ahead, or at least look into the possibilities, in other words when we have to pass the point of only you and I being involved, we let him know first. I said we would.

At any rate, here's the story. . . . Are you interested in pursuing this further? A lot of what he says has been said in so many places before. The exposé stuff sounds interesting, but to me at least, pretty undocumentable and therefore probably very libelous. But the more personal stuff on what Hoffa is like and how he behaves sounds pretty good. The basic situation of a fairly high Teamster official breaking publicly because of the corruption he's seen all around him is quite dramatic, and if he does it through us, it could be quite a piece. What he wants to do, if you show initial interest, is sit down and write something rough on his own. He's very verbose and my worry here would be that such a document might still not help you reach a final decision. You might prefer to have a collaborator go to work with him from the start. At any rate, he'd probably be agreeable to anything you suggest. Incidentally, I did not discuss money at all.

Of course this guy has an axe to grind and so, as you of course know, does Bobby Kennedy (see the Kennedy-Hoffa cartoon in yesterday's News of the Week in Review section of the *Times*).

Anyway, that's the story. If you'd like to have Graves or one of the text writers go into this more deeply with Baron, still just on an exploratory basis, I'm sure Kennedy and Baron will buy that.

Incidentally, since I have assurance I wouldn't handle any of this by phone, except in the most general way, could you respond on paper?

Please be sure the envelope is plainly marked P&C for while I trust BJ completely, I do want to keep my bargain with Kennedy, and her husband *is* in the Justice Department.

There followed, a few days later, a note dated simply "Thursday" which read:

DEAR ED:
I told Kennedy of your high interest and he is delighted. He makes the suggestion that the piece go into Baron's background and philosophy somewhat, to help explain his disgust with Hoffa and his motivation for breaking with the Teamsters. Kennedy believes deeply that this is not a case of sour grapes, but of a man acting out of conscience and principle. Kennedy thinks the break will be understood better in light of his total life in the labor movement.
Bob agrees that a ghost writer makes good sense, and is agreeable to Graves and a writer you trust being brought into the picture at this point.
Baron is out of town at the moment, but Kennedy thinks he'll be willing to return when I tell him we want to proceed. I assume you'd like to crank this up pretty quickly, so would you let me know who'll be doing it and when you'd like Baron back here to go to work. Since you'll only be talking about a writer and a date, I see no reason you can't phone me on this point.

Best,
Hank [sig.]
HANK SUYDAM

Kennedy's version of what happened came in the open when Senator Edward Long, a friend and business associate of Morris Shenker, Teamster attorney, revealed the correspondence. Testifying the next day, Kennedy said that he put Baron in touch with *Life* as a means of saving Baron's life and/or so that his story could be told in the event that something happened to him. Prior to Kennedy's testimony, I had been told by a Kennedy aide, "Baron, an honest Teamster, had been accused of disloyalty and knocked down by Hoffa. Baron wanted to tell his story, and he came to his friends at the Justice Department, to whom he had been giving information. He thought his life was in danger and based on the evidence you'd have to agree with him. We felt the one means by which he could stay alive was by putting out his story, which was given to *Life*—Sheridan gave it."
Kennedy told Long's committee:

First, as far as Mr. Hoffa is concerned, and *Life* magazine: There was a witness who was known to me while I was counsel of an investigating committee of the U.S. Senate, who was involved with Teamster activities. He reported to me and later to the Federal Bureau of Investigation regarding corruption and dishonesty within the Teamsters Union. He was in fear of his life. He felt that if anything happened to him, if he was killed, that he wanted to make sure that his story was told. He asked me to put him in touch with somebody who would relate what he had undergone as a Teamster official. I made that arrangement. I did nothing else. It is my understanding that if anything was published, it was going to be published—if something happened to him. If he was killed or in some way beaten. Nothing in fact was ever published until Mr. Baron, who is the Teamster official involved, was physically beaten by Mr. Hoffa. No story was ever published until he broke openly with the Teamsters Union and it was published [reported] in every magazine and every newspaper throughout the United States. . . .

I might say that the investigation of the Teamsters Union—of Mr. Hoffa particularly—a great deal of evidence was developed of violent beatings and terrorism in connection with those who opposed the international president of the Teamsters Union. There was testimony developed eventually of threats against me and against my family. So I knew what we were dealing with. . . . There was a connection between Mr. Baron and *Life* magazine over which I had no control and which was only to be published in case Mr. Baron was killed.

Kennedy objected to the implication of the facts placed on the record: "The implication was that after a meeting in March of 1961, some article was published in *Life* magazine in connection with Mr. Hoffa which was instigated by me. That is not true. That was the way the record was left yesterday. That in fact was not true."

The Baron contact was not an exception. It was the rule. It was one of the aspects of the anti-Hoffa operation. The idea was *not*, as Hoffa charged, to influence juries through out-of-court publicity—that would involve a possible obstruction of justice—but it was to create a climate in which Hoffa's effectiveness diminished, in which his lieutenants would be willing to testify against him, in which his union members might vote to throw him out of office, in which the public would recognize him for the evil influence that he was.

A less celebrated but perhaps more representative example of the Get-Hoffa Squad's method of using the press to anticipate or counter some of Hoffa's wild charges had to do with allegations made with reference to the Teamster bonding program.* In January of 1963 the

* A key provision of the 1959 Landrum-Griffin law called for all officers handling union trust funds and dues to be bonded by a government-approved bonding company against possible loss or theft of funds; violation of the bonding requirement carries a penalty on each offending official of up to a year in jail and a $10,000 fine.

Teamsters charged that "representatives of Bobby Kennedy" were going around talking bonding companies out of bonding him. Since bonding was a requirement under the Landrum-Griffin law, this—said the Teamsters—was Kennedy's way of trying to knock Hoffa out of office. Typical charges were made on a CBS interview with Hoffa conducted by Roger Mudd on Monday evening, January 28, 1963:

HOFFA: There is a pressure of the various departments of the government on the bonding companies, particularly those that have already bonded us, by telling them that if they continue the Teamsters' bond they will create problems for their bonding companies. . . .

MUDD: Do you regard this as a vendetta by the Attorney General against you?

HOFFA: This is another step of the Attorney General in an endeavor to remove the officers of the international union and local union officers by means other than court procedures—in which he has failed so far. And it is a continuation of the vendetta of Bob Kennedy using his office in violation of the oath he took to do by use of his powers rather than the court's ruling to accomplish what he has not been able to accomplish up to date, namely remove Hoffa from office. . . .

MUDD: What is the effective date that these bonding companies are going to cut you off?

HOFFA: February 8th. . . .

MUDD: Can you get a bond from some other company?

HOFFA: We will find some way how to comply with the law as we always have.

MUDD: Have all the bonding companies in the United States refused your request for new bond?

HOFFA: Every bonding company who writes this type of bond so far has refused and we've contacted them all.

MUDD: Well, how are you going to find another bonding company then?

HOFFA: We will, we will.

MUDD: What happens on February 9th, Mr. Hoffa, if you can't get a bond under the law?

HOFFA: We will take appropriate court action.

MUDD: Do you get thrown out of office according to . . . Landrum-Griffin?

HOFFA: Under the law you are not permitted to do certain acts that go with the administration of my office and certain other elective offices and we will find the necessary, the proper procedure by court to show that by interference of certain government representatives they are preventing us from complying with this law and I am sure no court in this land will allow one agency to set aside the will of Congress, namely the bonding by certain certified companies because of the vendetta of the Attorney General.

MUDD: You have no intention then of vacating your office as president?

HOFFA: None whatsoever.

If true, of course, the Attorney General's actions would have been inexcusable, unethical, probably illegal—certainly evidence of a "vendetta," "ruthlessness," a Hoffa-as-target notion of justice. In fact, contended the Department of Justice, it had not sought to discourage any company from providing the Teamsters with bonds for officers as required by law. The fundamental reason for the Teamsters' bonding problems was their insistence on seeking bondage only through a specific brokerage which had changed its name five times since September 1959 when the bonding requirement was enacted and which had ties to the underworld and an unfavorable reputation in the insurance business. FBI investigation into possible illegal aspects of the brokerage is what scared off existing bondsmen.

Well and good, perhaps, except that (a) the FBI might never have made its rounds had it not been for the Sheridan squad, and (b) the Justice Department was not satisfied with putting out a simple denial. Favored reporters were supplemented with a "Background" memo quoted here in full because it explains the situation, but also because it captures the context of Kennedy's press relations where Hoffa was concerned:

BACKGROUND:

The principal figure in the background of the Teamster bonding brokerage is Allen Dorfman. He is the son of Paul Dorfman, a major figure in the Chicago underworld. The McClellan Committee investigation demonstrated that he and James Hoffa set up Allen Dorfman in the insurance business and in return for an introduction to the Chicago underworld, Hoffa turned over to this business the insurance for the giant Central Conference of Teamsters Welfare Fund. Allen Dorfman has collected hundreds of thousands of dollars in excessive profits. Both the Departments of Justice and Labor have had a continuing interest in the activities of the Dorfmans.

When the bond requirement went into effect in September, 1959, the Teamsters arranged to obtain their bonds from an agency whose officers were associates both of Allen Dorfman and the Chicago underworld (Sol Schwartz and Irwin Weiner). This brokerage originally was known as the Illinois Agency of the Summit Fidelity and Surety Company of Akron, Ohio. When the McClellan Committee released a letter publicizing the control of Teamster bond commissions by the Dorfmans and the Chicago mob, the Illinois Insurance Company withdrew

Summit, its subsidiary, from the program. Potential reinsurers, including Stuyvesant Insurance Company of Allentown, Pa., also withdrew their support at that time.

The brokerage subsequently was reorganized several times as Oxford Agency, Inc., Chicago, Titan Management Corporation, and the Oxford Agency, Inc., but Dorfman has remained connected, although not formally, throughout. The Chicago *Sun-Times* this morning reported that when Oxford sought backing for Teamster bonds early this month from the Citizens Casualty Co. of New York City, it was Allen Dorfman himself, who, despite no formal connection with the agency, conducted the negotiations.

Beyond shying away from Teamster business because of Mr. Dorfman's insurance background and underworld ties, there are strong indications that bonding firms also have been frightened off by the insurance business reputation of at least one other person connected with the same brokerage. (Confidentially, he is Stewart Hopps, now on trial in Baltimore on charges of making false statements in connection with fraudulent insurance for a number of now-collapsed Maryland savings and loan associations. Tax charges are pending against him in New York.)

We are informed that where Teamster locals, in the west, including some in the Central Conference, have sought bonding on their own or through other brokers—they have had no difficulty. Problems for the International have arisen only when it has insisted on dealing through the brokerage with which Dorfman (and others such as Hopps) have been connected.

Anybody who covers law enforcement has probably at one time or another received a "background" briefing, even from the most high-minded of prosecutors. That, of course, does not make it right since such briefings can constitute potential interference with the rights of the accused and even of the not-yet-accused. What distinguished the Kennedy (Guthman/Sheridan) background briefings was that they constituted a pattern with the Justice Department's secret ammunition, often drawn from the files of the Rackets Committee, always one-upping Hoffa's open charges.

A final aspect of the Get-Hoffa Squad deserves attention and indelibly stamps it as a Kennedy enterprise: the wholesale involvement of the Kennedy family itself in matters beyond its proper concern. Nowhere was this more evident than in the strange situation of Robert Vick, a Nashville policeman who had worked with Sheridan and whose undercover work resulted in the conviction of Hoffa attorney Z. T. Osborn for conspiring to give a $10,000 bribe to a prospective juror in connection with the Chattanooga jury-tampering trial!

Since Osborn was the most respectable lawyer in Hoffa's camp—as a private attorney he had argued the *Baker* v. *Carr* case and was in line for the presidency of the Nashville Bar Association—his conviction was a coup for Sheridan. Although Hoffa claimed entrapment, the evidence was irrefutable. The bribe had been recorded by a Minifon strapped to Vick's back, and there was no way Osborn could deny it. Vick was a former Alcohol and Tax Unit agent who was working for Osborn as an investigator and with whom Sheridan had established contact.

Sheridan told me how it happened: "He called me one day and said Osborn had called him that day and told him or rather asked him to offer a juror $10,000—$5,000 before and $5,000 after trial. Vick's reputation was bad. I believed him, but James Neal [the co-prosecutor in both Tennessee trials] didn't and I think John Hooker, Sr., [the other government lawyer and a leading member of the Tennessee bar specially recruited for the case] didn't believe it either. So we got an affidavit from Vick about his first conversation and went to the judge. He authorized the FBI to put a recording device on the small of Vick's back. That way we could find out if he was telling the truth. . . . He was this skinny little guy and when he sat down something went wrong with the recording device. But the second time, with the FBI surveilling him to make sure there was no funny business, it was as clear as it could be. Osborn told Vick to go tell the juror $5,000 now and $5,000 later." Osborn was disbarred, convicted and eventually committed suicide. Those of the public who knew about Vick forgot about him.

But in August of 1968, in a proceeding ancillary to an appeal in one of the jury-tampering cases, it was revealed that in mid-December of 1964, three months after Robert Kennedy and Walter Sheridan with him had left the U.S. Department of Justice, Walter Sheridan had asked for and received from Kennedy's brother-in-law Steve Smith a loan of $3,000, which he promptly turned over to Robert Vick, who was destitute because he had lost his job after testifying against the influential and popular attorney. Sheridan explained that the reason for lending the money was that he thought it was bad for law enforcement if people who testified for the government were permitted to suffer for it.

Two days later, on the advice of Sheridan's attorney, Martin O'Donahue, who had served as Chief of the Court-appointed Monitors who were overseeing the Teamsters, Vick returned the money to Sheridan and Sheridan gave it back to Smith, who hadn't asked any questions in the first place. Sheridan recalls, "After the trial there were periodic subsequent conversations with Vick. There was constant calling. He called me Christmas '64 saying you've got to do something. So I finally told him I'd try to loan him some money and went to Steve Smith and asked for $3,000 cash. Vick came out to my house and I gave it to him. He went back to the motel. I started thinking, 'Was I doing the right thing?' So the next morning I brought him down to Marty O'Donahue's to make it legal—on paper. Marty said you're out of your mind. It can be misinterpreted. So I decided not to do it. Vick was furious and left town mad as hell."

Sheridan, who says he had never before or since asked Mr. Smith for money, gave the following testimony: in his deposition of August 1968 filed in connection with one of the many appeals in the Teamster cases:

Q. Did Mr. Smith know what you were going to do with $3,000?
A. No, he did not. I told him I needed $3,000 and he gave it to me. It was a loan.
Q. Did you tell him when you would pay it back?
A. No, I didn't.
Q. Did he ask you when you would pay it back?
A. No, he didn't.

There is probably no more revealing fact about the Get-Hoffa Squad than the uncontradicted, oath-backed assertion that Steve Smith gave Sheridan the $3,000 cash with no questions asked. Steve Smith's life style and Walter Sheridan's life style are as different as Judge Julius Hoffman's and Abbie Hoffman's. Mr. Smith has functioned as the family's efficiency expert, its money manager, its bookkeeper. Walter Sheridan is elusive, a driven man on the chase. Smith is staff; Sheridan is line. It was, perhaps, the most natural thing in the world for Sheridan to receive cash moneys in a sealed envelope. But it would normally be unnatural for Smith (a) not to ask for an explanation, (b) not to ask for a receipt, (c) not to ask when he would be repaid, (d) not to ask if Bobby knew, (e) not to ask anything.

The transaction takes on credibility only in the context of the Kennedy overlap between family and official resources, and the emotional investment Sheridan—a dedicated and single-minded man—and the Kennedys had in their work, their witnesses, their informants, their people. That it took Sheridan two days and a lecture from his attorney to think twice about it suggests the permissive aura, the special expectations, the *sui generis* rules under which the Hoffa squad had operated. Would Attorney General Tom Clark's brother-in-law have lent $4,000 to David Greenglass, whose testimony put the

Rosenbergs in the electric chair? Would John Mitchell lend ten cents to one of his anti-Panther witnesses?

Men like Vick and Partin had, in Walter Sheridan's view, put their careers and perhaps their lives on the line. They had resisted enormous bribe-promises to change their stories, and in Vick's case lost a job. By so doing they had become, in effect, members of the family, and Sheridan felt he owed them something, he had a sense of obligation. What *is* a prosecutor's obligation to those who come forward and testify in criminal cases? That is the difficult question raised by the bizarre and unprofessional transaction with Vick.

At 1320 19th Street, N.W., in the District of Columbia there is a law firm known now as Miller, Cassidy, Larroca and Lewin. Miller was head of the Criminal Division, which sponsored the Get-Hoffa drive. Cassidy was part of the Labor and Racketeering Section, which worked in tandem with the Get-Hoffa drive. Lewin was a belated member of the Get-Hoffa Squad. Also affiliated with the firm is Courtney Evans, who served as FBI liaison to the Attorney General and as such was deeply enmeshed in Hoffa affairs throughout the Kennedy years. And, despite the fact that he is not a lawyer, Walter Sheridan has an office in the firm, and can be reached through the switchboard. "Not a week goes by," says Sheridan, "that I don't hear from Partin once or twice. That man has problems."

The Teamsters made literally hundreds of allegations that Kennedy, Sheridan's Get-Hoffa Squad and the FBI had violated their rights. They came forward with affidavits from ex-policemen free-lance wire-tappers, who claimed to have been paid to tap Teamster wires. They had other affidavits from the publisher of the *Manchester Union Leader* and from an old friend of John Hooker, Sr., who had argued the Chattanooga case, that they had been told, in one case by Cartha deLoach, then the number-three man in the FBI, and in another by Hooker, that bugging and tapping of Hoffa was rampant. (DeLoach and Hooker filed counter-affidavits.) They charged that U.S. marshals bribed Hoffa jurors with gifts, liquor and women. They alleged entrapment, illegal search and seizure and violation of the Fourth, Fifth and Sixth Amendment rights in connection with Edwin Grady Partin's evidence. None of these claims—nor any others of consequence—has been upheld in the courts.

Nevertheless, the Hoffa episode, like the episode of the Nazi saboteurs twenty years earlier, underscores several social, ethical and legal issues.

First, though the Kennedy system may work under the Kennedys, it creates precedents which outlast the Kennedys; if there is nothing inherently wrong with a Get-Hoffa Squad, then there is nothing inherently wrong with a Get-Vietniks Squad or a Get-Panthers Squad or a Get-Radical Liberals Squad or a Get-Birchers Squad. Such assassination bureaus can flourish most when tension is least between the President and his chief law officer.

Second, when asked if they thought Kennedy had done *any*thing improper with respect to Hoffa, Lou Oberdorfer and Burke Marshall independently gave the same answer: "No, not unless you want to quarrel with his allocation of resources." Precisely. There comes a point at which the disproportionate allocation of men, money and time moves from a matter of quantity to a matter of quality, from prosecution to persecution.

Third, there is the danger identified by Robert Jackson—that a prosecutor will pick people he thinks he should get instead of crimes that need to be prosecuted. The wisdom of this warning is apparent in an age of data banks, sophisticated information-retrieval systems and escalating technology.

Fourth, whatever his motives—to finish the work he had begun on the Rackets Committee, to win the game, to destroy an enemy, to bring a public law-breaker and menace to justice, to safeguard the American way, to expose and extirpate corruption in labor-management relations—Robert Kennedy allowed the pursuit of justice to look like the pursuit of Hoffa. "You can't have even-handed justice and personal justice at the same time," Ramsey Clark comments. Nowhere does this perception have more relevance than to the *mano a mano* spectacle of the Kennedy–Hoffa feud.

"He gave the appearance of not being as dispassionate as you would expect an Attorney General to be," observed one Justice Department old-timer with understatement. The consequence can be to undermine public confidence in the even-handed administration of justice and in the long run in law itself.

Fifth, there were some less visible byproducts, such as the morale factor.

"With all those other things he was doing like the Cuban missile crisis and counter-insurgency it was difficult to get to see the AG. But not if you were in the Hoffa thing," said one Justice Department lawyer who was not in the Hoffa thing. "It depleted the Department's manpower," said another. "Too many brilliant young men who might have been bringing Southern sheriffs or Eastern conglomerates to justice were out chasing Hoffa." To that degree it was a demoralizing factor in a department which generally tended to treat the Get-Hoffa Squad like a bad joke. "We didn't feel it had the prosecutorial ability to achieve convictions," said Tom McBride of the Organized Crime Section. "It made me queasy," said a member of the Solicitor General's office, now teaching law at one of America's great universities.

It is not without significance that after the Chattanooga conviction of James Riddle Hoffa on charges of jury-tampering, which was also after the assassination of President John F. Kennedy, Walter Sheridan went to see the Attorney General to ask him, now that his Tennessee work was done and the Chicago trial seemed well in hand, what was he to do next. And the Attorney General said, "See Burke Marshall." Shortly thereafter Walter Sheridan and his "Terrible Twenty" got themselves deputized as special marshals, a designation which entitled them to carry guns, and they were off to Mississippi, as Sheridan puts it, "To get something going on the Klan. It was May of '64. We were sent because the Bureau wasn't doing anything. There were twenty FBI guys in the state, mostly Southerners, but they weren't doing anything unless they had to. Talk to John Doar. He would do whatever was done. The Bureau would say it didn't have jurisdiction."

The final achievement of Walter Sheridan's group, little noted at the time, was perhaps its happiest one. By the time they got to Mississippi, Sheridan was in total disrepute with the FBI and, with JFK out of the White House, J. Edgar Hoover did not feel the need to indulge even the formal courtesy of dealing with or in any way accommodating his immediate superior, Robert Kennedy. "I didn't speak to Robert Kennedy his last six months in office," Hoover has said. As Sheridan recalls it, "The last real go-round was when we went to Mississippi. The agents were afraid to be seen with me. Roy Moore, the A-SAC [Assistant Special Agent in Charge], called to tell me they found the three kids. You remember—that's when they dug up that dam with a derrick and found the three bodies inside. I asked, 'How did you find them?' He said, 'A routine search.' A routine search with a derrick? He was not trusting me enough to tell me that they had an informant. The rumor is that they paid somebody $25,000 for that information, but he wouldn't say."

When Sheridan arrived in Mississippi, FBI man James Malley told John Doar, "Either the Bureau is going to be *the* investigative agency of the Department or it's not. Either it's going to do all of it or none of it." Doar said, "What the hell are you talking about, Jim? You know I've been investigating down here for years." Malley replied, "That's different. You don't investigate, John, they just talk to you."

The logic of the Bureau's position, however, in this as in so many other cases, was somewhat obfuscated by Bureau-speak. Agents started sending messages back to "the seat of government," which were transmitted over Hoover's signature to Burke Marshall and the Attorney General, which read, "There is a man in Mississippi named Walter Sheridan who claims to be doing investigative work for the Department of Justice. This is to inform you that he is not a member of the FBI."

Sheridan's squad worked with the Alcohol and Tax Unit and John Doar. And as one young attorney who was there recalls, "Walter had devised a mission of his own. We were sworn in as deputies and were supposed to carry .38s, but Walter's mission was to go to the different cities and talk to the white power structure people to see what they were doing to maintain order. We divided into pairs and went to all the cities. We were talking to the silent white power people scared by the Klan and the rednecks, but upset by the decline in law and order. We wrote up all our interviews and sent them to John Doar, or sometimes we gave them to him. You would run into him everywhere and he might travel with you. He's a unique person. Everybody knew who he was. The blacks loved him."

Civil Rights Division lawyers had no particular use for the Sheridan group. "It was a tough-guy operation," said one. "They were a bunch of hot rocks who were supposed to get into some of the violent organizations and harass them."

Whatever they did or didn't do, John Doar says that "Sheridan's people performed a function that the Bureau ultimately assumed." And that was, of course, the point. In July 1964 the Federal Bureau of Investigation for the first time in its history opened a field office in Jackson, Mississippi. It was staffed with 150 agents. The Get-Hoffa Squad had helped to do what the entire civil rights movement couldn't do—put the FBI into Mississippi.

Three months later Robert F. Kennedy resigned as Attorney General to run for the U.S. Senate in New York.

The Get-Hoffa Squad didn't define Robert Kennedy, but it represented an aspect of him, an authoritarian capability. Given his assessment of the threat Hoffa and the corrupt Teamsters posed to the polity, what alternative was there? Well, in light of the unfortunate *mano a mano* history of his pre-1961 exchanges with Hoffa, he might have disqualified himself from participation as he did in the Landis case. By appointing a non-lawyer to run the Hoffa Squad, however, and a non-criminal law man to head up the Criminal Division he foreclosed any possibility that he might distance himself from the chase.

The great achievement of the Kennedys, with their charismatic authority system, is that they were in many respects able to subvert the bureaucratic authority system that confronted them. Since they were, by and large, carriers of the ideal of excellence, the Kennedy impact on the Justice Department was therapeutic and the causes they championed worthy ones. The risk of the code of the Kennedys, however, to the extent that it accommodated the personalism and moralism which help account for the Get-Hoffa Squad, was that it transmitted to succeeding Justice Departments the precedent for a Get-Dissenters Squad.

The advantage of a network of honorary Kennedys, a national charisma distribution system, is that it multiplies the power normally available to the White House, not to mention the Attorney General. The limitation of this system, however, may have been the tendency for each man from Robert Kennedy on down, consistent with the code of the Kennedys, to put himself in the place of the President— a Department of role-players. By so doing the Justice Department sacrificed its opportunity to make its concerns a part of the system of pressures that help shape decisions at the top.

Finally, the Kennedy technique of converting problems into urgencies and proceeding from crisis to crisis on an emergency basis more than justified itself in one-to-one results. But the defect of crisis-reaction as a principle of government is that it tends to obfuscate long-range policy goals, to obscure one's sense of proportion. As Byron White once remarked, "It's nothing to come to an important job in government and be smart. The key is what you spend your time on."

EPILOGUE

Kennedy Justice

B Y 1968 the relatively radical junior Senator from New York had established authentic and irreparable bonds with the black underclass, discovered in decentralization of governmental power a common denominator with the New Left and put aside his earlier cold-war, counterinsurgency stance in favor of vocal and articulate opposition to the Vietnam war.

It would be aesthetically pleasing and altogether symmetrical to trace the evolution of Kennedy the compassionate exponent of black freedom and the rights of the poor from Kennedy the ruthless, Kennedy the wiretapper, Kennedy the Hoffa-chaser, in terms of his Justice Department experience. Under this theory Kennedy-frog became Kennedy-prince through a sort of shock therapy—successive exposure to the hypocrisy of the Southern power structure, the violence of the KKK, the assassination of Medgar Evers and then John F. Kennedy, and the misery, hunger and poverty of the ghettos that absorbed an increasing amount of his attention.

Unquestionably Robert Kennedy learned, grew and deepened in his Justice Department years. His 1962 wiretapping bill had more Constitutional safeguards than his 1961 wiretapping bill; his 1963 preoccupation with civil rights matched his earlier preoccupation with organized crime, and after his brother's assassination, which sent him reeling, he was forced to redefine himself and what he stood for. His exposure to and respect for men like Marshall, Katzenbach, Oberdorfer and John Douglas undoubtedly helped sensitize him to civil liberties issues.

But it does as little service to his memory to underestimate Kennedy's 1961 capabilities as to romanticize his post-1964 achievements. It is probably no accident that while young Turks like Peter Edelman, Adam Walinsky and Jeff Greenfield, who served Robert Kennedy on his Senate staff, felt he had come into his own only after he had broken away from the memories and nexus of his older brother, those who had worked with him on the Rackets Committee—men like Walter Sheridan and James J. P. McShane—thought he came into his own on the Rackets Committee; and those who worked with him at the Justice Department—men like Burke Marshall, Louis Oberdorfer and John Doar—thought he came into his own from the day he arrived at the Justice Department. Throughout his career he seems to have had the ability to instill confidence, inspire loyalty and stretch as well as exploit the capacity of those with whom he worked.

At his first press conference in April 1961 the new Attorney General's request that Congress enact a series of anti-racketeering laws (and incidentally enlarge the FBI's formal jurisdiction) got all the play in the press; but he also announced the formation of a committee of distinguished lawyers to study the problems of the poor in obtaining justice in the federal courts. That study ultimately led to the establishment of the Office of Criminal Justice within the Justice Department, the Criminal Justice Act and a National Conference on Bail, which triggered more than a score of bail reform projects. One need not deny that Robert Kennedy evolved in his job to recognize that it was the pre-evolutionary Robert Kennedy who attracted and hired the most talented top-level team on the New Frontier, certainly a rival to anything past Attorneys General, with the conceivable exception of Francis Biddle, had been able to muster. At a minimum, the early Kennedy anticipated the later one.

The office *did* enlarge the man. It alerted him to the agonies of the Negro, so that by late spring of 1963 he was the Administration's leading in-house proponent of strong civil rights legislation. It exposed him to the victimization of the young, so that by 1964 his Committee on Juvenile Delinquency, headed by his old Milton Academy roommate David Hackett, had created the basic model for the war on poverty— community coordinated attacks on social injustice, stimulated but not controlled by federal monies. And it awoke him to the social significance of due process, so that Kennedy-sponsored legislation, passed just before he resigned, provided for the first time paid counsel for indigent defendants in federal courts.

All of that said, it is realism rather than cynicism to add that the trade-in of Kennedy's pre-assassination image of toughness for a post-assassination image of compassion was also at least in part a response to changing national circumstances, changing institutional role, changing personal aspirations and changing speech writers. I remember standing amid the stench of stink bombs in Chicago's Conrad Hilton Hotel on the final day of the Democrats' disastrous convention of 1968 and seeing one of Robert Kennedy's most trusted friends and advisers sitting on his bags waiting for the limousine to take him to the airport, and I asked whether he thought Kennedy would really have made a difference. "I don't know if we could have pulled it off," he said, "but we would have played it for keeps, not like those Boy Scouts." For instance? "Take that nonsense about not letting anyone in the convention hall without special electronically treated passes which they were checking on those light machines at the entrances. We would have gone down to the basement and cut the power off." That aspect of Robert Kennedy's capability, then, survived even his death.

It was, to borrow David Halberstam's phrase, an "unfinished odyssey." But what, to return to our original inquiry, was the impact of that odyssey on the Justice Department and the quality of justice in America? When he resigned from the Justice Department to run for the Senate from New York in September of 1964, Robert Kennedy published a book called *The Pursuit of Justice*, a collection of his speeches and testimony, which featured "A Chronology of Significant Actions" he had taken as Attorney General. The list included such items as the drive against organized crime, the conviction of Hoffa, the protection of the freedom riders, the countless Kennedy improvisations on behalf of equal justice, the passage of the Civil Rights Bill of 1964 and the Criminal Justice Act of the same year. The statistics were impressive (fifty-nine voting discrimination suits filed, as compared with a handful by the previous Administration; 325 racketeers convicted in Kennedy's last year as compared with fourteen in 1960, the last year of the previous Administration), and although one might argue about the "significance" of the creation of the Communications Satellite Corporation or the settlement of the General Aniline case or the delivery of a 1961 speech at the University of Georgia promising to enforce the law, all of which were listed, by and large the chronology left little doubt that the Kennedy Administration had been on the side of social reform and equal justice. As Charles Morgan, Jr., the white integrationist and civil-libertarian who in 1963 evacuated Birmingham, Alabama, for Atlanta, Georgia, a victim of white racism, has remarked, "Don't forget. He was the guy all the hatred fell down on. He was concerned with *real* things. I was worried about what motel I could sleep in and could you get out of town alive? There was a war on, and they were our allies. That's the most important thing." This commitment is an achievement that should not be understimated, although it is somewhat diminished when one factors into the humanitarian quotient such derelictions as the appointment of segregationist judges, the lax approach to electronic surveillance and the refusal to protect civil rights workers.

At the same time the chronology suggests that at best the Kennedys were an excellent species of the conventional rather than any sort of radical breakthrough with tradition. It is an unwritten law of annual report writing in the federal bureaucracy that every agency's statistics are better than those of the previous year and far better than those of the previous Administration, so the statistics trotted out at such moments prove nothing. It is true that the Civil Rights Bill President Kennedy sent to Congress on June 19, 1963, was "the most extensive legislation in this field in ninety years," as the chronology puts it, but change the "ninety" to "eighty-four" and the same claim might have been made for Eisenhower's Civil Rights Bill in 1957, and it probably was. In other words, Kennedy's civil rights activities were, for the most part, a response to the dynamics of the situation—the protests and demonstrations of the early Sixties. As Jack Greenberg, director of the NAACP Legal Defense Fund, has observed, ultimately the thousands of nameless civil rights workers deserve credit for enacting the statute which actually saved 3,000 of them from unjust sit-in convictions.

It is true that the drive on organized crime would probably not have occurred—at least not at its significant level of intensity—without the Kennedy impetus. But the FBI "participation" that made it possible was predicated on an arrangement—FBI autonomy and parallel "cooperation"—that made it conventional. A radical approach would have necessitated terminating the employment of J. Edgar Hoover, who has thrived on the principle of FBI veto power over Justice Department activities.

Ironically, the Kennedy "Chronology" misses Kennedy's most lasting and least conventional contribution: his impact on those with

whom he worked and, through them, on the humdrum routines of the
Justice Department itself. Kennedy's detractors concede the high
quality of day-to-day law business in the Kennedy years but attribute
it to the high quality of his lieutenants. This is to miss the point.
Kennedy's strength was precisely his personal quest for excellence and
his ability to use the best ideas provided him. He had an inspirational
quality that brought out the best in others. He used his very youth
and inexperience to embolden other young men to speak their tentative ideas, and then, as they saw these notions picked up and transformed into policy, they themselves were transformed, their sense of
the possible was uplifted, the action-potential of the bureaucracy was
stretched. Operations like the Cuban prisoner ransom were important
less for what they achieved than as a demonstration project of what
government could do. By popular standards, the Kennedy campaign
against juvenile delinquency was a failure. Patrick Anderson, who
worked on it, points out, "The program was publicly branded a 'dismal
failure' by one of its chief Congressional sponsors, it caused political
and civil rights controversies in nearly every city it entered, its most
successful project [Mobilization for Youth] was crippled by highly
publicized charges of Communism and corruption, and it can nowhere
be shown to have actually reduced juvenile delinquency." Yet Anderson
numbers himself among those who consider the juvenile delinquency
program "the most exciting experiment carried out by the Kennedy
Administration" because it demonstrated, for the first time, that community agencies, which were supported but not controlled by federal
funds and which were otherwise in competition, could and would work
together to address common social problems.

Robert Kennedy once wrote of his father: "He has called on the
best that was in us. There was no such thing as half trying. Whether
it was running a race or catching a football, competing in school—we
were to try. And we were to try harder than anyone else. We might
not be the best, and none of us were, but we were to make the effort
to be the best. 'After you have done the best you can,' he used to say,
'the hell with it.' " * Robert Kennedy never learned to say the hell with
it; otherwise those words serve as a good description of the striving for
excellence that the Kennedys exemplified and that proved contagious
within the Justice Department.

Striving *per se* makes no more headlines than the countless in-

* In 1965 Robert F. Kennedy wrote a private tribute to his father, Joseph P.
Kennedy, from which this is taken. It was read as the eulogy at the funeral service
for their father by Senator Edward M. Kennedy.

significant cases that never find their way into "Significant Action" chronologies and never find their way into court, yet have everything to do with the quality of justice. Striving is process; results are product. Kennedy's reputation was for results. That he secured them in the short run—where Kennedy values dictated that he do so—must not be overlooked. But his major contribution in the long run—positive and negative—was to process. He imbued those he touched with the Kennedy ethic, with loftier aspirations; part of that ethic, however, permitted if it did not encourage such troublesome precedents as the Get-Hoffa Squad which distorted the same process he did so much to elevate and which lend themselves to easy exploitation by future Attorneys General.

Given the high ideals, given the White House tie, given the superb staff, given the rare combination of charisma and capability, given the uniquely open environment which Robert Kennedy created and encouraged, why did Kennedy Justice, in so many ways, fail to transcend the conventional? It is fashionable among Kennedy's critics to acknowledge his talent as an administrator and then to proceed to attack his character. Indeed, the character of this man seems to have been unimpeachable; the pursuit and punishment of evil and the reward of virtue may be insufficient as jurisprudence, but they will do for morality until something better comes along—and those were the boundaries of Robert Kennedy's moral universe. If defects of the Kennedy record are not traceable to defects of character or capacity, they may be traceable in part—as are some of the accomplishments— to the intersection and interaction of the three codes of conduct that dominated Kennedy Justice.

Often Kennedy charisma combined with Ivy League ingenuity to cancel out or circumvent or utilize FBI bureaucracy. That was the case with Kennedy Justice's response to the freedom riders: The FBI wouldn't protect the riders, but it *would* take 119 pictures of discriminatory signs at interstate bus terminals, which were key exhibits in the Ivy League lawyers' imaginative and original brief that convinced the ICC to issue a rule desegregating interstate bus facilities. But this victory was achieved only with the behind-the-scenes cooperation of William Tucker, a Kennedy-appointed ICC Commissioner whose self-image as an honorary Kennedy triumphed over his self-image as an independent member of the Interstate Commerce Commission.

Generally, the cautious Ivy League lawyers served as a restraining influence on the naturally activist Kennedy impulse. The code of the Ivy

Leaguers enriched the code of the Kennedys by contributing to it notions of procedural due process, helping to translate Kennedy compassion into concrete programs for bail and sentencing reform, legal representation to the poor and, especially at the outset, sensitizing the Kennedys to the demands and *Realpolitik* of the establishment civil rights organizations. But having infused the code of the Kennedys with the urgencies of the movement for equal justice, the same advisors proceeded to invent a philosophy which discouraged doing anything about it.

In civil rights, then, the various codes complemented each other to the disadvantage of the Negro. The FBI, which was not much interested in civil rights anyway, insisted that it was not a protection agency; the Kennedys, who were disinclined to confront the power structure of the South, contracted their vision of the possible based on the unavailability of the FBI; and the Ivy League lawyers, with their instinct for the artful compromise and their talent for intellectualization, rationalized the brutality that the white South visited on civil rights workers instead of ending it.

The net impact of the FBI was to keep the Kennedys from operating at full capacity. The virtue of an independent intelligence operation is that it cannot be used for "political" purposes—a Gestapo to carry out night raids on behalf of the Administration in power. Thus, to some extent the tension between the code of the Kennedys and the code of the FBI was a healthy one. But in areas like organized crime, the result of FBI independence and autonomy was not merely to frustrate the policies of the Kennedy Administration but also to undermine the integrity of, and public confidence in, the procedures of law enforcement. Kennedy priorities dictated escalated FBI involvement in rackets-busting; the FBI mystique of secrecy, combined with its insistence on self-government, insulated their illegal electronic surveillance activities from visibility; and the Ivy League assumption that gentlemen didn't get involved in such "dirty business" contributed to Kennedy's illusion that his war on organized crime was within the law.

The Kennedy spontaneity and charismatic authority system, which made so much possible, had the disadvantage of not leaving much time for the sorting out of priorities. Ivy League lawyers with status as honorary Kennedys spent their time improving wiretap legislation rather than considering whether it was worth pushing for. They contributed of their time and expertise to help make the Hoffa convictions irreversible rather than asking whether the whole anti-Hoffa enterprise ought to be scrapped in favor of, say, a more ambitious anti-trust enterprise. They made informal gestures toward getting better intelligence on prospective Southern judicial nominees, but never thought to mount a serious challenge to the FBI system that failed to serve up such intelligence.

Here is not the place to argue the virtues of spontaneous action versus the dangers of procedural irregularity, the virtues of federal self-restraint versus the dangers of unprotected individual rights, the virtues of effective results versus the dangers of defective procedures. Here is the place to note a difficulty with the code of the Kennedys as a principle of government administration: If the code of the FBI requires bureaucrats and the code of the Ivy League lawyers requires reasonable men, the code of the Kennedys requires Kennedys—at least one or two of them at the top—and Kennedys, like philosopher kings, are in short supply. Since a number of precedents of Kennedy Justice might lend themselves to easy abuse, this is not a reservation to be taken lightly.

Appendix to Chapter Two

May 4, 1961
To: Byron R. White
    Deputy Attorney General
From: The Director, Federal Bureau of Investigation
Subject: Technical and Microphone Surveillance

In connection with the Attorney General's contemplated appearance before the Senate Subcommittee on Constitutional Rights, our views on the use of microphone surveillances in FBI cases are set forth for your consideration. Under date of April 21, 1961, we furnished our comments on S. 1495, which is proposed legislation on wiretapping.

Our policy on the use of microphone surveillances is based upon a memorandum from former Attorney General Herbert Brownell dated May 20, 1954, in which he approved the use of microphone surveillances with or without trespass. In this memorandum Mr. Brownell said in part:

> "I recognize that for the FBI to fulfill its important intelligence function, considerations of internal security and the national safety are paramount and, therefore, may compel the unrestricted use of this technique in the national interest."

In light of this policy, in the internal security field, we are utilizing microphone surveillances on a restricted basis even though trespass is necessary to assist in uncovering the activities of Soviet intelligence agents and Communist Party leaders. In the interests of national safety, microphone surveillances are also utilized on a restrictive basis even though trespass is necessary, in our covering major criminal activities. We are using such coverage in connection with our investigations of the clandestine activities of top hoodlums and organized crime. From an intelligence standpoint, this investigative technique has produced results obtainable through no other means. The information so obtained is treated in the same manner as information obtained from wiretaps, that is, not from the standpoint of evidentiary value but for intelligence purposes.

There is no Federal legislation at the present time pertaining to the use of microphone surveillances. The passage of any restrictive legislation in this field would be a definite loss to our investigative operations, both in the internal security field and in our fight against the criminal elements. This is especially true in the case of organized crime where we have too few weapons at our command to give up the valuable technique of microphones.

UNITED STATES DEPARTMENT OF JUSTICE
Federal Bureau of Investigation
Washington, D.C. 20535

December 7, 1966

Honorable H. R. Gross
House of Representatives
Washington, D.C. 20515

My Dear Congressman:

I welcome the opportunity to answer your letter of December 5, 1966. The questions you raised were most incisive. I have always felt that the Congress, in representing the general public, has every right to know the true facts of any controversy. This is the policy I have always practiced when appearing before the appropriations committees of the Congress; consequently, I feel compelled to do likewise in replying to your letter.

Your impression that the FBI engaged in the usage of wiretaps and microphones only upon the authority of the Attorney General of the United States is absolutely correct. You are also correct when you state that it is your understanding that "full documentation" exists as proof of such authorizations.

All wiretaps utilized by the FBI have always been approved in writing, in advance, by the Attorney General.

As examples of authorization covering the period in which you were specifically interested, you will find attached to this letter a communication dated August 17, 1961, signed by former Attorney General Robert F. Kennedy, in which he approved policy for the usage of microphones covering both security and major criminal cases. Mr. Kennedy, during his term of office, exhibited great interest in pursuing such matters and, while in different metropolitan areas, not only listened to the results of microphone surveillances but raised questions relative to obtaining better equipment. He was briefed frequently by an FBI official regarding such matters. FBI usage of such devices, while always handled in a sparing, carefully controlled manner and, as indicated, only with the specific authority of the Attorney General, was obviously increased at Mr. Kennedy's insistence while he was in office.

I thought you might like to know that the Congress has been advised by the Department of Justice on occasion regarding FBI usage of electronic equipment, both in the internal security and organized crime fields. Senator Sam J. Ervin, Jr., wrote Mr. Kennedy's assistant, Herbert J. Miller,

Jr., Assistant Attorney General, Criminal Division, on May 19, 1961, relative to this matter. Mr. Miller, under date of May 25, 1961, in reply, indicated the complete knowledge of the Department of Justice in such matters in that the specific number and areas of usage were definitely pinpointed. A copy of Mr. Miller's letter is attached.

I had a conference with the then Attorney General Nicholas deB. Katzenbach on March 30, 1965, in which I made recommendations similar to those I had made to each successive Attorney General following the administration of Attorney General Tom C. Clark. Such recommendations concerned strong, simple control by the Attorney General of procedures affecting electronic devices utilized by all Federal investigative agencies. President Lyndon B. Johnson on June 30, 1965, issued a memorandum to all Executive departments and agencies prohibiting wiretapping in all cases except those related to the internal security of the United States. This prohibition included the fact that no interception was to be undertaken or continued without first obtaining the approval of the Attorney General. This, of course, is the practice which has always been followed by the FBI.

I can assure you, backed by the proven record of long years of service, both by myself and the many career personnel of this Bureau, that the FBI has never operated in an irresponsible, unauthorized or uncontrolled manner. To reiterate, the minute number of electronic devices used have been authorized by the Attorney General. I would not allow practices to exist otherwise.

It was good of you to write me, and your interest in our activities is deeply appreciated.

Sincerely yours,
J. Edgar Hoover

Enclosures (2)

AT&T
AMERICAN TELEPHONE & TELEGRAPH COMPANY
195 Broadway, New York, N.Y. 10007

William P. Mullane, Jr.
News Services Manager

September 9, 1969

[Communication to the author]

Dear Mr. Navasky:

I reply to your letter of July 14. I am happy to report that we have exhausted all available sources of research, both here at AT&T and at the New York Telephone Company and have obtained the following answers to your questions:

1. [Neither] the New York Telephone Company, nor AT&T, knows of (a) any instance where a special telephone line has been furnished to the

FBI or other federal agencies for use in connection with microphone surveillance, nor (b) have any procedures been established by the telephone company for the furnishing of such lines, whether by letter request or other means.

2. Inasmuch as there is no lease arrangement, we have no requirement that the Attorney General or other Department of Justice employee sign a non-existent agreement.

3. Neither New York Telephone nor AT&T has any knowledge of an August 17, 1961 communication from the Department of Justice; therefore, we can't supply a copy.

4. See previous statement #3.

I'm sorry for the delay in getting you this information, but in the cause of accuracy I believe the delays were necessary both for research reasons and the American public's indulgence in the pagan custom of vacations.

Hopefully, the information still will be helpful to you.

Cordially,
Bill Mullane

May 20, 1954 "CONFIDENTIAL"

To: Director
From: The Attorney General
Subj: Microphone Surveillance

The recent decision of the Supreme Court entitled *Irvine* v. *Calif.* 347 US 128, denouncing the use of microphone surveillances by city police in a gambling case makes appropriate a reappraisal of the use which may be made in the future by the Federal Bureau of Investigation of microphone surveillance in connection with matters relating to the internal security of the country.

It is clear that in some instances the use of microphone surveillance is the only possible way of uncovering the activities of espionage agents, possible saboteurs, and subversive persons. In such instances I am of the opinion that the national interest requires [that] microphone surveillance be utilized by the Federal Bureau of Investigation. This use need not be limited to the development of evidence for prosecution. The FBI has an intelligence function in connection with internal security matters equally as important as the duty of developing evidence for presentation to the courts and the national security requires that the FBI be able to use microphone surveillance for the proper discharge of both of such functions. The Department of Justice approves the use of microphone surveillance by the FBI under these circumstances and for these purposes.

I do not consider that the decision of the Supreme Court in *Irvine* v. *California* requires a different course. That case is really distinguishable on its facts. The language of the Court, however, indicates certain uses of microphones which it would be well to avoid, if possible, even in internal security investigations. It is quite clear that in the Irvine case the Justices of the Supreme Court were outraged by what they regarded as the indecency of installing a microphone in a bedroom. They denounced the utilization of such methods of investigation in a gambling case as shocking. The Court's action is a clear indication of the need for discretion and intelligent restraint in the use of microphones by the FBI in all cases, including internal security matters. Obviously, the installation of a microphone in a bedroom or in some comparably intimate location should be avoided wherever possible. It may appear, however, that if important intelligence or evidence relating to matters connected with the national security can only be obtained by the installation of [a microphone in such a location and under such] circumstances the installation is proper and is not prohibited by the Supreme Court's decision in the Irvine case.

Previous interpretations which have been furnished to you as to what may constitute a trespass in the installation of microphones, suggest that the views expressed have been tentative in nature and have attempted to predict the course which courts would follow rather than reflect the present state of the law. It is realized that not infrequently the question of trespass arises in connection with the installation of a microphone. The question of whether a trespass is actually involved and the second question of the effect of such a trespass upon the admissability in Court of the evidence thus obtained, must necessarily be resolved according to the circumstances of each case. The Department in resolving the problems which may arise in connection with the use of microphone surveillance will review the circumstances of each case in the light of the practical necessities of investigation and of the national interest which must be protected. It is my opinion that the Department should adopt that interpretation which will permit microphone coverage by the FBI in a manner most conducive to our national interest. I recognize that for the FBI to fulfill its important intelligence function, considerations of internal security and the national safety are paramount, and therefore, may compel the unrestricted use of the technique in the national interest.

cc: Records
    2 courtesy copies to FBI
    Mr. Hall

Appendix to Chapter Seven

Name of Company	ANTI-TRUST DIVISION Defendant	Investigation	F.T.C. Defendant	Investigation
American Cyanamid Co. (Lederle) Pearl River, N.Y.	x	x	x	
Eli Lilly & Co. Indianapolis, Ind.		x		x
Armour Pharmaceutical Co. Chicago, Ill.				x
Merck & Co. New York, N.Y.		x		x
Carter Products, Inc. New York, N.Y.		x		x
Cutter Products, Inc. Berkeley, Cal.				x
Richardson-Merrell Greensboro, N.C.				x
Upjohn Co. Kalamazoo, Mich.		x		x
Warner-Lambert Pharm. Co. Morris Plains, N.J.				x
Ethicon, Inc. Sommerville, N.J.		x		
Sandoz Pharmaceutical Hanover, N.J.				x
Sterling Drugs New York, N.Y.			x	x
Smith, Kline & French Lab. Philadelphia, Pa.		x		x

Name of Company	ANTI-TRUST DIVISION Defendant	Investigation	F.T.C. Defendant	Investigation
Bristol-Myers Co. Syracuse, N.Y.	x	x	x	x
Abbott Laboratories Chicago, Ill.		x		x
G. D. Searle & Co. Skokie, Ill.		x		
Ritter Co., Inc. Rochester, N.Y.				x
The Borden Co. New York, N.Y.	x		x	x
Chas. Pfizer & Co. New York, N.Y.	x	x	x	x
Averst Labs Rouses Point, N.Y.		x		
Ciba Phar. Co. Summit, N.J.		x		x
Hoffman-LaRoch, Inc. Nutley, N.J.		x		x
American Home Prod. Lab. Whitehall Div. Hammonton, N.J.		x		x
Pillsbury Co. Minneapolis, Minn.		x		x
Kendall Co. Boston, Mass.		x		
Wyeth Lab. Radnor, Pa.		x	x	
Taylor Instrument Co. Rochester, N.Y.				x
Mentholatum Co. Buffalo, N.Y.				x
Glenbrook Lab. New York, N.Y.				x
S.S.S. Co. Atlanta, Ga.				x
Pet Milk Co. St. Louis, Mo.				x

Name of Company	ANTI-TRUST DIVISION *Defendant/Investigation/Defendant/Investigation*		F.T.C.	
Becton-Dickinson Rutherford, N.J.	x			
Mennon Co. Morristown, N.J.		x		x
Miles Laboratory Elkhart, Ind.				x
American Hospital Evanston, Ill.		x		
General Foods, Inc. White Plains, N.Y.				x
General Mills Minneapolis, Minn.		x		x
McKesson-Robbins Bridgeport, Conn.		x		x
Lehn & Fink Product Corp. New York, N.Y.				x
Ex-Lax, Inc. New York, N.Y.				x
Parke-Davis Detroit, Mich.		x		x
American Optical Co. West Bridge, Mass.	x			x
Plough Inc. Memphis, Tenn.			x	x
Sterilon Buffalo, N.Y.		x		
Winn-Dixie Grocery Co. Jacksonville, Fla.				x
J. B. Williams Co., Inc. New York, N.Y.				x
Chesebrough-Pond's, Inc. New York, N.Y.		x		x
Corning Glass Works Corning, N.Y.		x		
Green Giant Co. Minneapolis, Minn.				x

Name of Company	ANTI-TRUST DIVISION Defendant/Investigation		F.T.C. Defendant/Investigation	
Owens-Illinois Glass Co. Toledo, Ohio	x			
Campbell Soup Co. Camden, N.J.				x
National Tea Co. Chicago, Ill.			x	x
Union Carbide Corp. New York, N.Y.	x		x	x
Bausch & Lomb, Inc. Rochester, N.Y.	x			
Standard Brands, Inc. Hoboken, N.J.				x
E. R. Squibb & Sons New Brunswick, N.J.		x		
Eastman Kodak Co. Rochester, N.Y.				x
Westinghouse Electric Baltimore, Md.	x	x	x	x
E. Leitz, Inc. New York, N.Y.		x		
Procter & Gamble Cincinnati, Ohio	x		x	x
General Electric Co. Milwaukee, Wis.		x	x	x
Corn Products New York, N.Y.	x			
Monsanto Chem. Co. St. Louis, Mo.	x	x		

ACKNOWLEDGMENTS

I cannot begin to acknowledge my gratitude to all of those who served in and around Kennedy Justice and extended themselves, sometimes to the margins of the law, on my behalf. I have been the beneficiary of hundreds of hours of interviews, thousands of pages of memoranda and, in two cases, chapter-readings of my manuscript. Since some have requested anonymity and would be conspicuous by omission if I listed others, I have resolved the dilemma by listing nobody. But my appreciation is boundless nonetheless.

I would also like to thank the John F. Kennedy Library for its cooperation in making selected oral history interviews available to me, and for its invitation to serve as repository for the *Kennedy Justice* papers.

Although I was not able to employ a full-time research assistant, I received valuable *ad hoc* research and administrative aid from Barbara Field, Jean Strouse, Danny Laylin, Roger Mills, Kay Harris, Kathy Paulsen, Casey Damme and Loren Ghiglione.

Special thanks go to *The Atlantic Monthly*, *The Saturday Evening Post* and *The New York Times Magazine*, which gave me assignments—when I was freelancing—that contributed to my research on *Kennedy Justice*.

Finally, there are four people without whom the book would not have happened: My agent, Lynn Nesbit, who made it possible. My editor, Richard Kluger, who was unsparing in enterprise, enthusiasm and constructive criticism. My friend, Michael Meltsner, whose idea this book was in the first place, and whose insights and wise counsel were a constant source of stimulation and encouragement. And my wife, Annie, who, in addition to not leaving, typed much of the manuscript.

V.S.N.

Bibliographic Notes

Although *Kennedy Justice* could not have been written without and frankly builds on the vast warehouse of Kennedy literature, I have taken pains to exclude from the text the paraphernalia of scholarship, and I refrain here from the redundancy of yet another Kennedy bibliography. Superb Robert F. Kennedy bibliographies are available for the asking at the Library of Congress.

The traditional parade of erudition seems inappropriate here for two reasons: First, not having had systematic access to either the Kennedy papers or the FBI files, I look upon *Kennedy Justice* as more in the nature of an interim speculation than any kind of definitive scholarship. Second, had I cluttered up the text with the hundreds of little numbers that the conventions of scholarly publishing seem to require, a good percentage of them would refer to anonymous interviewees (whose interviews, as indicated in the Preface, I have deposited with the John F. Kennedy Memorial Library for future inspection) and as such would be useless.

The paucity of footnotes, however, does not bespeak a lack of literary or intellectual debts. Consider, instead, that to repay them here might require a book half again as long as the one that precedes these afterthoughts. Nevertheless, I have not resisted the temptation to mention below, in conjunction with the few chapter notes that could not be avoided, a few of the books and articles which help account for the form that *Kennedy Justice* has taken and the importance of which may not be evident from the text. *A Thousand Days: John F. Kennedy in the White House*, by Arthur M. Schlesinger, Jr. (Houghton, Mifflin, 1965), and *Kennedy*, by Theodore C. Sorensen (Harper & Row, 1965), were, of course, indispensable. *The Heir Apparent*, by William V. Shannon (Macmillan, 1967), and *Robert Kennedy at 40*, by Nick Thimmesch and William Johnson (Norton, 1965), each saved me hundreds of hours of research.

PART I: THE CODE OF THE FBI

The literature on the FBI is thin indeed. On the one side are the quasi-official apologias like Don Whitehead's *The FBI Story: A Report to the People* (Random House, 1956) or Harry and Bonaro Overstreet's *The FBI in Our Open Society* (W. W. Norton, 1969). On the other are such embattled critiques as Max Lowenthal's *The Federal Bureau of Investigation* (William Sloane Associates, 1950) and Fred J. Cook's muckraking *The FBI Nobody Knows* (Macmillan, 1964). In addition there are a growing number of memoirs by disenchanted former FBI agents, such as Jack Levine, who wrote "Hoover and the Red Scare" for *The Nation* (October 20, 1962), Norman Ollestad, author of *Inside the FBI* (Lyle Stuart, 1967) and William Turner, who first put out his story on KPFA, Pacifica Radio, Berkeley, California (October, 1962).

I learned much from magazine writers and journalists like Douglas Kiker (in *The Atlantic*), Joseph Kraft (an essay in his book, *Profiles in Power*, New American Library, 1967) Tom Wicker (*The New York Times Magazine*), Louis Kohlmeier (*The Wall Street Journal*) and Richard Harwood (*The Washington Post*), who wrote about the Bureau and its Director before it was fashionable to do so; *Kennedy Justice* was already in final form when the current rash of exposés and analyses commenced.

The Valachi Papers, by Peter Maas (Putnam, 1968), and Kennedy's own *The Enemy Within* (Harper & Brothers, 1960) shed light on the FBI's attitude toward organized crime as does Donald Cressy's *Death of a Nation* (Harper & Row, 1969).

Climbing Jacob's Ladder, by Pat Watters and Reese Cleghorn (Harcourt, Brace and World, 1967), is indispensable for understanding the impact of the FBI on the civil rights movement, as are the reports of the Southern Regional Council and the reports of the U.S. Civil Rights Commission, especially "Enforcement: A Report on Equal Protection in the South" (United States Commission on Civil Rights, 1965); and, of course, there are the FBI's own monthly *Law Enforcement Bulletins*, which include a regular editorial feature signed by J. Edgar Hoover, and FBI press releases.

For perspective, I found it helpful to supplement my reading of FBI official documents with simultaneous readings in the sociology of organizations, particularly *Political Parties*, by Robert Michels (The Free Press, 1962), *The Sociology of Georg Simmel*, translated and edited by Kurt H. Wolff (The Free Press, 1950), and *The Sociology of*

Max Weber, by Julien Freund (Vintage Books, 1969).

Coretta Scott King's memoir, *My Life with Martin Luther King, Jr.* (Holt, Rinehart, Winston, 1970) was important to my understanding of Stanley Levison's role in Dr. King's life.

CHAPTER ONE

1. Robert Michels, *Political Parties* (New York: The Free Press, 1962), p. 221.
2. Pat Watters and Reese Cleghorn, *Climbing Jacob's Ladder: The Arrival of Negroes in Southern Politics* (New York: Harcourt, Brace & World, Inc., 1967), p. 215.
3. John Kenneth Galbraith, "How to Control the Military," *Harper's Magazine,* June 1969, p. 32.
4. See *FBI Law Enforcement Bulletins,* 1960's, *passim,* and Mr. Hoover's speeches through the years. "Young punks," "misguided sentimentalists" and "bleeding hearts" are recurring epithets.
5. See Louis M. Kohlmeier, "Focus on the FBI," *The Wall Street Journal,* October 10, 1968, p. 1, col. 1, and October 15, 1968, p. 1, col. 1.
6. Douglas Kiker, "Washington Reports," *Atlantic Monthly,* April 1967, p. 6.
7. Francis Biddle, *In Brief Authority* (New York: Doubleday & Company, Inc., 1962), pp. 258–59.
8. "Untold Story of the Freedom Rides; Telephone Conversation with George E. Cruit and Explanations," *U.S. News and World Report,* October 23, 1961, pp. 76–79.
9. United States Commission on Civil Rights, *Law Enforcement: A Report on Equal Protection in the South* (Washington: Government Printing Office, 1965), p. 166 n.
10. Quoted in Arthur M. Schlesinger, Jr., *A Thousand Days* (Boston: Houghton Mifflin Company, 1965), p. 697.
11. Max Weber, *The Theory of Social and Economic Organization,* Alexander M. Henderson, trans., and Talcott Parsons, trans. and ed. (New York: Oxford University Press, 1947), pp. 337 *et seq.*
12. Arthur Selwyn Miller, "The Attorney General as the President's Lawyer," in Luther A. Huston, Arthur Selwyn Miller, Samuel Krislov and Robert G. Dixon, Jr., *Roles of the Attorney General* (Washington, D.C.: American Enterprise Institute for Policy Research, 1962), p. 66.
13. Letter from Attorney General Tom Clark to Hon. Edward Reese, House of Representatives, April 21, 1947.
14. Richard Harwood, "J. Edgar Hoover: A Librarian with a Lifetime Lease," *The Washington Post,* February 25, 1968.
15. Don Whitehead, *The FBI Story: A Report to the People* (New York: Random House, Inc., 1956), p. 350.
16. William V. Shannon, "The J. Edgar Hoover Case," *Commonweal,* December 11, 1964, p. 375. New York *Post.*
17. March 19, 1961. Press statement on file at Office of Public Information, U.S. Department of Justice.

CHAPTER TWO

1. Gerald L. Goettel, "Why the Crime Syndicate Can't Be Touched," *Harper's Magazine,* November 1960, p. 33.

2. William V. Shannon, *The Heir Apparent: Robert Kennedy and the Struggle for Power* (New York: The Macmillan Company, 1967), p. 66.
3. William Surface, *Inside Internal Revenue* (New York: Coward-McCann, Inc., 1967), p. 123.
4. Robert F. Kennedy, *The Enemy Within* (New York: Harper & Bros., 1960), p. 264.
5. *Ibid.*, p. 174.
6. *The Wall Street Journal*, September 6, 1962.
7. Victor S. Navasky, "A Famous Prosecutor Talks About Crime," *The New York Times Magazine*, February 17, 1970, p. 30.
8. Edwin Guthman, *We Band of Brothers* (New York: Harper & Row, 1971), p. 260.
9. Francis Biddle, *In Brief Authority* (New York: Doubleday & Company, Inc., 1962), p. 167.
10. *American Bar Association Project on Minimum Standards for Criminal Justice: Standards Relating to Electronic Surveillance*, G. Robert Blakey, Reporter (New York: Institute of Judicial Administration, June 1968), p. 29.

CHAPTER THREE

1. James V. Bennett, *I Chose Prison* (New York: Alfred A. Knopf, 1970), p. 154.
2. *Newsweek*, December 7, 1964, p. 24.
3. See Jules Feiffer, "Matter of Conscience," *Commentary*, December 1964, pp. 52–54, and Jack Newfield, *Robert Kennedy: A Memoir* (New York: E. P. Dutton & Co., Inc., 1969).
4. Letter on file at U.S. Department of Justice.
5. Memorandum from Burke Marshall to Salvatore A. Andretta, September 1, 1964.
6. Watters and Cleghorn, *op. cit.*, p. 58.
7. *Ibid.*, p. 295.
8. Anonymous affidavit on file with the office of the Southern Regional Council, Atlanta, Georgia.
9. Coretta Scott King, *My Life with Martin Luther King, Jr.*, (New York: Holt, Rinehart and Winston, 1969), p. 186.
10. See Arthur Krock's column in *The New York Times*, November 19, 1953; and J. Edgar Hoover's testimony, Senate Internal Security Subcommittee, November 17, 1953.

PART II: THE CODE OF THE
IVY LEAGUE GENTLEMAN

Burke Marshall's "Federalism and Civil Rights" with a foreword by Robert F. Kennedy (Columbia University Press, 1964) is the clearest and most systematic statement of the civil rights philosophy vis-à-vis the federal system of the Kennedy Administration. In addition to Watters and Cleghorn, I found Simon Lazarus III's critique of this theory, "Theories of Federalism and Civil Rights," *Yale Law Journal*,

Vol. 75, No. 6 (May 1966) the most penetrating, and Heywood Burns' essay, "The Federal Government and Civil Rights," in Leon Friedman, ed., *Southern Justice* (Pantheon, 1965), extremely helpful.

Walter Lord's *The Past That Would Not Die* (Harper & Row, 1964) is indispensable for understanding the events surrounding James Meredith's admission to the University of Mississippi.

The best critique of the Kennedy Administration's civil rights performance is probably Harold Fleming's "The Federal Executive and Civil Rights: 1961–1965," which appeared in *Daedalus*, Fall 1965. Some helpful information is also contained in the doctoral dissertation of Donald Francis Sullivan of the University of Oklahoma, completed in 1965 under the title: "The Civil Rights Programs of the Kennedy Administration: A Political Analysis."

Other critical source material is to be found in *Portrait of a Decade*, by Anthony Lewis (Random House, 1964) and especially the research reports of the Southern Regional Council.

Mary Curzan's doctoral dissertation on judicial selection in the Fifth Circuit, on file at Yale University, is—judging from the excerpts she has made public—most directly on point. Because some of the material was given to her on a restricted-use basis, however, the dissertation has not been made public. *Southern Justice*, edited by Leon Friedman (Pantheon, 1965), is a valuable source book. And I learned much about judicial selection in general from an unpublished paper by Harold Chase, University of Wisconsin, and from *Lawyers and Judges: The ABA and the Politics of Judicial Selection*, by Joel B. Grossman (John Wiley & Sons, 1965).

Robert G. Dixon, Jr.'s exhaustive *Democratic Representation: Reapportionment in Law and Politics* (Oxford University Press, 1968) along with *Reapportionment: The Law and Politics of Equal Representation*, by Robert B. McKay (Twentieth Century Fund, 1965), helped provide some basic background in the sticky reapportionment thicket.

CHAPTER FOUR

1. Edwin Guthman, *We Band of Brothers* (New York: Harper & Row, 1971), p. 95.
2. Erwin O. Smigel, *The Wall Street Lawyer: Professional Organization Man?* (New York: Free Press of Glencoe, 1964).
3. Bronislaw Malinowski, *Magic, Science and Religion* (New York: Doubleday Anchor Books, 1954), p. 84.
4. *The Washington Post*, May 5, 1961.

5. Michael Dorman, *We Shall Overcome* (New York: Delacorte Press, 1964), pp. 199–200.

6. Transcript of May 1963 briefing by Attorney General Robert F. Kennedy, on file in Public Information Office, U.S. Department of Justice.

7. Murray Kempton, "Marching on Washington," in Alan F. Westin, ed., *Freedom Now! The Civil Rights Struggle in America* (New York: Basic Books, Inc., 1964), p. 271.

8. Richard Harris, *Justice* (New York: E. P. Dutton & Co., Inc., 1970), p. 185.

9. These recollections and the local press reports are quoted in Walter Lord's *The Past That Would Not Die* (New York: Harper & Row, 1964).

10. Harold Fleming, "Federal Executive and Civil Rights," *Daedalus*, Fall, 1965, p. 936.

11. Harold Wilensky, *Organizational Intelligence* (New York: Basic Books, 1967), p. 78.

CHAPTER FIVE

1. *The Wall Street Journal*, September 21, 1967.

2. Alexander M. Bickel, *Politics and the Warren Court* (New York: Harper & Row, 1965), p. 73.

3. Pat Watters and Reese Cleghorn, *Climbing Jacob's Ladder: The Arrival of Negroes in Southern Politics* (New York: Harcourt, Brace and World, 1967), pp. 142–43.

4. *The New York Times*, July 19, 1963, p. 8, col. 3.

5. Theodore C. Sorensen, *Kennedy* (New York: Harper & Row, 1965), p. 614.

CHAPTER SIX

1. Press conference at U.S. Supreme Court, July 5, 1968.

2. Paul Freund, "New Vistas in Constitutional Law," *University of Pennsylvania Law Review*, Vol. 112 (1962), p. 631.

3. Robert B. McKay, *Reapportionment: The Law and Politics of Equal Representation* (New York: Twentieth Century Fund, 1965), p. 118.

PART III: THE CODE OF THE KENNEDYS

In addition to the standard Kennedy histories and the various Robert Kennedy biographies, mention should be made of Joseph Kraft's "Riot Squad for the New Frontier," which appeared in *Harper's* magazine, August 1963, and *"An Honorable Profession": A Tribute to Robert F. Kennedy*, edited by Pierre Salinger, Edwin Guthman, Frank Mankiewicz and John Seigenthaler (Doubleday, 1968).

The indispensable book on the Bay of Pigs is Haynes Johnson's *The Bay of Pigs: The Leaders' Story of Brigade 2506* (W. W. Norton, 1964). Some interesting additional material is provided in Morton Mintz's *The Therapeutic Nightmare* (Houghton Mifflin, 1965).

Background on the role of the Attorney General may be found in

Federal Justice: Chapters in the History of Justice and the Federal Executive, by Homer Cummings and Carl McFarland (Macmillan, 1937), and "Roles of the Attorney General of the United States," a fascinating collection of essays by Luther A. Huston, Arthur Selwyn Miller, Samuel Krislov and Robert G. Dixon, Jr., sponsored by the American Enterprise Institute for Public Policy Research and published in July 1968.

The Founding Father by Richard Whalen (New American Library, 1964) is a good source on Joseph Kennedy's relationship with James Landis.

On Hoffa, the critical literature includes Robert Kennedy's own The Enemy Within; Clark R. Mollenhoff's anti-Hoffa brief, Tentacles of Power: The Story of Jimmy Hoffa (World Publishing Company, 1965), Robert Cipes's civil libertarian analysis in The Crime War: The Manufactured Crusade, Sidney Lens's essay in The Progressive (quoted in the text) and James R. Hoffa's own The Trials of Jimmy Hoffa; The Autobiography of James R. Hoffa, as told to Donald I. Rogers (Henry Regnery, 1970).

Good over-all perspective on Robert Kennedy's attorney generalship is assisted by a reading of The Pursuit of Justice, by Robert F. Kennedy, edited by Theodore J. Lowi (Harper & Row, 1964), a collection of Kennedy's speeches and articles as Attorney General; In Brief Authority, Francis Biddle's memoir of his days at the Justice Department (Doubleday, 1962); and the various task force reports of the President's Commission on Law Enforcement and Administration of Justice, published by the Government Printing Office in 1967. The Commission was chaired by Nicholas deB. Katzenbach.

CHAPTER SEVEN

1. Harold H. Martin, "The Amazing Kennedys," The Saturday Evening Post, September 7, 1957.
2. Harold L. Wilensky, Organizational Intelligence (New York: Basic Books, 1967), p. 76.
3. Robert C. Tucker, "The Theory of Charismatic Leadership," Daedalus, Vol. 97, No. 3 (Summer 1968), p. 742.
4. Haynes Johnson, The Bay of Pigs (New York: W. W. Norton & Company, 1964), p. 327.
5. Morton Mintz, The Therapeutic Nightmare (Boston: Houghton Mifflin Company, 1965), p. 373.
6. This story, which went out over The New York Times News Service, appeared in the Boston Herald, December 26, 1962.
7. Arthur M. Schlesinger, Jr., A Thousand Days (Boston: Houghton Mifflin Company, 1965), p. 840.

CHAPTER EIGHT

1. Quoted in Luther A. Huston, Arthur Selwyn Miller, Samuel Krislov and Robert G. Dixon, Jr., *Roles of the Attorney General* (Washington, D.C.: American Enterprise Institute for Policy Research, 1962), p. 51.
2. *Ibid.*, p. 52.
3. Joseph Kraft, "Riot Squad for the New Frontier," *Harper's Magazine*, August 1963, p. 69.
4. William V. Shannon, *The Heir Apparent: Robert Kennedy and the Struggle for Power* (New York: The Macmillan Company, 1967), p. 63.

CHAPTER NINE

1. Monroe H. Freedman, "The Professional Responsibility of the Prosecuting Attorney," *Georgetown Law Journal*, Vol. 55, No. 6 (May 1967), p. 1035.
2. Jacob Tanzer, *The New Republic*, March 9, 1968, in the "Correspondence" section, p. 33.
3. Adam Yarmolinsky, *New York Review of Books*, September 26, 1968, in the "Letters" section, p. 75.
4. Robert F. Kennedy, *The Enemy Within*, pp. 161–62.
5. Paul Jacobs, "Extracurricular Activities of the McClellan Committee," *California Law Review*, Vol. 51, No. 2 (May 1963), p. 310.
6. Quoted in John Bartlow Martin, "The Struggle to Get Hoffa, Part Five: Hoffa Confounds His Enemies," *The Saturday Evening Post*, July 25, 1959, p. 86.
7. William V. Shannon, *The Heir Apparent: Robert Kennedy and the Struggle for Power* (New York: The Macmillan Company, 1967), p. 67.
8. Ralph and Esther James, *Hoffa and the Teamsters* (Princeton, N.J.: D. Van Nostrand and Company, Inc., 1965), pp. 62–63.
9. David L. Wolper's production of "The Journey of Robert F. Kennedy," which premiered on ABC-TV on Tuesday, February 17, 1970.
10. Clark Mollenhoff, *Tentacles of Power* (Cleveland, O.: World Publishing Company, 1965), pp. 371–372.
11. Quoted in George Plimpton, ed., *American Journey: Interviews by Jean Stein* (New York: Harcourt Brace Jovanovich, Inc., 1970), pp. 56–57.

INDEX

VICTOR S. NAVASKY

VICTOR S. NAVASKY is a 39-year-old editor on *The New York Times Magazine*. A Phi Beta Kappa graduate of Swarthmore College, he earned his LL.B. at Yale Law School, where he taught legal research and founded *Monocle* magazine, an occasional journal of political satire. He has served as Special Assistant to the Governor of Michigan and has written and taught widely on politics, literature and the law. He lives in New York City with his wife, Anne, and their two children, Bruno and Miri. *Kennedy Justice* is his first book.